PENNSYLVANIA
AND THE FEDERAL CONSTITUTION
1787–1788

PENNSYLVANIA

AND THE

Federal Constitution
1787–1788

EDITED BY

John Bach McMaster
and Frederick D. Stone

LIBERTY FUND

Indianapolis

This book is published by Liberty Fund, Inc., a foundation established to encourage study of the ideal of a society of free and responsible individuals.

囗⧉ 𝄇⤬⤜

The cuneiform inscription that serves as our logo and as the design motif for our endpapers is the earliest-known written appearance of the word "freedom" (*amagi*), or "liberty." It is taken from a clay document written about 2300 B.C. in the Sumerian city-state of Lagash.

c 1 2 3 4 5 6 7 8 9 10
p 1 2 3 4 5 6 7 8 9 10

Cover art: "A New and Accurate Map of the Province of Pennsylvania in North America from the Best Authorities," from Universal Magazine (London: J. Hinton, April 1780). Used courtesy of www.mapsofpa.com.

Library of Congress Cataloging-in-Publication Data
Historical Society of Pennsylvania.
Pennsylvania and the Federal Constitution 1787–1788 / edited by John Bach McMaster and Frederick D. Stone.—A Da Capo Press reprint ed.
p. cm.
"This Da Capo Press edition of Pennsylvania and the Federal Constitution, 1787–1788, is an unabridged republication in two volumes of the one-volume first edition published in Philadelphia, in 1888."
Includes bibliographical references and index.
ISBN 978-0-86597-793-8 (hardcover: alk. paper) —
ISBN 978-0-86597-794-5 (pbk.: alk. paper)
1. United States. Constitution. 2. Pennsylvania. Convention (1787)
I. McMaster, John Bach, 1852–1932, ed. II. Stone, Frederick D. (Frederick Dawson), 1841–1897, joint ed. III. Title.
KF4512.P4P45 2011
342.7302'92—dc22
2010031570

LIBERTY FUND, INC.
8335 Allison Pointe Trail, Suite 300
Indianapolis, Indiana 46250-1684

PREFACE.

THE object of this book is to show the circumstances under which the Federal Constitution was ratified by Pennsylvania. She was the first of the large states to accept the plan that gave the states having a small population an equal representation in the Senate with the others, and her prompt action influenced the result. Had this action been less prompt or less decided, it would have opened the way to dissensions and amendments that would in all probability have caused the rejection of the Constitution, or have sunk it to the level of the Articles of Confederation. Preceded only by Delaware in taking final action on the Constitution, she was the first to undertake its consideration.

Twenty hours after the Continental Congress submitted the Constitution to the States, the Assembly of Pennsylvania called a convention to ratify or reject it. When formally sent out to the people of the State, the "New Plan" at once became the subject of a violent contest, which continued almost to the day when Washington was sworn into office.

The history of this contest has never been written. In 1830 Jonathan Elliot published a collection of the debates that took place in some of the state conventions, and in this collection Pennsylvania was given a place. But what is there set forth as a record of the debate is false to history and discreditable to the industry of Mr. Elliot. The Convention sat from November 21 to December 15, the debate was exhaustive, the adverse views were strongly and ably urged. Yet Mr. Elliot gives only the preliminary proceedings, the speeches of James Wilson and a single speech of Thomas McKean, each in defence of the Constitution. He simply reprinted the small volume published by Thomas Lloyd in 1788, in which all the arguments of the opposition were suppressed.

It is true, the majority of the Convention refused to have their verdict weakened by allowing the minority to enter their reasons of dissent on the Journal; but these reasons with proposed amendments were issued as a broadside, and spread all over the country. They show that the battle was fought out here and conclusions reached that in many cases commended themselves to the majority of the people. The amendments thus unofficially offered were the forerunners of those of Massachusetts and Virginia, and undoubtedly formed the basis of what Mr. Madison laid before the House of Representatives in 1789.

The material for a proper showing of the conduct of the people of Pennsylvania during the struggle over the Federal Constitution in 1787, is plentiful and of two sorts—the official proceedings and debates of the Assembly and the Convention, and the essays, squibs, letters, speeches, etc., that were published from day to day in the Journals and Gazettes.

Of the debates, unhappily, no complete report is in existence. The Convention employed no short-hand reporter to take down what was said, the report begun by Alexander J. Dallas for the Pennsylvania "Herald" was soon suppressed, and from November 30, 1787, the sources of information are some notes by James Wilson, some speeches reported by Thomas Lloyd, and the summaries that appeared in the newspapers. From such material has been constructed the account of the debates in the Convention given in Chapter Fourth, which is probably all that can ever be known. The Journal of the Convention—a bare record of meetings, motions, adjournments, and votes—has not been reprinted for lack of room.

From the squibs and essays, many exceedingly unwise and dry, but all showing forth the popular views of the Constitution, such a selection has been made as seems to fairly represent both the Federal and Antifederal side. Much has been omitted, but whatever has been omitted has generally been said somewhere else in better form.

To preserve the memoirs of the men who were thought fit to represent the people on this occasion, a series of biographical sketches have been added.

Philadelphia, June 9th, 1888.

CONTENTS

CHAPTER I.

THE constitution of the United States, as is well known, was framed during the summer of 1787, by a convention of delegates from twelve States. The convention sat in the old State House at Philadelphia, and after a stormy session of four months, ended its labors on September 17th, 1787. On the afternoon of that day, the constitution duly signed by thirty-nine of the members, some resolutions, and a letter from Washington, were ordered to be sent to Congress, to be by it transmitted to the States.

While these things were taking place in a lower room of the State House, the Legislature of Pennsylvania was in session in a room above, and to it, on the morning of September 18th, the constitution was read. Copies were then given to the press, and the next day the people of Philadelphia were reading the new plan in the "Packet," the "Journal," and the "Gazetteer." For a few days nothing but praise was heard. But, before a week was gone, a writer made bold to attack it in the "Freeman's Journal;" answers were made to him in the "Gazetteer;" more attacks followed, the community was split into two great parties, the names Federal and Antifederal were formally assumed, and a struggle, the most interesting in the early history of the constitution, was commenced.

The new frame of government meanwhile had been presented to Congress, and there, too, had been strongly opposed. Led on by Melanchthon Smith, the New York delegates opposed it to a man. William Grayson, of Virginia, denounced it as too weak. Richard Henry Lee hated it for being too strong, and with him went Nathan Dane, of Massachusetts. To submit such a document to Congress, they held, was absurd. Congress could give it no countenance whatever.

(1)

The proposed constitution was a plan for a new government; a new government could not be set up till the old had been pulled down, and to pull down the old was out of the power of Congress. They were reminded that Congress had sanctioned the meeting of the convention, and told that, if Congress could approve the convention, it could approve the work the convention did. But they would not be convinced, and on September 26th, Lee moved a bill of rights and a long list of amendments. He would have no Vice-President, a council of state to be joined with the President in making appointments, more representatives, and more than a majority to pass an act for the regulation of commerce. His bill and his amendments were not considered, and the next day Lee came forward with a new resolution. This was, that the acts of the convention should be sent to the executives of the States, to be by them laid before their legislatures. Instantly a member from Delaware moved to add the words: "In order to be by them submitted to conventions of delegates to be chosen agreeably to the said resolutions of the convention." The question was taken, and of the twelve States on the floor, all were for the motion save New York, and all save New York and Virginia were so unanimously. It was then moved to urge the legislatures to call state conventions with all the speed they could; but Congress rose, and the matter went over to the next day.

It was now quite clear that neither party could have its own way. The Federalists wished to send the new plan to the States by the undivided vote of Congress. But this they could not do while the New York delegates held out. Lee and his followers wished to send it, if sent at all, without one word of approval. But this they could not do unless the Federalists were willing. When, therefore, Congress again assembled at noon on the 28th, each party gave up something. The Federalists agreed to withhold all words of approval. The Antifederalists agree to unanimity. The amendments offered by Lee on the 26th, and the vote on the 27th, were then expunged from the journal, and the constitution, the resolutions of the convention, and the letter of Washington, were formally sent to the States.

William Bingham of Pennsylvania at once sent off an express to Philadelphia with the news. But the rider had not crossed the ferry to Paulus Hook when the Legislature of Pennsylvania began to act. The Assembly had resolved to adjourn *sine die* on Saturday, September 29th. But the Federalists had determined that before adjournment a state convention to consider the constitution should be called. When, therefore, the day drew near, and no word of approval came from Congress, they took the matter into their own hands, and on Friday morning George Clymer rose in his place, and moved that a state convention of deputies be called, that they meet at Philadelphia, and that they be chosen in the same manner and on the same day as the members of the next General Assembly. Mr. Whitehill, who sat for Cumberland, objected, moved to put off consideration of the matter till afternoon, and provoked a long and bitter debate. The people, it was said, in the State at large knew nothing about the new plan. To inform them before election would be impossible. The matter should be left to the next Assembly. Congress besides had taken no action, and till Congress did, no State could act: the articles of confederation forbade them; they must keep on federal ground. The motion again was unparliamentary. The custom of the Assembly had always been, when important business was to be brought on, to give notice beforehand, have the matter made the order of the day, and have the bill read three times. To now bring on business so important by surprise, and hurry it through without debate, was clearly to serve some bad end.

Such argument, however, could not bring over a single Federalist, and the first of the resolutions,* that calling the convention to meet at Philadelphia, was carried by a vote of forty-three to nineteen. The Assembly then adjourned till four in the afternoon.

Not a few of the minority lodged in the house of Major Boyd, on Sixth street, and there it is likely a plan was laid that came very near being successful. The Assembly consisted of sixty-nine members. Forty-six made a quorum. If, there-

*Chap. II., p. 28.

fore, nineteen kept away there would be no quorum, and if there was no quorum the house would be forced to adjourn with the day for the election of delegates unfixed, and the manner of choosing the members unsettled. It was accordingly arranged that not one of the nineteen should go to the afternoon session, and not one did.

At four o'clock the Assembly met, with the Speaker and every federal member in his place. But all told, they counted only forty-four, and the business could not go on. After waiting a while and no more coming in, the Speaker sent out the sergeant-at-arms to summon the absentees. None would obey, and the house was forced to adjourn to 9 o'clock on Saturday morning.

Meanwhile, the rider sent on by Mr. Bingham came spurring into town with the resolution of Congress submitting the constitution to the States. This, when the Speaker had taken the chair on Saturday, was read to the house. Hoping that the opposition of the minority would now be removed, the sergeant-at-arms and the assistant clerk were dispatched to hunt up the malcontents, show them the resolution, and summon them to attend. The two officers went first to Major Boyd's, where were James M'Calmont, who sat for Franklin, and Jacob Miley, from Dauphin. They were shown the resolution, and stoutly said they would not go. The people, however, decided that they should; broke into their lodgings, seized them, dragged them through the streets to the State House, and thrust them into the assembly room, with clothes torn and faces white with rage. The quorum was now complete.

When the roll had been called and a petition praying for a convention presented and read, Mr. M'Calmont rose, complained of his treatment, and asked to be excused. Some debate followed, in the course of which the rules touching the matter were read. It then appeared that every member who did not answer at roll-call was to be fined 2s. 6d. But when a quorum could not be formed without him, a fine of 5s. was to be imposed. Thereupon Mr. M'Calmont rose, and, taking some silver from his pocket, said, "Well, sir, here is your 5s.

to let me go.'' The gallery broke into a laugh, the Speaker refused the money, and the debate went on till the vote was about to be taken, when Mr. M'Calmont left his seat and made for the door. Instantly the gallery* cried out, ''Stop him.'' The crowd about the door did so; Mr. M'Calmont returned to his seat; the house refused to excuse him, and appointed the first Tuesday in November for the election of delegates.

While these things were happening in the Assembly, the minority were busy preparing an address to the people, which sixteen of the nineteen signed.

The objections of these men were ten in number. The new plan was offensive because it was too costly, because it was to be a government of three branches, because it would ruin state governments or reduce them to corporations, because power of taxation was vested in Congress, because liberty of the press was not assured, because trial by jury was abolished in civil cases, and because the federal judiciary was so formed as to destroy the judiciary of the States. There ought to have been rotation in office, in place of which representatives were to be chosen for two years and senators for six. There ought to have been a declaration of rights, and provision against a standing army. They were at once answered in verse, in squibs, in mock protests, in serious and carefully drawn replies. One such reply came from six of the majority. Another, the longest and the most elaborate of all, was written by Pelatiah Webster. Webster was born at Lebanon, Connecticut, in 1725, and seems to have possessed the traditional versatility of the New England people. At twenty-one he was graduated from Yale college, studied theology, and for two years preached in the town of Greenwich. Wearying of this he turned business man, and went to Philadelphia in 1755. Either the profits were small or the business not to his taste, for in 1763 he accepted the place of

* This word occurs in the newspapers of the day. But the Assembly room contained no gallery. The term, therefore, must be understood in a parliamentary sense, and as referring to the people who stood in a crowd along the wall and around the door.

second English master in the Germantown academy, on a salary of one hundred pounds, proclamation money, a year. This he gave up in 1766, after which time nothing is known concerning him till, in 1776, he published an essay in favor of taxation for the purpose of redeeming the continental bills of credit. The British in 1778 threw him into jail, where he staid six months. As soon as he was free he once more took up the study of continental finance, and began a series of seven essays on "Free Trade and Finance," of which the first appeared in 1779 and the last in 1785. "A Dissertation on the Political Union and Constitution of the Thirteen United States of North America," one of the early efforts towards a more perfect union, appeared in 1783. In 1795 Webster died.

But an answer more decisive than that of Mr. Webster was made by the people at the polls, when the day came for choosing the members of the new Assembly and Council. Then Robert Whitehill, who signed the address as one of the sixteen, and had, in return, been put up for a seat in the Council, was thrown out by the voters of Cumberland county. Samuel Dale, whose name likewise appeared at the foot of the address, and Frederick Antis, who, having voted for the convention in the memorable morning session, went out with the nineteen in the afternoon, each met a like fate in Northumberland.

The election, however, to which the factions looked forward with most concern was that of delegates to the convention. Four weeks were to come and go before this took place, and during these weeks the Antifederalists were all activity. A friend was early found in Eleazer Oswald, who then owned the "Independent Gazetteer, or Chronicle of Freedom," and a champion in the unknown author of the letters of "Centinel."

Who "Centinel" was cannot be known. His letters in their day were ascribed to Oswald, to George Bryan, to almost every Antifederalist of note. But it seems not unlikely that the writer was Samuel Bryan.* Be this as it may, the

* This statement is made on the authority of Mr. Paul Leicester Ford, who

letters deserve the same rank in the list of pieces opposing the constitution, that has been given to the "Federalist" in the list of pieces supporting the constitution.

Eleazer Oswald was a native of Great Britian, and came to this country just at the outbreak of the Revolutionary war. Young, romantic, deeply impressed with the rights of man, he instantly took the part of the colonies, joined their army and fought for them during half the war. He was with Ethen Allen when Ticonderoga was taken, marched with Benedict Arnold to the siege of Quebec, led the forlorn hope on the day Montgomery fell, and took part under Washington in the battle of Monmouth. Of war he now seems to have had enough, for he resigned his commission in 1778, went to Philadelphia, and there, after casting about for something to do, turned tavern keeper and printer, re-opened the London Coffee House, and began the publication of the "Independent Gazetteer." Like most Whigs, he firmly believed the articles of confederation needed to be improved; but the constitution he considered no improvement at all, pronounced it monarchical, and made his paper the receptacle of the fiercest attacks on the new plan and its supporters. It was to the "Gazetteer" that Columbus and Gouvero, Tom Peep and Bye-Stander contributed their squibs, that "Philadelphiensis" sent his observations, and that "Centinel" contributed his twenty-four letters.

Stripped of all bitterness, the arguments of the two parties may be briefly stated. The new plan, said the Antifederalists, is not only a confederation of States, which it ought to be; but a government over individuals, which it ought not to be. Not only may Congress overawe the States, but it can go

has kindly furnished the following piece of information: "At the time of their publication, George Bryan, of Pennsylvania, was charged with the authorship of the letters of Centinel, and as such was the subject of many attacks from the Federalist newspapers; but his son, Samuel Bryan, writing to George Clinton, says: 'I have not the honor of being personally known to your Excellency, but * * * I flatter myself that in the character of Centinel I have been honored with your approbation and esteem.' It appears, however, from the Belknap Papers (II. 24, 35), that Eleazer Oswald, printer of the 'Independent Gazetteer,' was the author of some of the shorter squibs over that pseudonym."

down and lay hold on the life, liberty and property of the meanest citizen in the land. Where powers so extensive are bestowed on a government, the limits of the powers and the rights of the people ought to be clearly defined. Does the constitution do this? Far from it. No safeguards whatever are provided. There is no bill of rights, while trial by jury, that great bulwark of liberty, is carefully done away with in civil cases. Liberty of the press is not secured. Religious toleration is not provided for. There are to be general search warrants, excise laws, a standing army which the constitution does not forbid being quartered on the people. This is serious. For, by one article the "constitution and the laws made in pursuance thereof," are to be "the supreme law of the land." They are, moreover, to be binding on the judges of each State, anything in the constitution or laws of that State to the contrary notwithstanding. Now, the state constitutions provide for liberty of the press, of speech, and of worship. The constitution of the United States does not. A law by Congress abolishing any of these would therefore be in pursuance of the constitution, would be "the supreme law of the land," and would be binding on every state judge in the union.

By another article Congress is to have power to lay taxes, imposts and duties. But so have the States power to lay taxes. How long will it be before all taxation is in the hands of Congress? For, is it not clear that when two powers are given equal command over the purses of the people, they will fight for the spoils? And is it not clear that the weaker will be found to yield to the stronger? And will not Congress be stronger? State sovereignty, so carefully preserved in the articles, is well nigh destroyed in the constitution. The people, not the States, are to be represented in the house, and there every delegate is to vote as a man. Lest the people should derive any benefit from this change, annual elections and rotation in office are to be swept away. A republican form of government is indeed guaranteed, but whoever will take the pains to look will see that it is the form, and not the substance. Innumerable acts of sovereignty are to be taken from the States. They can coin no money, nor regulate their trade, nor derive one shilling from impost duty.

Indeed, there was hardly a provision in the whole constitution of which the Antifederalists could approve. The number of representatives was too small. The Senate was too aristocratic. The jurisdiction of the supreme court was too extensive. The President had powers which, when joined with those of the Senate, were utterly incompatible with liberty.

To strictures such as these a number of replies were made by the Federalists. Some were sarcastic or foolish, and intended merely to provoke a laugh. Some were temperate, and well considered, and of such the best were the speech of James Wilson at the State House, and the essays of "A Federalist," and "Plain Truth."

The occasion of Mr. Wilson's speech was a public meeting in the State House yard, to nominate delegates to the next General Assembly. As it was well known that the business of the meeting would bring a great crowd, the Federalists induced Mr. Wilson to make an address by way of answer to the many charges the Antifederalists had brought against the constitution.

He began by calling on his hearers to recollect that the constitutions of the States were very different instruments from the constitution proposed for the United States. When the people set up their state governments, they gave to their legislatures every right and every power which they did not expressly withhold. But in giving powers to the federal government this principle had been reversed, and the authority of Congress would be determined not by tacit implication, but by positive grant expressed in the constitution. In the case of the state governments, every power not expressly reserved was given. In the case of the proposed federal government, every power not expressly given was reserved.

This distinction being recognized, the objection of those who wished for a bill of rights was answered. A bill of rights was prefixed to the constitution of Pennsylvania, because in such an instrument the reserved powers must be specified, and this specification was done in the bill of rights. No bill of rights had been added to the proposed constitution of the United States, because it was not necessary to sum up the reserved powers, because no power was given unless expressly given, and the collection of express powers was the constitution.

Another objection was that trial by jury in civil cases would be abolished. This was a mistake. The business of the convention that framed the constitution was not local, but general. Its duty was not to meet the views and usages of any one State, but the views and usages of thirteen States. These usages were not common. When, therefore, the federal convention was considering the matter of jury trial, the members found themselves beset with difficulties on every hand. Cases open to a jury in one State were not open to a jury in another. Nowhere were admiralty cases, and such as came up in courts of equity, sent to a panel of twelve. To lay down a general rule was therefore impossible, and the convention wisely gave up the task, and left the matter as it stood, feeling sure no danger could arise.

The charge that the constitution would destroy the state governments was, Mr. Wilson held, refuted by the constitution itself. Was not the President to be chosen by electors? and was not the manner of choosing the electors to be determined by the legislatures of the States? Were not the senators to be elected by the state legislatures? Were not the qualifications of an elector of representatives to be the same as "the qualifications requisite for electors of the most numerous branch of the state legislature?" Did it not follow then that if the legislatures were destroyed no President could be chosen, no senators elected, no represenatives voted for?

Mr. Wilson then went on to refute the charges of "a standing army in time of peace," and of "the baleful aristocracy in the United States Senate." He ended his speech with the statement that the men who opposed the constitution did so from personal, not patriotic motives. They were, he said, placemen, tax collectors and excisemen, who, should the new plan go into effect, would be turned out of office by the abolition, or transfer to the federal government of the places they held under the State.*

The speech was hailed by the Federalists as final, and provoked the Antifederalists to make innumerable replies. "Centinel" devoted a whole letter to answering it. From New York came a series of long letters in reply. "A Democratic Federalist" labored hard to refute him.

Others, who could not answer, began to call names. "An officer of the late Continental army" described the speech as a "train of pitiful sophistries, unworthy of the man who uttered them." One bitter lampooner nick-named him "James de Caledonia." Another vilified him as "Jimmy." A third summed up his objections to the constitution with the remark that such a haughty aristocrat as Mr. Wilson having approved the new plan, was the best reason in the world why the people should reject it.

This, it was said, might possibly be so, if Mr. Wilson were the only signer of the constitution. But he was not. His was but one name in a long list of great names. Had it not been signed by a Washington, and did there live a villain so black-hearted as to assert that the American Fabius was now seeking to destroy the liberties he had done so much to secure? Had not Franklin signed it, and did any one suppose that he would close a long and splendid career by recommending to his countrymen an infamous constitution? Had it not been signed by a Morris and a Sherman? The Antifederalists admitted that it had, but warned the people not to be blinded by the glamour of great names. Were there not names, as great as any at the foot of the constitution, to be seen at the foot of the articles of confederation articles

---

*Gouverneur Morris in a letter to Washington makes the same statement. There had, he wrote, been reason to "dread the cold and sour temper of the back counties, and still more the wicked industry of those who have long habituated themselves to live on the public, and cannot bear the idea of being removed from the power and profit of State government, which has .been and still is the means of supporting themselves, their families and dependents, and (which perhaps is equally grateful) of depressing and humbling their political adversaries."

now declared to be thoroughly bad? Nay, had not some of the very men who put their hands to the one, put their hands to the other? Had not Roger Sherman, and Robert Morris, and Gouverneur Morris, recommended the confederation? What, then, was the value of these boasted great names? If these patriots had erred once, what was to hinder them from erring twice? "Centinel" went so far as to make some remarks on Washington and Franklin, which the Federalists interpreted to mean that Washington was a fool from nature and Franklin a fool from old age. The abuse of the "great names" once begun, no one was spared. The whole list of signers was gone through with. Robert Morris was "Bobby the Cofferer," and was said to be for the constitution because he hoped the new government would wipe out the debts he owed the old. Thomas Mifflin was "Tommy the Quartermaster General," and gave his support because his accounts were 400,000 dollars short. Gouverneur Morris was "Gouvero the cunning man." Few was sneered at as a bricklayer. Telfair was accused of having been a Tory. Baldwin was twitted with having once been steward of Princeton college, which was false. To the convention was given the nickname of the dark conclave.

The hatred was most bitter, however, toward the eight who signed for Pennsylvania. Indeed, so loud was the outcry against them, that when the time came to nominate delegates to the state convention, it was thought best that James Wilson should be the only one put up. The precaution was unnecessary, for in Philadelphia the Federalists carried everything.

Election day was the sixth of November. Five delegates were to be chosen from the city of Philadelphia, and when the polls were closed at the State House, it appeared that the Antifederalists had suffered a crushing defeat. The name standing highest on the federal ticket received twelve hundred and fifteen votes, and the name that stood lowest, eleven hundred and fifty-seven votes. For Pettit, who headed the antifederal ticket, one hundred and fifty votes were cast, while Irvine, who stood at the bottom, was given one hundred and thirty-two. Franklin, it is true, ran far ahead of Pettit; but he was in no sense an Antifederalist, and was well known to have little sympathy for the party that used his name. He had not been nominated by the Federalists, partly, as was explained, because he was old and feeble, but chiefly because he was still president of the commonwealth, and it was not thought fit that any officer of the State should sit in the convention. The Antifederalists accordingly used his great name in the hope of drawing votes. But the ruse was detected, and though some votes were drawn, they were for him and not for the ticket. He received two hundred and thirty-five.

The Federalists were greatly elated over their victory, and after midnight on election day a score or so of tipsy revellers went to the house of Major Boyd, where lived John Smilie, John Baird, Abraham Smith, James M'Calmont, James Mc-Lean, John Piper and William Findley, members of the legislature and noted Antifederalists, every one of them. Four had signed the address of the sixteen dissenting assemblymen. All had strongly opposed the calling of a state convention; all were detested by the mob which gathered before the house, broke the door, flung stones through the windows, and went off reviling the inmates by name. Enraged at the insult, they complained to the legislature. The Assembly asked the "Executive Council" to offer a reward. The council did so, and Franklin promptly issued a proclamation offering three hundred dollars for the capture and punishment of the offenders. The proclamation was mere matter of form. No search was made, no rioter was arrested, and the delegates chosen to the convention met at the State House on Wednesday, the twenty-first of November, when sixty of the sixty-nine members were present.

The sixty who, on that day, answered to their names, made up a body as characteristic of the State as has ever been gathered. Scarcely a sect, or creed, or nationality in the commonwealth, but had at least one representative on the floor of the convention. Some were Moravians; some were Lutherans; some Episcopalians; some Quakers; most were Presbyterians. Some were of German descent. The ances-

tors of others had but a generation or two before come over
from Scotland or England, or Ireland, or that part of Ireland
made famous by the Scotch.   One had sat in the "Council of
Censors."   Three had been members of Assembly.   Eleven
had been judges, or justices of the peace.   As many more had
been Revolutionary officers.   Scarce one but had taken some
part in the struggle for Independence.   One had received subscriptions to the continental loan.   Others had served on committees of observation, or had been members of the "Flying
Camp."   One had served with Washington and Braddock.
Another had been turned out of meeting for taking arms in
the good cause.   Five in time acquired national fame.   From
the city of Philadelphia came Benjamin Rush, and James
Wilson, and Thomas M'Kean.   Chester sent Anthony Wayne.
From Luzerne came Timothy Pickering, postmaster general,
secretary of war, and secretary of state under Washington,
secretary of state under Adams, senator from Massachusetts,
and to the day of his death the bitterest, the most implacable
of Federalists.

   Of the proceedings of the convention no full and satisfactory record is known to exist.   For our knowledge of what
was said and done we are indebted to the journal kept by the
secretary of the convention, to the report of a few speeches
taken down in shorthand by Thomas Lloyd, to the reports
and summaries of the debates that appeared in the newspapers, and to the notes jotted down by Wilson and intended
to be used by him as the subjects of replies and speeches.
The minutes are exceedingly meagre; but from them it appears
that Thomas Lloyd applied to the convention for the place of
assistant clerk.   Lloyd was a shorthand writer of considerable
note, and, when the convention refused his request, determined
to report the debates and print them on his own account.   His
advertisement promised that the debates should be accurately
taken in shorthand, and published in one volume octavo at
the rate of one dollar the hundred pages.   These fine promises, however, were never fulfilled.   Only one thin volume ever
came out, and that contains merely the speeches of Wilson
and a few of those of Thomas M'Kean.   The reason is not

far to seek. He was bought up by the Federalists, and, in order to satisfy the public, was suffered to publish one volume containing nothing but speeches made by the two federal leaders.

That the debates were thus suppressed may be considered as reasonably well-established. When the convention began its work, the "Packet" and the "Gazetteer," the "Journal" and the "Gazette" printed short summaries of each day's doings. The "Herald," however, published long and full reports, now known to have been the work of Alexander James Dallas. Mr. Dallas was then a young man, and was employed by William Spotswood to edit his two publications, the "Pennsylvania Herald" and the "Columbian Magazine." So good were his reports that all the newspapers copied them, till January 6, 1788, having reached the debate of November 30th, they suddenly stopped. No word of explanation was offered by the "Herald;" but "Centinel" declares they were stopped by the efforts of the Federalists, a charge which gains much likelihood from the facts that in February, 1788, the "Herald" ceased to be published and that the Federalists withdrew their subscriptions from every publication that warmly supported the Antifederal cause.*

* Benjamin Rush, himself a Federalist, asserts in a letter to Noah Webster (Febeuary 13, 1788): "From the impudent conduct of Mr. Dallas in misrepresenting the proceedings and speeches in the Pennsylvania convention, as well as from his deficiency of matter, the "Columbian Magazine," of which he is editor, is in the decline." For this extract we are again indebted to Mr. Paul Leicester Ford.

Complaints of the same kind are made by Mr. Oswald day after day in the "Gazetteer:" "The printer, having most pressing calls for money, is again impelled to request that the subscribers to his newspaper be so kind as to discharge their respective balances. And those who have been so *very liberal* as to withdraw their subscriptions and support (and having NOT settled) because he chose, in the present great political controversy, to act with his usual impartiality, by publishing freely on both sides the question, are particularly requested to call and pay off their arrearages.

"He, however, for the present, chooses to suppress the ideas that occur to him on this occasion and shall therefore only remind those *high-flying* tools, *pigmies*, and tiffanies of power and the prevailing party, those boasted friends of freedom and liberty of the press, that 'the tables' may, in the course of human events, be again turned, and that 'the race is not always to the *swift*, nor the battle to the strong.'"

From the first it was plain that in the convention the burden of debate would fall upon the Antifederalists, and by them the lead was gladly given to Whitehill, Findley and Smilie, who came from the counties of Cumberland, Westmoreland and Fayette. The Federalists looked up for leadership to Wilson and M'Kean. Indeed, it was M'Kean who, when a speaker had been chosen, and the rules approved, opened the business of the convention by moving that the constitution be adopted as the federal convention had framed it. Wilson supported him in a long and characteristic oration. Smilie attacked him in a speech which made up in bitterness what it lacked in length. Others followed, and a whole week was spent in debating motions to take up the constitution article by article in convention; to take it up by articles and sections in committee of the whole; to give each member the right when the yeas and nays were called to enter the reasons of his vote on the journals. The first alone prevailed. On each the vote was twenty-four to forty-four; nor did it, on any question that came before the convention at any time, materially change. Never did the majority have more than forty-six. Never did the minority have less than twenty-three.

These questions settled, Mr. Wilson took up the preamble, and opened a long debate on the kind of government proposed to be set up. Findley and Smilie and Whitehill declared that it would be a consolidation, and not a confederation of the States, and gave reasons for this belief. It would be a consolidated government because in the preamble were the words "We the People," and not "We the States," which showed it to be a compact between individuals forming a society, and not between sovereign States forming a government; because in Congress the votes were cast by individuals, and not by States; because the taxing power of the federal body would destroy state sovereignties, as two independent and sovereign taxing powers could not exist in one community; because Congress could regulate elections; because the judiciary was co-extensive with the legislative power; because congressmen were to be paid out of the national, and not out of the state treasury; because there was no bill of rights, no annual elections, and power to make all laws necessary to put the constitution into effect. Under such a plan it was simply impossible for a confederation to exist. The moment it went into operation, that moment state sovereignty was ended. Stripped of every lucrative source of taxation, deprived of innumerable rights and powers, the States would sink to mere corporations doing such things as the laws and treaties of Congress would permit.

To this one ardent Federalist made reply that he hoped they would sink to mere corporations. Plurality of sovereignty was in politics what plurality of gods was in religion. It was the idolatry, the heathenism of government. But the duty of defending the constitution fell chiefly to Mr. Wilson, and the arguments of Mr. Wilson were more forcible and direct. Those, he said, who opposed the new plan did so on the ground that the sovereign power was in the States as governments. Those who supported the constitution, on the other hand, did so because they believed that sovereignty was in the people; that the people had not, meant not, and ought not to part with it to any government on earth; that, having it in their own hands, the people could delegate it in such quantity, to such bodies, and on such terms, and under such limitations, as they saw fit. This doctrine was far from new. Indeed, the people had boldly asserted it in that grand passage of the Declaration of Independence which says: "We hold these truths to be self evident, that all men are created equal; that they are endowed of their creator with certain unalienable rights; that among these, are life, liberty, and the pursuit of happiness. That, to secure these rights, *governments* are instituted among men, *deriving their just powers from the consent of the governed;* that, whenever any form of government becomes destructive of these ends, it is the *right of the people* to *alter* or *abolish* it, and to institute a *new* government, laying its foundation on such principles, and *organizing its powers in such form* as to them shall seem most likely to effect their safety and happiness." On this broad basis independence was asserted and on this basis the people had acted ever since. Exercising the rights there affirmed, they had first set up state governments, and then a government of confederated States, which, again using their old rights, they now proposed to supplant by a new government " *laying its foundation on such principles, organizing its powers in such form* as to them" seemed fitting. That the world might know by whose act this was done, a preamble had been added to the new plan distinctly stating that " *We, the People,*" the people in whose hands is all sovereignty, the people who, under God, alone have the right to pull down and set up governments, do ordain, and establish the constitution. To say then, that the new plan is one for a consolidated, and not a confederated government, because it comes from "We, the People" and not from "We, the States," was to talk nonsense. The words were there to express two great truths, that all governments are created by the people, and for the people, and that this particular form of government had been so formed.

Again and again Mr. Wilson called on the opposition to define what they meant by a consolidated government. Mr. Findley answered that it was a government "which put the thirteen States into one." Mr. Smilie defined it as one that took the sovereignty from the state governments and gave it to a general government. Mr. Whitehill would give no definition at all. Taking up such as were given, Mr. Wilson declared that the States possessed no sovereignty, and that, therefore, none could be taken from them. They were governments of delegated powers, and nothing more. Some of these powers were, indeed, to be taken away, or recalled, by the sovereign people. But in every case a power so transferred was a power that had been long and shamefully abused. They could issue no more paper money; make no more tender laws; no longer treat the just requisitions of Congress with contempt. Weary of seeing Congress enact laws which no one obeyed, pass judgments the States refused to heed, the people had given to the new government executive and judicial as well as legislative power. Weary of seeing the States taxing, and burdening, and ruining the commerce of each other, the people had recalled the delegated right to lay impost duties, and in the new plan had given it to Congress.

The clamor raised about a bill of rights was pronounced idle. Were the States sovereign, doling out to the people such rights as the people could exact, the need of such a bill would indeed have been great. But they were not sovereign, they possessed no power not given. What reason was there then for the people to demand that they should be left secure in the enjoyment of their sovereign, undelegated powers?

From the character of the constitution as a whole the debate drifted off to the particular articles, and objection after objection was raised by the opposition. The Vice-President was a needless and dangerous officer. The Senate ought not to make treaties, nor try impeachments, nor have a share in the appointing power; nor its members be elected for so long a term as six years. Representation in the house was too small. The power of Congress was too great. It could borrow money, keep up a standing army, lay taxes, deprive electors of a fair choice of their representatives, call out the militia, and make all laws necessary to put these powers into execution. The President ought not to have the pardoning power. Trial by jury was not secure. It seemed, indeed, as if the whole plan of government was, in the opinion of the opposition, bad. This Mr. Findley protested was not the case. The opposition had no wish to reject it. A few amendments would remove every objection, and these Mr. Whitehill presented to the convention on the morning of the twelfth of December. They were fifteen in number, and are remarkable as containing the substance of the ten amendments afterwards added to the constitution. Similarity so marked cannot be accidental. There is much reason, therefore, to believe that when Madison, in 1789, drew up the amendments for the House of Representatives, he made use of those offered by the minority of the convention of Pennsylvania.

But the majority of the convention had no wish to use them, and, when the motion was made to adjourn to some future day, that the people might consider them, it was voted down by forty-six to twenty-three. By precisely the same vote, the constitution, just as it came from the body that framed it, was ratified a few minutes later. Without waiting to sign,

the convention, joined by the President and Vice-President of
the State, the constables, the sub-sheriffs, the high-sheriff,
the judges, the members of council, and all the state dignita-
ries, both civil and military, went in procession the following
day to the State House, and there read the ratification to a
great gathering of the people.   On Saturday the 15th of December the convention adjourned.

And now the minority published their address and reasons
of dissent.   It was not, they said, till the close of the late
glorious contest that any fault was found with the articles of
confederation.   Then the wants which, during the war, had
been supplied by the virtue and patriotism of the people, began to be apparent.   Then it was felt on every hand that
it would be well for the union to enlarge the powers of Congress, and suffer that body to regulate commerce, and lay and
collect duties throughout the United States.   With this in
view, Virginia proposed and Congress urged a convention of
deputies to revise and amend the articles of confederation,
and make them suited to the needs of the union.   So hastily
and eagerly did the States comply, that their legislatures, without the slightest authority, without ever stopping to consult
the people, appointed delegates, and the conclave met at Philadelphia.   To it came a few men of character, some more
noted for cunning than patriotism, and some who had always
been enemies to the independence of America.

The doors were shut, secrecy was enjoined, and what then
took place no man could tell.   But it was well known that the
sittings were far from harmonious.   Some left the dark conclave before the instrument was framed.   Some had the firmness to withhold their hands when it was framed.   But it
came forth in spite of them, and was not many hours old
when the meaner tools of despotism were carrying petitions
about for the people to sign, praying the legislature to call a
convention to consider it.   The convention was called by
a legislature made up in part of members who had been
dragged to their seats and kept there against their wills, and
so early a day was set for the election of delegates that many
a voter did not know of it till it was passed.   Others kept

away from the polls because they were ignorant of the new plan; some because they disliked it, and some because they did not think the convention legally called. Of the seventy thousand freemen entitled to vote but thirteen thousand voted.

Having given a history of the two conventions, the addressers repeated the fifteen amendments they offered in convention, and summed up their reasons of dissent under three general heads. They dissented because so wide a domain could never be governed save by a confederation of republics having all the powers of internal government, but united in the management of their general and foreign concerns. They dissented because the powers vested in Congress would break down the sovereignty of the States, and put up on their ruins a consolidated government, "an iron-handed despotism." They dissented because there was no bill of rights securing trial by jury, *habeas corpus*, liberty of conscience, and freedom of the press. Twenty-one of the twenty-three minority signed the address.

An examination of this list reveals the fact that the little band of malcontents was made up of all the delegates from the counties of Cumberland, Berks, Westmoreland, Bedford, Dauphin, Fayette, half of those from Washington, half from Franklin, and John Whitehill, of Lancaster. The reason is plain. The constitution proposed for the United States was in many ways the direct opposite of the constitution of Pennsylvania. The legislature of Pennsylvania consisted of a single house. The legislature of the United States was to consist of two houses. The President of Pennsylvania was chosen by the Assembly. The President of the United States was chosen by special electors. The constitution of Pennsylvania had a bill of rights, provided for a body of censors to meet once each seven years to approve or disapprove the acts of the legislature; for a council to advise the President; for annual elections; for rotation in office, all of which were quite unknown to the proposed constitution for the United States. But the Pennsylvania constitution of 1776 was the work of the patriot party; of this party a very considerable number were Presbyterians; and the great Presbyterian counties were Cumberland, Westmoreland, Bedford, Dauphin and Fayette. In opposing the new plan these men simply opposed a system of government which, if adopted, would force them to undo a piece of work done with great labor, and beheld with great pride and satisfaction. Every man, therefore, who gave his vote for the ratification of the national constitution, pronounced his state constitution to be bad in form, and this its supporters were not prepared to do. By these men, the refusal of the convention to accept the amendments they offered was not regarded as ending the matter. They went back to the counties that sent them more determined than ever but failed to gain to their side the great body of Presbyterians.

Elsewhere the action of the convention was heartily approved. At Lancaster the delegates were received with bell ringing and discharge of cannon. At Easton the delegates from Northampton county held a meeting, and issued an address to their constituents giving nine reasons why they voted for ratification. The state of the union required a concentration of the powers of government for general purposes. The proposed constitution provided for such a concentration in the best form that could be agreed on. Under it commerce would be restored to its former prosperity, agriculture would flourish, taxes be cut down, manufactures and the arts would be recognized, and the public creditors duly paid. There would be no more bloody contests between neighboring States over boundaries and territories; no more paper money and tender laws; no more partial laws of any kind. The delegates from Northampton were sure their constituents could not fail to approve so good a plan of government, and in this belief they were not mistaken.

While these things were happening in Pennsylvania, the convention of New Jersey met and ratified the constitution without one dissenting voice. Delaware had already done so, and these two with Pennsylvania made one-third of the number of States necessary to put the new plan into force. This continued success the Federalists of Carlisle determined should be duly celebrated, and chose the last Wednesday in December as the day, secured a cannon, and made a great pile of barrels for a bonfire on the public square; but no sooner were they assembled than a mob of Antifederalists attacked them, drove them from the ground, spiked the cannon, burned a copy of the constitution, and went off shouting "Damnation to the forty-six; long live the virtuous twenty-three." On the morrow the Federalists, fully armed, again met and carried out their celebration. When they had finished, the Antifederalists in turn appeared and burned two effigies, labelled, "Thomas M'Kean, Chief Justice," and "James Wilson, the Caledonian." Twenty of the rioters were in time arrested, but were speedily set at liberty by men chosen for that purpose by the companies of militia.

Thus stirred up, the excitement spread over all the antifederal counties. The country beyond the mountains was wholly in the hands of the Antifederalists. While the legislature was in session in September, a petition against the state convention was passed round in the two counties of Franklin and Cumberland, and soon bore four thousand signatures. So overwhelming was the number of the Antifederalists that the few Federalists did not think it worth while to make any demonstration at all. In Fayette county, at a great county meeting, but two supporters of the constitution appeared; in Bedford county, in the mountains, the number was estimated at twenty; in Huntingdon county not above thirty; in Dauphin, in the middle country, less than one hundred; in Berks, where the taxable inhabitants were nearly five thousand, the number of active Federalists was put down at fifty*. Through all these counties associations and societies were formed for the purpose of opposing the constitution, and committees of correspondence appointed to secure unity of action. Such action was greatly needed, for their chances of success grew smaller and smaller every day. In January came news that Georgia had ratified unanimously, and hard upon this the news that Connecticut had accepted the constitution by a vote of more than three to one. February 6th

* "Centinel," Letter 18.

the convention of Massachusetts approved the constitution by a majority of nineteen. This was most disheartening; for in no State did the chances of the Antifederalists seem better than in Massachusetts. There was the home of Shays, and there the people had within a year risen up in armed resistance to the authority of the State.

Amazed and angry at their defeat in New England, the Antifederalists began to cast about them for the cause, and soon found it in the management of the post-office. As the law then stood, newspapers were not mailable. The postmasters could officially have nothing to do with them. Neither could the post-riders be forced to carry newspapers in their portmanteaux. For the convenience to the public, however, the postmaster had suffered the riders to carry the Gazetteer and Packet, bargain with the printers about the postage, and put the money thus received in their own pockets. For a like reason the postmasters in the great towns undertook to distribute the newspapers, and were given, as the price of their labor, a paper by each printer. The suppression of a batch of Gazetteers or Journals was therefore an easy matter, and a question merely of money on the one hand and honesty on the other. If the bribe were large enough, and the rider or the postmaster dishonest enough, the thing could be done. That it was done in this particular instance is doubtful. The charge of the Antifederalists rested on three counts. The first was that while the convention of Pennsylvania was in session, New York newspapers full of most important reading had been stopped, and held back for weeks. To refute this the Federalists drew up a paper stating that while the convention was sitting the newspapers had come as usual. Most of the Philadelphia printers signed it. But the printer of the Freeman's Journal refused, and named seven consecutive numbers of Greenleaf's New York Journal which he stoutly maintained had not reached the city till the convention had risen. Some of these were most important, as they contained the essays of Brutus, Cato, and Cincinnatus. That containing the fifth number of the address of Cincinnatus to James Wilson was, he claimed, especially hateful to the Federalists, as it was full of information about the way in which " Bobby the Cofferer " had conducted the finances of the union. This paper was printed in the New York Journal of November twenty-ninth; but not a copy reached Philadelphia till December fifteenth, two days after the ratification of the constitution had been proclaimed from the State House.

The second count was, that information which would surely have changed many votes in the conventions of Massachusetts and Connecticut was purposely held back. Since the new year came in, printers in the eastern States had not seen a newspaper published south of New York. No one in Boston, therefore, had read a line of the masterly address and reasons of dissent of the minority of the convention of Pennsylvania, or so much as knew that there had been a minority.

The third count was, that the address and reasons of dissent of the minority of the convention of Pennsylvania had been published in pamphlet form, and a copy sent through the post-office to the address of every printer in the United States; yet not a copy, so far as could be learned, had ever been received by the persons to whom it had been sent. The post-office was clearly the cause of this. It was in the hands of the " well born," and these sons of power were determined that no newspaper should get out of the office in which it was dropped unless it contained fulsome praise of the new roof about to be put up to cover them and all the office-seekers of the continent. So much was made of this charge that the postmaster found it necessary to send out a circular in which he reminded the people that the post-office had nothing to do with the delivery of newspapers, and if they went astray the printers must look to the riders for redress, and not to him.

That the strictures of Cincinnattus could have changed a vote in the Pennsylvania convention, or the reasons of dissent have had any effect on the convention of Massachusetts, had both been promptly delivered, is not at all likely. Yet neither party ceased to strive to win supporters in the still doubtful States. The Federalists filled the columns of their newspapers with squibs and essays, and collected money

to send hundreds of copies to New York, to Virginia, to
Maryland, and even to South Carolina. Now it was the
New Roof by Francis Hopkinson; now the letters of "Conciliator," and a "Freeman," a series of essays the Antifederalists declared could have been the work of no one but
James Wilson. The Antifederalists seem to have made use
chiefly of committees of correspondence, a piece of political
machinery so effective in the early days of the Revolution.

Their efforts, however, were vain, and not a month went
by but another pillar, as the phrase went, was added to the
New Roof. Maryland ratified in April, and South Carolina
in May. In June came New Hampshire, and Virginia, and
the needed list of nine States was more than completed.

It was on the evening of the second of July that a post-
rider brought to Philadelphia the news that Virginia, the
tenth State, had accepted the new plan. The Federalists
had already determined that the coming fourth of July should
be a day of unusual rejoicing. But their zeal now burned
more fiercely than ever, and it was resolved that besides the
toasts and the speeches there should be a procession, and the
finest procession the city had ever beheld.

Though the "New Roof" was now up and Pennsylvania
under it, the Antifederalists were not disheartened. The societies, the committees and the associations in the western
counties were as active as ever, and a call for a state convention at Harrisburg was soon passing about among them.
September 3d was fixed as the day, and on that day thirty-
three delegates, representing every county of the State save
York and Montgomery, were present in the convention. Before they adjourned resolutions were adopted and an address
prepared, urging the legislature to apply to Congress for a
revision and amendment of the constitution by a new federal
convention. With this their active opposition ended.

CHAPTER II.

ON Friday, September 28th, after the House of Assembly had attended to some minor business, Mr. George Clymer rose and said:* The House cannot, Sir, have forgotten a business of the highest magnitude, which was recommended to their attention by the federal convention, and I am persuaded they will readily concur in taking the necessary measures for calling a convention of the citizens of Pennsylvania, to deliberate upon that plan of government which has been presented to this house; for which reason I shall submit the following resolutions:†

WHEREAS the convention of deputies from the several States composing the Union lately held in this city, have published a constitution for the future government of the United States, to be submitted to conventions of deputies chosen in each State by the people thereof, under recommendation of its Legislature, for their assent and ratification.

And whereas it is the sense of great numbers of the good people of this State, already signified in petitions and declarations to this House, that the earliest step should be taken to assemble a convention within the State, for the purpose of deliberating and determining on the said constitution.

Resolved, That it be recommended to such inhabitants of the State as are entitled to vote for representatives to the General Assembly, that they choose suitable persons to serve as Deputies in a State convention, for the purpose herein before mentioned; that is, for the city of *Philadelphia* and the counties respectively, the same number of Deputies that each is entitled to of representatives in the General Assembly. That the election for Deputies as aforesaid be held at the several places in the said city and counties, as are fixed by law for holding the elections of representatives to the General Assembly, and that they be conducted under the same officers, and according to the regulations prescribed by law for holding the elections for

---

* From Proceedings and Debates of the General Assembly of Pennsylvania, taken in short-hand by Thomas Lloyd. Philadelphia, 1787. Vol. I., p. 115.

† These Resolutions are copied from the Minutes of the Assembly. Those in Lloyd's debates are given in the language in which the resolutions were finally passed, with the exception of the time of holding the election.

said Representatives, and at the times herein mentioned, viz. For the city of *Philadelphia*, the counties of *Philadelphia, Chester, Bucks, Lancaster, Berks, Montgomery, Northampton, Northumberland, Dauphin, Luzerne, York, Cumberland and Franklin* on the day of the general election of Representatives to the General Assembly. For the counties of *Bedford, Huntingdon, Westmoreland, Fayette* and *Washington*, on the —— day of *October*. That the persons so elected to serve in Convention shall assemble on the last day of *November*, at the State House in the city of *Philadelphia*. That the proposition submitted to this House by the Deputies of *Pennsylvania* in the General Convention of the States, of ceding to the United States a district of country within this State, for the seat of the General Government, and for the exclusive legislation of Congress, be particularly recommended to the consideration of the Convention.

That it be recommended to the succeeding House of Assembly, to provide for the payment of any extraordinary expenses which may be incurred by holding the said election of Deputies.

These resolutions being seconded by Mr. Wynkoop, they were by agreement stated as distinct propositions, and on the question will the House agree to the following:

Resolved, That it be recommended to such of the inhabitants of the State as are entitled to vote for representatives to the General Assembly, that they choose suitable persons to serve as deputies in a State Convention, for the purpose hereinbefore mentioned; that is, for the city of Philadelphia and the counties respectively, the same number of deputies that each state is entitled to of representatives in the General Assembly.

Resolved, That the elections for Deputies as aforesaid be held at the several places in the said city and counties, as are fixed by law for holding the elections of representatives to the General Assembly, and that the same be conducted by the officers who conduct the said elections of representatives, and agreeably to the rules and regulations thereof.

Mr. Whitehill answered *No*. He then rose and said: The House, Sir, ought to have time to *consider* on this subject before they determine; for which reason I move to postpone *the consideration* until we meet again, and that may be this afternoon, as the session is drawing so near to a close.

Mr. Fitzsimons. I will submit it to the House whether it is proper to delay this business for the reason assigned by the member from Cumberland.* If the gentlemen are not prepared to say what time the election for delegates shall be held, at least the general principle, or that such convention is proper, must be well enough understood to warrant an im-

* Mr. Whitehill.

mediate determination. It will be observed that the ordinary business of the state is pretty well gone through, and the House likely to dissolve to-morrow. But the subject brought forward by my worthy colleague is a business of the highest consequence, and the House must see how eligible it will be to give it the sanction of the Legislature. The only object of consideration is, whether the election shall be held with that propriety which may perhaps be best effected by the representatives pointing out the mode for the conduct of the people. We are not, I conceive, to consider whether calling a convention is proper or improper, because that I look upon as a measure inevitable, even should not the Assembly consent —but it will be well for us to appoint the mode by which such choice shall be conducted. These are distinct propositions, and on the first every gentleman must have determined, but on the other every member will have an opportunity of offering his reasons, when it comes before us in the next resolution. Perhaps, Sir, it may be necessary to alter the times, from what is there mentioned, to more distant periods; of this the gentlemen from the several counties will be better able to judge than I can pretend to, and I am sure I shall give no opposition to every reasonable extension of the time. I hope it will not be thought necessary that anything should be said in commendation of the new constitution prepared for the government of the United States. This, Sir, is not the object of our discussion or deliberation, and was it, I think, Sir, my abilities could not enable me to do justice to the subject; but the feelings of every member will more forcibly convince his judgment than all the argument which could be offered. From the number of petitions on your table, it may be clearly inferred that it is the wish and expectation of the people that this House should adopt speedy measures for calling a convention: I do not, therefore, see a necessity for saying much on a subject so well felt and understood within and without, but cheerfully submit it to the members to say whether they will proceed now or in the afternoon.

Mr. D. Clymer. The worthy gentleman * from the city has

* Mr. Fitzsimons.

submitted the subject to the feelings of the House, and I
agree with him argument will not more clearly show the advantage that must result from the adoption of the federal
constitution, than what suggests to the mind of every person
within these walls; nor have I a doubt, Sir, but every member will do justice to those feelings, and cheerfully assent to
calling a convention for their own as well as for the future
happiness and welfare of the citizens of Pennsylvania. The
gentleman observes it is the general wish of the people that
we should go forward in the measure. Here, Sir, I firmly
believe him, for I think it has but few opposers, very few indeed. I have heard, Sir, that only four or five leading party-
men in this city are against it, whose names I should be glad
to know, that their characters might be examined; for I am
confident they will be hereafter ashamed to show their faces
among the good people whose future prosperity they wish to
blast in the bud. The reason of their opposition, though not
positively known, can be well conjectured; and let them be
careful, lest they draw upon themselves the odium of that
people who have long indulged their rioting upon public
favor. But, Sir, the adoption of this measure is a matter of
so much consequence to America that I am satisfied it will
meet the hearty concurrence of this House.

Mr. Findley. Whatever gentlemen say with respect to the
importance of this subject, is argument to prove that we
should go into it with deliberation. And if it is of so much
importance, and so well understood out of doors, the House
then certainly ought not to be surprised into it. The gentleman from Berks has spoken warmly against opposing the
present measure in a manner as if intended to prevent men
from speaking their minds. He has charged some leading
characters in this city with giving opposition; if he means me
as one of them—(Mr. D. Clymer interrupted him, addressing
the Speaker with No, Sir, upon my honor, I did not mean
him.) Well then, I don't consider that part of his speech as
not addressed to the House, but merely to the gallery. But,
Sir, I consider what has been said of the wishes of the people
as applying to the plan of government, and not to the present

question. If I understand it right, we are not at present to
judge of the merits of the plan, but on the proper and adequate measure of conducting the people into it. Of the plan I
believe there can be no doubt of its being wisely calculated
for the purposes intended; but nothing is perfect, and this
may be as well as could be expected, and I consider it as very
deserving the commendation it received. But this can be no
reason for hurrying on the measure with such precipitancy;
if it is of the importance it is said to be, surely the House will
not refuse to postpone for the present, in order that there may
be time to make it as agreeable as possible.

Mr. D. Clymer. I said, Sir, the matter was well understood, if we might judge from the sentiments of the people,
and there was but little opposition, and that from a few men,
who will be ashamed hereafter to come forward and avow
their secret machinations; so, Sir, I say still—nor can any gentleman aver to the contrary. With respect to the postponement of the business till the afternoon, I will ask where is
the necessity? Every member must be confident, that with
or without his consent, the measure will be adopted; for it is
too generally agreeable, and too highly recommended, to be
assassinated by the hand of intrigue and cabal. And if it
must be adopted, why can it not be done as well this morning
as in the afternoon? Or do some gentlemen want an opportunity of consulting with their associates, how far it is agreeable? If there are objections to the time of holding elections,
it may be altered. I think sufficient time is not allowed to
the county which I am honored by representing; many others
may be in the same predicament, but this can be accommodated—yet the general principle is so clear that nothing is
left for consideration or discussion.

Mr. Wynkoop. I suppose, Sir, there is not a member in
this House but what has pretty fully considered the present
business. This I am led to believe from its importance, and
the length of time which has elapsed since it was communicated to the House. Now if every member has made up his
mind, what reason can there be for further consideration?
And if the members do not declare they have not yet made

up their minds on the propriety of calling a convention, I shall vote for going on with the business.

Mr. Whitehill. It is very well known, that this business is a matter of great importance, and deserves the serious attention of the House—But however well the people may be said to be acquainted with the design and intention, yet I don't know how far that may be the case. This, Sir, is a very large and extensive State, and I may venture to say, that so far from being the general voice of the people, that not one in twenty know any thing about it. I believe a great many people in and about the city, have signed petitions in favor of it—but that is but a small part of the whole State.

But to waive the question on the propriety of the measure, it will appear clear, Sir, when we come to consider whether it should be held in so many distant counties on the day of the general election, that it cannot be done; and the members ought to have an opportunity of asking or consulting themselves on that, which would be more proper.

The gentlemen that have brought forward this motion, must have some design, as they cannot digest the postponement, or why not leave the members at liberty to consult, or acquire further information? If this is a concerted plan, and it must go through as it stands, we cannot help it; but if it is to be made agreeable to what may be right, on due consideration, why not allow time to consider of it? I believe if time is allowed, we shall be able to show that this is not the proper time for calling a convention; and I don't know any reason there can be for driving it down our throats, without an hour's preparation. It appears to me to be a plan not fit for discussion, or why refuse to allow it to be postponed? I hope, when the House comes to consider how it has been introduced, they will allow us the time we desire.

Mr. D. Clymer. The gentleman has misunderstood me, for I did not speak of the State at large, when I said the people understood it, and were in favor of it; though I have not the smallest doubt but it will receive their warmest approbation, when they hear of it.

Mr. Fitzsimons. I did wish, and still hope, the House will pretty unanimously agree to the resolutions which are before us. When we took the business up, I flattered myself the decision would not be delayed, because every member had time enough to consider this subject, since it was first introduced to our attention; but if it is the opinion of any considerable number of gentlemen, that it should lay over till the afternoon, I will not press it; I am sure the arguments made use of by the member from Cumberland,* offer no sufficient inducement for a delay. The plan of the new confederation has laid upon your table near a fortnight, and it can be nothing more or less than a confession of inattention, not to say neglect of duty, for gentlemen to plead they have not considered it; for surely the subject was so important, that they must have turned it in their minds, and know what is proper to decide on this occasion. The House is also so near its dissolution, that if the measure is to be effected, very little time remains for it; though as I observed before, I do not think it lies with the House to determine, whether a convention shall be called or no. This I think, Sir, forms no part of our deliberations. But it is my wish, that the legislature should take the lead, and guide the people into a decent exercise of their prerogative; and surely, Sir, it cannot be a matter of such high consideration, as to require much time in determining the day, on which elections should be held for nominating persons to form a State convention— And, I conceive, this is the single point which we have to consider; for I repeat again, that I do not think it is in our power, nay, I am sure it is not in our power, to prevent the people from adopting what may be a lasting benefit to themselves, and a certain treasure to posterity. But I think that taking the lead in this business, will be an honor not only to this legislature, but to the State also. It is not only honorable but convenient and advantageous; and I submit it to the majority of this House to conclude, whether we shall, by proceeding, obtain for ourselves and constituents these advantages, which even our neglect cannot prevent.

* Mr. Whitehill.

Mr. G. Clymer. The resolutions, Mr. Speaker, which I presented to you, contain separate and distinct propositions. Directing the elections to be held at a short day, goes upon the supposition that there is time to communicate the necessary information—if this is not well founded, of consequence it must be altered; but I hope no kind of hesitation can be made, as to the propriety of adopting the first, which goes on the principle, that such a convention is necessary for the better union and happiness of the several States of America. To hesitate upon this proposition will give a very unfavorable aspect to a measure, on which our future happiness, nay, I may almost say, our future existence, as a nation, depends. If the time, Sir, is not agreeable for holding elections, as mentioned in the second resolution, it cannot operate to prevent our entering upon the first: I therefore hope, gentlemen will withdraw their opposition, and let a degree of unanimity prevail, which may be an inducement to others steadily to co-operate in perfecting a work, that bids fair to relieve our embarassments, and carry us to a height of prosperity we have hitherto been strangers to.

Mr. Brackenridge. Before the division of the propositions, I had made up my mind to be in favor of the postponement; but it now appears clear to me, that we may decide upon the general principle, to wit, shall a convention of the people be called? With respect to this point, every member must have made up his mind fully, because it is a measure, that from the first was apparent, and must have occupied the attention of every individual who had but seen the plan. This, as was remarked before, has been on your table many days, and from its magnitude and importance must have been a subject of reflection to the members, who wished to perform the duty they owed to their God, their conscience, and fellow-citizens —so that voting now on a subject already understood, cannot be difficult, and in my opinion, we are as well prepared to determine upon the principle, as we shall be after dinner.

Mr. Whitehill. The gentleman from Westmoreland,* as well as the others who have spoken in favor of the resolu-

---

* Mr. Brackenridge.

tions, seemed generally of opinion, that they ought to be adopted without farther consideration, concluding that every member is prepared to determine on the propriety thereof. But this, Sir, is not the case; for I own, that I have not prepared myself to take up this business, because I did not expect any notice would be taken of it; for Congress ought to send forward the plan, before we do anything at all in this matter. For of what use was sending it forward to them, unless we meant to wait their determination—Now as these measures are not recommended by Congress, why should we take them up? Why should we take up a thing, which does not exist? For this does not exist, that is before us—nor can it until it is ratified by Congress. I have no doubt for my part, but Congress will adopt it; but if they should make alterations, and amendments in it, is there any one can say then, what sort of a plan it will be? And as this may happen, I hope the House, when they come to consider seriously, will see the impropriety of going on at present. It will appear, that it is necessary to give time for Congress to deliberate, before they recommend. It does appear that Congress have not recommended it; and the recommendation of Congress ought to be waited for in a matter that concerns the liberties and rights of the people of the United States. I say this recommendation is not come forward to the House, nor we don't know when (if ever,) it will. We do not know that Congress may be able to go thro' with it this long time yet, and why are we to determine on it, before we know whether they will allow of such change of the confederation? We do not know that Congress are even sitting, or whether they will be in session. And before we proceed to measures of this importance, do let us know what we are going on, and let us not sport away the rights and liberties of the people altogether. I say, is it not better to go safely on the business, and let it lie over till the next House; when we have adjourned, let our constituents think of it, and instruct their representatives to consider of the plan proper to be pursued. Will not the next House be as able to determine as we are? And I would wish the members to consider, that it never was supposed at our election, that we had the power to determine on such a measure. When we come to consider, it does appear to me better to leave it over to the next House, and they will be better able, and better instructed, what to do in this case. And what is the consequence the gentlemen propose by this hurry? That the State of Pennsylvania shall have the honor of taking the lead. This may be preserved, Sir, as well by letting it lie over; for, can the other states go into it before us? Can the State of Georgia receive it as soon, and send it forward for ratification, as we can? No, to be sure they cannot—therefore this hurry does appear too great in my opinion; because, if it is delayed, our determination can still be brought forward sooner than that of any other state. If there are any objections of moment against calling the convention at present, let us be prepared to make them; we may do that better, perhaps, by deferring only till the afternoon—for tho' gentlemen say they have had time, and have made up their minds, yet that has not been my case, and I don't see why the business should be hurried upon us at this rate. I hope when gentlemen consider, they will agree to postpone for the present.

Mr. Brackenridge. I conceive, Sir, that the member has wandered from the point, whenever he went into remarks upon the new constitution; but I did not interrupt, nor do I mean now to reply to those observations, because I would not follow him in a subject which is not before the House—but if it should be necessary to speak on the general principles, I trust that he would be fully answered. At present, Sir, I understand the question to be, whether sufficient time has not elapsed to give every member, who respects his duty, sufficient opportunity to have made up his mind on the propriety of calling a convention of the people; if this is the case, the House will not surely postpone.

Mr. D. Clymer. The member from Cumberland* seems to think it highly improper, that we should proceed in this business until Congress shall recommend it to our attention, and have given it the stamp of their approbation, but this,

* Mr. Whitehill.

Sir, is extremely fallacious. For if Congress are to determine the point, where was the necessity for the federal convention to recommend calling state conventions? Or pray, Sir, were the delegates to that important undertaking ordered even to report to Congress? No, Sir, they were not—but I take it that their reason for having done so, was, that as they meant to report to the people of the United States at large, they thought Congress would be a proper channel to convey it to every part, from New Hampshire to Georgia, and I think the mode of conveyance very proper; but I never entertained an idea that it was submitted to their cognizance, as the gentleman says, for alteration or amendment. He supposes, too, that the convention of the state may adopt some part of the frame of government, and refuse the other. But not so, Sir: they must adopt *in toto*, or refuse altogether: for it must be a plan that is formed by the United States; which can be agreeable to all, and not one formed upon the narrow policy and convenience of any one particular state. Such, Sir, is the constitution lately presented to you, framed by the collective wisdom of a continent, centered in a venerable band of patriots, worthies, heroes, legislators and philosophers—the admiration of a world. This, Sir, is a subject the member from the city did well to submit to your feelings. Vain is every attempt to do justice to its merits. No longer shall thirty thousand people engage all our attention—all our efforts to procure happiness. No!—the extended embrace of fraternal love shall enclose three millions, and ere fifty years are elapsed thirty millions, as a band of brothers! And will the State of Pennsylvania—will a few of her inhabitants, I should say—attempt to defeat this long-expected and wished-for moment, by entering into a discussion of the minutiæ— how her interest is preserved? Why, Sir, to form a happy union, the weakest eye must perceive the necessity of mutual concessions—mutual sacrifices. Had the late convention not been composed of gentlemen of liberal sentiments, patriotism, and integrity, it might never have been perfected. Had each been studious of accommodating the constitution to the circumstances and wishes of the state they represented, noth-

ing could have been effected. Do we not hear, that disposed
as they were to make a sacrifice of the local interests to the
general welfare, that five weeks elapsed before they could
determine the proportion of representation? If these gentlemen met with such difficulties, who possessed the information and knowledge of the continent, can it be supposed the
United States would submit to the amendments and alterations to be made by a few inhabitants of Pennsylvania?
Could it be expected that Virginia (the Dominion of Virginia,
as some people in derision call it—though I say it is a land
of liberty, a land of patriots, and the nurse of science)—I say
will you expect, Sir, that Virginia and the southern states
shall coincide with alterations made only for the benefit of
Pennsylvania? No!—away with such ideas, and let that unanimity prevail at its adoption that it did at its formation.
It is improper for gentlemen to say, we ought not to enter on
this business until it is ratified by Congress. This, Sir, is
not the case—and let me, as setting my argument on a foundation of solidity, call your attention to the recommendation
made by the united sense and wisdom of our continent to
this legislature. Remember how strong the language of the
venerable Franklin, when he addressed you to enforce this
recommendation. Remember the advantage and prosperity
held out to Pennsylvania, for her early and cheerful concurrence in a measure, whose perfections are so clearly seen as to
make hesitation criminal. Will all the art of sophistry prove
an inferiority to the present confederation, which, upon trial,
is found to be loose and ineffectual? Shall we, by chicane
and artful procrastination, defeat the measure so loudly demanded by every circumstance of happiness or preservation?
Better would it be, Mr. Speaker, to join in the glorious sentiment of that gallant officer, who having quitted his station,
and gained a signal victory over his enemy, and when called
to account for his breach of orders, answered, "That man
holds his life too dear, who would not sacrifice it for his country's safety."

If it is the interest of a few individuals to keep up the weak
and shattered government, which brings on us the contempt

of every surrounding tribe, and the reproach and obloquy of every nation, let them exert their opposition; but it will be all in vain, for should even this House refuse, I think it the duty of the people, as they value their present and future welfare, to come forward, and do that justice to themselves, which others would deny them.

As this subject is now before us, let us not hesitate, but eagerly embrace the glorious opportunity of being foremost in its adoption. Let us not hesitate, because it is damping the ardor with which it should be pursued. Sir, it is throwing cold water on the flame that warms the breast of every friend of liberty, and every patriot who wishes this country to acquire that respect to which she is justly entitled.

As we have taken up this matter, let us go through; for our determination may have weight with our sister states, and they will follow, where we take the lead, the honor of agreeing first to a measure, that must entitle to posterity security for their property—no longer subject to the fluctuation of faithless paper money and party laws—security to their liberty, and security to their personal safety. These are blessings which will engage the gratitude of posterity to venerate your ashes. Excuse me, Sir, for being warm; it is a matter I have much at heart, and a subject which I almost adore; and let the consequences to me be what they may, I must give it my support; for it has my most hearty concurrence, and to every part and particle I do pronounce a willing and a grateful *Amen.*

I am against the postponement of the question as to the principle; but as to that part of the resolution relating to the time, I shall move for an alteration, as my colleagues and myself think the period too short.

Mr. Fitzsimons. I was inclined to delay the business until the afternoon; but from all that has been said, I believe it must be the opinion of the House that it will be proper to decide upon the first resolution before we adjourn. As to the constitution itself, I believe the proper place for discussing that will be in the convention, so that nothing need be added on that head. If the time mentioned for the elections is supposed improper, that may be accommodated to the gentleman's wishes by amendments.

The question, Will the House agree to the postponement? was put, and only nine rose in favor of it. So it was determined in the negative.

Mr. Brackenridge. You will please to recollect, Sir, that when I was up last I observed that one of the arguments of the member from Cumberland might easily be obviated. As that was an improper time to reply to him, I declined doing it; but I mean now to enter on this subject, as I consider it fully before us.

Mr. Whitehill interrupted him with saying he had said nothing against the principles of the proposed plan, but that we were not ready to take it up.

Mr. Brackenridge. The gentleman must suppose me a fool to think I was going into a defence of the principles of the new form of government. No, Sir, that I take to be seated above either the reach of his arguments or information.

It is wholly upon another point I mean to remark. He has said, if I could select what he said, that we ought not to take up the present question nor adopt the resolution until we heard from Congress; and his argument was that this should be left to a future House to complete. Now this I mean to answer, and hope to show perfectly that neither premise or conclusion is well founded. There is also another question which seems to lie at the bottom of his argument, namely, that it is necessary at the same time for the state to wait until an improvement of the congressional government is recommended by Congress. This, Sir, I conceive would be a question lying at the bottom of the subject, which occupies our present consideration. But I have not been able to discover any principle on which an idea of this nature can be founded. What particular right have Congress to recommend an improvement of the federal government? They may recommend, but I should suppose it comes under no part of the authority delegated to them; and therefore that it was going wholly out of the province assigned to them. I should suppose it indelicate for the superior *bower* to solicit more. We know they are invested with the power of recommending by the confederation; but who would recommend from that body, that it should be gratified with more extensive power? I should, I say, presume it must come from them, not with the highest degree of delicacy. In the next place, taking it for granted that it should come entirely from them, what is the foundation or what must be the foundation of a recommendation of that nature? Is it because they have become sensible, that the present powers are not sufficient to conduct the affairs of the United States, and that a more vigorous and energetic government became necessary? Who ought to be the best judges of this necessity?—men in Congress reflecting abstractedly, or the body of the people on this continent, feeling and knowing this necessity? I therefore think it would be advisable to be guided in an alteration rather by this maxim than by the other. If a thing, Sir, ought to be done, it is little matter whether it be from the reflection of Congress or the feeling and sensibility of the people; and I own that I always feel a contempt for those languid and trammeled sentiments which move but like a piece of mechanism. And what are the consequences of taking up the subject without waiting the result of Congressional deliberation? We lead the way, and do great honor to ourselves in marking the road to obtain the sense of the people on a subject that is of the greatest moment to them and to their posterity. How did this business first originate? Did Virginia wait the recommendation of Congress? Did Pennsylvania, who followed her in the appointment of delegates, wait the recommendation of Congress? The assembly of New York, when they found they had not the honor of being foremost in the measure, revived the idea of its being necessary to have it recommended by Congress, as an excuse for their tardiness (being the seat of the federal government) —and Congress to humor them complied with their suggestions. How it happened to take effect in the other states I do not positively say; but I am rather inclined to believe it was adopted from the influence of example, rather than from the recommendation of Congress which happened to take place in the interval between the sittings of the legislatures.

But we never heard that it was supposed necessary to wait their recommendations. No such argument was made use of on this floor when the law was passed. The delegates to the convention were appointed without the recommendation of Congress, and they reported the result of their deliberations to this House. What reason then is there for waiting any longer to determine whether it is proper to call a convention to consider of it or not? I don't see for my part what Congress have to do with it; though doubtless I should not object to waiting a few days to hear their opinion. This has been done even until now, which is so near the close of our session as to make a longer delay improper, therefore waiting their recommendation is no argument for prolonging the consideration of the subject before us. But there are certainly strong reasons why we should call up and determine the question, whether a convention should be called or not? The advantages to the state are that it will be to her honor to take the lead in adopting so wise a plan, and it will be an inducement for other states to follow. We no doubt remember the influence the example of Virginia and Pennsylvania had in getting a general delegation appointed, and that example will no doubt as generally be followed in adopting the result, for it is everywhere fully and sensibly felt that an alteration in the federal government is requisite; and I think there can be little hesitation in agreeing to the resolution for calling a convention. As for the day of election, that is but a secondary consideration, and may be determined when it comes before us. We surely shall unanimously agree to the first resolution at this time, for delay would argue a lukewarmness that must be injurious to the cause. Every person who should hear we had the subject ten days before us, and notwithstanding avoided entering upon it, must conclude we are unfriendly to it; and it will be cause of triumph to our enemies, who wait only to see us refuse that government which alone can save us from their machinations.

As it is fully in our power to appoint the mode and manner of calling the convention, I hope gentlemen will turn their thoughts, and say what is the proper time; for if it is delayed until the next House, it will be some time far advanced into another year, before a convention can sit to ratify the plan of our future government; by which means the force of example would be for delay, and a measure so extremely necessary would be left exposed or perhaps neglected, unless the ardor of our citizens should induce them to do what our timidity would decline. The influence which this state may acquire by decision will be lost, and many of the advantages lessened by an unnecessary delay.

Mr. Findley. I do not intend to reply to the arguments used in favor of the present measure, but only examine the ground on which we stand. When the question was on postponement, I did not think it right that gentlemen should have introduced the observations which they did, nor that the manner of speaking which some used was proper. It was only addressed to the passions, and in my reply I do not mean to justify such language by using what may be similar. No, Sir, I intend to address the judgment, and not the passions of any man. I have no doubt *but a convention might be called, and will be called. That it ought to be called, and will be called,* is seen so clearly, that I shall add nothing to enforce it; therefore I take it that the propriety of calling a convention is not the question before us. After declaring my sentiments so far, I shall proceed, Sir, now to examine the ground on which we stand: I believe we stand on federal ground; therefore we are not in a state of nature. If we were in a state of nature, all the arguments produced for hastening this business would apply; but as we are not, I would observe that the most deliberate manner of proceeding is the best manner. But the manner in which this subject has been introduced is an indeliberate manner, and seems to argue that we are not on federal ground. The design of carrying this through, I say, Sir, is a presumption that we are in a state of nature. If that is the case, then it can only be proper to use this expedition. What I mean, Sir, by a state of nature is with respect to the confederation or union of the states, and not any wise alluding to our particular state government. Now my opinion is, Sir, that we are on federal ground: that the federal convention was a federal convention; that it had the powers of a federal convention, and that they were limited to act federally; that they have acted agreeably to the limitation, and have acted federally.   I know by some of the arguments which have been used that some gentlemen suppose otherwise.   Well then, Sir, we will have recourse to the confederation itself, and then to the law which appointed delegates to the convention, and let them decide whether we are on federal ground or not.

The sixth article of the confederation says: "No two or more states shall enter into any treaty, confederation, or alliance whatever between them, without the consent of the United States in Congress assembled, specifying accurately the purposes for which the same is to be entered into, and how long it shall continue." It may be said this don't apply. Well, let us examine what it says further in the thirteenth article: "The articles of confederation shall be inviolably observed by every state, and the union shall be perpetual; nor shall any alteration at any time hereafter be made in any of them, unless such alteration be agreed to in a Congress of the United States, and be afterwards confirmed by the legislatures of every state."   Now, did we act in conformity with these articles by passing the law appointing delegates to the convention, or did we not?   I say we did.   I know the contrary has been said, but let us have recourse to our own act.   I don't mean, as I said before, to reply particularly to any arguments, but to establish the point that we have all along acted upon federal principles, and that we ought to continue federal, and I have no doubt but we shall.   But what says the preamble of the law?   Hear our own words, Sir: "Whereas, the general assembly of this commonwealth, taking into their serious consideration the representations heretofore made to the legislatures of the several states in the union, by the United States in Congress assembled," etc. It has been mentioned that we took it up in consequence of Virginia's having engaged in the measure; and as the reasons are only mentioned in the preamble, they may not deserve much attention, but the second section of the law decides this point. The words are, after enumerating the persons, that they are hereby constituted and appointed deputies from this state, with powers to meet such deputies as may be appointed and authorized by the other states to assemble in the said convention at the city aforesaid, and to join with them in devising, deliberating on, and discussing all such alterations and further provisions as may be necessary to render the federal constitution fully adequate to the exigencies of the Union; and in reporting such act or acts for that purpose to the United States in Congress assembled, as, when agreed to by them and duly confirmed by the several states, will effectually provide for the same.

Now I consider it as a question of importance, whether we are to take up the new constitution, as being in a state of nature, or, acting on federal ground, whether we stand unconnected or subordinate to the present confederation; if we are bound by that, it obliges us to continue on federal ground. I should conceive that we are still bound by the confederation, and that the conduct of the House has hitherto been federal; that the convention was federal, as appears by their appointment and their report to Congress. Did they, Sir, address their report to this House? No, Sir, they did not. It is true, Sir, we were honored with a report from our own delegates. No, Sir, I retract the word—the delegates were honored; they did themselves the honor of communicating the result of their deliberations. But did the convention address this House? No, Sir, they did not. They addressed Congress, as they were ordered to do. Hitherto the business has been in a federal channel, and this, Sir, is the first step that places us upon unfederal ground. The report is before Congress, and it is to be presumed Congress will agree to it; but has such a length of time elapsed, as to induce us to suspect they will not concur, or to justify our going into it without their recommendation? We may act, Sir, without due deliberation, and hurry on without consideration, but Congress will not. I know the propriety of waiting to hear from them must have weight with every member, and I ask every gentleman in this House, will they take upon themselves to doubt of the acquiescence of Congress, in order to furnish an argument for dispatch? If any will, let him say so, and take the consequences upon his character. No doubt can be entertained, but Congress will recommend, as the acquisition of power is a desirable object with them. Their disposition must be to promote the present plan, but they must wish to preserve the appearance of decency on such a subject. I ask, can any gentleman suppose but what Congress will come readily into it? They who have been many years recommending and requiring, nay, I may say, begging for such powers as are now proposed to be given them, cannot change their disposition, and decline receiving an increase. Well, what does all this tend to prove? have we not all along been a federal State, remarkably so? And shall we be the first to step out of our way wantonly, and without any reason? Certainly we will not.

However, I suppose some gentleman will say, it is necessary for Pennsylvania to show a ready compliance on the present occasion—that it is absolutely necessary to supersede the existing confederation. Why, Sir, we know that nothing, no argument, no opposition, can withstand the plea of necessity. Well, but the absolute necessity must arise from the dangers we are in. Now where are any dangers to be avoided, while Congress are going only through their usual forms to recommend this measure? They must have time to read and consider the plan; it must go through the usual course of business. Circular letters must be prepared and sent with authenticated copies of the new form of government. I am of opinion all this will be done with proper speed, and the communications will be made as soon as possible. Why send the plan to Congress at all, if we must act upon it without their approbation? If the present confederation is not adequate to the great national purposes, it is fair to put it in competition with the proposed one. We know it was framed by good and wise men, and so was this. Wise and great men were employed in framing both. Nay, some of the same men prepared them—but as time and experience have shown a revision to be necessary, has it not been entered into on federal ground? And will the State of Pennsylvania quit this to answer the concealed purposes of those who urge on the present measure? No, I hope not,—but they will agree to leave it to another House, by which time the usual formalities may be given it by the United States. Surely Pennsylvania can take it up early enough to prevent any damage that is feared. In doing so we act federally. What are held out as inducements to act with such precipitation? As some members say the *honor* of being foremost; but I would rather say the *dishonor* of acting unfederally; and will any federal purposes be answered by a breach of the confederation, which can counterbalance the disgrace of being the first to dissolve the union? And, Sir, it is not convenient that one State should enter into this measure any length of time before the others. This is one reason of waiting the recommendation of Congress—for then the new constitution comes officially and all are prepared to go hand in hand in perfecting the work—but will a name justify us for a breach of faith unnecessarily? and no necessity is alleged to justify the measure. Sir, in acting the part I do in supporting federal measures, I am justified by every citizen who will think with deliberation on a subject of this importance. I have supposed the gentlemen who support the resolutions before you, have some object in view which is not understood. I have a right for such suspicion, or why was it delayed to the last but one day of the sessions? We do not treat this subject which is allowed to be of importance with any respect; we treat it rather as a matter of no importance when we hurry it on in this manner. Why, Sir, even the trifling business of appointing a prothonotary, or register, is made the order of the day. Certainly then we treat this with indignity.

There must be some reasons for this, but though I cannot see it, I may suppose it, and I would ask the gentlemen whether it is that they may have the merit of promoting a business which appears to be very popular; but will this consist with our federal engagements? I would go further and assign another reason against it, but I may be supposed to touch it with indelicacy. It may be asked, was this House elected with a view of entering into matters of this importance? I say this may be indelicate, as the House have elected delegates to convention—but then, Sir, I have showed they had that right by the articles of confederation, so that the House so far did their duty. It is true they happened, in their choice of delegates, to choose a number of their own members, but in this they were also justified for one reason: perhaps they thought them better judges of what would be for the benefit of a State they regulated by their legislation. I believe nothing was improper in this; but, I remember, it was lamented that some persons were not chosen better to represent the country interest. And it is these very men who now come forward with the resolutions. They, no doubt, are able to decide; but I think they should indulge others with time for a like consideration—therefore, I hope they will agree to let it lie over to the next House. I don't think that it will be then too late, and few or none of the other States can be forwarder than ourselves in calling a convention.

Mr. G. Clymer. We now, Mr. Speaker, have heard all the commonplace arguments against adopting the federal constitution; and among this mass of matter, what has the gentleman attempted to establish? I think, Sir, it may be reduced to these two points: first, that the legislature of Pennsylvania is not adequate to calling a convention, though generally desired; and the other is, that the measure of calling a convention, if gone into, is anti-federal, and shows an impropriety in the conduct of the House, in not waiting the result of the deliberations of Congress. Sir, I have as great respect for federal measures, and for Congress, as that gentleman can pretend to. But waiting their report, Sir, I believe will be to attend to forms, and lose the substance. A little calculation will serve to demonstrate this, and show the impropriety of waiting the report of that body. At the same time a due regard to decency has been had by postponing this business to so late an hour. If this House order a convention, it may be deliberated and decided some time in November, and the constitution may be acted under by December. But if it is left over to the next House, it will inevitably be procrastinated until December, 1788. No man, I presume, would be willing that our union and existence should remain so long in jeopardy, or run the risk of a final ruin.

If this business is neglected by the present House, and suffered to pass over to the next, it will undoubtedly have the appearance of our being unfriendly to the new constitution, or will be owning to the world that we are not willing to decide in its favor. The gentleman supposes wrong, when he says, that the reason for bringing it forward now is, that Congress are not favorable to the measure. It originated on no such apprehension; on the contrary, we know that Congress are favorable, and I have been informed by a gentleman of information, lately from York, that the members of Congress were unanimous in approving it; but that the formality which accompanies their decisions is of such a nature as to require a longer time for making official communications.

The other argument, that it is unfederal to call a convention without the approbation of Congress, is not supported; for he agrees, that should Congress disapprove, there is still a way left of laying it before the people, which amounts to a full proof that Congress is considered only as a vehicle to communicate the information generally to the United States. In this light the gentleman will find the convention addressed them; if he turns over to the resolutions accompanying the constitution, it is there declared as their opinion, that it should be addressed to a convention of delegates, chosen in each State by the people thereof, under the recommendation of its legislature; and when agreed to in such manner by nine States, it shall then be in force. Thus we see there is no power vested in Congress, to prevent the States going into it separately and independently. The idea which he has taken up, may be traced undoubtedly in the original confederation, but he will not find it at all attended to by the convention. Waiting to receive a recommendation of the measure from Congress, must even by that gentleman be esteemed merely as a compliment, which I think, by the delay already made, has been fully complied with; so that I think little remains but that the House patronize the calling a convention by agreeing to the first resolution, and no man, I apprehend, in favor of federal measures, will oppose this; and when the second comes before us, we may determine the time for holding the election.

Mr. Robinson. The argument of the gentleman, who objects to the present measure, is not against the propriety of calling a convention, but only that this is an improper time; and it appears that he supposes farther, that we are not acting consistent with our federal engagements in deciding on this subject before it is recommended by Congress: because, as he says, we quit the federal ground on which we have hitherto trodden, and act as if we were in a state of nature with respect to the confederation existing between the thirteen States. Now, Sir, I must oppose these arguments by asserting, in the first place, that we have not acted hitherto on federal ground; that the appointment made by this House of delegates to convention, was not federal, nor any one step taken by us has been in conformity with the articles of confederation. And all this I think, Sir, I shall be able to prove to your satisfaction, and to a full refutation of every pretext which the gentleman from Westmoreland has set up to defeat the proposed measure at the present. The gentleman has introduced to your attention the thirteenth article of the confederation, and concludes from it that we are acting unfederally, if we do not wait their decision. Now I mean to prove by this article, that we have not acted hitherto in conformity with it—but that at the very first onset, we entered new ground, and the articles of this confederation (it says) shall be *inviolably observed*, and the union shall be *perpetual*, nor shall any alteration, at any time hereafter be made in any of them, unless such alteration be agreed to in a Congress of the United States and be afterwards *confirmed* by the LEGISLATURE OF EVERY STATE.

From this is plainly inferred, that alterations ought to have *originated* with *Congress*, and by them been *recommended* to the several LEGISLATURES. Here is no provision for leaving it to *another body of men*, to recommend *alterations to State Conventions*—here is no provision for making an engagement binding, as soon as entered into by nine States assembled in *conventions*. No, sir, the constitution proposed is no *alteration* of any *particular article* of the *confederation*, which is the only thing provided for. The federal convention did not think of amending and altering the present confederation, for they saw the impropriety of vesting one body of men with the necessary powers. Hence resulted the necessity of a different organization. America has been taught by dear-bought experience, that she could never hope for security or prosperity under articles of union that were no longer binding than suited the convenience of each particular state, and were slighted or contemned as petulance or caprice dictated. America has seen the confederation totally inadequate to the purposes of an equal general government, incapable of affording security either within or without. Attempts in vain have been made to obtain the assent of all the States, to measures which have at one time or another been agreed by them severally, yet retracted by some when a prospect of success appeared. Hence resulted the necessity of taking up this business on original ground. Hence resulted the necessity of having again recourse to the AUTHORITY OF THE PEOPLE. *Under this impression, Sir, the* CONVENTION *originated*. Virginia passed a law appointing delegates to join with the delegates of such other States as, influenced by her example, and convinced of the necessity of having a more effective federal government, should concur therein. Virginia, Sir, was not authorized by Congress to make such appointment, nor did Pennsylvania wait for that authority; but this reason, which is inserted in the preamble of the bill, was thought sufficient to justify our conduct, and was the real inducement for passing the law: " And whereas the legislature of the State of Virginia have already passed an act of that commonwealth, empowering certain commissioners to meet at the city of Philadelphia, in May next, a convention of commissioners, or deputies, from the different States; and the legislature of this State are fully sensible of the important advantages which may be derived to the United States, and every of them, from *co-operating with the commonwealth of Virginia,* and the other States of the confederation, in the said design.''

Finally, Sir, the recommendation of Congress was obtained for calling the convention; but this was a power not vested in them by any article of the confederation, under which they ought to act. In this, Sir, they departed from that federal conduct, which the member from Westmoreland, by mistake, asserts has hitherto been pursued. Having, Sir, not hitherto proceeded one step on federal ground, is it to be expected that federal ground should now be resumed? But, Sir, if we were to proceed under the most earnest recommendation of Congress, to call a *state convention,* we proceed contrary to the principle laid down in the 13th article, which declares the alteration must be CONFIRMED BY THE LEGISLATURE: so whether Congress recommend, or do not recommend—if a *convention is called,* (which every gentleman agrees is proper) we act inconsistent with the articles of confederation. For is it any where said, that *conventions of the people* shall be called to determine such alterations as are submitted by Congress? No, Sir, THE LEGISLATURES are to decide, and moreover, it must be confirmed by *all of them* before it can have effect. Now is this a circumstance that can be reasonably expected after the disunion and obstinacy which has heretofore taken place? The new constitution declares, when nine States concur, it shall be binding on them; so that whatever way we proceed in, it must be clear we proceed without regard to the confederation.

With respect to the recommendation of Congress, I think it is generally believed they will recommend, but it is only mere formality that could require us to wait it—even was it federal—which it is not. Let us suppose that Congress were to refuse recommending, would it drop to the ground? And suppose we decline calling a convention, will not the people call one themselves? They surely will, and have an undoubted right so to do. And the only question before us is, what advantage will arise from calling that *convention now?* The people who reside near the seat of government have generally applied to you to direct this affair—now should we treat their application with a silent neglect, it will argue that the general assembly are unfriendly to a more federal and effective government. If it should not carry that idea to the people about us, who may have fuller information, it certainly will to the extremes of the State, and other distant places. It will tend to damp that ardor, which the proposed plan has universally inspired. The State of Pennsylvania is of great weight, her influence would be extended, nor has she ever relaxed her federal exertions; she would become still of greater importance in the union, and her example on the present question may fix the liberty, prosperity and happiness of united America, while sun and moon endureth.

A tardiness will lose us these advantages, and by referring to another House, we may not see it effected until many other States that have formed a better judgment of its importance, shall have acceded and eclipsed our fame.

Mr. Fitzsimons. I think too highly of the good sense of this House, to suppose it necessary to say anything to prove to them, that their *agreement* to calling a convention is *not unfederal*, as every member must have fully considered the point before this time; nor I do not think a single gentleman supposes, that it would be unfederal—though the member from Westmoreland has taken some pains to persuade us, that Pennsylvania has been hitherto a federal State, and that we are about to depart from that conduct, and to run before even prosperity itself. I think it greatly to the honor of Pennsylvania, that she deserves the gentleman's commendation, by having always stood foremost in support of federal measures; and I think it will redound still more to her honor, to enter foremost into this new system of confederation, seeing the old is so dissolved or rotten as to be incapable of answering any good purpose whatsoever. Has the gentleman ever looked at the new constitution? If he has, he will see, it is not an alteration of an article in the old, but that it departs in every principle from the other. It presupposes, Sir, that no confederation exists; or if it does exist, it exists to no purpose: as it can answer no useful purpose, it cannot provide for the common defence, nor promote the general welfare.

Therefore, arguments that are intended to reconcile one with the other, or make the latter an appendage to the former, are but a mere waste of words. Does the gentleman suppose that the convention thought themselves acting under any provision made in the confederation for altering its articles? No, Sir, they had no such idea. They were obliged, in the first instance, to begin with the destruction of its greatest principle, *equal representation.* They found the confederation without vigor, and so decayed that it was impossible to graft a useful article upon it; nor was the *mode*, Sir, as prescribed by that confederation, which requires alterations to originate with Congress. They found at an early period, that no good purpose could be effected by making such alterations as were provided by the first articles of union. They also saw, that what alterations were necessary could not be ratified by the legislatures, as they were incompetent to ordaining a form of government. They knew this belonged to the people only, and that the people only would be adequate to carry it into effect. What have Congress and the legislatures to do with the proposed constitution? Nothing, Sir,— they are but the mere vehicles to convey the information to the people. The convention, Sir, never supposed it was necessary to report to Congress, much less to abide their determination: they thought it decent to make the compliment to them of sending the result of their deliberations— concluding the knowledge of that would be more extensively spread through their means. Not that I would infer there is the least doubt of the most hearty concurrence of that body; but, should they decline, and the State of Pennsylvania neglect calling a convention, as I said before, the authority is with the people, and they will do it themselves; but there is a propriety in the legislatures providing the mode by which it may be conducted in a decent and orderly manner.

The member from Westmoreland agrees, that a convention ought to take place. He goes further and declares, that it must and will take place, but assigns no reason why it should not early take place. He must know that any time after the election will be proper, because at that time, the people being collected together, have full opportunity to learn each other's sentiments on this subject. Taking measures for calling a convention in a very different thing from deciding on the plan of government. The sentiments of the people, so far as they have been collected, have been unanimously favorable to its adoption, and its early adoption, if their representatives think it a good one. If we set the example now, there is a great prospect of its being generally come into; but if we delay, many ill consequences may arise. And I should suppose, if no better arguments are offered for the delay that what has been advanced by the gentleman on the other side of the House, that we will not agree to it. As to the time of election, that has been all along conceded, and gentlemen will propose such time as they think proper.

Mr. Findley. I wish to make a few observations, Sir, on what has been said by the several gentlemen who support the motion, and to offer some further reasons in favor of delay. One gentleman says, it will be procrastinated, if laid over to the next House, into another year—in that, Sir, I will agree with him, if he means the beginning, but not if the middle or latter end. The same gentleman says, that no one, in favor of federal measures, would oppose it. Now, Sir, I profess myself in favor of federal measures, and I believe the members of the House are generally so; and it is for that very reason that I wish to defer it, in order that we may accomplish in a federal manner. The gentleman further says, that if Congress disapprove of it, there is still a way left of having it adopted: but if Congress should disapprove—will it be contended, that we have acted properly, in agreeing to a measure without consideration. Congress certainly take no more time than is necessary, and they must know how the legislature of Pennsylvania is circumstanced: they know we are near our dissolution, and never can imagine that even if they were to determine on recommending, that we have time to decide on that recommendation.

As to what the gentleman from the county (Mr. Robinson) says of the federal convention's not being a federal convention, I have but little to reply. I stated some facts to prove they were a federal convention, acting under the confederation both by its injunctions and by the law. He charges Congress also with not having acted agreeable to the confederation; but he has not shown us why that body should wantonly step out of the way, when, by the 13th section, they were able to effect every alteration which was required. But for my part, I think their conduct was federal, and their resolution conformable to the confederation. Neglecting to adopt the measure of calling a convention is said by him to carry the idea of this state's being unfriendly to the proposed constitution. But why should it have this effect? Is it not known that the usual method of determining any matter of a public nature is by a due consideration and repeated deliberation conformable with our constitution? Can a hasty decision be expected? No; it is expressly prohibited. Why, then, must it be inferred from delay that we are unfriendly?

The member from the city (Mr. Fitzsimons) says that every member must have considered this subject. I will say that every member has not considered it; for my part I have read it over not with a view of considering it in this house, and as for the object before us—I never thought of it at all, taking it for granted that the session was so far expired that time was not left to receive it from Congress or deliberate upon it. I know that it is the province of the convention to consider of the merits of the plan, and I suppose that they will have good reasons assigned for their determination, whether it be to reject or adopt it, so that I shall add nothing on this head. The gentleman goes further, and informs us that the federal convention did not act under the confederation, which he says is dissolved and rotten, and they paid no respect to it in their deliberations. I know this matter does not come properly before the House, but, Sir, I cannot forbear remarking upon these words. I should think it unwise to throw out the dirty water, Sir, before we get clean. If the confederation is dissolved, there is no bond to keep us together even while we deliberate on the new. But, Sir, our confederation is not dissolved, though it may be defective. We remember it was framed in time of war, and every requisite for the time of peace may not have been adverted to; and we should remember it served, and served us faithfully, through a difficult and protracted war. Let us, therefore, not censure it too highly, as we have been advantaged by it, nor despise it, and say it is dissolved and rotten: for, Sir, when I go into my new house, I wait till it is finished and furnished, before I quit the humble cabin that has served me many a cold and weary day; and when I bid it an adieu, it is becoming to speak respectfully of it, because it was true and faithful to the last.

Now with respect to the propriety of waiting the recommendations of Congress, and whether we are acting federally or not, are questions, in my opinion, of high importance. The gentlemen say also that the subject is important—but how do they treat it? They treat it, Sir, as a trifle, whilst we, by desiring due deliberation, treat it as important. Ask the gentlemen, Sir, what they are about to do? They mean to summon an election of delegates at so short a day, that people have not the least time to consult together even on a proper representation. Perhaps the city and county of Philadelphia may have time sufficient, but no other can. If a majority of the people of Pennsylvania are favorable to the new constitution, how can they find out the sentiments of those whom they wish to represent them? Perhaps they may elect persons who will give it every opposition; and it may be, Sir, that the very persons who are pressing this business forward, do it to inspire a confidence that they are its supporters, when they mean, if opportunity shall offer, to destroy it. I ask the members of this House, Is it reasonable to suppose proper time is allowed? Let every member ask himself if the people can choose delegates with any kind of judgment? The people generally are disposed to have a government of more energy. How far the proposed one may answer their idea, I think we ought to let them consider. They have a right to think and choose for themselves. Shall we then deprive them of their right? Surely not. Let them then have time, and they no doubt will act right, and refuse or adopt the plan of government held out to them.

Mr. Brackenridge. With respect to the expediency of im-

mediate decision on this question, it has been sufficiently observed, that the example of Pennsylvania would be a great
inducement to the other States to come speedily into its adoption—on the contrary, a delay with us will occasion a delay
in the other legislatures. The gentleman allows we labor
under inconveniences by the present mode of government;
let his object then be to remove the difficulties and hasten
their termination, by a speedy application of the only remedy
the case admits of. I cannot see, Mr. Speaker, whence the
gentlemen (Messrs. Whitehill and Findley) are so averse to a
measure that the one owns is necessary and the other cannot
state a single objection against.

All efforts to restore energy to the federal government have
proved ineffectual, when exerted in the mode directed by the
13th article of the confederation, and it is in consequence of
this that recourse is once more had to the *authority of the
people.* The first step toward obtaining this was anti-federal;
the acquiescence of Congress was anti-federal; the whole process has been anti-federal so far as it was not conducted in
the manner prescribed by the articles of union. But the first
and every step was *federal*, inasmuch as it was sanctioned by
the PEOPLE OF THE UNITED STATES. The member from
Westmoreland pleases his fancy with being on federal ground,
pursuing federal measures, and being a very federal sort of
person; he concludes we are not in a state of nature, because
we are on federal ground. But, Sir, we are not on federal
ground, but on the wild and extended field of nature, unrestrained by any former compact, bound by no peculiar tie; at
least so far are we disengaged, as to be capable of forming a
constitution which shall be the wonder of the universe. It is
on the principle of self-conservation that we act. The former
articles of confederation have received sentence of death, and
though they may be on earth, yet are inactive, and have no
efficacy. But the gentleman would still have us to be bound
by them, and tells you your acts must correspond with their
doctrine. This he proves, Sir, from the 13th article: but in
this he is like some over-studious divines, who in comment-
ing on their text, turn it to different shapes, and force it to
prove what it never meant, or in the words of the poet.

As critics, learned critics view,
In Homer, more than Homer knew.

He will not suffer the old to be dissolved until the new is adopted; he will not quit his old cabin, till the new house is furnished, not if it crumbles about his ears. But, Sir, we are not now forsaking our tenement, it has already been forsaken: and I conceive we have the power to proceed independent of Congress or Confederation. But as to the second object, whether the time is proper as stated in the resolution, I do not say that it is, because I conceive it too short for several counties distant from this city; but this subject will come forward with propriety after the present question is agreed to.

Mr. Findley. The proposed plan is not now before us; therefore we have nothing to say on that subject. But, Sir, I would still suppose the old confederation is in existence— the new says that when nine States agree, it shall be binding on them;—that is to say, we shall not go out of the old, until the new is so far completed. Then, Sir, for my part I would retire from under the old, but not till then, when I would bid it an honorable and friendly adieu for its meritorious services; then I would cheerfully pay that attention to the new, which a more perfect edifice deserves; I would then support or act under it, as occasion might require.

Mr. Whitehill. I shall make but a very few observations on this business as enough has already been said, I apprehend, to convince the house of the propriety of delay, if any consideration can effect it. I believe, Sir, we are under the confederation, and when we come to consider the articles of that confederation, as well as the law passed appointing delegates to Congress, we shall have reason to conclude that we are on federal ground, and not in a state of nature. In the sixth article it is expressly declared that no State shall enter into any confederation without the consent of Congress; this is sufficient to satisfy the house that they ought not to proceed without the approbation of Congress. I say, when we come to consider, that the States appointed delegates in consequence of the recommendation of Congress, and that they reported to Congress agreeably to their orders, every member must be convinced that it is a federal measure, and this way of going out of it must be contrary to all right and propriety. We have articles of confederation, Sir, and we are bound by them. We are acting, Sir, a very wrong part to deny this—they are our government. They have the necessary powers by the confederation, and I say their recommendation is necessary; and unless we have it, nothing can be done toward establishing the new constitution.

Mr. D. Clymer said the new constitution had nothing to do with the present question which was simply, Will the house take the proper means to have a convention of the people called to deliberate on the propriety of receiving or refusing the new plan of confederation?

The question was now put, Will the house agree to the resolution? And the yeas and nays being called by Messrs. D. Clymer and Fitzsimons, are as follows:

YEAS.—Will, Fitzsimons, Clymer, Hiltzeimer, Gray, Robinson, Salter, Logan, Foulke, Wynkoop, Chapman, Upp, Moore, Willing, Ralston, Evans, Thomas, Wheelen, Lowry, Hubley, Carpenter, Work, Ross, Clemson, M'Conaghy, Schmyser, M'Clellan, Lilley, G. Hiester, Kreemer, J. Hiester, Davis, D. Clymer, Trexler, Burkhalter, Cannon, Antis, Brackenridge, Moore, Wheeler, Hockley, Risse, Carson—43.

NAYS.—Whitehill, Kennedy, Mitchell, Brown, Piper, Powell, Dale, Findley, Barr, Wright, M'Dowel, Flenniken, Allison, Phillips, Gilchrist, Smith, M'Calmont, Clarke, Miley—19.

After which the house adjourned till 4 o'clock in the afternoon.

Eodem die, p. m.

Mr. Speaker took the chair, when it appeared there were but 44 members met, which, not being a quorum,

Mr. Wynkoop observed that the house had under their conideration a business of the highest importance, and as he remarked the absent members were mostly those who had given it opposition in the forenoon, he suspected they had withdrawn themselves by design, he would therefore move that the Sergeant of Arms be sent for them. This being unanimously agreed to, the Sergeant was dispatched in search of the following members of the general Assembly of Pennsylvania, namely:

From Cumberland—*Robert Whitehill, Thomas Kennedy, David Mitchell.*

From Bedford—*John Piper, Joseph Powell.*

From Northumberland—*Frederick Antis,* (who voted in favor of calling the convention), *Samuel Dale.*

From Westmoreland—*William Findley, James Bar.*

From Washington—*Alexander Wright, John M' Dowel, John Flenniken, James Allison.*

From Fayette—*Theophilus Phillips, John Gilchrist.*

From Franklin—*Abraham Smith, James M' Calmont.*

From Dauphin—*Robert Clarke* and *Jacob Miley.*

The Speaker left the chair until the return of the Sergeant at Arms, who was immediately examined at the bar of the house.

Mr. Speaker. Well, Sergeant, have you seen the absent members? Sergeant. Yes, Sir, I saw R. Whitehill, Kennedy, Mitchell, Piper, Powell, Dale, Findley, Bar, Wright, M'Dowel, Flenniken, Allison, Gilchrist, M'Calmont, R. Clarke, Antis and Miley.

Mr. Speaker. What did you say to them? Sergeant. I told the gentlemen that the Speaker and the house had sent for them, and says they, There is no house.

Mr. Speaker. Did you let them know they were desired to attend? Sergeant. Yes, Sir, but they told me they could not attend this afternoon, for they had not made up their minds yet.

Mr. D. Clymer. How is that? Sergeant. They had not made up their minds this afternoon to wait on you.

Mr. Speaker. Who told you this? Sergeant. Mr. Whitehill told me the first.

Mr. Speaker. Where did you see them? Sergeant. At a house in Sixth street; Major Boyd's, I think.

D. Clymer. You say Mr. Whitehill told you first there was no house; who told you afterward? Sergeant. Mr. Clarke said they must go *electioneering* now.

D. Clymer. I would be glad to know what conversation there was among them, and who was there? Sergeant. There was a member of council with them, Mr. M'Laine, and he asked me, Who sent you?

Mr. Speaker. Was no other person in the room? Sergeant. Yes, I saw Mr. Smiley there.

D. Clymer. Was there no private citizens? Sergeant. No, Sir.

D. Clymer. There was none then but MEN IN PUBLIC OFFICES? Sergeant. No.

D. Clymer. Well; and pray what did the honorable Mr. Smiley say? Sergeant. He said nothing.

D. Clymer. Could all the persons in the room hear Mr. M'Laine's question. Sergeant. Yes, Sir.

D. Clymer. And did they seem pretty unanimous in their determination not to come? that is, did it appear so to you? Sergeant. Yes, Sir, as I understood it, nearly.

D. Clymer. Did you hear of any one willing to come? Sergeant. No, Sir.

Sergeant, you may retire.

The Speaker now recapitulated the unfinished business, and wished to know what the members would choose to do.

Mr. Wynkoop would be glad to know, if there was no way to compel men, who deserted from the duty they owed their country, to a performance of it, when they were within the reach of the House. If there is not, then *God be merciful to us! ! !*

Mr. Lowry believed there was a law to compel the absent members to serve, which was passed in the year 1777; but upon investigation, this law was found wholly inadequate, and upon search it appeared, that the only penalty to which such men were liable, was a forfeiture of one third of one day's pay, being the sum of five shillings Pennsylvania currency; and this is inflicted under one of the rules for the regulation of the members' conduct.

Mr. Robinson. I believe, Sir, that punishment is not in our power, nor can we compel their presence, so that we have nothing left but to adjourn; but before this I would wish to make a few observations. This House, Sir, have this afternoon agreed to call a convention of the people of this State, in order to deliberate upon a new form of confederation. I would remark, that this business is not of such a nature as to require a law to carry it into effect, it being merely to lay down the mode by which the citizens may proceed in their choice in a manner best suited to their convenience. This business, Sir, is of that important nature to all the citizens of the United States, that it must not be suffered to fail by the secession of nineteen of your members—though sorry I am that our journals are again to be stained by recording the conduct of an unmanly minority. But passing this over, I think there will be a propriety of meeting again, and under our respective signatures recommend this measure to our constituents. Fully impressed with the idea of its importance and necessity, I cannot but strongly recommend its adoption, and leave these men to suffer the stings of conscience, and that contempt and displeasure of their constituents, which they have drawn upon themselves.

Adjourned until to-morrow half past nine.

Saturday, September 29, A. M.

Mr. Speaker took the chair, and on calling over the roll, it appeared there were but forty-four members present; namely, all those who appeared yesterday, but Mr. ROBERT BROWN FROM NORTHAMPTON, who has now withdrawn himself. And by order, the Sergeant of Arms, accompanied by the assistant clerk, was dispatched in pursuit of the seceding members. But first Mr. G. Clymer presented to the chair the unanimous resolution of Congress, which he said had been agreed to yesterday, and was forwarded by Mr. Bingham to him express, having chosen this mode in preference to the ordinary conveyance by post. Whereupon,

The following resolution was read, and sent by the assistant clerk to the seceding members, (as was observed by the Speaker,) in order to remove that objection, which they had taken yesterday against the measure.

Friday, September 28, 1787.

Present—New Hampshire, Massachusetts, Connecticut, New York, New Jersey, Pennsylvania, Delaware, Virginia, North Carolina, South Carolina, and Georgia, and from Maryland, Mr. Ross.

CONGRESS having received the report of the CONVENTION lately assembled in Philadelphia,

Resolved unanimonsly, That the said report, with the resolution and letter accompanying the same, be transmitted to the several legislatures, in order to be submitted to a convention of delegates, chosen in each State, by the people thereof, in conformity to the resolves of the convention, made and provided in that case.   CHARLES THOMSON, *Secretary.*

The Speaker left the chair, and in a few minutes Mr. James M'Calmont and Mr. Jacob Miley entered the house. The Speaker resumed the chair, and the roll was called, when the following gentlemen answered to their names:

From the City of Philadelphia—Messrs. *Will, Morris, Fitzsimons, G. Clymer,* and *Hiltzeimer.*

From the county of Philadelphia—Messrs. *Gray, Robinson, Salter* and *Logan.*

From Bucks—Messrs. *Foulke, Wynkoop, Chapman* and *Upp.*

From Chester—Messrs. *J. Moore, Willing, Thomas, Ralston, Evans,* and *Wheelen.*

From Lancaster—Messrs. *Lowry, Hubley, Carpenter, Work, Ross,* and *Clemson.*

From York—Messrs. *M'Conaghy, Schmyser, M'Clellan,* and *Lilley.*

From Cumberland—NONE.

From Berks—Messrs. *J. Hiester, Davis,* and *D. Clymer.*

From Northampton—Messrs. *Trexler,* and *Burkhalter.*

From Bedford—Mr. *Cannon.*

From Northumberland—NONE.

From Westmoreland—Mr. *Brackenridge.*

From Washington—NONE.

From Fayette—NONE.

From Franklin—Mr. *M'Calmont.*

From Montgomery—Messrs. *J. Wheeler, C. Moore, Hockley,* and *Risse.*

From Dauphin—Messrs. *F. Miley,* and *Carson.*

Being 45, and with the Speaker 46, the number which constitutes a quorum.

After reading over the minutes of yesterday.

Mr. Hockley presented a petition and memorial from forty-three inhabitants of the county of Montgomery, desiring the house would take the necessary measures to have a convention of the people assembled as speedily as possible.

Which was read, and ordered to lie on the table.

The Committee appointed to select such business from the files of the House, as would be proper to recommend to the attention of the succeeding General Assembly, made report, which was also read, and ordered to lie on the table.

Mr. M'Calmont informed the house, that he had been forcibly brought into the assembly room, contrary to his wishes, this morning by a number of the citizens, whom he did not know, and that therefore, he begged he might be *dismissed* the house.

Mr. Lowry. I hope, as the gentleman says, he was forcibly brought, he will give some reason why force was necessary to make him do his duty; and what reason can he give now he is here, that should induce us to part with him again? Surely his being brought by force and against his wishes, is not a reason that he should be suffered to go off again.

Mr. Fitzsimons would be glad to know, if any member of the house was guilty of forcing the gentleman from the determination of absenting himself; if there was, he thought it necessary that the house mark such conduct with their disapprobation. But we are to consider, Sir, that the member is now here, and that the business of the State cannot be accomplished, if any one is suffered to withdraw: from which consideration I conclude, it will be extremely improper for any member to leave this house, until the laws and other unfinished business, is completed.

Mr. Robinson. I believe my sentiments, Sir, are well known on the subject of the new federal constitution, and I yesterday declared my strong disapprobation of the conduct of those members, who, by leaving the house, have forsaken that obligation they owe their God, their country, and their

conscience. But at the same time, that I decidedly condemn
their conduct, I would not wish to act by any means unfair,
in completing that business which they have neglected. No,
Sir, I consider that there are but forty-five members here, if
the gentleman is retained by compulsion. He cannot, Sir,
be detained against his will; and if the member is so callous
as to refuse the calls of his country to do her service, and for-
sakes his duty, when much is required, he must stand responsible to his constituents, and to his God, and must suffer
the general odium and reproach of every friend to decency or
order. But, Sir, we have no authority to confine him within
these walls; if any gentlemen suppose so, they will find upon
a due consideration, that their opinion is not well founded.
If any improper method has been used to bring him here,
and he is detained against his will, I do conceive we are not
a house.

Mr. Brackenridge. It may be a proper question for the
house to discuss, whether their officers by force have brought
this member here, or whether other members have by
violence compelled him. I suppose in either of these cases,
the house might have cognizance. But if the member has
been conducted by the citizens of Philadelphia to his seat in
the legislature, and they have not treated him with the respect and veneration he deserves, it must lie with him to obtain satisfaction, but not with us. The gentleman by
answering to his name, when the roll was called, acknowledged himself present, and forms a part of the house. Well,
Sir, I conceive the question is, what is to be done now he is
here—for how he came here, can form no part of our enquiry.
Whether his friends brought him (and I should think they
could not be his enemies, who would compel him to do his
duty, and avoid wrong) I say, Sir, whether his friends
brought him, or by the influence of good advice persuaded
him to come, and he did come; or whether to ease his difficulty in walking to this room, they brought him in a sedan
chair, or by whatever ways or means he introduced himself
among us, all we are to know, is, that he is here, and it
only remains for us to decide whether he shall have leave of

absence. Now, if the gentleman can show, that his life will be endangered by staying with us (for I should think the loss of health, on the present occasion, an insufficient reason) we may grant him the indulgence he asks for, waiving the whole story of his coming, I presume the house can immediately decide whether he may retire or not.

Mr. M'Calmont. I desire that the rules may be read, and I will agree to stand by the decision of the house.

The rules were read accordingly, and it appeared, that every member who did not answer on calling the roll, should pay two shillings and six pence, or, if there was not a quorum without him, five shillings.

Mr. M'Calmont then rose from his place, and putting his hand in his pocket took out some loose silver, and said, Well, Sir, here is your five shillings to let me go.

This ludicrous circumstance occasioned a loud laugh in the gallery. And the speaker told him, that the person who had been appointed to receive the fines, was not in his place; but if he was, the member ought not to pay it, as he had not broke the rule, which declared those persons only finable, who did not appear and answer to their names; he had done both, and therefore might retain his money.

Mr. Fitzsimons hoped the member would not be dismissed; for he thought no one man ought to be allowed to break up the assembly of Pennsylvania, which could be done agreeable to constitution only by the time expiring for which it was chosen.

The Sergeant at Arms and assistant clerk had, by this time, returned from hunting up the seceding members, and appearing in the house, the clerk was examined at the bar, and related as follows:

I went, Sir, in the pursuance of your order, with the Sergeant at Arms, in search of the absent members. First, Sir, I went to Major Boyd's, and there saw Mr. Miley and Mr. M'Calmont. I informed them that the Speaker and members present had sent me for them, and showed them the resolution of Congress. They told me in answer that they *would not attend.* Before I got from that door I saw Col.

Piper and some other member, who I do not recollect, at a great distance. I went after them to the corner of Arch and Sixth streets. I saw Mr. Barr and Mr. Findley, Col. Piper and some other member, going toward Marke tstreet. *Mr. Findley looked round and saw me, as I supposed, for he mended his pace.* I followed Mr. Piper and Mr. Barr, who kept on to Market street, and soon turned the corner—before I got there. *I lost sight of Mr. Findley, who I supposed had got into some house.* I went forward after Piper and Bar and came up with them, and told them of the unanimous resolution of Congress, but they answered me in the same manner, that they *would not attend.* From them I went to Mr. Whitehill's lodging, and saw a woman that I supposed to be the maid of the house. *She informed me that Mr. Whitehill was upstairs; she went up, and staid some time, when she returned and told me he was not at home.* I saw also Mr. Clark and Mr. M'Dowell in the street, and Mr. M'Dowell told me he would consider of the matter, and he would do what he thought just. I saw Mr. Mitchell at Mr. Whitehill's lodging, and he said he *would not attend.* Mr. Dale and Mr. Antis I found at their lodgings, and Mr. Dale told me *he would not attend.* Mr. Antis said this resolution of Congress had not come officially, and therefore *he would not attend.*

D. Clymer asked if Mr. M'Calmont had offered any excuse when he was desired to attend?

Clerk. No, he said he had heard of the resolution of Congress, but *he would not attend.*

Thus ended the report of the clerk.

Mr. Logan entered into a long detail of the benefits and advantages which would result from the adoption of the proposed confederation, when several of the members desired he would confine himself to the question. He went on to remark that the member was a part of the house, he had answered to his name, and after this it lay entirely with the house whether they would dismiss him or no.

Mr. Robinson. I do not conceive the question to be, whether he shall be dismissed or not; but as the doors are open he may go out, and if he does he is only responsible to his constituents for his conduct. I conceive he cannot be detained as in prison, and it rests with the gentleman whether he will stay or not.

Mr. Wynkoop expressed some amaze at the argument of the gentleman. The member, Mr. M'Calmont, had sworn to do the duties he was delegated to; there had been nothing of force in that, and he should not for his part think himself at liberty to withdraw until the business was completed, nor could he think any member ought. He would call on the gentleman to assign his reasons for absconding from his duty at the bar of the house, where he might be heard as to his complaint; but the house could not be formed without him.

Mr. M'Calmont replied he was not to be called to the bar of this house, he had to answer for his conduct at another bar.

Mr. D. Clymer was of opinion the member was within the power of the house by being present, and instanced the case of General Ganfell, who was arrested by the sheriff's officers in a protected place. The determination of the judges was that as he was taken, he should be confined until the debt was paid, though he had his action for damages against the officers who had broken the law of the realm in arresting him. So he was for punishing every person who had ill-treated the gentleman; however faulty his conduct was, it belonged not to individuals to punish, that was to be left to the judges, who, no doubt, will see the law properly executed.

Mr. Fitzsimons was a friend to good order and decorum, but he believed the gentleman's complaint was not to be redressed by the house. The member himself had trespassed, may be inadvertedly, since he had taken his seat. He had perhaps offered the greatest indignity to the legislature of Pennsylvania, which could be offered. He has, Sir, tendered you a fine of five shillings in order to be permitted to destroy the business, if not the good government of the State. On this, Sir, I will make no reflection; the member is now here, and we may determine that he shall stay, not only on constitutional ground, but from the law of nature, that will not suffer any body to destroy its own existence prematurely.

Mr. Robinson. The question, Sir, is whether the member

shall have leave of absence. Now suppose the house determine that he shall not, and yet he should attempt to withdraw. Certainly you will not lock your doors. (Mr. Fitzsimons interrupted with, Yes, Sir, if no other method could
retain him.)

This can't be proper, Sir, for it appears to me inconsistent
with the rules of every house to return a person as a membei
by compulsion. With respect to calling a convention, I apprehend the recommendation of forty-four members will have
as good effect as if the consent of that gentleman was obtained; for the citizens of Pennsylvania will not lose their
rights or liberty because nineteen members absconded this
house. But, Sir, I can't admit the idea that there is a house
while the member declares he is retained by compulsion, but
as long as he answers to his name and keeps his seat there
surely is a house.

D. Clymer would ask if the power to refuse leave of absence
did not imply a power to detain the person, and whether in
that case, if it was necessary to lock the doors, the house
would not be justifiable? An anecdote had occurred to him
which he would wish to communicate, though somewhat foreign. *It was remarkable that three years back from yesterday, a similar session had taken place; the same number of
members, namely nineteen, had then absconded, and there was
the same number of laws ready to be compared at the table.*

Mr. G. Clymer was decidedly of opinion, even had not the
gentleman submitted himself to the decision of the house,
that they were competent to use measures to compel his stay.

The Speaker now stated the question.

Mr. Robinson had all along agreed that the member was
in the power of the house, after answering to his name—but
he had supposed him to be held by compulsion, and if so,
then they were not a house.

Mr. M'Calmont now rose and made towards the door. Mr.
Fitzsimons addressed him, but so as not to be heard; and the
gallery called out *stop him*, there being a number of citizens
at the door he went toward. The commotion subsided in a
few seconds, and Mr. M'Calmont returned to his seat to wait
the decision of the house.

Mr. Fitzsimons informed the Speaker that Mr. M'Calmont had told him he had occasion to go out, and was willing to go in company with the Sergeant at Arms; he thereupon hoped the gentleman's wish might be complied with.

The Speaker put the question, Shall Mr. M'Calmont have leave of absence? which was determined almost, if not quite, unanimously in the negative.

The house now proceeded to compare and enact a number of bills which were lying engrossed on the table.

On motion the house resumed the consideration of the unfinished resolutions which were presented yesterday by Mr. G. Clymer, when the one fixing the day for holding the election of delegates to convention was read.

Mr. Brackenridge moved to insert the first Tuesday in November to be the day throughout the State.

Mr. Wynkoop thought the last Tuesday in October would allow sufficient time, but Mr. D. Clymer approved of the most distant day. None of the gentlemen were anxious about the week, and therefore agreed the question should be on the first Tuesday in November.

Mr. M'Calmont thought this much too early, and moved successively for the last Tuesday, the third Tuesday, and second Tuesday in December, without being seconded.

The question was therefore taken on the *first Tuesday in November*, which was agreed to.

On appointing the place where the convention should sit, it was proposed by Mr. M'Calmont to alter it from the city of Philadelphia to Carlisle; but in this he was not seconded. He then moved for Lancaster, and after some time was seconded by Mr. Lowry. The yeas and nays were called by him on this question, and are:

YEAS. Lowry, Hubley, Carpenter, Work, Ross, Clemson, M'Conaghy, Schmyser, M'Clellan, J. Hiester, G. Hiester, Cannon, M'Calmont, Miley, Carson—15.

NAYS. Will, Morris, Fitzsimons, Clymer, Hiltzeimer, Gray, Robinson, Salter, Logan, Foulke, Wynkoop, Chapman, Upp, Moore, Willing, Ralston, Evans, Thomas, Wheelen, Lilley, Kreemer, Davis, D. Clymer, Trexler, Burkhalter, Brackenridge, Moore, Wheeler, Hockley and Risse—30.

So it was determined in the negative, and afterward the resolution was agreed to as it stood.

Mr. G. Clymer now moved to insert these words in the preamble: "And whereas Congress on Friday, the twenty-eighth instant, did unanimously resolve that the said constitution be transmitted to the several legislatures of the States to the intent aforesaid." Which was accordingly done.

The resolutions were finally passed in the following form:

WHEREAS, the Convention of Deputies from the several States composing the union, lately held in this city, have published a constitution for the future government of the United States, to be submitted to conventions of deputies chosen in each State by the people thereof, under the recommendation of its legislature, for their assent and ratification; and,

WHEREAS, Congress, on Friday, the 28th inst., did unanimously resolve that the said constitution be transmitted to the several legislatures of the States to the intent aforesaid; and,

WHEREAS, it is the sense of great numbers of the good people of this State, already signified in petitions and declarations to this house, that the earliest steps should be taken to assemble a convention within the State, for the purpose of deliberating and determining on the said constitution,

Resolved, That it be recommended to such of the inhabitants of the State as are entitled to vote for representatives to the general assembly, that they choose suitable persons to serve as deputies in a State convention, for the purpose hereinbefore mentioned, that is, for the city of Philadelphia and the counties respectively, the same number of deputies that each is entitled to of representatives in the general assembly.

Resolved, That the elections for deputies as aforesaid, be held at the several places in the said city and counties as are fixed by law for holding the elections of representatives to the general assembly, and that the same be conducted by the officers who conduct the said elections of representatives, and agreeably to the rules and regulations thereof; and that the election of deputies as aforesaid, shall be held for the city of Philadelphia, and the several counties of this State, on the first Tuesday of November next.

Resolved, That the persons so elected to serve in convention shall assemble on the third Tuesday of November, at the State House in the city of Philadelphia.

Resolved, That the proposition submitted to this house by the deputies of Pennsylvania in the general convention of the States, of ceding to the United States a district of country within this State for the seat of the general government, and for the exclusive legislation of Congress, be particularly recommended to the consideration of the convention.

Resolved, That it be recommended to the succeeding house of assembly to make the same allowance to the attending members of the convention as is made to the members of the general assembly, and also to provide for the extraordinary expenses which may be incurred by holding the said elections.*

*From the Minutes of the Assembly.

The sixteen seceding members attempted to justify their conduct, and issued the following address to their constituents:

An Address of the subscribers, members of the late House of Representatives of the Commonwealth of Pennsylvania, to their constituents.*

Gentlemen: When in consequence of your suffrages at the late election we were chosen to represent you in the general assembly of this commonwealth, we accepted of the important trust with a determination to execute it in the best manner we were able; and we flatter ourselves we have acted in such a manner as to convince you, that your interest, with that of the good of the State, has been the object of our measures.

During the fall and spring sessions of the legislature on the recommendation of the Congress of the United States your representatives proceeded to the appointment of delegates to attend a convention to be held in the city of Philadelphia, for the purposes of revising and amending the present articles of confederation, and to report their proceedings to Congress, and when adopted by them, and ratified by the several States, to become binding on them as part of the confederation of the United States. We lamented at the time, that a majority of our legislature appointed men to represent this State who were all citizens of Philadelphia, none of them calculated to represent the landed interest of Pennsylvania, and almost all of them of one political party, men who have been uniformly opposed to that constitution for which you have on every occasion manifested your attachment. We were apprehensive at the time of the ill-consequences of so partial a representation, but all opposition was in vain. When the convention met, members from twelve States attended, and after deliberating upwards of four months on the subject, agreed on a plan of government which was sent forward by them to Congress, and which was reported to the house by the delegates of Pennsylvania as mere matter of information, and

* From the Pennsylvania Packet, Oct, 4th, 1787.

printed in the newspapers of the city of Philadelphia; but the house had not received it officially from Congress, nor had we the least idea that, as the annual election was so near, we should be called upon to deliberate, much less to act on so momentous a business; a business of the utmost importance to you and your posterity. We conceived it required the most minute examination and mature consideration, and that it ought to be taken up by the next house. Judge then of our surprise on finding the last day but one in the sessions, a member of the house who had been a delegate in the convention, without any previous notice or any intimation of his intentions to the house, offer a resolution recommending the calling a convention to consider of the proposed constitution and to direct the electing members for the same, at so early a period as the day of your annual election, thus attempting to surprise you into a choice of members—to approve or disapprove of a constitution, which is to entail happiness or misery forever, without giving time to the greatest part of the State even to see, much less to examine, the plan of government.

Our duty to ourselves and our regard for your dearest interests induced us to oppose the measure by every possible argument that we could suggest at the time; but all our efforts were insufficient even to produce a postponement until the afternoon. We urged and urged in vain the constant practice of the house when any important business was to be brought on, of giving previous notice and making it the order of the day sometime beforehand; that no bill, however trifling, was passed without three readings, and without this formality which gave the members time and opportunity to think on the subject; that the rules were adhered to so strictly, that even the building of a bridge, or the laying out a road, could not be determined on without this form; but this, the most important of all matters, was to be done by surprise, and as we conceived with design to preclude you from having it in your power to deliberate on the subject. Our anxiety for your interests was great, but notwithstanding the firmest and most determined opposition, no respite could be obtained, and the first resolution was adopted by a majority of the house, when they adjourned till the afternoon to complete the business. In these circumstances we had no alternative; we were under a necessity of either returning to the house, and by our presence enabling them to call a convention before our constituents could have the means of information, or time to deliberate on the subject, or by absenting ourselves from the house, prevent the measure taking place. Our regard for you induced us to prefer the latter, and we determined not to attend in the afternoon. We conceived that at the time we were chosen you had no view to this business, and we could see no inconvenience nor loss of time from deferring a matter of such importance, and which would in its consequences affect or perhaps annihilate our own constitution, as well as that of every constitution in the union, to a house chosen after the people had some knowledge of the plan, especially as the next house will meet at so early a period, and a convention could be called by them time enough to meet in a few months, which would be as early as any State in the union, and would be allowing you time to make up your minds on a matter which appeared to us to require so much deliberation. Thus circumstanced and thus influenced, we determined the next morning again to absent ourselves from the house, when James M'Calmont, esq., a member from Franklin, and Jacob Miley, esq., a member from Dauphin, were seized by a number of citizens of Philadelphia, who had collected together for that purpose, their lodgings were violently broken open, their clothes torn, and after much abuse and insult they were forcibly dragged through the streets of Philadelphia to the State house, and there detained by force, and in the presence of the majority, who had the day before voted for the first of the proposed resolutions, treated with the most insulting language; while the house so formed proceeded to finish their resolutions, which they mean to offer to you as the doings of the legislature of Pennsylvania. On this outrageous proceeding we make no comment. The inhabitants of Franklin and Dauphin have been grossly insulted by the treatment of their members. We know the feelings of the people of these counties are sufficiently keen;

it becomes us not to add to them by dwelling longer on the subject; but as our conduct may, and we have no doubt will, be misrepresented, we thought it our duty to lay before our constituents, to whom alone we are accountable, a real state of facts, that they may judge for themselves. We need not tell you that we could have no interested motive to influence our conduct. A sense of that duty which we owed to you and to ourselves could have alone induced us to submit to the variety of abuse and insults which many of us have experienced for not consenting to a measure that might probably have surprised you into a surrender of your dearest rights. Our conduct has at least had the good effect to lengthen out the time of election, and induced them to postpone the election for members to the convention until the first Tuesday in November next; whereas, the resolution first proposed directed it to be holden for all the counties east of Bedford on the day of the annual election, nine days from the time of proposing the measure.

We cannot conclude without requesting you to turn your serious attention to the government now offered to your consideration: "We are persuaded that a free and candid discussion of any subject tends greatly to the improvement of knowledge, and that a matter in which the public are so deeply interested cannot be too well understood. A good constitution and government is a blessing from heaven, and the right of posterity and mankind; suffer then we intreat you no interested motive, sinister view, or improper influence to direct your determinations or bias your judgments." Provide yourselves with the new constitution offered to you by the convention, look it over with attention, that you be enabled to think for yourselves. We confess when the legislature appointed delegates to attend the convention, our ideas extended no farther than a revision or amendment of the present confederation, nor were our delegates, by the acts of assembly appointing them, authorized to do more, as will appear by referring to the said act, the second section of which describes their powers in the following words, viz.

"2. Be it enacted, and it is hereby enacted by the representatives of the freemen of the commonwealth of Pennsylvania in general assembly met, and by the authority of the same. That Thomas Mifflin, Robert Morris, George Clymer, Jared Ingersoll, Thomas Fitzsimons, James Wilson and Gouverneur Morris, Esquires, are hereby appointed deputies from this State to meet in the convention of the deputies of the respective States of North America, to be held at the city of Philadelphia, on the second day of the month of May next. And the said Thomas Mifflin, Robert Morris, George Clymer, Jared Ingersoll, Thomas Fitzsimons, James Wilson and Gouverneur Morris, Esquires, or any four of them, are hereby constituted and appointed deputies from this State, with powers to meet such deputies as may be appointed and authorized by the other States to assemble in the said convention at the city aforesaid, and to join with them in devising, deliberating on and discussing all such alterations and further provisions as may be necessary to render the federal constitution fully adequate to the exigencies of the union; and in reporting such act or acts for that purpose, to the United States in Congress assembled, as when agreed to by them, and duly confirmed by the several States, will effectually provide for the same.''

You will therefore perceive that they had no authority whatever from the legislature, to annihilate the present confederation and form a constitution entirely new, and in doing which they have acted as mere individuals, not as the official deputies of this commonwealth. If, however, after mature deliberation, you are of opinion that the plan of government which they have offered for your consideration is best calculated to promote your political happiness and preserve those invaluable privileges you at present enjoy, you will no doubt choose men to represent you in convention who will adopt it; if you think otherwise, you will, with your usual firmness, determine accordingly.

You have a right, and we have no doubt you will consider whether or not you are in a situation to support the expense of such a government as is now offered to you, as well as the expense of your State government? or whether a legislature

consisting of three branches, neither of them chosen annually, and that the senate, the most powerful, the members of
which are for six years, are likely to lessen your burthens or
increase your taxes? or whether in case your State government should be annihilated, which will probably be the case,
or dwindle into a mere corporation, the continental government will be competent to attend to your local concerns?
You can also best determine whether the power of levying
and imposing internal taxes at pleasure, will be of real use to
you or not? or whether a continental collector assisted by a
few faithful soldiers will be more eligible than your present
collectors of taxes? You will also in your deliberations on
this important business judge, whether the liberty of the
press may be considered as a blessing or a curse in a free government, and whether a declaration for the preservation of it
is necessary? or whether in a plan of government any declaration of rights should be prefixed or inserted? You will be
able, likewise, to determine whether in a free government
there ought or ought not to be any provision against a standing army in time of peace? or whether the trial by jury in
civil causes is becoming dangerous and ought to be abolished? and whether the judiciary of the United States is not
so constructed as to absorb and destroy the judiciaries of the
several States? You will also be able to judge whether such
inconveniencies have been experienced by the present mode
of trial between citizen and citizen of different States as to
render a continental court necessary for that purpose? or
whether there can be any real use in the appellate jurisdiction with respect to fact as well as law? We shall not dwell
longer on the subject; one thing however, it is proper you
should be informed of: the convention were not unanimous
with respect to men, though they were as States; several of
those who have signed did not fully approve of the plan of
government, and three of the members, viz. : Governor Randolph and Colonel George Mason, of Virginia, and Eldridge
Gerry, Esq., of Massachusetts, whose characters are very respectable, had such strong objections as to refuse signing.
The confederation, no doubt, is defective, and requires

amendment and revision, and had the convention extended their plan to the enabling the United States to regulate commerce, equalize the impost, collect it throughout the United States, and have the entire juristiction over maritime affairs, leaving the exercise of internal taxation to the separate States, we apprehend there would have been no objection to the plan of government.

The matter will be before you, and you will be able to judge for yourselves. "Show that you seek not yourselves, but the good of your country, and may He who alone has dominion over the passions and understandings of men enlighten and direct you aright, that posterity may bless God for the wisdom of their ancestors."

James M'Calmont,	John Gilchrist,
Robert Clark,	Abraham Smith,
Jacob Miley,	Robert Whitehill,
Alexander Wright,	David Mitchell,
John M'Dowell,	John Piper,
John Flenniken,	Samuel Dale,
James Allison,	William Findley,
Theophilus Philips,	James Barr.

Saturday, Sept. 29, 1787.

To this address a dozen replies came forth immediately. One was signed by six members of the Assembly, and appeared in the Pennsylvania Packet for October 8.

MESSRS. DUNLAP AND CLAYPOOLE.

Mr. Findley, Mr. Whitehill, and others, members of the late General Assembly, making a disorderly secession from the house, with intention to put an end to its deliberations upon the subject of calling a State Convention, for the purpose of considering the system offered for the general government of the United States, they have, in a public address, rested their justification on these two points:

1st. The irregularity of taking up the constitution framed by the convention without the special permission of Congress—the assembly having in the appointment of deputies to the convention, proceeded but upon the recommendation of Congress.

3d. The unfitness of the deputies appointed—the addressers lamenting at the time when the choice was made, that they were all citizens of Philadelphia, and none of them *calculated* to represent the landed interest of the State.

Having been also members of the house, and competent to judge with respect to these points of justification, we beg leave to state all the necessary facts concerning them for the information of the public.

As to the first—on a communication of the proposition of Virginia, for holding a general convention, a bill for the appointment of the deputies was reported by a committee, of which Mr. Findley and Mr. Whitehill were members, and passed into a law on the 30th of December last. The law, as set forth in the preamble, stood upon "*Representations of Congress heretofore made*," and on the proposition of Virginia; but the special recommendation of Congress, to send the deputies to the proposed convention, made no part of the preamble—this recommendation not having passed Congress until the 21st day of February following, when that body, for the first time, recognized the convention. In the next session, on the 28th of March, a supplementary law passed the house; but its only object was to add another deputy to the number already chosen, and its only reference was to the original act.

As the representations of Congress spoken of in the preamble to the law, of the first session, were only such as had been frequently made of the weakness of the general government, and of the necessity that arose of endowing it with greater powers, but gave no special license to the States to send deputies to the convention proposed by the State of Virginia, it follows that in the appointment of the deputies, the assembly acted independently of Congress or of its recommendation. It is in vain, for the reasons before mentioned, that the addressers attempt, by a general reference to the transactions of both sessions, to cover their assertion upon this head—it is an artifice more unworthy than the most naked falsehood.

As little can be said in support of the second, their disapprobation of the deputies, which a state of nominations and votes will evince. The original intention of the house was to send seven deputies, though afterwards that number was, by the supplementary law, increased to eight. To supply the seven places, twelve persons stood in nomination: they, with the votes for each, were as follows:

*Jared Ingersoll, 61; Charles Pettit, 25; *Robert Morris, 63; *George Clymer, 63; *Thomas Mifflin, 63; Thomas M'Kean, 26; John Bayard, 25; *Thomas Fitzsimons, 37; *James Wilson, 35; *Governeur Morris, 33; Benjamin Franklin, 10; William Findley, 2.

Of whom those marked with an * were elected.

As to four of these persons, there appears from the votes to have been a general agreement, 63 being the number composing the house; so that no real controversy took place but as to the remaining three. Between these opposite three then must have have lain the question with the house, with respect to the fitness to represent the landed interest; and for this they might all have been fit, except in the circumstance of city residence, the candidates generally holding considerable landed property within the State, the whole body of candidates, Mr. Findley excepted, being inhabitants of Philadelphia; and as to that gentleman, the solitary nominee from the country, he seems then, from the state of the votes, to have been out of the question, which is the more extraordinary, if, as the addressers must be understood, a country residence was indispensable to represent the landed interest of the State.

But the truth is, that at the time of election no such lamentation was made by the sixteen or any others that the candidates were citizens of Philadelphia, or otherwise unqualified to represent the landed interest; for it is well known, that both Mr. Findley and Mr. Whitehill were of opinion that the choice should be confined to the city of Philadelphia and its neighborhood, as it would not be convenient for persons living at a distance to attend a convention; the former declaring a seat there would not suit him, which, perhaps, may account for the fewness of his votes.

This being the state of facts relating to these points, can we suppose a depravation of mind equal to such impositions and deceptions, or ought we not rather to suppose, in these instances, that the addressers were not at the pains to read what was prepared to their hands?

It is urged, in argument against the house, that the deputies having exceeded the terms of their powers, the system they agreed to ought not to be taken up. It is not easy to determine to what the powers of the deputation from Pennsylvania, and from the other States (for they are in the same predicament), did really extend; but any argument brought from an excess in the exercise of the powers against the object of them cannot be that of good sense or integrity. A man of understanding, or a good patriot, will examine only whether or not the system actually offered is calculated to better the condition of our country. Indeed one would think, the system being no more than a proposition, which none are bound to yield to, though all ought to consider, that the convention have not really transgressed their powers: they certainly might make whatever propositions they pleased.

The addressers resent the harsh treatment of the house to the two of their body who were forced back to their seats, by some of the citizens from without. They suffered no such treatment; on the contrary, the house showed a wonderful good temper on so provoking an occasion. When a misdemeanor had been committed of a kind which, though it has hitherto escaped even the slightest punishment, is deserving of the highest. When the addressers had by their conduct violated the first condition of all political society, which obliges the few to give way to the many. When they had offended in the double capacity of citizens of the United States and of Pennsylvania, in setting a dangerous example of riot and turbulence to the continent; and, as much as lay in their feeble means, attempting to dissolve the government under which they live.

William Will,	Jacob Hiltzheimer,
Thomas Fitzsimons,	Daniel Clymer,
George Clymer,	William Robinson, Junr.

Dr. Franklin's not having been chosen at the first election, was owing to a misunderstanding among the members with respect to his willingness to serve; but on better information, in the next session, it was the unanimous desire of the house that he should be added, which gave occasion to the supplementary law.

Philadelphia, October 6, 1787.

Another was a mock protest entitled:

THE PROTEST OF THE MINORITY, WHO OBJECTED TO CALLING A CONVENTION FOR THE PURPOSE OF ADOPTING THE FEDERAL CONSTITUTION. *

Dissentient.

1. Because, by the diminution of the power of the State of Pennsylvania, we shall have fewer officers and smaller salaries to bestow upon our friends.

2. Because, like the declaration of independence, the measure, if a right one, is *premature.*

3. Because the new federal constitution puts an end to all future emissions of paper money, and to tender laws, to both of which many of us owe our fortunes, and all of us our prospects of extrication from debt and exemption from gaol, or the benefit of the bankrupt law.

4. Because, by the new constitution of the United States, we shall be compelled to pay our taxes . . . whereas we now pay nothing towards the support of the government, and yet are handsomely supported out of the State treasury.

5. Because, the new constitution was not submitted to the consideration of the anti-federal junto in Philadelphia, before it was sent to Congress, to each individual whereof America is under greater obligations than to General Washington.

6. Because, by the 6th section of the 1st article of the Constitution of the United States, it is made impossible for persons in power to create offices for themselves, or to appoint themselves to office. This we conceive to be an evident departure from the free and excellent constitution of Pennsylvania, by which it is lawful for assemblymen and councillors

* Pennsylvania Gazette, Oct. 3, 1787.

to appoint themselves or their sons to all, or to any of the offices of the State.

7. Because a disaffected member of the federal convention. from Virginia, in a closet conversation with R. Whitehill, disapproved of the federal government, and we hold it to be our duty rather to follow his advice, than the inclinations of our constituents.

8. Because, from the power claimed by the new constitution, Congress will have a right to suppress all "domestic insurrections" in particular States, by which means we shall be deprived of the only means of opposing the laws of this State, especially laws for collecting taxes.

F——y, W——ll & Co., Major B——d's cellar, Sept. 29, 1787.

A local poet furnished the following:

DUETTO.*

Sung by W—h–ll and F—dl–y, accompanied by G—e B—n with a Violincelo.—Tune Darby, in the Poor Soldier.

1.

Though rascals and rogues they may call,
    Right toll loll, etc.
Yet now we may laugh at them all ;
    Right, etc.
'Twas well we escaped with whole bones,
    Right, etc.
For we merited horsewhips and stones,
    Right, etc.

2.

In troth we have cut no great dash,
    Right, etc.
Run away and not compass the cash,
    Right, etc.
I am sure 'twas a damnable shame,
    Right, etc.
But on fear we may lay all the blame,
    Right, etc.

3.

They may call us the glorious sixteen,
    Right, etc.
Such glory I wish I'd not seen ;
    Right, etc.

* Independent Gazetteer, Oct. 5, 1787.

For of all rogues the greatest we are
    Right, etc.
That ever smelt feathers and tar,
    Right, etc.

4.

Then quietly let us jog on,
    Right, etc.
Drink in comfort our whisky grog strong,
    Right, etc.
Rejoice that we 'scaped without evil,
    Right, etc.
And go as we ought to the devil.
    Right, etc.

But more serious addresses were called forth, of which the following were the most important:

Fellow Citizens: *

Upon perusing the address of sixteen of the seceding members of the late General Assembly to their constituents, I was much surprised to find, that they had so far lost all sense of their own dignity, as representatives of a free people, as basely to assert what I am informed are absolute falsehoods with respect to the conduct of those citizens, who did them the honor to conduct them to that house. The manner in which they endeavored to interest the feelings of their constituents in the supposed insults offered, and fancied wrongs done them, must convince every impartial mind, that they were aware of the impropriety of their own conduct, and fearful lest the good sense of their constituents should doom them to future neglect if a true state of facts should reach them. They knew full well that first impressions are, generally, the strongest, and that injuries or insults offered the representatives of any part of the community, could not but deeply interest that part in their favor—they knew these things, and they wisely determined to be beforehand with their opponents.

But let us candidly examine into the conduct of both parties in this affair, and let us not fear to censure where blame is due. What were the reasons which induced the seceding

* Independent Gazetteer, Oct. 9, 1787.

members to swerve from that duty which they owed their constituents—from that duty which they owed themselves.

The first grievance which they complain of is, that there were no country members in the delegation of this State to the late convention. What occasioned this circumstance I presume not to say, although I have no doubt that the house by which they were appointed had ample reason for this part of their conduct, and such reason as would be perfectly satisfactory to the State at large. Their next complaint appears to be, that the House of Assembly did not wait for Congress officially to recommend to them the calling of a convention upon this great and truly interesting occasion; but they are not candid enough to mention, that an express arrived to them from that body (whilst that very business was yet before them) earnestly recommending the very mode of conducting this important affair which the assembly had had in contemplation, and which they have since adopted. From this statement of the case, our representatives in the General Assembly do not appear to have acted improperly, and the progress they had made in the business before they were officially called upon, is rather deserving of praise than censure; for it shows that they attended to the call of duty, without reflecting whether it might turn to their private emolument or not.

What good could have resulted from delay, or why should a calling of a convention require so much deliberation? No good I am bold to say could have been derived from the postponement, but much evil might have resulted from such a measure—and certainly no one will hesitate to say that the representatives of a people convened for the express purpose of examining a constitution proposed for the acceptance or refusal of the citizens of the United States, will be fully competent to the task assigned them, and be as much possessed of the confidence of their constituents as any assembly, which they might choose at any future day. But is it not probable that the seceding members might have had something else in view which they wished to give the appearance of public good? As an individual I must acknowledge that I think they had, and I fully believe that every candid man, and every impartial observer of public transactions and party cabals, will join me in this acknowledgment. For it is too evident from the meeting of the junto at a certain clergyman's house in the neighborhood of the university, as well as from the frequent passings of one of the judges of the supreme court from that house to the lodgings of Mr. W———, not long since, when Sunday's dinner was given by that clergyman to a chosen few, that private interest was deeply concerned in the decision, and that a scheme was laid to impose upon our fellow citizens in the back as well as neighboring counties, that by sowing dissensions amongst us, they may save from deserved censure and disgrace, those poor tools who had shown themselves ready to encounter the displeasure of all good men, to forward the sinister views and wicked designs of a wretched faction.

After much pretended regard for your interests (which by the bye is a convenient cloak for their ruinous, and I may add, detestable schemes) they wish to excuse their conduct in attempting to break up the house, at this important crisis, by asserting that they had no alternative left, that they must either abandon your interests or break up the house. But how would they sacrifice your interests by calling of a convention? It is true, that they are conceited enough to imagine, that you are not able to form a judgment without their assistance; and they treat you like children who must be closely watched, to prevent them from injuring themselves; at the same time, they do not neglect this opportunity of filling your ears with complaints against the citizens of Philadelphia, for injuries and insults offered you, as they pretend, through them your representatives. But the fact appears very different from what they have stated it to every impartial mind, and I have not the least doubt but that you will judge, upon calmly considering the action which hath excited their spleen, that the persons complained against by them, were induced by motives of necessity, and public good to exert themselves in bringing your servants as well as theirs, to that duty from which they had disgracefully absconded.

They wish to prejudice you also against the house of assembly, by representing their conduct as illegal, and of course insinuating, that you ought not to consider yourselves bound by their resolves for calling a convention. They must certainly have thought differently upon this subject, or at least those two who were conducted to that house, and who have joined in the address to you; for they made motions and proposed alterations in the same manner as they would have done, if they had considered that house, as it most certainly was, legally and constitutionally formed.

Shortly after they discover a little more of their true sentiments, and throwing off the mask, which they have worn too long for your good, discover themselves to be much opposed, nay utterly averse, to the constitution proposed by the convention. And in declaring the delegates from this state no ways authorized to accede to the constitution proposed, by the act of assembly in which they were appointed, they injudiciously point out what they would wish to conceal and discover as the author of their piece and as their prime mover and adviser upon all occasions, an hackneyed attorney, and an unnecessary judge.

Little do their constituents imagine that they are paying men to answer private purposes, and that the alarm which is sounded arises to seceding members from their fears that the offices under this commonwealth will be made less lucrative, and, instead of being confined to one party, will be more regularly diffused through the community. They fear lest their particular friends in this city, by being found unworthy of the posts they fill, should no longer eat the bread of idleness or riot in the spoils of their fellow-citizens; and that the Trenton hero, who mistook the march of his battalion, and claimed the place of vendue-master of this city, in a long parade of imaginary services rendered the state, should no longer fill offices for which he is totally unqualified.

They also fear for the descendants of their masters, and they lament that the great man in embryo, whose strut has long since announced his self-importance, will no longer have an opportunity of occasioning to disappear from the files of the house, such papers, as like the petition or rather demand of the Trenton hero, show their authors in their proper colors as vain, as useless, and as ignorant tools.

They declare themselves apprehensive that the constitution of this State should dwindle into a corporation, and that the Congress of the United States should levy contributions by an armed force, instead of collecting taxes by municipal officers. What part of the constitution offered to you gives them such a power? I am bold to say that there is no part, and that they have not the slightest apprehension of the kind. The fear that paper money, that engine of oppression, should be banished the land, and that honest industry should rise superior to fraud and deceit, makes them anxious of reserving the power within their own hands of defrauding the widow and the orphan, and of keeping persons better principled than themselves, within the humble limits in which they had rather move than rise to power and to wealth by disreputable means. The concluding prayer, I will venture to assume, as I am sure that if that is attended to, they will forever be neglected. "Show that you seek not yourselves, but the good of your country, and may He alone, who has dominion over the passions and understandings of men, enlighten and direct you aright, that posterity may bless God for the wisdom of their ancestors."

An Independent Citizen.

The Independent Citizen, following the custom then in vogue, never made known his name. But another citizen, quite as independent, who replied to the address of the discontented sixteen, thought his work good enough to own and republish after the constitution had been adopted, and the "new roof" firmly set up. He was Pelatiah Webster, well known for his essays on Free Trade and Finance, and his pamphlet he called : REMARKS* ON THE ADDRESS OF SIX-

---

*These remarks were printed in pamphlet form by Eleazer Oswald. They were subsequently included in a volume of Essays Mr. Webster published in 179-, and to them he then appended the following note :

"When the *new constitution* was laid before the Assembly of Pennsylvania, in *September*, 1787, a resolution passed the House (forty-three against nine-

TEEN MEMBERS OF THE ASSEMBLY OF PENNSYLVANIA TO THEIR CONSTITUENTS, DATED SEPTEMBER 29, 1787. WITH SOME STRICTURES ON THEIR OBJECTIONS TO THE CONSTITUTION RECOMMENDED BY THE LATE FEDERAL CONVENTION.

1. The sixteen members, as appears by their own showing, are a minority of the assembly, belonging to a party which is strongly overruled by a great majorty of the house, and very much out of humor.

2. They were duly *appointed* members of the assembly, had *accepted the trust*, and *were solemnly sworn* to discharge the duties of it *faithfully and to the best of their abilities.*

3. That at a crisis of great importance in the assembly, they *deserted their station, abdicated their duty*, and refused their attendance in the house, with the most *explicit* and *avowed intention* to put an absolute stop to any business of the house, which was a contrivance not only *mean and infamous*, a trick below the dignity of members of that house, but *ruinous to the public councils*, and might in effect annihilate the assembly itself; for our constitution requires two-thirds of the members elected to make a quorum of the house, and of course if every member elected was in the house (which very rarely happens), a minority of one more than a third, or (as very frequently happens, where a bare quorum, or perhaps two or three more, attend in the house) one single member, or at most three or four, by deserting the house,

teen) to call a *convention* to consider it, etc. Sixteen of the dissentients published an *address to their constituents, dated September 27*, 1787, stating their conduct, and assigning the reasons of it; but as there was very little in all this affair that reflected *much honor* on the *dissenting members* or on *the State to which they belonged*, and *nothing* that could *affect* or *concern* anybody out of that State, I have here omitted my remarks on all of it, but *their objections* to the *new constitution itself*, which being of general consequence to the States, inasmuch as that constitution (with a few amendments since adopted) is the same which now exists in full establishment through the Union, I therefore here insert, I say, *their objections and my remarks on them*, and leave out all the rest as matter of *local* concern at *that time*, but like to be little interesting to the public in general at this or any future time."

A copy of the original pamphlet is in the Boston Athenæum, and the librarian, Mr. Cutter, has kindly had copied the portions omitted in the collected Essays, and has collated the text with the original.

might leave less than a quorum behind, and of course render them incapable of doing business; this might be continued through the year, which would in effect annihilate the house, and of course the whole State would be deprived of all benefits from their assembly.

Had our sixteen members attended their duty in the house, they might by their arguments have convinced their opponents, or might by the reasoning of their opponents have been themselves convinced, or might at least have obtained some valuable amendment; which is a benefit they claim the honor of, though only two of them attended the house, when the amendment was made.

4. It further appears by their own showing that two of their number were *forcibly* dragged to the assembly, and there detained *by force*, i. e. they were compelled by force to attend their *place and duty* in the assembly, and were not suffered to run away again, till their *duty was done.* That they received any other force, insult or dragging, than a simple compulsion to attend their duty, I suppose is not true; but this I allow to be a considerable dishonor, and a very trying mortification; for it is certainly very dishonorable and insulting to a dignified character to be publicly *forced along the streets*, *and compelled* to attend on that duty, which honor and character ought to induce him to do voluntarily without any force at all.

However, I conceive the dishonor in this case does not consist in the force and insult offered by the citizens to the deserting members, so much as in the demonstration which the circumstance affords, that their own *internal* honor and sense of character was not sufficient to induce them to do their duty without the assistance of some *external* compulsion.

Whether compelling people to do their duty is a breach of peace and violation of law, must be left to the proper court to determine; but I conceive that it can never be deemed a *damage* to any man to be compelled to do his duty, and of consequence no *damages* can be given in such a case.

This was not the first time that the same party availed themselves of this fatal artifice, to obstruct the business of the assembly, and compel the house to break up, and leave much very important business unfinished; and our citizens were determined not to suffer the like again, and the exertions of private citizens became in a manner necessary, forasmuch as our constitution provides no remedy against such an intolerable abuse of the public trust and confidence. I perceive that the framers of our constitution never once imagined that members of a Pennsylvania assembly could ever be guilty of such scandalous artifice, and, therefore, thought it needless to insult and wound the honorable feelings of their constituents by any provision or remedies against such pitiful tricks.

But all this notwithstanding, it is possible perhaps that a case may happen of an assembly mad enough to run on in full career in forming some act of a nature so absurd, and of consequence so ruinous, that some indirect methods of suspending or stopping their proceedings, might be justified. This brings me to the object which induced them to sacrifice all character and regularity of business, *overleap* all bounds, and strike at one blow the great council of the commonwealth into a state of perfect inaction. By their own showing.

5. It appears the great object, the great motive of this desperate step was to render ineffectual a resolution of the house (carried by 43 against 19), "recommending the calling a convention to *consider* of the constitution proposed by the Federal Convention, and to approve or disapprove the same."

It is here to be noted that they all agreed that such a convention ought to be called, and their only objection was that the time proposed was too soon, because the people had not time to make up their minds, i. e. : 1. To consider and judge whether the constitution was a suitable one or not; and, 2. To pitch on suitable persons for delegates to the convention.

The first of these reasons was nugatory, because it was confessed by all, that a convention was to be called, and this was the only way of knowing whether the constitution would be approved by the people or not; for this was the only method agreed on by all parties of collecting the sense of the

people, and the convention could not be straitened for time
to consider enough; because, when met, they would be at
liberty to take as much time as they pleased.

The second reason is as trifling as the first; for the great
characters in every part of the State suitable for such a trust,
would be as well known to the people on the day of election
proposed, as they would be three or six months afterwards.

To these reasons for delay were opposed the weightiest reasons for expediting the matter, because the whole Union,
both in their domestic and foreign interests, suffered very
great evils for want of a good constitution and energetic government: all which evils and mischiefs ought to be remedied
as soon as possible. The mode of remedy first to be considered was the proposed constitution; if that was approved, we
ought to proceed to execute it, without any needless delay;
if it should be disapproved, something else must be adopted,
and the pressing necessities of all the States are so great, that
no time ought to be lost. But their surprise and reasons
against the precipitate haste of the assembly in calling the
convention, does not give all the heart and all the feelings of
the sixteen members. They are greatly dissatisfied with the
constitution proposed, and use every coloring, every artifice,
and every argument they can devise to prejudice everybody
against it; and in this they are very open and candid, and
this part of their address certainly deserves our attention
much more than all the rest.

As a kind of preface to their objections, they complain of
the appointment of our delegates to the Federal Convention,
and lament: 1. That none of them *are calculated to represent
the landed interest.* I do not know how this can be, for the
delegates own more land, that is, they possess more real estate on an average, than any eight of the sixteen complainants, and are as good economists in the management of it,
and, for aught I know, are as much attached to it as any of
them. 2. Their second lamentation is more weighty, viz.,
that almost none of them were of their party, for that I take
to be their meaning, when they say that *almost all of them
were of one political party,* and were *opposed to the constitu-*

tion of Pennsylvania, which most certainly needs great amendments in the opinion of *almost* everybody.

3. They further suggest that our delegates in convention exceeded their powers, which were to make and report such *alterations* and *further provisions* in the federal constitution, as would render it fully adequate to the exigencies of the Union, or in the language of the sixteen complainants, *to revise and amend it.* I suppose the whole force of their meaning must rest on the word *amend;* for I imagine that to revise without amending it, would not have come up to their ideas. Now *an amendment,* in the sense of legislative bodies, means either to strike out some words, clauses or paragraphs in a bill, without substituting anything in the place of them, or to insert new words, clauses or paragraphs where nothing was inserted before ; or to strike out some words, clauses or paragraphs, and insert others in their room, which will suit better. Now I challenge the whole sixteen members to show that the convention have done an iota more than this ; besides, the new constitution does not by any express words, repeal the old one; therefore I suppose every article of the old one stands good and valid, unless where they are changed or annulled by the alterations and provisions of the new one. But after all, if the constitution offered to us is either a good one or a bad one, I cannot see that it is of any consequence to us, whether it is *the old one* revised and amended, or *a new one* fresh made; nor is it material whether the delegates of this State were competent to the business or not: it is offered by the whole respectable body—a body dignified by the general election of the States—and therefore ought to be received with respect, and treated with candid attention; but in the discussion of it as a rule of government for us all, the merits of it ought to be the sole consideration, and it is the acceptance of the States alone which can give it the stamp of authority; therefore any little bickerings about the qualities, or views, or powers of this or that member, must be mere quibbles of no weight or consequence.

4. It is further objected with great parade, that three members of the convention refused to sign, and but thirty-nine of

them only did sign the constitution proposed to us; but I
think that so large a majority in its favor very far outweighs
the negative of three members against it, neither of which
has any pretensions of character superior to the thirty-nine
who signed it.

Further, 5. They object to the assembly's recommending
the calling a convention, *till they received the new constitution officially from Congress.* I answer, 1. The assembly
meant *to pursue the recommendation of the Federal Convention,* which does not make the official directions of Congress
necessary to calling the State conventions, under the recommendation of their legislatures; and had Congress refused to
issue any official directions at all to the assembly, I do not
know that the holding the State convention ought to have
been prevented thereby. 2. The assembly had *the most certain information of the fact,* and had no doubt *of receiving all
necessary official communications from Congress,* long before
the convention could meet, or if they never came, could very
well act without them. 3. Their not waiting for *official letters from Congress* did not proceed *from any want of respect
to Congress,* but merely from their being *straitened for time,*
as the end of the session drew very near.

I come now to consider the objections of our sixteen members to the constitution itself, which is much the most important part that lies on me.

1. Their first objection is, that the government proposed will
be too expensive. I answer that if the appointments of officers are not more, and the compensations or emoluments of
office not greater than is necessary, the expense will be by no
means burdensome; and this must be left to the prudence of
Congress, for I know of no way to control supreme powers
from extravagance in this respect. Doubtless many instances
may be produced of many needless offices being created, and
many inferior officers, who receive far greater emoluments of
office than the president of the state.

2. Their next objection is against a *legislature consisting of
three branches.* This is so far from an objection that I consider it as an advantage. The most weighty and important

affairs of the union must be transacted in congress; the most essential councils must be there decided, which must all go through three several discussions in three different chambers (all equally competent to the subject and equally governed by the same motives and interests, viz., the good of the great commonwealth, and the approbation of the people) before any decision can be made; and when disputes are very high, five discussions are necessary, all of which afford time for all parties to cool and reconsider.

This appears to me to be a very safe way, and a very likely method to prevent any sudden and undigested resolutions from passing, and though it may delay, or even destroy, a good bill, will hardly admit the passing of a bad one, which is by far the worst evil of the two. But if all this cannot stop the course of a bad bill, the negative of the president will at least give it further embarrassment, will furnish all the new light which a most serious discussion in a third House can give, and will make a new discussion necessary in each of the other two, where every member will have an opportunity to revise his opinion, to correct his arguments, and bring his judgment to the greatest maturity possible. If all this can not keep the public decision within the bounds of wisdom, natural fitness, right and convenience, it will be hard to find any efforts of human wisdom that can do it.

I believe it would be difficult to find a man in the union who would not readily consent to have congress vested with all the vast powers proposed by the new constitution, if he could be sure that those powers would be exercised with wisdom, justice, and propriety, and not be abused; and I do not see that greater precautions and guards against abuses can well be devised, or more effectual methods used to throw every degree of light on every subject of debate, or more powerful motives to a reasonable and honest decision can be set before the minds of congress than are here proposed; and if this is the best that can be obtained, it ought in all prudence to be adopted till better appears, rather than to be rejected merely because it is human, not perfect, and may be abused. At any rate, I think it very plain that our chance of a right decision in a congress of three branches, is much greater than in one of a single chamber; but, however all this may, be I can not see the least tendency in a legislature of three branches to increase the burdens or taxes of the people. I think it very evident that any proposition of extravagant expense would be checked and embarrassed in such an assembly, more than in a single house.

Further, the two houses being by their election taken from the body of the states, and being themselves principal inhabitants, will naturally have the interest of the commonwealth sincerely at heart: their principle must be the same, their differences must be (if any) in the mode of pursuing it, or arise from local attachments. I say, the great interest of their country, and the esteem, confidence, and approbation of their fellow citizens must be strong governing principles in both houses, as well as in the president himself; "whilst at the same time the emulation naturally arising between them will induce a very critical and sharp-sighted inspection into the motions of each other. Their different opinions will bring on conferences between the two houses, in which the whole subject will be exhausted in arguments pro and con, and shame will be the portion of obstinate convicted error. Under these circumstances a man of ignorance or evil design will be afraid to impose on the credulity, inattention or confidence of his house by introducing any corrupt or indigested proposition which he knows he must be called on to defend against the severe scrutiny and poignant objections of the other house. I do not believe the many hurtful and foolish legislative acts which first or last have injured all the states on earth, have originated so much in corruption as in indolence, ignorance, and a want of a full comprehension of the subject, which a full, prying and emulous discussion would tend in a great measure to remove: this naturally rouses the lazy and idle, who hate the pain of close thinking, animates the ambitious to excel in policy and argument, and excites the whole to support the dignity of their house and vindicate their own propositions. I am not of opinion that bodies of elective men which usually compose parliaments, diets, assemblies, congresses, etc., are commonly dishonest; but I believe it rarely happens that there are not designing men among them, and I think it would be much more difficult for them to unite their partisans in two houses and corrupt or deceive them both, than to carry on their designs where there is but one unalarmed, unapprehensive house to be managed; and as there is no hope of making these bad men good, the best policy is to embarrass them, and make their work as difficult as possible. In these assemblies are frequently to be found sanguine men, upright enough indeed, but of strong, wild projection, whose brains are always teeming with Utopian, chimerical plans and political whims, very destructive to society. I hardly know a greater evil than to have the supreme councils of a nation played off on such men's wires; such baseless visions at best end in darkness, and the dance, though easy and merry enough at first, rarely fails to plunge the credulous, simple followers into sloughs and bogs at last. Nothing can tend more effectually to obviate these evils and to mortify and cure such maggoty brains, than to see the absurdity of their projects exposed by the several arguments and keen satire which a full, emulous and spirited discussion of the subject will naturally produce. We have had enough of these geniuses in the short course of our politics, both in our national and provincial councils, and have felt enough of their evil effects, to induce us to wish for any good methods to keep ourselves clear of them in future.

"The consultations and decisions of national councils are so very important, that the fate of millions depends on them; therefore no man ought to speak in such assemblies, without considering that the fate of millions hangs on his tongue, and, of course, a man can have no right in such august councils to utter indigested sentiments, or indulge himself in sudden unexamined flights of thought; his most tried and improved abilities are due to the States, who have trusted him with their most important interests. A man must therefore be most inexcusable, who is either *absent* during such debates, or sleeps, or whispers, or catches flies during the argument, and just rouses when the vote is called to give his yea or nay, to the weal or woe of a nation. Therefore it is manifestly proper, that every natural motive that can operate on his understanding, or his passions, to engage his attention and utmost efforts, should be put in practice, and that his present feelings should be raised by every motive of honor and shame, to stimulate him to every practicable degree of diligence and exertion, to be as far as possible useful in the great discussion. I appeal to the feelings of every reader, if he would not (were he in either house) be much more strongly and naturally induced to exert his utmost abilities and attention to any question which was to pass through the ordeal of a spirited discussion of another house, than he would be, if the absolute decision depended on his own house without any further enquiry or challenge on the subject."—*Vide a Dissertation* on the Political Union and Constitution of the Thirteen United States, published *by a citizen of Philadelphia*, February 16, 1783, where the subject is taken up at large.

3. Another objection is, that the constitution proposed will *annihilate the state governments or reduce them to mere corporations.* I take it that this objection is thrown out (merely *invidiæ causa*) without the least ground for it; for I do not find one article of the constitution proposed, which vests congress, or any of their officers or courts, with a power to interfere in the least in the internal police or goverment of any one state, when the interests of some other state or strangers, or the union in general, are not concerned; and in all such cases it is absolutely and manifestly necessary that congress should have a controlling power, otherwise there would be no end of controversies and injuries between different states, nor any safety for individuals, nor any possibility of supporting the union with any tolerable degree of honor, strength or security.

4. Another objection is against *the power of taxation vested in congress.* But, I answer, this is absolutely unavoidable, from the necessity of the case; I know it is a tender point, a vast power, and a terrible engine of oppression and tyranny, when wantonly, injudiciously, or wickedly used, but must be

admitted; for it is impossible to support the union, or indeed any government, without expense—the congress are the proper judges of that expense—the amount of it, and the best means of supplying it; the safety of the states absolutely requires that this power be lodged somewhere, and no other body can have the least pretensions to it; and no part of the resources of the states can, with any safety, be exempt, when the exigencies of the union or government require their utmost exertion. The stronger we make our government, the greater protection it can afford us, and the greater will our safety be under it. It is easy enough here to harangue on the arts of a court to create occasions for money, or the unbounded extravagance with which they can spend it; but all this notwithstanding, we must take our courts as we do our wives, *for better or for worse.* We hope the best of an American congress, but if they disappoint us, we cannot help it; it is in vain to try to form any plan of avoiding the frailties of human nature. Would any man choose a *lame* horse, lest a *sound* one should run away with him? or will any man prefer a *small tent* to live in before a *large house*, which may fall down and crush him in its ruins? No man has any right to find fault with this article, till he can substitute a better in its room.

The sixteen members attempt to aggravate the horrors of this devouring power, by suggesting the rigid severity with which congress, with their *faithful soldiers*, will exact and collect the taxes. This picture, stripped of its black drapery, amounts to just this, viz: That whatever taxes are laid will be collected, without exception, from every person charged with them—which must look disagreeable, I suppose, to people who, by one shift or another, have avoided paying taxes all their lives. But it is a plain truth, and will be obvious to anybody who duly considers it, that nothing can be more ruinous to a state, or oppressive to individuals, than a partial and dilatory collection of taxes, especially where the tax is an impost or excise, because the man who avoids the tax can undersell, and consequently ruin, him who pays it, *i. e.* smuggling ruins the fair trader; and a remedy of this mischief, I cannot suppose, will be deemed by our people in general such a very awful judgment, as the sixteen members would make us believe their constituents will consider it to be.

5. They object that the *liberty of the press is not asserted* in the constitution. I answer, neither are any of the ten commandments, but I do not think that it follows that it was the design of the convention to sacrifice either the one or the other to contempt or to leave them void of protection and effectual support.

6. It is objected further that the constitution contains *no declaration of rights*. I answer, this is not true—the constitution contains a declaration of many rights, and very important ones, *e. g.*, that people shall be obliged to fulfil their contracts, and not avoid them by tenders of anything less than the value stipulated; that no *ex post facto* laws shall be made, &c.; but it was no part of the business of their appointment to make a code of laws—it was sufficient to fix the constitution right, and that would pave the way for the most effectual security of the rights of the subject.

7. They further object that no provision is made against *a standing army in time of peace*. I answer, that a standing army, *i. e.* regular troops are often necessary in time of peace, to prevent a war, to guard against sudden invasions, for garrison-duty, to quell mobs and riots, as guards to congress and perhaps other courts, &c., &c., as military schools to keep up the knowledge and habits of military discipline and exercise, &c., &c.; and as the power of raising troops is rightfully and without objection vested in congress, so they are the properest and best judges of the number requisite, and of the occasion, time and manner of employing them; if they are not wanted on military duty, they may be employed in making public roads, fortifications, or any other public works—they need not be a useless burden to the states. And for all this the prudence of congress must be trusted, and nobody can have a right to object to this, till they can point out some way of doing better.

8. Another objection is, that the new constitution *abolishes trials by jury in civil causes*. I answer, I do not see one word

in the constitution, which by any candid construction can support even the remotest suspicion that this ever entered the heart of one member of the convention; I therefore set down the suggestion for sheer malice, and so dismiss it.

9. Another objection is that the federal *judiciary is so constructed as to destroy the judiciaries of the several states*, and that the *appellate jurisdiction, with respect to law and fact, is unnecessary.* I answer, both the original and appellate jurisdiction of the federal judiciary are manifestly necessary, where the cause of action affects the citizens of different states, the general interest of the union, or strangers (and to cases of these descriptions only, does the jurisdiction of the federal judiciary extend); I say, these jurisdictions of the federal judiciary are manifestly necessary for the reasons just now given under the third objection, and I do not see how they can avoid trying any issues joined before them, whether the thing to be decided is law or fact; but I think no doubt can be made, that if the issue joined is on *fact*, it must be tried by a jury.

10. They object, that the *election of delegates* for the house of representatives *is for two years*, and of senators *for six years.* I think this a manifest advantage, rather than an objection. Very great inconveniences must necessarily arise from a too frequent change of the members of large legislative or executive bodies, where the revision of every past transaction must be taken up, explained and discussed anew for the information of the new members, when the settled rules of the house are little understood by them, &c., &c., all which ought to be avoided, if it can be with safety. Further, it is plain that any man who serves in such bodies, is better qualified the second year than he could be the first, because experience adds qualifications for every business, &c. The only objection is that long continuance affords danger of corruption, but for this the constitution provides a remedy by impeachment and expulsion, which will be a sufficient restraint, unless a majority of the house and senate should become corrupt, which is not easily presumable; in fine, there is a certain mean between too long and too short con-

tinuances of members of congress, and I cannot see but it is judiciously fixed by the convention.

Upon the whole matter, I think the sixteen members have employed an address-writer of great dexterity, who has given us a strong sample of ingenious malignity and ill-nature—a master-piece of high coloring in the scare-crow way; in his account of the conduct of the sixteen members, by an unexpected openness and candor, he avows facts which he certainly cannot expect to justify, or even hope that their constituents will patronize or even approve; but he seems to lose all candor when he deals in sentiments; when he comes to point out the nature and operation of the new constitution, he appears to mistake the spirit and true principles of it very much; or which is worse, takes pleasure in showing it in the worst light he can paint it in. I however agree with him in this, that this is the time for consideration and minute examination: and I think the great subject, when viewed seriously, without passion or prejudice, will bear and brighten under the severest examination of the rational inquirer. If the provisions of the law or constitution do not exceed the occasions, if the remedies are not extended beyond the mischiefs, the government cannot be justly charged with severity; on the other hand, if the provisions are not adequate to the occasions, and the remedies not equal to the mischiefs, the government must be too lax, and not sufficiently operative to give the necessary security to the subject; to form a right judgment, we must compare these two things well together, and not suffer our minds to dwell on one of them alone, without considering them in connexion with the other; by this means we shall easily see that the one makes the other necessary.

Were we to view only the gaols and dungeons, the gallows and pillories, the chains and wheel-barrows, of any state, we might be induced to think the government severe; but when we turn our attention to the murders and parricides, and robberies and burglaries, the piracies and thefts, which merit these punishments, our idea of cruelty vanishes at once, and we admire the justice, and perhaps clemency, of that government which before shocked us as too severe. So when we

fix our attention only on the superlative authority and energetic force vested in congress and our federal executive powers by the new constiution, we may at first sight be induced
to think that we yield more of the sovereignty of the states
and of personal liberty, than is requisite to maintain the federal government; but when on the other hand we consider
with full survey the vast supports which the union requires,
and the immense consequence of that union to us all, we shall
probably soon be convinced that the powers aforesaid, extensive as they are, are not greater than is necessary for our
benefit; for, 1. *No laws of any state, which do not carry in
them a force which extends to their effectual and final execution, can afford a certain and sufficient security to the subject;*
for, 2. *Laws of any kind, which fail of execution, are worse
than none*, because they weaken the government, expose it to
contempt, destroy the confidence of all men, both subjects
and strangers, in it, and disappoint all men who have confided
in it; in fine, our union can never be supported without definite and effectual laws which are coëxtensive with their occasions, and which are supported by authorities and powers
which can give them execution with energy; if admitting
such powers into our constitution can be called a sacrifice,
it is a sacrifice to safety, and the only question is whether our
union or federal government is worth this sacrifice.   Our
union, I say, *under the protection of which* every individual
rests secure against foreign and domestic insult and oppression; but *without it* we can have no security against invasions,
insults, and oppressions of foreign powers, or against the inroads and wars of one state on another, or even against insurrections and rebellions arising within particular states, by
which our wealth and strength, as well as ease, comfort and
safety, will be devoured and destroyed by enemies growing
out of our own bowels.   It is *our union alone* which can give
us respectability abroad in the eyes of foreign nations; and
secure to us all the advantages both of trade and safety, which
can be derived from treaties with them.

The Thirteen States all united and well cemented together,
are a strong, rich and formidable body, not of stationary,

maturated power, but increasing every day in riches, strength, and numbers; thus circumstanced, we can demand the attention and respect of all foreign nations, but they will give us both in exact proportion to the solidity of our union. For if they observe our union to be lax, from insufficient principles of cement in our constitution, or mutinies and insurrections of our own people (which are the direct consequence of an insufficient cement of union); I say, when foreign nations see either of these, they will immediately abate of their attention and respect to us and confidence in us.

And, as it appears to me, that the new constitution does not vest congress with more or greater powers than are necessary to support this important union, I wish it may be admitted in the most cordial and unanimous manner by all the states.

It is a human composition, and may have errors which future experience will enable us to discover and correct; but I think it is pretty plain, if it has faults, that the address-writer of the sixteen members has not been able to find them; for he has all along either hunted down phantoms of error, that have no real existence, or which is worse, tarnished real excellencies into blemishes.

I have dwelt the longer on these remarks on this writer, because I observe that all the scribblers in our papers against the new constitution, have taken their cue principally from him, all their lucubrations contain little more than his ideas dressed out in a great variety of forms; one of which colors so high as to make the new constitution strongly resemble the Turkish government (*vide Gazetteer* of the 10th instant), which, I think, comes about as near the truth as any of the rest, and brings to my mind a sentiment in polemical divinity, which I have somewhere read, that there were once great disputes and different opinions among divines about the mark which was set on Cain, when one of them very gravely thought it was a horn fully grown out on his forehead. It is probable he could not think of a worse mark than that.

On the whole matter there is no end of the extravagancies of the human fancy, which are commonly dictated by poignant feelings, disordered passions, or affecting interests; but I could wish my fellow-citizens, in the matter of vast importance before us, would divest themselves of bias, passion, and little personal or local interests, and consider the great subject with that dignity of reason and independence of sentiment, which national interests ever require. I have here given my sentiments with the most unbiased freedom, and hope they will be received with the most candid attention and unbiased discussion, by the states in which I live, and in which I expect to leave my children.

I will conclude with one observation, which I take to be very capital, viz: that the distresses and oppressions both of nations and individuals often arise from the powers of government being too limited in their principle, too indeterminate in their definition, or too lax in their execution, and of course the safety of the citizens depends much on full and definite powers of government, and an effectual execution of them.

Philadelphia, October 12, 1787.

To the PEOPLE of AMERICA:*

The present situation of the United States has attracted the notice of every country in Europe. By the discussions which led to the revolution, we have proved to the world, that we were intimately acquainted with the natural rights and political relations of mankind. By those discussions, and the subsequent conduct of America, her enemies must be well convinced that she is sincerely attached to liberty, and that her citizens will never submit to a deprivation of that inestimable blessing. To ensure the continuance of that real freedom in the spirit of which our State constitutions were universally formed; to ensure it from enemies within, then existing and numerous; to ensure it from enemies without, then and ever to be watched and repelled, the first confederation was formed. It was an honest and solemn covenant among our infant States, and virtue and common danger supplied its defects. When the immediate perils of

* From the Pennsylvania Packet, Oct. 12, 1787.

those awful times were removed by the valor and persevering fortitude of America, aided by the active friendship of France, and the follies of Great Britain, those defects were too easily seen and felt. They have been acknowledged at various times by all the legislatures of the Union; and often, very often indeed, represented by Congress. The Commonwealth of Virginia took the first step to obtain this object of universal desire, by applying to her sister States to meet her in the Commercial Convention in the last year. Some of the States immediately adopted the measure, Congress *afterwards* added their sanction, and a few more of the States concurred. A meeting of the deputies, though not a general one, took place at the appointed time. The members of that body, influenced, I am persuaded, by the purest considerations, added their voice to the general wish for another Convention, whose object should be the revision and amendment of the federal government. It is worthy of remark that these proceedings of the States were not conducted through those channels the confederation points out, but they were not inconsistent with it, they were certainly not improper: for it is not material in what manner the United States in Congress become possessed of the matter and form of changes *really desired by the* people of the Union. It is only necessary when that body shall determine on alterations, that they proceed constitutionally to obtain the adoption of them. It may be observed further, that the address of the Annapolis Convention, signed by the Hon. John Dickinson, Esq., was published in September, 1786, in the newspapers of all the Middle States, and particularly those of Pennsylvania, during the sitting of the Hon. the General Assembly of the Commonwealth. The people, therefore, throughout the Union, *and most certainly in Pennsylvania*, must have known that the important duty of amending our Federal constitution (so far as the legislatures could interfere in it) must come before the members they were then about to choose. I have drawn the attention of my fellow-citizens to this fact, and request they will observe it, because a contrary idea has been given by some members of our legislature.

The recommendation for calling the late convention for the purpose of giving the requisite efficiency to the Union, was adopted by Congress and all the States, *but Rhode Island.* I will not abuse that unhappy, fallen, lost sister. As a sincere relation, however, wounded by the dishonor to our family name—as an honest man, distressed at the injury she has done to the cause of public and private virtue—as a friend to liberty, alarmed at the arguments against our republican governments which she has furnished to royal tyrants—I solemnly conjure her to consider her late conduct, unexampled in the history of the world. She exhibits to mankind the unheard of spectacle of a *people*, possessed of a constitution containing all the principles of substantial justice, and of civil and religious liberty, disregarding the rights of property and obligations between man and man, and trampling under their feet a solemn compact with neighboring and *related* States, yet bleeding with wounds sustained in fighting by their side in a common cause, and infringing the established laws of nations and treaties with allies *most powerful* and *friendly.* Let them ask themselves, let them permit a friend to ask them, what they can hope from such a conduct, or in what fatal catastrophe it may not issue?

The twelve states which made the appointment, sent forward their deputies in due time. I waive all weight of names, but they were such in general as it became the states to appoint. Exceptions, perhaps just ones, may have been made to some of them; but remember these were not alone; they did not even form a majority of the representation of one state; much less could they affect the general views of the whole body. I am not acquainted with the situation of parties in the other states, but have had too much opportunity, with the rest of the world, of judging of them in Pennsylvania. I acknowledge, that in my mind there might have been more propriety in the appointment from this state. The gentlemen were individually fully competent to the duty. They were so collectively. Had some of the same men resided in the western counties, it would have been more satisfactory. In point of good policy, it should have been so. While candor forbids us to withhold these observations, *the public good* requires that even the just offence it may have given, should not interfere with a plan sincerely intended to promote the happiness of our country. I wish to avoid offence, but I beg to be indulged in remarking that the appointment of our deputies to the Convention, from the city and county of Philadelphia, does not appear to have made any painful impressions on *the people* of the western counties. Perhaps it is because they have not observed the fact. If that is the case, it cannot be of importance to the tranquility of the state, nor to the great business before us. I confess my wishes were strongly in favor of some western deputies, though it seems the seceding members themselves proposed but one. I believe, however, many persons wished at the time, he had been appointed. Yet the people of that part of the state have not complained, and it was the act of a real majority. Besides, I feel too independent a freeman to endure the idea, that any one man could be indispensably necessary to that appointment. The truth is that some members of the Pennsylvania Assembly, after seceding from their brethren, have brought the idea for the first time, at an ill-judged moment, before the public. They have suggested it to their constituents, not their constituents to them. Reflect dispassionately on these circumstances, my Pennsylvania readers. I mean not offensive censure, which I despise and condemn. The seceding members, I say, suggested the idea of offence at the appointment of our deputies, after an unlucky quarrel had taken place. Does it not seem to be a little in the way of apology? When these gentlemen say they were apprehensive of the consequences of the appointment, I can believe they spoke truly—but when they bring it forward to the people only after their own secession from the house, to the people who have never complained of it, does it not rather appear that the jealousy they entertained in their own minds, has by too much brooding over it, grown to a sore, and that their letting it out now, is rather a proof of their own feelings than of any discontent among the people. Is it consistent with the delicacy of one of those gentlemen,

that he should sign this sentiment among the sixteen, when
he was himself a candidate? It were to be wished his name
at least had not been there, or that the observation in their
address had been omitted. It is consistent with propriety,
that another gentleman should vote for calling the Convention, and afterwards secede from his brethren? How much
more becoming the honor of their private characters, and the
dignity of their public offices, was the conduct of the two
gentlemen who were brought to the house by the speaker's
order, in entering freely into the debates that ensued.
Though they have not accustomed themselves to speak often,
they, on this occasion, proposed matters for the good of their
constituents (which they could not have done if absent), and
their motions were adopted.

The address carries an idea that the new federal constitution has been only approved by what is called the republican
party. I would cheerfully rest the disproving this insinua-
tion upon any man of honor in the constitutional party. Dr.
Franklin and Mr. Ingersoll, who assisted to frame, and afterwards signed the act of the convention, never opposed our
state constitution. Messrs. Will, Foulke, G. Heister, Kreemer, J. Heister, Davis, Trexler, Burkhalter and Antis, and
other members of the house, who voted for the call of a State
Convention, are surely not republicans; and among the four
thousand petitioners for the adoption of the new federal government, will be found many of the most zealous, active and
respectable friends of the constitution of this commonwealth.
This I assert as an incontrovertible fact, of which every individual of the sixteen seceding gentlemen was fully possessed;
for the petitions, with a very great number of the names
of such persons, were presented to the house on Monday,
Wednesday and Thursday. The secession took place on Friday afternoon, and was repeated on Saturday morning. The
good men of Pennsylvania will satisfy themselves whether
their sixteen representatives have given this wrong idea from
want of temper or from want of virtue—it was indeed un-
guarded to pass upon their constituents a suggestion that the
friends of the new federal government were all of them ene-

mies to the constitution of the State of Pennsylvania, and
had all of them destructive designs on the State frame of government. Before I quit this point let me add one piece of
information, which is, that the gentleman alluded to in a
preceding paragraph, is the only unsuccessful candidate for a
seat in the convention who has not declared for the adoption
of the federal constitution.

But to return.—The twelve States which concurred sent
forward their deputies in due time. I shall not attempt, as
I have already said, to pass upon your understandings the
weight of names—determine that matter for yourselves. Suffer me to remark only, that the faithful, disinterested and
invaluable services of WASHINGTON—the incessant, faithful
and essential services of FRANKLIN—might have saved them
from the contemptuous insinuations of a late writer. Were
such compositions applauded, it might indeed be said "*that
republics are ungrateful.*"

The constitution which these gentlemen have offered to
their fellow citizens has been considered with manly freedom, such I am sure as they wished it to meet. If in some
cases it has been carried further, it is a proof at once of our
liberty, and of the passions which we know to prevail among
men; and as every cause is open to the friendship and enmity
of bad men, there can be no doubt but that very wicked and
dangerous motives influence some, both among the friends
and enemies of the new frame of government. Leaving all
observations upon such points, in treating which even truth
will appear uncertain, and candor may heat and inflame, I
recommend to all men of pure, honest intentions the utmost
moderation and forbearance. The object before us is indeed
great and interesting. We are to arrange affairs essential to
our own happiness, and highly important to the present and
future people of the earth. Though it must be admitted that
too much and too bitter contention has appeared in our affairs, yet it is no less true that the active and speculative
friends of liberty, throughout the world, consider us *at this
day* as the enlightened and sincere supporters of their cause,
and look to us for examples which the one expects to approve,

the other to imitate. Let us refrain then from these little, mean, bitter invectives; let us suppress those contemptible remains of narrow party spirit, and consider our critical situation with decency and candor, remembering that *the true sons of liberty are brothers to each other.*

Much observation has been made in regard to the omission of a bill of rights in the new frame of government. Such remarks, I humbly conceive, arise from a great inadvertency in taking up the subject. When the people of these States dissolved their connection with the crown of Great Britain, by the Declaration of Independence, they found themselves, as to government, *in a state of nature:* yet they were very sensible of the blessings of civil society. On *a recommendation* of Congress, who were then possessed of no authority, the inhabitants of each colony respectively formed a compact for themselves, which compacts are our State constitutions. These were original agreements among *individuals* before actually in a state of nature. In these constitutions a bill of rights (that is, a declaration of the unaliened rights of each individual) was proper, and indispensably necessary. When the several States were thus formed into thirteen separate and independent sovereignties, Congress, who managed their general affairs, and their respective legislatures, thought it proper (and it was surely absolutely necessary) that a confederation should be prepared and executed. The measure was accordingly adopted; and here let us observe this was *a compact among thirteen independent States* of the nature of a perpetual treaty. It was acceded to by the several States as sovereign. *No individuals* were parties to it. *No rights of individuals* could, therefore, be declared in it. The rights of *contracting parties* (the thirteen *States*) were declared. Those rights remain inviolate. No bill of the rights of *the freemen* of the Union was thought of, nor could be introduced. No complaint was made of the want of it, for it was a matter foreign from the nature of the compact. In articles of agreement *among a number of people forming a civil society*, a bill of the rights of individuals comes in of course, and *is indispensably* necessary. In articles of agreement *among a number of independent states*, entering into a union, a bill of the rights of individuals is *excluded* of course. As in the old confederation or compact among the thirteen independent sovereignties of America, no bill of rights of individuals could be or was introduced; so in the proposed compact among the same thirteen independent sovereignties, no bill of the rights of individuals has been or could be introduced. This would be to annihilate our state constitutions, by rendering them unnecessary. The liberty of the press, from an honest republican jealousy, which I highly applaud, has also been a subject of observation: but the right of writing for publication, and of printing, publishing and selling what may be written, are *personal* rights, *are part of the rights of individuals.* Thus we see when attempts have been made to restrain them in any country, *the individuals concerned* have only been, or indeed could be, the objects of attention. They are the rights of *the people in the states*, and can only be exercised by them. They are not the rights of the thirteen independent sovereignties, therefore could not enter into either the old or new compact among them. Every constitution in the union guards the liberty of the press. It has also become a part of the common law of the land. But who is to destroy it? Not the people at large, for it is their most invaluable privilege—the palladium of their happiness—not the state legislatures, for their respective constitutions forbid them to infringe it. Not the federal government, *for they have never had it transferred into their hands.* It remains amongst those rights *not conveyed to them.* But who are the federal government, that they should take away the freedom of the press, was it not out of their reach? *Are they not the temporary responsible servants of the people?* How then, my countrymen, is this favorite inestimable privilege in danger? It cannot be affected. It is understood by all men that it is never to be touched. It is guarded by insurmountable barriers, as you have already seen; and woe betide—the heaviest woe will betide the sacrilegious hand that shall attempt to remove them. A CITIZEN OF PENNSYLVANIA.

To the FREEMEN of PENNSYLVANIA:*

A publication has lately appeared in several of our papers, said to be signed by *sixteen* members of the late Assembly of Pennsylvania, which challenges a few remarks.

The first remark that occurs is, that the paper was neither written by any *one* of them, nor signed by *all* of them. They are too illiterate to compose such an address, and it can be proved that several of the persons whose names are subscribed to it left the city on Saturday, before there was time to collect the materials of the address, or to receive it from the *person* who is well known to have written it.

A second remark that occurs in this place is, that there was a fixed resolution of the anti-federal junto to oppose the federal government, *long before* it made its appearance. In the month of July last, at a meeting of this junto, it was agreed, "that if the new constitution of Congress interfered in the least with the constitution of Pennsylvania, it ought to be opposed and rejected, and that even the name of a WASHINGTON should not carry it down." Happily it requires a reduction of the enormous expenses, and some other alterations of our constitution. Hence the reason of their opposition. Had it been much more perfect, or had it, like the Jewish theocracy, been framed by the hand of the SUPREME BEING himself, it would have been equally unpopular among them, since it interferes with their expensive hobby-horse, the Constitution of Pennsylvania.

The address, and all the opposition to the new government, originate from the officers of government, who are afraid of losing their salaries or places. This will not surprise those of us who remember the opposition which our Independence received from a few officers of government in the years 1775 and 1776. Recollect the FRIENDLY ADDRESSES and the CATOS, which appeared in those years in all our newspapers. Remember too, that these publications came from men of as great understandings, and of more extensive influence,

* From the Independent Gazetteer, or the Chronicle of Freedom, October 15, 1787.

than Randolph, Mason or Gerry. Which of them is fit to be named with Hutchinson, Bernard, Tryon or Kemp?

The address begins with two palpable falsehoods. "We lamented (it says) at the time, that a majority of our legislature appointed men to represent this state, who were all citizens of Philadelphia, and none of them calculated to represent the landed interest of Pennsylvania."

It is a well-know fact, that a seat in the convention was offered to William Findley, and that he objected to it, because no wages were to be connected with it. It became, therefore, a matter of economy, as well as convenience, to fill up the delegation with members from Philadelphia. If this was a crime, the sixteen concurred in it, for they *all* voted for five of the delegation, and for three other men who were at that time citizens of Philadelphia, viz: Thomas M'Kean, Charles Pettit and John Bayard, esquires.

The story of the delegates from Pennsylvania having no interest in the landed property of the state is equally groundless with the foregoing. They are all landholders, and one of them alone owns a greater landed estate than the whole sixteen absconders; and has for many years past punctually and justly paid more taxes on it than are paid by the whole anti-federal junto, and, unfortunately, for the support of the men who compose this junto.

The address confesses that the sixteen absconded to prevent the majority of the house from calling a convention, to consider the new form of government. Is this right, freemen of Pennsylvania? Is it agreeable to democratic principles, that the *minority* should govern the *majority?* Is not this aristocracy in good earnest? Is it not tyranny, that a *few* should govern the *many?* By absconding, and thereby obstructing the public business, they dissolved the constitution. They annihilated the first principles of government, and threw the commonwealth into a *state of nature.* Under these circumstances, the citizens of Philadelphia appealed to the *first* of nature's laws, viz: self-preservation. They seized two of the sixteen absconders, and compelled them to form a House by their attendance. In this they acted wisely and justly—as much so as the man who seizes a highwayman, who is about to rob him. If they were wrong in this action, then the men who drove Galloway, Skinner, Delancey, and other miscreants, from our states, by force, in the year 1776, were wrong likewise. What justified all the outrages that were committed against the tories in the beginning of the war? Nothing but the dissolution of our governments. What was the foundation of the dissolution of these governments? Nothing but a resolution of Congress. What determined us to establish new governments on the ruins of the old? Nothing but a recommendation of Congress. Why, then, do these men fly in the faces of the convention and Congress? It was from similar bodies of men, similarly constituted, that their present form of government derived its independence. It cannot exist without a Congress—it is meet, therefore, that it should harmonize with it.

The objections to the federal government are weak, false and absurd. The neglect of the convention to mention the *liberty of the press* arose from a respect to the state constitutions, in each of which this palladium of liberty is secured, and which is guaranteed to them as an essential part of their republican forms of government. But supposing this had not been done, the *liberty of the press* would have been an inherent and polical right, as long as nothing was said *against* it. The convention have said nothing to secure the privilege of eating and drinking, and yet no man supposes that right of nature to be endangered by their silence about it.

Considering the variety of interests to be consulted, and the diversity of human opinions upon all subjects, and especially the subject of government, it is a matter of astonishment that the government formed by the convention has so few faults. With these faults, it is a phenomenon of human wisdom and virtue, such as the world never saw before. It unites in its different parts all the advantages, without any of the disadvantages, of the three well-known forms of government, and yet it preserves the attributes of a republic. And lastly, if it should be found to be faulty in any particular, it provides an easy and constitutional method of curing its faults.

I anticipate the praise with which this government will be viewed by the friends of liberty and mankind in Europe. The philosophers will no longer consider a republic as an impracticable form of government, and pious men of all denominations will thank God for having provided in our federal constitution, an Ark for the preservation of the remains of the justice and liberties of the world.

Freemen of Pennsylvania, consider the character and services of the men who made this government. Behold the venerable FRANKLIN, in the 70th year of his age, cooped up in the cabin of a small vessel, and exposing himself to the dangers of a passage on the ocean, crowded with British cruisers, in a winter month, in order to solicit from the court of France that aid, which finally enabled America to close the war with so much success and glory—and then say, is it possible that this man would set his hand to a constitution that would endanger your liberties? From this aged servant of the public, turn your eyes to the illustrious American hero, whose name has ennobled human nature—I mean our beloved WASHINGTON. Behold him, in the year 1775, taking leave of his happy family and peaceful retreat, and flying to the relief of a distant, and at that time an unknown part of the American continent. See him uniting and cementing an army, composed of the citizens of thirteen states, into a band of brothers. Follow him into the field of battle, and behold him the *first* in danger, and the *last* out of it. Follow him into his winter quarters, and see him sharing in the hunger, cold and fatigues of every soldier in his army. Behold his fortitude in adversity, his moderation in victory, and his tenderness and respect upon all occasions for the civil power of his country. But above all, turn your eyes to that illustrious scene he exhibited at Annapolis in 1782, when he resigned his commission, and laid his sword at the feet of Congress, and afterwards resumed the toils of an American farmer on the banks of the Potomac. Survey, my countrymen, these illustrious exploits of patriotism and virtue, and then say, is it possible that the deliverer of our country would have recommended an unsafe form of government for that liberty, for which he had for eight long years contended with such unexampled firmness, constancy and magnanimity.

Pardon me, if I here ask—Where were the sixteen absconders and their advisers, while these illustrious framers of our federal constitution were exposing their lives and exerting their talents for your safety and happiness? Some of them took sanctuary in offices, under the constitution of Pennsylvania, from the dangers of the year 1776, and the rest of them were either inactive, or known only on the muster-rolls of the militia during the war.

Look around you, my fellow citizens, and behold the confusion and distresses which prevail in every part of our country. Behold, from the weakness of the government of Massachusetts, the leaders of rebellion making laws to exempt *themselves* from punishment. See, in Rhode Island, the bonds of society and the obligations of morality dissolved by paper money and tender laws. See the flames of court-houses in Virginia, kindled by debtors to stop the course of justice. Hear the complaints of our farmers, whose unequal and oppressive taxes in every part of the country amount to nearly the rent of their farms. Hear too the complaints of every class of public creditors. Look at the records of bankruptcies that fill every newspaper. Look at the melancholy countenances of our mechanics, who now wander up and down the streets of our cities without employment. See our ships rotting in our harbors, or excluded from nearly all the ports in the world. Listen to the insults that are offered to the American name and character in every court of Europe. See order and honor everywhere prostrate in the dust, and religion, with all her attending train of virtues, about to quit our continent forever. View these things, my fellow citizens, and then say that we do not require a new, a protecting, and efficient federal government, if you can. The picture I have given you of the situation of our country is not an exaggerated one. I challenge the boldest enemy of the federal constitution to disprove any one part of it.

It is not to be wondered at, that *some* of the rulers and officers of the government of Pennsylvania are opposed to the new constitution of the United States. It will lessen their power, number and influence—for it will necessarily reduce the expenses of our government from nearly 50,000 l. to 10,000 l., or, at most, 15,000 l. a year. I am very happy in being able to except many worthy officers of our government from concurring in this opposition. Their names, their conduct, and their characters, are well-known to their fellow citizens, and I hope they will all be rewarded by a continuance and accumulation of public favor and confidence.

The design of this address is not to inflame the passions of my fellow citizens; I know the feelings of the people of Pennsylvania are sufficiently keen. It becomes me not, therefore (to use the words of the address of the sixteen absconders), to add to them, by dwelling longer "upon the distresses and dangers of our country. I have laid a real state of facts before you; it becomes you, therefore, to judge for yourselves."

The absconders have endeavored to sanctify their false and seditious publication by a solemn address to the Supreme Being. I shall conclude the truths I have written, by adopting some of their own words, with a short addition to them.

"May HE, who alone has dominion over the passions and understandings of men, preserve you from the influence of rulers, who have upon many occasions *held fellowship with iniquity, and established mischief by law.*"

The author of this Address is one of the FOUR THOUSAND Citizens of Philadelphia and its neighborhood, who subscribed the petition to the late Assembly, immediately to call a Convention, in order to adopt the proposed FEDERAL CONSTITUTION.

CHAPTER III.

[Between the day when the convention was called and the day when the convention met, a period of seven weeks elapsed. During this time both the friends and detractors of the constitution resorted to every known means of influencing public opinion. Appeals were made to the prejudices, to the fears, to the religious bigotry of the people. The Antifederalists, as they began to be called, found a friend in Eleazer Oswald, and filled his "Independent Gazetteer" with all manner of effusions. The mouth-piece of the Federal party was the "Pennsylvania Packet," and from these two journals the greater part of this chapter is taken. The champion of the Antifederalists was "Centinel," whose name is still unknown. The champion of the Federalists was James Wilson, whose speech in the State House yard was held to be unanswerable. The essays of "Centinel" and the speech of Wilson are, therefore, given in full. But the essays of "Philadelphiensis" and "Old Whig," who supported the Antifederal cause, and of "American Citizen," who wrote on the Federal side, have not, for lack of space, been reprinted.

In place of these will be found a few, and but a few, of the immense number of short pieces that appeared day after day in the "Packet" and the "Gazetteer," and set forth such popular opinions as might be heard any afternoon in the taverns and the coffee-houses. In writings of this sort the Antifederal greatly outnumbered the Federal, and justify the belief that the burden of proof was considered to be with the party of opposition.]

From the *Pennsylvania Gazette.*

(By particular desire.)

The former distinction of the citizens of America (says a

correspondent) into Whigs and Tories, should be lost in the more important distinction of *Federal* and *Antifederal* men. The former are the friends of liberty and independence; the latter are the enemies of liberty and the secret abettors of the interests of Great Britain.

Should the federal government be *rejected* (AWFUL WORDS), another correspondent has favored us with the following paragraphs, to be published in our paper in the month of June, 1789:

On the 30th ult., his Excellency, David Shays, Esq., took possession of the government of Massachusetts. The execution of —— ——, Esq., the late tyrannical governor, was to take place the next day.

Accounts from New Jersey grow every day more alarming. The people have grown desperate from the oppressions of their new masters, and have secretly, it is said, dispatched a messenger to the court of Great Britain, praying to be taken again under the protection of the British Crown.

We hear from Richmond, that the new state house, lately erected there, was burnt by a mob from Berkeley county, on account of the assembly refusing to emit paper money. From the number and daring spirit of the mob, government have judged it most prudent not to meddle with them.

Yesterday 300 ship-carpenters embarked from this city for Nova Scotia, to be employed in his Britannic Majesty's ship-yards at Halifax.

We hear from Cumberland, Franklin and Bedford counties, in this State, that immense quantities of wheat are rotting in stacks and barns, owing to the demand for that article having ceased, in consequence of our ships being shut out of all the ports of Europe and the West Indies.

We hear that 300 families left Chester county last week, to settle in Kentucky. Their farms were exposed to sale before they set off, but many of them could not be raised to the value of the taxes that were due on them.

On Saturday last were interred from the bettering-house the remains of Mrs. Mary ——. This venerable lady was once in easy circumstances; but having sold property to the amount of 5,000*l.* and lodged it in the funds, which, from the convulsions and distractions of our country, have unfortunately become insolvent, she was obliged to retire to the city poor-house. Her certificates were sold on the Monday following her interment, but did not bring as much cash as paid for her winding-sheet.

By a vessel just arrived from L'Orient, we learn that the partition treaty between Great Britain and the Emperor of Morocco was signed on the 25th of April last, at London. The Emperor is to have possession of all the States to the southward of Pennsylvania, and Great Britain is to possess all the States to the eastward and northward of Pennsylvania, inclusive of this middle State. Private letters from London add, that Silas Dean, Esq., is to be appointed Governor of Connecticut, and Joseph Galloway, Esq., is to be appointed Governor of Pennsylvania. The government of Rhode Island was offered to Brigadier-General Arnold, who refused to accept of it, urging, as the reason of his refusal, that he was afraid of being corrupted by living in such a nest of speculators and traitors.

But, adds our correspondent, should the federal government be *adopted*, the following paragraphs will probably have a place in our paper in the same month, viz., June, 1789:

Yesterday arrived in this city his Excellency the Earl of Surry, from the Court of Great Britain, as Envoy Extraordinary to the United States. He was received by the principal Secretary of State, and introduced to the President-General at the federal State House, who received him with great marks of politeness. His lordship's errand to America is to negotiate a commercial treaty with the United States. The foundation of this treaty is, that all British ports are to be opened to American vessels, duty free, and a proposal to build 200 ships every year in the ports of Boston, New York, Philadelphia and Charleston.

Last evening arrived at Billingsport the ship Van Berkel, Nicholas van Vleck, master, from Amsterdam, with 100 reputable families on board, who have fled from the commotions which now distress their unhappy country. It is said they have brought cash with them to the amount of 45,000*l.* sterling, to be laid out in purchasing cultivated farms in this and the neighboring States.

We learn from Cumberland county, in this State, that land in the neighborhood of Carlisle, which sold in the year 1787 for only 5*l.* has lately been sold for 10*l.* per acre at public vendue. This sudden rise in the value of estates is ascribed to the new mode of taxation adopted by the federal government, as well as to the stability of this government.

Such are the improvements in the roads in this State since the establishment of the federal government, that several loaded wagons arrived in this city in two days from the town of Lancaster.

By a gentleman just arrived from Tioga, we learn that the insurgents in that place were surprised and taken by a party of the federal militia, and that their leaders are on their way to Wyoming, to be tried for their lives.

It appears from the custom-house books of this city, that the exports from this State were nearly double last year, of the exports of the year 1786.

In the course of the present year, it appears that there have arrived in this state 18,923 souls from different parts of Europe.

Several foreigners who attended the debates in the federal Assembly and Senate last Wednesday, declare that they never saw half so much decorum nor heard more noble specimens of eloquence in the House of Lords and Commons, than they saw and heard in our illustrious republican assemblies.

We hear from Fort Pitt, that since the navigation of the Mississippi has been confirmed to the United States by the Court of Spain, the price of wheat has risen from 4*s.* to 7*s.* 6*d.* per bushel in all the counties to the westward of the Allegheny mountains.

In consequence of the new and successful modes of taxation adopted by the United States, public securities of all kinds have risen to par with specie, to the great joy of widows, orphans, and all others who trusted their property in the funds of their country.

We hear that the Honorable Thomas ———, Esq., is appointed to deliver the anniversary oration in September next, in honor of the birthday of our present free and glorious federal Constitution—a day that cannot fail of being equally dear to all Americans with the 4th of July, 1776—for while this day gave us *liberty*, the 17th of September, 1787, gave us, under the smiles of a benignant Providence, a *government*, which alone could have rendered that liberty safe and perpetual. *

———

Mr. Oswald.—Having stepped into Mr. ———'s beer-house, in ——— street, on Saturday evening last, I perceived the room filled with a number of decent tradesmen, who were conversing very freely about the members of the federal convention, who, it was said, like good workmen, had finished their work on a Saturday night. As the principles of this company were highly federal, and many of their remarks very shrewd, I took notes of them in my memorandum book, in short-hand, and have since copied them for the use of your truly federal paper.

1. *A Sea Captain.*—By George, if we don't adopt the federal government we shall all *go to wreck.*

2. *His Mate.*—Hold, hold, captain, we are in no danger; *Washington* is still *at the helm.*

3. *A Continental Lieutenant.*—If we don't adopt the new government—why *the hardest send off—promotion is always most rapid in a civil war.*

4. *A Cooper.*—If we reject the new government, *we shall all go to staves.*

5. *A Blacksmith.*—If we don't submit to the convention, *we shall all be burned into cinders.*

6. *A Shoemaker.*—If we do not adopt the alterations in the federal convention now, we shall never have such another opportunity of having it *mended.*

7. *A Mason.*—The old fabric must be *underpinned*, or we shall all go to the devil together.

8. *A House Carpenter.*—We shall never do well till all

* Independent Gazetteer, Sept. 20, 1787.

the little rooms in the federal mansion house *are thrown into one.*

9. *A Silversmith.*—I hate your party-colored metals—the sooner we are all *melted into one mass* the better.

10. *A Baker.*—Let me see the man that dares oppose the federal government, and I will soon *make biscuit of him.*

11. *A Butcher.*—And I would soon *quarter the dog.*

12. *A Barber.*—And I would *shave* the son of a ——.

13. *A Cook.*—And I would *break every bone* in his body.

14. *A Joiner.*—And I would make a *wooden jacket* for him.

15. *A Potter.*—And I would grind his dust afterward into a *chamber-pot.*

16. *A Tailor.*—And I would throw it *into hell.**

———

From a Correspondent.—I was walking the other day in Second street, and observed a child, of five or six years old, with a paper in his hand, and lisping, with a smile, "*Here's what the convention have done.*" Last evening I was walking down Arch street, and was struck with the appearance of an old man, whose head was covered with hoary locks, and whose knees bent beneath the weight of his body, stepping to his seat by the door, with a crutch in one hand and his spectacles and the *new federal constitution* in the other. These incidents renewed in my mind the importance of the present era to one-half of the world! I was pleased to see all ages anxious to know the result of the deliberations of that illustrious council, whose constitutions are designed to govern a world of freemen! The unthinking youth, who cannot realize the importance of government, seems to be impressed with a sense of our want of union and system; and the venerable sire, who is tottering to the grave, feels new life at the prospect of having everything valuable secured to posterity.

Ye spirits of ancient legislators! Ye ghosts of Solon, Lycurgus and Alfred! Of the members of the grand Amphictyonic Council of Greece! and of the illustrious Senate of Rome! attend and bear testimony, how important the task of making laws for governing empires! Attend, ye ghosts of Warren,

* Independent Gazetteer, Sept. 20, 1787.

Montgomery, Mercer, and other heroes who offered your lives upon the altar of freedom! Bear witness, with what solicitude the great council of America, headed by a *Franklin* and a *Washington*, the fathers of their country, have deliberated upon the dearest interests of men, and labored to frame a system of laws and constitutions that shall perpetuate the blessings of that independence which you obtained by your swords!

> "These are the fathers of this western clime!
>   Nor names more noble grac'd the walls of fame,
> When Spartan firmness braved the wrecks of time,
>   Or Rome's bold virtues fanned the heroic flame.
> Not deeper thought the immortal sage inspired
>   On Solon's lips when Grecian senates hung;
> Nor manlier eloquence the bosom fired
>   When genius thundered from the Athenian tongue."

Away, ye spirits of discord! ye narrow views! ye local policies! ye selfish patriots, who would damn your country for a sixpenny duty! In the present state of America, *local views* are *general ruin! Unanimity* alone is our *last resort.* Every other expedient has been tried, and unanimity *now* will certainly secure freedom, national faith and prosperity.*

———

[Extract of a letter from a gentleman in Montgomery county to his friend in Philadelphia, dated 24th September, 1787.]

"We hear the petitions which are handing about in favor of the federal constitution, have met with no opposition in your city, except by five persons, who have lived upon the distresses of the people for some time past; you may expect those gentlemen will in time, on finding their little opposition will not avail, become good subjects of the federal government. They were not decided characters in our late glorious revolution, until they found independence would be maintained; it is even said that one of them, who was in Europe early in the contest, was decidedly against us, but, on finding we were able to support our independence, they became the best street whigs you had, and got themselves fixed in fat of-

* Pennsylvania Packet, Sept. 22.

fices, which they cannot but with reluctance run the risk of losing. We also hear that the only machine for spinning cotton with facility in your city has been bought up by a British rider and put on board a vessel for London. It is to be hoped the Manufacturing Society will have spirit enough to furnish that enemy to our country with a coat of

"TAR AND FEATHERS."*

For the *Independent Gazetteer.*

Mr. Oswald: In searching among some old papers a few days ago, I accidentally found a London newspaper, dated in March, 1774, wherein a certain Dean Tucker, after stating several advantages attendent on a separation from the then colonies, now United States of America, proceeds thus: "After a separation from the colonies our influence over them will be much greater than ever it was, since they began to feel their own weight and importance." "The moment a separation takes effect, intestine quarrels will begin;" and "in proportion as their factious republican spirit shall intrigue and cabal, shall split into parties, divide and sub-divide, in the same proportion shall we be called in to become their general umpires and referees."

I stood aghast on perusing this British prophecy, and could not help reflecting how my infatuated countrymen are on the very verge of suffering it to be fulfilled. Already have they in several of the States spurned at the federal government, despised their admonitions, and absolutely refused to comply with their requisitions; nay, they have gone further, and have enacted laws in direct violation of those very requisitions; nor does the present federal constitution give Congress power to enforce a compliance with the most trifling measure they may recommend. Hence, liberty becomes licentiousness (for while causes continue to produce their effects, want of energy in government will be followed by disobedience in the governed). Hence, also, credit, whether foreign or domestic, public or private, hath been abused, and, of course, is reduced to the lowest ebb; Rhode Island faith in particular is become

---

* Independent Gazetteer, Sept. 26, 1787.

superlatively infamous, even to a proverb. Would to God
that censure in this respect were only due to that petty State!
Sorry I am to say, several others merit a considerable share
of it. Ship-building and commerce no more enrich our
country; agriculture is neglected, or what is just the same,
our produce, instead of being exported, is suffered to rot in
the fields. Britain has dared to retain our frontier posts,
whereby she not only deprives us of our fur trade, but is enabled to keep up a number of troops, to take every advantage
of any civil broils which may arise in these States; and to
close the dismal scene, rebellion, with all its dire concomi-
tants, has actually reared its head in a sister State—such have
been the deplorable effects of a weak and impotent government. Perhaps the present situation of America cannot be
better described than by comparing her to a ship at sea in a
storm, when the mariners tie up the helm and abandon her
to the fury of the winds and waves. O, America! arouse!
awake from your lethargy! bravely assert the cause of federal
unanimity! and save your sinking country! Let it not be
said that those men who heroically extirpated tyranny from
America, should suffer civil discord to undo all that they have
achieved, or to effect more than all the powers of Britain,
aided by her blood-thirsty mercenaries, were able to accomplish. Let not posterity say: "Alas, our fathers expended
much blood and treasure in erecting the temple of liberty;
and when nothing more was wanting but thirteen pillars to
support the stately edifice, they supinely neglected this essential part; so has the whole become one mighty heap of ruins,
and slavery is entailed on their unhappy offspring." God
forbid that this should ever be the case!

Do any of my fellow citizens ask, how may we avert the
impending danger? The answer is obvious; let us adopt that
federal constitution, which has been earnestly recommended
by a convention of patriotic sages, and which, while it gives
energy to our government, wisely secures our liberties. This
constitution, my friends, is the result of four months' deliberation, in an assembly composed of men whose known integrity, patriotism and abilities justly deserve our confidence; let

us also remember that the illustrious WASHINGTON was their President. And shall we, my fellow citizens, render all their measures ineffectual by withholding our concurrence? The preservation of ourselves and our country forbid it. Methinks I hear every hill from St. Croix to the Mississippi re-echo the praises of this simple but excellent constitution.

Having once adopted this truly federal form of government, Dean Tucker and all the divines in England may prophecy our downfall if they will, we shall not regard them. Then shall commerce revisit our shores; then shall we take a distinguished rank among the nations of the earth; then shall our husbandmen and mechanics of every denomination enjoy the fruits of their industry; and then, and not till then, shall we be completely happy. A PENNSYLVANIA FARMER.
Bucks County, Sept. 22, 1787.*

———

For the *Independent Gazetteer.*

Mr. Oswald: An anonymous scribbler, in the *Freeman's Journal* of last Wednesday, has daringly attacked the new federal constitution, in making objections to supposed faults or defects therein, which this *mock-patriot* himself acknowledges to be *trivial and of very small importance.* Why then in the name of wonder has he started them at this awful crisis, when the fate of America depends on the unanimity of all classes of citizens in immediately establishing this hitherto unequalled, and I am happy to add, this *popular* form of government? Certainly, with a design to sow dissensions among the weak, the credulous and the ignorant, since no other effect can be produced by his antifederal remarks at this stage of the business.

I repeat it, sir, the proposed Federal Constitution is a master-piece in politics, and loudly proclaims the wisdom of its authors. But, even if it were imperfect, none of my fellow-citizens are stupid enough to think it, like the laws of the Medes and Persians, irrevocable and unalterable—no, it has one article which wisely provides for future amendments and alterations whenever they shall appear necessary. I can easily

———

* Independent Gazetteer, Sept. 27, 1787.

perceive that the author of these silly remarks is the same
person who attacked the Convention, under the signature
of "Z," before the result of their deliberations was known.
Need we wonder, then, to find him carping at their works
when published?

This *antifederalist* should reflect that his name may yet be
known and himself branded with infamy as an enemy to the
happiness of the United States. I would therefore advise
him to choose some other subject for his remarks in future,
if he wishes to escape the just resentment of an incensed people, who perhaps may honor him with a coat of

TAR AND FEATHERS.*

For the *Independent Gazetteer.*

That the opinion of the people becomes of great moment,
either to impart applause or obtain condemnation on those
who have been signally employed in national service, is a
maxim established by experience; but it is generally best
understood and attended to by men of base intentions, who
to favor some deep design, take care to varnish out a scheme
of deception with apparent colors of truth, whereby the mul-
tudes seeing the object through false colors alone, are often
ensnared and led to adopt sentiments repugnant to their dearest interest. In the *Freeman's Journal* of Wednesday last,
a writer well acquainted with this principle has with daring
effrontery attempted to make strictures on our new constitution, in order to tarnish with his corrosive ink extracted
from an antifederal heart the lustre of our august Convention.
Instigated either by private designs of some party or by
hatred to the national character of America, he has set out,
with the nimble feet of counterfeit probity, to exhibit imaginary defects, and to raise in the mind of the unthinking citizens groundless conjectures, which, if not checked in time,
may become so deeply seated that the joint force of truth and
pure demonstration can scarce be able to erase them, or
until, perhaps, the injury done to our country be of such
magnitude that it will be equally indifferent whether the deception be or be not discovered.

* Independent Gazetteer, Sept. 28, 1787.

In the exordium he says: "The writer of the following remarks has the happiness and respectability of the United
States much at heart, and it is with pleasure he has seen a
system promulged by the late Convention, which promises to
ensure those blessings; but as perfection is not in the lot of
human nature, we are not to expect it in the new federal constitution. Candor must confess, however, that it is a well-
wrought piece of stuff, and claims upon the whole the approbation of all the States. Our situation is critical and demands our immediate care. It is therefore to be hoped that
every State will be speedy in calling a convention—speedy,
because the business is momentous and merits the utmost
deliberation." It is pleasant to observe with what affected
tenderness and diffidence this writer attempts to remark upon
the imperfections of our new constitution; but, with all his
candor in allowing it to be a *well-wrought piece of stuff,* I fear
there are some who will be apt to think that his design is to
seduce the people; as the devil is painted in his temptation
of Saint Anthony in the modest habit of a fair face and the
charming form of virgin innocence, but his cloven foot is
very visible to those who can take their eyes off the object of
seduction. "It is therefore to be hoped (says he) that every
State will be speedy in calling a convention"—but for
what? Why to follow the example of this writer, to remark
upon and to condemn several articles of the new constitution,
and finally to reject the whole of such a *well-wrought piece
of stuff.* I appeal to the understanding, and ask, is not this
the language and true meaning of the writer?

Before he begins his futile remarks, he says: "The following strictures on the proposed constitution are submitted with
diffidence. Excepting a single instance, they regard points
of an inferior magnitude only; and as the writer is not possessed of any of the reasons which influenced the convention,
he feels the more diffident in offering these remarks." Here
is a matter of curiosity, undoubtedly; this gentleman is *not
possessed of any of the reasons which influenced the convention,*
and yet, I affirm it, there is not another person in America
besides himself unacquainted with them. There is not a man

in America or even in Europe possessed of common sense that has heard of the meeting of that honorable body, but knows the reasons and motives which influenced every member of it. Yes, the very enemies of America known them well, and will, I trust, soon feel their effects to their mortification. The reasons and motives which influenced the convention were: "To form a more perfect union, establish justice, ensure domestic tranquillity, provide for the common defence, promote the general welfare, and to secure the blessings of liberty to themselves and their posterity, and to promote the lasting welfare of that country so dear to us all." These, I say, were their motives; and where is the wretch so base as to suppose they were influenced by any other. Perhaps the writer may pretend to say that he meant no more in this paragraph than *he is not possessed of any of the reasons which influenced the convention to adopt those articles on which he has thought proper to make his strictures.* Now if this were his meaning, the general answer given above will still apply; for the same motives which influenced the convention to frame the whole body of this noble constitution, must necessarily have influenced them in framing every article of it, namely, the good of their country. Is not such a writer either an insidious enemy to his country or wilfully wicked?

But let us examine what he has to say against the constitution, and we will find that his objections are groundless and absurd. His first remark is upon Art. I, Sec. 2: "The number of Representatives shall not exceed one for every 30,000." After exhibiting a long paragraph of unmeaning sentences in the discussion of this subject, he concludes: "In America representation ought to be in a ratio with population." Now the very article against which he objects manifestly provides that the representation shall be in the direct ratio of the population. It seems to me that this gentleman's idea of the term *ratio* is to be explained by some learned definition of his own, with which I hope he will soon favor the *literati;* and then perhaps he will demonstrate the representation in America must increase in the *duplicate* ratio or proportion of the number of inhabitants. Such a learned Antifederal gentleman! *O princeps asinorum!*

It would indeed be spending time in a useless manner to remark upon all his strictures, which are equally erroneous. I shall therefore pass over his second and third, and conclude with taking some notice of his fourth or last remark, which is on Art. III, Sec. 2: "*The trial of all crimes, except in cases of impeachment, shall be by jury.* I sincerely wished," says he, "the convention had said a jury of thirteen, a majority of whom shall determine the verdict. Is it not extravagantly absurd to expect that twelve men shall have but one opinion among them upon the most difficult case? Common sense revolts at the idea, while conscience shudders at the prostitution of an oath thus sanctioned by law! Starve or be perjured! say our courts. The monstrous attachment of the people to an English jury show how far the force of prejudice can go; and the encomiums which have been so incessantly lavished upon it should caution us against borrowing from others, without the previous conviction of our own minds." Here is a complete specimen of this man of diffidence and candor; here we see him throwing off the mask, and stepping forth with dauntless courage, and attacking, with philosophical declamation, the first privilege of freemen—the noblest article that ever entered the constitution of a free country—a jewel whose transcendant lustre adds dignity to human nature. No, sir, common sense does not revolt at the idea; common sense and experience confirm the excellency of this law every day; in short, your own condemnation of it is manifestly a negative proof of its goodness. *Sit perpetua hac lex.* But plunge this Janus, this double-faced wretch (who, under the pretence of patriotism and candor, writes only with a view to embarrass the mind, and so prevent the adoption of the new constitution), into the mines a thousand yards deep; and there let the injured ghost of Columbia incessantly torment the monster.   NESTOR.*

To the Printer of the *Independent Gazetteer.*

Sir: I am a FEDERAL MAN in the truest sense of the word. I wish to see the United States in possession of a general

* Independent Gazetteer, Sept. 29, 1787.

government, which may ensure to them strength and liberty at home and respectability abroad. But I do not agree with a writer in your paper of this day that every person who objects to some parts, or even to the whole of the *aristocratical* plan proposed by the late convention, ought to have "a coat of *tar and feathers.*" Tar and feathers, I believe, never made a convert to any system whatever, whether religious or political; and that must be a most noble form of government indeed which requires such infamous measures to support and establish it! That would be a *mob* government with a witness.

At the glorious period of our *Independence* the newspapers were filled with publications against as well as for that salutary measure, and I am clearly of opinion that the LIBERTY OF THE PRESS—the great bulwark of all the liberties of the people—ought never to be restrained (notwithstanding the honorable convention did not think fit to make the least declaration in its favor) and that on every occasion truth and justice should have   FAIR PLAY.*

28*th Sept.*, 1787.

————

The inhabitants of the Old World, says a correspondent, have long been looking at America to see whether liberty and a republican form of government are worth contending for. The United States are at last about to try the experiment. They have formed a constitution, which has all the excellencies, without any of the defects, of the European governments. This constitution has been pronounced by able judges to be the wisest, most free and most efficient of any form of government that ancient or modern times have produced. The gratitude of ages only can repay the enlightened and illustrious patriots for the toil and time they have bestowed in framing it.

It is remarkable that while the federal government lessens the power of the States it increases the privileges of individuals. It holds out additional security for liberty, property and life in no less than five different articles which have no

* Independent Gazetteer, Sept. 29, 1787.

place in any one of the State constitutions. It moreover provides an effectual check to the African trade in the course of one-and-twenty years. How honorable to America —to have been the first Christian power that has borne a testimony against a practice that is alike disgraceful to religion and repugnant to the true interests and happiness of society!

George Washington, Esq., has already been destined by a thousand voices to fill the place of the first President of the United States under the new frame of government. While the deliverers of a nation in other countries have hewn out a way to power with the sword or seized upon it by stratagems and fraud, our illustrious hero peaceably retired to his farm after the war, from whence it is expected he will be called by the suffrages of three millions of people to govern that country by his wisdom (agreeable to fixed laws) which he had previously made free by his arms. Can Europe boast of such a man? or can the history of the world show an instance of such voluntary compact between the deliverer and the delivered of any country as will probably soon take place in the United States?*

———

Mr. Oswald : I have never interested myself much in the politics of the State, from an idea that the difference between a Constitutionalist and a Republican was of so trifling a nature that it was not worth interesting myself in. I have asked some of the parties what they were contending for: was it the bare name, a shadow, or was there a substance in view? but found they could not tell. It then appeared to me like two men worshipping the same being, but different in the mode, as there were many valuable and worthy men in each party who were worthy members of Republican government.

I have seen with astonishment *"a land,"* I may say, *"flowing with milk and honey,"* a country that can boast of more natural advantages than perhaps any other on the face of the globe, a-going to destruction from the factions and bad policy of its inhabitants: I viewed with pleasure the meeting of the late Federal Convention; a convention composed of

* Pennsylvania Packet, Sept. 27, 1787.

our wisest and best men—men perhaps unequaled for wisdom and virtue, with *Washington* at their head, as the only thing that could save a distressed people from destruction, and from falling an easy prey to foreign powers. The Convention has given us a constitution perhaps superior to any upon earth, and notwithstanding its excellence, it meets the opposition of a factious few, whose lives and conduct have been filled with dissimulation and deceit. These few men have had address sufficient to sway the judgment of nineteen of their creatures, members of the late General Assembly, whose names will be handed down with infamy to posterity. On Friday last, when a vote was to be taken of the utmost importance to Pennsylvania, and to keep them from attending the house contrary to their positive oaths, contrary to religion and virtue, and contrary to the real interest of their constituents, who have unfortunately placed a mistaken confidence in their integrity and patriotism, and who were paying them for their attendance and service as their representatives.

The people will now be convinced that the leaders of this party have not, nor never had, the real interest of Pennsylvania in view; they have clearly shown that their attachments to the Constitution were from its elasticity—they have turned it, and twisted it, as their interest and party views required, into a thousand shapes; and all under the mask of supporting it, have created offices, officers, and place-men to strengthen their party. They have, under a funding bill, loaded the State with debts she never contracted, debts of the neighboring states, in order to enrich a few individuals in Philadelphia. In short, their conduct has been such as show the only spark of patriotism they have is the bare name; I would advise the leaders of this party to take care how they conduct themselves in future, to offer no more injuries—they are well known. The people of Pennsylvania are an easy, good people; but they are a spirited people. Let those enemies to the State and to the United States recollect how Doctor Kearsley was treated in 1775, for his abuses of the people. They may probably share the same fate he did.

The Federal constitution no doubt will put an end to all

parties, if it is adopted, as it clearly will. Offices and officers will not be so numerous, nor offices so valuable, as to make it the interest of the people to neglect their business in pursuit of them. The large sums of money paid to a set of supernumerary officers and members of Assembly and Executive Council, will serve to pay our foreign and domestic debts. Our credit at home and abroad will revive; our treasury will be enabled to pay the real creditor, and the Federal treasury, by imposts and indirect taxation, which will not be felt by the people, will be enabled to answer all demands that may be upon it. British gold could not have done more injury to Pennsylvania than a few party men in Philadelphia have done, under the mask of friends to the Constitution and friends to the people. The grievance is great, and must be redressed. The only cure for it is to lay hold of the heads of the faction, do justice to yourselves, inflict the punishment on their persons equal to their demerits, which, by the bye, will not be a small one, and you will soon settle and cure the disease, and afterwards be a happy people. A MECHANIC.*

To the Printer of the *Independent Gazetteer.*

Sir: When we had the honor of addressing you, a few days since, we hoped our caution to the modern Tories, alias Anti-Federalists, might not be amiss. It has, however, attracted the notice of your correspondent, "Fair Play," who observes that "we never made a convert, either in religion or politics." Well, sir, it is granted. We would ask this gentleman, whether the sword, either of war or of justice, has ever made proselytes to any opinion? Certainly not in a greater degree than we have. Yet it is often found expedient to use these means (in punishing those on whom remonstrance and reason were thrown away) for the same purpose that Jehovah sent the deluge in Noah's days. Laughable indeed would it be, to suppose that no villain, however dignified among villains, ought to be punished, but with a view to reclaim *him;* there is a point of more consequence to be considered, and that is to expel from society a monster who is unfit to associate with men, and thereby to deter others from

*Independent Gazetteer, Oct. 2, 1787.

treading in his steps.   That we have frequently, during the Revolution, terrified the *Tories,* or *Antifederalists* of those times, into a moderate line of conduct, is well known.   True, indeed, we did not make many converts to Whiggism (although we have often decorated the backs of those gentry); neither did the sword.

If you trace our history, sir, you will find that we have been faithful allies to America, throughout the late war; but were never well relished by the *Tories,* and a few sham, or luke-warm Whigs.   Should our country again demand our aid, we shall cheerfully obey the summons.   At the same time permit us to declare, that we will never attack any real friend to America, however different his sentiments may be from the throng; nor will we ever assist in shackling the liberty of the press, but on the contrary, will exert ourselves to the last, in defence of that most invaluable privilege of freemen.

When, on Friday last, eighteen or nineteen human asses, who are a disgrace to Pennsylvania, basely deserted the trust reposed in them, by an unwarrantable revolt from the assembly, we confess candidly that nothing could have given us more pleasure than to have been employed in chastising these disciples of Shays, wretches who were not influenced in their defection by the laudable motives which actuated the citizens of Rome, when they revolted, and were appeased by the institution of those popular magistrates, styled tribunes; nor by that patriotic spirit, which prompted the illustrious English Barons to extort " Magna Charta " from their tyrannical King John.   No, sir, those tools of sedition, whose ignorance is still greater than their obstinacy, evidently copied after those despicable incendiaries, Jack Straw and Wat Tyler, in endeavoring to introduce anarchy into these States, that they might be an easy prey to their lord and master, Daniel Shays. Against such traitors to their delegated trust, we would willingly be engaged.

To conclude, we cannot help lamenting the monstrous ingratitude of the Americans in neglecting many of the best friends of the revolution, and among the rest, their faithful allies.   TAR AND FEATHERS.*

* Independent Gazetteer, Oct. 2, 1787.

To the Printer of the *Independent Gazetteer.*

Sir: Your correspondent, who has assumed the signature of "Tar and Feathers," seems to allow that his mode of administering *justice* never made a convert, yet persists in his diabolical plan of endeavoring to inflame the minds of the people against those who happen to differ from him on political subjects. Perhaps, like the fox who lost his tail and strove to persuade the rest of his species to have theirs cut off also, he himself has undergone the *discipline* he is now so anxious to bestow on others. I wonder whether this gentleman (though I much doubt he has any claim to the epithet) ever had the honor of bearing either "the sword of war or of justice." One would be apt to conclude he never had; otherwise, he could not be so destitute of those excellent qualifications which constitute the character of a good soldier and an impartial judge. Generous minds will ever rouse with indignation against such monsters as wish to interrupt the peace of society by flying in the face of all law and authority; and I must confess the new constitution comes in a very "questionable shape," when attended with such furious advocates as "Tar and Feathers." Brave men and good citizens will never associate with the most abandoned of the humam species, for such we must deem those creatures who contend for *mob* govetnments, to abuse an individual because he entertains a different opinion from themselves, or because he has firmness and honesty enough to show his own sentiments. None but the mere echoes and tools of party and faction would engage in such dirty business.

It is a fact, I believe, that will not be denied, that many of those who arrange themselves under the banner of those who call themselves *Federalists,* were either *downright Tories, lukewarm Whigs,* or disaffected to the cause of America and the revolution, and who now eagerly wish to seize the present opportunity to gratify their revenge and to retaliate on the *real Whigs* of 1775 and 1776. And I am more inclined to espouse this opinion, because the author of "Tar and Feathers" aims to destroy the distinction of *Whig and Tory,* and to establish one more odious, viz.: *Federalists* and *Anti-Federalists.*

The new friends to the tarring and feathering system seem to direct their resentment against the *Tories*. "*Laughable indeed would it be to suppose*" that they had not well examined and sought for a *few* of that class of beings among their own party to begin with. Look at home first, Mr. *Tar and Feathers*, and try to work a reformation there before you begin to deal damnation abroad. There invoke the Great Jehovah to forgive thy past crimes and follies; and presume no more, thou blasphemous wretch, to compare your infamous doctrine of *expedients* with the purpose of that Deity, "who sent the deluge in the days of Noah."

I shall conclude for the present, Mr. Oswald, with observing that I consider this demon of discord as some cowardly "*villain*," "*however dignified among villains*"—some ferocious monster, whose nerves do not admit of his heading a *tarring and feathering mob*, but who, at the same time, would rejoice to see anarchy and confusion prevailing and triumphing over peace and good order among the citizens of Philadelphia.

FAIR PLAY.*

We are authorized to declare that the two first pieces published in our paper, signed *Tar and Feathers*, were received from a different quarter from the two last under the same signature; and that therefore no part of the reply by *Fair Play* was intended for the author of the two first. He only meant in general to reprobate the idea of raising a commotion among the citizens.†

A correspondent informs us that a letter has lately been written to the Stadtholder of Holland, inviting him to come over to America, where there is shortly to be a vacancy. It is to be hoped that, as he is so ill-treated by his own countrymen, he will be induced to accept the invitation.

Another correspondent observes that although the tide seems to run so high at present in favor of the new constitution, there is no doubt but the people will soon change their

* Independent Gazetteer, Oct. 4, 1787.
† Independent Gazetteer, Oct. 6, 1787.

minds when they have had time to examine it with coolness and impartiality.

Among the *blessings* of the new proposed government, our correspondent enumerates the following: 1. The *liberty of the press* abolished. 2. A standing army. 3. A Prussian militia. 4. No annual elections. 5. Five-fold taxes. 6. No trial by jury in civil cases. 7. General search warrants. 8. Excise laws, custom-house officers, tide and land waiters, cellar rats, etc. 9. A free importation of negroes for one and twenty years. 10. Appeals to the supreme continental courts, where the rich may drag the poor from the furthermost parts of the continent. 11. Elections for Pennsylvania held at Pittsburg, or perhaps Wyoming. 12. Poll taxes for our heads, if we choose to wear them. 13. And *death* if we dare to complain.

A correspondent who sees with horror the low ribaldry which is daily published against Messrs. *Whitehill, Findley* and other virtuous characters, cannot but lament the blindness of those who smile at such wretched productions. Let us suppose for a moment that the scene is reverted and that a piece is published in which *Robert Morris* is styled a rascal, *Thomas Fitzsimons* a scoundrel, *George Clymer* a vain fool, etc., a cry of *scandalum magnatum* will immediately be raised—the people will take the part of the *well-born*, not from respect or love for their *virtues*, but from reverence for their WEALTH. *O altitudo divitiarum!*

A correspondent with pleasure informs the public that *John Franklin*, of *Luzerne county, a refractory member* of our late Assembly, was taken a few days ago by a few of the old continental officers, and is now safely lodged with Captain Reynolds in the gaol of this city, where he is to remain without bail or main-prize, until he is *impeached* with the infamous nineteen members who had the audacity to attempt the breaking up of the late House of Assembly at the close of the last session, after wasting £1067 10s. of the public's money, without finishing any part of the business the House had been sitting upon.*

* Independent Gazetteer, Oct. 6, 1787.

Mr. Oswald: I have put on my spectacles and read with attention the proposed federal constitution, and find that the right of citizenship, if it is adopted, will meet with a very material change in one clause in the tenth section, "No person except a natural born citizen of the United States, at the time of the adoption of this constitution, shall be eligible to the office of President; neither shall any person be eligible to that office who shall not have attained to the age of thirty-five years and been fourteen years a resident within the United States." Now, I would only ask if this is not very improper? The Americans ought not to be governors, they ought to be governed—let them cultivate the soil, and Europeans govern. What American in the United States is capable of governing or being President? O! it is a *horrid* constitution! Methinks the whole of it is *damnable.* What do you think, Mr. Oswald? A GAUL.*

According to advertisement, a very great concourse of people attended at the state-house on Saturday evening, to fix on a ticket of representatives for the ensuing General Assembly.

Mr. Nixon was chosen chairman and Mr. Tench Coxe secretary of the meeting.

Mr. Jackson having spoken, Mr. Gurney reported from a committee that had been previously appointed, the following names, which were separately offered to the consideration of the citizens and approved of, viz.: William Will, Thomas Fitzsimons, George Clymer, Jacob Hiltzheimer, William Lewis.

On motion of Mr. Donaldson, the citizens of the respective wards were requested to meet on Monday evening to appoint proper persons for making out and circulating a sufficient number of tickets in favor of the above persons.

Mr. Wilson then rose and delivered a long and eloquent speech upon the principles of the federal constitution as proposed by the late convention. The outlines of this speech we shall endeavor to lay before the public, as tending to re-

* Independent Gazetteer, Oct. 9, 1787.

flect great light upon the interesting subject now in general discussion.

Mr. Chairman and Fellow Citizens: Having received the honor of an appointment to represent you in the late convention, it is perhaps my duty to comply with the request of many gentlemen whose characters and judgments I sincerely respect, and who have urged that this would be a proper occasion to lay before you any information which will serve to explain and elucidate the principles and arrangements of the constitution that has been submitted to the consideration of the United States. I confess that I am unprepared for so extensive and so important a disquisition; but the insidious attempts which are clandestinely and industriously made to pervert and destroy the new plan, induce me the more readily to engage in its defence; and the impressions of four months' constant attention to the subject, have not been so easily effaced as to leave me without an answer to the objections which have been raised.

It will be proper, however, before I enter into the refutation of the charges that are alleged, to mark the leading discrimination between the State constitutions and the constitution of the United States. When the people established the powers of legislation under their separate governments, they invested their representatives with every right and authority which they did not in explicit terms reserve; and therefore upon every question respecting the jurisdiction of the House of Assembly, if the frame of government is silent, the jurisdiction is efficient and complete. But in delegating federal powers, another criterion was necessarily introduced, and the congressional power is to be collected, not from tacit implication, but from the positive grant expressed in the instrument of the union. Hence, it is evident, that in the former case everything which is not reserved is given; but in the latter the reverse of the proposition prevails, and everything which is not given is reserved.

This distinction being recognized, will furnish an answer to those who think the omission of a bill of rights a defect in the proposed constitution; for it would have been superfluous and absurd to have stipulated with a federal body of our own creation, that we should enjoy those privileges of which we are not divested, either by the intention or the act that has brought the body into existence. For instance, the liberty of the press, which has been a copious source of declamation and opposition—what control can proceed from the Federal government to shackle or destroy that sacred palladium of national freedom? If, indeed, a power similar to that which has been granted for the regulation of commerce had been granted to regulate literary publications, it would have been as necessary to stipulate that the liberty of the press should be preserved inviolate, as that the impost should be general in its operation. With respect likewise to the particular destrict of ten miles, which is to be made the seat of federal government, it will undoubtedly be proper to observe this salutary precaution, as there the legistive power will be exclusively lodged in the President, Senate, and House of Representatives of the United States. But this could not be an object with the Convention, for it must naturally depend upon a future compact, to which the citizens immediately interested will, and ought to be, parties; and there is no reason to suspect that so popular a privilege will in that case be neglected. In truth, then, the proposed system possesses no influence whatever upon the press, and it would have been merely nugatory to have introduced a formal declaration upon the subject—nay, that very declaration might have been construed to imply that some degree of power was given, since we undertook to define its extent.

Another objection that has been fabricated against the new constitution, is expressed in this disingenious form—"The trial by jury is abolished in civil cases." I must be excused, my fellow citizens, if upon this point I take advantage of my professional experience to detect the futility of the assertion. Let it be remembered then, that the business of the Federal Convention was not local, but general—not limited to the views and establishments of a single State, but co-extensive with the continent, and comprehending the views and establishments of thirteen independent sovereignities. When, therefore, this subject was in discussion, we were involved in difficulties which pressed on all sides, and no precedent could be discovered to direct our course. The cases open to a trial by jury differed in the different States. It was therefore im practicable, on that ground, to have made a general rule The want of uniformity would have rendered any reference to the practice of the States idle and useless; and it could not with any propriety be said that, "The trial by jury shall be as heretofore," since there has never existed any federal system of jurisprudence, to which the declaration could relate. Besides, it is not in all cases that the trial by jury is adopted in civil questions; for cases depending in courts of admiralty, such as relate to maritime captures, and such as are agitated in courts of equity, do not require the intervention of that tribunal. How, then was the line of discrimination to be drawn ? The Convention found the task too difficult for them, and they left the business as it stands, in the fullest confidence that no danger could possibly ensue, since the proceedings of the Supreme Court are to be regulated by the Congress, which is a faithful representation of the people; and the oppression of government is effectually barred, by delaring that in all criminal cases the trial by jury shall be preserved.

This constitution, it has been further urged, is of a pernicious tendency, because it tolerates a standing army in the time of peace. This has always been a topic of popular declamation; and yet I do not know a nation in the world which has not found it necessary and useful to maintain the appearance of strength in a season of the most profound tranquility. Nor is it a novelty with us; for under the present articles of confederation, Congress certainly possesses this reprobated power, and the exercise of that power is proved at this moment by her cantonments along the banks of the Ohio. But what would be our national situation were it otherwise? Every principle of policy must be subverted, and the government must declare war, before they are prepared to carry it on. Whatever may be the provocation, however important the object in view, and however necessary dispatch and secrecy may be, still the declaration must precede the preparation, and the enemy will be informed of your intention, not only before you are equipped for an attack, but even before you are fortified for a defence. The consequence is too obvious to require any further delineation, and no man who regards the dignity and safety of his country can deny the necessity of a military force, under the control and with the restrictions which the new constitution provides.

Perhaps there never was a charge made with less reasons than that which predicts the institution of a baneful aristocracy in the federal Senate. This body branches into two characters, the one legislative and the other executive. In its legislative character it can effect no purpose, without the co-operation of the House of Representatives, and in its executive character it can accomplish no object without the concurrence of the President. Thus fettered, I do not know any act which the Senate can of itself perform, and such dependence necessarily precludes every idea of influence and superiority. But I will confess that in the organization of this body a compromise between contending interests is descernible; and when we reflect how various are the laws, commerce, habits, population and extent of the confederated States, this evidence of mutual concession and accommodation ought rather to command a generous applause, than to excite jealousy and reproach. For my part, my admiration can only be equalled by my astonishment in beholding so perfect a system formed from such heterogeneous materials.

The next accusation I shall consider is that which represents the federal constitution, as not only calculated, but designedly framed, to reduce the State governments to mere corporations, and eventually to annihilate them. Those who have employed the term corporation upon this occasion are not perhaps aware of its extent. In common parlance, indeed, it is generally applied to petty associations for the ease and convenience of a few individuals; but in its enlarged sense, it will comprehend the government of Pennsylvania, the existing union of the States, and even this projected system is nothing more than a formal act of incorporation.

But upon what pretence can it be alleged that it was designed to annihilate the State governments? For I will undertake to prove that upon their existence depends the existence of the Federal plan. For this purpose, permit me to call your attention to the manner in which the President, Senate and House of Representatives are proposed to be appointed. The President is to be chosen by electors, nominated in such manner as the legislature of each State may direct; so that if there is no legislature there can be no electors, and consequently the office of President cannot be supplied.

The Senate is to be composed of two Senators from each State, chosen by the Legislature; and, therefore, if there is no Legislature, there can be no Senate. The House of Representatives is to be composed of members chosen every second year by the people of the several States, and the electors in each State shall have the qualifications requisite for electors of the most numerous branch of the State Legislature; unless, therefore, there is a State Legislature, that qualification cannot be ascertained, and the popular branch of the federal constitution must be extinct. From this view, then, it is evidently absurd to suppose that the annihilation of the seperate governments will result from their union; or, that having that intention, the authors of the new system would have bound their connection with such indissoluble ties. Let me here advert to an arrangement highly advantageous, for you will perceive, without prejudice to the powers of the Legislature in the election of Senators, the people at large will acquire an additional privilege in returning members to the House of Representatives; whereas, by the present confederation, it is the Legislature alone that appoints the delegates to Congress.

The power of direct taxation has likewise been treated as an improper delegation to the federal government; but when we consider it as the duty of that body to provide for the national safety, to support the dignity of the union, and to discharge the debts contracted upon the collected faith of the States for their common benefit, it must be acknowledged that those upon whom such important obligations are imposed, ought in justice and in policy to possess every means requisite for a faithful performance of their trust. But why should we be alarmed with visionary evils? I will venture to predict that the great revenue of the United States must, and always will, be raised by impost, for, being at once less obnoxious and more productive, the interest of the government will be best promoted by the accommodation of the people. Still, however, the objects of direct taxation should be within reach in all cases of emergency; and there is no more reason to apprehend oppression in the mode of collecting a revenue from this resource, than in the form of an impost, which, by universal assent, is left to the authority of the federal government. In either case, the force of civil institutions will be adequate to the purpose; and the dread of military violence, which has been assiduously disseminated, must eventually prove the mere effusion of a wild imagination or a factious spirit. But the salutary consequences that must flow from thus enabling the government to receive and support the credit of the union, will afford another answer to the objections upon this ground. The State of Pennsylvania particularly, which has encumbered itself with the assumption of a great proportion of the public debt, will derive considerable relief and advantage; for, as it was the imbecility of the present confederation which gave rise to the funding law, that law must naturally expire, when a competent and energetic federal system shall be substituted—the State will then be discharged from an extraordinary burthen, and the national creditor will find it to be his interest to return to his original security.

After all, my fellow-citizens, it is neither extraordinary or unexpected that the constitution offered to your consideration should meet with opposition. It is the nature of man to pursue his own interest in preference to the public good, and I do not mean to make any personal reflection when I add that it is the interest of a very numerous, powerful and respectable body to counteract and destroy the excellent work produced by the late convention. All the officers of government and all the appointments for the administration of justice and the collection of the public revenue, which are transferred from the individual to the aggregate sovereignty of the States, will necessarily turn the stream of influence and emolument into a new channel. Every person, therefore, who enjoys or expects to enjoy a place of profit under the present establishment, will object to the proposed innovation; not, in truth, because it is injurious to the liberties of his country, but because it affects his schemes of wealth and consequence. I will confess, indeed, that I am not a blind admirer of this plan of government, and that there are some parts of it which, if my wish had prevailed, would certainly have been altered. But, when I reflect how widely men differ in their opinions, and that every man (and the observation applies likewise to every State) has an equal pretension to assert his own, I am satisfied that anything nearer to perfection could not have been accomplished. If there are errors, it should be remembered that the seeds of reformation are sown in the work itself, and the concurrence of two-thirds of the Congress may at any time introduce alterations and amendments. Regarding it, then, in every point of view, with a candid and disinterested mind, I am bold to assert that it is the best form of government which has ever been offered to the world.

Mr. Wilson's speech was frequently interrupted with loud and unanimous testimonies of approbation, and the applause which was reiterated at the conclusion evinced the general sense of its excellence, and the conviction which it had impressed upon every mind.

Dr. Rush then addressed the meeting in an elegant and pathetic style, describing our present calamitous situation, and enumerating the advantages which would flow from the adoption of the new system of federal government. The advancement of commerce, agriculture, manufactures, arts and sciences, the encouragement of emigration, the abolition of paper money, the annihilation of party, and the prevention of war, were ingeniously considered as the necessary consequences of that event. The doctor concluded with an emphatic declaration—"Were this the last moment of his existence, his dying request and injunction to his fellow citizens would be, to accept and support the offered constitution.''

Mr. Gurney moved that a committee be appointed to write and publish answers, under the authority of their names, to the anonymous pieces against the federal constitution. But Mr. Donaldson observing that it would be improper to expose any particular gentleman to a personal attack, Col. Gurney's motion was withdrawn.

The thanks of the meeting being presented to the chairman, the business of the evening was closed.*

Messers. Printers—Please to republish the following, and oblige ''A Constant Reader:''

The arguments of the Honorable Mr. Wilson, expressed in the speech that he made at the State House on the Saturday preceding the general election, although extremely *ingenious*, and the best that could be adduced in support of so bad a cause, are yet extremely *futile*, and will not stand the test of investigation.

In the first place, Mr. Wilson pretends to point out a leading discrimination between the State constitution and the constitution of the United States. In the former, he says, every power which is not *reserved* is *given*, and in the latter, every power which is not *given* is *reserved*. And this may furnish an answer, he adds, to those who object that a bill of rights has not been introduced in the proposed federal constitution. If this doctrine is true, and since it is the only security that we are to have for our natural rights, it ought at least to have been clearly expressed in the plan of government. The second section of the present articles of confederation says: *Each State retains its sovereignty, freedom and independence, and every power, jurisdiction and right which is not by this confederation expressly delegated to the United States in Congress assembled.* This declaration (for what purpose I know not) is entirely omitted in the proposed constitution. And yet there is a material difference between this constitution and the present confederation, for Congress

* Pennsylvania Packet, Oct. 10, 1787.

in the latter are merely an executive body; it has no power
to raise money, it has no *judicial jurisdiction.* In the other,
on the contrary, the federal rulers are vested with each of the
three essential powers of government—their laws are to be
paramount to the laws of the different States: what then will
there be to oppose to their encroachments? Should they ever
pretend to tyrannize over the people, their *standing army*
will silence every popular effort; it will be theirs to explain
the powers which have been granted to them; Mr. Wilson's
distinction will be forgot, denied or explained away, and the
liberty of the people will be no more.

It is said in the second section of the third article of the
federal plan: "The judicial power shall extend to all cases in
law and equity arising under this constitution." It is very
clear that under this clause, the tribunal of the United States
may claim a right to the cognizance of all offences against the
general government, and libels will not probably be excluded. Nay, those offences may be by them construed, or
by law declared, misprision of treason, an offence which
comes literally under their express jurisdiction. Where is
then the safety of our boasted liberty of the press? And in
case of a conflict of jurisdiction between the courts of the
United States, and those of the several commonwealths, is
it not easy to foresee which of the two will obtain the advantage?

Under the enormous power of the new confederation, which
extends to the individuals as well as to the States of America,
a thousand means may be devised to destroy effectually the
liberty of the press. There is no knowing what corrupt and
wicked judges may do in process of time, when they are not
restrained by express laws. The case of John Peter Zenger,
of New York, ought still to be present to our minds, to convince us how displeasing the liberty of the press is to men in
high power. At any rate, I lay it down as a general rule,
that wherever the powers of a government extend to the lives,
the persons and properties of the subject, all of their rights
ought to be clearly and expressly defined; otherwise, they
have but a poor security for their liberties.

The second and most important objection to the federal plan, which Mr. Wilson pretends to be made in a disingenuous form, is the entire abolition of the trial by jury in civil cases. It seems to me that Mr. Wilson's pretended answer is much more disingenuous than the objection itself, which I maintain to be strictly founded in fact. He says, "that the cases open to trial by jury differing in the different States, it was therefore impracticable to have made a general rule." This answer is extremely futile, because a reference might easily have been made to the common law of England, which obtains through every State, and cases in the maritime and civil law courts would, of course, be excepted. I must also directly contradict Mr. Wilson when he asserts that there is no trial by jury in the courts of chancery. It cannot be unknown to a man of his high professional learning, that whenever a difference arises about a matter of fact in the courts of equity in America or England, the fact is sent down to the courts of common law to be tried by a jury, and it is what the lawyers call a feigned issue. This method will be impracticable under the proposed form of judicial jurisdiction for the United States.

But setting aside the equivocal answers of Mr. Wilson, I have it in my power to prove that under the proposed federal constitution, *the trial of facts in civil cases by a jury of the vicinage* is entirely and effectually abolished, and will be absolutely impracticable. I wish the learned gentleman had explained to us what is meant by the appellate jurisdiction as to law and fact which is vested in the superior court of the United States? As he has not thought proper to do it, I shall endeavor to explain it to my fellow citizens, regretting at the same time that it has not been done by a man whose abilities are so much superior to mine. The word *appeal*, if I understand it right, in its proper legal signification includes the fact as well as the law, and precludes every idea of a trial by jury. It is a word of foreign growth, and is only known in England and America in those courts which are governed by the civil or ecclesiastical law of the Romans. Those courts have always been considered in England as a grievance, and have all been established by the usurpations of the eclesiastical over the civil power. It is well known that the courts of chancery in England were formerly entirely in the hands of ecclesiastics, who took advantage of the strict forms of the common law, to introduce a foreign mode of jurisprudence under the specious name of equity. Pennsylvania, the freest of the American States, has wisely rejected this establishment, and knows not even the name of a court of chancery. And, in fact, there cannot be anything more absurd than a distinction between *law* and *equity*. It might perhaps have suited those barbarous times when the law of England, like almost every other science, was perplexed with quibbles and Aristotelian distinctions, but it would be shameful to keep up in these more enlightened days. At any rate, it seems to me that there is much more equity in a trial by jury than in an appellate jurisdiction from the fact.

An appeal, therefore, is a thing unknown to the common law. Instead of an appeal from facts, it admits of a second or even third trial by different juries, and mistakes in points of law are rectified by superior courts in the form of a writ of error; and to a mere common lawyer, unskilled in the forms of the civil law courts, the words appeal from law and fact are mere nonsense and unintelligible absurdity.

But, even supposing that the superior court of the United States had the authority to try facts by juries of the vicinage, it would be impossible for them to carry it into execution. It is well known that the supreme courts of the different States, at stated times in every year, go round the different counties of their respective States to try issues of fact, which is called riding the circuits. Now, how is it possible that the supreme continental court, which we will suppose to consist at most of five or six judges, can travel at least twice in every year through the different counties of America, from New Hampshire to Kentucky and from Kentucky to Georgia, to try facts by juries of the vicinage? Common sense will not admit of such a supposition. I am therefore right in my assertion, that *trial by jury in civil cases is by the proposed constitution entirely done away and effectually abolished.*

Let us now attend to the consequences of this enormous innovation and daring encroachment on the liberties of the citizens. Setting aside the oppression, injustice and partiality that may take place in the trial of questions of property between man and man, we will attend to one single case, which is well worth our consideration. Let us remember that all cases arising under the new constitution and all matters between *citizens of different States* are to be submitted to the new jurisdiction. Suppose, therefore, that the military officers of Congress, by a wanton abuse of power, imprison the free citizens of the United States of America; suppose the excise or revenue officers (as we find in Clayton's Reports, page 44, Ward's case)—that a constable, having a warrant to search for stolen goods, pulled down the clothes of a bed in which there was a woman and searched under her shift—suppose, I say, that they commit similar or greater indignities, in such cases a trial by jury would be our safest resource, heavy damage would at once punish the offender and deter others from committing the same; but what satisfaction can we expect from a lordly court of justice, always ready to protect the officers of government against the weak and helpless citizens, and who will perhaps sit at the distance of many hundred miles from the place where the outrage was committed? What refuge shall we then have to shelter us from the iron hand of arbitrary power? O! my fellow-citizens, think of this while it is yet time, and never consent to part with the glorious privilege of trial by jury but with your lives.

But Mr. Wilson has not stopped here. He has told us that a standing army, that great support of tyrants, not only was not dangerous, but was absolutely necessary. O, my much respected fellow citizens! and are you then reduced to such a degree of insensibility, that assertions like these will not rouse your warmest resentment and indignation? Are we then, after the experience of past ages, and the result of the enquiries of the best and most celebrated patriots have taught us to dread a standing army above all earthly evils—are we then to go over all the threadbare, common-place arguments that have been used without success by the advocates of tyranny, and which have been for a long time past so gloriously refuted? Read the excellent Burgh in his political disquisitions on this hackneyed subject, and then say whether you think that a standing army is necessary in a free country. Even Mr. Hume, an aristocratical writer, has candidly confessed that *an army is a moral distemper in a government, of which it must at last inevitably perish* (2d Burgh, 349), and the Earl of Oxford (Oxford the friend of France and the Pretender, the attainted Oxford), said in the British parliament, in a speech on the mutiny bill, that, "While he had breath he would speak for the liberties of his country, and against courts martial and a standing army in peace, as dangerous to the Constitution." (Ibid., page 455.) Such were the speeches even of the enemies of liberty when Britain had yet a right to be called free. But, says Mr. Wilson, "It is necessary to maintain the appearance of strength even in times of the most profound tranquillity." And what is this more than a thread-bare hackneyed argument, which has been answered over and over in different ages, and does not deserve even the smallest consideration? Had we a standing army when the British invaded our peaceful shores? Was it a standing army that gained the battles of Lexington and Bunker Hill, and took the ill-fated Burgoyne? Is not a well-regulated militia sufficient for every purpose of internal defence? And which of you, my fellow citizens, is afraid of any invasion from foreign powers that our brave malitia would not be able immediately to repel?

Mr. Wilson says, that he does not know of any nation in the world which has not found it necessary to maintain the appearance of strength in a season of the most profound tranquillity. If by this equivocal assertion he has meant to say that there is no nation in the world without *a standing army in time of peace*, he has been mistaken. I need only adduce the example of Switzerland, which, like us, is a republic, whose thirteen cantons, like our thirteen States, are under a federal government, and which besides is surrounded by the most powerful nations in Europe, all jealous of its liberty and prosperity. And yet that nation has preserved its freedom for many ages, with the sole help of a militia, and has never been known to have a standing army, except when in actual war. Why should we not follow so glorious example, and are we less able to defend our liberty without an army, than that brave but small nation, which, with its militia alone has hitherto defied all Europe?

It is said likewise, that a standing army is not a new thing in America—Congress even at this moment have a standing army on foot. I answer that *precedent* is not *principle*. Congress have no right to keep up a standing army in time of peace. If they do, it is an infringement of the liberties of the people—wrong can never be justified by wrong: but it is well known that the assertion is groundless—the few troops that are on the banks of the Ohio, were sent for the express purpose of repelling the invasion of the savages and protecting the inhabitants of the frontiers. It is our misfortune that we are never at peace with those inhuman butchers of their species, and while they remain in our neighborhood, we are always, with respect to them, in a state of war—as soon as the danger is over, there is no doubt but Congress will disband their handful of soldiers; it is therefore not true that Congress keep up a standing army in a time of peace and profound security.

The objection to the enormous powers of the President and Senate is not the least important of all, but it requires a full discussion and ample investigation. I shall take another opportunity of laying before the public my observations upon this subject, as well as upon every other part of the new constitution. At present I shall only observe that it is an established principle in America, which pervades every one of our State constitutions, that the legislative and executive powers ought to be kept forever separate and distinct from each other; and yet in this new constitution we find there are two executive branches, each of which has more or less control over the proceedings of the Legislature. This is an innovation of the most dangerous kind upon every known principle of government, and it will be easy for me to convince my fellow citizens that it will, in the first place, create a Venetian aristocracy, and, in the end, produce an absolute monarchy.

Thus I have endeavored to answer to the best of my abilities the principal arguments of Mr. Wilson. I have written this in haste, in a short interval of leisure from my usual avocations. I have only traced the outlines of the subject, and I hope some abler hand will second my honest endeavors.

A DEMOCRATIC FEDERALIST.*

From a Correspondent.—A medical gentleman speaking to one of his frinds about the piece signed *Centinel*, asked him if he had seen the couching needle. It seems that that gentleman is justly apprehensive that many citizens are afflicted with the cataract, and that this excellent piece will be of great use to remove the inspissation of the crystalline humor of their eyes. (Johnson.)

Those who say that the petition presented to the Legislature, praying them to call a convention to adopt the new federal plan, assert what is not strictly true. There were not above 3,000 signatures from the whole city and Liberties, and it is well known that the city alone contains 5,000 taxables; the districts of Southwark and the Northern Liberties may contain about 2,000, which makes 7,000. Here then are 4,000 who have not signed; and now deduct from the number of signers the minors, foreigners and old women, who have subscribed this famous petition, and see whether there is any ground for the assertion that was made in the House of Assembly, and echoed and re-echoed afterwards out of doors, and judge also whether there are no more than five persons opposed to this *precious* new plan.

THE COUCHING NEEDLE.†

For the *Independent Gazetteer.*

Mr. Printer : The *Centinel* in your paper of last Friday, compliments the citizens of Philadelphia when he says, " A frenzy of enthusiasm has actuated them in their approbation of the proposed federal constution, before it was possible that

* Pennsylvania Packet, Oct. 23, 1787.

† Independent Gazetteer, Oct. 10, 1787.

it could be the result of a rational investigation." This, however, is trivial, compared with the sequel, wherein he charges the worthy and very patriotic characters of whom the late convention was composed, with a conspiracy against the liberty of their country. Not even the immortal Washington, nor the venerable Franklin, escapes his satire; but both of them, says this insidious enemy to his country, were *non compos mentis* when they concurred in framing the new federal constitution. When he ventured to make these assertions against characters so very respectable, he should have been able to support the charge. One of his objections to this constitution is, that each State is to have two senators, and not a number proportioned to its inhabitants. Here he has fallen into a terrible inconsistency, not recollecting that such is the mode of electing members of the Supreme Executive Council in this State, where every county appoints one, and only one, without any regard had to the number of taxble inhabitants in the respective counties. Yet he has gone so far in panegyrics upon the constitution of this State, as to maintain that a similar one would be the best that could be devised for the United States.

Had the different members of the Convention entertained sentiments thus narrow, local, contracted and selfish, each would have proposed the constitution of his own State, and they would never have united in forming that incomparable one which is now exhibited to our view, and which, without partiality to any particular State, is adapted to the general circumstances of all.

I am happy to find the distinction of Republican and Constitutionalist in this city has given way to the more important one of Federalist and Antifederalist. Such a worthy example will, I trust, be imitated through every part of this State.

To conclude, sir, if some person of better abilities should not step forth in defence of the form of government proposed by the Convention, I shall hold myself bound, in duty to the welfare of my country, to expose upon a future occasion the weakness and futility of *Centinel's* arguments, together with the motives which urged him to undertake the infamous job.

I shall not, however, retort his torrents of personal invective, but shall take notice of the sophistry he has made use of, so far as it is calculated to mislead the citizens of Pennsylvania, or of the adjacent states.   A FEDERALIST.*

For the *Independent Gazetteer.*

Mr. Oswald: I have read without spectacles the proposed Federal Constitution, and I see with the most heartfelt pleasure the resemblance that it bears to that of our much admired Sublime Porte. Your President general will greatly resemble in his powers the mighty Ahdul Ahmed, our august Sultan—the senate will be his divan—your standing army will come in the place of our janizaries—your judges unchecked by vile juries may with great propriety be styled cadis ; and bishop Seabury will be your mufti. Oh ! I am delighted with this new Constitution—is it not a charming, a beautiful form of government? What do you think, Aga Oswald? What do you say, you Christian dog?

Allah ekber, allah illallah, Mohammed resul allah !

A TURK.†

For the *Independent Gazetteer.*

Mr. Printer: The authors of a late publication in your paper, signed *Centinel*, which has represented Doctor Franklin as a fool from age, and General Washington as a fool from nature, and which is replete with the grossest falsehoods and absurdities, have concluded their address with some lines from Shakespeare. The only answer that such an infamous libel upon distinguished merit, truth and liberty, is entitled to, may be taken from the works of a British poet of equal fame.

The Convention

> "Did but teach the age to quit their clogs,
>   By the plain rules of ancient liberty :
>   When lo ! a barbarous noise surrounded them—
>   Of owls, and cuckows, asses, apes, and dogs."   MILTON.†

Montgomery County, October 8th, 1787.

*Independent Gazetteer, Oct. 10, 1787.
† Independent Gazetteer, Oct. 10, 1787.

Extract of a letter from Sussex (Delaware), September 29.

"I must not forget to mention by way of postscript, that one of the newspapers of your city, some time in August last, by the accidental transposition of a single letter, occasioned an explanation that has afforded some merriment. The paper, instead of the words United States read *Untied* States. A farmer of my acquaintance in reading over the paper was at a loss what to make of the matter. "Untied States, Untied States, (said he) what can this mean? certainly it cannot mean that our governments are dissolved." The same evening he carried the paper to old Mr. G——, who, you know, keeps a school in the neighborhood, and desired an explanation. Mr. G——, after putting on his spectacles to prevent a possibility of deception, examined the paragraph, and found what the man said to be true. " It is even as you say, John, (replied he) and I think it can mean nothing more than that the States are, or shortly will be, no longer bound by their old Constitutions : that is, they will be completely untied from them, as soon as the new Constitution comes abroad !"*

A correspondent observes that the opposers of the federal constitution are secretly affecting delay in order to prevent its adoption. In the mean time, they are moving heaven and earth to prejudice the public mind against it. They do not reason, but abuse—General *Washington*, they (in effect) say, is a dupe, and Doctor *Franklin*, an old fool—vide the *Centinel*. They will doubtless in their next publications, assert that *Daniel Shays* is the best patriot in the United States, and that *John Franklin* should be king of Pennsylvania.

He further observes, that as delay is the means by which they are contriving to carry their point, they are about sending deputies to find out Lycurgus, the ancient lawgiver of the Spartans, whose death has never been clearly ascertained. Their errand is to invite him among us, that he may form another federal constitution. That until Lycurgus shall come, it will not be proper to adopt the constitution proposed

* Independent Gazetteer, Oct. 11, 1787.

by the convention, as he having lived two thousand years, will be able to frame a better one. They have agreed that when he shall come, they will renounce their offices as too profitable for his frugal plan of government, or will at least take their fees and salaries in iron, instead of gold and silver, pound for pound. But until Lycurgus come, they will hold their present offices and take their fees and salaries in gold and silver, as will be very convenient.

He further asks, whether any man of common sense believes we shall have another federal convention if the present plan is not adopted?—whether the complying States can believe Pennsylvania to be serious in her federal professions, if she rejects a plan recommended by men so experienced, able and upright, as the late convention, especially after so full a consideration of the subject?

He is curious to know what men will be named who are likely to form a better plan—and whether the nineteen seceding members, the *Centinel* and the *Old Whig*, are to be of the number—lastly, if they are, whether they are prepared to give security to their constituents that they will not desert their duty and make another secession when the salvation of their country depends on their keeping their posts. *

For the *Independent Gazetteer.*

Were it possible to suppress the honest indignation of patriotism, or to stifle that resentment which arises against the foes of persecuted America, while we behold the boasted freedom of her press prostituted to the purposes of her bitterest enemies—yet would the soldier, who has fought and bled by the side of his beloved chief (while many of these miscreants mingled in the opposing ranks), have cause to reproach himself did he silently suffer his respected name to be thus vilified by the base agents of Europe, or the baser parricides of America, who (under the cloak of concern lest the liberties of this land should be exposed to danger from the determinations of a *Washington*, a *Franklin*, a *Livingston*, a *Rutledge*, a *Dick-*

* Independent Gazetteer, Oct. 13, 1787.

inson, a *Madison*, a *Morris*, a *Hamilton*), are allowed to act a part for which the laws of Athens would have consigned them to the gibbet. No, Mr. Printer, the honest American, who, in asserting the freedom of the western world, wasted his youth and impaired his fortune, has a right to look for protection from the government in his old age—and he will rather rise in vengeance than submit to be thus abused by the Briton, the Gaul, the Spaniard, the Turk, or the *turn-coat American*—and whether they act in their distinct capacities of agents for their several countries, or are leagued with the detestable placemen of our own country, in opposing the establishment of the Federal Constitution, that first production of political wisdom and integrity, they are alike the objects of a just resentment, from which neither the gold of Europe, nor the friendship of apostate Americans, will be able to protect them.   DENTATUS.*

Mr. Oswald: Methinks by this time you are more fully convinced of the justice of my remarks on the federal constitution. I am astonished that so many of the Americans were so stupidly ignorant of their real interest as to run headlong with an enthusiastic spirit or mistaken zeal, and sign petitions to the late House of Assembly praying for the calling of a State convention, for the adoption of so wild a system of government; for the Americans, as I observed before, are unfit to govern themselves. *Judge B——n, Dr. E——g, C—— P——t, J——n, B. S——b* and *Johnny S——y*, who are the only men of good sense in Pennsylvania, were convinced of the absurdity of such a constitution the moment I discovered to them its design. A writer under the signature of *A Turk*, shows clearly what designing men would be at. He says: "I see with heart-felt pleasure the resemblance that it † bears to our much admired Sublime Porte. Your President-general will greatly resemble in his powers the mighty Abdul Ahmed, our august Sultan; the Senate will be his Divan;

* Independent Gazetteer, Oct. 13, 1787.
† The Federal Constitution.

your standing army will come in the place of our janizaries; your judges unchecked by vile juries,'' &c. Such a government no doubt would be pleasing to him, provided he should be chosen the Sultan of the empire. O! methinks it is *damnable.* I love our present government from its extensive liberty; as our Supreme Executive Council of this State can appoint me sworn interpreter of the English as well as the foreign languages, with a salary of £500 a year, to expound the laws to them, and let the people pledge themselves to each other to support and carry into execution the wholesome and wise laws that are made under the present constitution, and there needs be no new form of government in Pennsylvania. What do you think, Mr. Oswald? A GAUL.*

Mr. Oswald: I wish your correspondent, *Dentatus*, would be pleased to tell us who are those bitterest enemies of America, who, while the American soldier fought by the side of his beloved chief, mingled in the opposing ranks, and who now are writing against the proposed federal constitution? Is it not a shame to have recourse to such base lies in order to support the cause of tyranny and aristocratic power? But, Mr. Oswald, to confound your toothless *Dentatus* and his compeers, I think I am well grounded to assure you that many of the paragraphs and pieces which have appeared in the newspapers in favor of the new constitution, were written by a person who was, during the late war, a *sergeant in the British army in America.* MORSUS.†

For the *Independent Gazetteer.*

Mr. Oswald: It is a pretty cunning trick of the aristocratical party to fill the papers with ludicrous pieces under the signatures of ''Britons,'' ''Gauls,'' ''Spaniards,'' and even ''Turks,'' against the proposed federal constitution, in order to make you believe that the opposition that is made to it arises chiefly from foreigners and foreign agents. But I hope my fellow citizens will not suffer themselves to be deceived

* Independent Gazetteer, Oct. 13, 1787.
† Independent Gazetteer, Oct. 15, 1787.

by this thread-bare piece of political jockeyism. Look around you, Mr. Oswald, ask the British and other foreign agents their opinion of the new constitution, and you will find them all open-mouthed, bellowing forth its praises. How could it be otherwise, when its principles are so similiar to those of the constitutions of their own respective countries, which they have sucked with their milk? It is well known that all the foreign ministers at New York have declared in favor of this new form of government, and it is suspected that they have not been inactive in endeavoring to bring it about. What say the British Consuls in every part of the continent? Are they ever seen to mix or keep company with those who oppose the pretended federal plan? No; they would think themselves polluted to mix with any of the brave Whigs, who after having defended their liberties from the British tyrant, will not suffer them to be laid prostrate by tyrants of their own creating. This new proposed form of government is much better suited to their views than any other, because it will be much easier for them to deal with a single magistrate and a handful of senators, who are to remain six years in office, and may be re-elected during their lives, than with a a numerous Congress, annually elected, who cannot preserve their appointment longer than three years in six, and consequently are in a constant state of fluctuation. Away then with such perfidious insinuations! Those who are intent upon pursuing the interest of foreign princes in America will never suffer this country to preserve its liberties. Their most earnest wish is to see us under a tyrannical government, lest we should become too formidable.

AN AMERICAN CITIZEN.*

To the Freemen of Pennsylvania.

Friends and Fellow Citizens: Conscious of no other motives than those with which the love of my country inspires me, permit me to request your candid, impartial and unprejudiced attention, while I address you on business of the utmost importance to every honest American—a business

* Independent Gazetteer, Oct. 15, 1787.

of no less magnitude than the salvation of the United States.

I need hardly tell you, what is universally allowed, that our situation is now more precarious than it ever has been, even at that time when our country was laid waste by the sanguinary armies of Britain and her mercenary allies, and when our coasts were infested with her hostile fleets. Then a sense of the common danger united every heroic, every patriotic soul in the great cause of liberty. Even selfishness itself, forgetting every narrow, contracted idea, gave way to that diffusive liberality of sentiment, which was so instrumental in procuring peace and independence to America.

But ever since that memorable epoch, unanimity, the great source of national happiness and glory, has been banished from among us, and discord, with all its cursed attendants, has succeeded in its stead. Such a train of calamities issued from this fatal change as at length aroused the virtuous citizens of the different States from their lethargy, and excited in them a desire of exploring, and of removing the cause. Nor was the former a different task. Our distresses were immediately discovered to be inevitable effects of a weak, a disunited, and a despicable federal government. To effect the latter, delegates were sent by twelve of the States to the late Federal Convention, who, after four months' deliberation, at length agreed upon a plan of government for the United States, which is now submitted to your consideration. Upon this proposed federal constitution I mean not to bestow my useless panegyrics at this time. My slender praise might cast an odium upon what is in itself truly excellent, and needs but a candid reading to be admired. Suspended, as the fate of the United States now is, how immensely base must the wretch be, who strains every nerve to disunite his fellow-citizens, and by a long train of sophistical arguments. strives to establish antifederal sentiments in this State! Yet, however strange it may seem, such there are among us. One antifederal piece signed "Centinel," which is replete with glaring absurdities and complete nonsense, has been industriously circulated among you, in the newspapers and in hand-bills. The author (I should have said authors) of this illiberal and scandalous performance, remarks that a "frenzy of enthusiasm," not "a rational investigation into its principles, actuated the citizens of Philadelphia in their approbation of the proposed plan" of government. As some drunken men think every person they see is intoxicated, and as an illiterate observer on this earth is apt to believe in the sun's motion, not discerning that its apparent revolution is the effect of his own real motion, so has "Centinel" charged others with neglecting that rational investigation, to which he has paid very little attention. For if he carefully examines the proposed constitution, he will find that he has either ignorantly, or designedly, perverted its plain and simple construction. He seems to think that the citizens of Philadelphia ought to have suspended their judgment till they had know the result of his *rational investigation*. For, says the profound politician, "Those who are competent to the task of developing the principles of government ought to be encouraged to come forward, and thereby the better enable the people to make a proper judgment. For the science of government is so abstruse, that few are able to judge for themselves." He certainly must have forgot that he was addressing American freemen, who enjoy the darling prerogative of thinking for themselves. Such political priestcraft might have answered some purpose in the early ages of ignorance and superstition, when a set of artful and designing monks assumed an absolute control over both the purses and consciences of the people. But thanks to heaven! we live in an enlightened age, and in a free country, where such pernicious doctrine has long since been treated with deserved contempt.

He begins with enumerating "certain privileges secured to you by the constitution of this Commonwealth," which, notwithstanding his groundless assertions, are not infringed in the smallest degree by the proposed federal constitution, which obliges Congress to guarantee to each State its respective republican form of government. Whatever he may think of the matter, a firm union of all the States is certainly necessary to procure happiness and prosperity to America. In vain do we look up to the constitution or legislature of this State; they cannot alleviate our distresses.

Is it in the power of Pennsylvania to protest her own trade, by entering into commercial treaties with the nations of Europe, and thereby to secure a West India or an European market for her produce? No. Is it in her power to treat with and obtain from Spain a free navigation of the river Mississippi, to which God and nature have given us an un-doubted right? The impoverished state of our Western country, where the luxuriant crops of a fertile soil are suffered to rot in the fields, for want of exportation, answers No. Is it in her power to encourage our infant manufactures, to give sustenance to our starving mechanics, to prevent a general bankruptcy, or to raise a revenue, by laying an impost on foreign goods imported into this State? No. All her at-tempts are liable to be counteracted by any neighboring State; for it is well known that the imposts have been frequently evaded in this State, and always will while Jersey and Dela-ware open free ports for the reception of foreign wares. So that the exigencies of government must necessarily be pro-vided for by a heavy land tax, which you, my fellow citizens, have groaned under for some years past with surprising patience and resignation. Should some desperate ruffians, as a Shays or a Wyoming Franklin, with an armed banditti at his back, proceed to murder our defenceless inhabitants, has Pennsylvania the means of speedily repelling their ravages? No. Before the necessary steps could be taken for a defence, her towns might be laid in ruins and her fields deluged with the blood of her helpless citizens. And oh! distracting thought! the citizens of the neighboring States would aban-don us to our unhappy fate; nor would they deign to shed a tear of pity on our funeral urn. It would be an endless talk to give a detail of all the cases in which the exertions of in-dividual States cannot afford the smallest relief. An idea of thirteen neighboring States being able to exist independent of each other, without a general government, to control, con-nect and unite the whole, is no less absurd than was the con-duct of the limbs, in the fable, which refused to contribute to the support of the belly, and by working its downfall, accelerated their own ruin. Of this every State in the Union is fully convinced, by awful experience, unless we except Rhode Island; for the meridian of which "Centinel" has calculated his Antifederal remarks, which he has had the presumption to address to the freemen of Pennsylvania.

Afraid of investigating the constitution itself, he previously attempts to prejudice you against it by charging the patriotic members of the convention with a design "of lording it over their fellow-creatures" and with "long meditated schemes of power and aggrandizement." Is it possible that the freemen of America would appoint such men as these to so important a trust? No. The public characters of the gentlemen who were chosen by my respectable fellow-citizens in the different States are such as at once justify their conduct in the choice, and contradict the unjust and ungenerous assertion. This defamer has even dared to let fly his shafts at a *Washington* and a *Franklin*, who, he tells you, have been so mean, ignorant and base as to be dupes to the designs of the other members. Is not every man among you fired with resentment against the wretch who could undertake a job thus low, infamous and vile, and who was so prone to slander as wantonly to traduce names dear to every American—names, if not respected and esteemed, at least admired even by their enemies?

After having striven to inflame your passions against these worthy men, he then makes a general objection to different branches in government; here again he advances doctrine which has long since been exploded as dangerous and despotic. That a single legislative body is more liable to encroach upon the liberties of the people than two who hold an useful check upon the proceedings of each other he does not attempt to deny, but asserts that one body will be more responsible to the people than two or more can be; therefore, after this body shall have erred, the people can immediately take vengeance of its members, that is, if I may be indulged with a trite saying, after the steed is stolen lock the stable door. Had he proceeded in the same mode of reasoning, he might have proved that an elective monarchy is the best government, for it is certainly the most responsible, since one man is accountable for every grievance. In truth, my friends, you will easily perceive that this responsibility, which he lays so much stress on, is by no means sufficient to secure your liberties. If you enquire into the effects of sanguinary punishments upon criminals, you will find that instead of reforming they have increased the wickedness of the people.

But the convention, not content with providing punishments for the misdemeanors of government, have done wiser, in endeavoring to prevent these misdemeanors, which was evidently their intention in new modeling the federal government.

He next complains of the too extensive powers of Congress. "It will not be controverted," says he, "that the legislative is the highest delegated power in government, and that all others are subordinate to it." In this I perfectly agree with him, and am apt to believe, that had he paused here one moment, he would not have been so ready to fear an aristocracy in any branch of the new federal government; since the most essential parts of legislation are to be vested in the House of Representatives, the immediate servants of the people, with whom all money bills must originate.

He is ready to allow Congress to pay the debts of the Union; but then, they are to have power to lay and collect duties, imposts, &c., which the new constitution declares shall be uniform throughout the United States; here the word *collect* seems to stick in his stomach. What! says he, will they have power to enforce the payment of taxes? Oh! it is dangerous to invest them with such authority; they ought to call upon us as heretofore, and leave it at our option to comply with their requisitions or not. Such is the reasoning of this advocate for delinquency, the absurdity of whose political creed is self-apparent, and needs no comment. Happy would it be for Pennsylvania, if the different States were obliged to pay their proportions of the foreign and domestic debt; she would not then be struggling under an enormous land tax, to pay much more than her just quota of the public burthens. But, says he, there is a possibility of having standing armies too. This is quite wrong; let Congress have power to make war, crush insurrections, &c., but let them have no troops for these purposes, unless each State shall think proper to furnish its quota of men; or if we vest the power of raising armies in Congress, let them be tied down, and not permitted to raise a single regiment, until an invasion shall have actually taken place, and the enemy shall have ravaged and spread desolation over five or six of the States; it will then be time enough. Indeed I think we ought immediately to disband the troops stationed on the Ohio, and not raise a man for that service before the savages shall have laid our country waste, as far as Susquehanna at least. Why need we trouble ourselves about the inhabitants on the frontiers? Such truly is the substance of his arguments.

He has further discovered that the trial by jury in civil cases is abolished—that the liberty of the press is not provided for—and that the judicial and legislative powers of the respective States will be absorbed by those of the general government.

As to the first of these, it is well known that the cases which come before a jury, are not the same in all the States; that therefore the Convention found themselves unequal to the task of forming a general rule, among so many jarring interests, and left it with Congresss to regulate the conduct of the judiciary in all civil cases. It may not be improper here to remark, that Congress can at any time propose amendments to this Constitution, which shall become a part of it when ratified by the legislatures or Conventions of three-fourths of the States.

True, no declaration in favor of the liberty of the press is contained in the new Constitution, neither does it declare that children of freemen are also born free. Both are alike the unalienable birthright of freemen, and equally absurd would it have been, in the Convention, to have meddled with either.

The *ne plus ultra* of the powers of Congress, and of the judiciary of the United States, is expressly fixed—therefore, no danger can arise to the legislative or judicial authority of any State in the union. *Centinel*, in discussing this point, has ransacked his brains, tortured, twisted, and preverted the new plan of government, to support his blundering assertions ; especially where he has quoted sect. 4 of the 1st Art. "The times, places, and manner, of holding elections, for senators, and representatives, shall be prescribed, in each State, by the legislature thereof ; but the Congress may at any time, by law, make or alter such regulations, except as to the place of choosing senators."

"The plain construction of which," says Centinel, "is, that when the State legislatures drop out of sight, from the necessary operation of this government, then Congress are to provide for the election and appointment of representatives, and senators." O amazing result of *a rational investigation!* I confess he understands the meaning of words much better than I do, if his construction of that section be just. What may Congress "make or alter?" The times, places and manner of holding elections, in the different States. But why is the place of choosing senators excepted? Who are to appoint them? Certainly, the legislatures of the respective States, who are to elect the senators in any place they may think proper, which probably will be, where they meet in their legislative capacity. The existence of every branch of the Federal government depends upon the State legislatures, and both must stand or fall together.

He next attacks the construction of the federal government, says the number of representatives is too few. Others have thought it too many. How was it possible that the Convention, in this, or indeed in any other instance, could please everybody? For my part I am of opinion that the number fixed by the Convention (one for every 30,000) is fully adequate to the task of effectually representing the people ; and that a greater number would only clog the wheels, and add to the expenses of government, in which the strictest economy is at all times necessary. That two years is too long a time to continue in office is a mistaken notion ; much more inconvenience and expense would be attendant on annual elections throughout this extensive continent. The most strenuous advocates for a parliamentary reform, in Great Britain, never stickled for more than triennial elections, which they deemed fully sufficient to secure the liberties of the people. This body may justly be called the guardians of our liberties, since they are not chosen by the State legislatures, as Congress has hitherto been, but by the freemen at large, in every State. No undue influence can be exercised over them, nor the Senate, for no placemen, or officers of government, can have a seat among them.

He says the senate is constituted on the most unequal principles, since the smallest State in the Union sends as many senators as the largest. Here is a small concession to the smaller States, which proclaims the liberality of sentiment that prevailed in the convention. Let us, my friends, in the larger States, be satisfied with our superior influence in the House of Representatives. As to the senate being composed of the *better sort*, the *well-born*, etc., it is a most illiberal reflection thrown out by this antifederal demagogue against the freemen of America, who, I trust, will always elect to this important trust men of integrity and abilities. But how is there any danger of this body becoming an aristocracy? In their executive capacity they are checked by the President, and in their legislative capacity are checked by the House of Representatives, and of themselves cannot do a single act. He seems apprehensive that the President may form a coalition with the senate, "whose influence might secure his re-election to office." I cannot conceive how they can exercise any influence in his favor, for both senators and representatives are expressly excluded from being electors.

The only objection he makes to the power of the President is that he can grant pardons and reprieves. This prerogative must be and always is vested somewhere in all free governments; to whom then can it be given with more safety than to this officer, who never can have any interest in exercising it to evil purposes? If he should, he will be liable to impeachment, etc.

Previous to his conclusion he attempts to lull us into security; but his sophistry can never operate so far upon our senses as to make us believe that our situation is not "critically dreadful." The most ignorant among us severely feel the miseries which surround us on all sides. That he may be very well pleased with his present situation, I have not the smallest doubt; for it is notorious that the Antifederal junto in Philadelphia is composed of a few self-interested men, who, in the midst of our distresses, are receiving most enormous sums out of the public treasury, and like ravens are preying upon our very vitals. A FEDERALIST.*

Extract of a letter from a gentleman in the Western country to his friend in this city:

"It hath been reported that a great number of copies of the proposed constitution was directed to be printed in the English and German languages, to be distributed throughout the State. I wish it were done, that the people might have an opportunity of reading it, and judging for themselves. Much time elapses before information can reach the industrious yeomanry of the State that are distant from the seat of government. If a convention is to be chosen, the great body of the people will be ignorant of the plan to be decided upon, and be therefore unable to determine whether they ought to vote for persons who would oppose it or advocate it. If it will bear the examination of the people, who are to be bound thereby, why is such preciptancy used?"†

For the *Independent Gazetteer.*

The humble address of the *low-born* of the United States of America, to their fellow slaves scattered throughout the world—greeting:

Whereas, it hath been represented unto us that a most dreadful disease hath for these five years last past infected,

* Independent Gazetteer, Oct. 25, 1787.
† Pennsylvania Packet; Nov. 1, 1787.

preyed upon and almost ruined the government and people of this our country; and of this malady we ourselves have had perfect demonstration, not mentally, but bodily, through every one of the five senses: For although our sensations in regard to the mind be not just so nice as those of the *well born*, yet our feeling, through the medium of the plow, the hoe and the grubbing ax, is as acute as any nobleman's in the world. And, whereas, a number of skillful physicians having met together at Philadelphia last summer, for the purpose of exploring, and, if possible, removing the cause of this direful disease, have, through the assistance of John Adams, Esq., in the profundity of their great political knowledge, found out and discovered that nothing but a new government, consisting of three different branches, namely, king, lords and commons, or, in the American language, President, Senate and Representatives, can save this, our country, from inevitable destruction; and, whereas, it hath been reported that several of our *low-born* brethren have had the horrid audacity to think for themselves in regard to this new system of government, and, dreadful thought! have wickedly begun to doubt concerning the perfection of this evangelical constitution, which our political doctors have declared to be a panacea, which (by inspiration) they know will infallibly heal every distemper in the confederation, and finally terminate in the salvation of America.

Now we the *low born*, that is, all the people of the United States, except 600 or thereabouts, *well born*, do by this our humble address, declare and most solemnly engage, that we will allow and admit the said 600 *well born*, immediately to establish and confirm this most noble, most excellent and truly divine constitution: and we further declare that without any equivocation or mental reservation whatever we will support and maintain the same according to the best of our power, and after the manner and custom of all other slaves in foreign countries, namely by the sweat and toil of our body: nor will we at any future period of time ever attempt to complain of this our royal government, let the consequences be what they may.   And although it appears to us that a standing army, composed of the purgings of the jails of Great Britain, Ireland and Germany, shall be employed in collecting the revenues of this our king and goverment; yet, we again in the most solemn manner declare, that we will abide by our present determination of non-assistance and passive obedience; so that we shall not dare to molest or disturb those military gentlemen in the service of our royal government. And (which is not improbable) should any one of those soldiers when employed on duty in collecting the taxes, strike off the arm (with his sword) of one of our fellow slaves, we will conceive our case remarkably fortunate if he leaves the other arm on. And morever, because we are aware that many of our fellow slaves shall be unable to pay their taxes, and this incapacity of theirs is a just cause of impeachment of treason; wherefore in such cases we will use our utmost endeavors, in conjunction with the standing army, to bring such atrocious offenders before our federal judges, who shall have power, without jury or trial, to order the said miscreants for immediate execution; nor will we think their sentence severe unless after being hanged they are also to be both beheaded and quartered. And finally we shall henceforth and forever leave all power, authority and dominion over our persons and properties in the hands of the *well born*, who were designed by Providence to govern. And in regard to the liberty of the press, we renounce all claim to it forever more, Amen ; and we shall in future be perfectly contented if our tongues be left us to lick the feet of our *well born* masters.

Done on behalf of three millions of low-born American slaves. JOHN HUMBLE, Secretary.*

To the Printers of the United States.

Gentlemen: I have been delighted with the noble struggle which the brave and virtuous throughout America have been and still are making to establish the new frame of government. I am charmed with the good sense and humanity of the people at large, who, though they are very generally

* Independent Gazetteer, Oct. 29, 1787.

warmly attached to it, yet they bear with uncommon patience all the insults hitherto thrown out against it and the gentlemen of the late convention.

The friends of the new system are not ashamed to avow their principles and their writings on the subject, while its enemies take every prudent measure to prevent detection.

I know a gentleman in this city, high in office, who has written much against the new system, notwithstanding he has never in company uttered a syllable against it. Hence I conclude that the antifederal junto are conscious of the wickedness of their proceedings—that their cause is that of the devil, and of it they are truly ashamed. It appears by a late eastern paper that the publisher of the Massachusetts *Gazette* is determined to publish no sentiments on this important subject unless the writers leave their names with the printers, "that any one who may be desirous of knowing the author may be informed." No honest man, no true friend of America or to the liberty or happiness of mankind, can object to this.

For your imitation, gentlemen, I humbly propose the conduct of this your worthy brother, the publisher of the Massachusetts *Gazette*.   A PENNSYLVANIA MECHANIC.*
26th October, 1787.

———

Mr. Oswald: Since the new constitution of Congress has been published, I have made a journey into the three counties adjoining to us, in which I had many acquaintances among honest men of both the old parties which formerly divided this State. Good manners induced me, where I was hospitably entertained, to avoid broaching the subject of our new federal constitution, as I might possibly spoil the social happiness which I (who am no party man) had been used to enjoy with my good friends, constitutionalists and republicans. My hosts could not bear this my reserve—one and the other exclaimed, "Why do you not talk to me of the new constitution?—I have seen and read it, and though I liked the men who made it, I like the constitution they have given to us much

* Independent Gazetteer, Oct. 29, 1787.

more." Others observed that the good men who have been so
often tried and approved by us, may go off this uncertain
stage in the course of a few passing years, but they have left
a legacy which will make us and our children and our children's children as happy as a good government can make
them, for hundreds of years after the framers of it are no more.
"God be praised!" said an old man (whose benevolence I shall
long remember) "my neighbors of the Jerseys, of Delaware,
New York and Maryland, will be as happy as myself." He
then addressed himself to his younger child, a daughter:
"Dolly, my girl, you will not go from home when you go with
Jersey Dick, for we are all now one people; I shall not fear as
I have done, that we who lie on the borders shall be cutting
each other's throats, about bounds, smuggling and trade."
One man, indeed, in a corner of one of our friendly circles,
who after hunting for an office twenty years, had at last got
the office of excise in his county, muttered something of *Old
Whig*, *Centinel*, sixteen assemblymen, Governor *Randolph*,
lawyer *Mason*, one *Gerry*, liberty of the press, jurymen, and
that officers who had served but a few years and who had
not been paid for their services should be continued for life,
and many other things of the same kind, in a sullen, grumb-
ling, ill-natured way, was at length interrupted by a decent
elderly man, who as I learned had ever been a friend to his
country, never a placeman, a whig from benevolence to his
family, his neighbors and all whom he knew, an honest man
in the worst of times, who wished the farmer might reap
plentiful crops and have a good market, and that trade might
flourish, that we might make as many things among ourselves as possible, that tradesmen might fare well, and as he
said that the President and Senate might be able to make
and keep good and sufficient treaties to insure all these solid
benefits to us—says this good man, "My friend the exciseman,
there in yon corner, talks of old whigs: no body can doubt
of my being one of that sort, for I am an old man and always
was a whig since the name was known, and have been, I am
bold to say, as good a centinel among our militia in the field
of battle, as any man who calls himself a Centinel in a news-

paper. I think sixteen men should submit in their opinions to forty-three, when all our States approve of the conduct of the forty-three, and condemn the sixteen: and I will say the men were right who, with the sergeant of the assembly, brought the two men of the sixteen runaways back to the assembly; for if they had not done so sixteen men would have overthrown our government of Pennsylvania. Though I am no scholar, I think the speaker and the forty-three had a power from the good rule of preventing greater evils to force the whole sixteen to attend in their seats. If they have not this power, my friend the exciseman there in the corner, must lose his office, as the government and all offices, and the constitution and all, would be at an end immediately. As to Governor Randolph, I am told he is a cunning man, but no enemy to the new constitution ; he only wanted to overreach another man in politics. Lawyer Mason may plead his own cause in Virginia, where it is a chance of about four hundred thousand (that being the number of people in that State) to one, that is lawyer Mason, that he is in the wrong. Besides, I may say, he has the delegates of every State against him into the bargain. That Geary will never get on farther than Rhode Island, where the bad people will keep him, as the only man they can find out of their State, who is as bad as themselves. The liberty of printing, I find, from Burns' justice and our State constitution, is a thing quite safe already, and so is our trial by jurymen. If so, our convention would have wasted their time and our patience, my friends, if they had spent their time in making new fences where the old ones were strong enough. They had enough to do that was necessary, God knows ! My friend, the exciseman, thinks that a man once in office, should continue so for his life. I must needs say, I think he may if he be a good officer; I would give him my vote that he remain exciseman as long as he lives, and longer if it was possible, if that will make him listen to reason; for neither myself nor my children, I hope, will covet any office unless it be such in which we may fight the enemies of our United States. As we begun, my friends, so let us continue united. I have often told my children of the bundle of fagots; you may break each of them apart like the stem of this pipe (taking hold of the pipe he was then smoking), but if you bind them together, Goliah nor Sampson cannot break them.'' Wherever I went in this my journey I found all the good people talking in the same honest sensible way; this pleased me I will confess, for it favored an old opinion, that where passion does not twist our understandings, all upright and sensible men think in the same way. In short, that plain downright good sense which governs the honest farmer, miller, tradesman and merchant, governed the honest, tried and approved men, who sat in the late convention of these our United States.

HOMESPUN.*

Mr. Oswald: By inserting the following in your impartial paper, you will oblige yours, &c.

To the Citizens of Philadelphia.

Friends, countrymen, brethren and fellow-citizens: The important day is drawing near when you are to elect delegates to represent you in a convention, on the result of whose deliberations will depend in a great measure your future happiness.

This convention is to determine whether or not the commonwealth of Pennsylvania shall adopt the plan of government proposed by the late convention of delegates from the different States which sat in this city.

With a heart full of anxiety for the preservation of your dearest rights, I presume to address you on this important occasion. In the name of sacred liberty, dearer to us than our property and our lives, I request your most earnest attention.

The proposed plan of continental government is now fully known to you. You have read it, I trust, with the attention it deserves. You have heard the objections that have been made to it. You have heard the answers to these objections.

If you have attended to the whole with candor and un-biased minds, as becomes men that are possessed and deserv-

* Independent Gazetteer, Oct. 31, 1787.

ing of freedom, you must have been alarmed at the result of your observations. Notwithstanding the splendor of names which has attended the publication of the new constitution, notwithstanding the sophistry and vain reasonings that have been urged to support its principles, alas! you must at least have concluded that great men are not always infallible, and that patriotism itself may be led into essential errors.

The objections that have been made to the new constitution are these:

1. It is not merely (as it ought to be) a Confederation of States, but a Government of individuals.

2. The powers of Congress extend to the lives, the liberties and the property of every citizen.

3. The sovereignty of the different States is *ipso facto* destroyed in its most essential parts.

4. What remains of it will only tend to create violent dissensions between the State government and the Congress, and terminate in the ruin of the one or the other.

5. The consequence must therefore be, either that the union of the States will be destroyed by a violent struggle, or that their sovereignty will be swallowed up by silent encroachments into a universal aristocracy; because it is clear, that if two different sovereign powers have a coëqual command over the purses of the citizens, they will struggle for the spoils, and the weakest will be in the end obliged to yield to the efforts of the strongest.

6. Congress being possessed of these immense powers, the liberties of the States and of the people are not secured by a bill or Declaration of Rights.

7. The sovereignty of the States is not expressly reserved; the form only, and not the substance of the government, is guaranteed to them by express words.

8. Trial by Jury, that sacred bulwark of liberty, is abolished in civil cases, and Mr. W——, one of the convention, has told you, that not being able to agree as to the form of establishing this point, they have left you deprived of the substance. Here are his own words: "The subject was involved in difficulties. The convention found the task too difficult for them, and left the business as it stands."

9. The Liberty of the Press is not secured, and the powers of Congress are fully adequate to its destruction, as they are to have the trial of libels, or pretended libels against the United States, and may by a cursed abominable Stamp Act (as the Bowdoin administration has done in Massachusetts) preclude you effectually from all means of information. Mr. W—— has given no answer to these arguments.

10. Congress have the power of keeping up a standing army in time of peace, and Mr. W—— has told you that it was *necessary*.

11. The Legislative and Executive powers are not kept separate, as every one of the American constitutions declares they ought to be; but they are mixed in a manner entirely novel and unknown, even in the constitution of Great Britain; because,

12. In England the king only has a nominal negative over the proceedings of the legislature, which he has never dared to exercise since the days of King William, whereas by the new constitution, both the President-General and the Senate, two executive branches of Government, have that negative, and are intended to support each other in the exercise of it.

13. The representation of the lower house is too small, consisting only of 65 members.

14. That of the Senate is so small that it renders its extensive powers extremely dangerous; it is to consist only of 26 members, two-thirds of whom must concur to conclude any treaty or alliance with foreign powers. Now we will suppose that five of them are absent, sick, dead, or unable to attend; twenty-one will remain, and eight of these (one-third, and one over) may prevent the conclusion of any treaty, even the most favorable to America. Here will be a fine field for the intrigues and even the bribery and corruption of European powers.

15. The most important branches of the executive department are to be put into the hands of a single magistrate, who will in fact be an *elective king*. The military, the land and naval forces, are to be entirely at his disposal, and therefore,

16. Should the senate, by the intrigues of foreign powers,

become devoted to foreign influence, as was the case of late in Sweden, the people will be obliged, as the Swedes have been, to seek their refuge in the arms of the monarch or President-General.

17. Rotation, that noble prerogative of liberty, is entirely excluded from the new system of government, and the great men may and probably will be continued in office during their lives.

18. Annual elections are abolished, and the people are not to re-assume their rights until the expiration of two, four and six years.

19. Congress are to have the power of fixing the time, place and manner of holding elections, so as to keep them forever subjected to their influence.

20. The importation of slaves is not to be prohibited until the year 1808, and *slavery* will probably resume its empire in Pennsylvania.

21. The militia is to be under the immediate command of Congress, and men conscientiously scrupulous of bearing arms may be compelled to perform military duty.

22. The new government will be *expensive* beyond any we have ever experienced; the judicial department alone, with its concomitant train of judges, justices, chancellors, clerks, sheriffs, coroners, escheators, State attorneys and solicitors, constables, etc., in every State and in every county in each State, will be a burden beyond the utmost abilities of the people to bear, and upon the whole,

23. A government partaking of *monarchy* and aristocracy will be fully and firmly established, and liberty will be but a name to adorn the short historic page of the halcyon days of America.

These, my countrymen, are the objections that have been made to the new proposed system of government, and if you read the system itself with attention you will find them all to be founded in truth. But what have you been told in answer?

I pass over the sophistry of Mr. W——, in his equivocal speech at the state-house. His pretended arguments have been echoed and re-echoed by every retailer of politics, and victoriously refuted by several patriotic pens. Indeed, if you read this famous speech in a cool dispassionate moment, you will find it to contain no more than a train of pitiful sophistry and evasions, unworthy of the man who spoke them. I have taken notice of some of them in stating the objections, and they must, I am sure, have excited your pity and indignation. Mr. W—— is a man of sense, learning and extensive information; unfortunately for him, he has never sought the more solid fame of patriotism. During the late war he narrowly escaped the effects of popular rage, and the people seldom arm themselves against a citizen in vain. The whole tenor of his political conduct has always been strongly tainted with the spirit of *high aristocracy;* he has never been known to join in a truly popular measure, and his talents have ever been devoted to the patrician interest. His lofty carriage indicates the lofty mind that animates him—a mind able to conceive and perform great things, but which unfortunately can see nothing great out of the pale of power and worldly grandeur; despising what he calls the inferior order of the people, popular liberty and popular assemblies offer to his exalted imagination an idea of meanness and contemptibility, which he hardly seeks to conceal. He sees at a distance the pomp and pageantry of courts, he sighs after those stately palaces and that apparatus of human greatness which his vivid fancy has taught him to consider as the supreme good. Men of sublime minds, he conceives, were born a different race from the rest of the sons of men; to them and them only, he imagines, high heaven intended to commit the reins of earthly government; the remaining part of mankind he sees at an immense distance; they, he thinks, were born to serve, to administer food to the ambition of their superiors and become the footstool of their power. Such is Mr. W——, and fraught with these high ideas, it is no wonder that he should exert all his talents to support a form of government so admirably contrived to carry them into execution. But when the people, who possess collectively a mass of knowledge superior to his own, inquire into the principles of that government on the establishment or rejection of which depend their dearest concerns, when he is called upon by the voice of thousands to come and explain that favorite system which he holds forth as an object of their admiration, he comes—he attempts to support by reasoning what reason never dictated, and finding the attempt vain, his great mind, made for nobler purposes, is obliged to stoop to mean evasions and pitiful sophistry; himself not deceived, he strives to deceive the people, and the treasonable attempt delineates his true character, beyond the reach of the pencil of a West or Peale, or the pen of a Valerius.

And yet that speech, weak and insidious as it is, is the only attempt that has been made to support by argument that political monster, the proposed constitution. I have sought in vain amidst the immense heap of trash that has been published on the subject, an argument worthy of refutation, and I have not been able to find it. If you can bear the disgust which the reading of those pieces must naturally occasion, and which I have felt in the highest degree, read them, my fellow citizens, and say whether they contain the least shadow of logical reasoning, say (laying your hands upon your hearts) whether there is anything in them that can impress unfeigned conviction upon your unprejudiced minds.

One of them only I shall take notice of, in which I find that argument is weakly attempted. This piece is signed "An American Citizen," and has appeared with great pomp in four succeeding numbers in several of our newspapers. But if you read it attentively, you will find that it does not tell us what the new constitution is, but what it is not, and extols it on the sole ground that it does not contain all the principles of tyranny with which the European governments are disgraced.

But where argument entirely failed, nothing remained for the supporters of the new constitution but to endeavor to inflame your passions. The attempt has been made, and I am sorry to find not entirely without effect. The great names of *Washington* and *Franklin* have been taken in vain and shockingly prostituted to effect the most infamous purposes. What! because our august chieftain has subscribed his name in his capacity of president of the convention to the plan offered by them to the States, and because the venerable sage of Pennsylvania has testified by his signature that the majority of the delegates of this State assented to the same plan, will any one infer from this that it has met with their entire approbation, and that they consider it as the master-piece of human wisdom? I am apt to think the contrary, and I have good reason to ground my opinion on.

In the first place we have found by the publication of *Charles Cotesworth Pinckney*, esquire, one of the *signing* members of the convention, who has expressed the most pointed disapprobation of many important parts of the new plan of government, that all the members whose names appear at the bottom of this instrument of tyranny have not concurred in its adoption. Many of them might conceive themselves bound by the opinion of the majority of their State, and leaving the people to their own judgment upon the form of government offered to them, might have conceived it impolitic by refusing to sign their names, to offer to the world the lamentable spectacle of the disunion of a body on the decisions of whom the people had rested all their hopes. We know, and the long sitting of the convention tells us, that (as it is endeavored to persuade us) concord and unanimity did not reign exclusively among them. The thick veil of secrecy with which their proceedings have been covered, has left us entirely in the dark, as to the debates that took place, and the unaccountable *suppression of their journals*, the highest insult that could be offered to the majesty of the people, shows clearly that the whole of the new plan was entirely the work of an aristocratic majority.

But let us suppose for a moment that the proposed government was the unanimous result of the deliberations of the convention—must it on that account preclude an investigation of its merits? Are the people to be dictated to without appeal by any set of men, however great, however dignified? Freedom spurns at the idea and rejects it with disdain. We appeal to the collective wisdom of a great nation, we appeal

to their general sense, which is easily to be obtained through
the channel of a multitude of free presses, from the opinions
of thirty-nine men, who secluded from the rest of the world,
without the possibility of conferring with the rest of their
fellow-citizens, have had no opportunity of rectifying the
errors into which they may have been led by the most designing among them.   We have seen names not less illustrious
than those of the members of the late convention, subscribed
to the present reprobated articles of confederation, and if
those patriots have erred, there is no reason to suppose that
a succeeding set should be more free from error.   Nay, the
very men who advocate so strongly the new plan of government, and support it with the infallibility of Doctor Franklin,
affect to despise the present constitution of Pennsylvania,
which was dictated and avowed by that venerable patriot.
They are conscious that he does not entirely approve of the
new plan, whose principles are so different from those he
has established in our ever-glorious constitution, and there
is no doubt that it is the reason that has induced them to
leave his respected name out of the ticket for the approaching
election.

Now then my fellow-citizens, my brethren, my friends; if
the sacred flame of liberty be not extinguished in your breasts,
if you have any regard for the happiness of yourselves, and
your posterity, let me entreat you, earnestly entreat you by
all that is dear and sacred to freemen, to consider well before
you take an awful step which may involve in its consequences
the ruin of millions yet unborn.   You are on the brink of a
dreadful precipice—in the name therefore of holy liberty, for
which I have fought and for which we have all suffered, I call
upon you to make a solemn pause before you proceed.   One
step more, and perhaps the scene of freedom is closed forever
in America.   Let not a set of aspiring despots, who make us
slaves, and tell us 'tis our charter, wrest from you those invaluable blessings, for which the most illustrious sons of
America have bled and died—but exert yourselves, like men,
like freemen, and like Americans, to transmit unimpaired to
your latest posterity those rights, those liberties, which have

ever been dear to you, and which it is yet in your power to preserve.

AN OFFICER OF THE LATE CONTINENTAL ARMY.*

Philadelphia, November 3, 1787.

[Reply to "An Officer, &c."]

Friend Oswald: Seeing in thy paper of yesterday twenty-three objections to the new plan of federal government, I am induced to trouble the public once more; and shall endeavor to answer them distinctly and concisely. That this may be done with candor, as well as perspicuity, I request thee to re-print them as they are stated by "an officer of the late Continental army," and to place my answers in the same order.

I shall pass over everything that is not in point, and leave the strictures on friend W—— to those who are acquainted with him: I will only observe that "his lofty carriage," is very like to be the effect of habit; for I know by experience that a man who wears spectacles, must keep his head erect to see through them with ease, and to prevent them from falling off his nose.

Now for the objections:

"1. It is not merely (as it ought to be) a *Confederation of States*, but a *Government of Individuals.*"

Answer 1. It is more a government of the people, than the present Congress ever was, because the members of Congress have been hitherto chosen by the Legislatures of the several States. The proposed representatives are to be chosen "*by the people.*" If therefore it be not a confederation of *the States*, it is a popular compact, something more in favor of liberty. Art. 1, Sect. 2.

"2. The powers of Congress extend to the lives, the liberties and the property of every citizen."

2. Is there a government on earth, where the life, liberty and property of a citizen may not be forfeited by a violation of the laws of God and man? It is only when justified by such crimes, that the new government has such power; and

* Independent Gazetteer, Nov. 6, 1787.

all crimes (except in cases of impeachment) are expressly to be *tried by jury, in the State where they may be committed.* Art. 3, Sect. 2.

"3. The sovereignty of the different states is *ipso facto* destroyed in its most essential parts."

3. Can the sovereignty of each state in all its parts exist, if there be a sovereignty over the whole? Is it not nonsense in terms, to suppose a united government *of any kind*, over thirteen co-existent sovereignties? "It is obviously impracticable in the federal government of these states, to secure all the rights of independent sovereignty to each, and yet provide for the interest and safety of all." (President's letter.)

"4. What remains of it, will only tend to create violent dissensions between the state governments and the Congress, and terminate in the ruin of the one or the other."

4. No such dissension can happen, unless some state oppose the interests of the whole collectively; and it is to overcome such opposition by a majority of 12 to 1, "to ensure domestic tranquillity, to provide for the common defence, promote the general welfare, and secure the blessings of liberty," that the union is now, and has ever been thought indispensable. (Introduction to the new plan.)

"5. The consequence must therefore be, either that the union of the states will be destroyed by a violent struggle, or that their sovereignty will be swallowed up by silent encroachments into a universal aristocracy; because it is clear, that if two different foreign powers have a co-equal command over the purses of the citizens, they will struggle for the spoils, and the weakest will be in the end obliged to yield to the efforts of the strongest."

5. The preceding petition being eradicated, this consequence falls to the ground. It may be observed, however, that the revenue to be raised by Congress, is not likely to interfere with the taxes of any state. Commerce is the source to which they will naturally apply, because that is one great and uniform object, and they cannot attend to detail. The burden, too, will in this way be scarcely felt by the people. All foreigners who may sell merchandise at a loss (and that

often has been, and often will be the case in an extensive degree,) will pay the impost in addition to that loss, and the duties on all that may be sold at a profit, will be eventually paid by the consumers: thus the taxes will be insensibly included in the price, and every man will have the power of refusal, by not consuming the taxed luxuries.

"6. Congress being possessed of these immense powers, the liberties of the states and of the people are not secured by a bill or declaration of rights."

6. Notwithstanding all that has been written against it, I must recur to friend W———'s definition on this subject. A state government is designed *for all cases whatsoever*, consequently what is not reserved, is tacitly given. A federal government is expressly *only for federal purposes*, and its power is consequently bounded by the terms of the compact. In the first case a Bill of Rights is indispensable, in the second it would be at best useless, and if one right were to be omitted, it might injuriously grant, by implication, what was intended to be reserved.

"7. The sovereignty of the states is not expressly reserved: the form only, and not the substance of their government, is guaranteed to them by express words."

7. When man emerged from a state of nature, he surely did not reserve the natural right of being the judge of his wrongs, and the executioner of the punishments he might think they deserved. A renunciation of such rights, is the price he paid for the blessings of good government; and for the same reason, state sovereignty (as I have before observed) is as incompatible with the federal union, as the natural right of human vengeance is, with the peace of society.

"The United States shall guarantee to every state a republican form of government." That is, they shall guarantee it against monarchical or aristocratical encroachments; Congress can go no further, for the states would justly think themselves insulted, if they should presume to interfere in other alterations which may be individually thought more consistent with the good of the people. Art. 4, Sec. 4.

"8. Trial by jury, that sacred bulwark of liberty, is abolished in civil cases, and Mr. W———, one of the convention, has told you, that not being able to agree as to the form of establishing this point, they have left you deprived of the substance. Here is his own words: 'The subject was involved in difficulties. The convention found the task too difficult for them, and left the business as it stands.'"

8. Trial by jury has been seen to be expressly preserved in criminal cases. In civil cases, the federal court is like a court of chancery, except that it has original jurisdiction only in state affairs; in all other matters it has "appellate jurisdiction both as to law and fact, with such exceptions and under such regulations as Congress shall make." Art. 3, Sec. 2. Nobody ever complained that trials in chancery were not by jury. A court of chancery "may issue injunctions in various stages of a cause," saith Blackstone, "and stay oppressive judgment." Yet courts of chancery are everywhere extolled as the most equitable; the federal court has not such an extent of power, and what it has is to be always under the exceptions and regulations of the United States in Congress.

Friend W——— has well observed that it was impossible to make one imitation of thirteen different models, and the matter seems now to stand as well as human wisdom can permit.

"9. The liberty of the press is not secured, and the powers of Congress are fully adequate to its destruction, as they are to have the trial of libels, or pretended libels against the United States, and may by a cursed abominable stamp act (as the Bowdoin administration has done in Massachusetts) preclude you effectually from all means of information. Mr. W——— has given you no answer to these arguments."

9. The liberty of the press in each state can only be in danger from the laws of that state, and it is everywhere well secured. Besides, as the new Congress can only have the defined powers given, it was needless to say anything about liberty of the press, liberty of conscience, or any other liberty that a freeman ought never to be deprived of. It is remarkable in this instance, that among all the cases to which the federal jurisdiction is to extend (art. 3), not a word is said of

"libels or pretended libels." Indeed, in this extensive continent, and among this enlightened people, no government whatever *could* control the press. For after all that is said about "balance of power," there is one power which no tyranny on earth could subdue if once roused by this great and general grievance, that is, the people. This respectable power has preserved the press in Great Britain in spite of government; and none but a madman could ever think of controlling it in America.

"10. Congress have the power of keeping up a standing army in time of peace, and Mr. W—— has told you that it is *necessary.*"

10. The power here referred to is this, "to raise and support armies, *but no appropriation of money to that use shall be for a longer term than two years.*"—Art. 1, Sect. 8. Thus the representatives of the people have it in their power to disband this army every two years, by refusing supplies. Does not every American feel that no standing army in the power of Congress to raise, could support despotism over this immense continent, where almost every citizen is a soldier? If such an apprehension came, in my opinion, within the bounds of possibility, it would not indeed become my principles to oppose this objection.

"11. The Legislative and Executive powers are not kept separate, every one of the American constitutions declares they ought to be; but they are mixed in a manner entirely novel and unknown, even to the constitution of Great Britain."

11. The first article of the constitution defines the legislative, the second, the executive, and the third the judicial powers; this does not seem like mixing them. It would be strange indeed if a professed democratist should object, that the president's power is made subject to "the advice and consent of two-thirds of the Senate." Art. 2, Sect. 2.

"12. In England, the king only has a nominal negative over the proceedings of the legislature, which he has never dared to exercise since the days of King William, whereas by the new constitution, both the President-General and the Senate, two executive branches of the government, have the negative, and are intended to support each other in the exercise of it."

12. Whoever will read the 7th section of the 4th article, will see that the president has only a conditional negative, which is effectual or not as two-thirds of the Senate and two-thirds of the Representatives may on reconsideration determine. If the "two executive branches" (as they are here called) should agree in the negative, it would not be novel, as to the power of the Senate; for I believe every senate on the continent, and every upper house in the world, may refuse concurrence, and quash a bill before it arrives at the executive department. The king of England has an unconditional negative, and has often exercised it in his former colonies.

"13. The representation of the lower house is too small, consisting only of 65 members."

13. The Congress on the old plan had but 13 voices, and of these, some were frequently lost by equal divisions. If 65 voices be yet too few, it must follow that the new plan has made some progress towards perfection.

"14. That of the Senate is so small that it renders its extensive powers extremely dangerous: it is to consist only of 26 members, two-thirds of whom must concur to conclude any treaty or alliance with foreign powers. Now we will suppose that five of them are absent, sick, dead, or unable to attend, twenty-one will remain, and eight of these (one-third, and one over) may prevent the conclusion of any treaty, even the most favorable to America. Here will be a fine field for the intrigues and even the bribery and corruption of European powers."

14. This like the former objection is mere matter of opinion. The instance as to supposed vacancies does not apply, for "if vacancies happen by resignation or otherwise during the recess of the Legislature of any State, the executive thereof may make temporary appointments until the meeting of the Legislature, which shall then fill such vacancies." Art. 1, Sec. 3. This provision expressly implies that accidental vacancies shall be immediately filled.

"15. The most important branches of the executive department are to be put into the hands of a single magistrate, who
will be in fact an *elective king.* The military, the land and
naval forces are to be entirely at his disposal."

15. It was mentioned as a grievance in the 12th objection
that this supposed "elective king" had his powers clogged
by the conjunction of another branch; here he is called a
"single magistrate." Yet the new constitution provides that
he shall act "by and with the advice and consent of the Senate," Art. 2, Sec. 2, and can in no instance act alone, except
in the cause of humanity by granting reprieves or pardons.

"16. Should the Senate, by the intrigues of foreign powers,
become devoted to foreign influence, as was the case of late
in Sweden, the people will be obliged, as the Swedes have
been, to seek their refuge in the arms of the monarch or President-General."

16. The comparison of a little kingdom to a great republic, cannot be just. The revolution in Sweden was the affair
of a day, and the success of it was owing to its confined
bounds. To suppose a similar event in this extensive country, 3000 miles distant from European intrigues, is, in the
nature of things, a gross absurdity.

"17. Rotation, that noble prerogative of liberty, is entirely
excluded from the new system of government, and great men
may and probably will be continued in office during their
lives."

17. How can this be the case, when at stated periods the
government reverts to the people, and to the representatives
of the people, for a new choice in every part of it?

"18. Annual elections are abolished, and the people are
not to re-assume their rights until the expiration of two, four
and six years."

18. Annual changes in a federal government would beget
confusion; it requires years to learn a trade, and men in this
age are not legislators by inspiration. One-third of the Senate, as well as all of the Representatives, are to be elected
every two years. Art. 1, Sec. 3.

"19. Congress are to have the power of fixing the time,

place, and manner of holding elections, so as to keep them forever subjected to their influence."

19. Congress are not to have power to fix the place of choosing Senators: and the time, place, and manner of electing Representatives are to be fixed by each State itself. Congress, indeed, are to have control to prevent undue influence in elections, which we all know but too often happens through party zeal. Art. 1, Sec. 4.

"20. The importation of slaves is not to be prohibited until the year 1808, and slavery will probably resume its empire in Pennsylvania."

20. This is fully answered in my letter to Timothy, but it may not be amiss to repeat that Congress will have no power to meddle in the business until 1808. All that can be said against this offending clause is, that we may have no alteration in this respect for twenty-one years to come; but twenty-one years is fixed as a period when we may be better, and in the meantime we cannot be worse than we are now. Art. 1, Sec. 9.

"21. The militia is to be under the immediate command of Congress, and men conscientiously scrupulous of bearing arms, may be compelled to perform military duty."

21. Congress may "provide for calling forth the militia, and may provide for organizing, arming, and disciplining it." But the states respectively can only raise it, and they expressly reserve the right of "appointment of officers and of training it." Now we know that men conscientiously scrupulous by sect or profession are not forced to bear arms in any of the States, a pecuniary compensation being accepted in lieu of it. Whatever may be my sentiments on the present state of this matter is foreign to the point. But it is certain that whatever redress may be wished for, or expected, can only come from the State Legislature, where, and where only, the dispensing power, or enforcing power, is in the first instance placed. Art. I, Sec. 8.

"22. The new government will be *expensive* beyond any we have ever experienced; the judicial department alone, with its concomitant train of judges, justices, chancellors, clerks, sheriffs, coroners, escheators, state attorneys and solicitors, constables, etc., in every state, and in every county in each state, will be a burden beyond the utmost abilities of the people to bear.''

22. This mighty expense would be paid by about one shilling a man throughout the states. The other part of this objection is not intelligible; nothing is said in the new constitution of a judicial department in "states and counties," other than what is already established.

"23. A government partaking of *monarchy* and aristocracy will be fully and firmly established, and liberty will be but a name to adorn the short historic page of the halcyon days of America.''

23. The 5th article expressly provides against every danger, by pointing out a mode of amendment when necessary. And liberty will thus be a name to adorn the long historic page of American virtue and happiness.

Thus I have answered all the objections, and supported my answers by fair quotations from the new constitution; and I particularly desire my readers to examine all the references with accurate attention. If I have mistaken any part, it will, I trust, be found to be an error of judgment, not of will, and I shall thankfully receive any candid instruction on the subject. One quotation more and I have done: "In all our deliberations on this subject (saith *George Washington*) we kept steadily in our view, that which appears to us the greatest interest of every true American, the consolidation of our union, in which is involved our prosperity, felicity, safety, perhaps our national existence. This important consideration, seriously and deeply impressed on our minds, led each State in the convention to be less rigid on points of inferior magnitude, than might have been otherwise expected; and thus the constitution which we now present is the result of a spirit of amity, and of that mutual deference and concession which the peculiarity of our political situation rendered indispensable.'' PLAIN TRUTH.*

* Independent Gazetteer, Nov. 10, 1787.

[One of the Dissenting Assemblymen.]

From *The Pennsylvania Packet* and *Daily Advertiser*, Nov. 14, 1787.

Messrs. Printers: As the Constitution framed by the late Continental Convention is an object of the greatest magnitude, and upon the adoption or rejection of which the happiness or misery of this country greatly depends, I am happy to find it has become a subject of general discussion, and that many able pens are employed in the investigation of its nature and principles; everything, therefore, that hath any relation to this business must be interesting and of importance to the public. The secession of the minority of the late house of assembly having connection with this matter, and being severely reprobated by many who are, perhaps, ignorant of the principles which influenced their conduct, I have taken the liberty, as one of that minority, of stating to the public, through the medium of your paper, the motives which induced us to take such a measure.

In the formation of every good government, every innovation should be carefully guarded against, as it is much easier to prevent than to remedy evils; therefore, in every free government, the power of putting a negative upon particular laws is lodged in such a man or body of men, as have not the power of enacting laws. Thus, in Britain, a complete negative is vested not only in each house of parliament, but also in the king, whereas the concurrence of king, lords, and commons are necessary to enact a law. The despotism of the French monarchy is much restrained by the powers lodged with the parliament of Paris, of preventing the operation of any new laws, by refusing to register them. When the Roman Republic was in the zenith of its glory, the negative of a single tribune was sufficient to prevent the enacting of a law, but the concurrence of twelve tribunes was necessary to make any new law or innovation. In the Republic of Genoa, four-fifths of the Senate must assent to any new law, consequently if even forty should concur in the measure, it might be prevented by eleven.

But to come nearer home. In our neighboring States, the

majority of the Senate or upper house have a complete negative over the whole Legislature, which amounts in most cases
to one exercising a complete negative over eight, ten, or
twelve.

The framers of the Constitution of Pennsylvania, sensible
of the necessity of preventing innovations, have also provided sufficient checks; and though our legislature consists
of but one branch, and it is not in the power of a single
magistrate, or a majority of a small upper house, to put a
negative on our laws, or prevent what they might think improper innovations; yet, even in this government which derives its greatest security from responsibility and necessary
rotation, no bills can be enacted into laws, except in cases of
sudden necessity, without being published for consideration
from session to session, and thus laying them before the people, together with the yeas and nays, and reasons for the vote,
if any two members require it; but as the house are necessarily judges of the sudden necessity which may exist for enacting laws hastily, the constitution has carefully guarded
against any attempt of designing men, who may, from the
prevailing influence of some improper or dangerous interest,
prostitute the cry of public necessity to cloak their ambition,
and thus attempt such innovations as the minority may think
unconstitutional and highly mischievous, to prevent which
our form of government provides, that a quorum of not less
than two-thirds of the whole number elected shall be necessarily present, in order to do business.   Thus, a negative
check is clearly erected, and the exercise thereof vested in
such a minority as shall exist of a little more than one-third
of the whole number elected.   This is clearly a constitutional
check; the legislature have not the power of preventing it,
and the members who shall exercise it are responsible to their
constituents only for their conduct.

This negative has been often put in practice; there is an
instance of its having been done twice in one day; but as,
perhaps, the house was not of the greatest importance, or
what is more probable, that the majority were not aided by a
mob, these instances made very little noise, nor was the ex-

ercise of this negative ever attempted to be prevented, until the —— day of ——, 1784; when near the close of the last session of the house, a bill was brought forward for reviving the test laws. This the minority considered as a matter in which their constituents ought to be consulted, and for the enacting of which there was no sudden necessity; they, therefore, considered the enacting thereof in such a manner as a wilful breach of the constitution, and judged it to be their duty to avail themselves of every means which the constitution itself put in their power to preserve it inviolable, and consequently put a stop to the business, until it comes before their constituents; but on this occasion the doors were attempted to be shut, and force was used to detain the members, therefore they did not return to finish the business of the house, apprehending that if they acted under compulsion or the power of a mob, whatever was done would not be binding on the citizens, because freedom of acting is indispensable to the exercise of legislative authority. The case, of course, came before the people, and they decided, by approving of and returning the members who dissented, and by rejecting the majority of those who urged on the business.

The next occasion when this negative was exercised was on the 28th day of September last, being expected (at least by many of the members) to be the last day of the house sitting, when a resolution was proposed by one of the members (who had also been a member of the late Federal Convention) for calling a state convention, to be elected in the greatest part of the State within about ten days, for the purpose of examining and adopting the proposed new constitution for the government of the United States. To offer a resolution of such importance at that late hour, to take it up instantly without giving the members who did not expect such an attempt, and were consequently wholly unprepared, time even until the afternoon for advisement, was truly extraordinary. But, when it is considered that the adopting of the proposed plan may, in its consequences, alter, or even annihilate the constitution of our own State under which we act, and which is the rule and measure of our legislative authority, and to preserve which inviolate we had, in the presence of God, and of each other, solemnly plighted our faith; every unprejudiced person will allow we ought to have taken time to deliberate. Even the Council of Censors, who have the constitutional right to propose alterations or amendments to the constitution, yet are strictly prohibited from calling a convention to adopt such alterations or amendments, until they are published at least six months for the consideration of the people. But in the present instance, the assembly were called upon by surprise to propose essential alterations in the forms of government, without having received any new powers for that purpose from the people, but being expressly guarded from doing it, both by the powers delegated to them and by their own solemn oaths, and without permitting the people to know or judge of the importance of those alterations in their government, which they were thus called upon to adopt or reject, or the relative fitness of the persons whom they were about to elect for the proposed convention, or without the shadow of necessity for going into the measure with precipitation, as no injury could arise from deferring the business until the meeting of the new house, who would at least enjoy implied powers for that purpose, and might have sufficient information from the people to enable them to go into the business with a degree of understanding suited to its importance. But taking the matter up at that time and manner was an express violation of the existing confederation, for it is now well known that Congress did not transmit the new constitution to this State until the week after the last house finally rose, and that it was not officially before the legislature until after the present house met. In this situation we, who were of the minority, saw no alternative but either by our presence to assist in breaking the constitution of this State and the confederation of the United States, or else to avail ourselves of that negative check which the constitution itself hath instituted, by constituting a large quorum, and secured the exercise of by preventing the doors from being shut.

If the constitution had not pointed out such an alternative, or if the minority had not thought proper to make use of it, necessity dictated the measure; for before the business was brought forward, and before many of us knew any such matter was designed, the gallery and doors were so unusually crowded as to give ground of surprise, though we had no suspicion of the design until the extraordinary resolution was offered, and the still more extraordinary language that was used to support it, viz.:

"'That the citizens who had declined to sign an approbation of the new plan would shortly be dragged forth with public infamy and disgrace; that none would dare to oppose it; that the confederation was dissolved and rotten, and did not exist,'' etc.   I was by that time fully convinced that we were surrounded with a mob, probably collected there for the occasion by those who, being members of the house, had the address to procure seats in the Federal Convention; and these having exceeded the powers delegated to them were intoxicated with such fondness for the creature of their own production, or perhaps for the enjoyment of those offices which they had so liberally provided in the proposed plan, as not only to break through the rules of decency and good order, but every obligation they were under to their constituents.

Under the full persuasion that we were acting under such restraint as was inconsistent with the free exercise of legislative authority, and entirely subversive of the powers with which we were entrusted, when the first paragraph of the plan was pretty largely debated and adopted, and the remaining paragraphs were before us, the house adjourned until the afternoon, which was the only instance of that session in which we were to sit twice in one day.   I then determined in my own mind not to return to the house until I could do it with confidence of enjoying personal freedom, steadfastly believing that no law enacted under the evident restraint of a mob could be binding or admitted in a court of justice; but such of us who had opportunity proposed to the speaker of the house, and to the members who moved that hasty business, for to return to the house and finish the business that was regularly brought before the house, upon those gentlemen engaging that the new plan should not be further urged until it would come officially and orderly before them, but this was refused; and it is now notorious, that upon the next day after the resolution was introduced, the mob, after rendezvousing at the State House, marched to and entered by force the lodging of some of the members, and carried off two of them (which was all that fell into their hands), unto the assembly room—then become the guard house of the mob—and after putting them into it kept them there, and when under this restraint they assumed the form of a legislative assembly, and counting upon the imprisoned members as a necessary part of their number, proceeded to complete the resolutions, but with some alteration, for they did not then dare to give so short a day for the election as on the preceding day, and they added an idea to delude the people, as if the proposed plan of government had been transmitted to the house from Congress; but this I have already noticed, and it is now universally known to be true, whilst proceeding on this business the two members who were forced there by the mob were not only under restraint, but one of them prevented from his freedom of going even to the door by one who was both a member of the late Federal Convention and of the assembly, laying forcible hands upon him, and by the mob-cry "stop, stop," &c., and during those transactions so far was the discipline of the house from being exerted, that there was not even a call to order by the Speaker.

Thus it appears that the dissenting members only availed themselves of this constitutional negative in a case where the Constitution itself and the confederation were both at stake, as well as the people's right to information in a case wherein they are to judge for themselves and posterity. The magnitude of the case invited, and forcible necessity drove them to appeal to their constituents, who have already given an uncontrovertible decision in favor of our conduct by re-electing all those members who dissented that had not already served four years in the house, except one man who was left out through a mistaken division of votes, occasioned by a recent erection of a county. Thus the people have given the strongest testimony of their approbation which the case admits of.

It is the glory of the American revolution that the respective governments underwent a free and rational discussion, were the fruit of deliberation and choice, and were not dictated by a chieftain, nor hatched in a secret conclave, where the depraved and intriguing generally overreach and circumvent the disinterested and virtuous: they were also generally left open to a regular course of alteration or amendment, according as experience and circumstances dictate the propriety. But who would then have believed that at this early period, within the remembrance, and even when the feelings of the revolution were yet fresh on every sensible patriotic mind, that an attempt should be made in a legislative body to preclude the people who accomplished the revolution, and whose wounds have yet scarcely ceased to bleed, from the means of understanding and judging of the amendments or alterations by which they are to be bound. Future generations will justly censure those who precipitated this business, when the dark designs and ambitious intrigues which have fomented the embarrassments of the Union, and paved the way for the aristocratic attempts of the present day, shall be fully unfolded.

The worst that even an improper exertion of this negative by a minority can do is to postpone the business in question, be it what it will, and so to give further time for advisement.

But what will be the opinion of freemen of the precedent set by the majority of the late house, if a mob may be employed or countenanced in compelling members to attend and act who are necessarily responsible only to the rules of their own house and their constituents. May not the mob by the same rule, if they dislike a business which is likely to be enacted into a law, take out what number of members they please so as to turn the majority to their wishes? or may they not by all the terrors of riot oblige the members to vote as they think fit? But the consequences are too plain and too dreadful to be dwelt upon.

In some other free countries, mobs have had the audacity to interrupt the legislature, and prevent for a time the progress of some business obnoxious to the populace; but it remained for the legislature of Pennsylvania to suffer, and for the mob of Philadelphia to commit, that kind of outrage which puts an end to constitutional government, and the peace and confidence of society at once: for who can think a deliberative body free in their decisions, which sits in reach of the operations and terrors of such a set of desperadoes?

One of the evils prevalent in the controversies of the present times is, that the supposed merit or demerit of names are urged instead of reason, and detraction instead of argument. For this cause I shall not at present give my real name, but subscribe myself what I really have been,

ONE OF THE DISSENTING ASSEMBLYMEN.

CHAPTER IV.

The election of delegates to represent Philadelphia in the State Convention to consider the constitution took place at the State House on Tuesday, November 6th. All went quietly during the day. But at midnight a crowd gathered, and a riot occurred before the now famous house of Mr. Alexander Boyd on Sixth street. The occasion of the riot was the presence in the house of the Anti-Federal Junto against whom the voters had been muttering threats all day. What happened was stated to the Assembly a few days later by one of the members insulted.

GENERAL ASSEMBLY.

Saturday, November 10th.

The house met pursuant to adjournment.

The order of the day for electing a state treasurer was called up, but Mr. M'Lean expressing a desire to state a subject of some importance, that order was postponed to give him an opportunity to address the house, which he did in the following manner:

Mr. M'Lean. It is with the greatest diffidence I rise to represent some facts, which in my opinion, respect more the dignity, and honor of this house, than the personal safety and resentments of those who are individually interested. As a member of the legislature, it is my duty to guard and protect its privileges in whatever form they may be attacked; and even Mr. Speaker, when so humble a member as he that now addresses you, has been made the means of offering an insult to the house, the offence, which is but trivial when we consider the man, becomes of great importance when we consider his office. For these reasons therefore, I think myself bound to lay before the house, the circumstances of complaint

(204)

to which I have alluded; but to their wisdom I shall implicitly submit the measures which are proper to be pursued upon the occasion. About midnight on Tuesday last, a great concourse of people assembled opposite to the house of Mr. Alexander Boyd, in which myself, several other members of this house, and several members of the supreme executive council lodged, and at that time had retired to our respective chambers. The persons thus assembled made a considerable noise in the streets, and at length assailed Mr. Boyd's house, beating loudly at the door, and breaking the windows, thro' which they threw some very large stones, etc., exclaiming repeatedly, "here the damned rascals live who did all the mischief," and using other words highly reproachful to the members of this house and of the executive council. What were the motives of the rioters for this conduct, I do not know, nor am I solicitous to enquire; but having stated these facts, I am confident every gentleman here is ready to express his disapprobation of the proceedings, so grossly in violation of the law of the land, and the established privilege of this house.

Mr. Findley. Though I am aware, Mr. Speaker, that the fullest credit will be given to the information of the member who has just spoken, and that upon this subject no other evidence is necessary to support his allegation, yet I have been solicitous to put the authenticity of the facts which have been stated beyond all doubt, and therefore beg leave to present two affidavits, one made by Mr. Boyd, whose house has been attacked, and the other by Mr. Baird, a member of the supreme executive council.

The clerk then read the affidavits, which were as follows:

" *Philadelphia, ss.* "

On this ninth day of November, in the year of our Lord one thousand seven hundred and eighty-seven, before me Plunket Fleeson, Esquire, being one of the justices of peace, in the city and county of Philadelphia, residing in the said city; cometh Alexander Boyd, of Sixth street, from Delaware river in the said city, Esquire, who being solemnly sworn with uplifted hand, doth depose, testify and say that on the night of Tuesday last, being the sixth of this present month of November, this dependent, together with the honorable John Smilie, John Baird and Abraham Smith, members of the supreme executive council; and James M'Calmont, James M'Lean, John Piper and William Findley, Esquires, representatives in the general Assembly of the State of Pennsylvania, who lodge with this deponent, were gone to bed in his dwelling in Sixth street aforesaid: that this deponent was fallen asleep, when about 12 o'clock at midnight, a great noise in the adjoining street, awaked this deponent, who thereupon immediately jumped out of his bed, and raising the sash of a window towards the street of the the the third floor of the house, he saw a considerable number of men in the street, of whom twelve or fifteen were nigh to the door of this deponent's dwelling, and that divers of the persons, so as aforesaid assembled, did then and there speak reproachfully of the gentlemen who were lodged with this deponent, and did say that here is the house where the damned rascals lodge who do all the devilment, or words to the like effect; adding that they ought to be all hanged. That hearing the window rise and seeing this deponent at the window, as this deponent believes, this deponent hear one of the same persons say. 'There is one of the damned rascals putting his head out of the window.' That a man who lives nigh to this deponent, at this moment coming out of this dwelling, and approaching the mob aforesaid, the persons who composed the same ran northerly towards Mulberry street, and this deponent saw them no more. That this deponent was awaked as aforesaid, by the noise aforesaid, and by the throwing of large stones against the front door of his dwelling, some of which stones drove in the sash over the same door and fell in his entry, and one of them was at least ten pounds in weight. And that this deponent was not able to distinguish any of the aforesaid rioters, so as to know their names, or who they or any of them were. And further this deponent saith not.''

"*Philadelphia, ss.*

"On this ninth day of November, Anno Domini one thousand seven hundred and eighty-seven, before me, Plunket

Fleeson, Esq., being one of the justices of the peace in and for the city and county of Philadelphia, and residing in the same city, cometh the Honorable John Baird, who is one of the members of the supreme executive council of this commonwealth, and the said John, being duly sworn on the holy gospel, doth depose, testify and say, that he, this deponent, doth lodge with Alexander Boyd, and that being in bed at the dwelling of the said Alexander, in Sixth street from Delaware river, in the city of Philadelphia, on Tuesday night last, the 6th instant, and being fallen asleep, he was disturbed and awaked by a confused noise, at first seeming to him to be the report of guns fired, made by riotous persons in the street, at and near the same dwelling, and heard the glass of the lower story of the house breaking, by the throwing of stones against the same; that this deponent, still lying in his bed and not rising, heard some persons in the street say, 'Here the damned rascals live who do all the mischief,' or words to like effect; that the disturbance aforesaid did not continue after this deponent awaked, as aforesaid, above a minute, after which this deponent heard the rioters aforesaid departing hastily, as the sound of their feet indicated, towards Mulberry street; and that the Honorable John Smilie and Abraham Smith, together with James M'Calmont, James M'Lean, John Piper and William Findley, Esquires, representatives in the general assembly of this state, do also lodge with the said Alexander Boyd, and were all in bed, as this deponent hath good reason to believe, in the dwelling of the said Alexander aforesaid, at the time of the outrage and riot so as aforesaid committed, and further saith not.''

Mr. Kennedy. Sir, the outrage that has been committed against the public peace, and against the privilege of this house, being thus authenticated, I beg leave to offer a resolution upon the subject, in which I expect the unanimous concurrence of the members.

[The resolution was prefaced with a recital of the injury stated in the depositions and complained of by the members, and concluded with authorizing the executive council to offer a reward for the discovery of the offenders, and requiring them to direct the attorney general to prosecute the offenders when discovered.]

Mr. Peters. I am very ready Mr. Speaker, to declare that the transaction represented to the house is of an unwarrantable and scandalous nature, for the punishment of which I shall cheerfully unite with the movers of this resolution. But I profess, sir, to be at a loss in what manner we ought to proceed in order to maintain the dignity of the legislature, and to give efficacy to our decisions upon this subject, which is certainly of great importance, not only as it respects the present object, but as it is to establish a precedent for the future. I wish therefore to have a short time for reflection, and move that the resolution before us be referred to a committee—not, Mr. Speaker, to create unnecessary delay, but as I said before, to enable us to proceed with propriety and effect.

Mr. M'Lean. I do not perceive the least reason for referring this business to a committee: It is a plain, easy, and consistent proposition that lies before us, and the honor of the house requires that an explicit and immediate determination shall take place. The very reference to a committee will propagate an opinion that we are indifferent and in doubt as to the offence which has been committed, and it is probable that the executive council will have proceeded upon the complaint of their members, while we are indulging this useless spirit of procrastination. I cannot suppose that it is the wish of any member to defeat the question in this manner; and as it seems to be agreed that the disapprobation of the house ought to be expressed, there can be no reason given for not expressing it at this time, since every objection either to the form or substance of the proposed resolution may be obviated by immediate alteration or amendment. It was with reluctance that I consented to delay calling the attention of the house to this business so long, but as any further delay will I am confident be injurious to the legislative character, I shall oppose the motion for a commitment.

Mr. Lewis. It is difficult upon questions of importance suddenly to form an opinion which will be satisfactory to the mind; and therefore, though I shall never consent to sacrifice a moment to mere delay, I shall always be desirous to obtain the time that is necessary for deliberation. The subject before us is certainly of great moment, and therefore deserves consideration; but it is likewise of a complex nature, and therefore demands it. In the account which has been given to the house, we discover an offence that may either be considered as a riot and breach of the public peace, in which case the common course of the law is competent to punish the offenders, or it may be regarded as an infringement of the privilege of this house, in which case it becomes our duty to investigate the circumstances, for it is in our power alone to punish the delinquency. Connected with this distinction are many enquiries which it is impossible to ascertain by an instantaneous recourse to the memory; and therefore I shall vote for the commitment, which is intended, I am confident, to provide the proper means of redressing the injury, and not to divert our attention from the complaint which has been made to the house.

Mr. Fitzsimons. I have taken a cursory view of the depositions, and in my opinion, Mr. Speaker, they do not support the resolution which has been offered to the house. I should certainly therefore vote for the commitment upon that ground alone; but I conceive likewise, that in point of justice the legislature will not pass a vote which tends highly to reflect upon the city and its police, without a perfect investigation of the grounds on which they proceed. If the committee shall find the charge sufficiently supported, I shall concur in any proper measure for punishing the offenders; but to vindicate the conduct of the house, it is certainly necessary to enquire into the subject before we decide upon it.

Mr. Findley. Sir, I may be thought personally interested in the question, and therefore I shall not animadvert upon the means which the house ought to pursue, in order to declare their disapprobation of the transaction complained of; but I beg leave to observe, that I hope no other proofs will be called for in this case, than could be called for in any other case of a similar nature. According to parliamentary usage, the complaint of a member, Mr. Speaker, need only be supported by his own assertion, and the affidavits which have been produced on this occasion were superfluous and unnecessary. I claim no personal compliment or distinction, but possessing the honor of a seat in this house, I hope it will not be deemed arrogant or improper to claim the privileges and credit that belong to it.

Here the Speaker declared that Mr. Findley was certainly right in his ideas upon the subject, and Mr. Fitzsimons observed, that not being present when the business was introduced, he did not know that it came in the form of a complaint from any member of the house.

After some further debate, the question for commitment was carried by a small majority.

In due time the committee reported, the house accepted the report, and the President issued the following proclamation:

Pennsylvania, ss.

By the President and the Supreme Executive Council of the Commonwealth of Pennsylvania.

A Proclamation.

WHEREAS, It appears to us that about midnight between Tuesday the sixth and Wednesday the seventh instant, a most daring riot was committed by a large company of disorderly and evil-minded persons unknown, at and on the dwelling of Major Alexander Boyd, in Sixth street, in the city of Philadelphia, which company violently assaulted the same house by throwing stones thereat and damaging the same, to the great disturbance and annoyance of the honorable John Baird, Abraham Smith, and John Smilie, members of Council, and of James M'Lean, James M'Calmont, William Findley and John Piper, esquires, members of the General Assembly of this Commonwealth, who were there asleep within the same dwelling; and

Whereas, It is manifest that the said rioters did perpetrate the riot and outrage aforesaid, with design to affront and injure the gentlemen aforesaid, in as much as they at the same time declared that they knew that they were lodgers with the said Alexander Boyd, and did speak concerning them in the most contumelious and threatening terms; and

Whereas, The General Assembly of this state have transmitted to Council the following resolutions entered into by them on this occasion, viz. :

"Saturday, November 10th, 1787.

"The committee to whom was referred, this forenoon, the motion respecting the insult offered to some members of this House, made report which was read and on motion and by special order the same was read the second time and unanimously adopted as follows. viz:

"WHEREAS, Complaint hath been made to this House by James M'Calmont James M'Lene, John Piper and William Findley, esquires, members thereof, that on the night of Tuesday the sixth instant, the house of major Boyd, of this city, in which they resided, was riotously attacked by a number of persons, to the said members unknown, and themselves abused and insulted by reproachful language.

"*Resolved*, That such outrageous proceedings is highly disapproved of by this House, and is a breach of the privilege of its members.

"*Resolved*, That this resolution, together with the affidavits which the said members have thought proper to produce on the subject, be transmitted to the Supreme Executive Council, and that Council be requested to issue a proclamation, offering such rewards as they may deem necessary for apprehending the perpetrators of the said outrage, in order that they may be brought to punishment, and that this House will provide for the payment of such rewards;" and

Whereas, It is highly proper that the authors of such high contempts, so inconsistent with the dignity and good order of government, and of the most pernicious example, should be immediately discovered and brought to condign punishment; WE DO, therefore, by this our proclamation, offer and promise the reward of THREE HUNDRED DOLLARS for the discovery of the rioters aforesaid, so that they be duly convicted of the same offence, to be paid out of the public treasury of this commonwealth, to the person or persons who shall furnish the necessary information concerning the premises. And we do hereby charge and require all judges, justices, sheriffs and constables to make diligent search and enquiry after and to use their utmost endeavors to apprehend and secure the said rioters, their aiders, abettors and comforters, so that they may be dealt with according to law.

Given in Council, under the hand of the President, and the seal of the State, at Philadelphia, this twelfth day of November, in the year of our Lord one thousand, seven hundred and eighty-seven.

BENJAMIN FRANKLIN.

Attest: CHARLES BIDDLE, Sec'ry.

God save the Commonwealth.

The proclamation was matter of form; neither the Judges, nor the Justices, the Sheriffs nor the Constables exerted themselves to find the rioters, and the delegates chosen throughout the State assembled at the State House on the 21st of November.

STATE CONVENTION.

Wednesday, November 21 ?

Sixty* of the gentlemen elected to serve in the convention met; the returns of the elections held for the city of Philadelphia and the several counties of this State were read, by

* From the Pennsylvania Packet, Nov. 27.

which it appeared that the following gentlemen were returned as delegates to the convention* for the said city and counties respectively, viz:

Philadelphia City.	*Chester.*
George Latimer	Thomas Bull
Benjamin Rush	Anthony Wayne
Hilary Baker	William Gibbons
James Wilson	Richard Downing
Thomas M'Kean.	Thomas Cheyney
Philadelphia County.	John Hannum.
William Macpherson	*Lancaster.*
John Hunn	Stephen Chambers
George Gray	Robert Coleman
Samuel Ashmead	Sebastian Graff
Enoch Edwards.	John Hubley
Bucks.	Jasper Yeates
Henry Wynkoop	John Whitehill.
John Barclay	*York.*
Thomas Yardley	Henry Slagle
Abraham Stout	Thomas Campbell

*The minutes of the convention give but a meagre account of its proceedings, nor is there any complete report of the debates, that took place, known to exist. At first the Philadelphia papers furnished short accounts of the proceedings, but before long they reprinted from the Pennsylvania Herald what appears to have been a tolerably full report. Unfortunately this report was suspended after bringing the debates down to November 30th, and if the statement of "Centinel," is accepted it was suppressed through the efforts of the Federalists. There is but little doubt that it was prepared by Alexander James Dallas, then a young man engaged by William Spotswood, proprietor of the Pennsylvania Herald and Columbian Magazine, to edit those publications.

Thomas Lloyd, a short-hand writer of some note, proposed to take down the debates and print them as soon as the convention should adjourn. But one volume of his work however appeared, and that contains little else than the speeches of Wilson and a few of those of M'Kean. The language of some of these differs from the reports made by Dallas, and has evidently been subjected to revision. Nevertheless this volume was used by Elliot, and contains all he publishes as the Debates in the Pennsylvania Convention. To give as full an account as is now possible of what was said in the Convention, the Reports of Dallas, and what else appeared in the papers of the day, have been carefully arranged, and the omissions from Lloyd's volume in part supplied, indicating in each case the authority drawn from.

Thomas Hartley
David Grier
John Black
Benjamin Pedan.

Cumberland.

John Harris
John Reynolds
Robert Whitehill
Jonathan Hoge.

Berks.

Nicholas Lutz
John Ludwig
Abraham Lincoln
John Bishop
Joseph Hiester.

Northampton.

John Arndt
Stephen Balliet
Joseph Horsfield
David Deshler.

Bedford.

James Martin
Joseph Powell.

Northumberland.

William Wilson
John Boyd.

Westmoreland.

William Findley
John Baird
William Todd.

Washington.

James Marshel
James Edgar
Thomas Scott
John Neville.

Fayette.

Nathaniel Breading
John Smilie.

Franklin.

Richard Bard
John Allison.

Montgomery.

Jonathan Roberts
John Richards
Fred. A. Muhlenberg
James Morris.

Dauphin.

William Brown
Adam Orth
John Andre Hannah.

Luzerne.

Timothy Pickering

Huntingdon.

Benjamin Elliott.

The members then proceeded by ballot* to the election of a president, when there appeared 30 votes for Mr. Muhlenberg, 29 for Mr. M'Kean, and one for Mr. Gray. General Wayne doubted whether 30 votes could be deemed the sense of the meeting, as it was not a majority of 60, the number of delegates present, which occasioned a short conversation upon the subject; but at length, the question being taken

* From the Pennsylvania Herald, Nov. 27. Same in Independent Gazetteer, Nov. 27.

whether Mr. Muhlenberg should be conducted to the chair? it was determined in the affirmative. It was then proposed to proceed to the choice of a clerk, but that business was deferred on motion of Mr. Smilie. Dr. Rush moved "that a committee be appointed to request the attendance of some minister of the gospel to-morrow morning, in order to open the business of the convention with prayer." This was considered by several gentlemen as a new and unnecessary measure, which might be inconsistent with the religious sentiments of some of the members, as it was impossible to fix upon a clergyman to suit every man's tenets, and it was neither warranted by the example of the general assembly or of the convention that framed the government of Pennsylvania. To these observations Dr. Rush replied, that he hoped there was liberality sufficient in the meeting to unite in prayers for the blessing of Heaven upon their proceedings, without considering the sect or persuasion of the minister who officiated; and with respect to precedent, he remarked that it might be taken from the conduct of the first, and every succeeding Congress, who certainly deserved our imitation. "That the convention who framed the government of Pennsylvania, did not preface their business with prayer, is probably the reason," added the Doctor, "that the state has ever since been distracted by their proceedings." Mr. Smilie objected to the absurd superstition of that opinion, and moved a postponement, which was accordingly agreed to. An invitation was read from the trustees of the university, requesting the attendance of the members at the ensuing Commencement, which was unanimously accepted, and the convention adjourned to meet to-morrow morning at 9 o'clock, in order to proceed in a body to the college-hall.

Thursday, November 22, 10 o'clock, a. m.

The Convention met* agreeably to their adjournment, and on motion of Mr. Whitehill, the members proceeded in a body to the Commencement of the University. After the

* From the Pennsylvania Herald, Nov. 24. Same in the Independent Gazetteer, Nov. 27.

exercises were concluded, the Convention returned to the State-house.

On motion of Mr. Wayne,* seconded by Mr. Whitehill, a committee was appointed to report rules and regulations for conducting the business of the convention: the committee consisted of Benjamin Rush, James Wilson, George Gray, Anthony Wayne, and Robert Whitehill.

Adjourned until half after 9 o'clock to-morrow.

Friday, November 23.

The Convention† being met, pursuant to adjournment, on motion of Mr. M'Kean, they proceeded to the choice of a Secretary, when Mr. James Campbell was duly elected. Mr. Burt was afterwards appointed Messenger, and Mr. Fry, Doorkeeper. An application from Thomas Lloyd to be made Assistant Clerk, was read, and a motion, complying with the same, was postponed.

The committee‡ appointed yesterday to bring in rules and regulations made report, and the same being read, was, by special order, taken up, read by paragraphs, and agreed to, as follows:

1st. When the President assumes the chair, the members shall take their seats.

2d. At the opening of the convention each day, the minutes of the preceding day shall be read, and are then in the power of the convention to be corrected, after which any business addressed to the chair may be proceeded to.

3d. Every petition, memorial, letter, or other matter of the like kind, read in the convention, shall be deemed as lying on the table for further consideration, unless any special order be moved therein.

4th. A motion made and seconded shall be repeated by the President. A motion shall be reduced to writing, if the President or any two members require it. A motion may be

* From the Pennsylvania Packet, Nov. 27, 1787.

† From the Pennsylvania Herald, Nov. 24. Same in Independent Gazetteer, Nov. 27.

‡ From the Pennsylvania Packet, Nov. 27.

withdrawn by the member making it before any decision is had on it.

5th. No member speaking shall be interrupted but by a call to order by the President, or by a member through the President.

6th. No member to be referred to in debate by name.

7th. The President himself, or by request, may call to order any member who shall transgress the rules. If a second time, the President may refer to him by name. The convention may then examine and censure the member's conduct, he being allowed to extenuate or justify.

8th. Every member actually attending the convention shall be in his place at the time the convention stands adjourned to, or within half an hour thereof.

9th. The name of him who makes, and the name of him who seconds a motion, shall be entered on the minutes.

10th. No member shall speak more than twice to a question without leave.

11th. Every member of a committee shall attend at the call of his chairman.

12th. The yeas and nays may be called, and entered on the minutes when any two members require it.

On motion* of Mr. M'Kean, seconded by Mr. Smilie, resolved that the doors of the Convention be kept open.

On motion of Mr. M'Kean, the Constitution proposed for the federal government, was taken up and read by the Clerk.

Mr. Wilson then moved that the time of meeting and adjourning should be fixed, observing that with respect to the time of adjournment, it had been found necessary in the Federal Convention to make a rule that at 4 o'clock they should break up, even if a member was in the middle of his speech, and he proposed that two o'clock should be the hour now limited for adjournment; but, after a short conversation, it was agreed that the Convention should meet at 10 o'clock each morning, leaving the hour of adjournment unspecified.

The Convention adjourned to meet to-morrow morning at 10 o'clock.

---

* From the Pennsylvania Herald, Nov. 24, 1787. Same in Independent Gazetteer, Nov. 27.

Saturday, November 24th.

The Convention met pursuant to adjournment.

The Minutes of yesterday being read, the proposed Constitution of Federal Government was taken up for a second reading, after which the following proceedings took place:

Mr. M'Kean.* Mr. President, there will perhaps be some difficulty in ascertaining the proper mode of proceeding to obtain a decision upon the important and interesting subject before us. We are certainly without precedent to guide us; but the utility of the forms observed by other public bodies, will be an inducement to adhere to them where a variation of circumstance does not render a variation of the mode essentially necessary. As far, therefore, as the rules of the Legislature of Pennsylvania will apply to the Constitution and business of this body, I shall recommend their adoption; but I perceive that in a very great degree we shall be obliged, for conveniency and propriety, to resort to new regulations,

---

*This version of Wilson's speech on M'Kean's motion is taken from a pamphlet entitled "The Substance of a Speech delivered by James Wilson, Esq. Explanatory of the General Principles of the Proposed Federal Constitution Upon Motion made by the Honorable Thomas M'Kean, in the Convention of the State of Pennsylvania. On Saturday, the 24th of November, 1787. Philadelphia. Printed by Thomas Bradford, in Front Street, four doors below the Coffee House. MDCCLXXXVII."

It appears to have been prepared by Dallas, as the language attributed to M'Kean is almost exactly the same as that given in his report in the Pennsylvania Herald. The publication of the speech excited the jealousy of Lloyd, who appended to his proposals to print the Debates the following:

Several of the editor's friends having supposed a pamphlet printed by Thomas Bradford, entitled, "The Substance of a Speech delivered by James Wilson, Esq., &c." was written by him, he conceives himself under the necessity of counteracting any impression such an opinion may have made upon the public, by assuring them he was not the writer, but pledges himself to give that address in the forementioned volume, without mutilation or misrepresentation.

December 3, 1787.

In Lloyd's Debates the speech is erroneously given under date of Nov. 26th, and is so copied by Elliot. The language differs, but the argument is the same. Notwithstanding Lloyd's card, we believe the pamphlet version to be the nearer correct. The language used in it and the style are more those of a speech, and as it was in the hands of the people long before Lloyd's volumes, and at a critical time, it is given in preference. In Dallas' Report, printed in the Herald of Nov. 28th, there is only an abstract of Wilson's speech.

arising from the singularity of the subject offered to our consideration. For the present, however, I shall move you, Sir, that we come to the following resolution:

Resolved, That this Convention do adopt and ratify the Constitution of Federal Government as agreed upon by the Federal Convention at Philadelphia on the 17th day of September, 1787.

This measure, Mr. President, is not intended to introduce an instantaneous decision of so important a question, but merely to bring the object of our meeting fully and fairly into discussion. It is not my wish that it should be determined this day, nor do I apprehend it will be necessary that it should be determined this day week; but it is merely preparatory to another motion with which I shall hereafter trouble you, and which, in my opinion, will bring on that regular and satisfactory investigation of the separate parts of the proposed Constitution, which will finally enable us to determine upon the whole.

Mr. Wilson. As the only member of this respectable body, who had the honor of a seat in the late Federal Convention, it is peculiarly my duty, Mr. President, to submit to your consideration the general principles that have produced the national Constitution, which has been framed and proposed by the assembled delegates of the United States, and which must finally stand or fall by the concurrent decision of this Convention and of others acting upon the same subject, under similar powers and authority. To frame a government for a single city or State, is a business both in its importance and facility, widely different from the task entrusted to the Federal Convention, whose prospects were extended not only to thirteen independent and sovereign States, some of which in territorial jurisdiction, population, and resource, equal the most respectable nations of Europe, but likewise to innumerable States yet unformed, and to myriads of citizens who in future ages shall inhabit the vast uncultivated regions of the continent. The duties of that body therefore, were not limited to local or partial considerations, but to the formation of a plan commensurate with a great and valuable portion of the globe.

I confess, Sir, that the magnitude of the object before us, filled our minds with awe and apprehension. In Europe, the opening and extending the navigation of a single river, has been deemed an act of imperial merit and importance; but how insignificant does it seem when we contemplate the scene that nature here exhibits, pouring forth the Potowmack, the Rapahannock, the Susquehanna, and other innumerable rivers, to dignify, adorn, and enrich our soil. But the magnitude of the object was equalled by the difficulty of accomplishing it, when we considered the uncommon dexterity and address that were necessary to combat and reconcile the jarring interests that seemed naturally to prevail, in a country which, presenting a coast of 1500 miles to the Atlantic, is composed of 13 distinct and independent States, varying essentially in their situation and dimensions, and in the number and habits of their citizens—their interests too, in some respects really different, and in many apparently so; but whether really or apparently, such is the constitution of the human mind, they make the same impression, and are prosecuted with equal vigor and perseverance. Can it then be a subject for surprise that with the sensations indispensably excited by so comprehensive and so arduous an undertaking, we should for a moment yield to despondency, and at length, influenced by the spirit of conciliation, resort to mutual concession, as the only means to obtain the great end for which we were convened? Is it a matter of surprise that where the springs of dissension were so numerous, and so powerful, some force was requisite to impel them to take, in a collected state, a direction different from that which separately they would have pursued?

There was another reason, that in this respect, increased the difficulties of the Federal Convention—the different tempers and dispositions of the people for whom they acted. But, however widely they may differ upon other topics, they cordially agree in that keen and elevated sense of freedom and independence, which has been manifested in their united and successful opposition to one of the most powerful kingdoms of the world. Still it was apprehended by some, that

their abhorrence of constraint, would be the source of objection and opposition; but I confess that my opinion, formed
upon a knowledge of the good sense, as well as the high
spirit of my constituents, made me confident that they would
esteem that government to be the best, which was best calculated eventually to establish and secure the dignity and happiness of their country. Upon this ground, I have occasionally supposed that my constituents have asked the reason of
my assent to the several propositions contained in the plan
before us. My answer, though concise, is a candid and I
think a satisfactory one—because I thought them right; and
thinking them right, it would be a poor compliment indeed
to presume they could be disagreeable to my constituents—
a presumption that might occasion a retort to which I wish
not to expose myself, as it would again be asked, "Is this
the opinion you entertain of those who have confided in your
judgment? From what ground do you infer that a vote
right in itself would be disagreeable to us?" and it might
with justice be added, "this sentiment evinces that you deserved not the trust which we reposed in you." No, Sir!
I have no right to imagine that the reflected rays of delegated power can displease by a brightness that proves the
superior splendor of the luminary from which they proceed.

.The extent of country for which the New Constitution was
required, produced another difficulty in the business of the
Federal Convention. It is the opinion of some celebrated
writers, that to a small territory the democratical, to a midling territory (as Montesquieu has termed it) the monarchical,
and to an extensive territory the despotic form of government, is best adapted. Regarding then, the wide and almost
unbounded jurisdiction of the United States, at first view the
hand of despotism seemed necessary to control, connect and
protect it ; and hence the chief embarrassment arose. For
we knew that, although our constituents would cheerfully
submit to the legislative restaints of a free government, they
would spurn at every attempt to shackle them with despotic
power.

In this dilemma, a Federal Republic naturally presented

itself to our observation, as a species of government which secured all the internal advantages of a republic, at the same time that it maintained the external dignity and force of a monarchy. The definition of this form of government may be found in Montesquieu, who says, I believe, that it consists in assembling distinct societies which are consolidated into a new body, capable of being increased by the addition of other members—an expanding quality peculiarly fitted to the circumstances of America.

But while a federal republic removed one difficulty, it introduced another, since there existed not any precedent to assist our deliberations; for, though there are many single governments, both ancient and modern, the history and principles of which are faithfully preserved and well understood, a perfect confederation of independent states is a system hitherto unknown. The Swiss cantons, which have often been mentioned in that light, cannot properly be deemed a federal republic, but merely a system of united states. The United Netherlands are also an assemblage of states; yet, as their proceedings are not the result of their combined decisions, but of the decisions of each state individually, their association is evidently wanting in that quality which is essential to constitute a federal republic. With respect to the Germanic Body, its members are of so disproportionate a size, their separate governments and jurisdictions so different in nature and extent, the general purpose and operation of their union so indefinite and uncertain, and the exterior power of the House of Austria so prevalent, that little information could be obtained or expected from that quarter. Turning, then, to ancient history, we find the Achæan and Lycian leagues and the Amphyctionic council bearing a superficial resemblance to a federal republic; but of all these, the accounts which have been transmitted to us are too vague and imperfect to supply a tolerable theory, and they are so destitute of that minute detail from which practical knowledge may be derived, that they must now be considered rather as subjects of curiosity, than of use or information.

Government, indeed, taken as a science, may yet be considered in its infancy; and with all its various modifications, it has hitherto been the result of force, fraud, or accident. For, after the lapse of six thousand years since the creation of the world, America now presents the first instance of a people assembled to weigh deliberately and calmly, and to decide leisurely and peaceably, upon the form of government by which they will bind themselves and their posterity. Among the ancients, three forms of government seem to have been correctly known—the monarchical, aristocratical, and democratical; but their knowledge did not extend beyond those simple kinds, though much pleasing ingenuity has occasionally been exercised in tracing a resemblance of mixed government in some ancient institutions, particularly between them and the British constitution. But, in my opinion, the result of these ingenious refinements does more honor to the moderns in discovering, than to the ancients in forming the similitude. In the work of Homer, it is supposed by his enthusiastic commentators, the seeds of every science are to be found; but, in truth, they are first observed in subsequent discoveries, and then the fond imagination transplants them to the book. Tacitus, who lived towards the close of that period which is called ancient, who had read the history of all antecedent and contemporary governments, who was perfectly competent to judge of their nature, tendency, and quality—Tacitus considers a mixed government as a thing rather to be wished than expected; and if ever it did occur, it was his opinion that it could not last long. One fact, however, is certain, that the ancients had no idea of representation, that essential to every system of wise, good, and efficient government. It is surprising, indeed, how very imperfectly, at this day, the doctrine of representation is understood in Europe. Even Great Britain, which boasts a superior knowledge of the subject, and is generally supposed to have carried it into practice, falls far short of its true and genuine principles. For, let us enquire, does representation pervade the constitution of that country? No. Is it either immediately or remotely the source of the executive power? No. For it is not any part of the British constitution, as practiced at this time, that the king derives his authority from the people. Formerly that authority was claimed by hereditary or divine right; and even at the revolution, when the government was essentially improved, no other principle was recognized but that of an original contract between the sovereign and the people—a contract which rather excludes than implies the doctrine of representation. Again, is the judicial system of England grounded on representation? No. For the judges are appointed by the king, and he, as we have already observed, derives not his majesty or power from the people. Lastly, then, let us review the legislative body of that nation, and even there, though we find representation operating as a check, it cannot be considered as a pervading principle. The lords, acting with hereditary right, or under an authority immediately communicated by regal prerogative, are not the representatives of the people, and yet they, as well as the sovereign, possess a negative power in the paramount business of legislation. Thus the vital principle of the British constitution is confined to a narrow corner, and the world has left to America the glory and happiness of forming a government where representation shall at once supply the basis and the cement of the superstructure. For representation, Sir, is the true chain between the people and those to whom they entrust the administration of the government; and though it may consist of many links, its strength and brightness never should be impaired. Another, and perhaps the most important obstacle to the proceedings of the Federal Convention, arose in drawing the line between the national and the individual governments of the states.

On this point a general principle readily occurred, that whatever object was confined in its nature and operation to a particular State, ought to be subject to the separate government of the States; but whatever in its nature and operation extended beyond a particular State, ought to be comprehended within the federal jurisdiction. The great difficulty, therefore, was the application of this general principle, for it was found impracticable to enumerate and distinguish the various objects to which it extended; and as the mathematics only are capable of demonstration, it ought not to be thought extraordinary that the convention could not develop a subject involved in such endless perplexity. If, however, the proposed constitution should be adopted, I trust that in the theory there will be found such harmony, and in the practice such mutual confidence between the national and individual governments, that every sentiment of jealousy and apprehension will be effectually destroyed. But, Sir, permit me to ask whether, on the ground of a union, the individual or the national government ought most to be trusted? For my part, I think it more natural to presume that the interest of each would be pursued by the whole, than the reverse of the proposition that the several States would prefer the interest of the confederated body; for in the general government each is represented, but in the separate governments, only the separate States.

These difficulties, Mr. President, which embarrassed the Federal Convention, are not represented to enhance the merit of surmounting them, but with a more important view, to show how unreasonable it is to expect that the plan of government should correspond with the wishes of all the States, of all the citizens of any one State, or of all the citizens of the united continent. I remember well, Sir, the effect of those surrounding difficulties in the late Convention. At one time the great and interesting work seemed to be at a stand, at another it proceeded with energy and rapidity, and when at last it was accomplished, many respectable members beheld it with wonder and admiration. But having pointed out the obstacles which they had to encounter, I shall now beg leave to direct your attention to the end which the Convention proposed.

Our wants, imperfections, and weakness, Mr. President, naturally incline us to society; but it is certain, society cannot exist without some restraints. In a state of nature each individual has a right, uncontrolled, to act as his pleasure or his interest may prevail, but it must be observed that this license extends to every individual, and hence the state of nature is rendered insupportable, by the interfering claims and the consequent animosities of men, who are independent of every power and influence but their passions and their will. On the other hand, in entering into the social compact, though the individual parts with a portion of his natural rights, yet it is evident that he gains more by the limitation of the liberty of others, than he loses by the limitation of his own,—so that in truth, the aggregate of liberty is more in society, than it is in a state of nature.

It is then, Sir, a fundamental principle of society, that the welfare of the whole shall be pursued and not of a part, and the measures necessary to the good of the community must consequently be binding upon the individuals that compose it. This principle is universally allowed to be just with respect to single governments, and there are instances in which it applies with equal force to independent communities; for the situation and circumstances of states may make it as necessary for them as for individuals to associate. Hence, Mr. President, the important question arises: Are such the situation and circumstances of the American States?

At this period, America has it in her power to adopt either of the following modes of government: She may dissolve the individual sovereignty of the States, and become one consolidated empire; she may be divided into thirteen separate, independent and unconnected commonwealths; she may be erected into two or more confederacies; or, lastly, she may become one comprehensive Federal Republic.

Allow me, Sir, to take a short view of each of these suppositions. Is it probable that the dissolution of the State governments, and the establishment of one consolidated empire, would be eligible in its nature, and satisfactory to the people in its administration? I think not, as I have given reasons to show that so extensive a territory could not be governed, connected and preserved but by the supremacy of despotic power. All the exertions of the most potent Emperors of Rome were not capable of keeping that Empire together, which in extent was far inferior to the dominion of America. Would an independent, an unconnected situation, without any associating head, be advantageous or satisfactory? The consequences of this system would at one time expose the States to foreign insult and depredations, and at another, to internal jealousy, contention and war. Then let us consider the plan of two or more confederacies which has often been suggested, and which certainly presents some aspects more inviting than either of the preceding modes, since the subjects of strife would not be so numerous, the strength of the confederates would be greater, and their interests more united. But even here, when we fairly weigh the advantages and the disadvantages, we shall find the last greatly preponderating; the expenses of government would be considerably multiplied, the seeds of rivalship and animosity would spring up, and spread the calamities of war and tumult through the country; for tho' the sources of rancour might be diminished, their strength and virulence would probably be increased.

Of these three species of government, however, I must observe, that they obtained no advocates in the Federal Convention, nor can I presume that they will find advocates here, or in any of our sister States. The general sentiment in that body, and, I believe, the general sentiment of the citizens of America, is expressed in the motto which some of them have chosen, UNITE OR DIE; and while we consider the extent of the country, so intersected and almost surrounded with navigable rivers, so separated and detached from the rest of the world, it is natural to presume that Providence has designed us for an united people, under one great political compact. If this is a just and reasonable conclusion, supported by the wishes of the people, the Convention did right in proposing a single confederated Republic. But in proposing it they were necessary led, not only to consider the situation, circumstances, and interests of one, two, or three States, but of the collective body; and as it is essential to society, that the welfare of the whole should be preferred to the accommodation of a part, they followed the same rule in promoting the national advantages of the Union, in preference to the separate advantages of the States. A principle of candor, as well as duty, led to this conduct; for, as I have said before, no government, either single or confederated, can exist, unless private and individual rights are subservient to the public and general happiness of the nation. It was not alone the State of Pennsylvania, however important she may be as a constituent part of the union, that could influence the deliberations of a convention formed by a delegation from all the United States to devise a government adequate to their common exigencies and impartial in its influence and operation. In the spirit of union, inculcated by the nature of their commission, they framed the constitution before us, and in the same spirit they submit it to the candid consideration of their constituents.

Having made some remarks upon the nature and principles of civil society, I shall now take a cursory notice of civil liberty, which is essential to the well-being of civil government. The definition of civil liberty is, briefly, that portion of natural liberty which men resign to the government, and which then produces more happiness than it would have produced if retained by the individuals who resign it; still, however, leaving to the human mind the full enjoyment of every privilege that is not incompatible with the peace and order of society. Here I am easily led to the consideration of another species of liberty, which has not yet received a discriminating name, but which I will venture to term Federal liberty. This, Sir, consists in the aggregate of the civil liberty which is surrendered by each state to the national government; and the same principles that operate in the establishment of a single society, with respect to the rights reserved or resigned by the individuals that compose it, will justly apply in the case of a confederation of distinct and independent States.

These observations have been made, Mr. President, in order to preface a representation of the state of the Union, as it appeared to the late convention. We all know, and we have all felt, that the present system of confederation is inadequate to the government and the exigencies of the United States. Need I describe the contrasted scene which the revolution has presented to our view? On the one hand, the arduous struggle in the cause of liberty terminated by a glorious and triumphant peace; on the other, contention and poverty at home, discredit and disgrace abroad. Do we not remember what high expectations were formed by others and by ourselves on the return of peace? And have those honorable expectations from our national character been realized? No! What then has been the cause of disappointment? Has America lost her magnanimity or perseverance? No! Has she been subdued by any high-handed invasion of her liberties? Still I answer no; for dangers of that kind were no sooner seen than they were repelled. But the evil has stolen in from a quarter little suspected, and the rock of freedom, which stood firm against the attacks of a foreign foe, has been sapped and undermined by the licentiousness of our own citizens. Private calamity and public anarchy have prevailed; and even the blessing of independency has been scarcely felt or understood by a people who have dearly achieved it.

Shall I, Sir, be more particular in this lamentable history? The commencement of peace was likewise the commencement of our distresses and disgrace. Devoid of power, we could neither prevent the excessive importations which lately deluged the country, nor even raise from that excess a contribution to the public revenue; devoid of importance, we were unable to command a sale for our commodities in a foreign market; devoid of credit, our public securities were melting in the hands of their deluded owners, like snow before the sun; devoid of dignity, we were inadequate to perform treaties on our own part, or to compel a performance on the part of a contracting nation. In short, Sir, the tedious tale disgusts me, and I fondly hope it is unnecessary to proceed. The years of languor are over. We have seen dishonor and destruction, it is true, but we have at length penetrated the cause, and are now anxious to obtain the cure. The cause need not be specified by a recapitulation of facts; every act of Congress, and the proceedings of every State, are replete with proofs in that respect, and all point to the weakness and imbecility of the existing confederation; while the loud and concurrent voice of the people proclaims an efficient national government to be the only cure. Under these impressions, and with these views, the late convention were appointed and met; the end which they proposed to accomplish being to frame one national and efficient government, in which the exercise of beneficence, correcting the jarring interests of every part, should pervade the whole, and by which the peace, freedom, and happiness of the United States should be permanently ensured. The principles and means that were adopted by the convention to obtain that end are now before us, and will become the great object of our discussion. But on this point, as upon others, permit me to make a few general observations.

In all governments, whatever is their form, however they may be constituted, there must be a power established from which there is no appeal, and which is therefore called absolute, supreme, and uncontrollable. The only question is, where that power is lodged?—a question that will receive different answers from the different writers on the subject. Sir William Blackstone says, it resides in the omnipotence of the British Parliament, or in other words, corresponding with the practice of that country, it is whatever the British Parliament pleases to do: so that when that body was so base and treacherous to the rights of the people as to transfer the legislative authority to Henry the Eighth, his exercising that authority by proclamations and edicts could not strictly speaking be termed unconstitutional, for under the act of Parliament his will was made the law, and therefore his will became in that respect the constitution itself. But were we to ask some politicians who have taken a faint and inaccurate view of our establishments, where does this supreme power reside in the United States? they would probably answer, in their Constitutions. This however, though a step nearer to the fact, is not a just opinion; for in truth, it remains and flourishes with the people; and under the influence of that truth we, at this moment, sit, deliberate, and speak. In other countries, indeed, the revolutions of government are connected with war, and all its concomitant calamities. But with us, they are considered as the means of obtaining a superior knowledge of the nature of government, and of accomplishing its end. That the supreme power, therefore, should be vested in the people, is in my judgment the great panacea of human politics. It is a power paramount to every constitution, inalienable in its nature, and indefinite in its extent. For I insist, if there are errors in government, the people have the right not only to correct and amend them, but likewise totally to change and reject its form; and under the operation of that right, the citizens of the United States can never be wretched beyond retrieve, unless they are wanting to themselves.

Then let us examine, Mr. President, the three species of simple government, which as I have already mentioned, are the monarchical, aristocratical and democratical. In a monarchy, the supreme power is vested in a single person; in an aristocracy, it is possessed by a body not formed upon the principle of representation, but enjoying their station by descent, by election among themselves, or in right of some personal or territorial qualification; and lastly, in a democracy, it is inherent in the people, and is either exercised by themselves or by their representatives. Each of these systems has its advantages and its disadvantages. The advantages of a monarchy are strength, dispatch, and unity; its disadvantages are expense, tyranny, and war. The advantages of an aristocracy are experience, and the wisdom resulting from education; its disadvantages are the dissension of the governors, and the oppression of the people. The advantages of a democracy are liberty, caution, industry, fidelity, and an opportunity of bringing forward the talents and abilities of the citizens, without regard to birth or fortune; its disadvantages are dissension and imbecility, for the assent of many being required, their exertions will be feeble, and their counsels too soon discovered.

To obtain all the advantages, and to avoid all the inconveniences of these governments, was the leading object of the late convention. Having therefore considered the formation and principles of other systems, it is natural to enquire, of what description is the constitution before us? In its principles, Sir, it is purely democratical; varying indeed, in its form, in order to admit all the advantages, and to exclude all the disadvantages which are incidental to the known and established constitutions of government. But when we take an extensive and accurate view of the streams of power that appear through this great and comprehensive plan, when we contemplate the variety of their directions, the force and dignity of their currents, when we behold them intersecting, embracing, and surrounding the vast possessions and interests of the continent, and when we see them distributing on all hands beauty, energy and riches, still, however numerous and wide their courses, however diversified and remote the blessings they diffuse, we shall be able to trace them all to one great and noble source, THE PEOPLE.

Such, Mr. President, are the general observations with which I have thought it necessary to trouble you. In discussing the distinct propositions of the federal plan, I shall have occasion to apply them more particularly to that subject; but at present I shall conclude with requesting the pardon of the convention for having so long intruded upon their patience.

When Mr. Wilson had concluded,* Mr. Smilie rose and entered into a severe animadversion upon the nature of the motion offered by Mr. M'Kean, which however, he observed, was consistent with the system of precipitancy that had uniformly prevailed in respect to the important subject before the Convention. He observed that we were repeatedly told of the peculiar advantages which we enjoy in being able deliberately and peaceably to decide upon a government for ourselves and our posterity, but we find every measure that is proposed leads to defeat those advantages, and to preclude all argument and deliberation, in a case confessedly of the highest consequence to the happiness of a great portion of the globe. What, continued he, can be the object of the motion? Is it to bring on a hasty and total adoption of the constitution? Let it be remembered that the Federal Convention

* From the Pennsylvania Herald, Nov. 28, 1787.

consumed four months in framing it, and shall we not employ a few days in deciding upon it? If it is that noble, that perfect system, we have been told it is, why interfere with the fullest investigation of its principles, since, in that case, the better they are understood, the more they will be approved. The most common business of a legislative body is treated with greater delicacy, being submitted to repeated discussion, upon different days, and are we on a point of such magnitude to determine without information, to agree in toto to so complicated a system, before we have weighed and examined its constituent parts? No, Sir, it is our duty to go coolly and circumstantially into the consideration of this business, and by comparing it, at least, with the circumstances and exigencies of our country, ask with firmness, is such a sacrifice of civil liberty necessary to the national honor and happiness of America? For my part, I think otherwise, though at the same time I am sensible of the expediency of giving additional strength and energy to the Federal head. But we are not so situated as to be obliged to accept any terms; and if this plan is such as we ought no to accept, I hope this convention will have candour and fortitude enough to reject it.

Mr. M'Kean followed Mr. Smilie, and remarked that the object of his motion was declared when it was proposed: it was not to preclude, but promote a free and ample discussion of the federal plan. But as to the precedents which are pointed out from the legislature of Pennsylvania to guide our proceedings, if they were always right, which I do not think they are, still no parallel can be drawn between the nature of their business and ours, consequently their rules cannot apply. We do not come here to legislate; we have no right to inquire into the power of the late convention, or to alter and amend their work; the sole question before us is, whether we will ratify and confirm, or, upon due consideration, reject in the whole, the system of federal government that is submitted to us. But because this is the only question which we can decide, does it follow that we are not minutely to investigate its principles in every section and sentence? No, Sir; that will be our duty before we conclusively say whether we will ratify or reject; but precedents in point of proceeding cannot be drawn from any part of the world, for we are the first people who have ever peaceably assembled upon so great and interesting an occasion.

Mr. Whitehill stated that, in his opinion, the object of the motion had been misunderstood by the member from Fayette, which was undoubtedly intended to bring the subject fairly before the convention. Indeed, I cannot perceive how we can decide upon the whole without having first considered every part, and in order to do that with convenience and effect, I presume a motion to go into a committee of the whole convention, which I mean to propose, will be adopted. Notwithstanding the arrangements, there may be reasonable objections urged against the proposed plan, and if it is found that it conveys to the federal government rights and liberties which the people ought never to surrender, I hope no speculative argument will seduce us into a confirmation, which binds ourselves and our posterity forever.

The convention then adjourned to meet on Monday afternoon at 3 o'clock.

[The following comments on Mr. Wilson's speech appeared in the Pennsylvania Packet of Nov. 27th.]

Mr. Wilson attracted the attention of the house by a speech which the celebrated Roman orator would not have blushed to own. He began by pointing out the difficulties that the late convention had to encounter; the diversity of opinion, interest and prejudice they had to combat. He sketched the different forms of ancient and modern republics, and showed how imperfect models they were for our imitation; he proved to demonstration that there was not among them one confederated republic. He mentioned these difficulties (he said) not to make a parade of the merits of the convention in surmounting them, but to show how visionary—how idle it is to expect that under them a government could be framed unexceptionable in all its parts to each individual of so extensive an empire. He forcibly contrasted the imbecility of our present confederation with the energy which must result from the proffered constitution. After defining (with an accuracy which marked his acquaintance with governmental history) the different kinds of government, and pointing out their respective advantages and wants, he concluded a speech which had justly won the admiration of his audience, by saying that the late convention had in view, and he hoped had in some measure executed, a constitution whose energy would pervade the union and restore credit and happiness to a distracted empire.

Monday, November 26th.

The convention* met agreeably to adjournment.

It was moved by Mr. M'Kean, seconded by Mr. Chambers, that the convention do now proceed to consider the proposed constitution by articles.

This motion occasioned a long and desultory debate, in which it was contended, on the one hand, that the restraints of proceeding in convention, under fixed rules, precluding any member from speaking oftener than twice on the same question, and the advantages of reconsideration afforded by going into a committee of the whole, would be sufficient reasons for dissenting from the proposed motion.

On the other side, the expense and delay of going twice over the same ground was insisted on; and in order to obviate the difficulty arising from the rule of debate, it was proposed to rescind that, and leave it in the power of each member to speak as often as he pleased.

The rule was accordingly rescinded, and the question being taken on a motion made by Mr. Whitehill, for postponing the resolution proposed by Mr. M'Kean, in order to introduce a motion for going into a committee of the whole, was lost, there being 43 against it, and 24 in favor of it.

While the convention were debating† on the propriety of referring the constitution to a committee of the whole, Mr. Wilson made the following observation: "Shall we, Sir,

* From the Pennsylvania Herald, Nov. 28, 1787. Same in Independent Gazetteer, Nov. 29.

† From Independent Gazetteer, Nov 29, 1787.

while we contemplate a great and magnificent edifice, condescend like a fly, with its microscopic eye, to scrutinize the imperfections of a single brick?'' Mr. Findley, retorting the metaphor, said ''Shall we not, Sir, when we are about to erect a large and expensive fabric (for as far as it respects us, we are about to erect this mighty fabric of government in Pennsylvania) examine and compare the materials of which we mean to compose it, fitting and combining the parts with each other, and rejecting every thing that is useless and rotten?'' ''That,'' concluded Dr. Rush, ''is not our situation. We are not, at this time, called upon to raise the structure. The house is already built for us, and we are only asked, whether we choose to occupy it? If we find its apartments commodious, and, upon the whole, that it is well calculated to shelter us from the inclemencies of the storm that threatens, we shall act prudently in entering it ; if otherwise, all that is required of us is to return the key to those who have built and offered it for our use.''

It was observed in the convention, that the Federal convention had exceeded the powers given to them by the several legislatures; but Mr. Wilson observed, that however foreign the question was to the present business, he would place it in its proper light. The Federal convention did not act at all upon the powers given to them by the States, but they proceeded upon original principles, and having framed a constitution which they thought would promote the happiness of their country, they have submitted it to their consideration, who may either adopt or reject it, as they please.

Yesterday afternoon,* in the convention of this State, it was moved by Mr. M'Kean, seconded by Mr. Chambers, that this convention do now proceed to consider the proposed constitution by articles.

After some debate it was moved by Mr. R. Whitehill, seconded by Mr. Lincoln, that the aforesaid motion be postponed in order to introduce the following, viz.—That this convention resolve itself into a committee of the whole, for

---

* The following account is from the Pennsylvania Packet, Nov. 27, 1787.

the purpose of investigating and considering the aforesaid constitution by articles and sections, and to make report thereon.

A debate of considerable length now took place, which turned principally on the expediency of resolving the convention into a committee of the whole. In favor of this measure it was urged, that it would subject the constitution to a more free and candid discussion—that it would allow more time for the members to make up their minds—and that it would be more consonant to the practice of the Legislature of Pennsylvania. Against the motion was urged that by going into a committee of the whole, no minutes could be taken of the proceedings, and that the people at large would thereby be kept in ignorance of them—that as full liberty was given to each to speak as often as he pleased, there would be the same time given for deliberation in convention as in the committee —that the practice of the Assembly of Pennsylvania was no precedent for the convention—that this was a body without a precedent in the history of mankind—and that as the whole constitution was a single proposition, and that proposition alone before the convention, it was unnecessary to go into a committee, especially as no question could be taken upon any part of the constitution, nor any additions made to it, agreeably to the recommendation of the Assembly under which the convention sat; although objections to every part of it might be made before the question of ratification was proposed.

The question being at length put, Mr. Whitehill's motion for postponement was lost, the yeas and nays being as follows:

YEAS.	YEAS.
John Whitehill,	Abraham Lincoln,
John Harris,	John Bishop,
John Reynolds,	Joseph Hiester,
Robert Whitehill,	James Martin,
Jonathan Hoge,	Joseph Powell,
Nicholas Lutz,	William Findley,
John Ludwig,	John Baird,

William Todd,
James Marshall,
James Edgar,
Thomas Scott,
Nathaniel Breading,

John Smilie,
Richard Bard,
William Brown,
Adam Orth,
John Andre Hannah.—24.

NAYS.

George Latimer,
Benjamin Rush,
Hilary Baker,
James Wilson,
Thomas M'Kean,
William Macpherson,
John Hunn,
George Gray,
Samuel Ashmead,
Enoch Edwards,
Henry Wynkoop,
John Barclay,
Thomas Yardley,
Abraham Stout,
Thomas Bull,
Anthony Wayne,
William Gibbons,
Richard Downing,
Thomas Cheyney,
John Hannum,
Stephen Chambers,
Robert Coleman,

NAYS.

Sebastain Graff,
John Hubley,
Jasper Yeates,
Henry Slagle,
Thomas Campbell,
Thomas Hartley,
David Grier,
John Black,
Benjamin Pedan,
John Arndt,
Stephen Balliet,
Joseph Horsfield,
David Deshler,
William Wilson,
John Boyd,
John Neville,
John Allison,
Jonathan Roberts,
John Richards,
F. A. Muhlenberg,
James Morris,
Timothy Pickering.—44.

The question on Mr. M'Kean's motion was then put, and the motion adopted.

The speakers in favor of the motion for a committee were Mr. Findley, Mr. Smilie and Mr. Whitehill. The speakers against it were Mr. M'Kean, Mr. Wilson, Dr. Rush and Mr. Chambers.

Tuesday, November 27.

The convention* being met pursuant to adjournment, Mr.

* From the Pennsylvania Herald, Dec. 1st, 1787.

M'Kean moved that they should proceed to the consideration of the first article of the proposed constitution.

The convention chose Messrs. Hall and Sellers and Mr. Steiner the printers of their journals—3,000 copies to be in English, and 2,000 in German.

Mr. Whitehill offered a resolution, declaring that "upon all questions where the yeas and nays were called, any member might insert the reason of his vote upon the journals of the convention."

Mr. Hartley. Sir, before the question on this motion is decided, I should wish to understand how far it extends, and whether, contrary to what I have thought was the sense of the convention, more than one question will be taken upon the proposed constitution? If the questions are to be multiplied, and protests are to be admitted on each, I shall certainly object to the source of embarrassment, delay and expense which this motion will open. But if we are limited to the comprehensive question, will you ratify or reject the plan? then I think it may be reasonable to allow every man that pleases, to justify his assent or dissent by the motives upon which it may be founded.

Mr. M'Kean. When we were choosing our printers a few minutes ago, Mr. President, I did not think it a matter of so much importance as the adoption of the motion before us would render it; for, if every member whenever he pleases shall be at liberty to load our journals with long and labored arguments, it will be a profitable business indeed for those gentlemen that are appointed to publish them. There can, sir, but one question arise in the discussion of the plan that is submitted to us, which is simply whether we will ratify or reject it; and if the motion were narrowed to that point, I should have no objection to give it my approbation. But on its present ground we would expose ourselves to a scene of altercation highly unbecoming the character and dignity of this body.

Mr. Whitehill. I hope, Sir, the measure I have proposed, will upon consideration meet with the favor of the convention, since the arguments by which it is opposed arise chiefly from a presumption that the liberty it affords will be abused. This, Mr. President, ought not to be presumed, but rather that every member entertains so just a sense of his duty to himself and to this honorable convention, as to forbear every thing, in language or in argument, which will be unbecoming a place in your journals. In truth, Sir, unless we are allowed to insert our reasons, the yeas and nays will be a barren document, from which the public can derive no information, and the minority no justification for their conduct. On the other hand, if we are allowed to state the foundation of our votes, the merits of the constitution may be proved by the arguments of its advocates, and those who do not consider it to be an immaculate, or even salutary system, will have an opportunity to point out the defects from which their opposition originates. I think, Sir, the public have a right in so important a transaction to know the principles upon which their delegates proceed; and it is the just right of every man who is bound by his vote to be permitted to explain it. I cannot therefore withdraw or reduce the object of my motion.

Mr. Hartley. Then, Sir, if I comprehend the sense of the convention: we are limited to the one great question which shall decide the fate of the constitution; and upon that I agree in the propriety of permitting a protest. Let the opponents of the new system state their reasons fully and fairly; it will be the duty of its advocates to refute them upon the same terms, and the record of the whole will be preserved for the information of our constituents. This seems indeed to open a door for the renewal of all the arguments which have been previously advanced, but it will answer the same purpose as if protests were entered on each distinct proposition.

Mr. Whitehill. We are now, Mr. President, in the full enjoyment of the powers of the mind, and I hope we shall adopt no measure that will tend to curtail the exercise of our faculties. Upon every question that arises, it is in the power of any member to call the yeas and nays, and whenever a vote is registered in that permanent form, it is of no consequence whether it is in the intermediate or conclusive stages of the business, we ought to be permitted to promulge the reasons which have influenced our decisions. Every argument (and gentlemen seem to have conceded the propriety in one case) that will apply to entitle us to protest on the last question, will entitle us to that privilege on any preceding one: for I consider it rather as a right than an indulgence. But, Mr. President, it is said that we can only have one question in the business before us. If this is true, I see no cause to proceed further. It will be a great public saving to recur to that question at once, and we shall by such means escape the absurdity of arguing upon distinct propositions without determining anything with respect to them. Sir, there is no reason to suppose an improper use will be made of this necessary privilege. It is intended as the means of justifying to the people the conduct of those with whom they have entrusted their dearest interests, and if in the manner or the substance it is deficient or improper, the people will pronounce its condemnation. Let them therefore judge; but since we are answerable to them, let us not suppress the means of justification.

Doctor Rush. I shall certainly, Sir, object to any protest, but upon the great question, and even there it is hardly in my opinion proper or necessary. Those, Mr. President, who are in favor of the constitution, will be as anxious to vindicate their opinions as those who are against it; hence, whatever is advanced on one side, will draw on a reply upon the other, till the whole debates of the convention are intruded upon the journals. The expense and procrastination of this transaction would be intolerable. But, Sir, the proceedings of the convention are stamped with authenticity, and it would be dangerous to suffer protests to be inserted in them, which might contain insinuations not founded, and consequently produce here what has disgraced the legislature of Pennsylvania, a majority defending themselves from the assertions and misrepresentations of a minority. We know, Sir, of what nature the protests will be, and if they bear the complexion of the publications that have lately teemed from the press, I am sure they would not be honorable to this body. The proceedings of the convention cannot be compared in this respect to the proceedings of the legislature, where protests may lay the foundation of a future revision or repeal of the law to which they object by laying the necessary information before the people; but we can have no view either to a revision or a repeal, and therefore protests can only serve to distract and perplex the state. If, Sir, the proposed plan should be adopted by this convention, it will be the duty of every man, particularly those who have opposed it, on the fundamental principles of society, to promote its interests among the people. But if, contrary to my opinion of what is their duty, the minority should persevere in their opposition, I hope they will be left to publish in their own way, without our authority, the motives of their conduct, and let them enjoy all the advantages they may derive from the effects of that publication.

Mr. M'Kean. I shall be satisfied, Mr. President, if the object of the motion is confined to the final question; and, indeed, I do not perceive to what other motions it can extend. But it is said no harm will proceed from its adoption agreeably to its present general terms. Sir, all laws are made to prevent evil, upon a supposition that it may occur, and in the instance before us I do not only think it probable, but I have no doubt it will occur. We are again told of the conduct of the general assembly of Pennsylvania, which some gentlemen seem to imagine is an unanswerable argument upon every topic. But even there the practice of protesting has only been introduced since the revolution, nor was it before known in any province of America, or in any government in the world. Some compliment has on a former occasion been paid to my legal knowledge, with an intention however to depreciate my knowledge of parliamentary proceedings. But the truth is, Sir, that those proceedings have, both before and since the revolution, formed a great object of my studies, and it has been my lot to have been engaged likewise considerably in the practice. I therefore repeat, confidently, that no precedent of protesting is to be found anywhere but in Pennsylvania. The lords in England, indeed, enjoy, and frequently exercise the privilege; but the reason is, that they are not a representative body, nor accountable to any power for their legislative conduct but God and their consciences, and therefore from a desire to preserve their fame and honor free from suspicion and reproach, they render this voluntary account of their actions to the world. The same motive, however, does not prevail with a representative body the members of which are, from time to time, responsible to their constituents, and may be elected or removed from their trust according to the proof of their fidelity and industry in discharging it. I have seen, sir, language by such means intruded upon the journals of the legislature of Pennsylvania, which would have disgraced a private club at a tavern. But in the British house of lords, the language of the protest is under the control of the house, and it is not uncommon to erase sentences and paragraphs, and even whole protests, from their records. But, Mr. President, there cannot be any necessity for introducing the practice here, unless indeed to indulge the vanity of some gentlemen who wish to turn authors at the public expense, to write discourses upon government, and to give them a value and consequence by incorporating them with your proceedings, to which they are not intrinsically entitled. I therefore move, sir, that the motion before you be amended, so as to restrict the right of protesting to the last great question, to adopt or reject the proposed plan.

This motion was seconded by Mr. Chambers.

Mr. Wilson*. I am equally opposed, Mr. President, to the amendment and to the original motion. I do not wish, however, in any degree to suppress what may be spoken or done in this convention. On the contrary, I wish our proceedings may be fully known and perfectly understood by our constituents; and, to extend the scale, by all our fellow citizens of the United States. But we ought to pause and consider well before we communicate all this information at the public expense, for as the motion has been opened and explained, under the influence of that rule, our minutes may be increased

* From the Pennsylvania Herald, Dec. 5th, 1787.

to an immense volume, and yet we have just determined that 3,000 copies of them shall be printed. I certainly, sir, (as well as every other member) will have a right to enter my sentiments and arguments in the manner most satisfactory to myself, and therefore, not only what I may hereafter say, but what I have already said, in order to preserve connection and system in the reasoning, must be admitted. The press is undoubtedly free, but is it necessary to that freedom that every man's tenets on government should be printed at the public cost? Sir, we are here as upon many other occasions, referred to the constitution of Pennsylvania; but the privilege indulged in this respect, is, in my opinion, one of its exceptional parts, and the instances of its abuse alluded to by my honorable colleague, must excite the indignation of every friend to propriety and decency. Look at the journals of the legislature of Pennsylvania, and you will find altercations there which are adapted to the meridian of Billingsgate. In short, sir, the idea of a protest is not to be found in any other representative body, not even in that of the British house of commons; and if we must seek a lesson from other constitutions, we might, with great propriety, advert to the one before us, by which one-fifth of the members are enabled to call for the yeas and nays, but in no case is it permitted to record the reasons of a vote. Shall we then employ the whole winter in carrying on a paper war, at the expense of the state, in spreading clamor and dissension not only among our own citizens, but throughout the United States? My voice, Sir, never shall concur in rendering this room the centre from which so many streams of bitterness shall flow. Let the opponents of the proposed plan write as much as they please, let them print when they will, but I trust we shall not agree to indulge them at the expense of those who have sent us hither for a very different purpose.

Mr. Smilie. It appears, Mr. President, that on this question the gentlemen are divided among themselves.

Mr. M'Kean. No, Sir, there shall be no division. I thought the measure totally improper, and only proposed the amendment in compliment to the members who urged the general motion. I now withdraw my amendment, and leave the question upon its original ground.

Mr. Smilie. I am sorry, Sir, that the honorable member should so suddenly have retracted his amendment, for it was more satisfactory to me than the original motion, which I wish still to be narrowed down to the final question, as, indeed, I do not perceive how it can operate on any other subject, and it will then answer every purpose to which it can be applied, without leaving room for the objection on account of the extraordinary expense. It will, indeed, appear exceedingly strange upon this important subject, that we should be denied an opportunity of declaring the reasons that influence our votes—while we are responsible, it is our duty, and while we are bound, it is our right. Nor is it liberal or reasonable to presume that any harm can ensue from this privilege; for the apprehensions which are expressed, lest faction and clamor should be excited among the people, are highly unbecoming the citizens of a free government. An excellent author has observed, that slavery succeeds sleep, and the moment parties and political contentions subside among the people, from that moment liberty is at an end. I admit, Sir, that if the ferment rises to an extreme it is an evil; but as it originates from a blessing, those who wish to preserve their freedom must bear with its inconveniences. But what is the evil so much dreaded? We are told that protests in past times have been a dishonor and a discredit; but to whom have they been such? Certainly to those who wrote them; and so, if anything unworthy should appear in the protests upon your journals, the authors alone will be liable to the infamy and odium of their productions. But let us suppose, on the other hand, what I believe to be the real ground of opposition, that the protest should produce a change in the minds of the people, and incline them to new measures, is this an event proper either to be evaded or suppressed? I take it, Sir, that even after this convention shall have agreed to ratify the proposed plan, if the people on better information, and maturer deliberation, should think it a bad and improper form of government, they will still have a right to assemble another body, to consult upon other measures, and either in the whole, or in part, to abrogate this Federal work so ratified. If this is true, and that it is true a worthy member of the late convention admits, when he says the people have at all times a power to alter and abolish government, what cause is there to fear the operation of a protest? The reasons may easily be given in public newspapers, which circulate more widely and more expedtiously than our journals, and from whatever source the information is derived, as the people have the power, they may, and I believe they will exercise it, notwithstanding the determination of this body. The allusion to the conduct of the British commons will not apply, for they are in no instance called upon to enter their yeas and nays; and after all, it appears to me to be congenial with the spirit of a free government, and if the one before us is free, it will be congenial with the principles of the proposed constitution, that where men are bound by a solemn and recorded vote, their reasons should accompany their assent or dissent, and be together transmitted to posterity.

Mr. Wilson. It is one reason of my opposition to this measure, that its objects can be effected in another manner than by inserting them in our journals, and therefore there is no pretense to load the public with an expense for diffusing what is called necessary information, but which in my opinion will terminate in the acrimony of party. But, Sir, if there were no other cause of objection—if the thing were proper in itself—the enormous expense that it would occasion would be a conclusive ground for rejecting it. It is asked, however, what is there to fear? Sir, I repeat, that I have not the least dread at the most public and most general promulgation of what is done and spoken here. We know that the same things may as effectually, and perhaps more expeditiously, be disseminated through other channels, but let them not in their course either involve the public in expense, nor derive from our countenance a stamp of authenticity.

Mr. Whitehill. I do not think, Mr. President, that if there is any use in the proposed measure, the expense can be a sufficient reason to defeat it. The people ought to be informed of the principles upon which we have acted, and they ought to know in the clearest manner, what is the nature and tendency of the government with which we have bound them. The friends to the constitution will be pleased to receive arguments in favor of their opinions; those against it will be pleased to show to the world that their opposition does not arise merely from caprice, and the people at large will acknowledge with thanks the resulting information upon a subject so important to themselves and their latest posterity. But it is said that there are other means for accomplishing the same end, and that the press is open to those who chose to use it. This surely does not meet the object of the motion. A public paper is of a transient and perishable nature, but the journals of this house will be a permanent record for posterity, and if ever it becomes a question upon what grounds we have acted, each man will have his vote justified by the same instrument that records it. But this comparative view cannot take place through the medium of a common newspaper. As, however, it seems the general disposition, I am willing to reduce the motion to the last question, and this, at least, I hope will be acceded to. The expense cannot be so great as it is apprehended, and I really consider it essential to the discharge of the commission with which we are entrusted.

Mr. Hartley. On consideration, I do not think it necessary, Sir, to determine upon the motion at this time. It has been said on one hand, that there is no precedent but in the British house of lords, and in the legislature of Pennsylvania, for the practice of protesting; and on the other hand, it is insisted upon from the example of Pennsylvania and the important nature of the subject in discussion. But, Sir, it is certain that much misinformation and misrepresentation have at all times proceeded from public bodies. At present, therefore, I wish the question to be waived; otherwise, I shall vote against it, although at a future period, when the reasons are produced, I may be disposed to concur.

Mr. Whitehill. The gentleman's idea of a postponement amounts to this: If we like your reasons when we see them, we will permit you to enter them; if we do not, why we will withhold our consent. It is strange to observe how often members change their opinions on this subject. When I asked a general power to protest, it was said, we will not agree to that, but we think you ought to enjoy it on the last great question; then when we narrow our request to that point, even that is refused. Precedent, sir, cannot be adduced on this occasion, for a similar situation never had occurred before in the history of the world, nor do we know of any body of men assembled with similar powers to investigate so interesting a subject. The importance and singularity of the business must place it beyond any former rule.

Mr. Wayne. As it is probable this subject may hereafter be considered in a different and more proper point of view, I am in favor of the postponement. In the interim the usual channel of expressing their disapprobation of this system are open to the opposition. It has already been tried; and I cannot consent that discord and discontent should be propagated through the state at the public expense, particularly as every information may be given in another manner.

Mr. Wilson. Sir, I am against the postponement for two reasons—first, because I would not indulge a hope which it is not intended to gratify, and secondly, because I should wish as soon as possible to know the fate of the present motion, that every member may be prepared with his reasons if it should be adopted, and not have them to look for at the close of the business. But we are again asked, why suppress the species of information to be propagated by the proposed protests? I thought this question had already been answered satisfactorily, when it was said that the public ought not to be loaded with so extraordinary an expense. In truth, sir, the newspapers will answer every proper purpose; and though it is said they are of a transient nature, yet if the reasons are good they will even in that mode be preserved, and if they are bad, I hope we shall not agree to perpetuate at the public cost what ought to be consigned immediately to oblivion. It is added that the expense will be small. Let us enquire then, what will be the consequence of this vote? The minority, dissatisfied with the event of this important business, will first wish to file their reasons, and it would be improper and unjust to deny them the necessary time to digest and arrange them in the best manner. These reasons cannot be answered till they appear, and though they may not possess real merit, they may be plausible and specious, therefore some time will be necessarily given to the majority for framing a replication; and so on through an endless succession of assertion and reply. For my part, I shall certainly expect to be allowed a sufficient time to state my reasons, not only those I have already delivered, but likewise those I may hereafter, in the most accurate manner I can; but, as I am perhaps more accustomed to composition than other gentlemen, I shall not ask for that purpose more than two or three months. Shall we then, Sir, indulge this procrastinating plan at the expense of two or three hundred dollars a day, which is the daily expense of this meeting? I hope we shall have a greater regard for the interests of our constituents.

Mr. Whitehill and Mr. Smilie repeated some of the former arguments, and concluded with observing that if the motion was negatived, their constituents would at least observe that they were anxious to show the grounds of their conduct, which they were refused the opportunity of doing.

On taking the question there appeared a very great majority against the motion.

Mr. M'Kean then rose and recommended candor and forbearance in the investigation of this important subject. He stated that a difference of opinion was natural to the human mind, and was not only to be found in politics, but in religion. He then traced this difference through the various sects of the Christian faith, and concluded by expressing his approbation of a legislature constituted by two branches.

The convention adjourned to meet to-morrow at half past nine o'clock.

Wednesday, November 28.

The* convention met pursuant to adjournment.

Mr. Wilson. Mr. President, I shall now beg leave to

---

* From the Pennsylvania Herald, Dec. 8th, 1787.

trouble you with a few observations upon the preamble to the proposed constitution. In delivering my sentiments on a former day, I had occasion to show that the supreme power of government was the inalienable and inherent right of the people, and the system before us opens with a practical declaration of that principle. Here, Sir, it is expressly announced: "We, the people of the United States, do ordain, constitute, and establish." And those who can ordain and establish, may certainly repeal or annul the work of government, which in the hands of the people, is like clay in the hands of the potter, and may be moulded into any shape they please. This single sentence in the preamble is tantamount to a volume, and contains the essence of all the bills of rights that have been or can be devised; for it establishes at once, that in the great article of government, the people have a right to do what they please. It is with pride, Mr. President, I remark the difference between the terms of this constitution, and the British declaration of rights, or even their boasted Magna Charta. For, Sir, from what source does Magna Charta derive the liberties of the people? The very words of that celebrated instrument declare them to be the gift or grant of the king; and under the influence of that doctrine, no wonder the people should then and at subsequent periods wish to obtain some evidence of their formal liberties by the concessions of petitions and bills of right. But here, Sir, the fee simple of freedom and government is declared to be in the people, and it is an inheritance with which they will not part.

Mr. Smilie. I expected, Mr. President, that the honorable gentleman would have proceeded to a full and explicit investigation of the proposed system, and that he would have made some attempts to prove that it was calculated to promote the happiness, power and general interests of the United States. I am sorry that I have been mistaken in this expectation, for surely the gentleman's talents and opportunities would have enabled him to furnish considerable information upon this important subject; but I shall proceed to make a few remarks upon those words in the preamble of this plan, which he has considered of so super-excellent a quality. Compare them, Sir, with the language used in forming the state constitution, and however superior they may be to the terms of the great charter of England; still, in common candor, they must yield to the more sterling expressions employed in this act. Let these speak for themselves:

"That all men are born equally free and independent, and have certain natural, inherent and unalienable rights, among which are the enjoying and defending life and liberty, acquiring possessing and protecting property, and pursuing and obtaining happiness and safety.

"That the people of this state have the sole, exclusive and inherent right of governing and regulating the internal police of the same.

"That all power being originally inherent in, and consequently derived from the people; therefore all officers of government, whether legislative or executive, are their trustees and servants, and at all times accountable to them.

"That government is, or ought to be, instituted for the common benefit, protection and security of the people, nation or community; and not for the particular emolument or advantage of any single man, family, or set of men, who are a part only of that community. And that the community hath an indubitable, unalienable, and indefeasible right to reform, alter or abolish government in such manner as shall be by that community judged most conducive to the public weal."

But the gentleman takes pride in the superiority of this short preamble when compared with Magna Charta—why, sir, I hope the rights of men are better understood at this day than at the framing of that deed, and we must be convinced that civil liberty is capable of still greater improvement and extension, than is known even in its present cultivated state. True, sir, the supreme authority naturally rests in the people, but does it follow, that therefore a declaration of rights would be superfluous? Because the people have a right to alter and abolish government, can it therefore be inferred that every step taken to secure that right would be superfluous and nugatory? The truth is, that unless some criterion is established by which it could be easily and constitutionally ascertained how far our governors may proceed, and by which it might appear when they transgress their jurisdiction, this idea of altering and abolishing government is a mere sound without substance. Let us recur to the memorable declaration of the 4th of July, 1776. Here it is said:

"When in the course of human events, it becomes necessary for one people to dissolve the political bands which have connected them with another, and to assume among the powers of the earth the separate and equal station to which the laws of nature's God entitle them, a decent respect to the opinions of mankind requires that they should declare the causes which impel them to the separation.

"We hold these truths to be self-evident; that all men are created equal; that they are endowed by their Creator with certain unalienable rights; that among these are life, liberty, and the pursuit of happiness. That to secure these rights, governments are instituted among men, deriving their just powers from the consent of the governed; that when any form of government becomes destructive of these ends, it is the right of the people to alter or to abolish it, and to institute a new government, laying its foundation on such principles, and organizing its powers in such form, as to them shall seem most likely to effect their safety and happiness."

Now, Sir, if in the proposed plan, the gentleman can show any similar security for the civil rights of the people, I shall certainly be relieved from a weight of objection to its adoption, and I sincerely hope, that as he has gone so far, he will proceed to communicate some of the reasons (and undoubtedly they must have been powerful ones) which induced the late federal convention to omit a bill of rights, so essential in the opinion of many citizens to a perfect form of government.

Mr. M'Kean.—I conceived, Mr. President, that we were at this time to confine our reasoning to the first article, which relates to the legislative power composed of two branches, and the partial negative of the President. Gentlemen, however, have taken a more extensive field, and have employed themselves in animadverting upon what has been omitted, and not upon what is contained in the proposed system. It is asked, Sir, why a bill of rights is not annexed to the constitution? The origin of bills of rights has been referred to, and we find that in England they proceed upon the principle that the supreme power is lodged in the king and not in the people, so that their liberties are not claimed as an inherent right, but as a grant from the sovereign. The great charter rests on that footing, and has been renewed and broken above 30 times. Then we find the petition of rights in the reign of Charles I., and lastly, the declaration of rights on the accession of the Prince of Orange to the British throne. The truth is, Sir, that bills of rights are instruments of modern invention, unknown among the ancients, and unpractised but by the British nation, and the governments descended from them. For though it is said that Poland has a bill of rights, it must be remembered that the people have no participation in that government. Of the constitutions of the United States, there are but five out of the thirteen which have bills of rights. In short, though it can do no harm, I believe, yet it is an unnecessary instrument, for in fact the whole plan of government is nothing more than a bill of rights—a declaration of the people in what manner they choose to be governed. If, Sir, the people should at any time desire to alter and abolish their government, I agree with my honorable colleague that it is in their power to do so, and I am happy to observe, that the constitution before us provides a regular mode for that event. At present my chief object is to call upon those who deem a bill of rights so essential, to inform us if there are any other precedents than those I have alluded to, and if there is not, the sense of mankind and of nations will operate against the alleged necessity.

Mr. Wilson.* Mr. President, we are repeatedly called upon to give some reason why a bill of rights has not been annexed to the proposed plan. I not only think that enquiry is at this time unnecessary and out of order, but I expect, at least, that those who desire us to show why it was omitted, will furnish

* From the Pennsylvania Herald, Dec. 12th, 1787.

some arguments to show that it ought to have been inserted; for the proof of the affirmative naturally falls upon them. But the truth is, Sir, that this circumstance, which has since occasioned so much clamor and debate, never struck the mind of any member in the late convention till, I believe, within three days of the dissolution of that body, and even then of so little account was the idea that it passed off in a short conversation, without introducing a formal debate or assuming the shape of a motion. For, Sir, the attempt to have thrown into the national scale an instrument in order to evince that any power not mentioned in the constitution was reserved, would have been spurned at as an insult to the common understanding of mankind. In civil government it is certain that bills of rights are unnecessary and useless, nor can I conceive whence the contrary notion has arisen. Virginia has no bill of rights, and will it be said that her constitution was the less free?

Mr. Smilie. I beg leave to observe, Mr. President, that although it has not been inserted in the printed volume of state constitution, yet I have been assured by Mr. Mason that Virginia has a bill of rights.

Mr. Wilson. I do not rely upon the information of Mr. Mason or of any other gentleman on a question of this kind, but I refer to the authenticity of the volume which contains the state constitutions, and in that Virginia has no bill of rights. But, Sir, has South Carolina no security for her liberties?—that state has no bill of rights. Are the citizens of the eastern shore of the Delaware more secured in their freedom, or more enlightened on the subject of government, than the citizens of the western shore? New Jersey has no bill of rights, New York has none, Connecticut has none, and Rhode Island has none. Thus, Sir, it appears from the example of other states, as well as from principle, that a bill of rights is neither an essential nor a necessary instrument in framing a system of government, since liberty may exist and be as well secured without it. But it was not only unnecessary, but on this occasion it was found impracticable—for who will be bold enough to undertake to enumerate all the rights of the people?—and when the attempt to enumerate them is made, it must be remembered that if the enumeration is not complete, everything not expressly mentioned will be presumed to be purposely omitted. So it must be with a bill of rights, and an omission in stating the powers granted to the government, is not so dangerous as an omission in recapitulating the rights reserved by the people. We have already seen the origin of magna charta, and tracing the subject still further we find the petition of rights claiming the liberties of the people, according to the laws and statutes of the realm, of which the great charter was the most material, so that here again recourse is had to the old source from which their liberties are derived, the grant of the king. It was not till the revolution that the subject was placed upon a different footing, and even then the people did not claim their liberties as an inherent right, but as the result of an original contract between them and the sovereign. Thus, Mr. President, an attention to the situation of England will show that the conduct of that country in respect to bills of rights, cannot furnish an example to the inhabitants of the United States, who by the revolution have regained all their natural rights, and possess their liberty neither by grant nor contract. In short, Sir, I have said that a bill of rights would have been improperly annexed to the federal plan, and for this plain reason that it would imply that whatever is not expressed was given, which is not the principle of the proposed constitution.

Mr. Smilie. The arguments which have been urged, Mr. President, have not, in my opinion, satisfactorily shown that a bill of rights would have been an improper, nay, that it is not a necessary appendage to the proposed system. As it has been denied that Virginia possesses a bill of rights, I shall on that subject only observe that Mr. Mason, a gentleman certainly of great information and integrity, has assured me that such a thing does exist, and I am persuaded I shall be able at a future period to lay it before the convention. But, Sir, the state of Delaware has a bill of rights, and I believe one of the honorable members (Mr. M'Kean) who now contests the necessity and propriety of that instrument, took a very conspicuous part in the formation of the Delaware government. It seems, however, that the members of the federal convention were themselves convinced, in some degree, of the expediency and propriety of a bill of rights, for we find them expressly declaring that the writ of habeas corpus and the trial by jury in criminal cases shall not be suspended or infringed. How does this indeed agree with the maxim that whatever is not given is reserved? Does it not rather appear from the reservation of these two articles that everything else, which is not specified, is included in the powers delegated to the government? This, Sir, must prove the necessity of a full and explicit declaration of rights; and when we further consider the extensive, the undefined powers vested in the administrators of this system, when we consider the system itself as a great political compact between the governors and the governed, a plain, strong, and accurate criterion by which the people might at once determine when, and in what instance their rights were violated, is a preliminary, without which, this plan ought not to be adopted. So loosely, so inaccurately are the powers which are enumerated in this constitution defined, that it will be impossible, without a test of that kind, to ascertain the limits of authority, and to declare when government has degenerated into oppression. In that event the contest will arise between the people and the rulers: "You have exceeded the powers of your office, you have oppressed us," will be the language of the suffering citizen. The answer of the government will be short—"We have not exceeded our power; you have no test by which you can prove it." Hence, Sir, it will be impracticable to stop the progress of tyranny, for there will be no check but the people, and their exertions must be futile and uncertain; since it will be difficult, indeed, to communicate to them the violation that has been committed, and their proceedings will be neither systematical nor unanimous. It is said, however, that the difficulty of framing a bill of rights was insurmountable; but, Mr. President, I cannot agree in this opinion. Our experience, and the numerous precedents before us, would have furnished a very sufficient guide. At present there is no security even for the rights of conscience, and under the sweeping force of the sixth article, every principle of a bill of rights, every stipulation for the most sacred and invaluable privileges of man, are left at the mercy of government.

Mr. Whitehill. I differ, Sir, from the honorable member from the city,* as to the impropriety or necessity of a bill of rights. If, indeed, the constitution itself so well defined the powers of the government that no mistake could arise, and we were well assured that our governors would always act right, then we might be satisfied without an explicit reservation of those rights with which the people ought not, and mean not to part. But, Sir, we know that it is the nature of power to seek its own augmentation, and thus the loss of liberty is the necessary consequence of a loose or extravagant delegation of authority. National freedom has been, and will be the sacrifice of ambition and power, and it is our duty to employ the present opportunity in stipulating such restrictions as are best calculated to protect us from oppression and slavery. Let us then, Mr. President, if other countries cannot supply an adequate example, let us proceed upon our own principles, and with the great end of government in view, the happiness of the people, it will be strange if we err. Government, we have been told, Sir, is yet in its infancy: we ought not therefore to submit to the shackles of foreign schools and opinions. In entering into the social compact, men ought not to leave their rulers at large, but erect a permanent land-mark by which they may learn the extent of their authority, and the people be able to discover the first encroachments on their liberties. But let us attend to the language of the system before us. "We the people of the United States," is a sentence that evidently shows the old foundation of the union is destroyed, the principle of confederation excluded, and a new and unwieldy system of consolidated empire is set up, upon the ruins of the present compact between the states. Can this be denied? No, Sir: It is artfully indeed, but it is incontrovertibly designed to abolish

* Mr. Wilson.

the independence and sovereignty of the states individually, an event which cannot be the wish of any good citizen of America, and therefore it ought to be prevented, by rejecting the plan which is calculated to produce it. What right indeed have we in the manner here proposed to violate the existing confederation? It is declared, that the agreement of nine states shall be sufficient to carry the new system into operation, and consequently to abrogate the old one. Then, Mr President, four of the present confederated states may not be comprehended in the compact: shall we, Sir, force these dissenting states into the measure? The consequences of that attempt are evidently such as no man can either justify or approve. But reverse the idea—would not these states have a fair pretext to charge the rest with an unconstitutional and unwarrantable abandoment of the nature and obligation of the union of 1776? And having shown sufficient reason why they could not accede to the proposed government, would they not still be entitled to demand a performance of the orig-ginal compact between the states? Sir, these questions must introduce a painful anticipation of the confusion, contest, and a civil war, which, under such circumstances, the adoption of the offered system must produce. It will be proper, perhaps, to review the origin of this business. It was certainly, Mr. President, acknowledged on all hands, that an additional share of power for federal purposes ought to be delegated to Congress; and with a view to enquire how far it was necessary to strengthen and enlarge the jurisdiction of that body, the late convention was appointed under the authority, and by legislative acts of the several states. But how, Sir, did the convention act upon this occasion? Did they pursue the authority which was given to them? By the State of Pennsylvania that authority was strictly defined in the following words:

"And the said Thomas Mifflin, Robert Morris, George Clymer, Jared Ingersoll, Thomas Fitzsimons, James Wilson and Governeur Morris, Esqrs., or any four of them, are hereby constituted and appointed deputies from this state, with powers to meet such deputies as may be appointed and authorized by the other states to assemble in the said convention at the city aforesaid, and to join with them in devising, deliberating on and discussing all such alterations and further provisions as may be necessary to render the federal constitution fully adequate to the exigencies of the union; and in reporting such act or acts for that purpose to the United States in Congress assembled, as when agreed to by them, and duly confirmed by the several states, will effectually provide for the same.''

Thus, Sir, it appears that no other power was given to the delegates from this state (and I believe the power given by the other states was of the same nature and extent) than to increase in a certain degree the strength and energy of Congress; but it never was in the contemplation of any man that they were authorized to dissolve the present union, to abrogate the state sovereignties, and to establish one comprehensive government, novel in its structure, and in its probable operation oppressive and despotic. Can it then be said that the late convention did not assume powers to which they had no legal title? On the contrary, Sir, it is clear that they set aside the laws under which they were appointed, and under which alone they could derive any legitimate authority, they arrogantly exercised any powers that they found convenient to their object, and in the end they have overthrown that government which they were called upon to amend, in order to introduce one of their own fabrication.

True* it is, Mr. President, that if the people intended to engage in one comprehensive system of continental government, the power to frame that system must have been conferred by them; for the legislatures of the states are sworn to preserve the independence of their respective constitutions, and therefore they could not, consistently with their most sacred obligations, authorize an act which sacrificed the individual to the aggregate sovereignty of the states. But it appears from the origin and nature of the commission under which the late convention assembled, that a more perfect confederation was the only object submitted to their wisdom, and not, as it

*From the Pennsylvania Herald, Dec. 15th, 1787.

is attempted by this plan, the total destruction of the government of Pennsylvania, and of every other state. So far, Sir, the interference of the legislatures was proper and efficient; but the moment the convention went beyond that object, they ceased to act under any legitimate authority, for the assemblies could give them none, and it cannot be pretended that they were called together by the people; for, till the preamble was produced, it never was understood that the people at large had been consulted upon the occasion, or that otherwise than through their representatives in the several states, they had given a sanction to the proceedings of that body. If, indeed, the federal convention, finding that the old system was incapable of repair, had represented the incurable defects to Congress, and advised that the original and inherent power of the people might be called into exercise for the institution of a new government, then, Sir, the subject would have come fairly into view, and we should have known upon what principles we proceeded. At present we find a convention appointed by one authority, but acting under the arbitrary assumption of another; and instead of transacting the business which was assigned to them, behold! they have produced a work of supererogation, after a mysterious labor of three months. Let us, however, Sir, attend for a moment to the constitution. And here we shall find, in a single line, sufficient matter for weeks of debate, and which it will puzzle any one member to investigate and define. But, besides the powers enumerated, we find in this constitution an authority is given to make all laws that are necessary to carry it effectually into operation, and what laws are necessary is a consideration left for Congress to decide. In constituting the representative body, the interposition of the Congress is likewise made conclusive; for, with the power of regulating the place and manner of elections, it is easy to perceive that the returns will always be so managed as to answer their purpose. It is strange to mark, however, what a sudden and striking revolution has taken place in the political sentiments of America; for, Sir, in the opening of our struggle with Great Britain, it was often insisted

that annual parliaments were necessary to secure the liberties
of the people, and yet it is here proposed to establish a house
of representatives which shall continue for two, a senate for
six, and a president for four years! What is there in this
plan indeed, which can even assure us that the several departments shall continue no longer in office? Do we not
know that an English parliament elected for three years, by
a vote of their own body, extended their existence to seven,
and with this example, Congress possessing a competent
share of power may easily be tempted to exercise it. The advantages of annual elections are not at this day to be taught,
and when every other security was withheld, I should still
have thought there was some safety in the government, had
this been left. The seats of Congress being held for so short
a period, and by a tenure so precarious as popular elections,
there could be no inducement to invade the liberties of the
people, nor time enough to accomplish the schemes of ambition and tyranny. But when the period is protracted, an
object is presented worthy of contention, and the duration of
the office affords an opportunity for perpetuating the influence
by which it was originally obtained. Another power designed to be vested in the new government, is the superlative
power of taxation, which may be carried to an inconceivable
excess, swallowing up every object of taxation, and consequently plundering the several states of every means to support their governments, and to administer their laws. Then,
Sir, can it longer be doubted that this is a system of consolidation? That government which possesses all the powers of
raising and maintaining armies, of regulating and commanding the militia, and of laying imposts and taxes of
every kind, must be supreme, and will (whether in twenty
or in one year, it signifies little to the event) naturally
absorb every subordinate jurisdiction. It is in vain, Sir,
to flatter ourselves that the forms of popular elections will be
the means of self-preservation, and that the officers of the proposed government will uniformly act for the happiness of the
people—for why should we run a risk which we may easily
avoid? The giving such extensive and undefined power is

a radical wrong that cannot be justified by any subsequent merit in the exercise; for in framing a new system, it is our duty rather to indulge a jealousy of the human character, than an expectation of unprecedented perfection. Let us, however, suppose what will be allowed to be at least possible, that the powers of this government should be abused, and the liberties of the people infringed; do any means of redress remain with the states or with the people at large, to oppose and counteract the influence and oppression of the general government? Secret combinations, partial insurrections, sudden tumults may arise; but these being easily defeated and subdued, will furnish a pretence for strengthening that power which they were intended to overthrow. A bill of rights, Mr. President, it has been said, would not only be unnecessary, but it would be dangerous, and for this special reason, that because it is not practicable to enumerate all the rights of the people, therefore it would be hazardous to secure such of the rights as we can enumerate! Truly, Sir, I will agree that a bill of rights may be a dangerous instrument, but it is to the views and projects of the aspiring ruler, and not the liberties of the citizen. Grant but this explicit criterion, and our governors will not venture to encroach; refuse it, and the people cannot venture to complain. From the formal language of magna charta we are next taught to consider a declaration of rights as superfluous; but, Sir, will the situation and conduct of Great Britian furnish a case parallel to that of America? It surely will not be contended that we are about to receive our liberties as a grant or concession from any power upon earth; so that if we learn anything from the English charter, it is this: that the people having negligently lost or submissively resigned their rights into the hands of the crown, they were glad to recover them upon any terms; their anxiety to secure the grant by the strongest evidence will be an argument to prove, at least, the expediency of the measure, and the result of the whole is a lesson instructing us to do by an easy precaution, what will hereafter be an arduous and perhaps insurmountable task. But even in Great Britain, whatever may be the courtesy of their expressions, the matter stands substantially on a different footing, for we know that the divine right of kings is there, as well as here, deemed an idle and chimerical tale. It is true, the preamble to the great charter declares the liberties enumerated in that instrument, to be the grant of the sovereign, but the hyperbolical language of the English law has likewise declared that "the king can do no wrong," and yet, from time to time, the people have discovered in themselves the natural source of power, and the monarchs have been made painfully responsible for their action. Will it still be said, that the state governments would be adequate to the task of correcting the usurpations of Congress? Let us not, however, give the weight of proof to the boldness of assertion; for, if the opposition is to succeed by force, we find both the purse and the sword are almost exclusively transferred to the general government; and if it is to succeed by legislative remonstrance, we shall find that expedient rendered nugatory by the law of Congress, which is to be the supreme law of the land. Thus, Mr. President, must the powers and sovereignty of the several states be eventually destroyed, and when, at last, it may be found expedient to abolish that connection which, we are told essentially exists between the federal and individual legislatures, the proposed constitution is amply provided with the means in that clause which assumes the authority to alter or prescribe the place and manner of elections. I feel, Mr. President, the magnitude of the subject in which I am engaged, and although I am exhausted with what I have already advanced, I am conscious that the investigation is infinitely far from being complete. Upon the whole, therefore, I wish it to be seriously considered, whether we have a right to leave the liberties of the people to such future constructions and expositions as may possibly be made upon this system; particularly when its advocates, even at this day, confess that it would be dangerous to omit anything in the enumeration of a bill of rights, and according to their principle, the reservation of the habeas corpus, and trial by jury in criminal cases, may hereafter be construed to be the only privileges reserved by the people. I am not anxious, Mr. President, about forms—it is the substance which I wish to obtain; and therefore I acknowledge, if our liberties are secured by the frame of government itself, the supplementary instrument of a declaration of rights may well be dispensed with. But, Sir, we find no security there, except in the two instances referred to, and it will not, I hope, any longer be alleged that no security is requisite, since those exceptions prove a contrary sentiment to have been entertained by the very framers of the proposed constitution. The question at present, Sir, is, however, of a preliminary kind—does the plan now in discussion propose a consolidation of the states? and will a consolidated government be most likely to promote the interests and happiness of America? If it is satisfactorily demonstrated, that in its principles or in its operation, the dissolution of the state sovereignties is not a necessary consequence, I shall then be willing to accompany the gentlemen on the other side in weighing more particularly its merits and demerits. But my judgment, according to the information I now possess, leads me to anticipate the annihilation of the several state governments—an event never expected by the people, and which would, I fervently believe, destroy the civil liberties of America.

Mr. Wilson.* I am willing, Mr. President, to agree with the honorable member who has just spoken, that if this system is not calculated to secure the liberties and happiness of the United States, it should not be adopted; but, on the contrary, if it provides an adequate security for the general liberties and happiness of the people, I presume it ought not to be rejected. Before I comment upon the principles which have brought us to this issue, I beg leave to make one general remark. Liberty and happiness have, Sir, a powerful enemy on each hand;—on the one hand there is tyranny, on the other there is licentiousness. To guard against the latter, it is necessary that adequate powers should be given to the government, and to protect us from the former, it is requisite that that those powers should be properly distributed. Under this consideration, let us now regard the pro-

*From the Pennsylvania Herald, Dec. 19th 1787.

posed system; and I freely confess that if its adoption will necessarily be followed by the annihilation of the state governments, the objection is of very great force, and ought to be seriously weighed. The inference, however, appears rather unnatural that a government should be expressly calculated to produce the destruction of other governments, upon which its own existence must entirely depend; for, Mr. President, it is capable of demonstration, that if the state governments fall, the general government must likewise be involved in one common ruin. Is it not evident, Sir, when we particularly examine the structure of the proposed system, that the operation of the federal legislature necessarily presupposes the existence of the legislatures of the several States? Can the Congress, the president, or even the judiciary department, survive the dissolution of those powers in the separate governments, from which they essentially derive their origin, and on which they must forever depend for their renovation? No, sir! For, we find that the House of Representatives is to be composed of persons returned by the suffrage of freemen who are qualified to vote for the members of the most numerous branch of the state legislature, which legislature must necessarily exist, or the only criterion for supplying the popular department of the federal government will be extinct. The senate, which is to be chosen by the several legislatures, cannot consequently be appointed unless those legislatures exist; which is likewise the case in respect to the president, as this office is to be filled by electors nominated by the respective state legislatures; and, lastly, the judges are to be commissioned by the president and senate, who cannot appoint, unless they are themselves first appointed, and that, it appears, must depend upon the existence of the state legislatures. Thus, Mr. President, by a clear deduction, it is evident that the existence and efficiency of the general government presupposes the existence and full operation of the separate governments. For you can never prove a person to have been chosen, till you have proved that he was the choice of persons qualified to vote; you cannot prove any man to be entitled to elect a member of the house of representatives, till you have proved that he is qualified to elect a member of the most numerous branch of the state legislature. But, Sir, it has been intimated that the design of the federal convention was to absorb the state governments. This would introduce a strange doctrine indeed, that one body should seek the destruction of another, upon which its own preservation depends, or that the creature should eat up and consume the creator. The truth is, Sir, that the framers of this system were particularly anxious, and their work demonstrates their anxiety, to preserve the state governments unimpaired—it was their favorite object; and, perhaps, however proper it might be in itself, it is more difficult to defend the plan on account of the excessive caution used in that respect than from any other objection that has been offered here or elsewhere. Hence, we have seen each state, without regard to their comparative importance, entitled to an equal representation in the senate, and a clause has been introduced which enables two-thirds of the state legislature at any time to propose and effectuate alterations in the general system. But, Mr. President, though in the very structure of the plan the concomitant duration of the state governments is always pre-supposed, yet their power is not the only one intended to be recognized and established. The power of the people, Sir, is the great foundation of the proposed system, a power totally unknown in the present confederation, but here it mediately pervades every department and is immediately exercised in the house of representatives. I trust it is unnecessary to dwell longer upon this subject; for, when gentlemen assert that it was the intention of the federal convention to destroy the sovereignty of the states, they must conceive themselves better qualified to judge of the intention of that body than its own members, of whom not one, I believe, entertained so improper an idea. Intended it, Sir! how was this information obtained? I trust we shall not admit these visionary interpretations, but wisely judge of the tree by its fruit. The only pretence of proof, indeed, has been taken from the work itself—from that section which empowers the Congress to alter the place and manner of election, under which, it is said, the national government may be carried on after the state governments are totally eradicated.

This, Mr. President, is not only a proper, but a necessary power, for every government should possess the means of self-preservation. We have seen that the States may alter or amend the proposed system, if they should find it incompatible with their interest and independency, and the same reason justifies and requires that Congress should have an ultimate control over those elections, upon which its purity and existence must depend. What would otherwise be the consequence? One or more States might refuse to make any regulations upon the subject, or, might make such regulations as would be highly inconvenient and absurd—if the election were appointed to be held at Pittsburgh, or, if a minority, tumultuously breaking up the legislatures, should defeat the disposition of the majority to appoint any place for that purpose, shall Congress have no authority to counteract such notorious evils, but continue in absolute dependence upon the will of a refractory State? I say not, Sir, that these are probable events; but as they are certainly possible, it was the duty of the late convention to provide against the mischief, and to secure to the general government a power, in the dernier resort, for the more perfect organization of its constituent parts. In short, Sir, this system would be nugatory without the provision so much deprecated, as the national government must be laid prostrate before any State in the union, whose measures might at any time be influenced by faction and caprice. These, therefore, are the reasons upon which it is founded, and in spite of every perversion, it will be found only to contain the natural maxims of self-preservation. I shall take a future opportunity to remark upon the other points of the speech delivered by the member from Cumberland, and upon the general principles of the proposed constitution. Thus I have thought it proper to remark, in this early stage of the debate, because I am sensible that the imputation of subverting the State governments, either as a principle or a consequence of the plan, must if well founded prove a very important objection.

Mr. Smilie. I am happy, Mr. President, to find the argument placed upon the proper ground, and that the honorable member from the city has so fully spoken on the question, whether this system proposes a consolidation or a confederation of the states, as that is, in my humble opinion, the source of the greatest objection, which can be made to its adoption. I agree likewise with him, Sir, that it is, or ought to be, the object of all governments, to fix upon the intermediate point between tyranny and licentiousness; and therefore, it will be one of the great objects of our enquiry, to ascertain how far the proposed system deviates from that point of political happiness. For my part, I will readily confess, that it appears to be well guarded against licentiousness, but I am apprehensive it has deviated a little on the left hand, and rather invites than guards against the approaches of tyranny. I think however, Mr. President, it has been clearly argued, that the proposed system does not directly abolish, the governments of the several States, because its organization, and, for some time, perhaps, its operations, naturally pre-suppose their existence. But, Sir, it is not said, nor is thought, that the words of this instrument expressly announce that the sovereignty of the several States, their independency, jurisdiction, and power, are at once absorbed and annihilated by the general government. To this position and to this alone, the arguments of the honorable gentlemen can effectually apply, and there they must undoubtedly hold as long as the forms of State Government remain, at least, till a change takes place in the federal constitution. It is, however, upon other principles that the final destruction of the individual governments is asserted to be a necessary consequence of their association under this general form,—for, Sir, it is the silent but certain operation of the powers, and not the cautious, but artful tenor of the expressions contained in this system, that can excite terror, or generate oppression. The flattery of language was indeed necessary to disguise the baneful purpose, but it is like the dazzling polish bestowed upon an instrument of death; and the visionary prospect of a magnificent, yet popular government, was the most specious mode of rendering the people accessory to the ruin of those systems which they have so recently and so ardently labored to establish. Hence, Sir, we may trace that passage which has been pronounced by the honorable delegate to the late convention with exultation and applause; but when it is declared that "We the people of the United States do ordain and establish this constitution," is not the very foundation a proof of a consolidated government, by the manifest subversion of the principle that constitutes a union of States, which are sovereign and independent, except in the specific objects of confederation? These words have a plain and positive meaning, which could not be misunderstood by those who employed them; and therefore, Sir, it is fair and reasonable to infer, that it was in contemplation of the framers of this system, to absorb and abolish the efficient sovereignty and independent powers of the several States, in order to invigorate and aggrandize the general government. The plan before us, then, explicitly proposes the formation of a new constitution upon the original authority of the people, and not an association of States upon the authority of their respective governments. On that ground, we perceive that it contains all the necessary parts of a complete system of government, the executive, legislative and judicial establishments; and when two separate governments are at the same time in operation, over the same people, it will be difficult indeed to provide for each the means of safety and defence against the other; but if those means are not provided, it will be easily foreseen, that the stronger must eventually subdue and annihilate the weaker institution. Let us then examine the force and influence of the new system, and enquire whether the small remnant of power left to the States can be adequate even to the trifling charge of its own preservation. Here, Sir, we find the right of making laws for every purpose is invested in the future governors of America, and in this is included the uncontrolled jurisdiction over the purses of the people. The power of raising money is indeed the soul, the vital prop of legislation, without which legislation itself cannot for a moment exist. It will, however, be remarked that the power of taxation, though extended to the general government, is not taken from the States individually. Yes, Sir!—but it will be remembered that the national government may take from the people just what they please, and if anything should afterwards remain, then indeed the exigencies of the State governments may be supplied from the scanty gleanings of the harvest. Permit me now, Sir, to call your attention to the powers enumerated in the 8th section of the first article, and particularly to that clause which authorizes the proposed Congress, "to lay and collect taxes, duties, imposts and excises, to pay the debts and provide for the common defence and general welfare of the United States." With such powers, Mr. President, what cannot the future governors accomplish? It will be said, perhaps, that the treasure, thus accumulated, is raised and appropriated for the general welfare and the common defence of the States; but may not this pretext be easily perverted to other purposes, since those very men who raise and appropriate the taxes, are the only judges of what shall be deemed the general welfare and common defence of the national government? If then, Mr. President, they have unlimited power to drain the wealth of the people in every channel of taxation, whether by imposts on our commercial intercourse with foreign nations, or by direct levies on the people, I repeat it, that this system must be too formidable for any single State, or even for a combination of the States, should an attempt be made to break and destroy the yoke of domination and tyranny which it will hereafter set up. If, indeed, the spirit of men, once inflamed with the knowledge of freedom, should occasionally blaze out in remonstrance, opposition and force, these symptoms would naturally excite the jealousy of their rulers, and tempt them to proceed in the career of usurpation, till the total destruction of every principle of liberty should furnish a fit security for the exercise of arbitrary power. The money which has been raised from the people, may then be effectually employed to keep them in a state of slavish subjection: the militia, regulated and commanded by the officers of the general government, will be warped from the patriotic nature of

their institution, and a standing army, that most prevailing
instrument of despotism, will be ever ready to enforce obedience to a government by which it is raised, supported and
enriched.   If, under such circumstances, the several States
should presume to assert their undelegated rights, I ask again
what balance remains with them to counteract the encroachments of so potent a superior?   To assemble a military force
would be impracticable; for the general government, foreseeing
the attempt would anticipate the means, by the exercise of its
indefinite control over the purses of the people; and, in order
to act upon the consciences as well as the persons of men, we
find it is expressly stipulated, that every officer of the State
government shall be sworn to support the constitution of the
United States.   Hence likewise, Sir, I conclude that in every
point of rivalship, in every contention for power on the one
hand and for freedom on the other, the event must be favorable to the views and pretensions of a government gifted with
so decisive a pre-eminence.   Let us, however, regard this
subject in another light.   What, Mr. President, will be the
feelings and ideas of the people, when by the operation of the
proposed system, they are exposed to such accumulated expense, for the maintenance of the general government?   Is
it not easy to foresee, that however the States may be disposed individually to preserve the parade of independence
and sovereignty, the people themselves will become indifferent, and at last, averse to the continuance of an expensive
form, from which they derive no advantage?   For, Sir, the
attachment of citizens to their government and its laws is
founded upon the benefits which they derive from them, and
it will last no longer than the duration of the power to confer those benefits.   When, therefore, the people of the respective States shall find their governments grown torpid, and
divested of the means to promote their welfare and interests,
they will not, Sir, vainly idolize a shadow, nor disburse their
hard earned wealth without the prospect of a compensation.
The constitution of the States having become weak and useless to every beneficial purpose, will be suffered to dwindle
and decay, and thus if the governors of the Union are not

too impatient for the accomplishment of unrivalled and absolute dominion, the destruction of State jurisdiction will be produced by its own insignificance. Having now, Mr. President, shown that eventually this system will establish a consolidated government, though the intention is not expressly avowed, I will take some notice of the honorable member's principle, culled from the mode of election which is here prescribed. Sir, we do not upon this occasion contend for forms, which it is certain may exist long after the substance has forever perished. It is well remembered that the Roman senate continued to meet in all its ceremonies, long after they had lost their power, and the liberty of Rome had been sacrificed to the most horrid tyranny. Such, Sir, must be the case with the State legislature, which will necessarily degenerate into a mere name, or at most settle in a formal board of electors, periodically assembled to exhibit the servile farce of filling up the Federal representation.

Mr. M'Kean. The first objection offered, Mr. President, to the adoption of the proposed system, arises from the omission of a bill of rights, and the gentlemen in the opposition have gone (contrary, I think, to their former wishes, which were to discuss the plan minutely, section after section,) from the immediate objects of the first article into an investigation of the whole system. However, as they have taken this wide and extensive path, I shall, though reluctantly, pursue them. It appears then, Sir, that there are but seven nations in the world which have incorporated a bill or declaration of rights into their system of government. The ancients were unacquainted with any instrument of that kind and till the recent establishment of the thirteen United States, the moderns, except Great Britain and Poland (if the *Pacta Conventa* of that kingdom may be considered), have not recognized its utility. Hence, Sir, if any argument is to be drawn from the example of other countries, we find that far the greatest number, and those most eminent for their power and wisdom, have not deemed a declaration of rights in any degree essential to the institution of government or the preservation of civil liberty. But, Sir, it has already been incontrovertibly shown that on the present occasion a bill of rights was totally unnecessary, and that it might be accompanied with some inconveniency and danger, if there was any defect in the attempt to enumerate the privileges of the people. This system proposes a union of thirteen sovereign and independent states, in order to give dignity and energy to the transaction of their common concerns; it would be idle therefore to countenance the idea that any other powers were delegated to the general government than those specified in the constitution itself, which, as I have before observed, amounts in fact to a bill of rights—a declaration of the people in what manner they choose to be governed. I am happy, Mr. President, to find that no objection has been taken to the forms and structure of the proposed system, to the two branches of legislation, the unity of the executive power, and the qualified negative upon laws which is vested in the president. Objections upon the subject, indeed, might have easily been answered, since it is evident without the distribution of powers here made, the legislature would naturally have absorbed the authority of every other department, but particularly of the executive. It has, I am persuaded, been satisfactorily proved by my honorable colleague, that the suggestion which represent this system as being expressly calculated to annihilate the soverignty and independence of the States, is groundless and delusive; for he made it evident the existence of the States is a thing without which the federal functions cannot be organized and supplied, and therefore, the dissolution of the individual and general government must be concurrent—if the state legislatures fail, the Congress of the United States must likewise be at an end, inasmuch as the annihilation of that power which is alone competent to elect, must be followed by the annihilation of the body which is the object of its election. But it is argued that the power of changing the time and place of elections, transfers to Congress an authority which ought exclusively to reside in the respective states, and which will eventually enable that body to act independent of the several governments. In this respect, Sir, it must be remembered that in the first instance the states are authorized to regulate the time, place and proceedings of elections, and while they act with propriety, there can be little reason to suppose Congress will officiously interfere. But if, as it has been suggested by the honorable member from the city, an inconvenient situation should be appointed for holding the election, or if the time and manner should be made inconsistent with the principles of a pure and constitutional election, can it be doubted that the federal government ought to be enabled to make the necessary reform in a business so essential to its own preservation and prosperity? If, for instance, the states should direct the suffrage of their citizens to be delivered *viva voce*, is it not necessary that the Congress should be authorized to change that mode, so injurious to the freedom of election, into the mode by ballot so happily calculated to preserve the suffrages of the citizens from bias and influence? This was one object, I am persuaded, which weighed with the late convenaion in framing this clause; and we farther collect their solicitude to prevent as much as possible, an undue influence of wealth and talents in the important choice of representatives, from the regulation which expressly declares that the day of election shall be the same throughout the United States. By this means it is evident that the influence which is naturally acquired by extraordinary talents, activity and wealth, will be restricted in its operation, and the great men of one district deprived of all opportunity to interfere in the elections of another. Reviewing then, Sir, the objections to the power given to the proposed government for superintending the time, place and manner of choosing its members, they seem to be the offspring of fancy, unsupported by real or probable argument, while the power itself is proved to be a wise and rational subject of delegation. It is next said, Mr. President, and it is reasoned upon as a fact, that the Congress will enjoy over the thirteen States an uncontrolled power of legislation in all cases whatsoever; and it is repeated, again and again, in one common phrase, that the future governors may do what they please with the purses of the people, for there is neither restriction nor reservation in the constitution which they will be appointed to administer. Sir, there is not a power given in the article before us that is not in its expression, clear, plain, and accurate, and in its nature proper and absolutely necessary to the great objects of the union. To support this assertion, permit me to recapitulate the contents of the article immediately before us. First, then, it is declared that "the Congress shall have power to lay and collect taxes, duties, imposts and excises, to pay the debts and provide for the common defence and general welfare of the United States." Thus, Sir, as it is not the object of this government merely to make laws for correcting wicked and unruly men; but to protect the citizens of an extensive empire from exterior force and injury, it was necessary that powers should be given adequate to the discharge of so important a duty. But the gentlemen exclaim that here lies the source of excessive taxation, and that the people will be plundered and oppressed. What is there, however, that should render it a more dangerous trust in the hands of the general than of a particular government? For, is it not as much in the power of the State legislatures at this day to do all this mischief, as it will be hereafter in the power of Congress? The truth is, Sir, that the great restraint upon excessive taxation arises from this consideration, that the same act by which a representative imposes a tax upon his constituents, extends to himself and all his connections, friends and acquaintance, so that he never will attempt to lay a greater burthen upon the people than he is convinced is necessary for the public service and easy to be borne. Besides this natural security, which applies equally to the individual and the general government of the States, the people will, from time to time, have it in their power to remove those persons who have promoted any measure that tends to injure and oppress them. In short, Sir, it seems that the honorable members are so afraid the Congress will do some mischief, that they are determined to deny them the power to do any good. But we must divest ourselves of this extravagant jealousy, and remember that it is necessary to repose some degree of confidence in the administration of a government, from which we expect the revival of commerce, the encouragement of arts, and the general happiness of the people. To whose judgment, indeed, could be so properly referred the determination of what is necessary to accomplish those important objects, as the judgment of a Congress elected, either directly or indirectly, by all the citizens of the United States? For if the people discharge their duty to themselves, the persons that compose that body will be the wisest and best men amongst us;—the wisest to discover the means of common defence and general welfare, and the best to carry those means into execution, without guile, injustice or oppression. But it is not remarkable, Mr. President, that the power of raising money which is thought dangerous in the proposed system, is, in fact, possessed by the present Congress, tho' a single house without checks, and without responsibility. Let us now proceed, Sir, to the succeeding detail of the powers of the proposed government. That Congress shall have the power to borrow money on the credit of the United States, is not objected to; nor are the powers to regulate trade, to establish a general rule of naturalization, and to enact uniform laws on the subject of bankruptcies. The power to coin money and regulate its value, must be esteemed highly advantageous to the States, for hitherto its fluctuation has been productive of great confusion and fraudulent finesse. But when this power has established a certain medium throughout the United States, we shall know the extent and operation of our contracts, in what manner we are to pay or to be paid; no illicit practice will expose property to a sudden and capricious depreciation, and the traveller will not be embarrassed with the different estimates of the same coin in the different districts through which he passes. The punishment of forgery, and the establishment of post-offices and post roads, are subjects confessedly proper to be comprehended within the federal jurisdiction; and the power of securing to authors and inventors the exclusive right to their writings and discoveries, could only with effect be exercised by the Congress. For, Sir, the laws of the respective States could only operate within their respective boundaries, and therefore, a work which had cost the author his whole life to complete, when published in one State, however it might there be secured, could easily be carried into another State, in which a republication would be accompanied with neither penalty nor punishment—a circumstance manifestly injurious to the author in particular, and to the cause of science in general. The next powers enumerated are those for constituting tribunals inferior to the Supreme Court, for defining and punishing piracies and offences against the law of nations, and for declaring war, to which no objection has been made, and, I am persuaded, none can be made with reason and propriety. But, Sir, the power to raise and support armies has occasioned infinite opposition, and has been clothed in all the terrors which a jealous and heated imagination could conceive. Is it not necessary, however, Mr. President, that some power should exist capable of collecting and directing the national strength against foreign force, Indian depredations, or domestic insurrection? If that power is necessary, where could it otherwise reside, what other body is competent to carry it effectually into operation! For my part, Sir, I can perceive that the power is absolutely necessary to support the sovereignty and preserve the peace of the union, and, therefore, I will not idly argue against its use, from the possible abuse—an argument which, as it applies to every other power as well as that under our immediate consideration, would supersede all the attributes of government, and defeat every purpose of society. Having thus,* Mr. President, recapitulated the powers delegated by the proposed constitution, it appears to me that they are necessary to the objects of the union, and therefore entitled to our confirmation. Nor am I, Sir, impressed with the opinion which has given so much pain to the worthy gentlemen in the opposition, that the powers are so vaguely expressed, so indefinite and extensive in their nature, that they may hereafter be stretched to every act of legislation, and construed to imply something beyond what is here specified. To evince that the powers enumerated in this article are all the powers given to the proposed Congress,

* From the Pennsylvania Herald, December 26, 1787.

we need only refer to the clause in the section which I have just discussed, that grants to that body a right of exclusive jurisdiction in any district of ten miles, which shall hereafter with the consent of the inhabitants become the seat of federal government. Does not this clearly prove, Sir, that their right of exclusive jurisdiction is restricted to that district, and with respect to the United States at large, their jurisdiction must be measured by the powers actually contained in the instrument before us? For no proposition can surely be more clear than this, that in every grant whatever is not mentioned must, from the nature of the thing, be considered as excluded. But, Sir, we are repeatedly told that however specious the enumeration may be, yet by the sixth article, a general authority is given to the acts of the proposed government, which renders its powers supreme and unlimited. Let us attend to this assertion and compare it with the article referred to. There it is said, Mr. President, that "this constitution and the laws of the United States which shall be made in pursuance thereof, and all treaties made, or which shall be made under the authority of the United States, shall be the supreme law of the land; and the judges in every state shall be bound thereby, anything in the constitution or laws of any state to the contrary notwithstanding." Now, Sir, what does this prove? The meaning which appears to be plain and well expressed, is simply this, that Congress have the power of making laws upon any subject over which the proposed plan gives them a jurisdiction, and that those laws thus made in pursuance of the constitution, shall be binding upon the States. With respect to treaties, I believe there is no nation in the world in which they are not considered as the supreme law of the land, and consequently, obligatory upon all judges and magistrates. They are a common concern, and obedience to them ought to be a common duty. As, indeed, the interest of all the States must be uniformly in the contemplation of Congress, why should not that body be authorized to legislate for all? I earnestly hope, Sir, that the statutes of the federal government will last till they become the common law of the land, as excellent and as much valued as that which we have hitherto fondly denominated the birth-right of an American. Such, Mr. President, are the objects to which the powers of the proposed government extend. Nor is it entirely left to this evident principle, that nothing more is given than is expressed, to circumscribe the federal authority. For, in the ninth section of the first article, we find the powers so qualified that not a doubt can remain. In the first clause of that section, there is a provision made for an event which must gratify the feelings of every friend to humanity. The abolition of slavery is put within the reach of the federal government. And when we consider the situation and circumstances of the southern states, every man of candor will find more reason to rejoice that the power should be given at all, than to regret that its exercise should be postponed for twenty years. Though Congress will have power to declare war, it is here stipulated that "the privilege of the writ of habeas corpus shall not be suspended, unless when in cases of rebellion or invasion, the public safety may require it;" and men will not be exposed to have their actions construed into crimes by subsequent and retrospective laws, for it is expressly declared that "no bill of attainder or *ex post facto* law shall be passed." Though Congress will have the power to lay duties and taxes, yet, "no capitation or other direct tax shall be laid, unless in proportion to the census or actual enumeration of the states, nor can any tax or duty be laid on articles of exportation." This wise regulation, Sir, has been successfully practiced by England and Ireland, while the commerce of Spain by a different conduct has been weakened and destroyed. The next restriction on the powers of Congress respects the appropriation of the public funds. "For no money shall be drawn from the treasury, but in consequence of appropriations made by law; and a regular statement and account of the receipts and expenditures of all public money shall be published from time to time." What greater security could be required or given upon this important subject? First, the money must be appropriated by law, then drawn for according to that appropriation, and lastly, from time to time, an account of the receipts and expenditures must be submitted to the people, who will thus be enabled to judge of the conduct of their rulers, and, if they see cause to object to the use or the excess of the sums raised, they may express their wishes or disapprobation to the legislature in petitions or remonstrances, which, if just and reasonable, cannot fail to be effectual. Thus, Sir, if any power is given, you cannot in my opinion give less— for less would be inadequate to the great objects of the government, and would neither enable Congress to pay the debts, or provide for the common defence of the Union. The last restriction mentioned prohibits Congress "from granting titles of nobility, and the officers of the proposed government from accepting, without the consent of Congress, any present, emolument, office or title of any kind whatever, from any king, prince, or foreign State." The section which follows these qualifications of the powers of Congress, prescribes some necessary limits to the powers of the several States; among which, I find with particular satisfaction, it is declared that "no State shall emit bills of credit, or make anything but gold and silver coin a tender in payment of debts." By this means, Sir, some security will be offered for the discharge of honest contracts, and an end put to the pernicious speculation upon paper emissions—a medium which has undermined the morals, and relaxed the industry of the people, and from which one-half of the controversies in our courts of justice has arisen. Upon the whole, Mr. President, I must repeat, that I perceive nothing in this system which can alarm or intimidate the sincerest friend to the liberties of his country. The powers given to the government are necessary to its existence, and to the political happiness of the people—while the objections which are offered, arise from an evident perversion of its principles, and the presumption of a meaning which neither the framers of the system, nor the system itself, ever meant. True it is, Sir, that a form more pleasing, and more beneficial to the State of Pennsylvania, might be devised; but let it be remembered that this truth likewise applies to each of our sister States, whose separate interests have been proportionally sacrificed to the general welfare. And after all Mr. President, though a good system is certainly a blessing, yet the wealth, the prosperity, and the freedom of the people, must ultimately depend upon the administration of the best government. The wisdom, probity and patriotism of the rulers, will ever be the criterion of public prosperity; and hence it is, that despotism, if well administered, is the best form of government invented by human ingenuity. We have seen nations prosperous and happy under monarchies, aristocracies, and governments compounded of these, and to what can we ascribe their felicity, but the wise and prudent conduct of those who exercise the powers of government? For experience will demonstrate that the most perfect system may be so perverted as to produce poverty and misery, and the most despotic so executed as to disseminate affluence and happiness among the people. But, Sir, perfection is not to be expected in the business of this life, and it is so ordered by the wisdom of Providence, that as our stay in this world seldom exceeds three score and ten years, we may not become too reluctant to part with its enjoyments, but by reflecting upon the imperfections of the present, learn in time to prepare for the perfections of a future state. Let us then, Mr. President, be content to accept this system as the best which can be obtained. Every man may think, and many a man has said, that he could make it better; but, Sir, as I observed on a former occasion with respect to religion, this is nothing more than opinion, and every person being attached to his own, it will be difficult indeed to make any number of men correspond in the same objects of amendment. The excellent letter which accompanies the proposed system, will furnish a useful lesson upon this occasion. It deserves to be read with attention, and considered with candor. Allow me therefore, Sir, to close the trouble which I have given you in discussing the merits of the plan, with a perusal of this letter—in the second paragraph of which the reason is assigned for deviating from a single body for the federal government.

IN CONVENTION.

SIR: We have now the honor to submit to the consideration of the United States in Congress assembled, that Constitution which has appeared to us the most adviseable.

The friends of our country have long seen and desired that the power of making war, peace and treaties, that of levying money and regulating commerce, and the correspondent executive and judicial authorities, should be fully and effectually vested in the general government of the Union; but the impropriety of delegating such extensive trust to one body of men is evident. Hence results the necessity of a different organization.

It is obviously impracticable in the federal government of these States, to secure all rights of independent sovereignty to each and yet provide for the interest and safety of all. Individuals entering into society must give up a share of liberty to preserve the rest. The magnitude of the sacrifice must depend as as well on situation and circumstances, as on the object to be obtained. It is at all times difficult to draw with precision the line between those rights which must be surrendered and those which may be reserved; and on the present occasion this difficulty was increased by a difference among the several States as to their situation, extent, habits and particular interests. In all our deliberations on this subject we kept steadily in our view that which appears to us the greatest interest of every true American, the consolidation of our Union, in which is involved our prosperity, felicity, safety, perhaps our national existence. This important consideration, seriously and deeply impressed on our minds, led each State in the convention to be less rigid on points of inferior magnitude than might have been otherwise expected, and thus the Constitution which we now present is the result of a spirit of amity, and of that mutual deference and concession which the peculiarity of our political situation rendered indispensable.

That it will meet the full and entire approbation of every State is not, perhaps, to be expected; but each will doubtless consider that, had her interests been alone consulted, the consequences might have been particularly disagreeable or injurious to others; that it is liable to as few exceptions as could reasonably have been expected, we hope and believe; that it may promote the lasting welfare of that country so dear to us all, and secure her freedom and happiness, is our most ardent wish. With great respect, we have the honor to be, Sir,   Your Excellency's most obedient humble servants.

GEORGE WASHINGTON, President.
By the unanimous Order of Convention.

I confess, Sir, that reading this letter and examining the work to which it refers, though there are some points that I might wish had been otherwise, yet upon the whole, I am struck with wonder and admiration that this Constitution should have been rendered so unexceptionable as it is, and that so many men, the representatives of States differing essentially in their views and interests, should have concurred in presenting it to their country.

The convention adjourned till Friday at half past nine o'clock, having first agreed to meet in the convention room to-morrow morning, in order to attend to the exercises performed at the German Lutheran church.

On Wednesday [28th]* Mr. M'Kean closed a long speech on the legislative article of the new constitution with this striking observation: "Though a good system of government is certainly a blessing, yet it is on the *administration* of the best system that the freedom, wealth and happiness of the people depend. DESPOTISM, if wisely administered, *is the best form of government invented by the ingenuity of man,* and we find that the people under absolute and limited monarchies, under aristocracies and mixed governments, are as contented and as prosperous as we are, owing, undoubtedly, to the wisdom and virtue of their rulers. In short, the best government may be so conducted as to produce misery and disgrace, and the worst so administered as to ensure dignity and happiness to a nation."

On the same day Mr. Smilie, in an elegant, ingenious and argumentative speech, traced some of the leading defects in the constitution, and endeavored to show that, if not in express terms, yet by inevitable consequence, it would terminate in a consolidation and not a confederation of the States. To this objection (which Mr. Wilson agreed if taken upon true grounds was a very serious and important one), the argument respecting the necessary relation between the State legislatures and the federal branches of government was repeated, the latter of which could not exist, it was said, if the former were annihilated. "But (added Mr. Smilie) let us review the history of Rome and we shall find, after the most absolute and horrid tyranny was established on the imperial throne, the ancient forms of the commonwealth were preserved; its senate still met and were flattered with a show of authority, but we know the power and dignity of that once illustrious body were dwindled to a name. So here, Mr. President, the shadow of State government may long be retained when the substance is totally lost and forgotten."

* From the Pennsylvania Packet, December 3d, 1787.

"Liberty and happiness (says Mr. Wilson) have a powerful enemy on each hand; on the one hand tyranny, on the other licentiousness. To guard against the latter, it is necessary to give the proper powers to government; and to guard against the former, it is necessary that those powers should be properly distributed."

"I agree (replies Mr. Smilie) that it is, or ought to be, the object of all governments to fix upon the intermediate point between tyranny and licentiousness; and I confess that the plan before us is perfectly armed to repel the latter; but I believe it has deviated too much on the left hand, and rather invites than guards against the approaches of tyranny."

Thursday, November 29.

The members of the convention being assembled proceeded agreeably to their resolution of yesterday to the church in Race street, where they were entertained with the exercises of the young gentlemen belonging to the German Lutheran Academy.

Friday, November 30.

The Convention* met pursuant to adjournment.

Mr. Whitehill. I confess, Mr. President, that after the full exercise of his eloquence and ingenuity, the honorable delegate to the late convention† has not removed those objections which I formerly submitted to your consideration, in hopes of striking, indeed, from his superior talents and information, a ray of wisdom to illuminate the darkness of our doubts, and to guide us in the pursuit of political truth and happiness. If the learned gentleman, however, with all his opportunities of investigating this particular system, and with all his general knowledge in the science of government, has not been able to convert or convince us, far be it from me to impute this failure to the defects of his elocution, or the languor of his disposition. It is no impeachment of those abilities which have been eminently distinguished in the abstruse disquisitions of law, that they should fail in the insidious task of supporting, on popular principles, a government which origi-

* From the Pennsylvania Herald, December 29, 1787.
† Mr. Wilson.

nates in mystery, and must terminate in despotism. Neither can the want of success, Sir, be ascribed to the want of zeal; for we have heard with our ears, and our eyes have seen, the indefatigable industry of the worthy member in advocating the cause which he has undertaken. But, Mr. President, the defect is in the system itself; there lies the evil which no argument can palliate, no sophistry can disguise. Permit me, therefore, Sir, again to call your attention to the principles which it contains, and for a moment to examine the ground upon which those principles are defended. I have said, and with increasing confidence I repeat, that the proposed constitution must eventually annihilate the independent sovereignty of the several states. In answer to this, the forms of election for supplying the offices of the federal head have been recapitulated; it has been thence inferred that the connection between the individual and the general governments is of so indissoluble a nature, that they must necessarily stand or fall together, and, therefore, it has been finally declared to be impossible, that the framers of this constitution could have a premeditated design to sow, in the body of their work, the seeds of its own destruction. But, Sir, I think it may be clearly proved that this system contains the seeds of self-preservation independent of all the forms referred to — seeds which will vegetate and strengthen in proportion to the decay of state authority, and which will ultimately spring up and overshadow the thirteen commonwealths of America with a deadly shade. The honorable member from the city has, indeed, observed that every government should possess the means of its own preservation; and this constitution is possibly the result of that proposition. For, Sir, the first article comprises the grants of powers so superlative in their nature, and so unlimited in their extent, that without the aid of any other branch of the system, a foundation rests upon this article alone, for the extension of the federal jurisdiction to the most extravagant degree of arbitrary sway. It will avail little to detect and deplore the encroachments of a government clothed in the plenitude of these powers; it will afford no consolation to reflect that we are not enslaved by the positive dereliction of our rights; but it will be well to remember at this day, Sir, that, in effect, we rob the people of their liberties, when we establish a power, whose usurpations they will not be able to counteract or restrict. It is not alone, however, the operative force of the powers expressly given to Congress that will accomplish their independence of the States, but we find an efficient auxiliary in the clause that authorizes that body "to make all laws which shall be necessary and proper for carrying into execution the foregoing powers and all other powers vested by this constitution in this government of the United States or in any department or office thereof." Hence, Sir, if it should happen, as the honorable members from the city have presumed, that by the neglect or delinquency of the States, no place and manner, or an improper place and manner for conducting the elections should be appointed, will it not be said that the general government ought not for this reason to be destroyed? and will it not therefore be necessary for carrying the powers of this constitution into execution, that the Congress should provide for its elections in such manner as will prevent the federal business from being frustrated by the listless or refractory disposition of the States individually? This event is in a great measure provided for, indeed, by the plan itself; for "the Congress may (constitutionally) at any time by law make or alter such regulations (that is the times, places and manner of holding elections prescribed in each State by the legislature thereof) except as to the places of choosing senators." If the power here given was necessary to the preservation of the proposed government, as the honorable members have contended, does it not, at the same time, furnish the means to act independent of the connection which has been so often represented as the great security for the continuance of the State sovereignties? Under the sanction of this clause, the senators may hold their seats as long as they live, and there is no authority to dispossess them. The duration of the house of representatives may likewise be protracted to any period, since the time and place of election will always be adapted to the objects of the Congress or its leading demagogues; and as that body will ultimately declare what shall constitute the qualifications of its members, all the boasted advantages of representation must terminate in idle form and expensive parade. If the voice of complaint should not then be silenced by the dread of punishment, easy it is, nevertheless, to anticipate the fate of petitions or remonstrances presented by the trembling hand of the oppressed to the irritated and ambitious oppressor. Solicitation will be answered by those statutes which are to be the supreme law of the land, and reproach will be overcome by the frown of insolent authority. This, Mr. President, is but a slight view of the calamities that will be produced by the exercise of those powers which the honorable members from the city have endeavored to persuade us it is necessary to grant to the new government in order to secure its own preservation and to accomplish the objects of the Union. But in considering, Sir, what was necessary to the safety and energy of the government, some attention ought surely to have been paid to the safety and freedom of the people. No satisfactory reason has yet been offered for the omission of a bill of rights; but on the contrary, the honorable members are defeated in the only pretext which they have been able to assign, that everything which is not given is excepted, for we have shown that there are two articles expressly reserved, the writ of habeas corpus and the trial by jury in criminal cases, and we have called upon them in vain to reconcile this reservation with the tenor of their favorite proposition. For if there was danger in the attempt to enumerate the liberties of the people, lest it should prove imperfect and destructive, how happens it that in the instances I have mentioned, that danger has been incurred? Have the people no other rights worth their attention, or is it to be inferred, agreeably to the maxim of our opponents, that every other right is abandoned? Surely, Sir, our language was competent to declare the sentiments of the people and to establish a bar against the intrusion of the general government in other respects as well as these; and when we find some privileges stipulated, the argument of danger is effectually destroyed; and the argument of difficulty which has been drawn from the attempt to enumerate every right, cannot now be urged against the enumeration of more rights than this instrument contains. In short, Mr. President, it is our duty to take care that the foundation of this system is so laid that the superstructure, which is to be reared by other hands, may not cast a gloom upon the temple of freedom, the recent purchase of our toil and treasure. When, therefore, I consider it as the means of annihilating the constitutions of the several States, and consequently the liberties of the people, I should be wanting to my constituents, to myself and to posterity, did I not exert every talent with which heaven has endowed me to counteract the measures that have been taken for its adoption. That it was the design of the late federal convention to absorb and abolish the individual sovereignty of the States, I seek no other evidence but this system; for as the honorable delegate to that body has recommended, I am also satisfied to judge of the tree by its fruit. When, therefore, I behold it thus systematically constructed for the accomplishment of that object, when I recollect the talents of those who framed it, I cannot hesitate to impute to them an intention corresponding with the principles and operation of their own work. Finally, Sir, that the dissolution of our State constitutions will produce the ruin of civil liberty is a proposition easy to be maintained, and which I am persuaded in the course of these debates will be incontrovertibly established in the mind of every member whose judgment is open to conviction, and whose vote has not been conclusively pledged for the ratification of this constitution before its merits were discussed.

Mr. Wilson. It is objected* that the number of members in the House of Representatives is too small. This is a subject something embarrassing, and the convention who framed the article felt the embarrassment. Take either side of the question, and you are necessarily led into difficulties. A large representation, Sir, draws along with it a great expense. We all know that expense is offered as an objection to this

* From Lloyd's Debates.

system of government, and certainly had the representation been greater, the clamor would have been on that side, and perhaps with some degree of justice. But the expense is not the sole objection; it is the opinion of some writers, that a deliberative body ought not to consist of more than one hundred members. I think, however, that there might be safety and propriety in going beyond that number; but certainly there is some number so large, that it would be improper to increase them beyond it. The British House of Commons consists of upwards of five hundred. The senate of Rome consisted, it is said, at some times of one thousand members. This last number is certainly too great.

The convention endeavored to steer a middle course, and when we consider the scale on which they formed their calculation, there are strong reasons why the representation should not have been larger. On the ratio that they have fixed, of one for every thirty thousand, and according to the generally received opinion of the increase of population throughout the United States, the present number of their inhabitants will be doubled in twenty-five years, and according to that progressive proportion, and the ratio of one member for thirty thousand inhabitants, the House of Representatives will, within a single century, consist of more than six hundred members. Permit me to add a further observation on the numbers—that a large number is not so necessary in this case as in the cases of state legislatures. In them there ought to be a representation sufficient to declare the situation of every county, town and district, and if of every individual, so much the better, because their legislative powers extend to the particular interest and convenience of each; but in the general government its objects are enumerated, and are not confined in their causes or operations to a county, or even to a single state. No one power is of such a nature as to require the minute knowledge of situations and circumstances necessary in state governments possessed of general legislative authority. These were the reasons, Sir, that I believe had influence on the convention to agree to the number of thirty thousand; and when the inconveniences and conveniences on both sides are compared, it would be difficult to say what would be a number more unexceptionable.

Friday, November 30th.

Mr. Hartley.* It has been uniformly admitted, Sir, by every man who has written or spoken upon the subject, that the existing confederation of the States is inadequate to the duties of a general government. The lives, the liberties and the property of the citizens are no longer protected and secured, so that necessity compels us to seek beneath another system, some safety for our most invaluable rights and possessions. It is then the opinion of many wise and good men, that the constitution presented by the late federal convention, will in a great measure afford the relief which is required by the wants and weakness of our present situation, but, on the other hand, it has been represented as an instrument to undermine the sovereignty of the States and destroy the liberties of the people. It is the peculiar duty of this convention to investigate the truth of those opinions, and to adopt or reject the proposed constitution, according to the result of that investigation. For my part I freely acknowledge, Mr. President, that impressed with a strong sense of the public calamities, I regard the system before us as the only prospect which promises to relieve the distresses of the people and to advance the national honor and interests of America. I shall therefore offer such arguments in opposition to the objections raised by the honorable delegates from Cumberland and Fayette, as have served to establish my judgment, and will, I hope, communicate some information to the judgment of the worthy members who shall favor me with a candid attention. The first objection is, that the proposed system is not coupled with a bill of rights, and therefore, it is said, there is no security for the liberties of the people. This objection, Sir, has been ably refuted by the honorable members from the city, and will admit of little more animadversion than has already been bestowed upon it, in the course of their arguments. It is agreed, however, that the situation of a British subject, and that of an American citizen in the year 1776, were essentially different; but it does not appear to be accurately under-

---

* From the Pennsylvania Herald, January 2, 1788.

stood in what manner the people of England became enslaved before the reign of King John. Previously to the Norman conquest, that nation certainly enjoyed the greatest portion of civil liberty then known in the world. But when William, accompanied by a train of courtiers and dependents, seized upon the crown, the liberties of the vanquished were totally disregarded and forgotten, while titles, honors and estates, were distributed with a liberal hand among his needy and avaricious followers. The lives and fortunes of the ancient inhabitants became thus subject to the will of the usurper, and no stipulations were made to protect and secure them from the most wanton violations. Hence, Sir, arose the successful struggles in the reign of John, and to this source may be traced the subsequent exertions of the people for the recovery of their liberties, when Charles endeavored totally to destroy, and the Prince of Orange at the celebrated era of British revolution, was invited to support them, upon the principles declared in the bill of rights. Some authors, indeed, have argued that the liberties of the people were derived from the prince, but how they came into his hands is a mystery which has not been disclosed. Even on that principle, however, it has occasionally been found necessary to make laws for the security of the subject—a necessity that has produced the writ of habeas corpus, which affords an easy and immediate redress for the unjust imprisonment of the person, and the trial by jury, which is the fundamental security for every enjoyment that is valuable in the contemplation of a freeman. These advantages have not been obtained by the influence of a bill of rights, which after all we find is an instrument that derives its validity only from the sanction and ratification of the prince. How different then is our situation from the circumstances of the British nation?

As soon as the independence of America was declared, in the year 1776, from that instant all our natural rights were restored to us, and we were at liberty to adopt any form of government to which our views or our interest might incline us. This truth, expressly recognized by the act declaring our independence, naturally produced another maxim, that whatever portion of those natural rights we did not transfer to the government, was still reserved and retained by the people; for, if no power was delegated to the government, no right was resigned by the people; and if a part only of our natural rights was delegated, is it not absurd to assert that we have relinquished the whole? Where then is the necessity of a formal declaration, that those rights are still retained, of the resignation of which no evidence can possibly be produced? Some articles, indeed from their pre-eminence in the scale of political security, deserve to be particularly specified, and these have not been omitted in the system before us.

The definition of treason, the writ of habeas corpus, and the trial by jury in criminal cases, are here expressly provided for; and in going thus far, solid foundation has been laid.

The ingenuity of the gentlemen who are inimical to the proposed constitution may serve to detect an error, but can it furnish a remedy? They have told us that a bill of rights ought to have been annexed; but, while some are for this point, and others for that, is it not evidently impracticable to frame an instrument which will be satisfactory to the wishes of every man who thinks himself competent to propose and obviate objections? Sir, it is enough for me that the great cardinal points of a free government are here secured without the useless enumeration of privileges, under the popular appellation of a bill of rights. The second objection which I have been able to collect from the arguments of the honorable members in opposition is this, that annual elections are not recognized and established by this constitution. I confess, Mr. President, the business of elections is a very important object in the institution of a free government; but I am of opinion, that their frequency must always depend upon the circumstances of the country. In a small territory, an annual election is proper and convenient; but in a jurisdiction extending 1,500 miles, through various climates, even if practicable, it would be an idle and burthensome arrangement. If, for instance, a delegate to the Congress were obliged to travel 700 or 800 miles to Georgia and Carolina, he could scarcely have entered upon the duties of his appointment, before the year would be past, and his authority annulled. Let us look at the nations in Europe, and, by way of illustration, let us suppose particularly that it was necessary in Denmark to meet in Copenhagen, the seat of government, from districts at the distance of seven hundred miles, would it not be proper to extend the period of service in proportion to the time required for collecting the scattered members of the body politic? In England, indeed, a compact and cultivated country, through which the communication is never interrupted, an annual election might be productive of great advantages, and could be attended with few inconveniences; but, as I have already represented, the case must here be essentially different. If, then, this objection is answered, so likewise must be the objection which has been next offered, that the appropriation of public moneys for the maintenance of a military force, may be for a period of ten years, whereas in England it is only for one; since the same reasons which made it necessary to deviate from annual elections, must render it necessary to extend those appropriations.

The power granted to levy taxes is another subject for opposition; and at first view, indeed, it may naturally excite some astonishment. But, Mr. President, it is necessary that those who are authorized to contract debts upon the public faith should likewise be invested with the means for discharging those debts. We have fatally experienced that recommendations are incompetent to that object, for what part of our foreign obligations have they hitherto been able to discharge? Let us, however, suppose that by the operation of federal recommendation, it is possible to accomplish the payment of our existing debts; where is the faith so credulous that will advance us another shilling upon the same security? But on the other hand, establish a power which can discharge its engagement, and you insure the confidence and friendship of the world. The power of taxation is then a great and important trust; but we lodge it with our own representatives, and as long as we continue virtuous we shall be safe, for they will not dare to abuse it. We now come, Sir, to the objection which seems to spread the greatest alarm, and in support of which much labor and ingenuity have been displayed. That the rights now possessed by the States will in some degree be abridged by the adoption of the proposed system, has never been denied; but it is only in that degree which is necessary and proper to promote the great purposes of the Union. A portion of our natural rights are given up in order to constitute society; and as it is here, a portion of the rights belonging to the States individually is resigned in order to constitute an efficient confederation. But, Mr. President, I do not know any instance in ancient history exactly similar to the situation of this country. The allusion which was made by the honorable member from Fayette to the Roman annals, is incapable of a just application to the subject in discussion; for the senate at the period to which he has referred was not created by election, but appointed by the mandate of the prince. The power of life and death was exclusively possessed by the Emperor, and the senate had no authority but what he pleased to bestow. In modern history there is indeed one event which seems to be in point. When the Union was about to be formed between Scotland and England in the reign of Queen Anne, wise men of all descriptions opposed the transaction, and particularly it was the subject of clamor among the clergy of every denomination. Lord Peterborough compared it to Nebuchadnezzar's image of iron and clay; and then, as it is now, the annihilation of the inferior power was warmly predicted by the wise men of the north. But, Sir, those fears and prognostications have been dissipated and disappointed by the event, and every liberal Scotchman will acknowledge he has gained by the bargain. Let it now be remarked that though Scotland sends only fifty-five members to the British Parliament, yet its judiciary and religious establishments being secured to them by the union, it has never been alleged that the superintending power has in any degree intruded upon those rights, or infringed the general tenor of the compact. Here then is an instance of a kingdom preserved even where the law is made and proceeds from a different and distant country. With respect to the German confederation, if anything can thence be drawn, it is an inference contrary to the doctrine contended on the part of the opposition. There, Sir, a number of deputies meet in general diet and make certain laws which are to prevade the Germanic body. But has this general head subverted the independence and liberties of its constituent members? No:

for, on the reverse, we find the House of Austria, a single branch, has become superior to the whole, except the King of Prussia, who is likewise formidable, but it is in his power and influence over the general system. Upon the whole, Mr. President, I sincerely think that the opinions of the worthy gentlemen are mistaken, and that their fears are vain and extravagant; for it is necessary that something should be done, and this plan, waiving any compliment to its excellence, is at least an eligible one.

Doctor Rush.* I believe, Mr. President, that of all the treaties which have ever been made, William Penn's was the only one, which was contracted without parchment; and I believe, likewise, it is the only one that has ever been faithfully adhered to. As it has happened with treaties, so, Sir, has it happened with bills of rights, for never yet has one been made which has not, at some period or other, been broken. The celebrated magna charta of England was broken over and over again, and these infractions gave birth to the petition of rights. If, indeed, the government of that country has not been violated for the last hundred years, as some writers have said, it is not owing to charters or declarations of rights, but to the balance which has been introduced and established in the legislative body. The constitution of Pennsylvania, Mr. President, is guarded by an oath, which every man employed in the administration of the public business is compelled to take; and yet, Sir, examine the proceedings of the council of censors, and you will find innumerable instances of the violation of that constitution, committed equally by its friends and enemies. In truth, then, there is no security but in a pure and adequate representation; the checks and all the other desiderata of government are nothing but political error without it, and with it, liberty can never be endangered. While the honorable convention, who framed this system, were employed in their work, there are many gentlemen who can bear testimony that my only anxiety was upon the subject of representation; and when I beheld a legislature constituted of three branches, and in so

* From the Pennsylvania Herald, January 5, 1788.

excellent a manner, either directly or indirectly, elected by the people, and amenable to them, I confess, Sir, that here I cheerfully reposed all my hopes and confidence of safety. Civilians having taught us, Mr. President, that occupancy was the origin of property, I think it may likewise be considered as the origin of liberty; and as we enjoy all our natural rights from a pre-occupancy, antecedent to the social state, in entering into that state, whence shall they be said to be derived? Would it not be absurd to frame a formal declaration that our natural rights are acquired from ourselves? and would it not be a more ridiculous solecism to say, that they are the gift of those rulers whom we have created, and who are invested by us with every power they possess? Sir, I consider it as an honor to the late convention, that this system has not been disgraced with a bill of rights; though I mean not to blame or reflect upon those States which have encumbered their constitutions with that idle and superfluous instrument. One would imagine, however, from the arguments of the opposition, that this government was immediately to be administered by foreigners—strangers to our habits and opinions, and unconnected with our interests and prosperity. These apprehensions, Sir, might have been excused while we were contending with Great Britain; but at this time they are applicable to all governments, as well as that under consideration; and the arguments of the honorable member are, indeed, better calculated for an Indian council-fire, than the meridian of this refined and enlightened convention.

Mr. Yeates. The objections hitherto offered to this system, Mr. President, may, I think, be reduced to these general heads: first, that there is no bill of rights, and secondly, that the effect of the proposed government will be a consolidation and not a confederation of the States. Upon the first head it appears to me that great misapprehension has arisen, from considering the situation of Great Britain to be parallel to the situation of this country; whereas the difference is so essential, that a bill of rights which was there both useful and necessary, becomes here at once useless and unnecessary. In England a power (by what means it signifies little) was established paramount to that of the people, and the only way whic..

they had to secure the remnant of their liberties, was, on every opportunity, to stipulate with that power for the uninterrupted enjoyment of certain enumerated privileges. But our case is widely different, and we find that upon the opinion of this difference, seven of the thirteen United States have not added a bill of rights to their respective constitutions. Nothing, indeed, seems more clear to my judgment than this, that in our circumstances, every power which is not expressly given is in fact reserved. But it is asked, as some rights are here expressly provided for, why should not more? In truth, however, the writ of habeas corpus, and the trial by jury in criminal cases, cannot be considered as a bill of rights, but merely as a reservation on the part of the people, and a restriction on the part of their rulers. And I agree with those gentlemen who conceive that a bill of rights, according to the ideas of the opposition, would be accompanied with considerable difficulty and danger; for it might be argued at a future day by the persons then in power, You undertook to enumerate the rights which you meant to reserve; the pretension which you now make is not comprised in that enumeration, and consequently our jurisdiction is not circumscribed. The second general head respects the consolidation of the States; but I think, Sir, candor will forbid us to impute that design to the late convention, when we review the principles and texture of their work. Does it not appear that the organization of the new government must originate with the States? Is not the whole system of federal representation dependent upon the individual governments? For we find that those persons who are qualified to vote for the most numerous branch of the State legislatures, are alone qualified to vote for delegates to the house of representatives: the senators are to be chosen immediately by the legislatures of the States; and those legislatures likewise are to prescribe the manner for the appointment of electors who are to elect the President. Thus, Sir, is the connection between the States in their separate and aggregate capacity preserved, and the existence of the Federal government made necessarily dependant upon the existence and actual operation of its constituent members. Lest anything, indeed, should be wanting to assure us of the intention of the framers of this constitution to preserve the individual sovereignty and independence of the States inviolate, we find it expressly declared by the 4th section of the 4th article, that "the United States shall guarantee to every State in this Union, a republican form of government"—a constitutional security far superior to the fancied advantages of a bill of rights. It is urged, however, that all the security derived from this clause, and from the forms of representation, may be defeated by the exercise of the power which is vested in Congress to change the times, places, and manner of election. Sir, let it be remembered that this power can only operate in a case of necessity, after the factious or listless disposition of a particular State has rendered an interference essential to the salvation of the general government. But is it fair, is it liberal, that every presumption should impute to Congress an abuse of the powers with which they are entrusted? We might surely, on the ground of such extravagent apprehensions, proscribe the use of fire and water—for fire may burn, and water may drown us. Is it, indeed, possible to define any power so accurately, that it shall reach the particular object for which it was given, and yet not be liable to perversion and abuse? If it is too much restrained it will certainly be incompetent; and I am free to declare the opinion, that it is much better under a limited government, to trust something to the discretion of the rulers, than to attempt so precise a definition of power as must defeat every salutary object which it is intended to produce. In what instance does it appear, after all, that the jurisdiction of the States will be abridged, except, indeed, in those respects from which the universal sense of mankind must forever exclude them? The general government will, and incontrovertibly should, be possessed of the power to superintend the general objects and interests of the country; the particular objects and interests of the States will still be subject to the power of the particular governments—and is this not a natural and necessary distribution of authority? What single State, for instance, is equal to the regulation of commerce? Have we not seen a sister republic, by an obstinate refusal of the 5 per cent impost, involve the whole union in difficulties and disgrace? To that refusal, indeed, may be ascribed our present embarrassments, and the continuance of a heavy debt, which must, otherwise, have been long since discharged. But what are the particular restrictions which this system imposes upon the authority of the States? They are contained, Sir, in the tenth section of the first article; and I appeal, cheerfully, to the candor of every man who hears me, whether they are not such as ought, for the sake of public honor and private honesty, to be imposed. "No State shall enter into any treaty, alliance, or confederation; grant letters of marque and reprisal; coin money; emit bills of credit; make anything but gold and silver coin a tender in payment of debts; pass any bill of attainder, ex post facto law, or law impairing the obligation of contracts, or grant any title of nobility." These, Sir, and some restraints in commercial affairs, are the restrictions on the several States; we have little information from the fatal experience of past years, if we cannot perceive their propriety, and rejoice in the anticipation of the beneficial consequences they must produce. What, Mr. President, has hitherto been the effect of tender laws, paper money, and the iniquitous speculations these excrescences of a weak government naturally engendered? I wish not, Sir, to afflict you with a painful recollection upon this subject; but it will be well to remember how much we have suffered, that we may properly estimate the hand which rescues us from poverty and disgrace. If virtue is the foundation of a republican government, has it not been fatally sapped by these means? The morals of the people have been almost sunk into depravity; and the government of laws has been almost superseded by a licentious anarchy. The day of reformation and happiness, however, rapidly approaches, and this system will be, at length, the glorious instrument of our political salvation. For, under the authority here given, our commerce will be rendered respectable among the nations of the world; the product of the impost will ease the weight of internal taxation; the land tax will be diminished; and the luxuries and conveniences of life bear a proportionate share in the public expenses. In short, Sir, I perceive nothing in this system to terrify, but everything to flatter the hopes of a friend to his country, and I sincerely hope it will be adopted.

On Friday 30th* the convention proceeded in their deliberations upon the first article of the proposed constitution, and Mr. Wynkoop moved, after some debate, that the second article should be taken into consideration. On this Mr. Smilie observed, that he hoped so precipitate a measure would not be adopted, for, in his opinion, they had not yet got over the first six words of the preamble. He then reduced the present subject of discussion to two general heads, viz. 1st. The necessity of a declaration of rights; and 2d. Whether the plan was a consolidation, or a confederation of the United States? After these points are ascertained, he observed, it would be proper to consider each section of the first article particularly, in order to state the objections to the powers delegated to the Congress for imposing internal taxation, raising a poll tax, and maintaining a standing army in time of peace. The convention adjourned at two o'clock.

Mr. M'Kean said on Friday, in the convention, that he wished the opponents of the proposed constitution would not merely find out its defects, but state the remedies. Since they consider a bill of rights so essential, why do they not show us one, that we may judge of its necessity? To this Mr. Smilie answered, he was happy to hear the idea suggested, for he had understood that the convention did not mean to admit either additions or amendments; but let them agree to do this, and he pledged himself to produce such a declaration of rights, and such other amendments, as would conciliate the opponents of the plan in its present state, who wished not to reject it altogether, but to make it as secure as possible, in favor of the civil liberties of the people.

Saturday, December 1st.

Doctor Rush† (on the subject of the new government tending to abridge the States of their respective sovereignty) observed in the convention, that this passion for separate sover-

* From the Pennsylvania Packet, Dec. 3, 1787.
† From the Pennsylvania Packet, Dec. 5th, 1787.

eignty had destroyed the Grecian Union.   This plurality of
sovereignty is in politics what plurality of gods is in religion
—it is the idolatry, the heathenism of government.   In
marking the advantages which are secured to us by the new
government, the Doctor principally enforced the following:
The citizens under it will have an immediate voice in delega-
tions to Congress: that an unoffending posterity will not (as
is now the case on commission of treason) be punished for the
sins of offending ancestors; that an eternal veto will be
stamped on paper emissions; that religious tests would be
abolished; that Commerce will hold up her declining head,
under the influence of general, vigorous, uniform regulations;
that a system of infinite mischief to this State would be counteracted; that the adopted certificates would devolve back to
the continent.   The Doctor concluded an animated speech by
holding out the new constitution as pregnant with an increase
of freedom, knowledge and religion.

On Saturday [Dec. 1st]* Mr. Findley delivered an eloquent
and powerful speech, to prove that the proposed plan of government amounted to a consolidation, and not a confederation
of the states.   Mr. Wilson had before admitted that if this was
a just objection, it would be strongly against the system; and
it seems from the subsequent silence of all its advocates upon
that subject (except Doctor Rush, who on Monday insinuated
that he saw and rejoiced at the eventual annihilation of the
state sovereignties) Mr. Findley has established his position.
Previous to an investigation of the plan, that gentleman
animadverted upon the argument of necessity, which had
been so much insisted upon, and showed that we were in an
eligible situation to attempt the improvement of the Federal
Government, but not so desperately circumstanced as to be
obliged to adopt any system, however destructive to the liberties of the people, and the sovereign rights of the states.   He
then argued that the proposed constitution established a
general government and destroyed the individual governments, from the following evidence taken from the system it-

* From the Pennsylvania Packet, Dec. 6th.

self: 1st. In the preamble, it is said, *We the People*, and not *We the States*, which therefore is a compact between individuals entering into society, and not between separate states enjoying independent power, and delegating a portion of that power for their common benefit. 2d. That in the legislature each member has a vote, whereas in a confederation, as we have hitherto practised it, and from the very nature of the thing, a state can only have one voice, and therefore all the delegates of any state can only give one vote. 3d. The powers given to the Federal body for imposing internal taxation will necessarily destroy the state sovereignties, for there cannot exist two independent sovereign taxing powers in the same community, and the strongest will of course annihilate the weaker. 4th. The power given to regulate and judge of elections is a proof of a consolidation, for there cannot be two powers employed at the same time in regulating the same elections, and if they were a confederated body, the individual states would judge of the elections, and the general Congress would judge of the credentials which proved the election of its members. 5th. The judiciary power, which is co-extensive with the legislative, is another evidence of a consolidation. 6th. The manner in which the wages of the members is paid, makes another proof; and lastly, The oath of allegiance directed to be taken establishes it incontrovertibly; for would it not be absurd, that the members of the legislative and executive branches of a sovereign state should take a test of allegiance to another sovereign or independent body?

Mr. Wilson.* The secret is now disclosed, and it is discovered to be a dread that the boasted state sovereignties will, under this system, be disrobed of part of their power. Before I go into the examination of this point, let me ask one important question: Upon what principle is it contended that the sovereign power resides in the state governments? The honorable gentleman has said truly, that there can be no subordinate sovereignty. Now if there can not, my position is, that the sovereignty resides in the people. They have not

* From Lloyd's Debates.

parted with it; they have only dispensed such portions of power as were conceived necessary for the public welfare. This constitution stands upon this broad principle. I know very well, Sir, that the people have hitherto been shut out of the federal government, but it is not meant that they should any longer be dispossessed of their rights. In order to recognize this leading principle, the proposed system sets out with a declaration that its existence depends upon the supreme authority of the people alone. We have heard much about a consolidated government. I wish the honorable gentleman would condescend to give us a definition of what he meant by it. I think this the more necessary, because I apprehend that the term, in the numerous times it has been used, has not always been used in the same sense. It may be said, and I believe it has been said, that a consolidated government is such as will absorb and destroy the governments of the several States. If it is taken in this view, the plan before us is not a consolidated government, as I showed on a former day, and may, if necessary, show further on some future occasion. On the other hand, if it is meant that the general government will take from the state governments their power in some particulars, it is confessed and evident that this will be its operation and effect.

When the principle is once settled that the people are the source of authority, the consequence is that they may take from the subordinate governments powers with which they have hitherto trusted them, and place those powers in the general government, if it is thought that there they will be productive of more good. They can distribute one portion of power to the more contracted circle called State governments: they can also furnish another proportion to the government of the United States. Who will undertake to say as a state officer that the people may not give to the general government what powers and for what purposes they please? how comes it, Sir, that these State governments dictate to their superiors?—to the majesty of the people? When I say the majesty of the people, I mean the thing, and not a mere compliment to them. The honorable gentleman went a step further and said that the State governments were kept out of this government altogether. The truth is, and it is a leading principle in this system, that not the States only but the people also shall be here represented. And if this is a crime, I confess the general government is chargeable with it; but I have no idea that a safe system of power in the government, sufficient to manage the general interest of the United States, could be drawn from any other source or rested in any other authority than that of the people at large, and I consider this authority as the rock on which this structure will stand. If this principle is unfounded, the system must fall. If honorable gentlemen, before they undertake to oppose this principle, will show that the people have parted with their power to the State governments, then I confess I cannot support this constitution. It is asked, can there be two taxing powers? Will the people submit to two taxing powers? I think they will, when the taxes are required for the public welfare, by persons appointed immediately by their fellow citizens.

But I believe this doctrine is a very disagreeable one to some of the State governments. All the objections that will furnish an increase of revenue are eagerly seized by them; perhaps this will lead to the reason why a State government, when she was obliged to pay only about an eighth part of the loan-office certificates, should voluntarily undertake the payment of about one-third part of them. This power of taxation will be regulated in the general government upon equitable principles. No State can have more than her just proportion to discharge—no longer will government be obliged to assign her funds for the payment of debts she does not owe. Another objection has been taken that the judicial powers are co-extensive with the objects of the national government. So far as I can understand the idea of magistracy in every government, this seems to be a proper arrangement; the judicial department is considered as a part of the executive authority of government. Now, I have no idea that the authority should be restrained so as not to be able to perform its functions with full effect. I would not have the legislature sit to make laws which cannot be executed. It is not meant here

that the laws shall be a dead letter; it is meant that they shall
be carefully and duly considered before they are enacted; and
that then they shall be honestly and faithfully executed.
This observation naturally leads to a more particular consideration of the government before us.　In order, Sir, to give
permanency, stability and security to any government, I conceive it of essential importance that its legislature should be
restrained; that there should not only be what we call a *passive*, but an *active* power over it; for of all kinds of despotism,
this is the most dreadful and the most difficult to be corrected.
With how much contempt have we seen the authority of the
people treated by the legislature of this State—and how often
have we seen it making laws in one session that have been
repealed the next, either on account of the fluctuation of
party or their own impropriety!

This could not have been the case in a compound legislature; it is therefore proper to have efficient restraints upon
the legislative body.　These restraints arise from different
sources: I will mention some of them.　In this constitution
they will be produced in a very considerable degree by a division of the power in the legislative body itself.　Under this
system they may arise likewise from the interference of those
officers, who will be introduced into the executive and judicial departments.　They may spring also from another source,
the election by the people, and finally, under this constitution, they may proceed from the great and last resort—from
the PEOPLE themselves.　I say, under this constitution, the
legislature may be restrained and kept within its prescribed
bounds by the interposition of the judicial department.　This
I hope, Sir, to explain clearly and satisfactorily.　I had occasion on a former day to state that the power of the constitution was paramount to the power of the legislature acting
under that constitution.　For it is possible that the legislature,
when acting in that capacity, may transgress the bounds assigned to it, and an act may pass in the usual *mode* notwithstanding that transgression; but when it comes to be discussed
before the judges, when they consider its principles, and find
it to be incompatible with the superior powers of the consti-

tution, it is their duty to pronounce it void; and judges independent, and not obliged to look to every session for a continuance of their salaries, will behave with intrepidity and
refuse to the act the sanction of judicial authority. In the
same manner the President of the United States could shield
himself and refuse to carry into effect an act that violates the
constitution.

In order to secure the President from any dependence upon
the legislature as to his salary, it is provided that he shall, at
stated times, receive for his services a compensation that shall
neither be increased nor diminished during the period for
which he shall have been elected, and that he shall not receive
within that period any other emolument from the United
States or any of them.

To secure to the judges this independence, it is ordered that
they shall receive for their services a compensation which
shall not be diminished during their continuance in office.
The Congress may be restrained by the election of its constituent parts. If a legislature shall make a law contrary to the
constitution or oppressive to the people, they have it in their
power, every second year in one branch, and every sixth
year in the other, to displace the men who act thus inconsistent with their duty; and if this is not sufficient, they have
still a further power; they may assume into their own hands
the alteration of the constitution itself—they may revoke the
lease, when the conditions are broken by the tenant. But
the most useful restraint upon the legislature, because it
operates constantly, arises from the division of its power
among two branches, and from the qualified negative of the
president upon both. As this government is formed, there
are two sources from which the representation is drawn,
though they both ultimately flow from the people. *States*
now exist and others will come into existence; it was thought
proper that they should be represented in the general government. But gentlemen will please to remember, this constitution was not framed merely for the States; it was framed
for the PEOPLE also; and the popular branch of the Congress
will be the objects of their immediate choice.

The two branches will serve as checks upon each other; they have the same legislative authorities, except in one instance. Money bills must originate in the house of representatives. The senate can pass no law without the concurrence of the house of representatives; nor can the house of representatives without the concurrence of the senate. I believe, Sir, that the observation which I am now going to make, will apply to mankind in every situation; they will act with more caution, and perhaps more integrity, if their proceedings are to be under the inspection and control of another, than when they are not. From this principle, the proceedings of Congress will be conducted with a degree of circumspection not common in single bodies, where nothing more is necessary to be done, than to carry the business through amongst themselves, whether it be right or wrong. In compound legislatures, every object must be submitted to a distinct body, not influenced by the arguments, or warped by the prejudices of the other. And, I believe, that the persons who will form the Congress, will be cautious in running the risk, *with a bare majority*, of having the negative of the president put on their proceedings. As there will be more circumspection in forming the laws, so there will be more stability in the laws when made. Indeed one is the consequence of the other; for what has been well considered, and founded in good sense, will, in practice, be useful and salutary, and of consequence will not be liable to be soon repealed. Though two bodies may not possess more wisdom or patriotism than what may be found in a single body, yet they will necessarily introduce a greater degree of precision. An undigested and inaccurate code of laws, is one of the most dangerous things that can be introduced into any government. The force of this observation is well known by every gentleman that has attended to the laws of this State. This, Sir, is a very important advantage, that will arise from this division of the legislative authority.

I will proceed now to take some notice of a still further restraint upon the legislature: I mean the qualified negative of the president. I think this will be attended with very important advantages, for the security and happiness of the people of the United States. The president, Sir, will not be a stranger to our country, to our laws, or to our wishes. He will, under this constitution, be placed in office as the president of the whole union, and will be chosen in such a manner that he may be justly styled THE MAN OF THE PEOPLE; being elected by the different parts of the United States, he will consider himself as not particularly interested for any one of them, but will watch over the whole with paternal care and affection. This will be the natural conduct to recommend himself to those who placed him in that high chair, and I consider it as a very important advantage, that such a man must have every law presented to him before it can become binding upon the United States. He will have before him the fullest information of our situation, he will avail himself not only of records and official communications, foreign and domestic, but he will have also the advice of the executive officers in the different departments of the general government.

If in consequence of this information and advice, he exercise the authority given to him, the effect will not be lost —he returns his objections, together with the bill, and unless two-thirds of both branches of the legislature are *now* found to approve it, it does not become a law. But even if his objections do not prevent its passing into a law, they will not be useless; they will be kept together with the law, and, in the archives of congress, will be valuable and practical materials, to form the minds of posterity for legislation—if it is found that the law operates inconveniently, or oppressively, the people may discover in the president's objections the source of that inconvenience or oppression. Further, Sir, when objections shall have been made, it is provided, in order to secure the greatest degree of caution and responsibility, that the votes of both houses shall be determined by yeas and nays, and the names of the persons voting for and against the bill, shall be entered in the journal of each house respectively. Thus much I have thought proper to say, with regard to the distribution of the legislative authority, and the restraints under which it will be exercised.

The gentleman in opposition strongly insists, that the general clause at the end of the eighth section, gives to congress a power of legislating generally; but I cannot conceive by what means he will render the word susceptible of that expansion. Can the words, "the congress shall have power to make all laws which shall be necessary and proper to carry into execution the foregoing powers," be capable of giving them general legislative power? I hope that it is not meant to give to congress merely an illusive show of authority, to deceive themselves or constituents any longer. On the contrary, I trust it is meant, that they shall have the power of carrying into effect the laws which they shall make under the powers vested in them by this constitution. In answer to the gentleman from Fayette (Mr. Smilie,) on the subject of the press, I beg leave to make an observation: it is very true, Sir, that this constitution says nothing with regard to that subject, nor was it necessary, because it will be found that there is given to the general government no power whatsoever concerning it; and no law in pursuance of the constitution, can possibly be enacted, to destroy that liberty.

I heard the honorable gentleman make this general assertion, that the Congress was certainly vested with power to make such a law, but I would be glad to know by what part of this constitution such a power is given? Until that is done, I shall not enter into a minute investigation of the matter, but shall at present satisfy myself with giving an answer to a question that has been put. It has been asked, if a law should be made to punish libels, and the judges should proceed under that law, what chance would the printer have of an acquittal? And it has been said he would drop into a den of devouring monsters.

I presume it was not in the view of the honorable gentleman to say there is no such thing as a libel, or that the writers of such ought not to be punished. The idea of the liberty of the press, is not carried so far as this in any country—what is meant by the liberty of the press is, that there should be no antecedent restraint upon it; but that every author is responsible when he attacks the security or welfare of the government, or the safety, character and property of the individual.

With regard to attacks upon the public, the mode of proceeding is by a prosecution. Now if a libel is written, it must be within some one of the United States, or the district of congress. With regard to that district, I hope it will take care to preserve this as well as the other rights of freemen ; for whatever district congress may choose, the cession of it cannot be completed without the consent of its inhabitants. Now, Sir, if this libel is to be tried, it must be tried where the offence was committed; for under this constitution, as declared in the second section of the third article, the trial must be held in the State; therefore on this occasion it must be tried where it was published, if the indictment is for publishing; and it must be tried likewise by a jury of that State. Now, I would ask, is the person prosecuted in a worse situation under the general government, even if it had the power to make laws on this subject, than he is at present under the State government? It is true there is no particular regulation made, to have the jury come from the body of the county in which the offence was committed; but there are some States in which this mode of collecting juries is contrary to their established custom, and gentlemen ought to consider that this constitution was not meant merely for Pennsylvania. In some States the juries are not taken from a single county. In Virginia, the sheriff, I believe, is not confined even to the inhabitants of the State, but is at liberty to take any man he pleases, and put him on the jury. In Maryland I think a set of jurors serve for the whole Western Shore, and another for the Eastern Shore.

I beg to make one remark on what one gentleman has said, with respect to amendments being proposed to the constitution. To whom are the convention to make report of such amendments? He tells you, to the present congress. I do not wish to report to that body, the representatives only of the State governments; they may not be disposed to admit the people into a participation of their power. It has also been supposed, that a wonderful unanimity subsists among those who are enemies to the proposed system. On this point I also differ from the gentleman who made the observation. I have taken every pains in my power, and read every publication I could meet with, in order to gain information; and as far as I have been able to judge, the opposition is inconsiderable and inconsistent. Instead of agreeing in their objections, those who make them bring forward such as are diametrically opposite. On one hand, it is said that the representation in congress is too small; on the other, it is said to be too numerous. Some think the authority of the senate too great; some that of the house of representatives; and some that of both. Others draw their fears from the powers of the president; and like the iron race of Cadmus, these opponents rise only to destroy each other.

Monday, December 3.

On Monday [Dec. 3d] * it was urged by Mr. Findley, that Congress, under the new system, would have it in their power to lay an impost upon emigrants. Doctor Rush said he thought there was no reason to object to its being laid on the importation of indented servants, and Mr. Wilson said that the emigration of freemen was an object of commerce.

Doctor Rush having frequently alluded with disapprobation to the funding system, in a late debate, Mr. Findley observed that the Doctor was one of the committee of public creditors who had conferred with a committee of the General Assembly upon this measure, and was at that time active in promoting it. The Doctor, for fear any unfavorable impression should be made by that assertion, observed that he did not think the system would have extended so far.

Mr. Wilson said that the manner in which the opposition treated the proposed constitution, taking it by piece-meal, without considering the relative connection and dependence of its parts, reminded him of an anecdote which occurred when it was the practice in churches to detail a single line of Sternhold and Hopkins's psalms, and then set the verse to

* From the Pennsylvania Packet, Dec. 6th.

music. A sailor entered the church, when the clerk gave out the following line:

> The Lord will come, and he will not

The sailor stared, but when he heard the next line,

> Hold peace, but speak aloud,

he instantly left the congregation, convinced that it was an assembly of lunatics.

Mr. Wilson.* Much fault has been found with the mode of expression used in the first clause of the ninth section of the first article. I believe I can assign a reason why that mode of expression was used, and why the term slave was not directly admitted in this constitution:—and as to the manner of laying taxes, this is not the first time that the subject has come into the view of the United States, and of the legislatures of the several States. The gentleman (Mr. Findley) will recollect, that in the present Congress, the quota of the federal debt and general expenses was to be in proportion to the value of LAND and other enumerated property within the States. After trying this for a number of years, it was found on all hands to be a mode that could not be carried into execution. Congress were satisfied of this, and in the year 1783 recommended, in conformity with the powers they possessed under the articles of confederation, that the quota should be according to the number of free people, including those bound to servitude, and excluding Indians not taxed. These were the very expressions used in 1783, and the fate of this recommendation was similar to all their other resolutions. It was not carried into effect, but it was adopted by no fewer than eleven out of thirteen States; and it cannot but be a matter of surprise to hear gentlemen who agreed to this very mode of expression at that time, come forward and state it as an objection on the present occasion. It was natural, Sir, for the late convention to adopt the mode after it had been agreed to by eleven States, and to use the expression which

* From Lloyd's Debates.

they found had been received as unexceptionable before. With respect to the clause restricting Congress from prohibiting the migration or importation of such persons as any of the States now existing shall think proper to admit, prior to the year 1808, the honorable gentleman says that this clause is not only dark, but intended to grant to Congress, for that time, the power to admit the importation of slaves. No such thing was intended; but I will tell you what was done, and it gives me high pleasure that so much was done. Under the present confederation, the States may admit the importation of slaves as long as they please; but by this article, after the year 1808, the Congress will have power to prohibit such importation, notwithstanding the disposition of any State to the contrary. I consider this as laying the foundation for banishing slavery out of this country; and though the period is more distant than I could wish, yet it will produce the same kind, gradual change which was pursued in Pennsylvania. It is with much satisfaction I view this power in the general government, whereby they may lay an interdiction on this reproachful trade. But an immediate advantage is also obtained, for a tax or duty may be imposed on such importation not exceeding ten dollars for each person; and this, Sir, operates as a partial prohibition. It was all that could be obtained. I am sorry it was no more; but from this I think there is reason to hope that yet a few years, and it will be prohibited altogether. And in the meantime, the new States which are to be formed will be under the control of Congress in this particular, and slaves will never be introduced amongst them. The gentleman says that it is unfortunate in another point of view: it means to prohibit the introduction of white people from Europe, as this tax may deter them from coming amongst us. A little impartiality and attention will discover the care that the convention took in selecting their language. The words are, the *migration or* IMPORTATION of such persons, etc., shall not be prohibited by Congress prior to the year 1808, but a tax or duty may be imposed on such IMPORTATION. It is observable here that the term migration is dropped when a tax or duty is mentioned, so that Congress have power to impose the tax only on those imported.

Tuesday December 4, 1787.

Mr. Wilson.* I shall take this opportunity of giving an answer to the objections already urged against the constitution; I shall then point out some of those qualities, that entitle it to the attention and approbation of this convention; and after having done this, I shall take a fit opportunity of stating the consequences which I apprehend will result from rejecting it, and those which will probably result from its adoption. I have given the utmost attention to the debates and the objections that from time to time have been made by the three gentlemen who speak in opposition. I have reduced them to some order, perhaps not better than that in which they were introduced. I will state them; they will be in the recollection of the house, and I will endeavor to give an answer to them—in that answer, I will interweave some remarks that may tend to elucidate the subject.

A good deal has already been said, concerning a bill of rights; I have stated, according to the best of my recollection, all that passed in convention relating to that business. Since that time, I have spoken with a gentleman, who has not only his memory, but full notes, that he had taken in that body; and he assures me, that upon this subject no direct motion was ever made at all; and certainly, before we heard this so violently supported out of doors, some pains ought to have been taken to have tried its fate within; but the truth is, a bill of rights would, as I have mentioned already, have been not only unnecessary, but improper. In some governments it may come within the gentleman's idea, when he says it can do no harm; but even in these governments, you find bills of rights do not uniformly obtain; and do those States complain who have them not? Is it a maxim in forming governments, that not only all the powers which are given, but also that all those which are reserved, should be enumerated? I apprehend that the powers given and reserved, form the whole rights of the people, as men and as

* From Lloyd Debates.

citizens. I consider, that there are very few who understand
the *whole* of these rights. All the political writers, from Gro-
tius and Puffendorf, down to Vattel, have treated on this
subject; but in no one of those books, nor in the aggregate
of them all, can you find a complete enumeration of rights
appertaining to the people as men and as citizens.

There are two kinds of government; that where general
power is intended to be given to the legislature, and that
where the powers are particularly enumerated. In the last
case, the implied result is, that nothing more is intended to
be given than what is so enumerated, unless it results from
the nature of the government itself. On the other hand,
when general legislative powers are given, then the people
part with their authority, and on the gentleman's principle
of government, retain nothing. But in a government like
the proposed one, there can be no necessity for a bill of rights.
For, on my principle, the people never part with their power.
Enumerate all the rights of men! I am sure, Sir, that no
gentleman in the late convention would have attempted such
a thing. I believe the honorable speakers in opposition on
this floor were members of the assembly which appointed
delegates to that convention; if it had been thought proper
to have sent them into that body, how luminous would
the *dark conclave* have been! So the gentleman has been
pleased to denominate that body. Aristocrats as they were,
they pretended not to define the rights of those who sent
them there. We are asked repeatedly, what *harm* could the
addition of a bill of rights do? If it can do no *good*, I think
that a sufficient reason to refuse having anything to do with
it. But to whom are we to report this bill of rights, if we
should adopt it? Have we authority from those who sent us
here to make one?

It is true we may propose, as well as any other private persons; but how shall we know the sentiments of the citizens
of this State and of the other States? are we certain that
any one of them will agree with our definitions and enume-
rations?

In the second place, we are told, that there is no check

upon the government but the people; it is fortunate, Sir, if their superintending authority is allowed as a check: but I apprehend that in the very construction of this government, there are numerous checks. Besides those expressly enumerated, the two branches of the legislature are mutual checks upon each other. But this subject will be more properly discussed, when we come to consider the form of government itself; and then I mean to show the reason, why the right of habeas corpus was secured by a particular declaration in its favor.

In the third place we are told, that there is no security for the rights of conscience. I ask the honorable gentleman, what part of this system puts it in the power of congress to attack those rights? When there is no power to attack, it is idle to prepare the means of defence.

After having mentioned, in a cursory manner, the foregoing objections, we now arive at the leading ones against the proposed system.

The very manner of introducing this constitution, by the recognition of the authority of the people, is said to change the principle of the present confederation, and to introduce a *consolidating* and absorbing government!

In this confederated republic, the sovereignty of the States, it is said, is not preserved. We are told that there cannot be two sovereign powers, and that a subordinate sovereignty is no sovereignty.

It will be worth while, Mr. President, to consider this objection at large. When I had the honor of speaking formerly on this subject, I stated, in as concise a manner as possible, the leading ideas that occurred to me, to ascertain where the supreme and sovereign power resides. It has not been, nor, I presume, will it be denied, that somewhere there is, and of necessity must be, a supreme, absolute and uncontrollable authority. This, I believe, may justly be termed the sovereign power; for from that gentleman's (Mr. Findley) account of the matter, it cannot be sovereign, unless it is supreme; for, says he, a subordinate sovereignty is no sovereignty at all. I had the honor of observing, that if the question was asked, where the supreme power resided, different answers would be given by different writers. I mentioned that Blackstone will tell you, that in Britain it is lodged in the British parliament; and I believe there is no writer on this subject on the other side of the Atlantic, but supposes it to be vested in that body. I stated further, that if the question was asked, some politician, who had not considered the subject with sufficient accuracy, where the supreme power resided in our governments, would answer, that it was vested in the State constitutions. This opinion approaches near the truth, but does not reach it; for, the truth is, that the supreme, absolute and uncontrollable authority, *remains* with the people. I mentioned also, that the practical recognition of this truth was reserved for the honor of this country. I recollect no constitution founded on this principle: but we have witnessed the improvement, and enjoy the happiness, of seeing it carried into practice. The great and penetrating mind of Locke seems to be the only one that pointed towards even the theory of this great truth.

When I made the observation, that some politicians would say the supreme power was lodged in our State constitutions, I did not suspect that the honorable gentleman from Westmoreland (Mr. Findley) was included in that description; but I find myself disappointed; for I imagined his opposition would arise from another consideration. His position is, that the supreme power resides in the States, as governments; and mine is, that it *resides* in the PEOPLE, as the fountain of government; that the people have not—that the people mean not—and that the people ought not, to part with it to any government whatsoever. In their hands it remains secure. They can delegate it in such proportions, to such bodies, on such terms, and under such limitations, as they think proper. I agree with the members in opposition, that there cannot be two sovereign powers on the same subject.

I consider the people of the United States as forming one great community, and I consider the people of the different States as forming communities again on a lesser scale. From this great division of the people into distinct communities it will be found necessary that different proportions of legislative powers should be given to the governments, according to the nature, number and magnitude of their objects.

Unless the people are considered in these two views, we shall never be able to understand the principle on which this system was constructed. I view the States as made *for* the people as well as *by* them, and not the people as made for the States. The people, therefore, have a right, whilst enjoying the undeniable powers of society, to form either a general government, or state governments, in what manner they please; or to accommodate them to one another, and by this means preserve them all. This, I say, is the inherent and unalienable right of the people, and as an illustration of it, I beg to read a few words from the Declaration of Independence, made by the representatives of the United States, and recognized by the whole Union.—

"We hold these truths to be self-evident, that all men are created equal; that they are endowed by their Creator with certain unalienable rights; that among these are life, liberty, and the pursuit of happiness. That to secure these rights, *governments* are instituted among men, *deriving their just powers from the consent of the governed;* that whenever any form of government becomes destructive of these ends, it is the RIGHT of the people to alter or to abolish it, and institute a new government, laying its foundation on such principles, and organizing its powers in such forms, as to them shall seem most likely to effect their safety and happiness."

This is the broad basis on which our independence was placed. On the same certain and solid foundation this system is erected.

State sovereignty, as it is called, is far from being able to support its weight. Nothing less than the authority of the people could either support it or give it efficacy. I cannot pass over this subject without noticing the different conduct pursued by the late federal convention, and that observed by the convention which framed the constitution of Pennsylvania. On that occasion you find an attempt made to deprive the people of this right, so lately and so expressly asserted in

the Declaration of Independence.   We are told in the preamble to the Declaration of Rights, and frame of government,
that "*we* do, by virtue of the authority vested in *us*, ordain,
declare, and establish, the following Declaration of Rights
and frame of government to be the constitution of this commonwealth, and to remain in force therein UNALTERED, except in such articles as shall hereafter on experience be found
to require improvement, and which shall, by the same authority of the people, fairly delegated *as this frame of government directs*"—An honorable gentleman (Mr. Chambers) was
well warranted in saying that all that could be done was done
to cut off the people from the right of amending; for if it be
amended by any other mode than that which it directs, then
any number more than one-third may control any number
less than two-thirds.

But I return to my general reasoning.   My position is, Sir,
that in this country the supreme, absolute, and uncontrollable power resides in the people at large; that they have
vested certain proportions of this power in the State governments, but that the fee simple continues, resides and remains
with the body of the people.   Under the practical influence
of this great truth we are now sitting and deliberating, and
under its operation, we can sit as calmly, and deliberate as
coolly in order to change a constitution, as a legislature can
sit and deliberate under the power of a constitution in order
to alter or amend a law.   It is true, the exercise of this power
will not probably be so frequent, nor resorted to on so many
occasions, in one case as in the other; but the recognition of
the principle cannot fail to establish it more firmly.   Because
this recognition is made in the proposed constitution, an exception is taken to the whole of it, for we are told it is a violation of the present confederation—a CONFEDERATION of
SOVEREIGN STATES.   I shall not enter into an investigation
of the present confederation, but shall just remark, that its
principle is not the principle of free governments.   The PEO-
PLE of the United States are not as such represented in the
present Congress; and considered even as the component
parts of the several States, they are not represented in proportion to their numbers and importance.

In this place I cannot help remarking on the general inconsistency which appears between one part of the gentleman's objections and another. Upon the principle we have now mentioned, the honorable gentleman contended, that the powers ought to flow from the States; and that all the late convention had to do, was to give additional powers to Congress. What is the present form of Congress? A single body, with some legislative, but little executive, and no effective judicial power. What are these additional powers that are to be given? In some cases legislative are wanting, in other judicial, and in others executive; these, it is said, ought to be allotted to the general government; but the impropriety of delegating such extensive trust to one body of men is evident; yet in the same day, and perhaps the same hour, we are told, by honorable gentlemen, that these three branches of government are not kept sufficiently distinct in this constitution; we are told also that the senate, possessing some executive power, as well as legislative, is such a monster that it will swallow up and absorb every other body in the general government, after having destroyed those of the particular States.

Is this reasoning with consistency? Is the senate under the proposed constitution so tremendous a body, when checked in their legislative capacity by the house of representatives, and in their executive authority by the president of the United States? Can this body be so tremendous as the present congress, a single body of men possessed of legislative, executive and judicial powers? To what purpose was Montesquieu read to show that this was a complete tyranny? The application would have been more properly made by the advocates of the proposed constitution, against the patrons of the present confederation.

It is mentioned that this federal government will annihilate and absorb all the State governments. I wish to save as much as possible the time of the house: I shall not, therefore, recapitulate what I had the honor of saying last week on this subject; I hope it was then shown, that instead of being abolished (as insinuated) from the very nature of things, and from the organization of the system itself, the State governments must exist, or the general government must fall amidst their ruins; indeed, so far as to the forms, it is admitted they may remain, but the gentlemen seem to think their power will be gone.

I shall have occasion to take notice of this power hereafter, and, I believe, if it was necessary, it could be shown that the State governments, as States, will enjoy as much power, and more dignity, happiness and security, than they have hitherto done. I admit, Sir, that some of the powers will be taken from them, by the system before you; but it is, I believe, allowed on all hands, at least it is not among us a disputed point, that the late convention was appointed with a particular view to give more power to the government of the union: it is also acknowledged, that the intention was to obtain the advantage of an efficient government over the United States; now, if power is to be given to that government, I apprehend it must be taken from some place. If the State governments are to retain all the powers they held before, then, of consequence, every new power that is given to Congress must be taken from the people at large. Is this the gentleman's intention? I believe a strict examination of this subject will justify me in asserting that the States, as governments, have assumed too much power to themselves, while they left too little to the people. Let not this be called cajoling the people—the elegant expression used by the honorable gentleman from Westmoreland (Mr. Findley)—it is hard to avoid censure on one side or the other. At some time it has been said, that I have not been at the pains to conceal my contempt of the people; but when it suits a purpose better, it is asserted that I cajole them. I do neither one nor the other. The voice of approbation, Sir, when I think that approbation well earned, I confess is grateful to my ears; but I would disdain it, if it is to be purchased by a sacrifice of my duty, or the dictates of my conscience. No, Sir, I go practically into this system; I have gone into it practically when the doors were shut, when it could not be alleged that I cajoled the people; and I now endeavor to show that the true and only safe principle for a free people, is a practical recognition of their original and supreme authority.

I say, Sir, that it was the design of this system, to take some power from the State government, and to place it in the general government. It was also the design, that the people should be admitted to the exercise of some powers which they did not exercise under the present confederation. It was thought proper that the citizens, as well as the States, should be represented; how far the representation in the senate is a representation of States, we shall see by and by, when we come to consider that branch of the federal government.

This system, it is said, ''unhinges and eradicates the State governments, and was systematically intended so to do;'' to establish the *intention*, an argument is drawn from Art. 1st sect. 4th, on the subject of elections. I have already had occasion to remark upon this, and shall therefore pass on to the next objection—that the last clause of the 8th sect. of the 1st article, gives the power of self-preservation to the general government, *independent* of the States. For in case of their *abolition*, it will be alleged in behalf of the general government, that self-preservation is the first law, and necessary to the exercise of *all other* powers.

Now let us see what this objection amounts to. Who are to have this self-preserving power? The Congress. Who are Congress? It is a body that will consist of a senate and a house of representatives. Who compose this senate? Those who are *elected* by the *legislatures* of the different States. Who are the electors of the house of representatives? Those who are *qualified* to *vote* for the most numerous branch of the *legislature* in the separate States. Suppose the State legislatures annihilated, where is the criterion to ascertain the qualification of electors? and unless this be ascertained, they cannot be admitted to vote; if a state legislature is not elected, there can be no senate, because the senators are to be chosen by the *legislatures only*.

This is a plain and simple deduction from the constitution,

and yet the objection is stated as conclusive upon an argument expressly drawn from the last clause of this section.

It is repeated, with confidence, "that this is not a *federal* government, but a complete one, with legislative, executive and judicial powers: it is a *consolidating* government." I have already mentioned the misuse of the term; I wish the gentleman would indulge us with his definition of the word. If, when he says it is a consolidation, he means so far as relates to the general objects of the union—so far it was intended to be a consolidation, and on such a consolidation, perhaps, our very existence, as a nation, depends. If, on the other hand (as something which has been said seems to indicate) he (Mr. Findley) means that it will absorb the governments of the individual States, so far is this position from being admitted, that it is unanswerably controverted. The existence of the State government, is one of the most prominent features of this system. With regard to those purposes which are allowed to be for the general welfare of the union, I think it no objection to this plan, that we are told it is a complete government. I think it no objection, that it is alleged the government will possess legislative, executive and judicial powers. Should it have only legislative authority? We have had examples enough of such a government, to deter us from continuing it. Shall Congress any longer continue to make requisitions from the several States, to be treated sometimes with silent, and sometimes with declared contempt? For what purpose give the power to make laws, unless they are to be executed? and if they are to be executed, the executive and judicial powers will necessarily be engaged in the business.

Do we wish a return of those insurrections and tumults to which a sister State was lately exposed? or a government of such insufficiency as the present is found to be? Let me, Sir, mention one circumstance in the recollection of every honorable gentleman who hears me. To the determination of Congress are submitted all disputes between States, concerning boundary, jurisdiction, or right of soil. In consequence of this power, after much altercation, expense of time, and considerable expense of money, this State was successful enough to obtain a decree in her favor, in a difference then subsisting between her and Connecticut; but what was the consequence? the Congress had no power to carry the decree into execution. Hence the distraction and animosity, which have ever since prevailed, and still continue in that part of the country. Ought the government then to remain any longer incomplete? I hope not; no person can be so insensible to the lessons of experience as to desire it.

It is brought as an objection "that there will be a rivalship between the State governments and the general government; on each side endeavors will be made to increase power."

Let us examine a little into this subject. The gentlemen tell you, Sir, that they expect the States will not possess any power. But I think there is reason to draw a different conclusion. Under this system their respectability and power will increase with that of the general government. I believe their happiness and security will increase in a still greater proportion. Let us attend a moment to the situation of this country: it is a maxim of every government, and it ought to be a maxim with us, that the increase of numbers increases the dignity, the security, and the respectability of all governments; it is the first command given by the Deity to man, increase and multiply; this applies with peculiar force to this country, the smaller part of whose territory is yet inhabited. We are representatives, Sir, not merely of the present age, but of future times; nor merely of the territory along the sea coast, but of regions immensely extended westward. We should fill, as fast as possible, this extensive country, with men who shall live happy, free and secure. To accomplish this great end ought to be the leading view of all our patriots and statesmen. But how is it to be accomplished, but by establishing peace and harmony among ourselves, and dignity and respectability among foreign nations? By these means, we may draw numbers from the other side of the Atlantic, in addition to the natural sources of population. Can either of these objects be attained without a protecting head?

When we examine history, we shall find an important fact, and almost the only fact, which will apply to all confederacies.

They have all fallen to pieces, and have not absorbed the subordinate governments.

In order to keep republics together they must have a strong binding force, which must be either external or internal. The situation of this country shows, that no foreign force can press us together; the bonds of our union ought therefore to be indissolubly strong.

The power of the States, I apprehend, will increase with the population, and the happiness of their inhabitants. Unless we can establish a character abroad, we shall be unhappy from foreign restraints, or internal violence. These reasons, I think, prove sufficiently the necessity of having a federal head. Under it the advantages enjoyed by the whole union would be participated by every State. I wish honorable gentlemen would think not only of themselves, not only of the present age, but of others, and of future times.

It has been said, "that the State governments will not be able to make head against the general government;" but it might be said with more propriety, that the general government will not be able to maintain the powers given it against the encroachments and combined attacks of the State governments. They possess some particular advantages, from which the general government is restrained. By this system, there is a provision made in the constitution, that no senator or representative shall be appointed to any civil office under the authority of the United States, which shall have been created, or the emoluments whereof shall have been increased, during the time for which he was elected; and no person holding any office under the United States can be a member of either house; but there is no similar security against State influence, as a representative may enjoy places and even sinecures under the State governments. On which side is the door most open to corruption? If a person in the legislature is to be influenced by an office, the general government can give him none unless he vacate his seat. When the influence of office comes from the State government, he can retain his seat and salary too. But it is added, under this head, "that State governments will lose the attachment of the people, by losing the power of conferring advantages, and that the people will not be at the expense of keeping them up." Perhaps the State governments have already become so expensive as to alarm the gentlemen on that head. I am told that the civil list of this State amounted to £40,-000, in one year. Under the proposed government, I think it would be possible to obtain in Pennsylvania every advantage we now possess, with a civil list that shall not exceed one-third of that sum.

How differently the same thing is talked of, if it be a favorite or otherwise! When advantages to an officer are to be derived from the general government, we hear them mentioned by the name of *bribery*, but when we are told of the State governments losing the power of conferring advantages, by the disposal of offices, it is said they will lose the *attachment* of the people. What is in one instance corruption and bribery, is in another the power of conferring advantages.

We are informed that "the State elections will be ill attended, and that the State governments will become mere boards of electors." Those who have a due regard for their country, will discharge their duty, and attend; but those who are brought only from interest or persuasion had better stay away; the public will not suffer any disadvantage from their absence. But the honest citizen, who knows the value of the privilege, will undoubtedly attend, to secure the man of his choice. The power and business of the State legislatures relates to the great objects of life, liberty and property; the same are also objects of the general government.

Certainly the citizens of America will be as tenacious in the one instance as in the other. They will be interested, and I hope will exert themselves, to secure their rights not only from being injured by the State governments, but also from being injured by the general government.

"The power over election, and of judging of elections,

gives absolute sovereignty;" this power is given to every State legislature, yet I see no necessity that the power of absolute sovereignty should accompany it. My general position is, that the absolute sovereignty never goes from the people.

We are told, "that it will be in the power of the senate to prevent any addition of representatives to the lower house."

I believe their power will be pretty well balanced, and though the senate should have a desire to do this, yet the attempt will answer no purpose; for the house of representatives will not let them have a farthing of public money, till they agree to it. And the latter influence will be as strong as the other.

"Annual assemblies are necessary" it is said—and I answer, in many instances they are very proper. In Rhode Island and Connecticut they are elected for six months. In larger States, that period would be found very inconvenient, but in a government as large as that of the United States, I presume that annual elections would be more disproportionate, than elections for six months would be in some of our largest States.

"The British Parliament took to themselves the prolongation of their sitting to seven years. But even in the British Parliament the appropriations are annual."

But Sir, how is the argument to apply here?—how are the congress to assume such a power? They cannot assume it under the constitution, for that expressly provides "the members of the house of representatives shall be chosen every two years, by the people of the several States, and the senators for six years." So if they take it at all, they must take it by usurpation and force.

"Appropriations may be made for two years,—though in the British Parliament they are made but for one." For some purposes, such appropriations may be made annually, but for every purpose they are not; even for a standing army, they may be made for seven, ten, or fourteen years—the civil list is established during the life of a prince. Another objection is "that the members of the senate may enrich themselves—

they may hold their office as long as they live, and there is
no power to prevent them; the senate will swallow up everything.'' I am not a blind admirer of this system. Some of
the powers of the senators are not with me the favorite parts
of it, but as they stand connected with other parts, there is
still security against the efforts of that body: it was with
great difficulty that security was obtained, and I may risk the
conjecture, that if it is not now accepted, it never will be
obtained again from the same States. Though the senate
was not a favorite of mine, as to some of its powers, yet it
was a favorite with a majority in the Union, and we must submit to that majority, or we must break up the Union. It is
but fair to repeat those reasons, that weighed with the convention; perhaps I shall not be able to do them justice, but
yet I will attempt to show, why additional powers were given
to the senate, rather than to the house of representatives.
These additional powers, I believe, are, that of trying impeachments, that of concurring with the President in making
treaties, and that of concurring in the appointment of officers.
These are the powers that are stated as improper. It is fortunate, that in the exercise of every one of them, the Senate
stands controlled; if it is that monster which it said to be, it
can only show its teeth, it is unable to bite or devour. With
regard to impeachments, the senate can try none but such as
will be brought before them by the house of representatives.

The senate can make no treaties; they can approve of none
unless the President of the United States lay it before them.
With regard to the appointment of officers, the President
must nominate before they can vote. So that if the powers of
either branch are perverted, it must be with the approbation
of some one of the other branches of government: thus
checked on each side, they can do no one act of themselves.

''The powers of Congress extend to taxation, to direct taxation, to internal taxation, to poll taxes, to excises, to other
State and internal purposes.'' Those who possess the power
to tax, possess all other sovereign power. That their powers
are thus extensive is admitted; and would any thing short of
this have been sufficient? is it the wish of these gentlemen?

If it is, let us hear their sentiments, that the general government should subsist on the bounty of the States. Shall it have the power to contract, and no power to fulfil the contract? Shall it have the power to borrow money, and no power to pay the principal or interest? Must we go on, in the track that we have hitherto pursued? and must we again compel those in Europe, who lent us money in our distress, to advance the money to pay themselves interest on the certificates of the debts due to them?

This was actually the case in Holland, the last year. Like those who have shot one arrow, and cannot regain it, they have been obliged to shoot another in the same direction, in order to recover the first. It was absolutely necessary, Sir, that this government should possess these rights, and why should it not as well as the State governments? Will this government be fonder of the exercise of this authority, than those of the States are? Will the States, who are equally represented in one branch of the legislature, be more opposed to the payment of what shall be required by the future, than what has been required by the present Congress? Will the people, who must indisputably pay the whole, have more objections to the payment of this tax, because it is laid by persons of their own immediate appointment, even if those taxes were to continue as oppressive as they now are?—but under the general power of this system, that cannot be the case in Pennsylvania. Throughout the union, direct taxation will be lessened, at least in proportion to the increase of the other objects of revenue. In this constitution, a power is given to Congress to collect imposts, which is not given by the present articles of confederation. A very considerable part of the revenue of the United States will arise from that source; it is the easiest, most just, and most productive mode of raising revenue; and it is a safe one, because it is voluntary. No man is obliged to consume more than he pleases, and each buys in proportion only to his consumption. The price of the commodity is blended with the tax, and the person is often not sensible of the payment. But would it have been proper to have rested the matter there? Suppose the funds should not prove sufficient, ought the public debts to remain unpaid?—or the exigencies of government be left unprovided for? Should our tranquility be exposed to the assaults of foreign enemies, or violence among ourselves, because the objects of commerce may not furnish a sufficient revenue to secure them all? Certainly Congress should possess the power of raising revenue from their constituents, for the purpose mentioned in the eighth section of the first article, that is "to pay the debts and provide for the common defence and general welfare of the United States." It has been common with the gentlemen, on this subject, to present us with frightful pictures. We are told of the hosts of tax-gatherers that will swarm through the land; and whenever takes are mentioned, military force seems to be an attending idea. I think I may venture to predict, that the taxes of the general government (if any shall be laid) will be more equitable, and much less expensive, than those imposed by the State government.

I shall not go into an investigation of this subject; but it must be confessed, that scarcely any mode of laying and collecting taxes can be more burdensome than the present.

Another objection is, "that Congress may borrow money, keep up standing armies, and command the militia." The present Congress possesses the power of borrowing money and of keeping up standing armies. Whether it will be proper at all times to keep up a body of troops, will be a question to be determined by Congress; but I hope the necessity will not subsist at all times; but if it should subsist, where is the gentleman that will say that they ought not to possess the necessary power of keeping them up?

It is urged, as a general objection to this system, that "the powers of Congress are unlimited and undefined, and that they will be the judges, in all cases, of what is necessary and proper for them to do." To bring this subject to your view, I need do no more than point to the words in the constitution, beginning at the 8th sect. art. 1st. "The Congress (it says) shall have power, &c." I need not read over the words, but I leave it to every gentleman to say whether the powers are not as accurately and minutely defined, as can be well done on the same subject, in the same language. The old constitution is as strongly marked on the subject; and even the concluding clause, with which so much fault has been found, gives no more, or other powers; nor does it in any degree go beyond the particular enumeration; for when it is said, that Congress shall have power to make all laws which shall be necessary and proper, those words are limited, and defined by the following, "for carrying into execution the foregoing powers." It is saying no more than that the powers we have already particularly given, shall be effectually carried into execution.

I shall not detain the house, at this time, with any further observations on the liberty of the press, until it is shown that Congress have any power whatsoever to interfere with it, by licensing it, or declaring what shall be a libel.

I proceed to another objection, which was not so fully stated as I believe it will be hereafter; I mean the objection against the judicial department. The gentleman from Westmoreland only mentioned it to illustrate his objection to the legislative department. He said "that the judicial powers were so co-extensive with the legislative powers, and extend even to capital cases." I believe they ought to be co-extensive, otherwise laws would be framed, that could not be executed. Certainly, therefore, the executive and judicial departments ought to have power commensurate to the extent of the laws; for, as I have already asked, are we to give power to *make* laws, and no power to *carry them into effect?*

I am happy to mention the punishment annexed to one crime. You will find the current running strong in favor of humanity. For this is the first instance in which it has not been left to the legislature, to extend the crime and punishment of treason so far as they thought proper. This punishment, and the description of this crime, are the great sources of danger and persecution, on the part of government against the citizen. Crimes against the state! and against the officers of the state! History informs us, that more wrong may be done on this subject than on any other whatsoever. But under this constitution, there can be no treason against the United States, except such as is defined in this constitution. The manner of trial is clearly pointed out; the positive testimony of two witnesses to the same overt act, or a confession in open court, is required to convict any person of treason. And after all, the consequence of the crime shall extend no further than the life of the criminal; for no attainder of treason shall work corruption of blood, or forfeiture, except during the life of the person attainted.

I come now to consider the last set of objections that are offered against this constitution. It is urged, that this is not such a system as was within the powers of the convention; they assumed the *power of proposing*. I believe they might have made proposals without going beyond their powers. I never heard before, that to make a proposal was an exercise of power. But if it is an exercise of power, they certainly did assume it; yet they did not act as that body who framed the present constitution of Pennylvania acted; they did not by an ordinance attempt to rivet the constitution on the people, before they could vote for members of assembly under it. Yet such was the effect of the ordinance that attended the constitution of this commonwealth. I think the late convention have done nothing beyond their powers. The fact is, they have exercised no power at all. And in point of validity, this constitution proposed by them for the government of the United States, claims no more than a production of the same nature would claim, flowing from a private pen. It is laid before the citizens of the United States, unfettered by restraint; it is laid before them, to be judged by the natural, civil and political rights of men. By their FIAT, it will become of value and authority; without it, it will never receive the character of authenticity and power. The business, we are told, which was entrusted to the late convention, was merely to amend the present articles of confederation. This observation has been frequently made, and has often brought to my mind a story that is related of Mr. Pope, who it is well known, was not a little deformed. It was customary with him, to use this phrase, "God mend me,'' when any little incident happened. One evening a link boy was lighting him along, and coming to a gutter, the boy jumped nimbly over it—Mr. Pope called to him to turn, adding, "God mend me:'' The arch rogue turned to light him—looked at him, and repeated, "God mend you! he would sooner make a half-a-dozen new ones.'' This would apply to the present confederation; for it would be easier to make another than to mend this. The gentlemen urge, that this is such a government as was not expected by the people, the legislatures, nor by the honorable gentlemen who mentioned it. Perhaps it was not such as was expected, *but it may be* BETTER; and is that a reason why it should not be adopted? It is not worse, I trust, than the former. So that the argument of its being a system not expected, is an argument more strong in its favor than against it. The letter which accompanies this constitution, must strike every person with the utmost force. ''The friends of our country have long seen and desired the power of war, peace and treaties, that of levying money and regulating commerce, and the corresponding executive and judicial authorities, should be fully and effectually vested in the general government of the union; but the impropriety of delegating such extensive trust to one body of men, is evident. *Hence results the necessity of a different organization.*'' I therefore do not think it can be urged as an objection against this system, that it was not expected by the people. We are told, to add greater force to these objections, that they are not on local, but on general principles, and that they are uniform throughout the United States. I confess I am not altogether of that opinion; I think some of the objections are inconsistent with others, arising from a different quarter, and I think some are inconsistent even with those derived from the same source. But, on this occasion, let us take the fact for granted, that they are all on general principles, and uniform throughout the United States. Then we can judge of their full amount; and what are they, BUT TRIFLES LIGHT AS AIR? We see the whole force of them; for according to the sentiments of opposition, they can no where be stronger, or more fully stated, than here. The conclusion, from all these objections, is reduced to a point, and the plan is declared to be inimical to our liberties. I have said nothing, and mean to say nothing, concerning the dispositions or characters of those that framed the work now before you. I agree that it ought to be judged by its own intrinsic qualities. If it has not merit, weight of character ought not to carry it into effect. On the other hand, if it has merit and is calculated to secure the blessings of liberty and to promote the general welfare, then such objections as have hitherto been made ought not to influence us to reject it.

I am now led to consider those qualities that this system of government possesses, which will entitle it to the attention of the United States. But as I have somewhat fatigued myself, as well as the patience of the honorable members of this house, I shall defer what I have to add on this subject until the afternoon.

Before I proceed to consider those qualities in the constitution before us, which I think will endure in our approbation, permit me to make some remarks, and they shall be very concise, upon the objections that were offered this forenoon, by the member from Fayette (Mr. Smilie). I do it at this time, because I think it will be better to give a satisfactory answer to the whole of the objections, before I proceed to the other part of my subject. I find that the doctrine of a single legislature is not to be contended for in this constitution. I shall therefore say nothing on that point. I shall consider that part of the system, when we come to view its excellencies. Neither shall I take particular notice of his observation on the qualified negative of the president; for he finds no fault with it; he mentions, however, that he thinks it a vain and useless power, because it can never be executed. The reason he assigns for this is, that the king of Great Britain, who has an absolute negative over the laws proposed by parliament, has never exercised it, at least not for many years. It is true, and the reason why he did not exercise it, was, that during all that time, the king possessed a negative before the bill had passed through the two houses; a much stronger power than a negative after debate. I believe, since the revolution, at the time of William the Third, it was never known that a bill disagreeable to the crown passed both houses. At one time in the reign of Queen Anne, when there appeared some danger of this being effected, it is well known that she created twelve peers, and by that means effectually defeated it. Again, there was some risk of late years in the present reign, with regard to Mr. Fox's East-India bill, as it is usually called, that passed through the house of commons, but the king had interest enough in the house of peers, to have it thrown out; thus it never came up for the royal assent. But that is no reason why this negative should not be exercised here, and exercised with great advantage. Similar powers are known in more than one of the States. The governors of Massachusetts and New York have a power similar to this; and it has been exercised frequently, to good effect.

I believe the governor of New York, under this power, has been known to send back five or six bills in a week; and I well recollect that at the time the funding system was adopted by our legislature, the people in that State considered the negative of the governor as a great security that their legislature would not be able to incumber them by a similar measure. Since that time an alteration has been supposed in the governor's conduct, but there has been no alteration in his power.

The honorable gentleman from Westmoreland (Mr. Findley) by his highly refined critical abilities, discovers an inconsistency in this part of the constitution and that which declares, in section first: "All legislative powers, herein granted, shall be vested in the Congress of the United States, which shall consist of a senate and a house of representatives," and yet here, says he, is a power of legislation given to the president of the United States, because every bill, before it becomes a law, shall be presented to him: thus he is said to possess legislative powers. Sir, the convention observed on this occasion strict propriety of language; "if he approve the bill when it is sent, he shall sign it, but if not, he shall return it;" but no bill passes in consequence of having his assent—therefore he possesses no legislative authority.

The effect of his power, upon this subject, is merely this: if he disapproves a bill, two-thirds of the legislature become necessary to pass it into a law, instead of a bare majority. And when two-thirds are in favor of the bill, it becomes a law, not by his, but by authority of the two houses of the legislature. We are told, in the next place, by the honorable gentleman from Fayette (Mr. Smilie) that in the different orders of mankind, there is that of a natural aristocracy. On some occasions, there is a kind of magical expression, used to conjure up ideas, that may create uneasiness and apprehension. I hope the meaning of the words is understood by the gentleman who used them. I have asked repeatedly of gentlemen to explain, but have not been able to obtain the explanation of what they meant by a consolidated government. They keep round and round about the thing, but never define. I ask now what is meant by a natural aristocracy? I am not at a loss for the etymological definition of the term, for, when we trace it to the language from which it is derived, an aristocracy means nothing more or less than a government of the best men in the community, or those who are recommended by the words of the constitution of Pennsylvania, where it is directed, that the representatives should consist of those most noted for wisdom and virtue. Is there any danger in such representation? I shall never find fault, that such characters are employed. Happy for us, when such characters can be obtained. If this is meant by a natural aristocracy, and I know no other, can it be objectionable that men should be employed that are most noted for their virtue and talents? And are attempts made to mark out these as the most improper persons for the public confidence?

I had the honor of giving a definition, and I believe it was a just one, of what is called an aristocratic government. It is a government where the supreme power is not retained by the people, but resides in a select body of men, who either fill up the vacancies that happen by their own choice and election, or succeed on the principle of descent, or by virtue of territorial possessions, or some other qualifications that are not the result of personal properties. When I speak of personal properties, I mean the qualities of the head and the disposition of the heart.

We are told that the representatives will not be known to the people, nor the people to the representatives, because they will be taken from large districts where they cannot be particularly acquainted. There has been some experience in several of the States upon this subject, and I believe the experience of all who have had experience, demonstrates that the larger the district of election, the better the representation. It is only in remote corners of a government, that little demagogues arise. Nothing but real weight of character, can give a man real influence over a large district. This is remarkably shown in the commonwealth of Massachusetts. The members of the house of representatives are chosen in very small districts, and such has been the influence of party cabal and little intrigue in them, that a great majority seem inclined to show very little disapprobation of the conduct of the insurgents in that State.

The governor is chosen by the people at large, and that State is much larger than any district need be under the proposed constitution. In their choice of their governor, they have had warm disputes; but however warm the disputes, their choice only vibrated between the most eminent characters. Four of their candidates are well known; Mr. Hancock, Mr. Bowdoin, General Lincoln, and Mr. Gorham, the late president of Congress.

I apprehend it is of more consequence to be able to know the true interest of the people, than their faces; and of more consequence still, to have virtue enough to pursue the means of carrying that knowledge usefully into effect. And surely when it has been thought hitherto, that a representation in Congress of from five to two members, was sufficient to represent the interest of this State, is it not more than sufficient to have ten members in that body? and those in a greater comparative proportion than heretofore? The citizens of Pennsylvania will be represented by eight, and the State by two. This, certainly, though not gaining enough, is gaining a good deal; the members will be more distributed through the State, being the immediate choice of the people, who hitherto have not been represented in that body. It is said that the house of representatives will be subject to corruption, and the senate possess the means of corrupting, by the share they have in the appointment to office. This was not spoken in the soft language of attachment to government. It is perhaps impossible, with all the caution of legislators and statesmen, to exclude corruption and undue influence entirely from government. All that can be done, upon this subject, is done in the constitution before you. Yet it behoves us to call out, and add, every guard and preventative in our power. I think, Sir, something very important, on this subject, is done in the present system. For it has been provided, effectually, that the man that has been bribed by an office, shall have it no longer in his power to earn his wages. The moment he is engaged to serve the senate, in consequence of their gift, he no longer has it in his power to sit in the house of representatives. For "no representative shall, during the term for which he was elected, be appointed to any civil office, under the authority of the United States, which shall have been created, or the emoluments whereof shall have been increased during such time." And the following annihilates corruption of that kind: "and no person holding any office under the United States, shall be a member of either house, during his continuance in office." So that the mere acceptance of an office as a bribe, effectually destroys the end for which it was offered. Was this attended to when it was mentioned, that the members of the one house could be bribed by the other? "But the members of the senate may enrich themselves," was an observation made as an objection to this system. As the mode of doing this has not been pointed out, I apprehend the objection is not much relied upon. The senate are incapable of receiving any money except what is paid them out of the public treasury.

They cannot vote to themselves a single penny, unless the proposition originates from the other house. This objection therefore is visionary like the following one, "that pictured group, that numerous host and prodigious swarm of officers, which are to be appointed under the general government." The gentlemen tell you that there must be judges of the supreme and judges of the inferior courts, with all their appendages. There will be tax-gatherers swarming throughout the land. Oh! say they, if we could ennumerate the offices and the numerous officers that must be employed every day in collecting and receiving and comptrolling the moneys of the United States, the number would be almost beyond imagination. I have been told, but I do not vouch for the fact, that there are not in some shape or another more than a thousand persons in this very state who get their living in assessing and collecting our revenues from the other citizens. Sir, when this business of revenue is conducted on a general plan, we may be able to do the business of the thirteen states with an equal, nay, with a less number—instead of thirteen comptroller generals, one comptroller will be sufficient; I apprehend that the number of officers under this system will be greatly reduced from the number now employed. For as congress can now do nothing effectually, the states are obliged to do everything. And in this very point, I apprehend that we shall be great gainers.

Sir, I confess I wish the powers of the senate were not as they are. I think it would have been better if those powers had been distributed in other parts of the system. I mentioned some circumstances in the forenoon, that I had observed on this subject. I may mention now, we may think ourselves very well off, Sir, that things are as well as they are, and that that body is even so much restricted. But surely objections of this kind come with a bad grace from the advocates, or those who prefer the present confederation, and who wish only to increase the powers of the present Congress. A single body, not constituted with checks like the proposed one, who possess not only the power of making treaties, but executive powers, would be a perfect despotism:

but, further, these powers are, in the present confederation, possessed without control.

As I mentioned before, so I will beg leave to repeat, that this senate can do nothing without the concurrence of some other branch of the government. With regard to their concern in the appointment to offices, the president must nominate before they can be chosen; the president must acquiesce in that appointment. With regard to their power in forming treaties, they can make none, they are only auxiliaries to the president. They must try all impeachments ; but they have no power to try any until presented by the house of representatives; and when I consider this subject, though I wish the regulations better, I think no danger to the liberties of this country can arise even from that part of the system. But these objections, I say, come with a bad grace from those who prefer the present confederation, who think it only necessary to add more powers to a body organized in that form. I confess, likewise, that by combining those powers, of trying impeachments, and making treaties, in the same body, it will not be so easy as I think it ought to be, to call the senators to an account for any improper conduct in that business.

Those who proposed this system, were not inattentive to do all they could. I admit the force of the observation, made by the gentleman from Fayette (Mr. Smilie) that when two-thirds of the senate concur in forming a bad treaty, it will be hard to procure a vote of two-thirds against them, if they should be impeached. I think such a thing is not to be expected; and so far they are without that *immediate* degree of responsibility, which I think requisite to make this part of the work perfect. But this will not be *always* the case. When a member of senate shall behave criminally, the criminality will not expire with his office. The senators may be called to account after they shall have been changed, and the body to which they belonged shall have been altered. There is a rotation; and every second year one-third of the whole number go out. Every fourth year two-thirds of them are changed. In six years the whole body is supplied by a new one. Considering it in this view, responsibility is not entirely lost. There is another view in which it ought to be considered, which will show that we have a greater degree of security. Though they may not be convicted on impeachment before the senate, they may be tried by their country: and if their criminality is established, the law will punish. A grand jury may present, a petty jury may convict, and the judges will pronounce the punishment. This is all that can be done under the present confederation, for under it there is no power of impeachment; even here then we gain something. Those parts that are exceptionable in this constitution, are improvements on that concerning which so much pains are taken to persuade us, that it is preferable to the other.

The last observation respects the judges. It is said that if they dare to decide against the law, one house will impeach them, and the other will convict them. I hope gentlemen will show how this can happen, for bare supposition ought not to be admitted as proof. The judges are to be impeached, because they decide an act null and void, that was made in defiance of the constitution! What house of representatives would dare to impeach, or senate to commit judges for the performance of their duty? These observations are of a similar kind to those with regard to the liberty of the press.

I will now proceed to take some notice of those qualities in this constitution, that I think entitle it to our respect and favor. I have not yet done, Sir, with the great principle on which it stands; I mean the practical recognition of this doctrine, that in the United States the people retain the supreme power.

In giving a definition of the simple kinds of government known throughout the world, I have occasion to describe what I meant by a democracy; and I think I termed it, that government in which the people retain the supreme power, and exercise it either collectively or by representation. This constitution declares this principle in its terms and in its consequences, which is evident from the manner in which it is announced—"WE, THE PEOPLE OF THE UNITED STATES. After all the examination which I am able to give the subject, I view this as the only sufficient and the most honorable basis, both for the people and government, on which our constitution can possibly rest. What are all the contrivances of states, of kingdoms and empires? What are they all intended for? They are all intended for man, and our natural character and natural rights are certainly to take place, in preference to all artificial refinements that human wisdom can devise.

I am astonished to hear the ill-founded doctrine, that States alone ought to be represented in the federal government; these must possess sovereign authority forsooth, and the people be forgot! No: let us *reascend* to first principles. That expression is not strong enough to do my ideas justice. Let us RETAIN first principles. The people of the United States are now in the possession and exercise of their original rights, and while this doctrine is known and operates, we shall have a cure for every disease.

I shall mention another good quality belonging to this system. In it the legislative, executive and judicial powers are kept nearly independent and distinct. I express myself in this guarded manner because I am aware of some powers that are blended in the senate. They are but few, and they are not dangerous. It is an exception, yet that exception consists of but few instances and none of them dangerous. I believe in no constitution for any country on earth is this great principle so strictly adhered to or marked with so much precision and accuracy as in this. It is much more accurate than that which the honorable gentleman so highly extols, I mean the constitution of England. There, Sir, one branch of the legislature can appoint the members of another. The king has the power of introducing members into the House of Lords. I have already mentioned that in order to obtain a vote, twelve peers were poured into that house at one time; the operation is the same as might be under this constitution if the president had a right to appoint the members of the senate. This power of the king's extends into the other branch, where, though he cannot immediately introduce a member, yet he can do it remotely by virtue of his prerogative as he may create boroughs with power to send members to the House of Commons. The House of Lords form a much stronger exception to this principle than the senate in this system; for the House of Lords possess judicial powers, not only that of trying impeachments, but that of trying their own members, and civil causes when brought before them from the courts of chancery and the other courts in England.

If we therefore consider this constitution with regard to this special object, though it is not so perfect as I would wish, yet it is more perfect than any other government that I know.

I proceed to another property which I think will recommend it to those who consider the effects of beneficence and wisdom. I mean the *division of this legislative authority* into two branches. I had an opportunity of dilating somewhat on this subject before, and as it is not likely to afford a subject of debate, I shall take no further notice of it, than barely to mention it. The next good quality that I remark is that the *executive authority is one;* by this means we obtain very important advantages. We may discover from history, from reasoning, and from experience, the security which this furnishes. The executive power is better to be trusted when it has no *screen.* Sir, we have a responsibility in the person of our president; he cannot act improperly and hide either his negligence or inattention; he cannot roll upon any other person the weight of his criminality. No appointment can take place without his nomination; and he is responsible for every nomination he makes. We secure *vigor.* We well know what numerous executives are; we know there is neither vigor, decision nor responsibility in them. Add to all this: That officer is placed high, and is possessed of power far from being contemptible, yet not a *single privilege* is annexed to his character; far from being *above the laws,* he is *amenable* to them in his *private character* as a *citizen,* and in his public character by impeachment.

Sir, it has often been a matter of surprise, and frequently

complained of even in Pennsylvania, that the independence of the judges is not properly secured. The servile dependence of the judges, in some of the States, that have neglected to make proper provision on this subject, endangers the liberty and property of the citizen; and I apprehend that whenever it has happened that the appointment has been for a less period than during good behaviour, this object has not been sufficiently secured; for if every five or seven years the judges are obliged to make court for a re-appointment to office, they cannot be styled independent. This is not the case with regard to those appointed under the general government, for the judges here shall hold their offices during good behaviour. I hope no further objections will be taken against this part of the constitution, the consequence of which will be that private property (so far as it comes before their courts) and personal liberty, so far as it is not forfeited by crimes, will be guarded with firmness and watchfulness.

It may appear too professional to descend into observations of this kind, but I believe that public happiness, personal liberty and private property, depend essentially upon the able and upright determinations of independent judges.

Permit me to make one more remark on the subject of the judicial department. Its objects are extended *beyond* the bounds of power of every particular State, and therefore must be proper objects of the general government. I do not recollect any instance where a case can come before the judiciary of the United States that could possibly be determined by a particular State, except one, which is, where citizens of the same state claim lands under the grant of different States, and in that instance the power of the two States necessarily comes in competition; wherefore there would be great impropriety in having it determined by either.

Sir, I think there is another subject with regard to which this constitution deserves approbation. I mean the *accuracy* with which the *line is drawn* between the powers of the *general government*, and that of the *particular State governments*. We have heard some general observations on this subject, from the gentlemen who conduct the opposition.

They have asserted that these powers are unlimited and un-defined. These words are as easily pronounced as limited and defined. They have already been answered by my honorable colleague (Mr. M'Kean) therefore, I shall not enter into an explanation; but it is not pretended, that the line is drawn with mathematical precision; the inaccuracy of language must, to a certain degree, prevent the accomplishment of such a desire. Whoever views the matter in a true light, will see that the powers are as minutely enumerated and defined as was possible, and will also discover that the general clause, against which so much exception is taken, is nothing more than what was necessary to render effectual the particular powers that are granted.

But let us suppose (and the supposition is very easy in the minds of the gentlemen on the other side) that there is some difficulty in ascertaining where the true line lies. Are we therefore thrown into despair? Are disputes between the general government and the State governments to be neces-sarily the consequence of inaccuracy? I hope, Sir, they will not be the enemies of each other, or resemble comets in conflicting orbits mutually operating destruction: but that their motion will be better represented by that of the plane-tary system, where each part moves harmoniously within its proper sphere, and no injury arises by interference or opposi-tion. Every part, I trust, will be considered as a part of the United States. Can any cause of distrust arise here? Is there any increase of risk? or rather are not the enumerated powers as well defined here as in the present articles of con-federation?

Permit me to proceed to what I deem another excellency of this system—all authority of every kind *is derived by* REP-RESENTATION *from the* PEOPLE *and the* DEMOCRATIC *principle is carried into every part of the government.* I had an opportunity when I spoke first of going fully into an elu-cidation of this subject. I mean not now to repeat what I then said.

I proceed to another quality that I think estimable in this system, *it secures in the strongest manner the right of suffrage.*

Montesquieu, book 2d, ch. 2d, speaking of laws relative to democracy, says:

"When the body of the people is possessed of the SUPREME POWER, this is called a *democracy*. When the SUPREME POWER is lodged in the hands of a part of the people, it is then an *aristocracy*.

"In a democracy the people are in some respects the sovereign, and in others the subject.

"There can be no exercise of sovereignty but by their suffrages, which are their own will. Now, the sovereign's will is the sovereign himself. The laws, therefore, which establish the right of suffrage are fundamental to this government. And indeed it is as important to regulate in a republic in what manner, by whom, to whom, and concerning what, suffrages are to be given, as it is in a monarchy, to know who is the prince, and after what manner he ought to govern."

In this system it is declared that the electors in each state shall have the qualification requisite for electors of the most numerous branch of the state legislature. This being made the criterion of the right of suffrage, it is consequently secured, because the same constitution *guarantees* to every state in the union a *republican* form of government. The right of suffrage is fundamental to republics.

Sir, there is another principle that I beg leave to mention. *Representation and direct taxation* under this constitution are to be according to numbers. As this is a subject which I believe has not been gone into in this house, it will be worth while to show the sentiments of some respectable writers thereon. Montesquieu, in considering the requisites in a confederate republic, book 9th, ch. 3d, speaking of Holland observes, "It is difficult for the United States to be all of equal power and extent. The Lycian * republic was an association of twenty-three towns; the large ones had three votes in the common council, the middling ones two, and the small towns one. The Dutch republic consists of seven provinces of different extent of territory which have each one voice.

* Strabo, lib. 14.

The cities of Lycia * *contributed to the expenses of the state according to the proportion of suffrages.* The provinces of the United Netherlands cannot follow this proportion; they must be directed by that of their power.

In Lycia† the judges and town magistrates were elected by the common council, *and according to the proportion already mentioned.* In the republic of Holland, they are not chosen by the common council, but each town names its magistrates. Were I to give a model of an excellent confederate republic, I should pitch upon that of Lycia.

I have endeavored, in all the books that I could have access to, to acquire some information relative to the Lycian republic, but its history is not to be found; the few facts that relate to it are mentioned only by Strabo; and however excellent the model it might present, we were reduced to the necessity of working without it. Give me leave to quote the sentiments of another author, whose peculiar situation and extensive worth throws a lustre on all he says—I mean Mr. Neckar— whose ideas are very exalted both in theory and practical knowledge on this subject. He approaches the nearest to the truth in his calculations from experience, and it is very remarkable that he makes use of that expression. His words are:‡ "Population can therefore be only looked on as an exact measure of comparison, when the provinces have resources nearly equal; but even this imperfect rule of proportion ought not to be neglected. And of all the objects which may be subjected to a determined and positive calculation, that of the taxes to the population approaches nearest to the truth."

Another good quality in this constitution is, that the members of the *legislature cannot hold offices under the authority of this government.* The operation of this, I apprehend, would be found to be very extensive and very salutary in this country, to prevent those intrigues, those factions, that corruption, that would otherwise rise here, and have risen so plentiful in every other country. The reason why it is necessary in England to continue such influence, is that the crown, in order to secure its own influence against two other branches of the

---

* Strabo, lib. 14.　　† Ibid.　　‡ Neckar on Finance. vol. i., p. 308.

legislature, must continue to bestow places, but those *places* produce the opposition which frequently runs so strong in the British Parliament.

Members who do not enjoy offices combine against those who do enjoy them. It is not from principle that they thwart the ministry in all its operations. No; their language is: Let us turn them out and succeed to their places. The great source of corruption in that country, is that persons may hold offices under the crown, and seats in the legislature at the same time.

I shall conclude at present, and I have endeavored to be as concise as possible, with mentioning that, in my humble opinion, the powers of the general government are necessary and well defined; that the restraints imposed on it, and those imposed on the State governments, are rational and salutary, and that it is entitled to the approbation of those for whom it was intended.

I recollect, on a former day, the honorable gentleman from Westmoreland (Mr. Findley), and the honorable gentleman from Cumberland (Mr. Whitehill), took exceptions against the first clause of the 9th sect., art. 1, arguing very unfairly, that because Congress might impose a tax or duty of ten dollars on the importation of slaves within any of the United States, Congress might therefore permit slaves to be imported within this State, contrary to its laws. I confess I little thought that this part of the system would be excepted to.

I am sorry that it could be extended no further; but so far as it operates, it presents us with the pleasing prospect that the rights of mankind will be acknowledged and established throughout the Union.

If there was no other lovely feature in the constitution but this one, it would diffuse a beauty over its whole countenance. Yet the lapse of a few years, and Congress will have power to exterminate slavery from within our borders.

How would such a delightful prospect expand the breast of a benevolent and philanthropic European! Would he cavil at an expression, catch at a phrase? No, Sir; that is only reserved for the gentleman on the other side of your chair to do. What would be the exultation of that great man, whose name I have just mentioned, we may learn from the following sentiments on this subject. They cannot be expressed so well as in his own words.*

"The colonies of France contain, as we have seen, near five hundred thousand slaves, and it is from the number of these wretches that the inhabitants set a value on their plantations. What a fatal prospect! and how profound a subject for reflection! Alas! how inconsequent we are, both in our morality and our principles. We preach up humanity, and yet go every year to bind in chains twenty thousand natives of Africa! We call the Moors barbarians and ruffians because they attack the liberty of Europeans at the risk of their own; yet these Europeans go without danger and as mere speculators to purchase slaves, by gratifying the cupidity of their masters, and excite all those bloody scenes which are the usual preliminaries of this traffic! In short, we pride ourselves on the superiority of man, and it is with reason that we discover this superiority in the wonderful and mysterious unfolding of the intellectual faculties; and yet a trifling difference in the hair of the head or in the color of the epidermis, is sufficient to change our respect into contempt, and to engage us to place beings like ourselves, in the rank of those animals devoid of reason, whom we subject to the yoke, that we may make use of their strength and of their instinct at command.

"I am sensible, and I grieve at it, that these reflections which others have made much better than me, are unfortunately of very little use! The necessity of supporting sovereign power has its peculiar laws, and the wealth of nations is one of the foundations of this power: thus the sovereign who should be the most thoroughly convinced of what is due to humanity, would not singly renounce the service of slaves in his colonies; time alone could furnish a population of free people to replace them, and the great difference that would exist in the price of labor would give so great an advantage to the nation that should adhere to the old custom that the others would soon be discouraged in wishing to be more vir-

*Vol. i., p. 329.

tuous. And yet, would it be a chimerical project to propose a general compact by which all the European nations should unanimously agree to abandon the traffic of African slaves! They would in that case find themselves exactly in the same proportion relative to each other as at present; for it is only on comparative riches that the calculations of power are founded.

"We cannot as yet indulge such hopes; statesmen in general think that every common idea must be a low one, and since the morals of private people stand in need of being curbed and maintained by the laws, we ought not to wonder if those of sovereigns conform to their independence.

"The time may nevertheless arrive when, fatigued of that ambition which agitates them and of the continual rotation of the same anxieties and the same plans, they may turn their views to the great principles of humanity; and if the present generation is to be witness of this happy revolution, they may at least be allowed to be unanimous in offering up their vows for the perfection of the social virtues and for the progress of public beneficial institutions."

These are the enlarged sentiments of that great man.

Permit me to make a single observation in this place on the restraints placed on the State governments. If only the following lines were inserted in this constitution, I think it would be worth our adoption: "No State shall hereafter *emit bills of credit;*—make anything but gold and silver coin a *tender* in payment of debts; pass any bills of attainder, ex post facto law, *or law impairing the obligation of contracts.*" Fatal experience has taught us, dearly taught us, the value of these restraints. What is the consequence even at this moment? It is true we have no tender law in Pennsylvania; but the moment you are conveyed across the Delaware you find it haunt your journey and follow close upon your heels. The paper passes commonly at twenty-five or thirty per cent. discount. How insecure is property!

These are a few of those properties in this system that I think recommend it to our serious attention, and will entitle it to receive the adoption of the United States. Others might be enumerated, and others still will probably be disclosed by experience.

[Of the debates on the 5th and 6th of December no report exists. Neither Lloyd nor the newspapers have preserved for us even a summary. As the convention was in session on each of these days, the lack of any report can only be explained by supposing that no shorthand writer was present. From the manuscript notes of James Wilson, however, it is possible to get some idea of what was said.]

Wednesday, December 5th.*

On the morning of the 5th, Mr. Findley seems to have made a long speech on the need of a Bill of Rights; the amount of sovereignty it was safe for the States to give up; how much the constitution would take from them, and ended with an appeal for a *federal* in preference to a *consolidated* government. To say that if the constitution were rejected evil would follow, was, in his opinion, improper. It was acting the tyrant's part and saying, "Take this or nothing."

In the afternoon, Mr. Findley spoke on the partial negative of the President, on the system of representation, on the need of annual elections, on the independence of the judges; declared the internal powers of the proposed new government inadmissible; said there was no guard against Congress making paper money, and insisted that if the amendments wanted were not obtained now, they never would be. Mr. Chambers then moved to pass to the consideration of Article 2d.

Thursday, December 6th.*

Mr. Smilie objected to the powers of Congress over the militia, thought that the representatives were too few; that the President should make all appointments with the advice of a council, and dwelt at great length on the evil of giving Congress command of the militia. In these views he was supported by Mr. Findley.

Friday, December 7th.*

According to the notes of Mr. Wilson, Mr. Whitehill opened with an attack on the Vice-President. He thought that officer dangerous, as he had a casting vote, and on that

* Manuscript notes of James Wilson.

vote might often depend his salary. The power of Congress to fix the time of choosing electors was improper; the power of the Senate to make treaties was dangerous.

Mr. Findley did not want the Senate to try impeachments, and objected to blending legislative and executive powers.

Messrs. Whitehill, Smiley and Findley, in turn, then discussed the provision touching the Supreme Court. Mr. Wilson, in his notes, makes no mention of a speech by himself, but Lloyd reports him to have spoken as follows:*

Mr. Wilson. This is the first time that the article respecting the judicial department has come directly before us. I shall therefore take the liberty of making such observations as will enable honorable gentlemen to see the extent of the views of the convention in forming this article, and the extent of its probable operation.

This will enable gentlemen to bring before this House their objections more pointedly than, without any explanation, could be done. Upon a distinct examination of the different powers, I presume it will be found that not one of them is unnecessary. I will go further—there is not one of them but will be discovered to be of such nature, as to be attended with very important advantages. I shall beg leave to premise one remark, that the convention, when they formed this system, did not expect they were to deliver themselves, their relations and their posterity, into the hands of such men as are described by the honorable gentlemen in opposition. They did not suppose that the legislature, under this constitution, would be an *association of demons*. They thought that a proper attention would be given by the citizens of the United States, at the general election, for members to the House of Representatives; they also believed, that the particular States would nominate as good men as they have heretofore done, to represent them in the Senate. If they should now do otherwise, the fault will not be in Congress, but in the people, or States themselves. I have mentioned oftener than once, that for a people wanting to themselves, there is no remedy.

The convention thought further (for on this very subject,

* Lloyd's Debates.

there will appear caution, instead of imprudence in their transactions) they considered, that if suspicions are to be entertained, they are to be entertained with regard to the objects in which government have separate interests and separate views from the interests and views of the people. To say that officers of government will oppress, when nothing can be got by oppression, is making an inferrence, bad as human nature is, that cannot be allowed. When persons can derive no advantage from it, it can never be expected they will sacrifice either their duty or their popularity.

Whenever the general government can be a party against a citizen, the trial is guarded and secured in the constitution itself, and therefore it is not in its power to oppress the citizen. In the case of treason, for example, though the prosecution is on the part of the United States, yet the Congress can neither define nor try the crime. If we have recourse to the history of the different governments that have hitherto subsisted, we shall find that a very great part of their tyranny over the people has arisen from the extension of the definition of treason. Some very remarkable instances have occurred, even in so free a country as England. If I recollect right, there is one instance that puts this matter in a very strong point of view. A person possessed a favorite buck, and on finding it killed, wished the horns in the belly of the person who killed it; this happened to be the king; the injured complainant was tried and convicted of treason, for wishing the king's death.

I speak only of free governments, for in despotic ones, treason depends entirely upon the will of the prince. Let this subject be attended to, and it will be discovered where the dangerous power of the government operates to the oppression of the people. Sensible of this, the convention has guarded the people against it, by a particular and accurate definition of treason.

It is very true, that trial by jury is not mentioned in civil cases; but I take it, that it is very improper to infer from hence, that it was not meant to exist under this government. Where the people are represented—where the interest of government cannot be separate from that of the people, (and this is the case in trial between citizen and citizen) the power of making regulations with respect to the mode of trial, may certainly be placed in the legislature; for I apprehend that the legislature will not do wrong in an instance from which they can derive no advantage. These were not all the reasons that influenced the convention to leave it to the future Congress to make regulations on this head.

By the constitution of the different States, it will be found that no particular mode of trial by jury could be discovered that would suit them all. The manner of summoning jurors, their qualifications, of whom they should consist, and the course of their proceedings, are all different, in the different States; and I presume it will be allowed a good general principle, that in carrying into effect the laws of the general government by the judicial department, it will be proper to make the regulations as agreeable to the habits and wishes of the particular States as possible; and it is easily discovered that it would have been impracticable, by any general regulation, to have given satisfaction to all. We must have thwarted the custom of eleven or twelve to have accommodated any one. Why do this, when there was no danger to be apprehended from the omission? We could not go into a particular detail of the manner that would have suited each State.

Time, reflection and experience, will be necessary to suggest and mature the proper regulations on this subject; time and experience were not possessed by the convention, they left it therefore to be particularly organized by the legislature —the representatives of the United States, from time to time, as should be most eligible and proper. Could they have done better?

I know in every part, where opposition has risen, what a handle has been made of this objection; but I trust upon examination it will be seen that more could not have been done with propriety. Gentlemen talk of bills of rights! What is the meaning of this continual clamor, after what has been urged, though it may be proper in a single State, whose legislature calls itself the sovereign and supreme power? yet it would be absurd in the body of the people, when they are delegating from among themselves persons to transact certain business, to add an enumeration of those things, which they are not to do. "But trial by jury is secured in the bill of rights of Pennsylvania; the parties have a right to trials by jury, which OUGHT to be held sacred," and what is the consequence? There have been more violations of this right in Pennsylvania, since the revolution, than are to be found in England, in the course of a century.

I hear no objection made to the tenure by which the judges hold their offices—it is declared that the judges shall hold them during good behavior; nor to the security which they will have for their salaries — they shall at stated times receive for their services, a compensation which shall not be diminished during their continuance in office.

The article respecting the judicial department, is objected to as going too far, and is supposed to carry a very indefinite meaning. Let us examine this—the judicial power shall extend to all cases in law and equity, *arising under this constitution and the laws of the United States.* Controversies may certainly arise under this constitution and the laws of the United States, and is it not proper that there should be judges to decide them? The honorable gentleman from Cumberland (Mr. Whitehill) says, that laws may be made inconsistent with the constitution, and that therefore the powers given to the judges are dangerous; for my part, Mr. President, I think the contrary inference true. If a law should be made inconsistent with those powers vested by this instrument in Congress, the judges, as a consequence of their independence, and the particular powers of government being defined, will declare such law to be null and void. For the power of the constitution predominates. Any thing therefore, that shall be enacted by Congress contrary thereto, will not have the force of law.

The judicial power extends to all cases arising under treaties made, or which shall be made, by the United States. I shall not repeat at this time, what has been said with regard to the power of the States to make treaties; it cannot be controverted, that when made, they ought to be observed. But it is highly proper that this regulation should be made; for the truth is, and I am sorry to say it, that in order to prevent the payment of British debts, and from other causes, our treaties have been violated, and violated too by the express laws of several States in the Union. Pennsylvania, to her honor be it spoken, has hitherto done no act of this kind; but it is acknowledged on all sides, that many States in the Union have infringed the treaty; and it is well known, that when the minister of the United States made a demand of Lord Carmarthen, of a surrender of the western posts, he told the minister, with truth and justice, "The treaty, under which you claim those possessions, has not been performed on your part; until that is done, those possessions will not be delivered up." This clause, sir, will show the world that we make the faith of treaties a constitutional part of the character of the United States; that we secure its performance no longer nominally, for the judges of the United States will be enabled to carry them into effect, let the legislatures of the different States do what they may.

The power of the judges extends to all cases affecting ambassadors, other public ministers, and consuls. I presume very little objection will be offered to this clause; on the contrary, it will be allowed proper and unexceptionable.

This will also be allowed with regard to the following clause, "all cases of admiralty and maritime jurisdiction."

The next is, "to controversies to which the United States shall be a party." Now I apprehend it is something very incongruous, that, because the United States are a party, it should be urged as an objection, that their judges ought not to decide, when the universal practice of all nations have and unavoidably must admit of this power. But, say the gentlemen, the sovereignty of the States is destroyed, if they should be engaged in a controversy with the United States, because a suitor in a court must acknowledge the jurisdiction of that court, and it is not the custom of sovereigns to suffer their names to be made use of in this manner. The answer is plain and easy: The government of each State ought to be subordinate to the government of the United States.

"To controversies between two or more States." This power is vested in the present congress, but they are unable, as I have already shown, to enforce their decisions. The additional power of carrying their decrees into execution, we find is therefore necessary, and I presume no exception will be taken to it.

"Between a state, and citizens of another State." When this power is attended to, it will be found to be a necessary one. Impartiality is the leading feature in this Constitution; it pervades the whole. When a citizen has a controversy with another State, there ought to be a tribunal where both parties may stand on a just and equal footing.

"Between citizens of different States, and between a State, or the citizens thereof, and Foreign States, citizens or subjects." This part of the jurisdiction, I presume, will occasion more doubt than any other part, and at *first view* it may seem exposed to objections well-founded and of great weight; but I apprehend this can be the case only *at first view.* Permit me to observe here, with regard to this power, or any other of the foregoing powers given to the Federal court, that they are not exclusively given. In all instances the parties may commence suits in the courts of the several States. Even the United States may submit to such decision if they think proper. Though the citizens of a State, and the citizens or subjects of foreign States, *may* sue in the federal court, it does not follow that they *must* sue. These are the instances in which the jurisdiction of the United States may be exercised; and we have all the reason in the world to believe, that it will be exercised impartially; for it would be improper to infer that the judges would abandon their duty, the rather for being independent. Such a sentiment is contrary to experience, and ought not to be hazarded. If the people of the United States are fairly represented, and the president and Senate are wise enough to choose men of abilities and integrity for judges, there can be no apprehension; because, as I mentioned before, the government can have no interest in injuring the citizens.

But when we consider the matter a little further, is it not necessary, if we mean to restore either public or private credit, that foreigners, as well as ourselves, have a just and impartial tribunal to which they may resort? I would ask, how a merchant must feel to have his property lie at the mercy of the laws of Rhode Island? I ask further, how will a creditor feel, who has his debts at the mercy of tender laws in other States? It is true, that under this Constitution, these particular iniquities may be restrained in future; but, Sir, there are other ways of avoiding payment of debts. There have been instalment acts, and other acts of a similar effect. Such things, Sir, destroy the very sources of credit.

Is it not an important object to extend our manufactures and our commerce? This cannot be done, unless a proper security is provided for the regular discharge of contracts. This security cannot be obtained, unless we give the power of deciding upon those contracts to the general governments.

I will mention further, an object that I take to be of particular magnitude, and I conceive these regulations will produce its accomplishment. The object, Mr. President, that I allude to, is the improvement of our domestic navigation, the instrument of trade between the several States. That decay of private credit which arose from the destruction of public credit, by a too inefficient general government, will be restored, and this valuable intercourse among ourselves, must give an encrease to those useful improvements, that will astonish the world. At present, how are we circumstanced? Merchants of eminence will tell you, that they can trust their correspondents without law; but they cannot trust the laws of the State in which their correspondents live. Their friend may die, and may be succeeded by a representative of a very different character. If there is any particular objection that did not occur to me on this part of the Constitution, gentlemen will mention it; and I hope when this article is examined, it will be found to contain nothing but what is proper to be annexed to the general government. The next clause, so far as it gives original jurisdiction in cases affecting ambassadors, I apprehend is perfectly unexceptionable.

It was thought proper to give the citizens of foreign States full opportunity of obtaining justice in the general courts, and this they have by its appellate jurisdiction; therefore, in order to restore credit with those foreign States, that part of the article is necessary. I believe the alteration that will take place in their minds, when they learn the operation of this clause, will be a great and important advantage to our country, nor is it anything but justice; they ought to have the same security against the State laws that may be made, that the citizens have; because regulations ought to be equally just in the one case as in the other. Further, it is necessary in order to preserve peace with foreign nations. Let us suppose the case, that a wicked law is made in some one of the States, enabling a debtor to pay his creditor with the fourth, fifth, or sixth part of the real value of the debt, and this creditor, a foreignor, complains to his prince or sovereign, of the injustice that has been done him: What can that prince or sovereign do? Bound by inclination as well as duty to redress the wrong his subject sustains from the hand of perfidy, he cannot apply to the particular guilty State, because he knows that by the articles of confederation, it is declared that no State shall enter into treaties. He must therefore apply to the United States: The United States must be accountable: "My subject has received a flagrant injury; do me justice, or I will do myself justice." If the United States are answerable for the injury, ought they not to possess the means of compelling the faulty State to repair it? They ought, and this is what is done here. For now, if complaint is made in consequence of such injustice, Congress can answer, "Why did not your subject apply to the general court, where the unequal and partial laws of a particular State would have had no force?"

In two cases the Supreme Court has original jurisdiction; that affecting ambassadors, and when a State shall be a party. It is true, it has appellate jurisdiction in more, but it will have it under such restrictions as the Congress shall ordain. I believe then any gentleman, possessed of experience or knowledge on this subject, will agree that it was impossible to go further with any safety or propriety, and that it was best left in the manner in which it now stands.

"In all the other cases before mentioned, the Supreme Court shall have appellate jurisdiction, both as to law and fact." The jurisdiction as to fact, may be thought improper; but those possessed of information on this head, see that it is necessary. We find it essentially necessary from the ample experience we have had in the courts of admiralty with regard to captures. Those gentlemen, who during the late war, had their vessels retaken, know well what a poor chance they would have had, when those vessels were taken into other States and tried by juries, and in what a situation they would have been, if the court of appeals had not been possessed of authority to reconsider and set aside the verdict of those juries. Attempts were made by some of the States to destroy this power, but it has been confirmed in every instance.

There are other cases in which it will be necessary; and will not Congress better regulate them as they rise from time to time, than could have been done by the convention? Besides, if the regulations shall be attended with inconvenience, the Congress can alter them as soon as discovered. But any thing done in convention must remain unalterable, but by the power of the citizens of the United States at large.

I think these reasons will show, that the powers given to the Supreme Court, are not only safe, but constitute a wise and valuable part of this system.

Saturday, December 8th.

The whole of this day was taken up with a debate on the failure of the Constitution to provide for trial by jury in civil cases. Twice in the course of it the members came to personalities, and once almost to blows.

The first occurred in the course of an argument to prove the dissolution of the trial by jury, if the proposed system was adopted, and the consequent sacrifice of the liberties of the people, Mr. Findley observed, that when the trial by jury which was known in Sweden so late as the middle of the last century, fell into disuse, the commons of that nation lost their freedom, and a tyrannical aristocracy prevailed. Mr. Wilson and Mr. M'Kean interrupted Mr. Findley, and called warmly for his authority to prove that the trial by jury existed in Sweden, Mr. Wilson declaring that he had never met with such an idea in the course of his reading; and Mr. M'Kean asserting, that the trial by jury was never known in any other country than England, and the governments descended from that kingdom. Mr. Findley answered, that he did not at that moment recollect his authority, but having formerly read histories of Sweden, he had received and retained the opinion which he now advanced, and would on a future occasion perhaps, refer immediately to the book. Accordingly, on Monday afternoon, he produced the Modern Universal History, and the 3d volume of Blackstone's Commentaries, which incontrovertibly established his position. Having read his authorities, he concluded in the following manner: "I am not accustomed, Mr. President, to have my word disputed in public bodies, upon the statement of a fact; but in this convention it has already occurred more than once. It is now evident however, that I was contradicted on this subject improperly and unjustly, by the learned Chief Justice and Counsellor from the city. That the account given in the Universal History should escape the recollection or observation of the best informed man, is not extraordinary, but this I will observe, that if my son had been at the study of the law for six months, and was not acquainted with the passage in Blackstone, I should be justified in whipping him. But the contradiction coming from the quarter known to this Convention, I am at a loss whether to ascribe it to the want of veracity, or the ignorance of the learned members." On Tuesday morning Mr. Wilson again adverted to the subject in the following manner. "I will, Mr. President, take some notice of a circumstance, which for want of something more important, has made considerable noise. I mean what respects the assertion of the member from Westmoreland, that trials by jury were known in Sweden. I confess, Sir, when I heard that assertion, it struck me as new, and contrary to my idea of the fact, and therefore, in as decent terms as I could, I asked for the honorable member's authority: the book in which it is found convinces me I must before have read it, but I do not pretend to remember everything I read. This remark is made more for the sake of my colleague, who supported my opinion, than for my own. But I will add, Sir, that those whose stock of knowledge is limited to a few items, may easily remember and refer to them; but many things may be overlooked and forgotten in a magazine of literature. It may therefore with propriety be said by my honorable colleague, as it was formerly said by Sir John Maynard to a petulant student, who reproached him with an ignorance of a trifling point, "Young man, I have forgotten more law than ever you learned."*

Hardly had this incident passed away when the Antifederal party, put into high spirits by the arguments of Findley, Smilie and Whitehill, on the question of trial by jury, began to call loudly for answers from the friends of the constitution. What followed is thus reported in the *Packet.*

On Saturday last a very warm altercation passed in the convention, of which we submit to our readers the following impartial statement.

Mr. M'Kean, rising in consequence of the repeated call of the opposition for an answer to their arguments, observed that the observations and objections were so often reiterated, that most of them had already been replied to, and in his opinion, all the objections which had been made to the proposed plan, might have been delivered in the space of two hours; so he concluded, that the excess of time had been consumed in trifling and unnecessary debate. In reply to these observations, Mr. Smilie remarked, that the honorable gentleman had treated the opposition with contempt; and with *a magisterial air* had condemned their arguments. He was about to proceed in his animadversion upon the conduct of the majority, who presumed thus, he added, upon their numbers, when several members started up, but at length Mr.

* Pennsylvania Packet, Dec. 13, 1787.

Chambers claimed the attention of the president: He began a speech of some length with terming Mr. Smilie's language *indecent,* because he said it alluded to Mr. M'Kean as a judge. He then proceeded with great heat to reprobate the behavior of the *three* gentlemen, who managed the arguments against the proposed system, and declared that they had *abused* the *indulgence* which the other side of the House had *granted* to them, in consenting to hear all their reasons. He next animadverted upon the characters of those who composed the opposition, and loudly asked, where had they been found in the day of danger? Thence drawing a contrast between them and the representatives of Pennsylvania in the late Federal Convention, who were, he remarked, men of as great talents and patriotism, as good generals and statesmen, as any that had appeared in the businesss of the revolution. From this ground he took an opportunity of saying something about those Englishmen who had arrived in this country since the peace, and who had presumed to judge for themselves respecting the politics of Pennsylvania. He referred to Mr. Findley's having no more than two votes as a delegate to the Federal Convention, in order to show the insignificance of his character, and the wisdom of Pennsylvania, which would not admit of his being elected on that occasion. He then adverted to the character of Mr. M'Kean, which he asserted was superior to all attacks, and concluded with declaring that everything which had been offered by the opposition was, in his judgment, trifling and unnecessary. When Mr. Chambers had finished, Mr. Smilie appealed to the candor of the convention, whether he had used a single word which could be deemed *indecent,* and which was not fairly justified by the conduct to which he had alluded. He feelingly exclaimed that he was pleading for the interests of his country, and that no character should influence, and no violence overawe his proceedings. For, he not only claimed the free exercise of speech as a right, but he would exercise it as a duty. Mr. Findley followed, promising that he should take very little notice of the speech delivered by Mr. Chambers, as indeed he had never found occasion to take much notice of anything that dropped from that quarter. He would observe, however, that the characteristic of the conduct of the honorable member in public bodies was to discourse without reason, and to talk without argument. Here a considerable cry of order arose, and Mr. Findley said he would only add, that he always wished to avoid an investigation of characters, but at least he would take care never to engage on that subject but with a competent judge. During some disturbance in the House, Mr. Chambers retorted, that he had a perfect contempt both for Mr. Findley's arguments and person, and Mr. Findley closed the altercation with declaring, that he saw no reason for dispute, since he and Mr. Chambers were in that respect so perfectly agreed. Mr. Macpherson stated to the chair the impropriety of such proceedings, and observed, that the member from Fayette had not satisfactorily shown in what manner the member from the city (Mr. M'Kean) had spoken indecent language, to justify the retort that had been made. Mr. Findley then remarked, that when a member undertook personally to dictate to the convention, he was an object of personal animadversion; for it was only by motion and resolve of the whole body, that their proceedings were to be governed.

Mr. Smilie said, he had in his opinion satisfactorily shown the ground upon which he had spoken, for he had referred to the recollection of the convention that Mr. M'Kean treated the arguments of the opposition as trifling and contemptible, and this with a *magisterial air*, which was all the retort he had made. To this Mr. Findley subjoined, that he did not rise to argue upon the question, but to claim what was just and right; he therefore referred it to the President to determine, whether he or his coadjutors had transgressed any of the established rules of the convention? Upon this the President said, it was true that no positive rule had been transgressed, but he could not avoid considering Mr. Smilie's language highly improper. On this there was an unanimous cry of adjourn, which at last put a stop to the altercation.*

* Pennsylvania Packet Dec. 13, 1787.

Monday, December 10th.

As soon as Mr. Findley had cited his authorities in support of his statement regarding trial by jury in Sweden, a number of memorials were on Monday last presented to the convention from the inhabitants of the county of Philadelphia, stating the advantages that county enjoys, and requesting it might be offered as the seat of Federal Government, in which the exclusive jurisdiction of Congress may be exercised. This done, Mr. M'Kean took the floor and replied at length to the objectors to the Constitution, having previously given notice that he should on Wednesday recur to his motion for the adoption of the proposed plan, and remarked that the State of Delaware had already entered into that resolution, to which Mr. Smilie replied, that the State of Delaware had indeed reaped the honor of having first surrendered the liberties of the people to the new system of government.*

The speech of Mr. M'Kean is summed up in the *Packet* as follows:

On Monday (10th) afternoon, Mr. M'Kean entered into an elaborate investigation of the leading objections made to the proposed constitution, and having ably defended it in all its parts, he concluded emphatically, that having served a routine in government, in the legislative, executive and judicial departments, he saw nothing in the system under consideration which his judgment could determine to be the object of terror or apprehension; but he anticipated from its adoption what had been his constant wish—permanency in the government, and stability in the laws.

As soon as Mr. M'Kean had closed his speech, a loud and general tribute of applause was expressed by the citizens in the gallery; which gave occasion to the following philippic from Mr. Smilie. "Mr. President, I confess that hitherto I have persuaded myself that the opposition had the best of the argument on the present important question; but I have found myself mistaken, for the gentlemen on the other side have indeed an argument which surpasses and supersedes all others,—a party in the gallery

* Pennsylvania Packet, Dec. 13, 1787.

prepared to clap and huzza in affirmance of their speeches. But, Sir, let it be remembered that this is not the voice of the people of Pennsylvania; for, were I convinced of that, I should consider it as a conclusive approbation of the proposed system, and give a ready acquiescence. No, Sir, this is not the voice of the people of Pennsylvania; and were this convention assembled at another place, the sound would be of a different nature, for the sentiments of the citizens are different indeed. Even there however it would pain me, were I to see the majority of this body treated with such gross insult and disrespect by my friends, as the minority now experience from theirs. In short, Mr. President, this is not the mode which will prevail on the citizens of Pennsylvania to adopt the proposed plan, let the decision here be what it may; and I will add, that such conduct, nay were the gallery filled with bayonets, such appearance of violence would not intimidate me, or those who act with me, in the conscientious discharge of a public duty.'' When Mr. Smilie had finished, Mr. M'Kean remarked that the worthy gentleman seemed mighty angry, merely because somebody was pleased.

Mr. M'Kean said, in the course of his speech on Monday, that the apprehensions of the opposition respecting the new plan, amounted to this, that *if the sky falls, we shall catch larks; if the rivers run dry, we shall catch eels:* and he compared their arguments to a sound, but then it was a mere sound, like *the working of small beer.*

[A better report has been preserved by Lloyd, who in his published debates, declared it was delivered on December 11th. The newspapers, however, and Mr. Wilson's notes where the whole speech is carefully summarized, prove it was delivered on December 10th.]

Mr. M'Kean.* Sir, you have under your consideration a matter of very great weight and importance, not only to the present generation but to posterity; for where the rights and liberties of the people are concerned, there certainly it is fit to proceed with the utmost caution and regard. You have done so hitherto. The power of this convention, being de-

* Lloyd's Debates.

rived from the people of Pennsylvania, by a *positive* and *voluntary* grant, cannot be extended farther than what this *positive grant* hath conveyed. You have been chosen by the people, for the sole purpose of "assenting to and ratifying the constitution, proposed for the future government of the United States, with respect to their general and common concerns," or of rejecting it. It is a sacred trust; and, as on the one hand, you ought to weigh well the innovations it will create in the governments of the individual States, and the dangers which may arise by its adoption; so upon the other hand, you ought fully to consider the benefits it may promise, and the consequences of a rejection of it. You have hitherto acted strictly conformably to your delegated power; you have agreed, that a single question can come before you; and it has been accordingly moved, that you resolve, "to assent to and ratify this constitution." Three weeks have been spent in hearing the objections that have been made against it, and it is now time to determine, whether they are of such a nature as to overbalance any benefits or advantages that may be derived to the State of Pennsylvania by your accepting it.

Sir, I have as yet taken up but little of your time; notwithstanding this, I will endeavor to contract what occurs to me on the subject: and in what I have to offer, I shall observe this method; I will first consider the arguments that have been used against this constitution, and then give my reasons, why I am for the motion.

The arguments against the constitution are, I think, chiefly these:

First. That the elections of representatives and senators are not frequent enough to ensure responsibility to their constituents.

Second. That one representative for thirty thousand persons is too few.

Third. The senators have a share in the appointment of certain officers, and are to be the judges on the impeachment of such officers. This is blending the executive with the legislative and judicial department, and is likely to screen the offenders impeached, because of the concurrence of a majority of the senate in their appointment.

Fourth. That the Congress may by law deprive the electors of a fair choice of their representatives, by fixing improper times, places and modes of election.

Fifth. That the powers of Congress are too large, particularly in laying internal taxes and excises, because they may lay excessive taxes, and leave nothing for the support of the State governments.

In raising and supporting armies, and that the appropriation of money for that use should not be for so long a term as two years.

In calling forth the militia on necessary occasions; because they may call them from one end of the continent to the other, and wantonly harass them; besides, they may coerce men to act in the militia, whose consciences are against bearing arms in any case.

In making all laws which shall be necessary and proper for carrying into execution the foregoing powers, and all other powers vested by this constitution in the government of the United States, or in any department or officer thereof.

And in declaring, that this constitution, and the laws of the United States which shall be made in pursuance thereof, and all treaties made, or which shall be made, under the authority of the United States, shall be the supreme law of the land.

That migration or importation of such persons, as any of the States shall admit, shall not be prohibited prior to 1808, nor a tax or duty imposed on such importation exceeding ten dollars for each person.

Sixth. That the whole of the executive power is not lodged in the President alone, so that there might be one responsible person.

That he has the sole power of pardoning offences against the United States, and may therefore pardon traitors, for treasons committed in consequence of his own ambitious and wicked projects, or those of the Senate.

That the Vice-President is a useless officer, and being an executive officer, is to be president of the Senate, and in case of a division is to have the casting voice.

Seventh. The judicial power shall be vested in one Supreme Court. An objection is made, that the *compensation* for the services of the judges shall not be *diminished* during their continuance in office, and this is contrasted with the compensation to the President, which is to be neither *increased* nor *diminished* during the period for which he shall have been elected: but that of the judges may be increased, and the judge may hold other offices of a lucrative nature, and his judgment be thereby warped.

That in all the cases enumerated, except where the Supreme Court has original jurisdiction, "they shall have *appellate* jurisdiction, both as to law and facts, with such exceptions, and under such regulations, as the Congress shall make." From hence is inferred that the trial by jury is not secured.

That they have jurisdiction between citizens of different States.

Eighth. That there is no bill or declaration of rights in this constitution.

Ninth. That this is a *consolidation* of the several States, and not a *confederation.*

Tenth. It is an *aristocracy*, and was intended to be so by the framers of it.

The first objection that I heard advanced against this constitution, I say, sir, was that the elections of representatives and senators are not frequent enough to ensure responsibility to their constituents.

This is a subject that most men differ about, but there are more considerations than that of mere responsibility. By this system the House of Representatives is composed of persons, chosen every second year by the people of the several States; and the senators every six years by the Legislatures: whether the one or the other of these periods are of too long duration, is a question to which various answers will be given; some persons are of opinion that three years in the one case, and seven in the other, would be a more eligible term than that adopted in this constitution. In Great Britain, we find the House of Commons elected for seven years; the House of

Lords is perpetual, and the king never dies. The Parliament of Ireland is octennial; in various other parts of the British dominions, the House of Representatives are during the royal pleasure, and have been continued twenty years; this, sir, is a term undoubtedly too long. In a single State, I think annual elections most proper, but then there ought to be more branches in the Legislature than one. An annual Legislature possessed of supreme power, may be properly termed an annual despotism—and, like an individual, they are subject to caprice, and act as party spirit or spleen dictates; hence that instability to our laws, which is the bane of republican governments. The framers of this constitution wisely divided the legislative department between two houses, subject to the qualified negative of the President of the United States, though this government embraces only enumerated powers. In a single State, annual elections may be proper, the more so when the legislative powers extend to all cases; but in such an extent of country as the United States, and when the powers are circumscribed, there is not that necessity, nor are the objects of the general government of that nature as to be acquired immediately by every capacity. To combine the various interests of thirteen different States, requires more extensive knowledge than is necessary for the Legislature of any one of them; two years are therefore little enough for the members of the House of Representatives to make themselves fully acquainted with the views, the habits and interests of the United States. With respect to the Senate, when we consider the trust reposed in them, we cannot hesitate to pronounce, the period assigned to them is short enough; they possess, in common with the House of Representatives, legislative power; with its concurrence they also have power to declare war; they are joined with the President in concluding treaties; it therefore behooves them to be conversant with the politics of the nations of the world, and the dispositions of the sovereigns, and their ministers; this requires much reading and attention. And believe me, the longer a man bends his study to any particular subject, the more likely he is to be the master of it. Experience and practice will assist genius

and education.   I therefore think the time allowed, under
this system, to both houses, to be extremely proper.   This
objection has been made repeatedly, but it can only have
weight with those who are not at the pains of thinking on
the subject.   When anything, sir, new or great, is done, it
is very apt to create a ferment among those out of doors, who,
as they cannot always enter into the depth and wisdom of
counsels, are too apt to censure what they do not understand;
upon a little reflection and experience, the people often find
that to be a singular *blessing* which at first they deemed a
curse.

Second.   "That one representative for thirty thousand persons is too few."

There will be, sir, sixty-five in the House of Representatives and twenty-six in the Senate, in all ninety-one, who,
together with the President, are to make laws in the several
particular matters entrusted to them, and which are all
enumerated and expressed.   I think the number sufficient at
the present, and in three years' time, when a census or actual
enumeration must take place, they will be increased, and in
less than twenty-five years they will be more than double.
With respect to this, different gentlemen in the several States
will differ, and at last the opinion of the majority must
govern.

Third.   "The senators have a share in the appointment of
certain officers, and are to be the judges on the impeachment
of such officers.   This is blending the executive with the
legislative and judicial department, and is likely to screen
the offenders impeached, because of the concurrence of a
majority of the Senate in their appointment."

The President is to nominate to office, and with the advice and consent of the Senate appoint officers, so that he is
the responsible person, and when any such impeachment
shall be tried, it is more than probable, that not one of the
Senate, who concurred in the appointment, will be a senator,
for the seats of a third part are to be vacated every two years,
and of all in six.

As to the senators having a share in the executive power,

so far as to the appointment of certain officers, I do not know where this restraint on the President could be more safely lodged. Some may think a privy-counsellor might have been chosen by every State, but this could little mend the matter if any, and it would be a considerable additional expense to the people. Nor need the Senate be under any necessity of sitting constantly, as has been alleged, for there is an express provision made to enable the President to fill up all vacancies that may happen during their recess; the commissions to expire at the end of the next sessions.

As to impeachments, the objection is much stronger against the supreme executive council of Pennsylvania.

The House of Lords in Great Britain are judges in the last resort in all civil causes, and besides have the power of trying impeachments.

On the trial of impeachments the senators are to be under the sanction of an oath or affirmation, besides the other ties upon them to do justice; and the bias is more likely to be against the officer accused than in his favor, for there are always more persons disobliged than the contrary when an office is given away, and the expectants of office are more numerous than the possessors.

Fourth. "That the Congress may by law deprive the electors of a fair choice of their representatives, by fixing improper times, places and modes of election."

Every House of Representatives is of necessity to be the judges of the elections, returns and qualifications of its own members. It is therefore their province, as well as duty, to see that they are fairly chosen, and are the legal members; for this purpose, it is proper they should have it in their power to provide, that the times, places and manner of election, should be such as to ensure free and fair elections.

Annual *congresses* are expressly secured; they have only a power given to them, to take care, that the *elections* shall be at convenient and suitable times and places, and conducted in a proper manner; and I cannot discover why we may not entrust these particulars to the representatives of the United States, with as much safety as to those of the individual States.

In some States the electors vote *viva voce*, in others by ballot; they ought to be uniform, and the elections held on the same day throughout the United States, to prevent corruption or undue influence. Why are we to suppose that Congress will make a bad use of this power, more than the representatives in the several States?

It is said "that the powers of Congress, under this constitution, are too large, particularly in laying internal taxes and excises, because they *may* lay excessive taxes, and leave nothing for the support of the State governments." Sir, no doubt but you will discover, on consideration, the necessity of extending these powers to the government of the Union. If they have to borrow money, they are certainly bound in honor and conscience to pay the interest, until they pay the principal, as well to the foreign as to the domestic creditor ; it therefore becomes our duty to put it in their power to be honest. At present, sir, this is not the case, as experience has fully shown. Congress have solicited and required the several States to make provision for these purposes; has one State paid its quota ? I believe not one of them ; and what has been the result ? Foreigners have been compelled to advance money, to enable us to pay the interest due them on what they furnished to Congress during the late war. I trust, we have had experience enough to convince us, that Congress ought no longer to depend upon the force of requisition. I heard it urged, that Congress ought not to be authorized to collect taxes, until a State had refused to comply with this requisition. Let us examine this position. The engagements entered into by the general government, render it necessary that a certain sum shall be paid in one year; notwithstanding this, they must not have power to collect it until the year expires, and then it is too late. Or is it expected that Congress would borrow the deficiency? Those who lent us in our distress, have little encouragement to make advances again to our government; but give the power to Congress to lay such taxes as may be just and necessary, and public credit will revive: yet, because they have the power to lay taxes and excise, does it follow that they *must?* For my part, I hope it may not be necessary; but if it is, it is much easier for the citizens of the United States to contribute their proportion, than for a few to bear the weight of the whole principal and interest of the domestic debt; and there is perfect security on this head, because the regulation must equally affect every State, and the law must originate with the immediate representatives of the people, subject to the investigation of the State representatives. But is the abuse an argument against the use of power? I think it is not ; and, upon the whole, I think this power wisely and securely lodged in the hands of the general government; though on the first view of this work, I was of opinion they might have done without it; but, sir, on reflection, I am satisfied that it is not only proper, but that our political salvation may depend upon the exercise of it.

The next objection is against "the power of raising and supporting armies, and the appropriation of money for that use, should not be for so long a term as two years." Is it not necessary that the authority superintending the general concerns of the United States, should have the power of raising and supporting armies? Are we, sir, to stand defenseless amidst conflicting nations? Wars are inevitable, but war cannot be declared without the consent of the immediate representatives of the people; there must also *originate* the law which appropriates the money for the support of the army, yet they can make no appropriation for a longer term than two years; but does it follow that because they *may* make appropriations for that period, that they *must* or even *will* do it? The power of raising and supporting armies, is not only necessary, but is enjoyed by the present Congress, who also judge of the expediency or necessity of keeping them up. In England there is a standing army; though in words it is engaged but for one year, yet is it not kept constantly up? is there a year that parliament refuses to grant them supplies? Though this is done annually, it might be done for any longer term. Are not their officers commissioned for life? and when *they* exercise this power with so much prudence, shall the representatives of this country be suspected the more, because they are restricted to two years?

It is objected that the powers of Congress are too large, because "they have the power of calling forth the militia on necessary occasions, and may call them from one end of the continent to the other, and wantonly harass them; besides, they may coerce men to act in the militia whose consciences are against bearing arms in any case." It is true, by this system, power is given to Congress to organize, arm, and discipline the militia, but everything else is left to the State governments; they are to officer and train them. Congress have also the power of calling them forth, for the purpose of executing the laws of the Union, suppressing insurrections and repelling invasions; but can it be supposed they would call them in such cases from Georgia to New Hampshire? Common sense must oppose the idea.

Another objection was taken from these words of the constitution: "to make all laws which shall be necessary and proper for carrying into execution the foregoing powers, and all other powers vested by this constitution in the government of the United States, or in any department, or officer thereof." And in declaring "that this constitution, and the laws of the United States which shall be made in pursuance thereof, and all treaties made, or which shall be made, under the authority of the United States, shall be the supreme law of the land." This has at last been conceded, that though it is explicit enough, yet it gives to Congress no further powers than those already enumerated. Those that first said it gave to Congress the power of superseding the State governments, cannot persist in it; for no person can, with a tolerable face, read the clauses over, and infer that such may be the consequence.

Provision is made that Congress shall have power to prohibit the importation of slaves after the year 1808, but the gentlemen in opposition accuse this system of a crime, because it has not prohibited them at once. I suspect those gentlemen are not well acquainted with the business of the diplomatic body, or they would know that an agreement might be made, that did not perfectly accord with the will and pleasure of any one person. Instead of finding fault with what has been gained, I am happy to see a disposition in the United States to do so much.

The next objections have been against the executive power; it is complained of, "because the whole of the executive power is not lodged in the President *alone*, so that there might be one responsible person; he has the *sole* powers of pardoning offences against the United States, and may therefore pardon traitors, for treasons committed in consequence of his own ambitious or wicked projects, or those of the Senate."

Observe the contradiction, sir, in these two objections; one moment the system is blamed for not leaving all executive authority to the President *alone*, the next it is censured for giving him the *sole* power to pardon traitors. I am glad to hear these objections made, because it forebodes an amendment in that body in which amendment is necessary. The President of the United States must nominate to all offices, before the persons can be chosen; he here consents and becomes liable. The executive council of Pennsylvania appoint officers by ballot, which effectually destroys responsibility. He may pardon offences, and hence it is inferred that he may pardon traitors, for treason committed in consequence of his own ambitious and wicked projects. The executive council of Pennsylvania can do the same. But the President of the United States may be impeached before the Senate and punished for his crimes.

"The vice-President is an useless officer;" perhaps the government might be executed without him, but there is a necessity of having a person to preside in the Senate, to continue a full representation of each State in that body. The Chancellor of England is a judicial officer, yet he sits in the House of Lords.

The next objection is against the judicial department. The judicial power shall be vested in one Supreme Court. An objection is made that the compensation for the services of the judges shall not be *diminished* during their continuance in office, and this is contrasted with the compensation of the President, which is to be neither *increased* nor *dimin-*

ished during the period for which he shall be elected. But that of the judges may be increased, and the judges may hold other offices of a lucrative nature, and his judgment be thereby warped.

Do gentlemen not see the reason why this difference is made? do they not see that the President is appointed but for four years, whilst the judges may continue for life, if they shall so long behave themselves well? In the first case, little alteration can happen in the value of money; but in the course of a man's life, a very great one may take place from the discovery of silver and gold mines, and the great influx of those metals; in which case an increase of salary may be requisite. A security that their compensation shall not be lessened, nor they have to look up to every session for salary, will certainly tend to make those officers more easy and independent.

"The judges may hold other offices of a lucrative nature." This part of the objection reminds me of the scheme that was fallen upon in Pennsylvania, to prevent any person from taking up large tracts of land: a law was passed restricting the purchase to a tract not exceeding three hundred acres; but all the difference it made, was, that the land was taken up by several patents, instead of one, and the wealthy could procure, if they chose it, three thousand acres. What though the judges could hold no other office? might they not have brothers, children and other relations, whom they might wish to see placed in the offices forbidden to themselves? I see no apprehensions that may be entertained on this account

That in all cases enumerated, except where the Supreme Court has original jurisdiction, "they shall have appellate jurisdiction both as to law and fact, with such exceptions and under such regulations as the Congress shall make." From this is inferred that the trial by jury is not secured; and an objection is set up to the system, because they have jurisdiction between citizens of different States. Regulations, under this head, are necessary, but the convention would form no one that would have suited each of the United States. It has been a subject of amazement to me to hear gentlemen contend that the verdict of a jury shall be without revision in all cases. Juries are not infallible because they are twelve in number. When the law is so blended with the fact as to be almost inseparable, may not the decision of a jury be erroneous? Yet notwithstanding this, trial by jury is the best mode that is known. Appellate jurisdiction, sir, is known in the common law, and causes are removed from inferior courts by writ of error into some court of appeal. It is said that the Lord Chancellor, in all cases, sends down to the lower courts when he wants to determine a fact, but that opinion is not well founded, because he determines nineteen out of twenty without the intervention of any jury. The power to try causes between citizens of different States was thought by some gentlemen invidious; but I apprehend they must see the necessity of it, from what has been already said by my honorable colleague.

"That there is no bill or declaration of rights in this constitution."

To this I answer, such a thing has not been deemed essential to liberty, excepting in Great Britain, where there is a king and a House of Lords, quite distinct with respect to power and interest from the rest of the people; or in Poland, the *pacta conventa*, which the king signs before he is crowned, and in six States of the American United States.

Again, because it is unnecessary; for the powers of Congress, being derived from the people in the mode pointed out by this constitution, and being therein enumerated and *positively* granted, can be no other than what this positive grant conveys. *

With respect to executive officers, they have no manner of authority, any of them, beyond what is, by *positive* grant and commission, delegated to them.

"That this is a *consolidation* of the several States, and not a *confederation*."

To this I answer, the name is immaterial—the thing unites the several States, and makes them like one in particular in-

* Locke on Civil Government, vol. 2, b. 2, chap. ii, sect. 141, and in the xiiith chap. sect. 152.

stances and for particular purposes, which is what is ardently desired by most of the sensible men in this country. I care not whether it is called a consolidation, confederation, or national government, or by what other name, if it is a good government, and calculated to promote the blessings of liberty, tranquillity and happiness.

"It is an *aristocracy*, and was intended to be so by the framers of it."

Here again, sir, the name is immaterial, if it is a good system of government for the general and common concerns of the United States. But after the definition which has already been given of an aristocratic government, it becomes unnecessary to repeat arguments to prove that this system does not establish an aristocracy.

There have been some other small objections to, or rather criticisms on this work, which I rest assured the gentlemen who made them, will, on reflection, excuse me in omitting to notice them.

Many parts of this constitution have been wrested and tortured, in order to make way for shadowy objections, which must have been observed by every auditor. Some other things were said with acrimony; they seemed to be personal; I heard the sound, but it was inarticulate. I can compare it to nothing better than the feeble noise occasioned by the working of small beer.

It holds in argument as well as nature, that *destructio unius est generatio alterius*—the refutation of an argument begets a proof.

The objections to this constitution having been answered, and all done away, it remains pure and unhurt, and this alone is a forcible argument of its goodness.

Mr. President, I am sure nothing can prevail with me to give my vote for ratifying this constitution, but a conviction from comparing the arguments on both sides, that the not doing it is liable to more inconvenience and danger than the doing it.

I. If you do it, you strengthen the government and people of these United States, and will thereby have the wisdom and assistance of all the States.

II. You will settle, establish and firmly perpetuate our independence, by destroying the vain hopes of all its enemies, both at home and abroad.

III. You will encourage your allies to join with you; nay to depend, that what hath been stipulated or shall hereafter be stipulated and agreed upon, will be punctually performed, and other nations will be induced to enter into treaties with you.

IV. It will have a tendency to break our parties and divisions, and by that means, lay a firm and solid foundation for the future tranquility and happiness of the United States in general, and of this State in particular.

V. It will invigorate your commerce, and encourage shipbuilding.

VI. It will have a tendency not only to prevent any other nation from making war upon you, but from offering you any wrong or even insult.

In short, the advantages that must result from it are obviously so numerous and important, and have been so fully and ably pointed out by others, that it appears to be unnecessary to enlarge on this head.

Upon the whole, sir, the law has been my study from my infancy, and my only profession. I have gone through the circle of office, in the legislative, executive and judicial departments of government; and from all my study, observation and experience, I must declare, that from a full examination and due consideration of this system, it appears to me the *best the world has yet seen.*

I congratulate you on the fair prospect of its being adopted, and am happy in the expectation of seeing accomplished, what has been long my ardent wish—that you will hereafter have a SALUTARY PERMANENCY in *magistracy* and STABILITY IN THE LAWS.

Tuesday, December 11th.

[Mr. Wilson occupied the entire day with his reply to the objections made to the constitution. Says the *Packet:*]

On Tuesday morning, Mr. Wilson entered into a general answer of all the objections urged by the opposition, but, being fatigued, the conclusion of his speech was postponed till the afternoon. The substance of this, and of the several speeches of the members on both sides, will be given in the regular course of the debates.*

[Lloyd's report of the speech is this:]†

Tuesday, December 11th.

Mr. Wilson. Three weeks have now elapsed since this convention met. Some of the delegates attended on Tuesday, the 20th of November, a great majority within a day or two afterwards, and all but one on the fourth day. We have been since employed in discussing the business for which we are sent here. I think it will now become evident to every person who takes a candid view of our discussions, that it is high time our proceedings should draw toward a conclusion. Perhaps our debates have already continued as long, nay longer than is sufficient for any good purpose. The business which we were intended to perform is necessarily reduc to a very narrow compass. The single question to be determined is, shall we assent to and ratify the constitution proposed? As this is the first State whose convention has met on the subject, and as the subject itself is of very great importance, not only to Pennsylvania but to the United States, it was thought proper fairly, openly and candidly, to canvass it. This has been done. You have heard, Mr. President, from day to day and from week to week, the objections that could be offered from any quarter. We have heard those objections once—we have heard a great number of them repeated much oftener than once. Will it answer any valuable end, sir, to protract these debates longer? I suppose it will not. I apprehend it may serve to promote very pernicious and destructive purposes. It may perhaps be insinuated to other States, and even to distant parts of this State, by people in opposition to this system, that the expediency of adopting is at most very doubtful, and that the business labors among the members of the convention.

* Pennsylvania Packet, Dec. 13, 1787.
† Lloyd's Debates.

This would not be a true representation of the fact; for there is the greatest reason to believe, that there is a very considerable majority, who do not hesitate to ratify the constitution. We were sent here to express the voice of our constituents on the subject, and I believe that many of them expected to hear the echo of that voice before this time.

When I consider the attempts that have been made on this floor, and the many misrepresentations of what has been said among us that have appeared in the public papers, printed in this city, I confess that I am induced to suspect that opportunity may be taken to pervert and abuse the principles on which the friends of this constitution act. If attempts are made here, will they not be repeated when the distance is greater, and the means of information fewer? Will they not at length produce an uneasiness, for which there is, in fact, no cause? Ought we not to prohibit any such uses being made of the continuance of our deliberations? We do not wish to preclude debate—of this our conduct has furnished the most ample testimony. The members in opposition have not been prevented a repetition of all their objections, that they could urge against this plan.

The honorable gentleman from Fayette (Mr. Smilie) the other evening claimed for the minority, the merit of contending for the rights of mankind; and he told us, that it has been the practice of all ages, to treat such minorities with contempt: he further took the liberty of observing, that if the majority had the power, they do not want the inclination to consign the minority to punishment. I know that claims, self-made, form no small part of the merit, to which we have heard undisguised pretences; but it is one thing to claim, and it is another thing, very different indeed, to support that claim. The minority, sir, are contending for the rights of mankind; what then are the majority contending for? If the minority are contending for the rights of mankind, the majority must be contending for the doctrines of tyranny and slavery. Is it probable that is the case? Who are the majority in this assembly? Are they not the people? are they not the representatives of the people, as well as the minority? Were they not elected by the people as well as by the minority? Were they not elected by the greater part of the people? Have we a single right separate from the rights of the people? Can we forge fetters for others, that will not be clasped round our own limbs? Can we make heavy chains, that shall not cramp the growth of our own posterity? On what fancied distinction shall the minority assume to themselves the merit of contending for the rights of mankind?

Sir, if the system proposed by the late convention, and the conduct of its advocates who have appeared in this house, deserve the declarations and insinuations that have been made concerning them—well may we exclaim—Ill fated America! thy crisis was approaching! perhaps it was come! Thy various interests were neglected—thy most sacred rights were insecure. Without a government! without energy! without confidence internally! without respect externally! the advantages of society were lost to thee! In such a situation, distressed but not despairing, thou desiredst to re-assume thy native vigor, and to lay the foundation of future empire! Thou selectedst a number of thy sons, to meet together for the purpose. The selected and honored characters met; but horrid to tell! they not only consented, but they combined in an aristocratic system, calculated and intended to enslave their country! Unhappy Pennsylvania! thou, as a part of the union, must share in its unfortunate fate! for when this system, after being laid before thy citizens, comes before the delegates selected by you for its consideration, there are found but three of the numerous members that have virtue enough to raise their voices in support of the rights of mankind! America, particularly Pennsylvania, must be ill-starred indeed, if this is the true state of the case! I trust we may address our country in far other language.

Happy America! thy crisis was indeed alarming, but thy situation was not desperate. We had confidence in our country; though on whichever side we turned, we were presented with scenes of distress. Though the jarring interests of the various States, and the different habits and inclinations of their inhabitants, all lay in the way, and rendered our prospect gloomy and discouraging indeed, yet such were the generous and mutual sacrifices offered up, that amidst forty-two members, who represented twelve of the United States, there were only three who did not attest the instrument as a confirmation of its goodness. Happy Pennsylvania! this plan has been laid before thy citizens for consideration, they have sent delegates to express their voice; and listen, with rapture listen! from only three opposition has been heard against it.

The singular unanimity that has attended the whole progress of their business will in the minds of those considerate men, who have not had opportunity to examine the general and particular interest of their country, prove to their satisfaction that it is an excellent constitution, and worthy to be adopted, ordained and established by the people of the United States.

After having viewed the arguments drawn from *probability*, whether this is a good or a bad system, whether those who contend for it, or those who contend against it, contend for the rights of mankind, let us step forward and examine the *fact*.

We were told some days ago, by the honorable gentleman from Westmoreland (Mr. Findley), when speaking of this system and its objects, that the convention, no doubt, thought they were forming a compact or contract of the greatest importance. Sir, I confess I was much surprised at so late a stage of the debate to hear such principles maintained. It was matter of surprise to see the great leading principle of this system still so very much misunderstood. "The convention, no doubt, thought they were forming 'a contract!'" I cannot answer for what every member thought; but I believe it cannot be said that they thought they were making a contract, because I cannot discover the least trace of a compact in that system. There can be no compact unless there are more parties than one. It is a new doctrine that one can make a compact with himself. "The convention were forming compacts!" With whom? I know no bargains that were made there. I am unable to conceive who the parties could be. The State governments make a bargain with one another; that is the doctrine that is endeavored to be established, by gentlemen in opposition; their State sovereignties wish to be represented! But far other were the ideas of this convention, and far other are those conveyed in the system itself.

As this subject has been often mentioned, and as often misunderstood, it may not be improper to take some further notice of it. This, Mr. President, is not a government founded upon compact; it is founded upon the power of the people. They express in their name and their authority, "*We the People do ordain and establish,*" &c., from their ratification, and their ratification alone it is to take its constitutional authenticity; without that it is no more than *tabula rasa*.

I know very well all the common-place rant of State sovereignties, and that government is founded in original compact. If that position was examined, it will be found not to accede very well with the true principle of free government. It does not suit the language or genius of the system before us. I think it does not accord with experience, so far as I have been able to obtain information from history.

The greatest part of governments have been founded on conquest; perhaps a few early ones may have had their origin in paternal authority. Sometimes a family united, and that family afterwards extended itself into a community. But the greatest governments which have appeared on the face of the globe have been founded in conquest. The great empires of Assyria, Persia, Macedonia and Rome, were all of this kind. I know well that in Great Britain, since the revolution, it has become a principle that the constitution is founded in contract; but the form and time of that contract no writer has yet attempted to discover. It was, however, recognized at the time of the revolution, therefore is politically true. But we should act very imprudently to consider our liberties as placed on such foundation.

If we go a little further on this subject, I think we see that the doctrine of original compact cannot be supported consistently with the best principles of government. If we admit it, we exclude the idea of amendment; because a contract once entered into between the governor and governed becomes obligatory, and cannot be altered but by the mutual consent of both parties. The citizens of United America, I presume, do not wish to stand on that footing, with those to whom, from convenience, they please to delegate the exercise of the general powers necessary for sustaining and preserving the Union. They wish a principle established, by the operation of which the legislatures may feel the direct authority of the people. The people possessing that authority, will continue to exercise it by amending and improving their own work. This constitution may be found to have defects in it; amendments hence may become necessary; but the idea of a government founded on contract, destroys the means of improvement. We hear it every time the gentlemen are up, "Shall we violate the confederation, which directs every alteration that is thought necessary to be established by the State legislatures only?" Sir, those gentlemen must ascend to a higher source; the people fetter themselves by no contract. If your State legislatures have cramped themselves by compact, it was done without the authority of the people, who alone possess the supreme power.

I have already shown, that this system is not a compact or contract; the system itself tells you what it is; it is an ordinance and establishment of the people. I think that the force of the introduction to the work, must by this time have been felt. It is not an unmeaning flourish. The expressions declare, in a practical manner, the principle of this constitution. It is ordained and established by the people themselves; and we, who give our votes for it, are merely the proxies of our constituents. We sign it as their attorneys, and as to ourselves, we agree to it as individuals.

We are told by honorable gentlemen in opposition, "that the present confederation should have been continued, but that additional powers should have been given to it: that such was the business of the late convention, and that they had assumed to themselves the power of proposing another in its stead; and that which is proposed, is such an one as was not expected by the legistatures nor by the people." I apprehend this would have been a very insecure, very inadequate, and a very pernicious mode of proceeding. Under the present confederation, Congress certainly do not possess sufficent power; but one body of men we know they are; and were they invested with additional powers, they must become dangerous. Did not the honorable gentleman himself tell us, that the powers of government, vested either in one man, or one body of men, formed the very description of tyranny? To have placed in the present, the legislative, the executive and judicial authority, all of which are essential to the general government, would indubitably have produced the severest despotism. From this short deduction, one of these two things must have appeared to the convention, and must appear to every man, who is at the pains of thinking on the subject. It was indispensably necessary, either to make a new distribution of the powers of government, or to give such powers to one body of men as would constitute a tyranny. If it was proper to avoid tyranny, it becomes requisite to avoid placing additional powers in the hands of a Congress, constituted like the present; hence the conclusion is warranted, that a different organization ought to take place.

Our next inquiry ought to be, whether this is the most proper disposition and organization of the necessary powers. But before I consider this subject, I think it proper to notice one sentiment, expressed by an honorable gentleman from the county of Cumberland (Mr. Whitehill); he asserts the extent of the government is too great, and this system cannot be executed. What is the consequence, if this assertion is true? It strikes directly at the root of the Union.

I admit, Mr. President, there are great difficulties in adapting a system of good and free governments to the extent of our country. But I am sure that our interests as citizens, as States and as a nation, depend essentially upon an Union. This constitution is proposed to accomplish that great and desirable end. Let the experiment be made, let the system be fairly and candidly tried, before it is determined that it cannot be executed.

I proceed to another objection; for I mean to answer those

that have been suggested, since I had the honor of addressing you last week. It has been alleged by honorable gentlemen, that this general government possesses powers, for *internal* purposes, and that the general government cannot exercise internal powers. The honorable member from Westmoreland (Mr. Findley) dilates on this subject, and instances the opposition that was made by the colonies against Great Britain, to prevent her imposing internal taxes or excises. And before the Federal Government will be able to impose the one, or obtain the other, he considers it necessary that it should possess power for every internal purpose.

Let us examine these objections; if this government does not possess internal as well as external power, and that power for internal as well as external purposes, I apprehend that all that has hitherto been done, must go for nothing. I apprehend a government that cannot answer the purposes for which it is intended, is not a government for this country. I know that Congress, under the present articles of confederation, possess no internal power, and we see the consequences: they can recommend; they can go further, they can make requisitions; but there they must stop. For as far as I recollect, after making a law, they cannot take a single step towards carrying it into execution. I believe it will be found in experience, that with regard to the exercise of internal powers, the general government will not be unnecessarily rigorous. The future collection of the duties and imposts, will, in the opinion of some, supersede the necessity of having recourse to internal taxation. The United States will not, perhaps, be often under the necessity of using this power at all; but if they should, it will be exercised only in a moderate degree. The good sense of the citizens of the United States, is not to be alarmed by the picture of taxes collected at the point of the bayonet. There is no more reason to suppose that the delegates and representatives in Congress, any more than the legislature of Pennsylvania, or any other State, will act in this manner. Insinuations of this kind, made against one body of men, and not against another, though both the representatives of the people, are not made with propriety, nor will they have the weight of argument. I apprehend the greatest part of the revenue will arise from external taxation. But certainly it would have been very unwise in the late convention to have omitted the addition of the other powers; and I think it would be very unwise in this convention to refuse to adopt this constitution, because it grants Congress power to lay and collect taxes, for the purpose of providing for the common defense and general welfare of the United States.

What is to be done to effect these great purposes, if an impost should be found insufficient? Suppose a war was suddenly declared against us by a foreign power, possessed of a formidable navy: our navigation would be laid prostrate, our imposts must cease; and shall our existence as a nation, depend upon the peaceful navigation of our seas? A strong exertion of maritime power, on the part of an enemy, might deprive us of these sources of revenue in a few months. It may suit honorable gentlemen, who live at the western extremity of this State, that they should contribute nothing, by internal taxes, to the support of the general government. They care not what restraints are laid upon our commerce; for what is the commerce of Philadelphia to the inhabitants on the other side the Alleghany Mountain? But though it may suit them, it does not suit those in the lower part of the State, who are by far the most numerous. Nor can we agree that our safety should depend altogether upon a revenue arising from commerce.

Excise may be a necessary mode of taxation; it takes place in most States already.

The capitation tax is mentioned as one of those that are exceptionable. In some States, that mode of taxation is used; but I believe in many, it would be received with great reluctance; there are one or two States, where it is constantly in use, and without any difficulties and inconveniences arising from it. An excise, in its very principles, is an improper tax, if it could be avoided; but yet it has been a source of revenue in Pennsylvania, both before the revolution and since; during all which time, we have enjoyed the benefit of free government.

I presume, sir, that the executive powers of government ought to be commensurate with the government itself, and that a government which cannot act in every part, is so far defective. Consequently it is necessary, that Congress possess powers to tax internally, as well as externally.

It is objected to this system, that under it there is no sovereignty left in the State governments. I have had occasion to reply to this already; but I should be very glad to know at what period the State governments became possessed of the supreme power. On the principle on which I found my arguments, and that is the principle of this constitution, the supreme power resides in the people. If they choose to indulge a part of their sovereign power to be exercised by the State governments, they may. If they have done it, the States were right in exercising it; but if they think it no longer safe or convenient, they will resume it, or make a new distribution, mere likely to be productive of that good, which ought to be our constant aim.

The power both of the general government, and the State governments, under this system, are acknowledged to be so many emanations of power from the people. The great object now to be attended to, instead of disagreeing about who shall possess the supreme power, is to consider whether the present arrangement is well calculated to promote and secure the tranquility and happiness of our common country. These are the dictates of sound and unsophisticated sense, and what ought to employ the attention and judgment of this honorable body.

We are next told, by the honorable gentlemen in opposition (as indeed we have been from the beginning of the debates in this convention, to the conclusion of their speeches yesterday) that this is a consolidated government, and will abolish the State governments. Definitions of a consolidated government have been called for; the gentlemen gave us what they termed definitions, but it does not seem, to me at least, that they have as yet expressed clear ideas upon that subject. I will endeavor to state their different ideas upon this point.

The gentleman from Westmoreland (Mr. Findley) when

speaking on this subject, says, that he means by a consolidation, that government which puts the thirteen States into one.

The honorable gentleman from Fayette (Mr. Smilie) gives you this definition: "What I mean by a consolidated government, is one that will transfer the sovereignty from the State governments to the general government."

The honorable member from Cumberland (Mr. Whitehill) instead of giving you a definition, sir, tells you again, that "it is a consolidated government, and we have proved it so."

These, I think, sir, are the different descriptions given us of a consolidated government. As to the first, that it is a consolidated government, that puts the thirteen United States into one; if it is meant, that the general government will destroy the governments of the States, I will admit that such a government would not suit the people of America: It would be improper for *this* country, because it could not be proportioned to *its extent* on the principles of freedom. But that description does not apply to the system before you. This, instead of placing the State governments in jeopardy, is founded on their existence. On this principle, its organization depends; it must stand or fall, as the State governments are secured or ruined. Therefore, though this may be a very proper description of a consolidating government, yet it must be disregarded as inapplicable to the proposed constitution. It is not treated with decency, when such insinuations are offered against it.

The honorable gentleman (Mr. Smilie) tells you, that a consolidating government "is one that will transfer the sovereignty from the State governments to the general government." Under this system, the sovereignty is not in the possession of the State governments, therefore it cannot be transferred from them to the general government. So that in no point of view of this definition, can we discover that it applies to the present system.

In the exercise of its powers will be insured the exercise of their powers to the State government; it will insure peace and stability to them; their strength will increase with its strength, their growth will extend with its growth.

Indeed, narrow minds, and some such there are in every government—narrow minds, and intriguing spirits—will be active in sowing dissentions and promoting discord between them. But those whose understandings and whose hearts are good enough to pursue the general welfare, will find, that what is the interest of the whole, must, on the great scale, be the interest of every part. It will be the duty of a State, as of an individual, to sacrifice her own convenience to the general good of the Union.

The next objection that I mean to take notice of is, that the powers of the several parts of this government are not kept as distinct and independent as they ought to be. I admit the truth of this general sentiment. I do not think, that in the powers of the Senate, the distinction is marked with so much accuracy as I wished, and still wish; but yet I am of opinion that real and effectual security is obtained, which is saying a great deal. I do not consider this part as *wholly* unexceptionable; but even where there are defects in this system, they are improvements upon the old. I will go a little further; though in this system, the distinction and independence of power is not adhered to with entire theoretical precision, yet it is more strictly adhered to than in any other system of government in the world. In the Constitution of Pennsylvania, the executive department exercises judicial powers, in the trial of public officers; yet a similar power in this system is complained of ; at the same time the constitution of Pennsylvania is referred to, as an example for the late convention to have taken a lesson by.

In New Jersey, in Georgia, in South Carolina, and in North Carolina, the executive power is blended with the legislative. Turn to their constitutions, and see in how many instances.

In North Carolina, the senate and house of commons elect the governor himself; they likewise elect seven persons, to be a council of State, to advise the governor in the execution of his office. Here we find the whole executive department under the nomination of the legislature, at least the most important part of it.

In South Carolina, the legislature appoint the governor and commander-in-chief, lieutenant governor and privy council. "Justices of the peace shall be nominated by the legislature, and commissioned by the governor," and what is more, they are appointed during pleasure. All other judicial officers are to be appointed by the senate and house of representatives. I might go further, and detail a great multitude of instances, in which the legislative, executive, and judicial powers are blended, but it is unnecessary; I only mention these to show, that though this constitution does not arrive at what is called perfection, yet it contains great improvements, and its powers are distributed with a degree of accuracy superior to what is termed accuracy, in particular States.

There are four instances in which improper powers are said to be blended in the Senate. We are told, that this government is imperfect, because the Senate possess the power of trying impeachments. But here, sir, the Senate are under a check, as no impeachment can be tried until it is made; and the House of Representatives possess the sole power of making impeachments. We are told that the share which the Senate have in making treaties, is exceptionable; but here they are also under a check, by a constituent part of the government, and nearly the immediate representative of the people—I mean the President of the United States. They can make no treaty without his concurrence. The same observation applies in the appointment of officers. Every officer must be nominated solely and exclusively by the President.

Much has been said on the subject of treaties, and this power is denominated a blending of the legislative and executive powers in the Senate. It is but justice to represent the favorable, as well as unfavorable side of a question, and from thence determine whether the objectionable parts are of a sufficient weight to induce a rejection of this constitution.

There is no doubt, sir, but under this constitution, treaties will become the supreme law of the land; nor is there any doubt but the Senate and President possess the power of making them. But though treaties are to have the force of laws, they are in some important respects very different from other acts of legislation. In making laws, our own consent alone is necessary. In forming treaties, the concurrence of another power becomes necessary; treaties, sir, are truly contracts, or compacts, between the different states, nations, or princes, who find it convenient or necessary to enter into them. Some gentlemen are of opinion, that the power of making treaties should have been placed in the legislature at large; there are, however, reasons that operate with a great force on the other side. Treaties are frequently (especially in time of war) of such a nature that it would be extremely improper to publish them, or even commit the secret of their negotiation to any great number of persons. For my part I am not an advocate for secrecy in transactions relating to the public; not generally even in forming treaties, because I think that the history of the diplomatique corps will evince, even in that great department of politics, the truth of an old adage, that "honesty is the best policy," and this is the conduct of the most able negotiators; yet sometimes secrecy may be necessary, and therefore it becomes an argument against committing the knowledge of these transactions to too many persons. But in their nature treaties originate differently from laws. They are made by equal parties, and each side has half of the bargain to make; they will be made between us and the powers at the distance of three thousand miles. A long series of negotiations will frequently precede them; and can it be the opinion of these gentlemen, that the legislature should be in session during this whole time? It well deserves to be remarked, that though the house of representatives possess no active part in making treaties, yet their legislative authority will be found to have strong restraining influence upon both President and Senate. In England, if the king and his ministers find themselves, during their negotiation, to be embarrassed, because an existing law is not repealed, or a new law is not enacted, they give notice to the legislature of their situation, and inform them that it will be necessary, before the treaty can operate, that some law be repealed, or some be made. And will not the same thing take place here? Shall less prudence, less caution, less moderation, take place among those who negotiate treaties for the United States, than among those who negotiate them for the other nations of the earth? And let it be attended to, that even in the making treaties the States are immediately represented, and the people mediately represented; two of the constituent parts of the government must concur in making them. Neither the President nor the Senate solely, can complete a treaty; they are checks upon each other, and are so balanced as to produce security to the people.

I might suggest other reasons, to add weight to what has already been offered, but I believe it is not necessary; yet let me, however, add one thing, the Senate is a favorite with many of the States, and it was with difficulty that these checks could be procured; it was one of the last exertions of conciliation, in the late convention, that obtained them.

It has been alleged, as a consequence of the small number of representatives, that they will not know as intimately as they ought, the interests, inclinations, or habits, of their constituents.

We find on an examination of all its parts, that the objects of this government are such as extend beyond the bounds of the particular States. This is the line of distinction between this government and the particular State governments.

This principle I had an opportunity of illustrating on a former occasion. Now when we come to consider the objects of this government, we shall find, that in making our choice of a proper character to be a member of the House of Representatives, we ought to fix on one, whose mind and heart are enlarged; who possesses a general knowledge of the interests of America, and a disposition to make use of that knowledge for the advantage and welfare of his country. It belongs not to this government to make an act for a particular township, county, or State.

A defect in *minute* information, has not certainly been an objection in the management of the business of the United States, but the want of enlarged ideas, has hitherto been chargeable on our councils; yet even with regard to minute knowledge, I do not conceive it impossible to find eight characters, that may be very well informed as to the situation, interests and views of every part of this State; and who may have a concomitant interest with their fellow citizens: they could not materially injure others, without affecting their own fortunes.

I did say, that in order to obtain that enlarged information in our representatives, a large district for election would be more proper than a small one. When I speak of large districts, it is not agreeble to the idea entertained by the honorable member from Fayette (Mr. Smilie), who tells you, that elections for large districts must be ill attended, because the people will not choose to go very far on this business. It is not meant, sir, by me, that the votes should be taken at one place; no, sir, the elections may be held through this State, in the same manner as elections for members of the general assembly, and this may be done too without any additional inconvenience or expense.

If it could be effected, all the people of the same society ought to meet in one place, and communicate freely with each other on the great business of representation. Though this cannot be done in fact, yet we find that it is the most favorite and constitutional idea. It is supported by this principle too, that every member is the representative of the whole community, and not of a particular part. The larger therefore the district is, the greater is the probability of selecting wise and virtuous characters, and the more agreeable it is to the constitutional principle of representation.

As to the objection, that the House of Representatives may be bribed by the Senate, I confess I do not see that bribery is an objection against *this system;* it is rather an objection against human nature. I am afraid that bribes in every government may be offered and received; but let me ask of the gentlemen who urge this objection, to point out where any power is given to bribe *under this Constitution?* Every species of influence is guarded against as much as possible. Can the Senate procure money to effect such design? All public moneys must be disposed of by law, and it is necessary that the House of Representatives originate such law. Before the money can be got out of the treasury, it must be appropriated by law. If the legislature had the effrontery to set aside three or four hundred thousand pounds for this purpose, and the people would tamely suffer it, I grant it might be done; and in Pennsyvania the legislature might do the same; for by a law, and that conformably to the Constitution, they might divide among themselves what portion of the public money they pleased. I shall just remark, Sir, that the objections which have repeatedly been made, with regard to "the number of representatives being too small, and that they may possibly be made smaller; that the districts are too large, and not within the reach of the people; and that the House of Representatives may be bribed by the Senate." These objections come with an uncommon degree of impropriety, from those who would refer us back to the articles of confederation. For under those the representation of this State cannot exceed seven members, and may consist of only two; and these are wholly without the reach or control of the people. Is there not also greater danger that the majority of such a body might be more easily bribed, than the majority of one, not only more numerous, but checked by a division of two or three distinct and independent parts? The danger is certainly better guarded against in the proposed system, than in any other yet devised.

The next objections which I shall notice, are, "that the powers of the Senate are too great, that the representation therein is unequal, and that the Senate, from the smallness of its number, may be bribed." Is there any propriety in referring us to the confederation on this subject? Because, in one or two instances, the Senate possess more power than the House of Representatives, are these gentlemen supported in their remarks, when they tell you they wished and expected more powers to be given to the present Congress, a body certainly much more exceptionable than any instituted under this system?

"That the representation in the Senate is unequal," I regret, because I am of opinion the States ought to be represented according to their importance; but in this system there is considerable improvement; for the true principle of representation is carried into the House of Representatives, and into the choice of the President; and without the assistance of one or the other of these, the Senate is inactive, and can do neither good or evil.

It is repeated again and again, by the honorable gentlemen, "that the power over elections, which is given to the general government in this system, is a dangerous power." I must own I feel myself surprised that an objection of this kind should be persisted in, after what has been said by my honorable colleague in reply. I think it has appeared by a minute investigation of the subject, that it would have been not only unwise, but highly improper in the late convention, to have omitted this clause, or given less power than it does over elections. Such powers, sir, are enjoyed by every State government in the United States. In some, they are of a much greater magnitude; and why should this be the only one deprived of them? Ought not this, as well as every other legislative body, to have the power of judging of the qualifications of its own members? "The times, places and manner of holding elections for representatives, may be altered by Congress." This power, sir, has been shown to be necessary, not only on some particular occasions, but even to the very existence of the federal government. I have heard some very improbable suspicions indeed, suggested with regard to the manner in which it will be exercised. Let us suppose it may be improperly exercised; is it not more likely so to be by the particular States, than by the government of the United States? because the general government will be more studious of the good of the whole, than a particular State will be; and therefore, when the power of regulating the time, place or manner of holding elections is exercised by the Congress, it will be to correct the improper regulations of a particular State.

I now proceed to the second article of this Constitution, which relates to the executive department.

I find, Sir, from an attention to the argument used by the

gentlemen on the other side of the house, that there are but few exceptions taken to this part of the system. I shall take notice of them, and afterwards point out some valuable qualifications, which I think this part possesses in an eminent degree.

The objection against the powers of the President, is not that they are too many or too great, but to state it in the gentlemen's own language, they are so trifling, that the President is no more than the *tool* of the Senate.

Now, Sir, I do not apprehend this to be the case, because I see that he may do a great many things independent of the Senate; and with respect to the executive powers of government in which the Senate participate, they can do nothing without him. Now I would ask, which is most likely to be the tool of the other? Clearly, Sir, he holds the helm, and the vessel can proceed neither in one direction nor another, without his concurrence. It was expected by many, that the cry would have been against the powers of the President as a monarchical power; indeed the echo of such sound was heard, some time before the rise of the late convention. There were men at that time, determined to make an attack upon whatever system should be proposed, but they mistook the point of direction. Had the President possessed those powers, which the opposition on this floor are willing to consign him, of making treaties, and appointing officers, with the advice of a council of State, the clamor would have been, that the House of Representatives, and the Senate, were the *tools* of the monarch. This, Sir, is but conjecture, but I leave it to those who are acquainted with the current of the politics pursued by the enemies to this system, to determine whether it is a reasonable conjecture or not.

The manner of appointing the President of the United States, I find, is not objected to, therefore I shall say little on that point. But I think it well worth while to state to this house, how little the difficulties, even in the most difficult part of this system, appear to have been noticed by the honorable gentlemen in opposition. The Convention, Sir, were perplexed with no part of this plan so much as with the mode of choosing the President of the United States. For my own part, I think the most unexceptionable mode, next after the one prescribed in this Constitution, would be that practised by the eastern States, and the State of New York; yet if gentlemen object, that an eighth part of our country forms a district too large for elections, how much more would they object, if it was extended to the whole Union? On this subject, it was the opinion of a great majority in Convention, that the thing was impracticable; other embarrassments presented themselves.

Was the President to be appointed by the legislature? was he to continue a certain time in office, and afterward was he to become ineligible?

To have the executive officers dependent upon the legislative, would certainly be a violation of that principle, so necessary to preserve the freedom of republics, that the legislative and executive powers should be separate and independent. Would it have been proper, that he should be appointed by the Senate? I apprehend that still stronger objections could be urged against that—cabal, intrigue, corruption— every thing bad would have been the necessary concomitant of every election.

To avoid the inconveniences already enumerated, and many others that might be suggested, the mode before us was adopted. By it we avoid corruption, and we are little exposed to the lesser evils of party and intrigue; and when the government shall be organized, proper care will undoubtedly be taken to counteract influence even of that nature—the constitution, with the same view, has directed that the day on which the electors shall give their votes, shall be the same throughout the United States. I flatter myself the experiment will be a happy one for our country.

The choice of this officer is brought as nearly home to the people as is practicable; with the approbation of the State legislatures, the people may elect with only one remove; for "each State shall appoint, in such manner as the legislature thereof may direct, a number of electors equal to the whole number of senators and representatives, to which the State may be entitled in Congress.'' Under this regulation, it will not be easy to corrupt the electors, and there will be little time or opportunity for tumult or intrigue. This, Sir, will not be like the elections of a Polish diet, begun in noise and ending in bloodshed.

If gentlemen will look into this article, and read for themselves, they will find that there is no well-grounded reason to suspect the President will be the *tool* of the Senate. "The President shall be commander in chief of the army and navy of the United States, and of the milita of the several States, when called into the actual service of the United States. He may require the opinion in writing of the principal officers in each of the executive departments, upon any subject relative to the duties of their respective offices; and he shall have power to grant reprieves and pardons, for offences against the United States." Must the President, after all, be called the *tool* of the Senate? I do not mean to insinuate that he has more powers than he ought to have, but merely to declare, that they are of such a nature as to place him above expressions of contempt.

There is another power of no small magnitude, entrusted to this officer: "He shall take care that the laws be faithfully executed."

I apprehend, that in the administration of this government, it will not be found necessary for the Senate always to sit. I know some gentlemen have insinuated and conjectured, that this will be the case, but I am inclined to a contrary opinion. If they had employment every day, no doubt but it might be the wish of the Senate to continue their session; but from the nature of their business, I do not think it will be necessary for them to attend longer than the House of Representatives. Besides their legislative powers, they possess three others, viz., trying impeachments, concurring in making treaties, and in appointing officers. With regard to their power in making treaties, it is of importance that it should be very seldom exercised—we are happily removed from the vortex of European politics, and the fewer and the more simple our negotiations with European powers, the better they will be;

if such be the case, it will be but once in a number of years, that a single treaty will come before the Senate. I think, therefore, that on this account it will be unnecessary to sit constantly. With regard to the trial of impeachments, I hope it is what will seldom happen. In this observation, the experience of the ten last years supports me. Now there is only left the power of concurring in the appointment of officers; but care is taken, in this constitution, that this branch of business may be done without their presence—the President is authorized to fill up all vacancies that may happen during the recess of the Senate, by granting commissions, which shall expire at the end of their next session. So that on the whole the Senate need not sit longer than the House of Representatives, at the public expense; and no doubt if apprehensions are entertained of the Senate, the House of Representatives will not provide pay for them one day longer than is necessary. But what (it will be asked) is this great power of the President? he can fill the offices only by temporary appointments. True: but every person knows the advantage of being once introduced into an office; it is often of more importance than the highest recommendation.

Having now done with the legislative and executive branches of this government, I shall just remark, that upon the whole of the executive, it appears that the gentlemen in opposition state nothing as exceptionable but the deficiency of powers in the President; but rather seem to allow some degree of political merit in this department of government.

I now proceed to the judicial department; and here, Mr. President, I meet an objection I confess I had not expected; and it seems it did not occur to the honorable gentleman (Mr. Findley) who made it, until a few days ago.

He alleges that the judges, under this constitution, are not rendered sufficiently independent, because they may hold other offices; and though they may be independent as judges, yet their other office may depend upon the legislature. I confess, sir, this objection appears to me to be a little wire-drawn in the first place; the legislature can appoint to no office, therefore the dependence could not be on them for the office, but rather on the President and Senate; but then these cannot add the salary, because no money can be appropriated but in consequence of a law of the United States.   No sinecure can be bestowed on any judge, but by the concurrence of the whole legislature and of the President; and I do not think this an event that will probably happen.

It is true, that there is a provision made in the Constitution of Pennsylvania, that the judges shall not be allowed to hold any other office whatsoever; and I believe they are expressly forbidden to sit in Congress; but this, sir, is not introduced as a principle into this constitution.   There are many States in the Union, whose constitutions do not limit the usefulness of their best men, or exclude them from rendering such services to their country, for which they are found eminently qualified.   New York, far from restricting their chancellor or judges of the Supreme Court from a seat in Congress, expressly provide for sending them there on extraordinary occasions.   In Connecticut, the judges are not precluded from enjoying other offices.   Judges from many States have sat in Congress.   Now it is not to be expected, that eleven or twelve States are to change their sentiments and practice on this subject, to accommodate themselves to Pennsylvania.

It is again alleged against this system, that the powers of the judges are too extensive; but I will not trouble you, sir, with a repetition of what I had the honor of delivering the other day; I hope the result of those arguments gave satisfaction, and proved that the judicial were commensurate with the legislative powers; that they went no further, and that they ought to go so far.

The laws of Congress being made for the Union, no particular State can be alone affected; and as they are to provide for the general purposes of the Union, so ought they to have the means of making the provisions effectual, over all that country included within the Union.

Eodem Die, 1787, P. M.

Mr. Wilson.   I shall now proceed, Mr. President, to notice the remainder of the objections that have been suggested, by the honorable gentlemen who oppose the system now before you.

We have been told, Sir, by the honorable member from Fayette (Mr. Smilie), "that the trial by jury was *intended* to be given up, and the civil law was *intended* to be introduced into its place, in civil cases."

Before a sentiment of this kind was hazarded, I think, Sir, the gentleman ought to be prepared with better proofs in its support, than any he has yet attempted to produce. It is a charge, Sir, not only unwarrantable, but cruel; the idea of such a thing, I believe, never entered into the mind of a single member of that convention; and I believe further, that they never suspected there would be found within the United States, a single person that was capable of making such a charge. If it should be well founded, Sir, they *must* abide by the consequences, but if (as I trust it will fully appear) it is ill founded, then he or they who make it, *ought* to abide by the consequences.

Trial by jury forms a large field for investigation, and numerous volumes are written on the subject; those who are well acquainted with it may employ much time in its discussion; but in a country where its excellence is so well understood, it may not be necessary to be very prolix, in pointing them out. For my part, I shall confine myself to a few observations in reply to the objections that have been suggested.

The member from Fayette (Mr. Smilie) has labored to infer, that under the articles of confederation, the Congress possessed no appellate jurisdiction; but this being decided against him, by the words of that instrument, by which is granted to Congress the power of "establishing courts for receiving and determining, finally, appeals in all cases of capture;" he next attempts a distinction, and allows the power of appealing from the decisions of the judges, but not from the verdict of a jury; but this is determined against him also, by the practice of the States; for in every instance which has occurred, this power has been claimed by Congress, and exercised, by the court of appeals; but what would be the consequences of allowing the doctrine for which he contends?

Would it not be in the power of a jury, by their verdict, to involve the whole Union in a war? They may condemn the property of a natural, or otherwise infringe the law of nations; in this case ought their verdict to be without revisal? Nothing can be inferred from this, to prove that trials by jury were intended to be given up. In Massachusetts, and all the Eastern States, these causes are tried by juries, though they acknowledge the appellate jurisdiction of Congress.

I think I am not now to learn the advantages of a trial by jury; it has excellencies that entitle it to a superiority over any other mode, in cases to which it is applicable.

When jurors can be acquainted with the characters of the parties and the witnesses, where the whole cause can be brought within their knowledge and their view, I know no mode of investigation equal to that by a jury: they hear every thing that is alleged; they not only hear the words, but they see and mark the features of the countenance; they can judge of weight due to such testimony; and moreover, it is a cheap and expeditious manner of distributing justice. There is another advantage annexed to the trial by jury; the jurors may indeed return a mistaken, or ill founded verdict, but their errors cannot be systematical.

Let us apply these observations to the objects of the judicial department, under this constitution. I think it has been shewn already, that they all extend beyond the bounds of any particular State; but further, a great number of the civil causes there enumerated, depend either upon the law of nations, or the marine law, that is, the general law of mercantile countries. Now, Sir, in such causes, I presume it will not be pretended that this mode of decision ought to be adopted; for the law with regard to them is the same here as in every other country, and ought to be administered in the same manner. There are instances, in which I think it highly probable, that the trial by jury will be found proper; and if it is highly probable that it will be found proper, is it not equally probable, that it will be adopted? There may be causes depending between citizens of different States, and as trial by jury is known and regarded in all the States, they will certainly prefer that mode of trial before any other. The Congress will have the power of making proper regulations on this subject, but it was impossible for the convention to have gone minutely into it; but if they could, it must have been very improper, because alterations, as I observed before, might have been necessary; and whatever the convention might have done would have continued unaltered, unless by an alteration of the Constitution. Besides, there was another difficulty with regard to this subject. In some of the States they have courts of chancery, and other appellate jurisdictions, and those State are as attached to that mode of distributing justice, as those that have none are to theirs.

I have desired, repeatedly, that honorable gentlemen, who find fault, would be good enough to point out what they deem to be an improvement. The member from Westmoreland (Mr. Findley) tells us, that the trial between citizens of different States ought to be by a jury of that State in which the cause of action arose. Now it is easy to see, that in many instances, this would be very improper and very partial; for beside the different manner of collecting and forming juries in the several States, the plaintiff comes from another State; he comes a stranger, unknown as to his character or mode of life, while the other party is in the midst of his friends, or perhaps his dependents. Would a trial by jury in such a case ensure justice to the stranger? But again; I would ask that gentleman, whether if a great part of his fortune was in the hands of some person in Rhode Island, he would wish that his action to recover it, should be determined by a jury of that country, under its present circumstances?

The gentleman from Fayette (Mr. Smilie) says, that if the convention found themselves embarrassed, at least they might have done thus much—they should have declared, that the substance should be secured by Congress; this would be saying nothing unless the cases were particularized.

Mr. Smilie. I said the convention ought to have declared, that the legislature should establish the trial by jury by proper regulations.

Mr. Wilson. The legislature shall establish it by proper regulations! So after all, the gentleman has landed us at the very point from which we set out. He wishes them to do the very thing they have done, to leave it to the discretion of Congress. The fact, sir, is, nothing more could be done.

It is well known, that there are some cases that should not come before juries; there are others, that in some of the States never come before juries, and in those States where they do come before them, appeals are found necessary, the facts re-examined, and the verdict of the jury sometimes is set aside; but I think in all cases, where the cause has come originally before a jury, that the last examination ought to be before a jury likewise.

The power of having appellate jurisdiction, as to facts, has been insisted upon as a proof, "that the convention *intended* to give up the trial by jury in civil cases, and to introduce the civil law." I have already declared my own opinion on this point, and have shown, not merely, that it is founded on reason and authority. The express declaration of Congress * is to the same purpose: They insist upon this power, as requisite to preserve the peace of the Union; certainly, therefore, it ought always to be possessed by the head of the confederacy.

We are told, as an additional proof, that the trial by jury was intended to be given up, "that appeals are unknown to the common law; that the term is a civil law term, and with it the civil law is intended to be introduced." I confess I was a good deal surprised at this observation being made; for Blackstone, in the very volume which the honorable member (Mr. Smilie) had in his hand and read us several extracts from, has a chapter entitled "of proceeding in the nature of appeals;" and in that chapter says, that the principal method of redress for erroneous judgments in the king's courts of record, is by writ of error to some superior "*court of appeal.*"† Now, it is well known, that his book is a commentary upon the common law. Here then is a strong refutation of the assertion, "that appeals are unknown to the common law."

* Journals of Congress, March 6, 1779.　　† III. Blackstone, 406.

I think these were all the circumstances adduced to show the truth of the assertion that in this constitution, the trial by jury was *intended* to be given up by the late convention in framing it. Has the assertion been proved? I say not, and the allegations offered, if they apply at all, apply in a contrary direction. I am glad that this objection has been stated, because it is a subject upon which the enemies of this constitution have much insisted. We have now had an opportunity of investigating it fully, and the result is, that there is no foundation for the charge, but it must proceed from ignorance or something worse.

I go on to another objection which has been taken to this system, "that the expense of the general government and of the State governments, will be too great, and that the citizens will not be able to support them." If the State governments are to continue as cumbersome and expensive as they have hitherto been, I confess it would be distressing to add to their expenses, and yet it might be necessary; but I think I can draw a different conclusion on this subject, from more conjectures than one. The additional revenue to be raised by a general government, will be more than sufficient for the additional expense; and a great part of that revenue may be so contrived as not to be taken from the citizens of this country; for I am not of opinion that the consumer always pays the impost that is laid on imported articles; it is paid sometimes by the importer, and sometimes by the foreign merchant who sends them to us. Had a duty of this nature been laid at the time of the peace, the greatest part of it would have been the contribution of foreigners. Besides, whatever is paid by the citizens is a voluntary *payment*.

I think, Sir, it would be very easy and laudable, to lessen the expenses of the State governments. I have been told (and perhaps it is not very far from the truth), that there are *two thousand* members of assembly in the several States; the business of revenue is done in consequence of requisitions from Congress, and whether it is furnished or not, it commonly becomes a subject of discussion. Now when this business is executed by the legislature of the United States, I leave it to those who are acquainted with the expense of long and frequent sessions of assembly, to determine the great saving that will take place. Let me appeal to the citizens of Pennsylvania how much time is taken up in this State every year, if not every session, in providing for the payment of an amazing interest due on her funded debt. There will be many sources of revenue, and many opportunities for economy, when the business of finance shall be administered under one government; the funds will be more productive, and the taxes, in all probability, less burthensome than they are now.

I proceed to another objection that is taken against the power given to Congress, of raising and keeping up standing armies. I confess I have been surprised that this objection was ever made, but I am more so that it is still repeated and insisted upon. I have taken some pains to inform myself how the other governments of the world stand with regard to this power; and the result of my enquiry is, that there is not one which has not the power of raising and keeping up standing armies. A government without the power of defence!—it is a solecism!

I well recollect the principle insisted upon by the patriotic body in Great Britain; it is that in time of peace a standing army ought not to be kept up without the consent of parliament. Their only apprehension appears to be that it might be dangerous, was the army kept up without the concurrence of the representatives of the people. Sir, we are not in the millennium. Wars may happen—and when they do happen, who is to have the power of collecting and appointing the force then become immediately and indispensably necessary?

It is not declared in this constitution that the Congress *shall* raise and support armies. No, Sir, if they are not driven to it by necessity, why should we suppose they would do it by choice, any more than the representatives of the same citizens in the State legislatures? for we must not lose sight of the great principle upon which this work is founded. The authority here given to the general government flows from the same source as that placed in the legislatures of the several States.

It may be frequently necessary to keep up standing armies in time of peace. The present Congress have experienced the necessity; and seven hundred troops are just as much a standing army as seventy thousand. The principle which sustains them is precisely the same. They may go further, and raise an army without communicating to the public the purpose for which it is raised. On a particular occasion they did this: When the commotions existed in Massachusetts, they gave orders for enlisting an additional body of two thousand men. I believe it is not generally known on what a perilous tenure we held our freedom and independence at that period. The flames of internal insurrection were ready to burst out in every quarter; they were fanned by the correspondents of some State officers (to whom an allusion was made on a former day) and from one end to the other of the continent, we walked on ashes, concealing fire beneath our feet: and ought Congress to be deprived of power to prepare for the defence and safety of our country? Ought they to be restrained from arming until they divulge the motive which induced them to arm? I believe the *power* of raising and keeping up an army in time of peace is essential to every government. No government can secure its citizens against dangers, internal and external, without possessing it, and sometimes carrying it into execution. I confess it is a power in the exercise of which all wise and moderate governments will be as prudent and forbearing as possible. When we consider the situation of the United States, we must be satisfied that it will be necessary to keep up some troops for the protection of the western frontiers and to secure our interest in the internal navigation of that country. It will be not only necessary, but it will be economical on the great scale. Our enemies finding us invulnerable, will not attack us, and we shall thus prevent the occasion for larger standing armies. I am now led to consider another charge that is brought against this system.

It is said, that Congress should not possess the power of calling out the militia, to execute the laws of the Union, suppress insurrections and repel invasions, nor the President have the command of them, when called out for such purposes.

I believe any gentleman who possesses military experience will inform you, that men without an uniformity of arms, accoutrements and discipline, are no more than a mob in a camp: that in the field, instead of assisting, they interfere with one another. If a soldier drops his musquet, and his companion, unfurnished with one, takes it up, it is of no service, because his cartridges do not fit it. By means of this system, a uniformity of arms and discipline will prevail throughout the United States.

I really expected that for this part of the system at least, the framers of it would have received plaudits, instead of censures, as they here discover a strong anxiety to have this body put upon an effective footing, and thereby, in a great measure, to supersede the necessity of raising, or keeping up, standing armies.

The militia formed under this system, and trained by the several States, will be such a bulwark of internal strength, as to prevent the attacks of foreign enemies. I have been told, that about the year 1744, an attack was intended by France upon Massachusetts Bay, but was given up on reading the militia law of that province.

If a single State could deter an enemy from such attempts, what influence will the proposed arrangement have upon the different powers of Europe!

In every point of view, this regulation is calculated to produce the best effects. How powerful and respectable must the body of militia appear, under general and uniform regulations! how disjointed, weak and inefficient are they at present! I appeal to military experience for the truth of my observations.

The next objection, Sir, is a serious one indeed; it was made by the honorable gentleman from Fayette (Mr. Smilie): "The Convention knew this was not a free government, otherwise they would not have asked the powers of the purse and sword." I would beg to ask the gentleman, what free government he knows that has not the powers of both? There was indeed a government under which we unfortunately were for a few years past, that had them not, but it does not now exist. A government without those powers, is one of the improvements with which the opposition wish to astonish mankind.

Have not the freest governments those powers? and are they not in the fullest exercise of them? This is a thing so clear, that really it is impossible to find facts or reason more clear, in order to illustrate it. Can we create a government without the power to act; how can it act without the assistance of men? and how are men to be procured without being paid for their services? is not the one power the consequence of the other?

We are told, and it is the last and heaviest charge, "that this government is an aristocracy, and was *intended* so to be by the late Convention;" and we are told (the truth of which is not disputed) that an aristocratical government is incompatible with freedom. I hope, before this charge is believed, some stronger reasons will be given in support of it, than any that have yet been produced.

The late Convention were assembled to devise some plan for the security, safety and happiness of the people of the United States; if they have devised a plan that robs them of their power, and constitutes an aristocracy, they are the parricides of their country, and ought to be punished as such. What part of this system is it that warrants the charge?

What is an aristocratic government? I had the honor of giving a definition of it at the beginning of our debates; it is, Sir, the government of a few over the many, elected by themselves, or possessing a share in the government by inheritance, or in consequence of territorial rights, or some quality independent of the choice of the people; this is an aristocracy, and this constitution is said to be an aristocratical form of government, and it is also said that it was intended so to be by the members of the late convention who framed it. What peculiar rights have been reserved to any class of men, on any occasion? Does even the first magistrate of the United States draw to himself a single privilege, or security, that does not extend to every person throughout the United States? Is there a single distinction attached to him in this system, more than there is to the lowest officer in the republic? Is there an office from which any one set of men whatsoever are excluded? Is there one of any kind in this system but is as open to the poor as to the rich? to the inhabitant of the country, as well as to the inhabitant of the city? and are the places of honor and emoluments confined to a few? and are these few the members of the late Convention? Have they made any particular provisions in favor of themselves, their relations, or their posterity? If they have committed their country to the demon of aristocracy, have they not committed themselves also, with everything they held near and dear to them?

Far, far other is the genius of this system. I have had already the honor of mentioning its general nature; but I will repeat it, Sir. In its principle, it is purely democratical; but its parts are calculated in such manner as to obtain those advantages also, which are peculiar to the other forms of government in other countries. By appointing a single magistrate, we secure strength, vigor, energy and responsibility in the executive department. By appointing a senate, the members of which are elected for six years, yet by a rotation already taken notice of they are changing every second year, we secure the benefit of experience, while, on the other hand, we avoid the inconveniences that arise from a long and detached establishment. This body is periodically renovated from the people, like a tree, which, at the proper season, receives its nourishment from its parent earth.

In the other branch of the legislature, the House of Representatives, shall we not have the advantages of benevolence and attachment to the people, whose immediate representatives they are?

A free government has often been compared to a pyramid. This allusion is made with peculiar propriety in the system before you: it is laid on the broad basis of the people; its powers gradually rise, while they are confined, in proportion as they ascend, until they end in that most permanent of all forms. When you examine all its parts, they will invariably be found to preserve that essential mark of free governments, a chain of connection with the people.

Such, Sir, is the nature of this system of government; but the important question at length presents itself to our view, Shall it be ratified, or shall it be rejected by this Convention? In order to enable us still further to form a judgment on this truly momentous and interesting point, on which all we have or can have dear to us on earth is materially depending, let us for a moment consider the consequences that will result from one or the other measure. Suppose we reject this system of government, what will be the consequences? Let the farmer say; he whose produce remains unasked for, nor can he find a single market for its consumption, though his fields are blessed with luxuriant abundance. Let the manufacturer and let the mechanic say; they can feel and tell their feelings. Go along the warves of Philadelphia, and observe the melancholy silence that reigns. I appeal not to those who enjoy places and abundance under the present government; they may well dilate upon the easy and happy situation of our country. Let the merchants tell you, what is our commerce; let them say what has been their situation, since the return of peace: an æra which they might have expected would have furnished additional sources to our trade, and a continuance, and even an increase to their fortunes. Have these ideas been realized, or do they not lose some of their capital in every adventure, and continue the unprofitable trade from year to year, subsisting under the hopes of happier times under an efficient general government? The ungainful trade carried on by our merchants, has a baneful influence on the interests of the manufacturer, the mechanic, and the farmer, and these I believe are the chief interests of the people of the United States.

I will go further—is there now a government among us that can do a single act, that a national government ought to do? Is there any power of the United States that can *command* a single shilling? This is a plain and a home question.

Congress may recommend; they can do more, they may require; but they must not proceed one step further. If things are bad now, and that they are not worse, is only owing to hopes of improvement, or change in the system. Will they become better when those hopes are disappointed? We have been told, by honorable gentlemen on this floor (Mr. Smilie, Mr. Findley and Mr. Whitehill), that it is improper to urge this kind of argument in favor of a new system of government, or against the old one. Unfortunately, Sir, these things are too severely felt to be omitted; the people feel them; they pervade all classes of citizens and every situation from New Hampshire to Georgia; the argument of necessity is the patriot's defence, as well as the tyrant's plea.

Is it likely, Sir, that if this system of government is rejected, a better will be framed and adopted? I will not expatiate on this subject, but I believe many reasons will suggest themselves to prove that such an expectation would be illusory. If a better could be obtained at a future time, is there anything essentially wrong in this? I go further: is there anything wrong that cannot be amended more easily by the mode pointed out in the system itself, than could be done by calling convention after convention before the organization of the government? Let us now turn to the consequences that will result if we assent to, and ratify the instrument before you; I shall trace them as concisely as I can, because I have trespassed already too long on the patience and indulgence of the house.

I stated on a former occasion one important advantage: by adopting this system we become a NATION; at present we are not one. Can we perform a single national act? can we do anything to procure us dignity, or to preserve peace and tranquility? can we relieve the distress of our citizens? can we provide for their welfare or happiness? The powers of our government are mere sound. If we offer to treat with a nation, we receive this humiliating answer, "You cannot in propriety of language make a treaty—because you have no power to execute it." Can we borrow money? There are too many examples of unfortunate creditors existing, both on this and the other side of the Atlantic, to expect success from this expedient. But could we borrow money, we cannot command a fund to enable us to pay either the principal or interest; for in instances where our friends have advanced the principal, they have been obliged to advance the interest also in order to prevent the principal from being annihilated in their hands by depreciation. Can we raise an army? The prospect of a war is highly probable. The accounts we receive by every vessel from Europe mention that the highest exertions are making in the ports and arsenals of the greatest maritime powers; but whatever the consequence may be, are we to lay supine? We know we are unable under the articles of confederation to exert ourselves; and shall we continue so until a stroke be made on our commerce, or we see the debarkation of an hostile army on our unprotected shores? Who will guarantee that our property will not be laid waste, that our towns will not be put under contribution, by a small naval force, and subjected to all the horror and devastation of war? May not this be done without opposition, at least effectual opposition, in the present situation of our country? There may be safety over the Appalachian mountains, but there can be none on our sea coast. With what propriety can we hope our flag will be respected while we have not a single gun to fire in its defence?

Can we expect to make internal improvement, or accomplish any of those great national objects which I formerly alluded to, when we cannot find money to remove a single rock out of a river?

This system, Sir, will at least make us a nation, and put it in the power of the Union to act as such. We will be considered as such by every nation in the world. We will regain the confidence of our own citizens, and command the respect of others.

As we shall become a nation, I trust that we shall also form a national character; and that this character will be adapted to the principles and genius of our system of government: as yet we possess none—our language, manners, customs, habits and dress, depend too much upon those of other countries. Every nation in these respects should possess originality. There are not on any part of the globe finer qualities, for forming a national character, than those possessed by the children of America. Activity, perseverance, industry, laudable emulation, docility in acquiring information, firmness in adversity, and patience and magnanimity under the greatest hardships; from these materials, what a respectable national character may be raised! In addition to this character, I think there is strong reason to believe that America may take the lead in literary improvements and national importance. This is a subject which I confess I have spent much pleasing time in considering. That language, Sir, which shall become most generally known in the civilized world, will impart great importance over the nation that shall use it. The language of the United States will in future times be diffused over a greater extent of country than any other that we now know. The French, indeed, have made laudable attempts toward establishing an universal language; but beyond the boundaries of France, even the French language is not spoken by one in a thousand. Besides the freedom of our country, the great improvements she has made and will make in the science of government will induce the patriots and literati of every nation, to read and understand our writings on that subject, and hence it is not improbable that she will take the lead in political knowledge.

If we adopt this system of government, I think we may promise security, stability and tranquility to the governments of the different States. They will not be exposed to the danger of competition on questions of territory, or any other that have heretofore disturbed them. A tribunal is here founded to decide, justly and quietly, any interfering claim; and now is accomplished, what the great mind of Henry the IV. of France had in contemplation, a system of government, for large and respectable dominions, united and bound together in peace, under a superintending head, by which all their differences may be accommodated, without the destruction of the human race! We are told by Sully, that this was the favorite pursuit of that good king during the last years of his life, and he would probably have carried it into execution, had not the dagger of an assassin deprived the world of his valuable life. I have, with pleasing emotion, seen the wisdom and beneficence of a less efficient power under the articles of confederation, in the determination of the controversy between the States of Pennsylvania and Connecticut; but, I have lamented that the authority of Congress did not extend to extinguish, entirely, the spark which has kindled a dangerous flame in the district of Wyoming.

Let gentlemen turn their attention to the amazing consequences which this principle will have in this extended country—the several States cannot war with each other; the general government is the great arbiter in contentions between them; the whole force of the Union can be called forth to reduce an aggressor to reason. What a happy exchange for the disjointed, contentious State sovereignties!

The adoption of this system will also secure us from danger, and procure us advantage from foreign nations. This, in our situation, is of great consequence. We are still an inviting object to one European power at least, and, if we cannot defend ourselves, the temptation may become too alluring to be resisted. I do not mean, that, with an efficient government, we should mix with the commotions of Europe. No, Sir, we are happily removed from them, and are not obliged to throw ourselves into the scale with any. This system will not hurry us into war; it is calculated to guard against it. It will not be in the power of a single man, or a single body of men, to involve us in such distress, for the important power of declaring war is vested in the legislature at large;—this declaration must be made with the concurrence of the House of Representatives; from this circumstance we may draw a certain conclusion, that nothing but our national interest can draw us into a war. I cannot forbear, on this occasion, the pleasure of mentioning to you the sentiments of the great and benevolent man whose works I have already quoted on another subject; Mr. Neckar has addressed this country, in language important and applicable in the strictest degree to its situation and to the present subject. Speaking of war, and the great caution that all nations ought to use in order to avoid its calamities, "And you, rising nation," says he, "whom generous efforts have freed from the yoke of Europe ! let the universe be struck with still greater reverence at the sight of the privileges you have acquired, by seeing you continually employed for the public felicity: do not offer it as a sacrifice at the unsettled shrine of political ideas, and of the deceitful combinations of warlike ambition; avoid, or at least delay participating in the passions of our hemisphere; make your own advantage of the knowledge which experience alone has given to our old age, and preserve for a long time, the simplicity of childhood: in short, honor human nature, by shewing that when lost to its own feelings, it is still capable of those virtues that maintain public order, and of that prudence which insures public tranquillity."

Permit me to offer one consideration more that ought to induce our acceptance of this system. I feel myself lost in the contemplation of its magnitude. By adopting this system, we shall probably lay a foundation for erecting temples of liberty in every part of the earth. It has been thought by many, that on the success of the struggle America has made for freedom, will depend the exertions of the brave and enlightened of other nations. The advantages resulting from this system will not be confined to the United States; it will draw from Europe, many worthy characters, who pant for the enjoyment of freedom. It will induce princes, in order to preserve their subject, to restore to them a portion of that liberty of which they have for so many ages been deprived. It will be subservient to the great designs of providence, with regard to this globe; the multiplication of mankind, their improvement in knowledge, and their advancement in happiness.

Wednesday, December 12, 1787.

[With the speeches of Wilson and M'Kean the report of Lloyd ceases. Of the proceedings on the 12th he makes no mention. The newspapers then are the only source of information, and of these the *Packet* is the fullest.]

On Wednesday Mr. Findley in the course of an eloquent and argumentative speech, suddenly introduced the following observation: "Mr. President, I have observed a person who has introduced himself among the members of this convention, laughing for some time at everything I have said. This conduct does not, Sir, proceed from a superiority of understanding, but from the want of a sense of decency and order. If he were a member, I should certainly call him to order; but as it is, I shall be satisfied with despising him.

"What," said Mr. Findley, "would we have thought of Congress, if at the time that body made the requisition for an impost of five per cent., the powers and jurisdiction contained in the proposed plan had been required? It would have been thought at once imprudent and ridiculous. How great then is the revolution of our sentiments in so short a space of time!"

In the course of the desultory debate which took place immediately before the vote of adoption and ratification, Mr. M'Kean pronounced an animated eulogium on the character, information and abilities of Mr. George Mason, but concluded that the exclusion of juries in civil causes was not among the objections which had governed his conduct. On this assertion Mr. Whitehill quoted the following passage from Mr. Mason's objections: "There is no declaration of any kind for preserving the liberty of the press, *the trial by jury in civil causes*, nor against the danger of standing armies in time of peace."

On Wednesday morning Mr. Findley closed his arguments in opposition to the proposed Federal system, and in the afternoon Mr. Smilie, taking a general view of the subject, stated briefly the leading principles which influenced his vote. The important question was now called for, when Doctor Rush requested the patience of the Convention for a few minutes. He then entered into a metaphysical argument, to prove that the morals of the people had been corrupted by the imperfections of the government; and while he ascribed all our vices and distresses to the existing system, he predicted a millennium of virtue and happiness as the necessary consequence of the proposed Constitution. To illustrate the depraved state of society, he remarked, among other things, the disregard which was notorious in matters of religion, so that between the congregation and the minister scarcely any com-

munication or respect remained; nay, the Doctor evinced
that they were not bound by the ties of common honesty, on
the evidence of two facts, from which it appears that several
clergymen had been lately cheated by their respective flocks
of the wages due for their pastoral care and instruction.
Doctor Rush then proceeded to consider the origin of the proposed system, and fairly deduced it from heaven, asserting
that he as much believed the hand of God was employed in
this work, as that God had divided the Red Sea to give a passage to the children of Israel, or had fulminated the ten commandments from Mount Sinai! Dilating sometime upon this
new species of *divine right*, thus transmitted to the future
governors of the Union, he made a pathetic appeal to the opposition, in which he deprecated the consequences of any
further contention, and pictured the honorable and endearing
effects of an unanimous vote, after the full and fair investigation which the great question had undergone.   " It is not,
Sir, a majority, (continued the Doctor) however numerous
and respectable, that can gratify my wishes—nothing short
of an unanimous vote can indeed complete my satisfaction.
And, permit me to add, were that event to take place, I could
not preserve the strict bounds of decorum, but, flying to the
other side of this room, cordially embrace every member, who
has hitherto been in opposition, as a brother and a patriot.
Let us then, Sir, this night bury the hatchet, and smoke the
calumet of peace!" When Dr. Rush had concluded, Mr.
Chambers remarked upon the Doctor's wish of conciliation
and unanimity, that *it was an event which he neither expected nor wished for.* Mr. Whitehill now rose, and having
animadverted upon Dr. Rush's metaphysical arguments, and
regretted that so imperfect a work should have been ascribed
to God, he presented several petitions from 750 inhabitants
of Cumberland county, praying, for the reasons therein specified, that the proposed Constitution should not be adopted
without amendments, and particularly, without a bill of
rights. The petitions being read from the chair, Mr. M'Kean
said he was sorry at this stage of the business so improper an
attempt should be made. He repeated that the duty of the

Convention was circumscribed to the adoption or rejection of the proposed plan, and such had certainly been the sense of the members, when it was agreed that only one question could be taken on the important subject before us. He hoped, therefore, that the petitions would not be attended to. Mr. Whitehill then read, and offered as the ground of a motion for adjourning to some remote day the consideration of the following articles, which, he said, might either be taken collectively, as a bill of rights, or, separately, as amendments to the general form of government proposed.

1. The rights of conscience shall be held inviolable, and neither the legislative, executive nor judicial powers of the United States shall have authority to alter, abrogate or infringe any part of the constitutions of the several States, which provide for the preservation of liberty in matters of religion.

2. That in controversies respecting property and in suits between man and man, trial by jury shall remain as heretofore, as well in the federal courts, as in those of the several States.

3. That in all capital and criminal prosecutions, a man has a right to demand the cause and nature of his accusation, as well in the federal courts, as in those of the several States; to be heard by himself or his counsel; to be confronted with the accusers and witnesses; to call for evidence in his favor, and a speedy trial, by an impartial jury of the vicinage, without whose unanimous consent he cannot be found guilty, nor can he be compelled to give evidence against himself; that no man be deprived of his liberty, except by the law of the land or the judgment of his peers.

4. That excessive bail ought not to be required, nor excessive fines imposed, nor cruel or unusual punishments inflicted.

5. That warrants unsupported by evidence, whereby any officer or messenger may be commanded or required to search suspected places, or to seize any person or persons, his or their property, not particularly described, are grievous and oppressive, and shall not be granted either by the magistrates of the federal government or others.

6. That the people have a right to the freedom of speech, of writing and of publishing their sentiments; therefore, the freedom of the press shall not be restrained by any law of the United States.

7. That the people have a right to bear arms for the defence of themselves and their own State, or the United States, or for the purpose of killing game; and no law shall be passed for disarming the people or any of them, unless for crimes committed, or real danger of public injury from individuals; and as standing armies in the time of peace are dangerous to liberty, they ought not to be kept up; and that the military shall be kept under strict subordination to and be governed by the civil power.

8. The inhabitants of the several States shall have liberty to fowl and hunt in seasonable times on the lands they hold, and on all other lands in the United States not inclosed, and in like manner to fish in all navigable waters, and others not private property, without being restrained therein by any laws to be passed by the legislature of the United States.

9. That no law shall be passed to restrain the legislatures of the several States from enacting laws for imposing taxes, except imposts and duties on goods exported and imported, and that no taxes, except imposts and duties upon goods imported and exported and postage on letters, shall be levied by the authority of Congress.

10. That elections shall remain free, that the house of representatives be properly increased in number, and that the several States shall have power to regulate the elections for senators and representatives, without being controlled either directly or indirectly by any interference on the part of Congress, and that elections of representatives be annual.

11. That the power of organizing, arming and disciplining the militia, (the manner of disciplining the militia to be prescribed by Congress) remain with the individual States, and that Congress shall not have authority to call or march any of the militia out of their own State, without the consent of such State, and for such length of time only as such State shall agree.

12. That the legislative, executive, and judicial powers be kept separate, and to this end, that a constitutional council be appointed to advise and assist the President, who shall be responsible for the advice they give (hereby, the senators would be relieved from almost constant attendance); and also that the judges be made completely independent.

13. That no treaties which shall be directly opposed to the existing laws of the United States in Congress assembled, shall be valid until such laws shall be repealed or made conformable to such treaty, neither shall any treaties be valid which are contradictory to the constitution of the United States, or the constitutions of the individual States.

14. That the judiciary power of the United States shall be confined to cases affecting ambassadors, other public ministers and consuls, to cases of admiralty and maritime jurisdiction, to controversies to which the United States shall be a party, to controversies between two or more States—between a State and citizens of different States—between citizens claiming lands under grants of different States, and between a State or the citizens thereof and foreign States, and in criminal cases, to such only as are expressly enumerated in the constitution, and that the United States in Congress assembled, shall not have power to enact laws, which shall alter the laws of descents and distributions of the effects of deceased persons, the title of lands or goods, or the regulation of contracts in the individual States.

15. That the sovereignty, freedom and independency of the several States shall be retained, and every power, jurisdiction and right which is not by this constitution expressly delegated to the United States in Congress assembled.

Some confusion arose on these articles being presented to the chair, objections were made by the majority to their being officially read, and, at last, Mr. Wilson desired that the intended motion might be reduced to writing, in order to ascertain its nature and extent. Accordingly, Mr. Whitehill drew it up, and it was read from the chair in the following manner:

"That this Convention do adjourn to the ——— day of ——— next, then to meet in the city of Philadelphia, in order that the propositions for amending the proposed constitution may be considered by the people of this State; that we may have an opportunity of knowing what amendments or alterations may be proposed by other States, and that these propositions, together with such other amendments as may be proposed by other States, may be offered to Congress, and taken into consideration by the United States, before the proposed constitution shall be finally ratified.''

As soon as the motion was read, Mr. Wilson said he rejoiced that it was by this means ascertained upon what principles the opposition proceeded, for, he added, the evident operation of such a motion would be to exclude the people from the government and to prevent the adoption of this or any other plan of confederation. For this reason he was happy to find the motion reduced to certainty, that it would appear upon the journals, as an evidence of the motives that prevailed with those who framed and supported it, and that its merited rejection would permanently announce the sentiments of the majority respecting so odious an attempt. Mr. Smilie followed Mr. Wilson, declaring that he too rejoiced that the motion was reduced to a certainty, from which it might appear to their constituents that the sole object of the opposition was to consult with and obtain the opinions of the people upon a subject, which they had not yet been allowed to consider. "If," exclaimed Mr. Smilie, "those gentlemen who have affected to refer all authority to the people, and to act only for the common interest, if they are sincere, let them embrace this last opportunity to evince that sincerity. They all know the precipitancy with which the measure has hitherto been pressed upon the State, and they must be convinced that a short delay cannot be injurious to the proposed government, if it is the wish of the people to adopt it; if it is not their wish, a short delay, which enables us to collect their real sentiments, may be the means of preventing future contention and animosity in a community, which is, or ought to be, equally dear to us." The question being taken on the motion, there appeared for it 23, against it 46. The great and conclusive question was then taken, that "this convention do assent to and ratify the plan of federal government, agreed to and recommended by the late federal convention?'' when the same division took place, and the yeas and nays being called by Mr. Smilie and Mr. Chambers, were as given in our paper of Thursday last. Yeas 46. Nays 23.

This important decision being recorded, Mr. M'Kean moved that the convention do to-morrow proceed in a body to the Court House, there to proclaim the ratification, and that the supreme executive council be requested to make the necessary arrangements for the procession on that occasion, which motion was agreed to, and the convention adjourned till the next morning at half-past nine o'clock.

From the minutes of the convention it appears that the vote of each member was,

YEAS.	YEAS.
George Latimer,	John Hubley,
Benjamin Rush,	Jasper Yeates,
Hilary Baker,	Henry Slagle,
James Wilson,	Thomas Campbell,
Thomas M'Kean,	Thomas Hartley,
William Macpherson,	David Grier,
John Hunn,	John Black,
George Gray,	Benjamin Pedan,
Samuel Ashmead,	John Arndt,
Enoch Edwards,	Stephen Balliet,
Henry Wynkoop,	Joseph Horsfield,
John Barclay,	David Deshler,
Thomas Yardley,	William Wilson,
Abraham Stout,	John Boyd,
Thomas Bull,	Thomas Scott,
Anthony Wayne,	John Neville,
William Gibbons,	John Allison,
Richard Downing,	Jonathan Roberts,
Thomas Cheyney,	John Richards,
John Hannum,	F. A. Muhlenberg,
Stephen Chambers,	James Morris,
Robert Coleman,	Timothy Pickering,
Sebastian Graff,	Benjamin Elliot. 46.

NAYS.

John Whitehill,
John Harris,
John Reynolds,
Robert Whitehill,
Jonathan Hoge,
Nicholas Lutz,
John Ludwig,
Abraham Lincoln,
John Bishop,
Joseph Hiester,
James Martain,
Joseph Powell,

NAYS.

William Findley,
John Bard,
William Todd,
James Marshall,
James Edgar,
Nathaniel Breading,
John Smilie,
Richard Baird,
William Brown,
Adam Orth,
John Andre Hannah.   23.

Thursday, December 13, 1787.

On Thursday, the convention being assembled, Mr. Whitehill remarked that the bill of rights, or articles of amendment, which he had the day before presented to the chair,
were not inserted upon the journals, together with the resolution which referred to them. This he declared an improper
omission, and desired they might be inserted. This was opposed by the majority, but as there was no motion before the
convention, the president did not see how a determination
could take place, though he wished to know the sense of the
members upon this occasion. Mr. Smilie, in consequence of
this intimation, moved for the insertion of Mr. Whitehill's
articles. Mr. Wilson continued his opposition, and called
upon Mr. Smilie to reduce his motion to writing. "Indeed,
sir," observed Mr. Smilie, "I know so well that if the honorable member from the city says the articles shall not, they
will not be admitted, that I am not disposed to take the useless trouble of reducing my motion to writing, and therefore
I withdraw it." Mr. Chambers exclaimed that the member
from Fayette and his friends might be accustomed to the arrangement which he alluded to, but neither Mr. Wilson, nor
those who agreed in sentiments with him, were to be led by a
mere *fiat*. The form being presented by Mr. M'Kean, who
with Mr. Wilson and Mr. Yeates were appointed as a committee to prepare it, it was agreed that the convention should

proceed to proclaim the ratification before it was signed, which was accordingly done.*

Joined by the President and Vice-President of the State, members of Congress, the faculty of the University, the magistrates and militia officers of the city, the convention then proceeded to the Court House, where the ratification was read to a great gathering of people.

In the procession went

Constables with their Staves.

Sub-Sheriffs with their Wands.

High Sheriff and Coroner with their Wands.

Judges of the Supreme Court, and Judges of the High Court of Errors and Appeals.

Attorney-General and Prothonotary of the Supreme Court.

Marshal of the Admiralty.

Judge and Register of the Admiralty.

Wardens of the Port of Philadelphia.

Naval Officers, Collectors of the Customs, and Tonnage Officer.

Treasurer and Comptroller-General.

Secretary of the Land Office.

Receiver-General and Surveyor-General.

Justices of the Peace.

Prothonotary of the Court of Common Pleas, and Clerk of the Court of Quarter Sessions.

Clerk of the City Court.

Master of the Rolls and Register of Wills.

Assistant Secretary of the Council.

Secretary of the Council.

His Excellency the PRESIDENT, and Honorable the VICE PRESIDENT.

Members of the Council, two and two.

Doorkeeper of the Council.

Sergeant-at-Arms, with the Mace.

Secretary of the Convention.

Honorable the President of the Convention.

* Pennsylvania Packet, December 14th.

Members of the Convention, two and two.
Doorkeeper of the Convention.
Provost and Faculty of the University.
Officers of the Militia.
Citizens.

RATIFICATION.

In the Name of the PEOPLE of PENNSYLVANIA:

BE it known unto all men—That we, the delegates of the Commonwealth of Pennsylvania, in general convention assembled, have assented to and ratified, and by these presents do, in the name and the authority of the same people, and for ourselves, assent to and ratify the foregoing constitution for the United States of America.

> Done in convention the 12th day of December, in the year 1787 and of the Independence of the United States of America the twelfth.
>
> In witness whereof, &c.

Thirteen cannon were then fired, and the bells were rung on this joyful occasion; after this the convention returned to the State House and subscribed the two copies of the ratification.

On the return of the members to the convention, Mr. Hartley hoped that the opposition might yet be induced to sign the ratification, as a fair and honorable acquiescence in the principle that the majority should govern. To which Mr. Smilie replied, that speaking for himself, he never would allow his hand, in so gross a manner, to give the lie to his heart and tongue. Two copies of the proposed constitution were then formally ratified by the members who voted in favor of it; Mr. Harris observing, that though he had voted against it, and would still abide by that vote so far as to decline putting his signature to the ratification, yet he did now, and always should, consider himself to be bound by the sense of the majority of any public body of which he had the honor to be appointed a member. The convention then adjourned till Friday morning at half past nine o'clock.

At three o'clock they met and dined with the members

of the supreme executive council, several members of Congress and a number of citizens, at Mr. Epple's tavern; where the remainder of the day was spent in mutual congratulations upon the happy prospect of enjoying, once more, order, justice and good government in the United States. The following is the list of the toasts given on the occasion:

1. The *People* of the United States.
2. The President and Members of the late Convention of the United States.
3. The President of the State of Pennsylvania.
4. May the citizens of America display as much wisdom in adopting the proposed Constitution to *preserve* their liberties, as they have shown fortitude in *defending* them.
5. May order and justice be the pillars of the American Temple of Liberty.
6. May the agriculture, manufactures and commerce of the United States speedily flourish under the new Constitution.
7. The Congress.
8. The virtuous minority of Rhode Island.
9. The powers of Europe in alliance with the United States.
10. May the flame, kindled on the Altar of Liberty in America, lead the nations of the world to a knowledge of their rights and to the means of recovering them.
11. The memory of the heroes who have sacrificed their lives in defence of the liberties of America.
12. May America diffuse over Europe a greater portion of political light than she has borrowed from her.
13. Peace and free governments to all the nations in the world.

Friday, December 14, 1787.

Friday the Convention appointed a committee to consider and report upon the overtures which have been made by the county of Philadelphia, and likewise by part of the county of Philadelphia, Montgomery and Bucks united, respecting the cession of 10 miles square to the future Congress of the United States. This the opposition to the federal system deemed a matter upon which the Convention could not, and ought not to act; for, they represented it as a violation of the constitution of the State, which still existed, and which while in existence, it was the duty of every citizen to support. Upon this principle they refused either to vote for or against the appointment of a committee, which produced a temporary embarrassment, as the majority were not at first agreed in the number, but ultimately concurred in making it nine. The Convention likewise appointed a committee to receive and state an account of their expenses, &c., and then adjourned till Saturday at half past nine o'clock.

Saturday December 15, 1787.

The Convention met pursuant to adjournment.

The committee appointed to consider the motion of Mr. Wilson relative to a cession, to the United States, of a district for the seat of the federal government, report the following resolution:

"That when the Constitution proposed by the late general Convention shall have been organized, this commonwealth will cede to the Congress of the United States the jurisdiction over any place in Pennsylvania, not exceeding ten miles square, which with the consent of the inhabitants, the Congress may choose for the seat of the government of the United States, excepting only the city of Philadelphia, the district of Southwark, and that part of the Northern-Liberties included within a line running parallel with Vine street, at the distance of one mile northward thereof, from the river Schuylkill to the southern side of the main branch of Cohocksink creek, thence down the said creek to its junction with the river Delaware. But the marsh land and so much of the adjoining bank, on the same side of the said creek, as shall be necessary for the erecting any dams and works to command the water thereof, are excluded from this exception.

"Resolved, That it is the opinion of this Convention, that until the Congress shall have made their election of a district, for the place of their permanent residence, and provided buildings for their accommodation, they have the use of such of the public buildings within the city of Philadelphia, or any other part of this State, as they shall find necessary.

" Unanimously Resolved, That the thanks of this Convention be presented to the President, for his able and faithful discharge of the duties of the Chair."

To which the President answered:

"GENTLEMEN,

" I feel with the utmost gratitude the honor you have just now done me, and I shall always esteem your approbation as my highest reward for performing my duty to you, or rendering any services to my fellow citizens."

The Convention then adjourned *sine die.*

CHAPTER V.

[As soon as the work of the Convention began, the press, and particularly the anti-federal press, teemed with letters, squibs, and essays from the people at large. Some were serious, some were intended to be satirical or funny, some were in verse, and some were exceedingly silly. Yet, taken as a whole, they form a running commentary on the work of the Convention from day to day, and must be considered as a fair expression of what the people as a body thought. To give them all is impossible ; a few therefore have been selected, and these, it is believed, may be safely regarded as samples of all. No attempt has been made to edit them, as they are too miscellaneous to allow of such treatment.

First, in point of time, was a petition drawn up and passed round the coffee-houses by those in favor of amending the Constitution, or referring it for amendment to a new Convention.]

Such of the citizens of Pennsylvania as are not clearly ascertained of the propriety of adopting the proposed constitution, without amendment or farther consideration, may think it proper to join in the following petition :

To the Honorable the Delegates of the STATE CONVENTION :
The Petition of the Citizens of Pennsylvania humbly showeth,

That your petitioners, highly sensible of the benefits arising from good government, and perceiving that there were defects in the federal compact established in the infancy of our independency, assented with alacrity to a revision of the articles of confederation, in full confidence that such amendments would be made therein as would give sufficient strength and energy to the federal head, without infringing those

(432)

rights of sovereignty in the several States which are necessary for the purposes of internal government, and the performance of their respective functions as members of a federal
union; or such rights of individuals as are necessary to distinguish free citizens from the subjects of despotism.

That the plan proposed by the general convention, instead
of offering to our consideration such amendments as were
generally expected and might be easily understood, contains
a total abolition of the existing confederation, and is in itself,
as a late writer expresses it, "a novelty in the practice of
legislation, essentially different, both in principles and organization, from any system of government heretofore formed."
And although it may be an improvement on all those which
have preceded it, and better calculated for political happiness
than our present system of confederation is capable of being
made, yet your petitioners conceive it is no less the *duty* than
the *right* of every citizen to examine it with care and attention, and deliberately consider its probable operations and
effects before he assents to the adoption of a system of such
infinite importance. Accident, fraud, or force, may impose
on a people a system of government to which they will yield
obedience no longer than they are restrained from opposition
by a power that deprives them of the freedom of citizens.
But when a free people deliberately frame a government for
themselves, or adopt as their deliberate choice a system which
they have carefully investigated and understand, they are
bound to the observance of it by other ties than those of fear:
confident of acting in general concert, and of deriving reciprocal benefits, every individual will then more cheerfully
yield obedience to the laws and perform the duties of a citizen. Hence it is of the highest importance that the proposed
system of government should be well understood by the people in every State before it be adopted.

But your petitioners conceive that the people of Pennsylvania have not yet had sufficient time and opportunity
afforded them for this purpose. Many of those who have
had the best opportunity that the shortness of the time would
admit, find their minds yet unsatisfied on some important

points, though they may highly approve of the general structure; others, who felt a general approbation at first view, now think some amendments essentially necessary: but the great bulk of the people, from the want of leisure from other avocations; their remoteness from information, their scattered situation, and the consequent difficulty of conferring with each other, cannot yet have duly investigated and considered a system of so much magnitude, which involves so many important considerations as to require not only more time than they have yet had since it was promulged, but the combined force of many enlightened minds, to obtain a right understanding of it.

Your petitioners hope they shall be excused if they mention on this occasion some other matters which have retarded the calm investigation which a subject of this importance ought to receive. The disorderly proceedings in the city, and the unaccountable zeal and precipitation used to hurry the people into a premature decision, spread an amazement through the country, which excited jealousies and suspicions from which they could neither easily nor speedily recover. Those who became partisans in the business had their minds too much agitated to act with deliberation, and the election of delegates was rushed into before the greater part of the people had sufficiently recovered from their surprise to know what part to take in it, or how to give their suffrages; they therefore remained inactive. Your petitioners wish to be understood, however, as being far from intending to invalidate the election, or to intimate any irregularity in the members chosen, whom they respect both individually and as a body, and in whose desire to promote the welfare and happiness of the people they have much confidence; but they conceive it will operate as a strong argument in favor of the measure they request.

Your petitioners beg leave to suggest that the suspension of your final determination for a few months will not occasion any delay to the union, as divers of the States, whose determinations are of equal importance with that of Pennsylvania, will not meet in convention on this business in less than five or six months. The people of these States have wisely determined to deliberate before they delegate the power of decision. But the people of Pennsylvania, deprived of this privilege, are reduced to the necessity of asking as a favor, what they ought to have enjoyed as a right, and they confide in your wisdom and prudence to afford them an opportunity of forming, collecting and expressing their sentiments by petitions or instructions before you come to a determination which may preclude farther deliberation.

Your petitioners therefore pray that the honorable Convention will be pleased to adjourn till some day in April or May next, in order to obtain the deliberate sense of the citizens of Pennsylvania on the plan of government proposed by the late general convention.*

––––––

[An essay by "Candid" defending the work of the Federal Convention.]
Fellow Citizens,

The object of our present attention is the establishment of a permanent government for ourselves and posterity; than which, except what immediately concerns eternal salvation, no object of greater magnitude can be offered to human consideration.

History does not afford an instance exactly parallel with the present—a people highly civilized, in an enlightened age, in profound peace, the wisdom of the world in their hands, all theory before their eyes, and all experiment within their knowledge, resolving themselves, as it were, into a state of nature, to institute a system of government, which is to characterize their country, and on which their political happiness and safety is to depend. I say, history does not furnish an instance of such a people, so employed, and under like circumstances.

The only practicable mode of commencing this important business has been adopted. Delegates have been appointed by the respective States for the purpose of framing a system

* From the Pennsylvania Packet, Dec. 11, 1787.

of government, and proposing it to the consideration of the people at large. In this first step you have shown a discretion and propriety not usual in popular elections. I mean as to the persons whom you appointed to this difficult and important service. Your most precious and admired characters were brought together on this occasion—men most eminent for wisdom and integrity—men whose judgments could not be warped by any personal interests whatever, who were themselves to partake of the good or evil of the fruits of their deliberations—men whose attachment to their country cannot be doubted, and whose competency to the business in hand has never been disputed. One partiality alone could influence the component parts of that most respectable body, the late Convention; and that I conceive to be a happy influence. The delegates from the respective States would naturally, and from a sense of duty, be jealous and watchful, that in the formation of a general government, no more of the specific rights or interests of each State should be sacrificed, than was absolutely necessary for the dignity, safety, and good government of the United States; and therefore, it may be supposed, as the fact really was, that they have made the best compromise of complicated interests, which the nature of the case would allow; so that the present question is not whether the government proposed is the best of all possible governments, theoretically considered–although if fairly investigated, it might stand even this test–but whether a better union of separate sovereignties can be obtained; or which is of still greater importance, whether if the proposed system should be rejected, the States will ever again make the same compromise.

The theory of government hath employed the pens of speculative and learned men in every age; and yet no system hath ever been formed which is not liable to many positive and many more probable evils and objections. A scheme of government which shall invest the rulers with efficient powers, without a possibility of these powers being in any instance abused or misapplied, should be sought for by those only who are looking for the phliosopher's stone, or the perpetual motion. But supposing it were possible to form a political system unexceptionable in theory, it would be found unexceptionable in theory only. The temper, genius, and internal circumstances of the country to which it is to be applied, must be considered, otherwise the people might be very unhappy under this best of all possible schemes.

In governments, two extremes are positively evil—an uncontrolled and unresponsible tyranny on the one hand, and such a relaxed state on the other, as is insufficient for defence or good order, in which all men are put upon a level, without regard to virtue, merit, or abilities, and in which he who can practise most upon the credulity and indolence of the multitude, will have the best opportunities of gratifying his ambition and avarice. Between these extremes are many degrees of excellence; many combinations of forms and dispositions of delegated power, which may be suited to the circumstances of different nations, and yet all liable to ingenious objections by those who may think it their interest to magnify possible evils, and hold up imaginary dangers.

If a people should remain without any government, until a system could be framed so seemingly perfect in itself as to be impregnable to all criticism, they would wait till fallible man should do that which the Deity at least hath not done. The government of the Jews, which was a pure *theocracy*, was not so perfect, but that people frequently murmured and rebelled.

After our struggles for liberty and independence were crowned with acknowledged success, the politicians of Europe looked to see the sun of our glory rise; but a long night hath followed. Our federal union hath become insignificant —almost contemptible. No one will be so hardy as to assert that our situation as a nation, is either happy or honorable. And how long shall we remain in this situation? Until all malcontents shall be satisfied? Until the *unanimous* consent of the people shall be obtained? Be not deceived—those who oppose this constitution, under a pretended zeal for the liberties of the people, would with equal zeal, and under the same pretences, oppose every other that could be offered. I know not how it may be in the other States, but in Pennsyl-

vania we need only look at the men to know their motives.
If we wait till these men are satisfied, we shall wait till some
Shays, some desperate adventurer, shall rise in the blast of
popular confusion into influence and importance, and frame
a government for us in a camp. And then, a very short answer will suffice for all objections real and imaginary.

It is time—it is high time—that we had an efficient government, in which the wisdom and strength of the United States
may be concentered. The fable of the man and his sons and
the bundle of sticks, may with propriety be extended beyond
the usual interpretation of mere mental concord. The moral
of the fable requires not only a bundle of sticks, but a bundle
of sticks *bound together*, for a union of strength. An efficient
federal government is the only cord that can bind our States
together for any length of time. For want of this bond of
union, Rhode Island, which is but a twig in the bundle, hath
already shewn symptoms of disaffection.

The establishment of a good and respectable government
for the United States, was an event which the leading men of
a party in Pennsylvania neither wished for, nor expected.
Their hope was, that the delegates from the different States
would never unite in any system. But when it was discovered
that a frame of government was indeed likely to be fixed upon,
and was nearly ripe for promulgation, some of the party were
so indiscreet as to declare their intended opposition, even
before they knew the system they were determined to oppose.
But the more cunning, though not less adverse, waited till
the Convention had announced their plan, and even then,
these politicians affected to be in its favor, and with its success, until by an unexpected motion in the House of Assembly, they were compelled to throw off the mask, and declare
themselves openly. They wished to prevent even the first
step for bringing the federal government into existence.
They saw plainly, that a majority of the House would be for
recommending it to the people of the State at large to appoint
delegates in their behalf to consider, and if proper, give the
assent of this State to the proposed plan. In this emergency
they played off a stroke of wicked policy, which the same

party had once before found successful. As many of the mal-contents, or rather tools of real malcontents, as were suffi-cient to break up the House, abandoned their seats; but even this manœuvre did not answer the purpose. An accident not looked for, defeated the pernicious intent, and the House have legally, and in complete organization, recommended that a State Convention should be called, and pointed out the time and mode of doing it.

The disappointed partisans are now filling the newspapers with loud outcries against the proposed constitution. They have invoked Hecate to their aid; called up spirits from the vasty deep, and presented raw-head and bloody-bones to the people; weak and nervous politicians are even terrified by their incantations. But the fallacy consists in this: These writers consider the proposed constitution as vesting govern-mental powers in strangers to be imported from God knows what country, whose interests and those of the people of the United States are not only separate from, but opposed to each other. And in this view they descant largely on the dangers and evils to be apprehended. Upon no other ground can their arguments prove of any force. But the truth is, that this Federal Assembly, this Senate, and this President of the United States, are to be composed of our own brethren, of men of our own appointment, taken from amongst ourselves; whose interests must go hand in hand with ours; who, if they do evil, must partake of that evil. If they enslave others, they cannot leave their own children free. If they involve the country in ruin, they cannot provide a *Goshen* for themselves, their families and friends; for their power will neither be perpetual nor hereditary. The constitution ordains a frequent recurrence to the people for the choice of their legislators and principal officers, all of whom are re-sponsible for their conduct, and the component parts of the system mutually control and check each other, in all cases where checks and controls are consistent with good govern-ment.

But this good constitution may be corrupted and abused, say the opposers; and so indeed it may. From a like argument, divine wisdom would have never made man, because his body is subject to disorders; much less would man have been entrusted with freedom of will, because it is too manifest that he can make a bad use of it. For the same reason, we should not eat for fear of indigestion, or drink for fear of a dropsy, should never travel lest we lose our way, or go to sea because we may be shipwrecked. Some hazard must attend all human transactions, and the event of the most simple pursuit cannot be ascertained with certainty.

Imagination has been wearied with efforts to vilify the Federal Constitution proposed by the late convention; but if nothing more substantial can be urged against it, we may well pronounce it to be most worthy of our acceptance. The irresistible voice of the people seems to be in its favor; and I hope, and I doubt not but that it will be established to the honor and safety of the United States, and to the confusion of their enemies internal and external.   CANDID.*

CATO'S SOLILOQUY PARODIED.

It must be so—K——m, thou reason'd well!
Else whence this pleasing hope, this fond desire,
This longing after offices of State?
Or whence this secret dread, and inward horror,
Of falling into nought? Why shrink our souls,
And startle at the Federal Government?
'Tis interest, dear self-interest stirs within us,
And tells us that a Federal government
Is bane, is prison to State demagogues.
A Federal government—O dreadful thought!
Through what variety of untried being,
Through what new scenes and changes must we pass?
The wide unbounded prospect lies before us;
But shadows, clouds, and darkness rest upon it.
State sovereignty we'll hold: for if there is
A power superior that we must submit to,
(And that there must be, reason cries aloud
Through all the land) it may be just and virtuous;
Defeat our views, and make a nation happy.
I fear! I fear!—This State is not for K——m.
But time must soon decide—My death and life,†

* From the Pennsylvania Packet, Nov. 27th.
† Pointing to the Federal system and State Constitution.

My bane and antidote, are both before me:
This in a moment brings me to an end,
And this informs me I shall still be great.
My interest well secur'd, I'll smile at those
Poor easy tools, I've dup'd to serve my purpose ;
And mock at all the clamors of good men.
Patriots may shrink away—Fabius himself,
And Franklin dim with age, lament with tears
Their toils, their cares, with virtues, all were vain,
If I but flourish in the general ruin,
Unhurt amidst the war of jarring States,
The wrecks of property, and crush of justice.
What means this heaviness that hangs upon me?
This lethargy that creeps through all my senses?
Nature oppress'd, and harrass'd out with care,
Sinks down to rest. I'll try to favor her,
That my awaken'd genius may arise,
With force renew'd to invent new fallacies
To puzzle and deceive. Let fears alarm
The patriot's breast—K——m knows none of them !
Indifferent in his choice, if good or ill
Betide his country, if he govern still.*

[Report of a Committee of Citizens.]

For the Independent Gazetteer.

Mr. Printer: It has been often said, concerning the proposed constitution, that those who complained of its faults, should suggest amendments. A number of citizens, warmly desirous of promoting the establishment of a well organized federal government; and perceiving in each other, sentiments inclining to harmony, formed a committee of their own members to examine and consider the proposed constitution, with instructions to report such amendments, and such only as they should deem absolutely necessary to safety in the adoption of it, paying equal regard to its practicability and efficiency as a system of government on the one hand, and to those rights which are essential to free citizens in a state of society on the other.

The report having been read, a motion was made to adopt it; but after some debate, in which some of the members declared that their minds had already undergone some changes,

* Independent Gazetteer, Nov. 27, 1787.

and that their opinions were not yet satisfactorily established, it was thought proper that further time should be taken to deliberate and advise with their fellow citizens on a subject of such high importance and general concernment. It was therefore agreed that the question should be postponed for further consideration, and that in the meantime the report be published. By giving it a place in your paper, you will oblige MANY CUSTOMERS.

The committee to whom was referred the plan proposed by the late general convention, for the government of the United States, report,

That in the examination of the said plan, they have conceived it to be their duty to exercise the freedom which the magnitude of the trust reposed in them required; at the same time, that they have kept constantly in mind the respect and deference due to the great characters who formed the plan, and that candor and liberality of construction which are necessary in forming a just opinion of a national compact is which the citizens of every State in the Union, having an equal interest, are equally parties.

Under these impressions, your committee have taken the said plan into their most serious consideration; and though they find much in it which merits approbation, yet the duty they owe to their constituents and to their country, obliges them to propose some alterations, which they should deem necessary, considering it merely with regard to practicability as a system of government; and when to this consideration are added the propriety of preserving to the respective States so much of their sovereignty as may be necessary to enable them to manage their internal concerns, and to perform their respective functions as members of a federal republic, and of preserving to individuals such rights as are essential to freemen in a state of society, the necessity of making such alterations appear to your committee irresistibly strong.

There are four points in which your committee apprehend alterations are absolutely necessary before the plan can with safety be put in operation, namely :

Respecting Elections.

Internal Taxation.

The Judicial Department.

The Legislative Power, so far as it is independent of the House of Representatives.

Divers other amendments might with propriety be proposed, some of which might be comprehended in a bill of rights, or table of fundamental principles, so declared and established as to govern the construction of the powers given by the constitution; but your committee avoid to mention them in detail, because if suitable amendments are made respecting the points enumerated, the necessity for going farther on the present occasion, though not entirely done away, will be so far diminished, as that it may be thought advisable to leave them to future consideration, on such suggestions as time and experience shall offer.

Your committee therefore proposes the following amendments—Art. 1, sect. 4, strike out these words—*but the Congress may at any time by law make or alter such regulations, except as to the place of choosing senators.*

Art. 1, sect. 8, strike out *tax* and *excises*—[and so throughout the plan make such amendments as may be necessary in conformity with this idea] at the end of the clause, add—" To make requisitions, in the proportion aforesaid, on the several States in the Union, for such supplies of money as shall be necessary, in aid of the other revenues, for these purposes; leaving to the States respectively, the mode of levying and collecting the same: Provided, that if any State shall neglect or refuse to pass an act for complying with any such requisition, or shall otherwise neglect or refuse to pay its quota of any such requisition within the time therein limited, it shall be in the power of the Congress on any such delinquency, by law, to direct the levying and collecting of such quota, together with such farther sum as may be necessary to defray the expense thereof, and interest from the time it ought to have been paid, from the persons and estates of the inhabitants of such delinquent State, according to the mode of assessment by law established in such State; or in default of such establishment, by such modes and means as the Congress shall by law establish for that purpose."

Art. 3, sect. 2, clause 1st.—Strike out the words *between citizens of different States.* After the words "between a State," strike out, *or the citizens thereof.*

Clause 2d—Strike out *both as to law and fact.*

These two clauses will then stand as follows:

"The judicial power shall extend to cases in law and equity, arising under this constitution, the laws of the United States, and treaties made or which shall be made, under their authority; to all cases affecting ambassadors, other public ministers and consuls; to all cases of admiralty and maritime jurisdiction; to controversies to which the United States shall be a party; to controversies between two or more States; between a State and citizens of another State; between citizens of the same State claiming lands under grants of different States; and between a State and foreign States, citizens or subjects.

"In all cases affecting ambassadors, other public ministers and consuls, and those in which a State shall be party, the Supreme Court shall have original jurisdiction. In all the other cases before-mentioned, the Supreme Court shall have appellate jurisdiction, with such exceptions and under such regulations as the Congress shall make."

Art. 6, clause 2—After the word "notwithstanding," insert "provided that every such treaty which shall hereafter be made shall have been laid before the House of Representatives, and have obtained the approbation of so many of the members of that House as shall be a majority of the whole number elected."

And your committee submit the following resolutions to consideration:

That the foregoing amendments to the plan of government formed by the late general convention, be transmitted to the United States in Congress assembled.

That Congress be requested to recommend to the several States in the union, that delegates be elected by the people of the said States respectively, to meet in general convention at   on the   day of   next, to take into consideration the said amendments, together with such amendments as shall be proposed by the several State conventions, and to revise and amend the said plan of government is such manner as they shall agree upon, not altering the form as it now stands, farther than shall be necessary to accommodate it to such of the amendments which shall be so proposed to them, as they, or the representatives of any nine or more States, shall agree to adopt; and that in case the plan so agree upon shall be assented to by the vote of every State which shall be represented in such Convention, they shall have power, without further reference to the people, to declare the same the Constitution or frame of government of the United States, and it shall thereupon be accepted and acted upon accordingly.*

[A criticism of the report by "Columbus."]
" *Be the workmen what they may be, let us speak of the work.*"   BACON'S ESSAYS.

A late publication in your paper, in the form of a Report of a Committee, has afforded both information and satisfaction to divers of your readers. It were to be wished that societies, of the kind of that to which the committee reported, were formed in every neighborhood, and that more time had been taken by the people, by such or other means, to possess themselves of a more accurate knowledge of a subject so highly interesting to every individual, before the men were fixed upon who should possess the power of deciding for them on a subject of the highest sublunary importance to them and their posterity.

The members of the general convention had the matter several months under daily discussion and debate. Every thought which occurred to any one was communicated to and examined by every one, so that every one had time and opportunity to trace the purport and tendency of every clause and sentence, separately considered, as well as the probable

*From the Independent Gazetteer, Dec. 1, 1787.

effect and influence of the combined whole; but these deliberations were kept within their own walls with the secrecy of a conclave. The people expected the result would be an amendment of the federal compact, on such points only as had been generally spoken of as defective. Their minds were prepared for such amendments as they could easily judge of, and come to a speedy decision upon. But instead of the old instrument being repaired and amended, we are called upon to consider it as totally dissolved, and its component party reduced to a state of nature.

The constitution proposed in its stead is confessedly, even by the framers of it, a *novelty* in the practice of legislation, essentially different, both in principles and organization, from any system of government heretofore formed, either by force, fraud, accident, or the deliberate consent of a people. It *may* be, as some of its sanguine advocates have asserted, the *best* form that was ever offered to a people; but we should remember, that what *may* be, may *not* be; and however ready *we* may be to adopt measures on the credit of others, in matters of lighter moment, the subject before us is certainly a matter of too much consequence to be decided upon without thorough examination, and more deliberation than the citizens of Pennsylvania have had an opportunity of exercising. For although a few individuals who were in the General Convention may have given it a sufficient degree of investigation to satisfy their own minds; yet it may be fairly said of the people at large, that they could not possibly have given it a due degree of examination at the time, that they were in a manner surprised into a kind of surrender of the right of further deliberation, by the election of delegates to express their final decision. It has been said, that a small proportion only of the voters in the State (hardly a sixth part) gave their suffrages on this occasion; and it may fairly be presumed, circumstances considered, that a large proportion of those who did not vote, declined it because they found themselves unqualified, from the mere want of such information as every citizen ought to possess, before he gives his weight on either side, on a question of so much importance.

Will the members of the State convention, thus possessed of the power, run hastily into the adoption, in *toto*, of a plan of government which, in the opinion of a large proportion of their constituents, cannot with safety be put in operation, without very essential amendments? Or will they not rather assent either to make the necesary amendments the condition of their agreeing to the plan, or to adjourn for a reasonable time, in order to obtain the deliberate sense of their constituents on a matter of so much importance? Those who mean to act fairly, can hardly withhold their assent to such an adjournment, except it be on the score of expense, and the trouble of reassembling. But surely these are considerations too light to be placed in opposition to the object. The delay can occasion no real loss of time as to the final event, because the accession of other States will be necessary to give operation to the plan; and we know that divers of the State conventions will not meet to deliberate upon it before May or June. Why then should we be denied a reasonable time for deliberation? If the system be a good one and calculated to promote the happiness of the people, the more it is examined and understood, the more generally will it be approved of; but if it should be otherwise, it can hardly be expected that the people would acquiesce in a determination, which they might suppose had been unfairly obtained.* COLUMBUS.

———

[A criticism of M'Kean.]

Mr. Oswald: What a contracted soul must that man have, who does not think that inestimable jewel, that greatest of blessings, *Liberty*, is worth contending for; who advises his fellow citizens, when they have the alternative within their reach, to submit to tyranny without a struggle, because the life of man is such a span, seldom more than three-score years.† Indeed the votaries of despotism must hereafter give the palm of superior merit to him, for he hath discovered that a good government is the greatest curse that can be inflicted

* Pennsylvania Packet, Dec. 8, 1787.

† This is the substance of a speech delivered by C——f J——e M'K——n in the Convention on Tuesday last.

on mankind ; for, says he, it attaches men too much to this sublunary scene, it makes them reluctant to quit their earthly tabernacles. On his principle the Turks are supremely blessed, who suffering under constant oppression, can have no inducement to wish their existance prolonged; they must be in a constant state of preparation to make their exit.*

A BYE-STANDER.

[A criticism of Mr. Whitehill.]

Substance of a speech, delivered by J. W—h—ll, Esquire, in convention, on last Monday evening.

Mr. President: It has been said that Congress will have power, by the new Constitution, to lay an impost on the *importation* of slaves into these States ; but that they will have no power to impose any tax upon the *migration* of Europeans. Do the gentlemen, sir, mean to insult our understandings, when they assert this ? Or are they ignorant of the English language? If, because of their ignorance, they are at a loss, I can easily explain this clause for them. The words "*migration*" and "*importation*," sir, being *connected* by the *disjunctive* conjunction "*or*," certainly mean either migration, or importation ; either the one, or the other ; or both. Therefore, when we say "a tax may be laid upon such *importation*, we mean, either upon the *importation*, or *migration ;* or upon both ; for, because they are *joined together*, in the first instance, by the *disjunctive* conjunction *or*, they are both synonymous terms for the same thing—therefore, "*such importation*," because the *comparative* word *such*, is used, means both importation and migration.

Mr. Oswald. As the above *learned exposition* may be a valuable acquisition to our English commentators, it may not be amiss, at this time, to demonstrate the truth of it, for the benefit of the ignorant, to whom it may seem rather paradoxical.

Suppose the Legislature of Pennsylvania should say— "French *or* British ships shall be allowed to come into our ports ; but such British ships shall be taxed," etc.—Here, it

----

*Independent Gazetteer, Dec. 1. 1787.

is evident, that the French ships, as well as the British, would be obliged to pay tax, imposed as above; for they are *connected* by the *disjunctive* conjunction *or*—*Ergo*, *French ships* and *British ships* are the same thing—also *importation* and *migration*—Q. E. D.

I shall conclude, sir, with observing that were all the the members of our convention capable, like Mr. W—h—ll, of dissecting, analyzing, and explaining, the new Constitution, they would be able in a few days to pass a judgment upon it: and thus there would be upwards of 14,000 dollars saved to the State; for, it is very probable they will sit nearly as long, in discussing the new Constitution, as the federal convention did in framing it. PUFF.*

[The Minority of the Convention denounced.]

Mr. Oswald: Who are those "24 virtuous characters who compose the minority in the Convention, whose souls have been *tried* in the late glorious war," we are told of in Mr. Bailey's paper of this day? In what manner have *their souls* been *tried*? Where was *Mr. S——y* the day of the battle of Brandywine? Did he command the right or left wing of the army of the United States? Did he dispute rank, on that day, with Major General Lord Sterling? Was that the cause of his Lordship's putting him in the guard-house? Or did his Lordship consider him a suspicious character? A Spy! Where was *Mr. F——y* and *Mr. R——t W——ll*, during the late glorious war? Go through the whole *antifederal junto*, and you will find few real whigs amongst them! No Sir, good whigs are good members and supports of good government! Sir, we have a Constitution offered us by the United States for our acceptance, in which all the real and disinterested whigs will unite: and which the good whigs will adopt. I believe, Sir, the only antifederalists in this or the neighboring States, are the street or sunshine whigs, and office holders who know that as the number of offices and officers will be lessened, they are unwilling to part with them. There will be no such thing under the federal Constitution as creat-

* Independent Gazetteer, Dec. 6, 1787.

ing offices for the purpose of making a favorite an officer, at the expense of the people.* A TRUE WHIG.

[Cost of the Convention.]

Mr. Oswald: I am afraid we have got into a scrape by putting so many counsellors, judges, assemblymen and lawyers into our State Convention. They are spending a wonderful deal of their time and our money. I wish we had put in plain folks, not so much used to talking in public. I would not wish to hurry them, but that I think, if they do not like the Constitution proposed, they should say so at once. A week would have been time enough to talk the matter over, and then they might have taken the question. Really, Sir, public expenses are so great, trade so hampered, for want of power in Congress, produce of course so low, and living so expensive, that any needless charge is death to us, however great the sport is to them, who spend the money. I hope therefore the House will take the question very soon.†

A FREEHOLDER.

Germantown Township, Dec. 4, 1787.

[A call for the question.]

Messrs. Dunlap and Claypoole: I have attended some of the debates of the convention, as well as your correspondent in this day's paper, who signs himself "One of the People."

I have listened with attention to the monotonous and pertinacious Whitehill, to the zealous Smilie, and to the candid, thoughtful Findley. On the other side of the room I have heard with conviction the clear and rational arguments of the Chief Justice, the good sense of Yeates, the fervency of Chambers, the pathos and imagination of Rush, the nervous thinking and correct eloquence of Wilson. I have heard in the gallery the whispers of approbation circulate, as true federal sentiments have been well expressed or happily introduced by the speakers; I have seen those who wished for the establishment of the proposed government return more zealous for it than before; I have seen those who went there

* Independent Gazetteer, Dec. 6, 1787.
† Independent Gazetteer, Dec. 6, 1878.

undetermined depart in full decision to support it. I have enquired abroad for the opponents of the plan, and have found them almost uniformly the possessors or expectants of office, with their nearest friends and connections. I have seen the presses loaded with anti-federal compositions and the federal government almost left to defend itself. I have sought for the effect so many publications must have had on the public mind, and have almost everywhere met with confessions, that, objectionable as it might be, in the present situation of things we could not expect a better. I have seen the farmer storing his grain, the merchant suspending his enterprises, and the men of ready money hoarding up their cash, till the operation of the government should give activity and confidence to the people of this country in their dealings abroad and with each other. I have seen the landholders assemble and make an offer of territory, and I have witnessed the hopes of the manufacturers and mechanics that their offer may be accepted. I have noticed an anxiety lest Pennsylvania, often the leader, and always amongst the foremost in useful and distinguished measures, should suffer two of her weakest sisters to anticipate her laurels. I have at length heard something like murmurs, that the people of Pennsylvania should spend their time in debates, which being conducted without order, promise no certain end, in which the issue of the argument can only be guessed at from the countenance of the members, and the final vote upon the acceptance or rejection of the whole cannot possibly (for the reasons given) be influenced by this discussion on its parts; and I have heard it said, that however suitable these disquisitions might be in an academy of petty critics, or a divan of trembling slaves—where the evidence and ingenuity in one, or the exercise of freedom by the other, might consist in the dissection of a sentence, or the explanation of a *synonima*; yet it would be more manly, more characteristic of a convention of freemen, at once to put the question: Shall we be happy or miserable, powerful or contemptible? Shall Pennsylvania adopt or reject the Federal Government? *

Wednesday, Dec. 5th.   Yours, E. G. O.

* Pennsylvania Packet, Dec. 8, 1787.

[Reply to James Wilson.]

Mr. Oswald: In your paper of the 16th instant, some person under the signature of Puff or *Froth*, I don't now recollect which, came forward in the shape of a critique, and demonstrated it very clearly that a gallon of air would be necessary to support him, while he carped at a grammatical error, which he pretended to have discovered in Mr. J—— Wh—h—ll's speech in Convention. But Mr. Oswald, how many gallons of air would it require to. support this *Dr. Froth*, while he described all the errors of a different complexion made by members on his side of the house—I will mention a few, such as when J——s W—ls—n, Esquire, declared that German or Irish indented servants, imported, were not articles of commerce, and therefore not subject to the tax of 10 dollars each —but that freemen were properly articles of commerce, (as well as blacks).

That Virgina and most of the other States had no bills of rights, and therefore we ought not to have one; and added he, "some member said there would be no harm in having one, but it is my opinion that there would be much harm in it, and it would also put it out of the power of our independent judges to show their firmness in checking the lawmakers" (who appoints them, and who have the power to impeach and discard them).

Now, Mr. Oswald, I thought it was a bill of rights ascertaining the bounds of the legislative power, that gave the judges a right to say when the laws were unconstitutional, and therefore void.

The bill of rights of our Constitution, Mr. W—ls—n declared had been of great hurt. Do not you remember that it was the only thing saved you, when *Judge Jeffries* called you to his bar;—it was jury trial and the declaration of the freedom of the press which checked him, and saved you and the press from being crushed, at that time. But Jefferies *hopes* soon to be *Judge and Jury*. He and Mr. W—ls—n Saturday in Convention interrupted a member while speaking, and declared that jury trial never existed in Sweden or in any other country, out of Great Britain and America. O Truth, where art thou gone? Fled from the councils of America! Are we thus to be fooled out of the transcendant privilege of freemen, trial by jury of our peers (or equals), and in the place of it be tried by corrupted judges?

It is thus that lawyers are allowed to rob us of our dearest privileges—to serve themselves? Law will become a *bottomless pit*, indeed, if our right worshipful judgeships are allowed to re-examine and judge of facts as well as law, in their continental courts.*   One of the People.

———

[Conduct of the Majority of the Convention.]

Mr. Oswald: I am a sober, orderly citizen, not wise enough to frame governments, nor weak enough to act contrary to my conscience. If any thing could induce me to oppose the new Constitution, it would be the indecent, supercilious carriage of its advocates towards its opponents, which I take to indicate the spirit of the system itself. Every insult offered to the minority is offered to the State, which they, as well as the majority, represent; and it surely will not be denied that for general reasoning the friends do not muster stronger than the enemies of this plan. I declare to you, Sir, that the management of this business has shaken the faith of
        A Federalist.†

* Independent Gazetteer, Dec. 11, 1787.
† Independent Gazetteer, Dec. 11, 1787.

CHAPTER VI.

[While the members of the Convention were eating their dinner and drinking their toasts at Epple's Tavern, some enthusiastic Federalists were busy in one of the ship-yards preparing a novel method of celebrating their victory. By evening all was ready, and what then took place was afterwards described in the *Gazetteer.*]

"On the evening of the public rejoicing for the ratification of the Federal Constitution, a number of ship carpenters and sailors conducted a boat, on a wagon drawn by five horses, through the city, to the great amusement of many thousand spectators. On their way through the different streets, they frequently threw a sounding line and cried out, "Three and twenty fathom—*foul* bottom," and in other places, "Six and forty fathom—sound bottom—safe anchorage," alluding to the numbers that composed the minority and majority of the late Convention of Pennsylvania which ratified the Federal Constitution."

[If the rejoicing Federalists supposed that all opposition to their new plan would stop, they were greatly mistaken. The Antifederalists were far from humbled, and, till well into the autumn of 1788, the Antifederal presses of the State teemed with assaults on the Constitution. First in time and importance came]

THE ADDRESS AND REASONS OF DISSENT OF THE MINORITY OF THE CONVENTION OF THE STATE OF PENNSYLVANIA TO THEIR CONSTITUENTS.*

It was not until after the termination of the late glorious contest, which made the people of the United States an independent nation, that any defect was discovered in the present

---

*From The Pennsylvania Packet and Daily Advertiser, Dec. 18, 1787.

(454)

confederation. It was formed by some of the ablest patriots in America. It carried us successfully through the war, and the virtue and patriotism of the people, with their disposition to promote the common cause, supplied the want of power in Congress.

The requisition of Congress for the five *per cent.* impost was made before the peace, so early as the first of February, 1781, but was prevented taking effect by the refusal of one State; yet it is probable every State in the Union would have agreed to this measure at that period, had it not been for the extravagant terms in which it was demanded. The requisition was new moulded in the year 1783, and accompanied with an additional demand of certain supplementary funds for twenty-five years. Peace had now taken place, and the United States found themselves laboring under a considerable foreign and domestic debt, incurred during the war. The requisition of 1783 was commensurate with the interest of the debt, as it was then calculated; but it has been more accurately ascertained since that time. The domestic debt has been found to fall several millions of dollars short of the calculation, and it has lately been considerably diminished by large sales of the Western lands. The States have been called on by Congress annually for supplies until the general system of finance proposed in 1783 should take place.

It was at this time that the want of an efficient federal government was first complained of, and that the powers vested in Congress were found to be inadequate to the procuring of the benefits that should result from the union. The impost was granted by most of the States, but many refused the supplementary funds; the annual requisitions were set at naught by some of the States, while others complied with them by legislative acts, but were tardy in their payments, and Congress found themselves incapable of complying with their engagements and supporting the federal government. It was found that our national character was sinking in the opinion of foreign nations. The Congress could make treaties of commerce, but could not enforce the observance of them. We were suffering from the restrictions

of foreign nations, who had suckled our commerce while we
were unable to retaliate, and all now agreed that it would be
advantageous to the union to enlarge the powers of Congress,
that they should be enabled in the amplest manner to regulate commerce and to lay and collect duties on the imports
throughout the United States.   With this view, a convention
was first proposed by Virginia, and finally recommended by
Congress for the different States to appoint deputies to meet in
convention, "for the purposes of revising and amending the
present articles of confederation, so as to make them adequate
to the exigencies of the union."   This recommendation the
legislatures of twelve States complied with so hastily as not
to consult their constituents on the subject; and though the
different legislatures had no authority from their constituents
for the purpose, they probably apprehended the necessity
would justify the measure, and none of them extended their
ideas at that time further than "revising and amending the
present articles of confederation."   Pennsylvania, by the act
appointing deputies, expressly confined their powers to this
object, and though it is probable that some of the members
of the assembly of this State had at that time in contemplation to annihilate the present confederation, as well as the
constitution of Pennsylvania, yet the plan was not sufficiently
matured to communicate it to the public.

The majority of the legislature of this commonwealth were
at that time under the influence of the members from the city
of Philadelphia.   They agreed that the deputies sent by them
to convention should have no compensation for their services,
which determination was calculated to prevent the election
of any member who resided at a distance from the city.   It
was in vain for the minority to attempt electing delegates to
the convention who understood the circumstances, and the
feelings of the people, and had a common interest with them.
They found a disposition in the leaders of the majority of the
house to choose themselves and some of their dependents.
The minority attempted to prevent this by agreeing to vote
for some of the leading members, who they knew had influence enough to be appointed at any rate, in hopes of carry-

ing with them some respectable citizens of Philadelphia, in whose principles and integrity they could have more confidence, but even in this they were disappointed, except in one member: the eighth member was added at a subsequent session of the assembly.

The Continental Convention met in the city of Philadelphia at the time appointed. It was composed of some men of excellent character; of others who were more remarkable for their ambition and cunning than their patriotism, and of some who had been opponents to the independence of the United States. The delegates from Pennsylvania were, six of them, uniform and decided opponents to the Constitution of this commonwealth. The convention sat upwards of four months. The doors were kept shut, and the members brought under the most solemn engagements of secrecy.* Some of those who opposed their going so far beyond their powers, retired, hopeless, from the convention; others had the firmness to refuse signing the plan altogether; and many who did sign it, did it not as a system they wholly approved, but as the best that could be then obtained, and notwithstanding the time spent on this subject, it is agreed on all hands to be a work of haste and accommodation.

Whilst the gilded chains were forging in the secret conclave, the meaner instruments of the despotism without were busily employed in alarming the fears of the people with dangers which did not exist, and exciting their hopes of greater advantages from the expected plan than even the best government on earth could produce. The proposed plan had not many hours issued forth from the womb of suspicious secrecy, until such as were prepared for the purpose, were carrying about petitions for people to sign, signifying their approbation of the system, and requesting the legislature to call a convention. While every measure was taken to intimidate the people against opposing it, the public papers teemed with the most violent threats against those who should dare to think for themselves, and *tar and feathers* were liberally promised to all those who would not immediately join in sup-

---

* The Journals of the conclave are still concealed.

porting the proposed government, be it what it would. Under such circumstances petitions in favor of calling a Convention were signed by great numbers in and about the city, before they had leisure to read and examine the system, many of whom—now they are better acquainted with it, and have had time to investigate its principles—are heartily opposed to it. The petitions were speedily handed in to the legislature.

Affairs were in this situation, when on the 28th of September last, a resolution was proposed to the assembly by a member of the house, who had been also a member of the federal convention, for calling a State convention to be elected within *ten* days for the purpose of examining and adopting the proposed Constitution of the United States, though at this time the house had not received it from Congress. This attempt was opposed by a minority, who after offering every argument in their power to prevent the precipitate measure, without effect, absented themselves from the house as the only alternative left them, to prevent the measures taking place previous to their constituents being acquainted with the business. That violence and outrage which had been so often threatened was now practised; some of the members were seized the next day by a mob collected for the purpose, and forcibly dragged to the house, and there detained by force whilst the quorum of the legislature *so formed*, completed their resolution. We shall dwell no longer on this subject: the people of Pennsylvania have been already acquainted therewith. We would only further observe that every member of the legislature, previously to taking his seat, by solemn oath or affirmation, declares "that he will not do or consent to any act or thing whatever, that will have a tendency to lessen or abridge their rights and privileges, as declared in the constitution of this State." And that constitution which they are so solemnly sworn to support, cannot legally be altered but by a recommendation of the council of censors, who alone are authorized to propose alterations and amendments, and even these must be published at least *six months* for the consideration of the people. The proposed system of government for the United States, if adopted, will alter and may annihilate the constitution of Pennsylvania; and therefore the legislature had no authority whatever to recommend the calling a convention for that purpose. This proceeding could not be considered as binding on the people of this commonwealth. The house was formed by violence, some of the members composing it were detained there by force, which alone would have vitiated any proceedings to which they were otherwise competent; but had the legislature been legally formed, this business was absolutely without their power.

In this situation of affairs were the subscribers elected members of the Convention of Pennsylvania—a Convention called by a legislature in direct violation of their duty, and composed in part of members who were compelled to attend for that purpose, to consider of a Constitution proposed by a Convention of the United States, who were not appointed for the purpose of framing a new form of government, but whose powers were expressly confined to altering and amending the present articles of confederation. Therefore the members of the continental Convention in proposing the plan acted as individuals, and not as deputies from Pennsylvania.* The assembly who called the State Convention acted as individuals, and not as the legislature of Pennsylvania; nor could they or the Convention chosen on their recommendation have authority to do any act or thing that can alter or annihilate the Constitution of Pennsylvania (both of which will be done by the new Constitution), nor are their proceedings, in our opinion, at all binding on the people.

The election for members of the Convention was held at so early a period, and the want of information was so great, that some of us did not know of it until after it was over, and we

---

* The continential Convention, in direct violation of the 13th article of the confederation, have declared "that the ratification of nine States shall be sufficient for the establishment of this Constitution, between the States so ratifying the same." Thus has the plighted faith of the States been sported with! They had solemnly engaged that the confederation now subsisting should be inviolably preserved by each of them, and the Union thereby formed should be perpetual, unless the same should be altered by mutual consent.

have reason to believe that great numbers of the people of Pennsylvania have not yet had an opportunity of sufficiently examining the proposed Constitution. We apprehend that no change can take place that will affect the internal government or Constitution of this commonwealth, unless a majority of the people should evidence a wish for such a change; but on examining the number of votes given for members of the present State Convention, we find that of upwards of *seventy thousand* freemen who are entitled to vote in Pennsylvania, the whole convention has been elected by about *thirteen thousand* voters, and though *two-thirds* of the members of the Convention have thought proper to ratify the proposed Constitution, yet those *two-thirds* were elected by the votes of only *six thousand and eight hundred* freemen.

In the city of Philadelphia and some of the eastern counties the junto that took the lead in the business agreed to vote for none but such as would solemnly promise to adopt the system *in toto*, without exercising their judgment. In many of the counties the people did not attend the elections, as they had not an opportunity of judging of the plan. Others did not consider themselves bound by the call of a set of men who assembled at the State-house in Philadelphia and assumed the name of the legislature of Pennsylvania; and some were prevented from voting by the violence of the party who were determined at all events to force down the measure. To such lengths did the tools of despotism carry their outrage, that on the night of the election for members of convention, in the city of Philadelphia, several of the subscribers (being then in the city to transact your business) were grossly abused, ill-treated and insulted while they were quiet in their lodgings, though they did not interfere nor had anything to do with the said election, but, as they apprehend, because they were supposed to be adverse to the proposed constitution, and would not tamely surrender those sacred rights which you had committed to their charge.

The convention met, and the same disposition was soon manifested in considering the proposed constitution, that had been exhibited in every other stage of the business. We were prohibited by an express vote of the convention from taking any questions on the separate articles of the plan, and reduced to the necessity of adopting or rejecting *in toto.* 'Tis true the majority permitted us to debate on each article, but restrained us from proposing amendments. They also determined not to permit us to enter on the minutes our reasons of dissent against any of the articles, nor even on the final question our reasons of dissent against the whole. Thus situated we entered on the examination of the proposed system of government, and found it to be such as we could not adopt, without, as we conceived, surrendering up your dearest rights. We offered our objections to the convention, and opposed those parts of the plan which, in our opinion, would be injurious to you, in the best manner we were able; and closed our arguments by offering the following propositions to the convention.

1. The right of conscience shall be held inviolable; and neither the legislative, executive nor judicial powers of the United States shall have authority to alter, abrogate or infringe any part of the constitution of the several States, which provide for the preservation of liberty in matters of religion.

2. That in controversies respecting property, and in suits between man and man, trial by jury shall remain as heretofore, as well in the federal courts as in those of the several States.

3. That in all capital and criminal prosecutions, a man has a right to demand the cause and nature of his accusation, as well in the federal courts as in those of the several States; to be heard by himself and his counsel; to be confronted with the accusers and witnesses; to call for evidence in his favor, and a speedy trial by an impartial jury of his vicinage, without whose unanimous consent he cannot be found guilty, nor can he be compelled to give evidence against himself; and, that no man be deprived of his liberty, except by the law of the land or the judgment of his peers.

4. That excessive bail ought not to be required, nor excessive fines imposed, nor cruel nor unusual punishments inflicted.

5. That warrants unsupported by evidence, whereby any officer or messenger may be commanded or required to search suspected places; or to seize any person or persons, his or their property not particularly described, are grievous and oppressive, and shall not be granted either by the magistrates of the federal government or others.

6. That the people have a right to the freedom of speech, of writing and publishing their sentiments; therefore the freedom of the press shall not be restrained by any law of the United States.

7. That the people have a right to bear arms for the defence of themselves and their own State or the United States, or for the purpose of killing game; and no law shall be passed for disarming the people or any of them unless for crimes committed, or real danger of public injury from individuals; and as standing armies in the time of peace are dangerous to liberty, they ought not to be kept up; and that the military shall be kept under strict subordination to, and be governed by the civil powers.

8. The inhabitants of the several States shall have liberty to fowl and hunt in seasonable time on the lands they hold, and on all other lands in the United States not inclosed, and in like manner to fish in all navigable waters, and others not private property, without being restrained therein by any laws to be passed by the legislature of the United States.

9. That no law shall be passed to restrain the legislatures of the several States from enacting laws for imposing taxes, except imposts and duties on goods imported or exported, and that no taxes, except imposts and duties upon goods imported and exported, and postage on letters, shall be levied by the authority of Congress.

10. That the house of representatives be properly increased in number; that elections shall remain free; that the several States shall have power to regulate the elections for senators and representatives, without being controlled either directly or indirectly by any interference on the part of the Congress; and that the elections of representatives be annual.

11. That the power of organizing, arming and disciplining

the militia (the manner of disciplining the militia to be prescribed by Congress), remain with the individual States, and that Congress shall not have authority to call or march any of the militia out of their own State, without the consent of such State, and for such length of time only as such State shall agree.

That the sovereignty, freedom and independency of the several States shall be retained, and every power, jurisdiction and right which is not by this Constitution expressly delegated to the United States in Congress assembled.

12. That the legislative, executive and judicial powers be kept separate; and to this end that a constitutional council be appointed to advise and assist the President, who shall be responsible for the advice they give—hereby the senators would be relieved from almost constant attendance; and also that the judges be made completely independent.

13. That no treaty which shall be directly opposed to the existing laws of the United States in Congress assembled, shall be valid until such laws shall be repealed or made conformable to such treaty; neither shall any treaties be valid which are in contradiction to the Constitution of the United States, or the constitution of the several States.

14. That the judiciary power of the United States shall be be confined to cases affecting ambassadors, other public ministers and consuls, to cases of admiralty and maritime jurisdiction; to controversies to which the United States shall be a party; to controversies between two or more States—between a State and citizens of different States—between citizens claiming lands under grants of different States, and between a State or the citizens thereof and foreign States; and in criminal cases to such only as are expressly enumerated in the constitution; and that the United States in Congress assembled shall not have power to enact laws which shall alter the laws of descent and distribution of the effects of deceased persons, the titles of lands or goods, or the regulation of contracts in the individual States.

After reading these propositions, we declared our willingness to agree to the plan, provided it was so amended as to meet those propositions or something similar to them, and finally moved the convention to adjourn, to give the people of Pennsylvania time to consider the subject and determine for themselves; but these were all rejected and the final vote taken, when our duty to you induced us to vote against the proposed plan and to decline signing the ratification of the same.

During the discussion we met with many insults and some personal abuse. We were not even treated with decency, during the sitting of the convention, by the persons in the gallery of the house. However, we flatter ourselves that in contending for the preservation of those invaluable rights you have thought proper to commit to our charge, we acted with a spirit becoming freemen; and being desirous that you might know the principles which actuated our conduct, and being prohibited from inserting our reasons of dissent on the minutes of the convention, we have subjoined them for your consideration, as to you alone we are accountable. It remains with you whether you will think those inestimable privileges, which you have so ably contended for, should be sacrificed at the shrine of despotism, or whether you mean to contend for them with the same spirit that has so often baffled the attempts of an aristocratic faction to rivet the shackles of slavery on you and your unborn posterity.

Our objections are comprised under three general heads of dissent, viz.:

We dissent, first, because it is the opinion of the most celebrated writers on government, and confirmed by uniform experience, that a very extensive territory cannot be governed on the principles of freedom, otherwise than by a confederation of republics, possessing all the powers of internal government, but united in the management of their general and foreign concerns.

If any doubt could have been entertained of the truth of the foregoing principle, it has been fully removed by the concession of *Mr. Wilson*, one of the majority on this question, and who was one of the deputies in the late general convention. In justice to him, we will give his own words; they are as follows, viz.: "The extent of country for which the new constitution was required, produced another difficulty in the business of the federal convention. It is the opinion of some celebrated writers, that to a small territory, the democratical; to a middling territory (as Montesquieu has termed it), the monarchical; and to an extensive territory, the despotic form of government is best adapted. Regarding then the wide and almost unbounded jurisdiction of the United States, at first view, the hand of despotism seemed necessary to control, connect and protect it; and hence the chief embarrassment rose. For we know that although our constituents would cheerfully submit to the legislative restraints of a free government, they would spurn at every attempt to shackle them with despotic power." And again, in another part of his speech, he continues: "Is it probable that the dissolution of the State governments, and the establishment of one *consolidated empire* would be eligible in its nature, and satisfactory to the people in its administration? I think not, as I have given reasons to show that so extensive a territory could not be governed, connected and preserved, but by the *supremacy of despotic power*. All the exertions of the most potent emperors of Rome were not capable of keeping that empire together, which in extent was far inferior to the dominion of America."

We dissent, secondly, because the powers vested in Congress by this constitution, must necessarily annihilate and absorb the legislative, executive, and judicial powers of the several States, and produce from their ruins one consolidated government, which from the nature of things will be *an iron handed despotism*, as nothing short of the supremacy of despotic sway could connect and govern these United States under one government.

As the truth of this position is of such decisive importance, it ought to be fully investigated, and if it is founded to be clearly ascertained; for, should it be demonstrated that the powers vested by this constitution in Congress will have such an effect as necessarily to produce one consolidated government, the question then will be reduced to this short issue, viz.: whether satiated with the blessings of liberty, whether repenting of the folly of so recently asserting their unalienable rights against foreign despots at the expense of so much blood and treasure, and such painful and arduous struggles, the people of America are now willing to resign every privilege of freemen, and submit to the dominion of an absolute government that will embrace all America in one chain of despotism; or whether they will, with virtuous indignation, spurn at the shackles prepared for them, and confirm their liberties by a conduct becoming freemen.

That the new government will not be a confederacy of States, as it ought, but one consolidated government, founded upon the destruction of the several governments of the States, we shall now show.

The powers of Congress under the new constitution are complete and unlimited over the *purse* and the *sword*, and are perfectly independent of and supreme over the State governments, whose intervention in these great points is entirely destroyed. By virtue of their power of taxation, Congress may command the whole or any part of the property of the people. They may impose what imposts upon commerce, they may impose what land taxes, poll taxes, excises, duties on all written instruments and duties on every other article, that they may judge proper; in short, every species of taxation, whether of an external or internal nature, is comprised in section the eighth of article the first, viz.:

"The Congress shall have power to lay and collect taxes, duties, imposts, and excises, to pay the debts, and provide for the common defence and general welfare of the United States."

As there is no one article of taxation reserved to the State governments, the Congress may monopolize every source of revenue, and thus indirectly demolish the State governments, for without funds they could not exist; the taxes, duties and excises imposed by Congress may be so high as to render it impracticable to levy farther sums on the same articles; but whether this should be the case or not, if the State governments should presume to impose taxes, duties or excises on the same articles with Congress, the latter may abrogate and repeal the laws whereby they are imposed, upon the allegation that they interfere with the due collection of their taxes, duties or excises, by virtue of the following clause, part of section eighth, article first, viz.:

"To make all laws which shall be necessary and proper for carrying into execution the foregoing powers, and all other powers vested by this constitution in the government of the United States, or in any department or officer thereof."

The Congress might gloss over this conduct by construing every purpose for which the State legislatures now lay taxes, to be for the "*general welfare*," and therefore as of their jurisdiction.

And the supremacy of the laws of the United States is established by article sixth, viz.: "That this constitution and the laws of the United States which shall be made in pursuance thereof, and *all treaties* made, or which shall be made under the authority of the United States, shall be the *supreme law* of the *land; and the judges in every State shall be bound thereby; anything in the constitution or laws of any State to the contrary notwithstanding.*" It has been alleged that the words "pursuant to the constitution," are a restriction upon the authority of Congress; but when it is considered that by other sections they are invested with every efficient power of government, and which may be exercised to the absolute destruction of the State governments, without any violation of even the forms of the constitution, this seeming restriction, as well as every other restriction in it, appears to us to be nugatory and delusive; and only introduced as a blind upon the real nature of the government. In our opinion, "pursuant to the constitution " will be co-extensive with the *will* and *pleasure* of Congress, which, indeed, will be the only limitation of their powers.

We apprehend that two co-ordinate sovereignties would be a solecism in politics; that, therefore, as there is no line of distinction drawn between the general and State governments, as the sphere of their jurisdiction is undefined, it would be contrary to the nature of things that both should exist together—one or the other would necessarily triumph in the fulness of dominion.   However, the contest could not be of long continuance, as the State governments are divested of every means of defence, and will be obliged by "the supreme law of the land" *to yield at discretion.*

It has been objected to this total destruction of the State governments that the existence of their legislatures is made essential to the organization of Congress; that they must assemble for the appointment of the senators and President-general of the United States.   True, the State legislatures may be continued for some years, as boards of appointment merely, after they are divested of every other function; but the framers of the constitution, foreseeing that the people will soon become disgusted with this solemn mockery of a government without power and usefulness, have made a provision for relieving them from the imposition in section fourth of article first, viz.: "The times, places and manner of holding elections for senators and representatives shall be prescribed in each State by the legislature thereof; *but the Congress may at any time by law make or alter such regulations, except as to the place of choosing senators.*"

As Congress have the control over the time of the appointment of the President-general, of the senators and of the representatives of the United States, they may prolong their existence in office for life by postponing the time of their election and appointment from period to period under various pretences, such as an apprehension of invasion, the factious disposition of the people, or any other plausible pretence that the occasion may suggest; and having thus obtained life-estates in the government, they may fill up the vacancies themselves by their control over the mode of appointment; with this exception in regard to the senators that as the place of appointment for them must, by the constitution, be in the particular State, they may depute some body in the respective States, to fill up the vacancies in the senate, occasioned by death, until they can venture to assume it themselves. In this manner may the only restriction in this clause be evaded.   By virtue of the foregoing section, when the spirit of the people shall be gradually broken, when the general government shall be firmly established, and when a numerous standing army shall render opposition vain, the Congress may complete the system of despotism, in renouncing all dependence on the people by continuing themselves and children in the government.

The celebrated *Montesquieu*, in his Spirit of Laws, vol. i., page 12, says, "That in a democracy there can be no exercise of sovereignty, but by the suffrages of the people, which are their will; now the sovereign's will is the sovereign himself—the laws, therefore, which establish the right of suffrage, are fundamental to this government. In fact, it is as important to regulate in a republic in what manner, by whom, and concerning what suffrages are to be given, as it is in a monarchy to know who is the prince, and after what manner he ought to govern." The *time, mode* and *place* of the election of representatives, senators and president-general of the United States, ought not to be under the control of Congress, but fundamentally ascertained and established.

The new Constitution, consistently with the plan of consolidation, contains no reservation of the rights and privileges of the State governments, which was made in the confederation of the year 1778, by article the 2d, viz.: "That each State retains its sovereignty, freedom and independence, and every power, jurisdiction and right which is not by this confederation expressly delegated to the United States in Congress assembled."

The legislative power vested in Congress by the foregoing recited sections, is so unlimited in its nature, may be so comprehensive and boundless in its exercise, that this alone would be amply sufficient to annihilate the State governments, and swallow them up in the grand vortex of general empire.

The judicial powers vested in Congress are also so various and extensive, that by legal ingenuity they may be extended to every case, and thus absorb the State judiciaries; and when we consider the decisive influence that a general judiciary would have over the civil polity of the several States, we do not hesitate to pronounce that this power, unaided by the legislative, would effect a consolidation of the States under one government.

The powers of a court of equity, vested by this constitution in the tribunals of Congress—powers which do not exist in Pennsylvania, unless so far as they can be incorporated with jury trial—would, in this State, greatly contribute to this event. The rich and wealthy suitors would eagerly lay hold of the infinate mazes, perplexities and delays, which a court of chancery, with the appellate powers of the Supreme Court in fact as well as law would furnish him with, and thus the poor man being plunged in the bottomless pit of legal discussion, would drop his demand in despair.

In short, consolidation pervades the whole constitution. It begins with an annunciation that such was the intention. The main pillars of the fabric correspond with it, and the concluding paragraph is a confirmation of it. The preamble begins with the words, "We the people of the United States," which is the style of a compact between individuals entering into a state of society, and not that of a confederation of States. The other features of consolidation we have before noticed.

Thus we have fully established the position, that the powers vested by this constitution in Congress will effect a consolidation of the States under one government, which even the advocates of this constitution admit could not be done without the sacrifice of all liberty.

3. We dissent, thirdly, because if it were practicable to govern so extensive a territory as these United States include, on the plan of a consolidated government, consistent with the principles of liberty and the happiness of the people, yet the construction of this Constitution is not calculated to attain the object; for independent of the nature of the case, it would of itself necessarily produce a despotism, and that not by the usual gradations, but with the celerity that has hitherto only attended revolutions effected by the sword.

To establish the truth of this position, a cursory investigation of the principles and form of this constitution will suffice.

The first consideration that this review suggests, is the omission of a BILL OF RIGHTS ascertaining and fundamentally establishing those unalienable and personal rights of men, without the full, free and secure enjoyment of which there can be no liberty, and over which it is not necessary for a good government to have the control—the principal of which are the rights of conscience, personal liberty by the clear and unequivocal establishment of the writ of *habeas corpus*, jury trial in criminal and civil cases, by an impartial jury of the vicinage or county, with the common law proeeedings for the safety of the accused in criminal prosecutions; and the liberty of the press, that scourge of tyrants, and the grand bulwark of every other liberty and privilege. The stipulations heretofore made in favor of them in the State constitutions, are entirely superseded by this Constitution.

The legislature of a free country should be so formed as to have a competent knowledge of its constitutents, and enjoy their confidence. To produce these essential requisites, the representation ought to be fair, equal and sufficiently numerous to possess the same interests, feelings, opinions and views which the people themselves would possess, were they all assembled; and so numerous as to prevent bribery and undue influence, and so responsible to the people, by frequent and fair elections, as to prevent their neglecting or sacrificing the views and interests of their constituents to their own pursuits.

We will now bring the legislature under this Constitution to the test of the foregoing principles, which will demonstrate that it is deficient in every essential quality of a just and safe representation.

The House of Representatives is to consist of sixty-five members; that is one for about every 50,000 inhabitants, to be chosen every two years. Thirty-three members will form a quorum for doing business, and seventeen of these, being the majority, determine the sense of the house.

The Senate, the other constituent branch of the legislature, consists of twenty-six members, being *two* from each State, appointed by their legislatures every six years; fourteen senators make a quorum—the majority of whom, eight, determines the sense of that body, except in judging on impeachments, or in making treaties, or in expelling a member, when two-thirds of the senators present must concur.

The president is to have the control over the enacting of laws, so far as to make the concurrence of two-thirds of the representatives and senators present necessary, if he should object to the laws.

Thus it appears that the liberties, happiness, interests, and great concerns of the whole United States, may be dependent upon the integrity, virtue, wisdom, and knowledge of twenty-five or twenty-six men. How unadequate and unsafe a representation! Inadequate, because the sense and views of three or four millions of people, diffused over so extensive a territory, comprising such various climates, products, habits, interests, and opinions, cannot be collected in so small a body; and besides, it is not a fair and equal representation of the people even in proportion to its number, for the smallest State has as much weight in the Senate as the largest; and from the smallness of the number to be chosen for both branches of the legislature, and from the mode of election and appointment, which is under the control of Congress, and from the nature of the thing, men of the most elevated rank in life will alone be chosen. The other orders in the society, such as farmers, traders, and mechanics, who all ought to have a competent number of their best informed men in the legislature, shall be totally unrepresented.

The representation is unsafe, because in the exercise of such great powers and trusts, it is so exposed to corruption and undue influence, by the gift of the numerous places of honor and emolument at the disposal of the executive, by the arts and address of the great and designing, and by direct bribery.

The representation is moreover inadequate and unsafe, because of the long terms for which it is appointed, and the mode of its appointment, by which Congress may not only control the choice of the people, but may so manage as to divest the people of this fundamental right, and become self-elected.

The number of members in the House of Representatives *may* be increased to one for every 30,000 inhabitants. But when we consider that this cannot be done without the consent of the Senate, who from their share in the legislative, in the executive, and judicial departments, and permanency of appointment, will be the great efficient body in this government, and whose weight and predominancy would be abridged by an increase of the representatives, we are persuaded that this is a circumstance that cannot be expected. On the contrary, the number of representatives will probably be continued at sixty-five, although the population of the country may swell to treble what it now is, unless a revolution should effect a change.

We have before noticed the judicial power as it would affect a consolidation of the States into one government; we will now examine it as it would affect the liberties and welfare of the people, supposing such a government were practicable and proper.

The judicial power, under the proposed constitution, is founded on well-known principles of the *civil law*, by which the judge determines both on law and fact, and appeals are allowed from the inferior tribunals to the superior, upon the whole question; so that *facts* as well as *law*, would be re-examined, and even new facts brought forward in the court of appeals; and to use the words of a very eminent civilian— "The cause is many times another thing before the court of appeals, than what it was at the time of the first sentence."

That this mode of proceeding is the one which must be adopted under this constitution, is evident from the following circumstances: 1st. That the trial by jury, which is the grand characteristic of the common law, is secured by the constitution only in criminal cases. 2d. That the appeal from both *law* and *fact* is expressly established, which is utterly inconsistent with the principles of the common law and trials by jury. The only mode in which an appeal from law and fact can be established, is by adopting the principles and practice of the civil law, unless the United States should be drawn into the absurdity of calling and swearing juries, merely for the purpose of contradicting their verdicts, which would render juries contemptible and worse than useless. 3d. That the courts to be established would decide on all cases *of law and equity*, which is a well-known characteristic of the civil law, and these courts would have conusance not only of the laws of the United States, and of treaties, and of cases affecting ambassadors, but of all cases of *admiralty and maritime jurisdiction*, which last are matters belonging exclusively to the civil law, in every nation in Christendom.

Not to enlarge upon the loss of the invaluable right of trial by an unbiased jury, so dear to every friend of liberty, the monstrous expense and inconveniences of the mode of proceeding to be adopted, are such as will prove intolerable to the people of this country. The lengthy proceedings of the civil law courts in the chancery of England, and in the courts of Scotland and France, are such that few men of moderate fortune can endure the expense of; the poor man must therefore submit to the wealthy. Length of purse will too often prevail against right and justice. For instance, we are told by the learned Judge *Blackstone*, that a question only on the property of an ox, of the value of three guineas, originating under the civil law proceedings in Scotland, after many interlocutory orders and sentences below, was carried at length from the court of sessions, the highest court in that part of Great Britain, by way of *appeal* to the House of Lords, where the question of law and fact was finally determined. He adds, that no pique or spirit could in the court of king's bench or common pleas at Westminster, have given continuance to such a cause for a tenth part of the time, nor have cost a twentieth part of the expense. Yet the costs in the courts of king's bench and common pleas in England, are infinitely greater than those which the people of this country have ever experienced. We abhor the idea of losing the transcendent privilege of trial by jury, with the loss of which, it is remarked by the same learned author, that in Sweden, the liberties of the commons were extinguished by an aristocratic Senate; and that *trial by jury* and the liberty of the people went out together. At the same time we regret the intolerable delay, the enormous expense, and infinite vexation, to which the people of this country will be exposed from the volumnious proceedings of the courts of civil law, and especially from the appellate jurisdiction, by means of which a man may be drawn from the utmost boundaries of this extensive country to the seat of the Supreme Court of the nation to contend, perhaps, with a wealthy and powerful adversary. The consequence of this establishment will be an absolute confirmation of the power of aristocratical influence in the courts of justice; for the common people will not be able to contend or struggle against it.

Trial by jury in criminal cases may also be excluded by declaring that the libeller for instance shall be liable to an action of debt for a specified sum, thus evading the common law prosecution by indictment and trial by jury. And the common course of proceeding against a ship for breach of revenue laws by informa (which will be classed among civil causes) will at the civil law be within the resort of a court, where no jury intervenes. Besides, the benefit of jury trial, in cases of a criminal nature, which cannot be evaded, will be rendered of little value, by calling the accused to answer far from home; there being no provision that the trial be by a jury of the neighborhood or country. Thus an inhabitant of Pittsburgh, on a charge of crime committed on the banks of the Ohio, may be obliged to defend himself at the side of the Delaware, and so *vice versa*. To conclude this head: we observe that the judges of the courts of Congress would not be independent, as they are not debarred from holding other offices, during the pleasure of the President and Senate, and as they may derive their support in part from fees, alterable by the legislature.

The next consideration that the constitution presents, is the undue and dangerous mixture of the powers of government; the same body possessing legislative, executive and judicial powers. The Senate is a constituent branch of the legislature, it has judicial power in judging on impeachments, and in this case unites in some measure the characters of judge and party, as all the principal officers are appointed by the president-general, with the concurrence of the Senate, and therefore they derive their offices in part from the Senate. This may bias the judgments of the senators, and tend to screen great delinquents from punishment. And the Senate has, moreover, various and great executive powers, viz., in concurrence with the president-general, they form treaties with foreign nations, that may control and abrogate the constitutions and laws of the several States. Indeed, there is no power, privilege or liberty of the State governments, or of the people, but what may be affected by virtue of this power. For all treaties, made by them, are to be the "supreme law of the land; anything in the constitution or laws of any State, to the contrary notwithstanding."

And this great power may be exercised by the President and ten senators (being two-thirds of fourteen, which is a quorum of that body). What an inducement would this offer to the ministers of foreign powers to compass by bribery *such concessions* as could not otherwise be obtained. It is the unvaried usage of all free States, whenever treaties interfere with the positive laws of the land, to make the intervention of the legislature necessary to give them operation. This became necessary, and was afforded by the parliament of Great Britain, in consequence of the late commercial treaty between that kingdom and France. As the Senate judges on impeachments, who is to try the members of the Senate for the abuse of this power! And none of the great appointments to office can be made without the consent of the Senate.

Such various, extensive, and important powers combined in one body of men, are inconsistent with all freedom; the celebrated Montesquieu tells us, that "when the legislative and executive powers are united in the same person, or in the same body of magistrates, there can be no liberty, because apprehensions may arise, lest the same monarch or *senate* should enact tyrannical laws, to execute them in a tyrannical manner."

"Again, there is no liberty, if the power of judging be not separated from the legislative and executive powers. Were it joined with the legislative, the life and liberty of the subject would be exposed to arbitrary control; for the judge would then be legislator. Were it joined to the executive power, the judge might behave with all the violence of an oppressor. There would be an end of everything, were the same man, or the same body of the nobles, or of the people, to exercise those three powers; that of enacting laws, that of executing the public resolutions, and that of judging the crimes or differences of individuals.''

The president general is dangerously connected with the senate; his coincidence with the views of the ruling junto in that body, is made essential to his weight and importance in the government, which will destroy all independency and purity in the executive department; and having the power of pardoning without the concurrence of a council, he may screen from punishment the most treasonable attempts that may be made on the liberties of the people, when instigated by his coadjutors in the senate. Instead of this dangerous and improper mixture of the executive with the legislative and judicial, the supreme executive powers ought to have been placed in the president, with a small independent council, made personally responsible for every appointment to office or other act, by having their opinions recorded; and that without the concurrence of the majority of the quorum of this council, the president should not be capable of taking any step.

We have before considered internal taxation as it would effect the destruction of the State governments, and produce one consolidated government. We will now consider that subject as it affects the personal concerns of the people.

The power of direct taxation applies to every individual, as Congress, under this government, is expressly vested with the authority of laying a capitation or poll tax upon every person to any amount. This is a tax that, however oppressive in its nature, and unequal in its operation, is certain as to its produce and simple in its collection; it cannot be evaded like the objects of imposts or excise, and will be paid, because all that a man hath will he give for his head. This tax is so congenial to the nature of despotism, that it has ever been a favorite under such governments. Some of those who were in the late general convention from this State, have labored to introduce a poll tax among us.

The power of direct taxation will further apply to every individual, as Congress may tax land, cattle, trades, occupations, etc., to any amount, and every object of internal taxation is of that nature that however oppressive, the people will have but this alternative, either to pay the tax or let their property be taken, for all resistance will be vain. The standing army and select militia would enforce the collection.

For the moderate exercise of this power, there is no control left in the State governments, whose intervention is destroyed. No relief, or redress of grievances, can be extended as heretofore by them. There is not even a declaration of RIGHTS to which the people may appeal for the vindication of their wrongs in the court of justice. They must therefore, implicitly obey the most arbitrary laws, as the most of them will be pursuant to the principles and form of the constitution, and that strongest of all checks upon the conduct of administration, *responsibility to the people*, will not exist in this government. The permanency of the appointments of senators and representatives, and the control the congress have over their election, will place them independent of the sentiments and resentment of the people, and the administration having a greater interest in the government than in the community, there will be no consideration to restrain them from oppression and tyranny. In the government of this State, under the old confederation, the members of the legislature are taken from among the people, and their interests and welfare are so inseparably connected with those of their constituents, that they can derive no advantage from oppressive laws and taxes; for they would suffer in common with their fellow-citizens, would participate in the burthens they impose on the community, as they must return to the common level, after a short period; and notwithstanding every exertion of influence, every means of corruption, a necessary rotation excludes them from permanency in the legislature.

This large State is to have but ten members in that Congress which is to have the liberty, property and dearest concerns of every individual in this vast country at absolute command, and even these ten persons, who are to be our only guardians, who are to supersede the legislature of Pennsylvania, will not be of the choice of the people, nor amenable to them. From the mode of their election and appointment they will consist of the lordly and high minded; of men who will have no congenial feelings with the people, but a perfect indifference for, and contempt of them; they will consist of those harpies of power that prey upon the very vitals, that riot on the miseries of the community. But we will suppose, although in all probability it may never be realized in fact, that our deputies in Congress have the welfare of their constituents at heart, and will exert themselves in their behalf, what security could even this afford? what relief could they extend to their oppressed constitutents? To attain this, the majority of the deputies of the twelve other States in Congress must be alike well disposed; must alike forego the sweets of power, and relinquish the pursuits of ambition, which, from the nature of things, is not to be expected. If the people part with a responsible representation in the legislature, founded upon fair, certain and frequent elections, they have nothing left they can call their own. Miserable is the lot of that people whose every concern depends on the *will* and *pleasure* of their rulers. Our soldiers will become Janissaries, and our officers of government Bashaws; in short, the system of despotism will soon be completed.

From the foregoing investigation, it appears that the Congress under this constitution will not possess the confidence of the people, which is an essential requisite in a good government; for unless the laws command the confidence and respect of the great body of the people, so as to induce them to support them when called on by the civil magistrate, they must be executed by the aid of a numerous standing army, which would be inconsistent with every idea of liberty; for the same force that may be employed to compel obedience to good laws, might and probably would be used to wrest from the people their constitutional liberties. The framers of this constitution appear to have been aware of this great deficiency—to have been sensible that no dependence could be placed on the people for their support: but on the contrary, that the government must be executed by force. They have therefore made a provision for this purpose in a permanent *standing army* and a *militia* that may be objected to as strict discipline and government.

A standing army in the hands of a government placed so independent of the people, may be made a fatal instrument to overturn the public liberties; it may be employed to enforce the collection of the most oppressive taxes, and to carry into execution the most arbitrary measures. An ambitious man who may have the army at his devotion, may step up into the throne, and seize upon absolute power.

The absolute unqualified command that Congress have over the militia may be made instrumental to the destruction of all liberty, both public and private; whether of a personal, civil or religious nature.

First, the personal liberty of every man, probably from sixteen to sixty years of age, may be destroyed by the power Congress have in organizing and governing of the militia. As militia they may be subjected to fines to any amount, levied in a military manner; they may be subjected to corporal punishments of the most disgraceful and humiliating kind; and to death itself, by the sentence of a court martial. To this our young men will be more immediately subjected, as a select militia, composed of them, will best answer the purposes of government.

Secondly, the rights of conscience may be violated, as there is no exemption of those persons who are conscientiously scrupulous of bearing arms. These compose a respectable proportion of the community in the State. This is the more remarkable, because even when the distresses of the late war, and the evident disaffection of many citizens of that description, inflamed our passions, and when every person who was obliged to risk his own life, must have been exasperated against such as on any account kept back from the common danger, yet even then, when outrage and violence might have been expected, the rights of conscience were held sacred.

At this momentous crisis, the framers of our State Constitution made the most express and decided declaration and stipulations in favor of the rights of conscience; but now, when no necessity exists, those dearest rights of men are left insecure.

Thirdly, the absolute command of Congress over the militia may be destructive of public liberty; for under the guidance of an arbitrary government, they may be made the unwilling instruments of tyranny. The militia of Pennsylvania may be marched to New England or Virginia to quell an insurrection occasioned by the most galling oppression, and aided by the standing army, they will no doubt be successful in subduing their liberty and independency; but in so doing, although the magnanimity of their minds will be extinguished, yet the meaner passions of resentment and revenge will be increased, and these in turn will be the ready and obedient instruments of despotism to enslave the others; and that with an irritated vengeance. Thus may the militia be made the instruments of crushing the last efforts of expiring liberty, of riveting the chains of despotism on their fellow-citizens, and on one another. This power can be exercised not only without violating the Constitution, but in strict conformity with it; it is calculated for this express purpose, and will doubtless be executed accordingly.

As this government will not enjoy the confidence of the people, but be executed by force, it will be a very expensive and burthensome government. The standing army must be numerous, and as a further support, it will be the policy of this government to multiply officers in every department; judges, collectors, tax-gatherers, excisemen and the whole host of revenue officers, will swarm over the land, devouring the hard earnings of the industrious—like the locusts of old, impoverishing and desolating all before them.

We have not noticed the smaller, nor many of the considerable blemishes, but have confined our objections to the great and essential defects, the main pillars of the constitution; which we have shown to be inconsistent with the liberty and happiness of the people, as its establishment will annihilate the State governments, and produce one consolidated government that will eventually and speedily issue in the supremacy of despotism.

In this investigation we have not confined our views to the interests or welfare of this State, in preference to the others. We have overlooked all local circumstances—we have considered this subject on the broad scale of the general good; we have asserted the cause of the present and future ages—the cause of liberty and mankind.

Nathaniel Breading,
John Smilie,
Richard Bard,
Adam Orth,
John A. Hannah,
John Whitehill,
John Harris,
Robert Whitehill,
John Reynolds,
Jonathan Hoge,
Nicholas Lutz,
John Ludwig,
Abraham Lincoln,
John Bishop,
Joseph Hiester,
Joseph Powell,
James Martin,
William Findley,
John Baird,
James Edgar,
William Todd.

The yeas and nays upon the final vote were as follows, viz.:

YEAS.	YEAS.
George Latimer,	John Barclay,
Benjamin Rush,	Thomas Yardley,
Hilary Baker,	Abraham Stout,
James Wilson,	Thomas Bull,
Thomas M'Kean,	Anthony Wayne,
William Macpherson,	William Gibbons,
John Hunn,	Richard Downing,
George Gray,	Thomas Cheyney,
Samuel Ashmead,	John Hannum,
Enoch Edwards,	Stephen Chambers,
Henry Wynkoop,	Robert Coleman,
Sebastian Graff,	David Deshler,
John Hubley,	William Wilson,

Jasper Yeates,
Henry Slagle,
Thomas Campbell,
Thomas Hartley,
David Grier,
John Black,
Benjamin Pedan,
John Arndt,
Stephen Balliet,
Joseph Horsfield,

John Boyd,
Thomas Scott,
John Neville,
John Allison,
Jonathan Roberts,
John Richards,
F. A. Muhlenberg,
James Morris,
Timothy Pickering,
Benjamin Elliott.

NAYS.

John Whitehill,
John Harris,
John Reynolds,
Robert Whitehill,
Jonathan Hoge,
Nicholas Lutz,
John Ludwig,
Abraham Lincoln,
John Bishop,
Joseph Hiester,
James Martin,
Joseph Powell,

NAYS.

William Findley,
John Baird,
William Todd,
James Marshel,
James Edgar,
Nathaniel Breading,
John Smilie,
Richard Bard,
William Brown,
Adam Orth,
John Andre Hannah.

Philadelphia December 12, 1787

[The example thus set by the minority was quickly followed by individual members of the majority. No sooner did they reach their homes than they too made appeals to their constituents under the form of reports to county meetings. The earliest of these was made at Easton.]

Philadelphia, January 7. *

At a meeting of sundry respectable inhabitants of the county of Northampton, held at Easton, the twentieth day of December, 1787.

Alexander Patterson, Esq. in the chair.

The meeting took into consideration the report made to the people of this county by their deputies to the State Convention. Whereupon

* Independent Gazetteer, Jan. 7, 1788.

Resolved unanimously, First. That we highly approve of the conduct of our deputies, in assenting to and ratifying the Constitution of the United States, as proposed by the late Federal Convention.

Second. That the chairman be requested to return our hearty thanks to the said deputies, for the patriotism, public spirit and faithful discharge of their duty, as representatives of this county.

Third. That their report, together with these resolutions, be transmitted by the chairman to Philadelphia, for publication. Signed, by order of the meeting,

ALEXANDER PATTERSON, Chairman.

Attest, JAMES PETTIGREW, Secretary.

Friends and Fellow-citizens of Northampton county.

The representatives of this county in the late convention of this State, think it their duty, as servants of the public, to lay before you, their constituents, the result of their deliberations upon the new Constitution for the United States, submitted to their consideration by a resolve of the legislature for calling a State Convention.

The debates at large we have reason to expect will be published, wherein those whose inclination may lead them to it, will find a detail of all the arguments made use of either for or against the adoption of the constitution. Our intention, therefore, is not to enter fully into an investigation of the component parts of it, but only to inform our constituents that it has been carefully examined in all its parts; that every objection that could be offered to it has been heard and attended to; and that upon mature deliberation, two-thirds of the whole number of deputies from the city and counties of this State, in the name and by the authority of the people of this State, fully ratified it, upon the most clear conviction:

1st. That the state of America required a concentration and union of the powers of government for all general purposes of the United States.

2d. That the constitution proposed by the late convention of the United States, held at Philadelphia, was the best form that could be devised and agreed upon.

3d. That such a constitution will enable the representatives of the different States in the Union to restore the commerce of all the States in general, and this in particular, to its former prosperity.

4th. That by a diminution of taxes upon real estates, agriculture may be encouraged, and the prices of lands, which have of late greatly declined, will be increased to their former value.

5th. That by imposing duties on foreign luxuries, not only arts and manufactures will be encouraged in our own country; but the public creditors of this State and the United States will be rendered secure in their demands, without any perceptible burthen on the people.

6th. That all disputes which might otherwise arise, concerning territory or jurisdiction, between neighboring States, will be settled in the ordinary mode of distributing justice, without war or bloodshed.

7th. That the support of government will be less expensive than under the present constitutions of the different States.

8th. That all partial laws of any particular State for the defeating contracts between parties, or rendering the compliance therewith on one part easier than was originally intended, and fraudulent to the other party, are effectually provided against, by a prohibition of paper money and tender laws; and

9th. That peace, liberty, and safety, the great objects for which the late United Colonies, now free independent States, expended so much blood and treasure, can only be secured by such an union of interests as this constitution has provided for.

In full confidence that our unanimous conviction and concurrence in favor of this constitution will meet the entire approbation of our constituents, the freemen and citizens of this county, we have the honor to subscribe ourselves,

Their devoted servants,

JOHN ARNDT,
STEPHEN BALLIET,
JOS. HORSFIELD,
DAVID DESHLER.

Easton, December 20, 1787.

[A similar meeting held at Carlisle a week later was the cause of a serious riot; described by a writer in the Independent Gazetteer.]

Mr. Oswald: As you may perhaps have heard of an affray which happened in this town, I send you the particulars:— On Wednesday the 26th of December last, a number of persons here, much in love with the new Constitution, formed a plan of rejoicing on account of its adoption by this State; they kept their purpose a profound secret from the rest of the inhabitants (who they knew were of a different opinion) until near night, at which time a cannon was brought from the public magazine, placed in the centre of the square, a drum beat and the bell rung; this collected a vast concourse of people, and a report having been propagated that whoever did not illuminate their windows would have them broke in pieces. This alarmed the people very much, who asked the rejoicers what they intended, and why they placed a cannon there at that time; they answered, it was to express their approbation of the adoption of the federal Constitution; they were then asked why they attempted to do so without calling a town meeting, to take the sense of the people on the subject. They replied that such as did not like it might let it alone— that they were determined, in spite of all opposition, to fire that cannon, and swearing most tremendously, if they would not clear the way, they would fire it through their bodies. A smart altercation now took place between both parties, when a number of barrels which had been piled for the bonfire, were thrown down; this provoked some of the most violent of the rejoicers to lay about them most unmercifully with such weapons as they were provided with, but the people defended themselves so well, and aimed their blows so successfully, that it soon converted the intended joy into mourning—the most forward of the rejoicing party were either carried off, or ran with the greatest precipitation, not caring longer to face the hardy cuffs of their enranged opponents, who they knew would pay no respect to their rank, nor make any allowance for their delicate constitutions; I assure you it was laughable to see lawyers, doctors, colonels, captains, etc., etc., leave the scene of their rejoicing in such haste, and run some one way and some another, so that in about three minutes from the first commencement of the battle, there was not one of the rejoicing party to be seen on the ground, except a few who skulked in the dark, in order to collect what they could hear, with a view of appearing as evidences on a future day.

When the fray was over, the rejoicing took a new turn; the fragments of the broken barrels were collected, piled and set fire to; the new constitution was then produced and committed to the flames, by the hands of the executor of the law, amidst the loudest acclamations, then followed three cheers in honor of the dissenting minority of twenty-three in the State convention. Immediately after this (the people having mostly dispersed) some fellows whom the rejoicers had employed to assist them in working the cannon (but who deserted their cause when they saw them defeated) went so far as to burn the carriage and every part of the cannon-mounting that would burn, contrary to the express prohibition of such of the people as were then present, but now too few to prevent the rabble, at the head of whom was one Ryan, a late wheelbarrow convict, whom the rejoicers had employed to work the cannon for them: he swore (when desired to desist and not destroy the carriage) that first he would burn one side of the cannon, and then turn it like a po-ta-tee, for he was captain now.

Next day at noon the rejoicers collected a number of men with fire-arms and ammunition, in order (as they expressed it) to rejoice at the risk of their lives; they fired a few rounds, but on hearing the people's drum beat to arms, they dispersed, appointing to meet at two o'clock, to finish their rejoicings: this, however, they prudently declined. Now in their turn the people met, and having dressed up the effigies of two of the most noted partisans and promoters of the new constitution, after carrying them in procession through the principal streets of the town, to the funeral pile which was burning in the square for their reception, committed them to the flames, with an indignation suitable to the opinion they entertained of men who could endeavor to undermine

the liberties of their country. From the first appearance of
the effigies the dead bell tolled until they were totally consumed to ashes: this ended the exercises of the day; however,
the lawyers are like to make something by the matter—the
rejoicers swear they will be avenged, they have summoned a
long train of evidences before a justice who they think
favors their party, and are endeavoring to injure a number of
respectable characters among the people; who in their turn
have it amply in their power to retaliate, but will only act
agreeably to the laws of their country, the nod of the great
not being yet the supreme law of the land.

ONE OF THE PEOPLE.

Carlisle, January 1, 1788.*

Carlisle, January 2.

As the riot on Wednesday last, and the burning of the
effigies of two of the most distinguished characters in the
State, in the public streets of Carlisle, by a mob on Thursday,
has already made a considerable noise in the county, an impartial spectator, desirous of furnishing the public with a just
and true state of facts, to enable them to form a proper judgment of the conduct of the parties concerned, begs leave to
lay before them the following representation, for the truth of
which he pledges himself, and which will appear by the
depositions of a cloud of reputable and respectable witnesses,
in the possession of John Agnew, esq.

About five o'clock on Wednesday afternoon, public notice
being given by ringing the bell and beating the drum, a
number of persons met at the public square, to testify their
approbation of the proceedings of the late convention, in the
most decent and orderly manner. A piece of artillery having
been brought to the ground, and materials collected for a
bonfire, a number of men armed with bludgeons, came in
regular order from one quarter of the town, while others
sallied forth from different streets armed in the same manner.
Major James A. Wilson (having been appointed with two
other gentlemen, to make the necessary arrangements for the
occasion) was preparing to have the gun loaded, when he was

* Independent Gazetteer, Feb. 7, 1788.

ordered by many of the armed party to desist, and many threats thrown out against any person who would attempt to kindle the bonfire; to which the Major replied, that those who were not disposed to rejoice, might withdraw; and that he hoped, people so pregnant with poverty as they appeared to be, would not wish to hinder their neighbors from showing marks of joy, when they were pleased. Immediately after a number of barrels and staves were thrown at him, one of which struck him on the breast; he then sprung forward to the persons who threw at him, and struck one of them with a small pine stick, to which a piece of pitch rope was fixed; he was then beat down by a number of blows from six or seven persons with bludgeons, who continued beating him after he fell. They would have taken his life had not a trusty old soldier thrown himself on the Major, and received the blows aimed at him. A general confusion took place. Mr. Robert Miller, jun, was attacked by a person who with both hands wielded a massy bludgeon, and while he was engaged with the first, received several blows from one who stood behind him. The persons met for the purpose of the celebration, altogether unprepared for such an assault (being even without walking canes) were forced to return. The armed party having accomplished their premeditated designs of preventing the public rejoicing, proceeded to spike the cannon, and having made a large fire, committed to the flames the cannon and its carriage, together with a sledge on which it had been drawn to the ground. They then sent for an almanac containing the Federal Constitution, which was formally burned. Loud huzzas were repeated, with "Damnation to the 46 members, and long live the virtuous 23."

On Thursday at 12 o'clock, I understood that the friends to government intended to carry into execution the resolution of the celebration of the event from which, the evening before they had been so violently prevented. I went to the place, found them, at the court house armed chiefly with muskets and bayonets; they discovered every pacific disposition, but at the same time the most determined resolution to repel, at the risk of their lives, any attack which might be made on them. A bonfire was made, and the ratification of the constitution by this State was read, accompanied by the acclamations of all the people present, repeated volleys of musketry and firing of cannon.

I cannot help giving my praise to the good order and coolness and determined spirit with which the business was conducted, although the mob made their appearance in several places, armed with guns and bludgeons, and even came close to where the federalists were firing the cannon, and used threatening language, which was treated with every possible contempt, and no violence offered to them. The federalists remained two hours on the ground, testified their joy, with every appearance of harmony and good humor, and returned without any disturbance to their homes. Immediately after a drum beat—the mob gathered, collected barrels, and proceeded to the court-house with noise and tumult, when there were brought from an adjacent lot two effigies with labels on their breasts, Thomas M'Kean, Chief Justice, and James Wilson, the Caledonian. They formed in order, had the effigies carried in front, preceded only by a noted captain of militia, who declared he was inspired from Heaven, paraded the streets, and with shouts and most dreadful execrations committed them to the flames. It is remarkable that some of the most active people in the riot of Wednesday evening, and the mob of Thursday, have come to this country within these two years—men perfectly unknown, and whose characters were too obscure to attract the notice of the inhabitants of this place, and others who but lately have stripped off the garb of British soldiers. I think it improper to prejudice the public by naming the persons concerned in these atrocious riots, as prosecutions are about to be commenced in the name of the State against them. Every lover of good order must lament the wound the dignity of the State has received in burning in the public street, in one of the largest towns in open day, the effigy of the first magistrate of the Commonwealth. Proceedings of this kind are really alarming, directly tend to the dissolution of all governments, and must receive the rebrobation of every honest citizen.

I was invited, being an old man, to spend the evening with the federalists at Mr. Joseph Postlethwait's tavern, where an elegant supper had been prepared—a number of the respectable inhabitants of Carlisle convened there and spent the evening with the most perfect harmony, good humor and conviviality.   After supper the following toasts were drank:

1. The Federal Constitution.
2. General Washington and the Federal Constitution.
3. The States who Acceded to the Federal Constitution.
4. A speedy accession and ratification of the Constitution by all the States.
5. The patriotic forty-six.
6. The president of the State.
7. The chief justice of Pennsylvania and member of the late convention.
8. The honorable James Wilson, Esq., of Philadelphia.
9. Major James Armstrong Wilson.
10. An increase of the agriculture, manufactures and commerce of America.
11. May the flag of the United States fly triumphant in all the ports of the world.
12. Our friends in Europe.*

Extract of a letter from Carlisle, dated January 4, 1788.

"I dare say you have heard of the unhappy rumpus which took place here on the 25th ult.   This spirit of rage and discord is increasing every hour; Squire *Agnew* issued warrants for some of the rioters, but none would venture to serve them.   A boy indeed was taken, but the people of the town threatening to rise again, he was discharged, and the country people declaring they would come in and pull down the houses of any who should attempt to issue or execute any warrants.   Nothing is or can be done!   You cannot conceive the violent language used here; the whole country is alive with wrath, and it is spreading from one county to another so rapidly that it is impossible to say where it will end, or how far it will reach, as the best and leading characters in

*Independent Gazetteer, Jan. 9, 1788.

all these counties during the late war are now the foremost in this unfortunate dispute. The county of Franklin is, if possible, they tell me, worse than ours; they also are forming themselves into societies and associations to oppose this new constitution. The order from council to repair the arms cannot be executed; it is the subject of much speculation.''*

[Some of the rioters, however, were arrested. What happened to them is set forth in the following narrative.]

Carlisle, March 5.

A narrative of facts, respecting the manner by which the prisoners were liberated from their confinement, in the gaol of Cumberland county, on Saturday the first of March instant.

It is presumed the public are already in full possession of the cause which gave rise to the following transactions, viz., the opposition made by some of the inhabitants of the borough of Carlisle, to the rejoicing intended to be celebrated by the new federalists, on the 26th and 27th of December last. It is already known that a number of depositions were taken in the office of John Agnew, Esquire, with an intention to criminate the several persons who were active in opposing said rejoicing, on which depositions or other information laid before the honorable the supreme justices of the State of Pennsylvania, a warrant was issued charging the said opposers with divers unlawful acts, &c., and commanding the Sheriff of this county to apprehend 20 persons therein named, and take them before some of the Justices of the Supreme Court, or any of the Justices of Cumberland county, to answer to the premises and be dealt with according to law. Some time after the Sheriff received the warrant, and called upon the defendants, and informed them such warrant was in his hands; each person willingly agreed to appear at any time he might think proper before any magistrate of this county: he thought proper to appoint Monday the 25th of February last for them to appear before John Agnew, Esq., which they readily complied with. The warrant being read, which ex-

* Independent Gazetteer, Jan. 12, 1788.

hibited the charge of a riot against the defendants, who demanded that they should be confronted with the witnesses, and offered, if permitted, to produce sufficient evidence to exculpate themselves from the charge alleged against them, which was refused, as the magistrate was of opinion that it was not in his power to supersede a warrant issued by the Supreme Justices. In the interim a country magistrate arrived, who had been previously sent for by John Agnew, Esquire; after a short consultation they came forth, and the country justice told the defendants that in his opinion the warrant admitted of a hearing, but added, that he was determined not to act in the matter, and advised the defendants to accept of a proposal made by Mr. Agnew, which was to remain in the custody of the Sheriff until the 25th of March next, at which time Mr. Agnew hoped to have instructions from the Supreme Justices. Seven of the defendants absolutely refused the proposal, unless they were assured of an investigation of the premises at the time mentioned, which was likewise refused. Bail was then demanded by the Justice; the defendants answered they were conscious that they were guilty of no crime against the laws of their country; and as they were prosecuted to gratify party spite, they were determined not to enter bail on the occasion, but would otherwise willingly comply with the orders of his worship; upon which Mr. Agnew wrote and signed their commitment, and gave it to the Sheriff, who conducted the prisoners to the county gaol. Immediately the country took the alarm, on hearing that a number of persons were confined in prison for opposing a measure that was intended to give sanction to the proposed Federal Constitution. The people who composed the different companies of militia in this county, thought proper to collect, and appointed to meet in Carlisle, on Saturday last, to inquire why those persons were confined, and at the same time determined to act agreeably to the opposition offered them by the rejoicing party. Accordingly about sunrise the bell began to ring, and the men under arms made their appearance from different quarters, who previously had appointed one person from each company to represent them in a committee, for the purpose of consulting on such measures as might be most expedient on the occasion. Previous to their meeting five persons with delegated power from the people of Dauphin county, had met a number of new federalists, and had proposed terms of accommodation. In one hour the new federalists promised to give them an answer, at which time they accordingly met, together with the committee appointed by the different companies, who immediately agreed on terms of accommodation, and mutually consented to transmit a petition to Council, signed by a number of respectable persons on both sides of the question; they then agreed that the Sheiff would sign the following discharge:

"Be it known that I, Charles Leeper, Esq., Sheriff of Cumberland county, do hereby discharge from their imprisonment in the jail of this county of Cumberland, the following persons, viz., James Wallace, William Petrikin, Thomas Dickson, Samuel Greer, Bartholomew White, Joseph Young, and Joseph Steel.

.‘‘CHARLES LEEPER, Sheriff.’’

After the above agreement was ratified, the militia were marched under their respective officers from the public square to the jail, where the sheriff conducted the prisoners to the street; having read the above discharge, they were restored to their former liberty with loud huzzas and a *feu de joie* from right to left of the companies, who then marched out of town in good order, without injuring any person or property, except two balls which were fired through a tavern-keeper's sign who is said to be a warm federalist.

It is with pleasure we announce to the public, that the militia who appeared on this occasion amounted to about 1,500 men, who are generally men of property and good characters, who all evinced both by words and actions, that they intended to persevere in every measure that would oppose the establishment of the new Constitution, at the risk of their lives and fortunes.

The following is a copy of the petition to Council alluded to above.

To the Honorable the Supreme Executive Council of the State of Pennsylvania.

We, the undersigned, being desirous of preserving the peace of the county of Cumberland, do hereby signify and declare our wishes and desire that the prosecutions commenced respecting certain riots said to have been committed upon Wednesday and Thursday the twenty-sixth and twenty-seventh of December last, should be discontinued; and that your honors will be pleased to direct the attorney-general to enter *noli prosequi* to the said prosecutions.

John Montgomery,	William Blair,
John Agnew,	John Wray,
Stephen Duncan,	William Brown,
James Hamilton,	Mathew Alison,
Samuel A. M. Coskery,	John Jordon,
Robert Magaw,	James Lemberton,
Joseph Thornburg,	Samuel Gray,
John Holmes,	George Logan.
John Creigh,	
Richard Butler.	

N. B. John Montgomery, etc., are in favor of the new constitution, and William Blair, etc., against it.*

[The Antifederalists of Carlisle meantime had not been idle. The Assembly was petitioned and the minority of the convention repeatedly thanked.]

From the Carlisle *Gazette*.

Messrs. Printers: By inserting the following in your useful *Gazette*, you will oblige a number of your constant readers.

An address to the Minority of the State Convention of Pennsylvania.

The history of mankind is pregnant with frequent, bloody and almost imperceptible transitions from freedom to slavery. Rome, after she had been long distracted by the fury of the patrician and plebeian parties, at length found herself reduced to the most abject slavery under a Nero, a Caligula,

* Independent Gazetteer, Mar. 14, 1788.

etc. The successive convulsions, which happened at Rome, were the immediate consequence of the aspiring ambition of a few great men, and the very organization and construction of the government itself. The republic of Venice, by the progressive and almost imperceptible encroachments of the nobles, has at length degenerated into an odious and permanent aristocracy. This we are convinced by indubitable demonstration, will be the final consequence of the proposed Federal Constitution; and because we prize the felicity and freedom of our posterity equally with our own, we esteem it our indispensable duty to oppose it with that determined resolution and spirit that becomes freemen. That fire for liberty which was kindled in every patriotic breast during the late glorious contention, though in a latent state, will be easily rekindled; and upon the contact of a very spark will devour by its direful explosion, not only the enemies of liberty, but both parties promiscuously.

Discontent, indignation and revenge already begin to be visible in every patriotic countenance; and civil discord already raises her snakey head. And we are well convinced that nothing less than a total recantation and annihilation of the proposed aristocratic delusion will appease the insulted and enraged defenders of liberty. If the lazy and great wish to ride, they may lay it down as an indubitable position or axiom, that the people of America will make very refractory and restive hackneys. Although the designing and artful Federalists have effected their scheme so far as to have the constitution adopted in this State by surprise, notwithstanding the people are pretty generally convinced of their delusion, and little less than the lives of their betrayers will satiate their revenge. Not even the authority of the clergy, who seem generally to have been a set of men decidedly opposed to popular freedom, can give sanction to such a government. The people of America understand their rights better than, by adopting such a constitution, to rivet the fetters of slavery; or to sacrifice their liberty at the shrine of aristocracy or arbitrary government. We, the subscribers, are a society united for the express purpose of reciprocal or mutual improvement; we meet once a week, and political matters are frequently the subjects of litigation and debate. We have read and endeavored fully to comprehend the proposed federal constitution, and also the arguments for and against it; and after mature deliberation, we unanimously acquiesce with, and cordially thank you the minority in the late State convention: First, for your patriotic and spirited endeavors to support the drooping cause of liberty, and rights of your constituents: Secondly, for your integrity and firmness in stemming the torrent of popular clamor, insult and flattery: Thirdly, for your unanswerable, solid, and well-founded arguments and reason of dissent: Lastly, we rejoice to think that your names will shine illustriously in the page of history, and will be read with honor and grateful remembrance in the annals of fame; while the names of the majority and their ignorant tools will be spurned and execrated by the succeeding generations as the pillars of slavery, tyranny and despotism.

James M'Cormick,	James Bell,
David Boyd,	Thomas Atchley,
William Gelson	William Irvin,
James Irvin,	William Douglass,
Andrew Irvin,	John Walker,
William Carothers, senior,	William Greason,
William Adams,	David Walker,
William Carothers, junior,	Jonathan Walker,
John Douglass,	John Buchanan,
Archibald Hamilton,	Francis M'Guire,
Joseph Junkin,	John Armstrong,
John Clandinen,	Benj. Junkin,
Thomas Henderson,	John Carothers, junior,
Robert Bell,	James Fleming,
John Junkin,	Thomas Carothers.*

Carlisle, February 13.

An Address to the Minority of the late State Convention—
From Union Society.

GENTLEMEN: After the most mature and deliberate consideration, we feel ourselves prompted by the most lively

*Independent Gazetteer, Jan. 9, 1788.

glow of gratitude, to tender you our unfeigned address of thanks for your able and spirited exertions in the late Convention, in behalf of liberty and your country, and with unwearied assiduity struggling through fatigue and opposition, in support of the unalienable rights of mankind, against the iron hand of despotism, which is the concomitant of slavery and oppression. Though baffled and disappointed in your late glorious contest, in contending for the blessing of freedom—we congratulate you that the happy day is not far off when your virtuous endeavors will illustriously shine in the annals of fame, and immortalize your names in the historic page. Believe it, gentlemen, as a truth, that it will redound to your honor, whose lot it was to fall into an age that asserted common liberty and the rights of your country, that you were possessed of undaunted courage to give us some proofs of it in this critical moment, a blessing which we wish with all our souls may be perpetuated to posterity; for as to what concerns ourselves, one day's experience is abundantly sufficient for our comfort and instruction, both young and old. Those that are in years will leave the world with less regret, when they shall better understand the advantages that attend liberty; and for those that are growing up, the very example will inflame them with a virtuous emulation of treading in the steps of their famous ancestors. Gentlemen, it is with great respect we offer this tribute of our acknowledgments due to your merits.

Signed by order of the Society,

JAMES STERRITT, Secretary.*

An address of thanks from a number of the inhabitants of the borough of Carlisle, to the minority of the late State Convention in general, and the representatives of Cumberland county in particular.

GENTLEMEN: We return you our hearty thanks for the magnanimous and spirited opposition which you made in the late State Convention to that instrument of oppression, injustice and tyranny, which was then the subject of your

* Independent Gazetteer, Feb. 27, 1788.

deliberations, viz.: The Proposed Constitution for the United States.

We assure you that your conduct meets with our most cordial approbation, and fully answers the expectation we formed of you when we voted you to represent us. Although we did not tie up your hands, by dictating to you how to behave or what side to take, nor did we preclude you from investigating its properties or discussing its principles in the most ample manner, according to the dictates of your own enlightened understanding, by extorting from you, previous to your election or afterwards, any promises or engagements to vote for or against the proposed plan. This would have been treating you like machines or tools, and for such a purpose as this parrots and magpies trained to prattle would have answered the purpose much better than freemen. Nevertheless, gentlemen, the measures you have taken have fully justified the confidence we reposed in you, and come up to our most sanguine wishes.

We, gentlemen, with you, deprecate the impending ruin, and deplore the unhappy state of our dear country and innocent posterity, should this engine of slavery ever be established. We sincerely grieve to see the people of this State plunge themselves into the jaws of destruction, and sacrifice their dearest interests to gratify the ambition of a few selfish despots. Yet we sorrow not as those who have no hope; we are happy to find that a formidable opposition is made to it in some of our sister States; we rejoice in the expectation of your cogent arguments and spirited protest being disseminated through America, and rousing multitudes from their supine lethargy, and opening the eyes of others who are blinded with prejudice, and misled by artful men; we comfort ourselves with the hope that your example will animate such citizens of our own State, whose generous souls recoil at the idea of slavery, and who have not yet degenerated so far from their original principles as to be content to live in fetters—to oppose it. We hope it is not yet too late, although the chains are making they are not yet riveted on, and their Constitution is not yet "the supreme law of the land," and we flatter ourselves it never will. When liberty was the grand question, America combated an infinitely more formidable power than the partisans of the proposed Constitution; when her rights and privileges were invaded by one of the most puissant monarchs on earth, she bravely resisted the attack, and laughed at the shaking of their spear—she despised their menaces and returned their threats with redoubled vengeance on their own heads. Will her brave freeborn yeomen, then, tamely submit to be circumvented or cajoled out of their freedom and invaluable rights by a few petty domestic tyrants? No, we are persuaded they never will.

It is, gentlemen, with the most agreeable surprise that we behold a very few country farmers and mechanics nonplus the great rabbis and doctors of the schools, who no doubt summoned in all the rhetoric, logic, and sophistry they were capable of on this occasion. We rejoice to see scholastic learning and erudition fly before simple reason, plain truth and common sense. But though you defeated them in argument, they exceeded you in numbers; however, should the worst happen (which heaven avert) this will be your consolation, that in the time of danger you exerted every effort to prevent the calamity; you exonerated your consciences by a faithful discharge of your duty; your names will descend to posterity with admiration and esteem, when those of your opponents will be loaded with infamy and execration: It will be said, these were the Demosthenes's, the Bruti, the Cato's of America, when your antagonists will be classed with the vilest tyrants that ever disgraced human nature. This will be a sufficient compensation for all the outrage and insult you have received from the senseless, ignorant rabble in Philadelphia, and the harsh rude treatment given you by such of the aristocratical junto as were members of the Convention; so that your reward is sure, suppose this Constitution should even be adopted universally, which we are persuaded will never be. The late glorious revolution is too recent in the memory of American freemen, to suffer this. It may occasion a small conflict, but the cause of liberty is worth contending for, and we firmly believe there are yet numbers who will account it their highest honor to unite with you in the glorious struggle. That the same spirit which actuated you from the first appearance of this baneful instrument, may predominate in the breast of every brave American, is, gentlemen, the most ardent desire of your inflexible adherents.*

Signed by order of the meeting,

WILLIAM BROWN, in the Chair.

GEORGE LOGUE, Clerk.

From the Carlisle *Gazette.*

Messrs. Kline and Reynolds: You will oblige a number of your customers by inserting the following address in your useful paper, and through it they ask the opportunity of soliciting the concurrence of their fellow-citizens.

To the Honorable the Representatives of the Freemen of the Commonwealth of Pennsylvania, in General Assembly met.

The petition of the subscribers, freemen of the county of Franklin, most respectfully showeth : That your petitioners are desirous that order and good government should prevail, and that the Constitution of this State should not be subverted nor altered in any other way than is therein provided.

That as the members of your honorable House are all sworn or affirmed to do no act or thing prejudicial or injurious to the Constitution or government as established by the Convention, by whom the same was framed, they look up to you as the guardians of the rights and liberties therein secured to your petitioners, and pray that they may be protected therein.

That your petitioners are much alarmed at an instrument called a Constitution for the United States of America, framed by a Convention that had been appointed by several of the States, solely for the purpose of revising the articles of confederation, and to report such alterations and provisions therein, as should, when agreed to in Congress and confirmed by the several States, render the federal Constitution adequate to the exigencies of government and the preservation of the union, inasmuch as the liberties, lives and property of your petitioners are not secured thereby.

*Independent Gazetteer, Feb. 14, 1788.

That the powers therein proposed to be granted to the government of the United States are too great, and that the proposed distribution of these powers is dangerous and inimical to liberty and equality amongst the people.

That they esteem frequent elections and rotation in offices as the great bulwark of freedom.

That they conceive standing armies in time of peace are dangerous to liberty, and that a well organized militia will be the proper security for our defence.

That the rights of conscience should be secured to all men, that none should be molested for his religion, and that none should be compelled contrary to his principles or inclination to hear or support the clergy of any one established religion.

That the liberty of the *Press* should not be insecure or in danger.

That the right of trial by jury should be secured in civil as well as in criminal cases.

That the government as proposed would be burthensome, expensive and oppressive, and that your petitioners from paying taxes to support a numerous train of offices erected thereby, which would be not only unnecessary but dangerous to our liberties.

That your petitioners observe this proposed Constitution hath not been approved of by the Congress of the United States, as directed by the articles of their confederation.

That your petitioners conceive the majority of the deputies of the General Convention, who have been appointed by the State, have assumed to exercise powers with which they were not delegated, that their conduct is reprehensible, and that they should be brought to account for the same, as the precedent is highly dangerous and subversive of all government.

And your petitioners desire that the said proposed plan of government may not be confirmed by the legislature of this State, nor adopted in the said United States, and that the delegates of Congress from this State be instructed for that purpose.

And your petitioners as in duty bound shall ever pray.*

* Independent Gazetteer, Feb. 19, 1788.

[The violence at Carlisle excited no comment and beyond the limits of the county in which it occurred was soon forgotten. In Philadelphia the antifederalists became more active than ever. To reprint all that was written is not necessary; but the following selection of pieces both wise and foolish may safely be taken as samples of the whole].

Mr. Oswald: I believe the leaders of the majority in our convention did not publish their address and reasons of assent on two accounts: First, because nearly one-half of their number were obliged to vote according to their solemn engagements and promises, (by which they were tied down before their election,) and not according to their judgments; therefore had not signed it.

Secondly, because when they found the address of the minority so ably drawn up, and so well supported by undoubted facts and unanswerable arguments, they despaired of their sophistical inflammatory address being of any service to them, therefore they resolved still to avoid the field of argument, and to depend on their old aids, detraction, scandal, and falsehoods.

However, I think they should have allowed their members (whom they detained from Wednesday till Tuesday, to sign and carry home their address) something towards extra expenses in that time.　　　　I am yours, etc.,

　　　　　　　　　　　　　　　　UNCLE TOBEY.*

Messrs. Dunlap and Claypoole: In answer to Mr. Findley's declaration on the day of the ratification, of only one-sixth part of the State of Pennsylvania having voted for the late convention, Colonel Hartley, or one of the federalists, observed that this was a very unfair mode of determining the strength or number of the friends of the new government—that the whole of the State seldom voted upon any occasion, except in contested elections, and that the reason why so few voted was because in the city of Philadelphia, and in all the large and populous counties, there was nearly a perfect unanimity upon the subject of the new constitution. The speaker added,

* Independent Gazetteer, Dec. 19, 1787.

that the convention that framed the Constitution of Pennsylvania was chosen only by about 6000 votes, and that the members of the first legislature that sat under it were elected by a little more than 1500 votes. A BYSTANDER.*

Mr. Oswald: The conduct of our fellow-citizens on the late glorious occasion, of solemnly proclaiming to the people the ratification and adoption of the proposed new constitution, by the convention of this State, does them no honor; for, notwithstanding due notice having been given by our friends in the convention and council, to the members of council, judges, justices and other State officers, the faculty of the University, militia officers, and citizens, of the order and time of the procession; yet few of any of these attended; the citizens and militia officers in particular were uncommonly scarce—they should at least have given their countenance to this very important business; it is not very unaccountable that more officers of government did not come forth, but that more of the professors, etc., in the University, the militia officers, and citizens did not appear to celebrate this grand affair which concerns them all so materially, is wonderful.

And the common people, I observed, were as inattentive as the others; they did not seem to show any attention to a fine little batteau (dressed off with colors) that was industriously carried on a cart through some of the back streets, as an emblem of our *future* commerce; although the sailors, etc. who conducted it, used all their generous endeavors to excite admiration: they huzzaed at the corners, had the sweet music of a fiddle, etc. I followed them many squares, and could not find any but children with them. O strange behavior! the people do not seem to know what grandeur is preparing for them and their posterity.

But to come to the point, our friends, the majority, after dining together, enjoyed much happiness in the pleasures of the social bottle till late at night, when our worthy Chief Justice, that great patron and protector of the press, was a little affected by the working of small beer, and so retired.

*Pennsylvania Packet, Dec. 25, 1787.

Some of the toasts that were drank were middling, but most of them were not to the purpose; for we should now forget our past national transactions, and it will be ridiculous to give thirteen toasts hereafter, as we are all to be united and bound together into one : for the same reason it was wrong to fire thirteen guns—one great gun ought only to have been fired: and we must immediately alter our flags and remove the thirteen stripes and stars, and in their places insert the spread eagle or some other great monster, emblematical of our future unison.

I think the conduct of our people in the majority in Convention was from the beginning a true emblem of our future unanimity and grandeur, they were from the first united in and under J. W——n, Esquire, without whose direction nothing was done or said: in short, none of our party attempted to argue except him, and he deserves much credit for his industry and ingenuity on the occasion; to be sure, he had the best right to defend it, for it was framed by him and our worthy friend, Mr. G——r M——s, in the Federal Convention. I think, Mr. Oswald, that if we had not put him in our Convention, the business would have been lost; the yellow whigs were so arch, and upon the whole, they both deserve great promotion and the highest offices. I am sure they shall have the vote of   A UNITARIAN.*

A few queries hnmbly submitted to the consideration of the people of Pennsylvania.

1. Was the *recommendation* of the late General Assembly to choose a Convention for the purpose of adopting the new Constitution, so binding upon the people, as that they were necessarily and legally obliged to comply with it at the time and in the manner then recommended? Or were not the people still at liberty to act according to their own judgment on this momentous question?

2. As no more than about one-sixth part of the freemen of this State have yet thought proper to appoint a convention for the above purpose, can the act of this small minority, or of

* Independent Gazetteer, Dec. 21, 1787.

the men chosen by them, be, with any propriety, considered as the act of the people of the State?

3. May not, therefore, the freemen of Pennsylvania, at any time before the new Constitution shall become the *supreme law of the land*, call a Convention by their own authority, to consider of this proposed plan of government; and give them power either to adopt, propose amendments to, or reject the same, as they shall, upon due deliberation, judge most proper?*

December 24, 1787.

Mr. Oswald: Please to insert the following in your paper and oblige,   *A Constant Reader.*

From the New-Haven *Gazette*, of Dec. 13, 1787.

ADVERTISEMENT.

Broke into the State of Connecticut on the evening of the 12th ult., a large overgrown creature, marked and branded *Centinel.* She appears to be of Pennsylvania extraction, and was lately in the keeping of J— L—, Esq., of New York, from whence she escaped to this State. She is well pampered for market, and at first was thought to be of great value, but upon more minute examination she is found to be a deception—Cock's head and tail at first sight, but is soon discovered to be lame in her *fore* feet. Nine hundred pounds (her late maker's salary under the present Constitution) written in small letters on her left hip, the hip which eminent farmers conjecture will soon be put out of joint. She has a large blaze in her forehead, in which is written in capitals, *Friends, Countrymen and Fellow Citizens.* She was considerably *galled* and *fretted* before she left Pennsylvania, by the lash of Mr. Wilson, which caused her to quit the place of her nativity. She is well enough spread for the people of this State, and they do not wish her to be spread any more, and therefore if her original proprietor, or her late protector, will take her away and pay charges, no questions will be asked; if not before the first Thursday in January next, she will be

---

* Independent Gazetteer, Dec. 22, 1787.

re-shipped for New York to pay duties, as we are determined not to winter her.

The advocates of the new system of government must be very much exhausted in point of argument indeed, when they have recourse to such wretched abuse as is contained in the above *advertisement.* Unfortunately for this horrid scribbler, the gentleman, at whom he has levelled his scurrility and low ribaldry, is held in the highest estimation by his fellow-citizens for his honor, integrity, and unshaken attachment to the cause of liberty. And the name of the patriotic LAMB of New York, "will be sweet in the mouths" of a grateful and applauding country, when those of his infamous political adversaries,—the upstarts and mushroons of an hour,—the *totos* and *major tiffanies*—the time-serving tools, the Phocions and Publiuses of our day,—"will stink in the very nostrils of posterity."*

From the *Daily Patriotic Register.*

How one story brings another to mind! Mr. Wilson's witticism (in the Pennsylvania Convention) about Sternhold and Hopkins's psalms, made me think of the following: A man who was ridiculed for the shortness of his coat smartly said, "It will be long enough before I get another." The person who ridiculed him was pleased with the reply, and treasured it up for the purpose of retailing it. He met with an opportunity, and said, he had heard one of the wittiest things lately that he ever met with. Upon being asked what it was, he replied he had been laughing at ―――― because his coat was so short; and ―――― told him it would be a long time before he would get another. His friend observed that he could not see any wit in it. "Why, really, nor I," said he, "now; but I remember it was a good story when I heard it." Mr. Wilson was equally unfortunate in retailing Sternhold and Hopkins; for the two lines he quoted are not in that version of the Psalms, nor I believe in any other.

SQUIB.*

* Independent Gazetteer, Dec. 27, 1787.

Mr. Oswald: As the publication of the debates of the late Convention promised by Mr. Lloyd, does not appear, I beg leave to present the public by anticipation with the new political maxims which have been delivered in the course of their speeches, by the members who spoke in support of the new Constitution (for it is well known that what was said by the members of the opposition is not worth recording). These maxims which are the *quintessence* of the arguments that have been urged to prove the excellence of that new form of government, which has been *sent down to us by God Almighty from Mount Sinai,* or in other words of the new political testament, I think ought to be published together, for the honor of Pennsylvania, and of human nature.

ARGUS.

MAXIMS.

1. An *aristocracy* is the best government on earth, because according to its *etymology,* it is the government of the *better sort of people.*

2. Whatever government is *best administered* is *best,* because the *form* or *species* of a government, and its *administration* are the *same thing,* and consequently *one* good *king* can make *monarchy* the best of all possible governments *forever* —Therefore we must say with *Pope,* who never was in the wrong:

> For forms of government let fools contest,
> Whate'er is best administered is best.

3. Government is not founded on a compact between the *governors* and the *governed,* nor indeed on any *compact* or *contract*; its foundations are *power* on the one hand, and *fear* on the other.

4. A *plan* of government submitted to the consideration of a popular convention, is like a *house ready built,* and ought to be adopted or rejected *in toto,* and it is not at all like the *plan* of a house *before* it is built, which may be altered or amended at pleasure; neither is it like a *watch* presented for inspection to a skilful artist, who would naturally take it to pieces, and examine *every spring separately,* before he gave his opinion upon the whole.

5. BILLS or *declaration of the* RIGHTS *of the people,* are always useless in a new Constitution, and are often dangerous to liberty; and this is very clear, because *Virginia has no bill of rights.*

6. The *liberty of the press* is not at all endangered by the new Constitution; first, because there is nothing said about it; and second, because the judicial officers of Congress alone will have the cognizance of libels against their government.

7. Trial by jury was *never known in Sweden,* and therefore we ought not to have it in America.

8. It is not true that *appeals* are unknown to the common law, because *Blackstone* has a chapter entitled "Of proceedings *in the nature* of appeals."

9. *Standing armies* are always necessary in time of peace.

10. Congress ought to have an absolute command over the militia of the United States, in order that *their muskets may be all of the same size.*

11. We must not be afraid of trusting too much power to our rulers, because we cannot suppose that they will be demons of tyranny.

12. A government which doubles the number of public officers, and which will require a standing army, must of course lessen the taxes and national expenses.

13. A *federal* government and a *consolidated* government are the same—*unum et idem.* *

Anecdote of Publius; who pants for a fat office under the new system of government.

A country relation of *Publius's* calling to see him in New York, at the time his 18th number appeared, the author inquired of him, what the people up in his part of the country said of the *Federalist;* the other, not suspecting he was the author of it, answered that he had read it, but heard little said about it, as the attention of the people was so much occupied on the subject of the *New Constitution,* they had no time or inclination to read any essay on *Foreign Affairs.* †

* Independent Gazetteer, Jan. 5, 1787.
† Independent Gazetteer, Jan. 5, 1787.

For the *Pennsylvania Packet.*
The New Roof.

The roof of a certain mansion house was observed to be in a very bad condition, and insufficient for the purpose of protection from the inclemencies of the weather. This was matter of surprise and speculation, as it was well known the roof was not more than 12 years old, and therefore, its defects could not be ascribed to a natural decay by time. Although there were many different opinions as to the cause of this deficiency, yet all agreed that the family could not sleep in comfort or safety under it. It was at last determined to appoint some skilful architects to survey and examine the defective roof, to make report of its condition, and to point out such alterations and repairs as might be found necessary. These skilful architects, accordingly went into a thorough examination of the faulty roof, and found

1st. That the whole frame was too weak.

2d. That there were indeed 13 rafters, but that these rafters were not connected by any braces or ties, so as to form a union of strength.

3d. That some of these rafters were thick and heavy, and others very slight, and as the whole had been put together whilst the timber was yet green, some had warped outwards, and of course sustained an undue weight, whilst others warping inwards, had shrunk from bearing any weight at all.

4th. That the lathing and shingling had not been secured with iron nails, but only wooden pegs, which, shrinking and swelling by successions of wet and dry weather, had left the shingles so loose, that many of them had been blown away by the winds, and that before long the whole would probably, in like manner, be blown away.

5th. That the cornice was so ill proportioned, and so badly put up, as to be neither of use, nor an ornament. And

6th. That the roof was so flat as to admit the most idle servants in the family, their playmates and acquaintance, to trample on and abuse it.

Having made these observations, these judicious architects gave it as their opinion, that it would be altogether vain and fruitless to attempt any alterations or amendments in a roof so defective in all points; and therefore proposed to have it entirely removed, and that a new roof of a better construction should be erected over the mansion house. And they also prepared and offered a drawing or plan of a new roof, such as they thought most excellent for security, duration and ornament. In forming this plan they consulted the most celebrated authors in ancient and modern architecture, and brought into their plan the most approved parts, according to their judgments, selected from the models before them; and finally endeavored to proportion the whole to the size of the building, and strength of the walls.

This proposal of a new roof, it may well be supposed, became the principal subject of conversation in the family, and the opinions upon it were various, according to the judgment, interest, or ignorance of the disputants.

On a certain day the servants of the family had assembled in the great hall to discuss this important point. Amongst these was James the architect, who had been one of the surveyors of the old roof, and had a principal hand in forming the plan of a new one. A great number of the tenants had also gathered out of doors and crowded the windows and avenues to the hall, which were left open that they might hear the arguments for and against the new roof.

Now there was an old woman known by the name of Margery, who had got a comfortable apartment in the mansion house. This woman was of an intriguing spirit, of a restless and inveterate temper, fond of tattle, and a great mischief maker. In this situation, and with these talents, she unavoidably acquired an influence in the family, by the exercise of which, according to her natural propensity, she had long kept the house in confusion, and sown discord and discontent amongst the servants. Margery was, for many reasons, an irreconcilable enemy to the new roof, and to the architects who had planned it; amongst these, two reasons were very obvious—1st, The mantle piece on which her cups and platters were placed was made of a portion of the great cornice, and she boiled her pot with the shingles that blew off from the defective roof: And 2dly, It so happened that in the construction of the new roof, her apartment would be considerably lessened. No sooner, therefore, did she hear of the plan proposed by the architects, but she put on her old red cloak and was day and night trudging amongst the tenants and servants, and crying out against the new roof and the framers of it. Amongst these she had selected William, Jack and Robert, three of the tenants, and instigated them to oppose the plan in agitation—she caused them to be sent to the great hall on the day of debate, and furnished them with innumerable alarms and fears, cunning arguments and specious objections.

Now the principal arguments and objections with which Margery had instructed William, Jack and Robert, were:

1st. That the architects had not exhibited a bill of scantling for the new roof as they ought to have done; and therefore the carpenters, under pretence of providing timber for it, might lay waste whole forests to the ruin of the farm.

2d. That no provision was made in the plan for a trap door for the servants to pass through with water, if the chimney should take fire, and that in case of such an accident, it might hereafter be deemed penal to break a hole in the roof for access to save the whole building from destruction.

3d. That this roof was to be guarded by battlements, which in stormy seasons would prove dangerous to the family, as the bricks might be blown down and fall on their heads.

4th. It was observed that the old roof was ornamented with twelve pedestals ranged along the ridge, which were objects of universal admiration; whereas, according to the new plan, these pedestals were only to be placed along the eaves of the roof, over the walls, and that a cupola was to supply their place on the ridge or summit of the new roof. As to the cupola itself, some of the objectors said it was too heavy and would become a dangerous burthen to the building, whilst others alledged that it was too light and would certainly be blown away by the wind.

5th. It was insisted that the thirteen rafters being so strongly braced together, the individual and separate strength of each rafter would be lost in the compounded and united strength of the whole; and so the roof might be considered as one solid mass of timber, and not as composed of distinct rafters like the old roof.

6th. That according to the proposed plan, the several parts of the roof were so framed as to mutually strengthen and support each other, and therefore there was great reason to fear that the whole might stand independent of the walls; and that in time the walls might crumble away and the roof remain suspended in air, threatening destruction to all that should come under it.

To these objections, James the architect, in substance, replied:

1st. As to the want of a bill of scantling, he observed, that if the timber for this roof was to be purchased from a stranger, it would have been quite necessary to have such a bill, lest the stranger should charge in account more than he was entitled to, but as the timber was to be cut from our own lands a bill of scantling was both useless and improper—of no use, because the wood always was and always would be the property of the family, whether growing in the forest, or fabricated into a roof for the mansion house—and improper, because the carpenters would be bound by the bill of scantling, which, if it should not be perfectly accurate—a circumstance hardly to be expected—either the roof would be defective for want of sufficient materials, or the carpenters must cut from the forest without authority, which is penal by the laws of the house.

To the second objection he said that a trap door was not properly a part in the frame of a roof, but there could be no doubt but that the carpenters would take care to have such a door through the shingling, for the family to carry water through, dirty or clean, to extinguish fire either in the chimney or on the roof, and that this was the only proper way of making such a door.

3d. As to the battlements, he insisted that they were absolutely necessary for the protection of the whole house. 1st. In case of an attack by robbers, the family would defend themselves behind these battlements, and annoy and disperse the enemy. 2dly. If any of the adjoining buildings should take fire, the battlements would screen the roof from the destructive flames; and 3dly. They would retain the rafters in their respective places in case any of them should from rottenness or warping be in danger of falling from the general union, and injuring other parts of the roof; observing that the battlements should always be ready for these purposes, as there would be neither time nor opportunity for building them after an assault was actually made, or a conflagration begun. As to the bricks being blown down, he said the whole was in the power of the family to repair or remove any loose or dangerous parts, and there could be no doubt but that their vigilance would at all times be sufficient to prevent accidents of this kind.

4th. With respect to the twelve pedestals, he acknowledged their use and elegance; but observed that these, like all other things, were only so in their proper places, and under circumstances suited to their nature and design, and insisted that the ridge of a roof was not the place for pedestals, which should rest on the solid wall, being made of the same materials and ought in propriety to be considered as so many projections or continuations of the wall itself, and not as component parts of the wooden roof. As to the cupola, he said that all agreed there should be one of some kind or other, as well for a proper finish to the building, as for the purposes of indicating the winds and containing a bell to sound an alarm in cases of necessity. The objections to the present cupola, he said, were too contradictory to merit a reply.

To the fifth objection he answered, that the intention really was to make a firm and substantial roof by uniting the strength of the thirteen rafters; and that this was so far from annihilating the several rafters and rendering them of no use individually, that it was manifest from a bare inspection of the plan, that the strength of each contributed to the strength of the whole, and that the existence of each and all was essentially necessary to the existence of the whole fabric as a roof.

Lastly, he said that the roof was indeed so framed that the parts should mutually support and check each other, but it was most absurd and contrary to the known laws of nature, to infer from thence that the whole frame should stand self-supported in air, for however its component parts might be combined with respect to each other, the whole must necessarily rest upon and be supported by the walls. That the walls might indeed stand for a few years in a ruinous and uninhabitable condition without any roof, but the roof could not for a moment stand without the support of the walls; and finally, that of all dangers and apprehensions, this of the roof's remaining when the walls are gone was the most absurd and impossible.

It was mentioned before that, whilst this debate was carrying on in the great hall, the windows and doors were crowded with attendants. Amongst these was a half crazy fellow who was suffered to go at large because he was a harmless lunatic. Margery, however, thought he might be a serviceable engine in promoting opposition to the new roof. As people of deranged understandings are easily irritated, she exasperated this poor fellow against the architects, and filled him with the most terrible apprehensions from the new roof, making him believe that the architects had provided a dark hole in the garret, where he was to be chained for life. Having by these suggestions filled him with rage and terror, she let him loose among the crowd, where he roared and bawled to the annoyance of all by-standers. This circumstance would not have been mentioned but for the opportunity of exhibiting the style and manner in which a deranged and irritated mind will express itself—one of his rhapsodies shall conclude this narrative:

"The new roof! the new roof! Oh! the new roof! Shall demagogues, despising every sense of order and decency, frame a new roof? If such bare-faced presumption, arrogance and tyrannical proceedings will not rouse you, the goad and the whip—the goad and the whip should do it; but you are careless and insecure sinners, whom neither admonitions, entreaties nor threatenings can reclaim—sinners con-

signed to unutterable and endless woe. Where is that pusil-
lanimous wretch who can submit to such contumely—oh! the
ultima Ratio Regium! [He got these three Latin words from
Margery.] Oh! the ultima Ratio Regium! Ah! the days of
Nero! ah! the days of Caligula! ah! the British tyrant and
his infernal junto—glorious revolution—awful crisis—self-
important nabobs—diabolical plots and secret machinations—
oh! the architects! the architects—they have seized the government, secured power, brow-beat with insolence and assume majesty—oh! the architects! they will treat you as con-
quered slaves, they will make you pass under the yoke, and
leave their gluttony and riot to attend the pleasing sport—
oh! that the glory of the Lord may be made perfect—that he
would show strength with his arm and scatter the proud in
the imaginations of their hearts—blow the trumpet—sound
an alarm! I will cry day and night—behold, is not this my
number five—attend to my words, ye women laboring of
child—ye sick persons and young children—behold—behold
the lurking places, the despots, the infernal designs—lust of
dominion and conspiracies—from battle and murder and from
sudden death, good Lord deliver us.

"Figure to yourselves, my good fellows, a man with a cow
and a horse—oh the battlements, the battlements, they will
fall upon his cow, they will fall upon his horse, and wound
them, and bruise them, and kill them, and the poor man will
perish with hunger. Do I exaggerate?—no truly—Europe
and Asia and Indostan, deny it if you can—oh God! what a
monster is man!—A being possessed of knowledge, reason,
judgment and an immortal soul—what a monster is man!
But the architects are said to be men of skill—then the more
their shame—curse on the villains!—they are despots, syco-
phants, Jesuits, tories, lawyers—curse on the villains! We
beseech thee to hear us—Lord have mercy on us—Oh!—Ah!
—Ah!—Oh!"——*

[The author of The New Roof was Francis Hopkinson.
This the anti-federalists quickly discovered, and set upon
him savagely. These pieces contain nothing but personal
abuse, and are therefore not inserted.]

* Pennsylvania Packet, Dec. 29, 1787.

Mr. Oswald: At this important crisis, when the sanction of the people is much wanted to the proceedings of our Convention, you will please insert the following recipe for making a county meeting; which upon trial,* I have found to be the best yet used in Pennsylvania, for the purpose of taking the sense of a county and obtaining their sanction to any measure. I am, etc., GOUVERO.

Draw up a set of resolves, enclose them, and (if you have any thing to do with a bank) a five-dollar note, in a letter to a partisan in the county (who must be promised an office, etc.), with the following directions to him, viz: Call on some few of your trusty friends and companions, and proceed as quietly as possible to some one of the little towns (the more out of the way the better), get all the townsmen you can into a tavern, and after laying out the five-dollar note in grog, beer, etc., and you are all grown cheerful, place a *hero* in the chair, who, after reading the resolves, must order those who do not dislike them to hold up their hands, and of course (*nemine contradicente*) let them sign them as the unanimous resolve of a meeting of sundry respectable (not disorderly) inhabitants of the county of ——, etc., but care must be taken that no stir be made during the time; ten or twelve persons will be sufficient for a meeting, sooner than make a stir about more; and the company must separate as soon as may be, as the farmers may hear of the meeting and give you interruption; but by all means avoid firing any cannon, as the reports will bring in and conjure up the antifederalists, etc., which may be attended with *dangerous* consequences.†

Mr. Printer: I think it my duty to inform the public, that the aristocrats held an *extraordinary* meeting, in consequence of a special convocation on Friday evening last, at the house of Mr. Epple, at the sign of the *Rainbow*. This assembly, which clearly proclaims their fears of the present spirit of the people, was not so numerous as was expected by

* Pittsburgh, Carlisle, and Easton.
† Independent Gazette, Jan. 10, 1788.

the chieftains. A great number of the persons invited did not attend, and *one-fourth* at least of those who attended, went there without any invitation. Mr. George Clymer was appointed chairman, and the meeting being organized, Mr. Wilson rose, and made a long pathetic speech, in which he observed that the Democratic party (to which to be sure he gave another name) was daily increasing in consequence of the publications which issued constantly from the press against the proposed constitution; that the aristocrats (to whom also he gave another denomination) had visibly relaxed of late in their efforts to complete the glorious work they had undertaken. That the press ought to be kept groaning with pieces, paragraphs, anecdotes, and skits of all kinds in favor of the new form of government. That as the publishing and circulating those pieces would be productive of some expense, they had been called together to consult on the propriety of raising money by subscription to defray those charges. In consequence he moved that committees might be appointed in the different wards of the city, to wait on the aristocrats and their dependents, and collect subscriptions among them, which motion was carried in the affirmative, and committees were consequently appointed.

The public will now no longer be at a loss to discover the origin of those numerous paragraphs, anecdotes, innuendos and falsehoods, which have begun to flow afresh with greater rapidity from the press; it was necessary to inform them of the means by which the aristocrats intend to carry their monstrous plan into execution, and of the effect which the present disposition of the people has begun to have upon them.*

Tom Peep.

Mr. Oswald: Your correspondent, Tom Peep, who has undertaken to give you an account of the proceedings of the aristocratic meeting at Epple's, has not been quite so particular as I could have wished. He mentions generally that on motion of Mr. Wilson, a committee was appointed to collect

---

*Independent Gazetteer, Jan. 10, 1788.

subscriptions in the different wards of the city, for the purpose of defraying the expense of printing pieces in favor of the new constitution. But it seems to me from other circumstances not mentioned by your correspondent, that printing and publishing are not the only uses for which the money is intended. The fact is, that a member of the above meeting, informed the aristocrats met, that 75*l.* had already been expended for the public service, and that a much larger sum was now wanted, which was no less than TWO THOUSAND POUNDS! It was accordingly agreed by the meeting to raise that sum by subscription, upon which 131*l.* were subscribed immediately on the spot, and committees were appointed to collect the remainder.

Now, Mr. Oswald, it appears to me very proper, that the public should inquire into the nature of those *services* which require such a large sum as 2000*l.* In my opinion, it can be no other than that great engine of gouveronian politics, bribery. Such a circumstance seems truly alarming, and will, I hope, convince the people of the necessity of opposing in the bud so dreadful a combination of the rich and well-born against the liberties of the nation. The means which they employ loudly proclaim their design, and loudly call for a speedy, manly, and spirited opposition from the free-born part of the community.* PEEP, JUNIOR.

Mr. Oswald, I blush for human nature; I tremble for the happiness of the United States, when I read such gross and shocking misrepresentation as that published in your paper of this day, under the signature of Peep, Junior. He says that two thousand pounds were mentioned by a person at that meeting, as necessary to be raised, and that 131*l.* was subscribed on the spot. Now I was present the whole time, and must and can declare both assertions to be absolutely untrue. Oh, my fellow citizens of Pennsylvania and of the union at large, how much are you abused by that wretched scribbler! how much is the inestimable privilege of a free press abused to alarm you with false and wanton charges of bribery, con-

* Independent Gazetteer, Jan. 14, 1788.

spiracy, and every thing that is fearful! Think for yourselves, and cast away far from you all the suggestions and
doctrines of men of such dreadful dispositions.*

A FREEMAN.

January 12, 1788.

To the People of America:

The subject now before you, like all other important matters, has excited much passion, and created innumerable misrepresentations.   Two writers in the Philadelphia papers
have most unwarrantably asserted, that the Quakers of this
state are opposed to the proposed federal constitution.   That
numerous and wealthy society are certainly more universally
in favor of it than any other society in this state.   It is one
of their known principles not to be much concerned in the
alterations of governments; wherefore one would naturally
suppose it would be difficult to adduce instances to prove
their sentiments on the present occasion.   It is, however, not
impossible, as will be found from the four following facts:

1st. When the last assembly determined to call a convention, there were seven Quakers members of the House; all of
whom attended and voted for the call of a convention, though
nineteen members opposed it, and urged that it would be better to leave it to the next House, then soon to be chosen.

2d. When some of the members absented themselves the
next day, in order to prevent the days of election and meeting of the convention from being fixed by that House of Assembly, the seven Quakers duly attended, and all voted with
the majority on the several points that were moved as necessary to arrange and prepare for the business of the convention.

3d. Eight Quakers were chosen members of the State convention, and all took their seats.   They all voted against
postponing the final determination on the constitution till the
spring, which was attempted by the minority.

4th. The same eight Quakers all voted for the adoption of
the proposed federal constitution in toto, and for the grant to
Congress of the jurisdiction of ten miles square within this
commonwealth for the seat of the federal government.

* Independent Gazetteer, Jan. 15, 1788.

If the Quakers were really opposed to the new constitution, they could have made up many times the number of votes that were given in at the election of members of convention in this city for the candidates who wished to alter the proposed federal form of government. The votes ran variously from 230 to 270 for the different persons of that description. The name of Dr. Franklin, whom the Quakers venerate, was put into the unsuccessful ticket, I am persuaded, without his permission. This the Quakers were convinced of, and not approving of the rest of the men, or approving of the successful members, the ticket of the antifederalists, as is evident from the number of votes, received neither their countenance nor support. *   UNDENIABLE FACTS.

Philadelphia, January 14.

To the People of the United States:

When we observe how much the several gentlemen of the late convention, who declined to sign the federal constitution, differ in their ground of opposition, we must see how improbable it is that another convention would unite in any plan. Colonel Mason and Mr. Gerry complain of the want of a bill of rights : Governor Randolph does not even mention it as desirable, much less as necessary. Colonel Mason objects to the powers of Congress to raise an army; Governor Randolph and Mr. Gerry make no objections on this point, but the former seems to think a militia an inconvenient and uncertain dependence, which is contrary to our opinions in Pennsylvania. Mr. Randolph gives up the objection against the power of Congress to regulate trade by a majority ; Mr. Mason complains of this, and says the objection is insuperable ; Mr. Gerry does not say one word against it. Mr. Randolph wishes the president ineligible after a given number of years ; Mr. Mason and Mr. Gerry do not make this one of their objections. Mr. Randolph objects to ambiguities of expression; Mr. Mason does not. Colonel Mason objects to the slave trade on the principles of policy merely; Mr. Gerry and Mr. Randolph make no such objection. Mr. Mason objects

*Independent Gazetteer, Jan. 15, 1788.

to the power of the president to pardon for treason; Mr. Gerry makes no such objection, and Mr. Randolph wishes only that the offender may be convicted before the president shall have power to pardon! This appears to be a legal solecism. Mr. Randolph objects to the power of Congress to determine their wages (the privilege of every legislature in the Union); but Mr. Gerry and Colonel Mason do not object to this power. Mr. Randolph objects to the president's power of appointing the judges ; Mr. Gerry and Colonel Mason do not. Mr. Gerry says the people have no security for the right of election; Colonel Mason and Mr. Randolph do not make this objection. Mr. Gerry and Mr. Mason think the representation not duly provided for; Mr. Randolph expresses no such idea. Mr. Mason objects to the want of security for the common law, to the power of the Senate to alter money bills, to originate applications of money, to regulate the officers' salaries, to the want of a privy council, to the vice-president, to the want of a clause concerning the press, and to the want of power in the States to lay imposts on exports, not one of which are stated as objections by Mr. Randolph or Mr. Gerry. Mr. Randolph objects to the want of a proper court of impeachment for Senators (though the State courts of impeachment can always take cognizance of them); Mr. Gerry and Colonel Mason do not hold this exceptionable. Colonel Mason objects to the States or Congress being restrained from passing ex post facto laws; Mr. Randolph and Mr. Gerry do not.

The minority of the Pennsylvania convention, on the other hand, differ from all these gentlemen. They say the defects of the old confederation were not discovered till after the peace, while Mr. Randolph says the short period between the ratification of the old constitution and the peace was distinguished by melancholy testimonies of its defects and faults.

The minority object because some of the persons appointed by Pennsylvania have disapproved of our State constitution, which differs from those of eleven States in the Union in the want of a division of the legislature, and in having nineteen persons to execute the office of governor, whose number will be increased by the addition of one more for every new county.

The minority object to the latitude taken by the convention. We find no such objection made by Mr. Randolph, Mr. Gerry, or Colonel Mason. Mr. Gerry says in his letter, it was necessary, and Mr. Mason insisted strongly in the house, that the convention could not do their business, unless they considered and recommended everything that concerned the interests of the United States, though the strict letter of their powers was supposed by some not to extend so far. The minority say religious liberty is not duly secured, which is omitted as an objection by all of the three gentlemen above named. The right of the people to fish, fowl and hunt, the freedom of speech, provision against disarming the people, a declaration of the subordination of the military to the civil power, annual elections of the representatives, and the organization and call of the militia, are considered by the minority of our convention as on an exceptionable footing; but none of these are even mentioned by Governor Randolph, Mr. Mason or Mr. Gerry.

The minority desire a declaration that such powers as are not expressly given shall be considered as retained; Mr. Randolph thinks this unnecessary, for that the States retain everything they do not grant; Mr. Gerry is silent on this head. The minority desire a constitutional council for the president; Mr. Gerry and Mr. Randolph do not. The minority except against powers to erect a court of equity being vested in the federal government, to which neither of the above gentlemen express any dislike. The minority desire a bill of rights, and object to the smallness of the representation, which Mr. Randolph does not. They object to the term of duration of the legislature, which none of the above gentlemen find fault with. Nor does the account of particulars end here. The objections severally made by the three honorable gentlemen, and the Pennsylvania minority are so different and even discordant in their essential principles, that all hope of greater unanimity of opinion either in another convention or in the people must be given up by those who know

the human heart and mind, with their infinitely varying feelings and ideas.   PHILANTHROPOS.
    January 15, 1788.*

————

Mr. Printer: Our two celebrated sowers of sedition, *Centinel*
and *Philadelphiensis*, the one in Mr. Oswald's, the other in
Mr. Bailey's paper of this day, exhibit a striking proof of
what falsehoods disappointed ambition is capable of using to
impose upon the public. The real patriot, sir, is the watchful guardian of the people's liberties. The designing incen-
diary, well aware of the reception his base undertakings
would meet with from an injured and insulted people, is
obliged to assume the appearance of the real patriot, and
fully pretend himself a friend to his country; but his infamous
designs will still appear through his hypocritical mask; for
truth being unfit for his purpose, he will be obliged to have
recourse to falsehood; and this is the best criterion for distinguishing between the mock and the real patriot—the dis-
guised enemy and the open friend of liberty.

What, sir, has been the conduct of the two incendiaries
above-mentioned? The one in a series of 12, the other in a
series of 8 performances, which for the sophistry of their
reasoning, and falsity of their assertions, are unparalleled in
ancient or modern times, have disgraced the enlightened capital of Pennsylvania.

These hireling writers and hackneyed drudges of tottering
power, jealous of the rising greatness of America, and convinced of the unstable ground on which they stand, have
dared, Sempronius-like, to bellow out for that country, the
happiness of which they fear will be their downfall. They
have told the public that the proprietor of the Pennsylvania
Herald has dismissed his editor, and that some of the subscribers to that paper have withdrawn their subscriptions—
for, what more is expressed by all the high-sounding, inflammatory bombast they have bellowed forth? What inference
do they attempt to draw from these positions? That the
conspirators, as they are pleased to term the federal citizens

* Independent Gazetteer, Jan. 16, 1788.

of Pennsylvania, are endeavoring to destroy the liberty of the press—for shame! ye illustrious citizens, who have braved every danger of establishing the freedom of your country, are you thus to be traduced and slandered with impunity? If the proprietor of a paper dismisses his editor, must your patriotism be called in question, by the villainous enemies of America! If some of you wish no longer to contribute to the support of a newspaper, (which, instead of debates in the convention of Pennsylvania, has contained the most glaring falsehoods, and the grossest misrepresentations which its editor was capable of inventing,) must you, in consequence of this, be branded with infamy, as enemies to the freedom of the press? If you must, I confess printers of newspapers have an exclusive privilege, enjoyed by no other set of men upon earth, of making the public pay them for what they neither wish to purchase nor to read. A REAL PATRIOT.

23d January, 1788.*

Mr. Oswald: The admirers of the new constitution are continually blazing away on the great names which are said to be in favor of the system; but it is hoped that the good sense of the people of these states is not to be deceived by such flimsy arguments. If great names were to be the test of truth, it would frequently make sad work in religion, philosophy and politics. The Divine Oracles assert that great men are not always wise, and the history of the world demonstrates there is no perfection in human beings. What so delusive and fascinating in its nature as power? Nothing more apt to prejudice and mislead our minds, and to render our conduct and temper inconsistent. Where ambition may be concerned, an Archangel is not to be trusted.

As these premises are true, I could wish there would be no more attempts to delude the people with the authority of names; for, if the favorers of the new leviathan persist in such a mode of reasoning, it will become necessary to investigate the characters of those who are thus held up as the greatest patriarchs to the admiration of the public. It has

* Independent Gazetteer, Jan. 28, 1788.

been observed, too, that those paragraphists do not always adhere to truth, as may be seen in some of our late prints, where it is said, that "the same characters which took the lead in each of the states, in the struggle for liberty, in the glorious years of 1775 and 1776, now take the lead in their exertions to establish the federal government."

Amongst the great names, Few, Telfair and Baldwin are mentioned as leading characters at this early period in Georgia. Now it is well known that Mr. Few was originally a bricklayer in North Carolina, removed to Georgia, and but lately of any consideration in public life. As to Telfair, he with Doctor Zubly and many others, was taken up and put in confinement by order of the governor of that state, in the year 1776, being deemed as inimical to the American cause.

Mr. Baldwin's political existence is of much later date. On Sunday, 24th December, 1780, I happened to be at Nassau Hall, Princeton, and heard Mr. Baldwin pray and read a sermon there, for want of a parson, the Reverend Mr. S—— being at Philadelphia. At that time he was unknown in the great world, and acted as college steward. There are some others among the great names that have been given us, who are not to be met with in the annals of 1775 and 1776, and who have no pretensions to be considered as leaders at this or any other period; neither did they endure any more "cold, hunger and nakedness," than ten thousand besides of their fellow citizens. It has long been an expensive folly of America to admire great names, and to make great men; hence it is that we have been sending commissioners, ambassadors, agents, etc., etc., to London, Paris, Madrid, Petersburgh, Amsterdam, and even to the Grand Duke of Tuscany, to borrow money and to spend it; and we want to repeat the same follies, though it is evident as the meridian glory of the sun, that nothing can save America but the weaning ourselves from European attachments.*

An Old American.

Philadelphia, February 8, 1788.

*Independent Gazetteer, Feb. 11, 1788.

Mr. Oswald: As the times are bad, and I am out of work, I have more leisure than I used to have to read newspapers. In reading your paper of this day, I observe a scribbler, who calls himself An Old American, attempts to derogate from the consequence of the worthy delegates from Georgia in the late Federal Convention. I have no knowledge of these gentlemen, except from character, but by their works I conclnde they are honest patriots. He particularly affects to despise the Honorable Mr. Few, saying he was a bricklayer. But tell this antifederal tool (a secret which he does not seem to know) that virtue alone ennobles human nature; and that an honest mechanic who serves his country faithfully is as well deserving of her favor as another. Tell him also, that if we judge of Mr. Few's mechanical by his political bricklaying, we shall think him an excellent artist, for he has helped to build a noble mansion for the residence of American liberty. A BRICKLAYER.

February 11th.*

———

Mr. Oswald: Having sometimes met in English newspapers with articles entitled "Bankruptcies this week," "Casualties this week," etc., etc., I once intended to publish in your Gazetteer, being a customer, a periodical list, in like manner, of all the falsehoods uttered in print by the Centinel, Philadelphiensis, and their associates, under the title of Antifederal lies this week, believing that if every lie was to be punished by clipping, as in the case of other forgeries, not an ear would be left amongst the whole party. From this undertaking, however, I was deterred on reflecting that in order to get at the said lies, the eye not being particularly solicited to them by italics, which would have saved an abundance of trouble, and which I therefore recommend to their future practice, I must at least have been under the necessity generally of going through a prodigious mass of heavy arguments and dull invective—a labor of most dreadful discouragement! Had the *Old American*, who certainly is young in the art of political lying, but been so prudent

* Independent Gazetter, Feb. 15, 1788.

as to mix up his falsified facts in a great bundle of other villainous ingredients, after the example of some of his brethren of long-winded memory, they would probably have passed off unnoticed, but I have to thank him for making his whoppers the single subject of the piece, and thus by expressing the whole, make it impossible for them to escape even the slightest glance.

His subject is three gentlemen of Georgia—Mr. Few he affirms to have been but of little account until late—but this gentleman was in Congress as long ago at least as the year 1781. Mr. Telfair (who by the bye was not in the federal convention) was it seems an enemy to his country in 1776. How is this reconcilable with the confidence reposed in him by his country so soon after, and in more trying and dangerous times? for we find Mr. Telfair's name to the first articles of confederation, in July, 1778. But the boldest whopper of all is what relates to Mr. Baldwin—who, says the writer, on Sunday, the 24th December, in the year of our Lord, 1780, occasionally read public prayers at Princeton College, being then the steward of the college. Now it is known to twenty lads here who have resided at that college, that Baldwin, the steward, had been a farmer in the neighborhood, and that he since removed to New York, where he at present keeps a boarding-house.

But if it be the general purpose to charge the new system upon the well born, why endeavor to show that Mr. Few was once a bricklayer, for which, indeed, we have only this Old American's blasted word. Indeed, on this subject of inconsistency I am surprised, considering how few are the antifederal writers, though the signatures be many, that they do not oftener lay their loggerheads together—this would at least save them from many contradictions, than which nothing can be more disreputable to a party—for instance, with respect to the conspiracy carrying on against B—n and Co., while the Centinel asserts that its authors are the powerful and the wealthy, Philadelphiensis affirms them to be men of no consideration and of desperate fortunes.* GOMES.

*Independent Gazetteer, Feb. 16, 1788.

ON THE NEW CONSTITUTION.

In evil hours his pen 'Squire Adams drew,
Claiming dominion to his well-born few:
In the gay circle of St. James's placed,
He wrote, and, writing, has his work disgraced.
Smit with the splendor of a British King,
The crown prevailed, so once despised a thing!
Shelburne and Pitt approved of all he wrote,
While Rush and Wilson echo back his note.
   Tho' British armies could not here prevail,
Yet British politics shall turn the scale;
In five short years of Freedom weary grown,
We quit our plain republics for a throne;
Congress and President full proof shall bring
A mere disguise for Parliament and King.
   A standing army!—hence the plan so base;
A despot's safety—liberty's disgrace.
Who sav'd these realms from Britain's bloody hand,
Who but the generous rustics of the land?
That free-born race, inured to every toil,
Who tame the ocean and subdue the soil,
Who tyrants banished from this injured shore,
Domestic traitors may expel once more.
   Ye who have bled in Freedom's sacred cause,
Ah, why desert her maxims and her laws?
When thirteen states are mouldered into one,
Your rights are vanished, and your honors gone
The form of Freedom shall alone remain,
As Rome had senates when she hugged the chain.
Sent to revise your systems—not to change—
Sages have done what reason deems most strange:
Some alterations in our fabric we
Calmly proposèd, and hoped at length to see—
Ah, how deceived!—these heroes in renown
Scheme for themselves, and pull the fabric down—
Bid in its place Columbia's tomb-stone rise,
Inscribed with these sad words—*Here freedom lies!* *

[The State of Massachusetts having adopted the constitution, the antifederalists asserted that newspapers expressing their views had been suppressed in the mails by the federalists. Newspapers at that time were not mailable, and the post offices could not be forced to take them. They were carried by the riders on such terms as they could make with

* Independent Gazetteer, Mar. 10, 1788.

the printers. After the charge of suppressing the newspapers had been repeated many times, the postmaster made this denial.]

General Post-Office, New York, March 19, 1788.

Several paragraphs having lately appeared in some of the newspapers, reflecting upon the conduct of the offices of this department, on account of irregularity in the transportation of newspapers, and indecent attacks of a more recent date, replete with illiberality and rancour, having been made upon the postmaster general, on the same account, he thinks it necessary to state the following facts in order to prevent any undue impressions being made upon the public mind; viz:

That the post-pffice was established for the purpose of facilitating commercial correspondence, and has, properly speaking, no connection with newspapers, the carriage of which was an indulgence granted to the post-riders, prior to the revolution in America.

That the riders stipulated with the printers for the carriage of their papers, at a price which was agreed upon between them, and this price was allowed as a perquisite to the readers.

That newspapers have never been considered as a part of the mail, nor (until within a very few years) admitted into the same portmanteau with it, but were carried in saddle-bags provided for that purpose by the riders, at their own expense.

That to promote general convenience, the postmasters (not officially) undertook to receive and distribute the newspapers brought by the riders, without any other compensation for their trouble than the compliment of a newspaper from each printer.

That although the United States in Congress assembled, from an idea that beneficial improvements might be made in the transportation of the mail, have directed alterations as to the mode of carrying it; yet they have not directed any to be made in the custom respecting newspapers; and

That the postmaster-general has given no orders or directions about them, either to the postmasters or to the riders.

From this succinct state of facts, the postmaster-general apprehends it will clearly appear, that so far as the post-office is concerned, the carriage of newspapers rests exactly on its original foundation; and that the attempts to excite clamor against the department must have some other source than a failure in duty on the part of the officers.*

For the *Independent Gazetteer.*

THE FALLACIES OF THE FREEMAN DETECTED BY A FARMER.

Some weeks since there was published in the Carlisle *Gazette* an address to the minority of the late convention of this State, under the signature of a Freeman, which I then supposed had been written by some well-meaning person of that place, who had not yet entered the porch of political knowledge, who was thus unacquainted with the nature of sovereignty, and incapable of distinguishing ministerial agency from the exercise of sovereignty; I therefore took no especial notice of it, until happening to see a Philadelphia newspaper, I found the address had originated there, and was ascribed to a gentleman who is far from being ignorant, as I had candidly supposed the author to be, but who hath habituated himself to presume much upon the supposed ignorance of the people, and whose expectation of future support and grandeur hath probably been very influential in framing and promoting the proposed system of government. Upon this discovery, I read the address again with more attention, and resolved to communicate, through your useful paper, the result of my observations thereon. I do not, however, design to answer the address in detail, but to establish and explain such general principles as may assist people in judging for themselves, and have a tendency to detect the sophistry which characterizes the performance. In order to do this, I shall explain:

First. The nature of sovereignty.

Second. Of a federal republic.

Third. Of a consolidated government.

Fourth. The nature of ministerial agency.

*The Freeman's Journal, March 26, 1788.

Fifth. Examine the address to the minority (the occasion of these enquiries).

Sixth. Conclude with some general observations on the times.

I return to the *first* then: From the very design that induces men to form a society that has its common interests, and to promote and secure which it ought to act to concert, it is necessary that there should be established a public authority, to order and direct what ought to be done by each individual as he stands in relation to the society itself, or to the individual members thereof; and this public authority, consisting of that portion of natural liberty which each member surrenders to the society, to be exercised for the common advantage, is the sovereignty which is often called political authority. If this sovereignty or political authority be vested in and exercised by the whole people, as in some of the ancient republics, or if it be delegated to representatives chosen by the people from among themselves, as in modern times, the government is called a democracy. If, on the contrary, the sovereignty be in a particular class of citizens who have not a common interest with the people at large, or body of the nation, it is called an aristocracy; and if in a single person, a monarchy or despotism; and these three kinds may be variously combined and modified, as in the British government and others; but every nation that governs itself by its own laws, let the form of government be what it may, is a sovereign state.

Sovereignty, therefore, consists in the understanding and will of the political society, and this understanding and will is originally and inherently in the people; the society having vested it where and in what manner it pleases, he or they to whom it is delegated is the sovereign, and is thus vested with the political understanding and will of the people, for their good and advantage solely.

The power of making rules or laws to govern or protect the society is the essence of sovereignty, for by this the executive and judicial powers are directed and contracted, to this every ministerial agent is subservient, and to this all corporate or privileged bodies are subordinate; this power not only regulates the conduct, but disposes of the wealth and commands the force of the nation. To keep this sovereign power, therefore, in due bounds, fundamental laws, which we call constitutions and bills of rights, have been made and declared. Scarcely hath the wisdom of man, matured by the experience of ages, been able with all the checks, negatives and balances, either of ancient or modern invention, to prevent abuses of this high sovereign authority.

Here I may possibly be misunderstood; it may perhaps be objected, that in Great Britain the *King* is called the Sovereign, and that he is an executive and not legislative officer. True, the king of Great Britain is the supreme executive of the nation, but it is not this alone that constitutes him a sovereign; he hath a negative over the legislative. The laws are made by and with his consent, and are called the King's Laws; he calls, prorogues and dissolves his Parliament when he pleases; the Parliament indeed so manage that the necessity of the case obliges him to convene them frequently, but he is not obliged to do it by the constitution; so that, properly speaking, it is the King and Parliament of Great Britain which is sovereign. However, if the legislative authority were to be distributed in various portions, that man, or body of men, who should be vested with the sole and uncontrolled power of taxation, would eventually become the sovereign; for whoever can command our whole property has the means in his power of ruling us as he pleases, because (as Montesquieu says) "sovereignty necessarily follows the power of taxation."

Secondly. I shall proceed to define a *federal republic.* A federal republic is formed by two or more single or consolidated republics, uniting together by a perpetual confederacy, and without ceasing to be distinct states or sovereignties, they form together a federal republic or an empire of states. As individuals in a state of nature surrender a portion of their natural liberty to the society of which they became members, in order to receive in lieu thereof protection and conveniency; so in forming a federal republic the individual states surrender a part of their separate sovereignty to the general government or federal head, in order that, whilst they respectively enjoy internally the freedom and happiness peculiar to free republics, they may possess all that external protection, security, and weight by their confederated resources, that can possibly be obtained in the most extended, absolute monarchies.

The peculiar advantages and distinctive properties of a federal republic are that each state or member of the confederation may be fully adequate for every local purpose, that it may subsist in a small territory, that the people may have a common interest, possess a competent knowledge of the resources and expenditures of their own particular government, that their immediate representatives in the state governments will know and be known by the citizens, will have a common interest with them, and must bear a part of all the burdens which they may lay upon the people; that they will be responsible to the people, and may be dismissed by them at pleasure; that therefore the government would be a government of confidence, and possess sufficient energy without the aid of standing armies; that the collectors of the revenue would at least have the bowels of citizens, and not be the off-scourings of Europe, or other states who have no interest in, or attachment to the people; that if one or more of the states should become the prey of internal despotism, or foreign foes, the other states may remain secure under the protection of their own state government; that if some popular and wealthy citizen should have influence enough to attempt the liberties of one state, he might be stopped in his career by the interposition of the others, for his influence could not be equally great in all the states; that if the general government should fail, or be revised or changed, yet the several state governments may remain entire to secure the happiness of the citizens; and that the members of a confederated republic may be increased to any amount, and consequently its external strength, without altering the nature of the government, or endangering the liberty of the citizens.

The perfection of a federal republic consists in drawing the proper line between those objects of sovereignty which are of a general nature, and which ought to be vested in the federal government, and those which are of a more local nature, and ought to remain with the particular governments; any rule that can be laid down for this must vary according to the situation and circumstances of the confederating states; yet still this general rule will hold good, viz: that all that portion of sovereignty which involves the common interest of all the confederating states, and which cannot be exercised by the states in their individual capacity without endangering the liberty and welfare of the whole, ought to be vested in the general government, reserving such a proportion of sovereignty in the state governments as would enable them to exist alone, if the general government should fail, either by violence or with the common consent of the confederates. The states should respectively have laws, courts, force and revenues of their own sufficient for their own security; they ought to be fit to keep house alone if necessary. If this be not the case, or so far as it ceases to be so, it is a departure from a federal to a consolidated government; and this brings me to the next particular, which is to show what is meant by a consolidated government.

Thirdly. The idea of a *consolidated government* is easily understood, where a single society or nation forms one entire separate government, and possesses the whole sovereign power; this is a consolidated or national government. Whether a government be of a monarchical, aristocratical or democratical nature, it doth not alter the case; it is either a federal or a consolidated government, there being no medium as to kind. The absoluteness of a despotic sovereignty is often restricted by corporate bodies, who are vested with peculiar privileges and franchises, and by a just distribution of the executive and ministerial powers; but although these may contribute to the happiness of the people, yet they do not change the nature of the government. Indeed, monarchies can never form a federal government; they may enter into alliances with each other; for monarchy cannot be divested of a competent proportion of sovereignty to form a general government without changing its nature. It is only free

republics that can completely and safely form a federal republic; I say free republics, for there are republics who are
not free, such as Venice, where a citizen carrying arms is
punished with instant death, and where even the nobles dare
not converse with strangers, and scarcely with their friends,
and are liable by law to be put to death secretly without
trial—or Poland, which, in much the same words that are
expressed in the new system, is by a league with the neighboring powers guaranteed to be forever independent and of a
republican form; yet a writer of their own says that the body
of the people are scarcely to be distinguished from brutes; and
again he says, "we have reduced the people of our kingdom
by misery to a state of brutes; they drag out their days in
stupidity," etc.   Free republics are congenial to a federal republic.   In order that a republic may preserve its liberty, it
must not only have a good form of government, but it must
be of small extent; for if it possess extensive territory, it
would be ruined by internal imperfection.   The authority of
government in a large republic does not equally pervade all
the parts; nor are the political advantages equally enjoyed
by the citizens remote from the capital as by those in the
vicinity; combinations consequently prevail among the members of the legislature, and this introduces corruption, and is
destructive of that confidence in government, without which
a free republic cannot be supported; besides, the high influential trusts which must be vested in the great officers of state,
would at particular times endanger the government, and are
necessarily destructive of that equality among the citizens,
which is the only permanent basis of a republic; in short, the
diversity of the situation, habits, manners, and interests of the
people in an extensive dominion, subjects the government to
a thousand accidents, which would embarrass a republican
government.   The experience of nations and the nature of
things, sufficiently prove that the government of a single
person, aided by armies and controlling influence, is necessary
to govern a large consolidated empire.

And on the other hand, if the territory be small, the republic is liable to be destroyed by external force, therefore, reason

and observation point out a confederation of republics, as the only method to preserve internal freedom, together with external strength and respectability. Small republics forming a federal republic on these principles, may be resembled to divers small ropes plaited together to make a large and strong one; if the latter is untwisted, the small ropes are still useful as such, but if the former are untwisted, they are reduced to hemp, the original state.

To apply these principles to our present situation without respect to the proposed plan of government: in order to render the federal government adequate to the exigencies of the confederating states, it is necessary not only that the general government should be properly constructed in its forms, but that it should be vested with powers relative to all the federal objects of government; these objects are not only the powers of making peace and war, etc., but also with the power of making treaties respecting commerce, regulating and raising revenues therefrom, etc., to make requisitions of money when necessity requires it, from each of the states, and a certain well-described power of compelling delinquent states to pay up their quota of such requisitions—perhaps if each State had its own share of the domestic debt quoted, so as they might each pay their own citizens, the general revenues would be sufficient for the other demands of the Union in times of peace, if the government itself be not made too expensive by too great a number of officers being created. Congress ought, however, to have all powers which cannot be exercised by one state without endangering the other states, such as the power of raising troops, treating with foreign nations, etc.—The power of levying imposts will, by the particular states, be irregularly exercised, and the revenue in a great degree lost or misapplied; therefore, it ought not to be left with the states, but under proper checks, vested in the general government. All these the minority were amongst the foremost willing to have vested in the federal head, and more than this had never been asked by Congress, nor proposed by the greatest advocates for congressional power, nor is more than this consistent with the nature of a federal republic. When

the existing confederation was adopted, powers were given
with a sparing hand, and perhaps not improperly at that
period, until experience should point out the discriminating
line with sufficient certainty, well knowing that it is easy
for a government to obtain an increase of power when common utility points out the propriety, but that powers once
vested in a government, however dangerous they may prove,
are rarely recovered without bloodshed, and even that awful
method of regaining lost liberty is seldom effectual. It is now,
however, evident that the power of regulating commerce, being of a general nature, ought to belong to the general government, and the burthen of debt incurred by the Revolution
hath rendered a general revenue necessary; for this purpose imposts upon articles of importation present themselves, not only
as a productive source of revenue, but as a revenue for which
the governments of the particular states are, for well-known
reasons, incompetent. The danger of entrusting a government
so far out of the people's reach as Congress must necessarily be,
strongly impressed the public mind about four or five years
since, but now a conviction of the advantage and probable
safety of such a measure pervades almost every mind, and
none are more willing for putting it in operation, under
proper guards, than the opposers of the new system; they are
also willing to admit what the majority of the states may
judge proper checks in the *form* of the general government,
as far as those checks, or the distribution of powers, and responsibility of those who be vested with those powers, may be
consistent with the security of the essential sovereignity of
the respective states. The minority of the convention (who
I really believe, in their address, express the serious sentiments of the majority of this state) opposed vesting such
powers in Congress as can be most effectually exercised by
the state governments in a full consistency with the general
interests of the confederating states, and which, not being of
a general nature, are not upon federal principles, objects of
the federal government. I mean the power of capitation, or
poll tax, by which the head, or in other words, the existence
of every person, is put in their power by the new system as a

property, subject to any price or tax that may be judged proper. I do not mean to say that this implies the power of life and death, although it certainly implies the power of selling the property, or if none is to be had, of imprisoning or selling the person for a servant, who doth not choose, or is not able to pay the poll tax; the minority also objected to vesting Congress with power to tax the property, real and personal, of the citizens of the several states, to what amount, and in what manner it may please, without any check or control upon its discretion; also to the unlimited power over the excise; if this could extend only to spirituous liquors, as is usual with us, the danger would be less; but the power of excise extends to everything we eat, drink, or wear, and in Europe it is thus extensively put in practice. Under the term duties, every species of indirect taxes is included, but it especially means the power of levying money upon printed books, and written instruments.

The Congress, by the proposed system, have the power of borrowing money to what amount they may judge proper, consequently to mortgage all our estates, and all our sources of revenue. The exclusive power of emitting bills of credit is also reserved to Congress. They have, moreover, the power of instituting courts of justice without trial by jury, except in criminal cases, and under such regulations as Congress may think proper to decide, not only in such cases as arise out of all the foregoing powers, but in the other cases which are enumerated in the system.

The absolute sovereignity in all the foregoing instances, as well as several others not here enumerated, is vested in the general government, without being subject to any constitutional check or control from the state governments.*

It remains to examine the nature of the powers which are left with the states, and on this subject it is not necessary to follow the *Freeman* through the numerous detail of particulars with which he confuses the reader. I shall examine only a few of the more considerable. The *Freeman* in his second number, after mentioning in a very delusory manner diverse

* Independent Gazetteer, Apr. 15, 1788.

powers which remain with the states, says we shall find many other instances under the constitution which require or imply the existence or continuance of the sovereignty and severalty of the states; he, as well as all the advocates of the new system, take as their strong ground the election of senators by the state legislatures, and the special representation of the states in the federal senate, to prove that internal sovereignty still remains with the States; therefore they say that the new system is so far from annihilating the state governments, that it secures them, that it cannot exist without them, that the existence of the one is essential to the existence of the other. It is true that this particular partakes strongly of that mystery which is characteristic of the system itself; but if I demonstrate that this particular, so far from implying the continuance of the state sovereignties, proves in the clearest manner the want of it, I hope the other particular powers will not be necessary to dwell upon.

The State legislatures do not chose senators by legislative or sovereign authority, but by a power of ministerial agency as mere electors or boards of appointment; they have no power to direct the senators how or what duties they shall perform; they have neither power to censure the senators, nor to supersede them for misconduct. It is not the power of chosing to office merely that designates sovereignty, or else corporations who appoint their own officers and make their own by-laws, or the heads of department who choose the officers under them, such as commanders of armies, etc., may be called sovereigns, because they can name men to office whom they cannot dismiss therefrom. The exercise of sovereignty does not consist in choosing masters, such as the senators would be, who, when chosen, would be beyond control, but in the power of dismissing, impeaching, or the like, those to whom authority is delegated. The power of instructing or superseding of delegates to Congress under the existing confederation hath never been complained of, although the necessary rotation of members of Congress hath often been censured for restraining the state sovereignties too much in the objects of their choice. As well may the electors who are to vote for the president under the new constitution, be said to be vested with the sovereignty, as the State legislatures in the act of choosing senators. The senators are not even dependent on the States for their wages, but in conjunction with the federal representatives establish their own wages. The senators do not vote by States, but as individuals. The representatives also vote as individuals, representing people in a consolidated or national government; they judge upon their own elections, and, with the Senate, have the power of regulating elections in time, place and manner, which is in other words to say, that they have the power of elections absolutely vested in them.

That the State governments have certain ministerial and convenient powers continued to them is not denied, and in the exercise of which they may support, but cannot control the general government, nor protect their own citizens from the exertion of civil or military tyranny, and this ministerial power will continue with the States as long as two-thirds of Congress shall think their agency necessary; but even this will be no longer than two-thirds of Congress shall think proper to propose, and use the influence of which they would be so largely possessed to remove it.

But these powers, of which the *Freeman* gives us such a profuse detail, and in describing which he repeats the same powers with only varying the terms, such as the powers of officering and training the militia, appointing State officers, and governing in a number of internal cases, do not any of them separately, nor all taken together, amount to independent sovereignty; they are powers of mere ministerial agency, which may, and in many nations of Europe are or have been vested, as before observed, in heads of departments, hereditary vassals of the crown, or in corporations; but not that kind of independent sovereignty which can constitue a member of a federal republic, which can enable a State to exist within itself if the general government should cease.

I have often wondered how any writer of sense could have the confidence to avow, or could suppose the people to be ignorant enough to believe, that, when a State is deprived of the power not only of standing armies (this the members of a confederacy ought to be), but of commanding its own militia, regulating its elections, directing or superseding its representatives, or paying them their wages; who is, moreover, deprived of the command of any property, I mean source of revenue or taxation, or what amounts to the same thing, who may enact laws for raising revenue, but who may have these laws rendered nugatory, and the execution thereof superseded by the laws of Congress. This is not a strained construction, but the natural operation of the powers of Congress under the new constitution; for every object of revenues, every source of taxation, is vested in the general government. Even the power of making inspection laws, which, for obvious conveniency, is left with the several States, will be unproductive of the smallest revenue to the State governments; for, if any should arise, it is to be paid over to the officers of Congress— besides, the words "to make all laws necessary and proper for carrying into execution the foregoing powers," etc., give, without doubt, the power of repelling or forbidding the execution of any tax law whatever, that may interfere with or impede the exercise of the general taxing power, and it would not be possible that two taxing powers should be exercised on the same sources of taxation without interfering with each other. May not the exercise of this power of Congress, when they think proper, operate not only to destroy those ministerial powers which are left with the States, but even the very forms? May they not forbid the state legislatures to levy a shilling to pay themselves, or those whom they employ, days' wages?

The State governments may contract for making roads (except post-roads), erecting bridges, cutting canals, or any other object of public importance; but when the contract is performed or the work done, may not Congress constitutionally prevent the payment? Certainly; they may do all this and much more, and no man would have a right to charge them with breaking the law of their appointment. It is an established maxim, that wherever the whole power of the revenue or taxation is vested, there virtually is the whole effective, influential, sovereign power, let the forms be what they may. By this armies are procured, by this every other controlling guard is defeated. Every balance or check in government is only so far effective as it hath a control over the revenue.

The State governments are not only destitute of all sovereign command of, or control over, the revenue or any part of it, but they are divested of the power of commanding or prescribing the duties, wages, or punishments of their own militia, or of protecting their life, property or characters from the rigors of martial law. The power of making treason laws is both a power and and an important defence of sovereignty; it is relative to and inseparable from it; to convince the States that they are consolidated into one national government, this power is wholly to be assumed by the general government. All the prerogatives, all the essential characteristics of sovereignty, both of the internal and external kind, are vested in the general government, and consequently the several States would not be possesed of any essential power or effective guard of sovereignty.

Thus I apprehend, it is evident that the consolidation of the States into one national government (in contradistinction from a confederacy) would be the necessary consequence of the establishment of the new constitution, and the intention of its framers—and that consequently the State sovereignties would be eventually annihilated, though the forms may long remain as expensive and burthensome remembrances of what they were in the days when (although laboring under many disadvantages) they emancipated this country from foreign tyranny, humbled the pride and tarnished the glory of royalty, and erected a triumphant standard to liberty and independence.

It is not my present object to decide whether the government is a good or a bad one, it is only to prove in support of the minority, that the new system does not in reality, whatever its appearances may be, constitute a federal but a consolidated government. From the distinguishing characteristics of these two kinds of government which I have stated, some assistance perhaps may be derived in judging which of them would be most suitable to our circumstances, and the best calculated to promote and secure the liberty and welfare of these United States.

A few general observations shall conclude this essay. It is commonly said by the friends of the system, that the dangers which we point out are imaginary, that we ought to depend more upon the virtue of those who shall exercise those powers; that we talk as if we supposed men would be possessed of a demon as soon as they should be vested with the proposed powers, etc. I shall in answer thereto join with a sensensible reasoner in saying that I will not abuse the new Congress until it exists, nor then until it misbehaves, nor then unless I dare; but it is a fact, that all governments that have ever been instituted among men, have degenerated and abused their power, and why we should conceive better of the proposed Congress than of all governments who have gone before us, I don't know; it is certainly incumbent on the supporters of this system, first to prove either that the uniform testimony of history, and experience of society, is false, or else that the new system will have the divine influence to inspire those who exercise the powers which it provides, with wisdom and virtue in an infallible degree. Surely the conduct of the framers and promoters of the new constitution do not present mankind as more worthy of confidence now, than they have been in other periods of society. For proof of this let us examine facts. The legislatures of the various States elected members for a federal convention, without having authority for that purpose from their constituents; this gave no alarm, as necessity perhaps justified the measure; but how dangerous is the smallest precedent of usurped power, for the general convention when met, far outdid the example. They were strictly bound by the law of their appointment to revise the confederation; the additional powers with which it ought to have been vested were generally understood, and would have been universally submitted to. This convention not only neglected the duty of their appointment, but assumed a power of the most extraordinary kind; they proceeded to destroy the very government which they were solemnly enjoined to strengthen and improve, and framed a system (to say no worse of it) that was destructive not only of the form, but of the nature of the government whose foundations were laid in the plighted faith and whose superstructure was cemented with the best blood of the United States. The legislature of this State, whose leading members were also self-chosen members of the general convention, no sooner had it in their power, than notwithstanding the solemn trust reposed in them, and still more solemn oath to preserve the constitution of this State inviolate, proceeded upon the expected last day of their session to call a convention, in order to adopt the proposed system of government before the people could be acquainted with it; and to carry this into execution, they added violence to perfidy, and by the aid of mob compelled members, sanctified by their presence that usurped exertion of power, which their faith and trust obliged them to discountenance.

The consequence was, that about one-sixth of the citizens only obeyed the irregular call of the Assembly, and elected members to the State convention: one-third of those members, and who were chosen by nearly one-half of the voters who did elect, voted against the adoption of the new constitution, and being refused the right of entering their testimony on the minutes, laid their conduct and their reasons before their constituents. About five out of six of the people, whether disdaining to obey a call which neither the general convention or Assembly were authorized to make, or whether being taken by surprise they were not sufficiently informed to act with decision, and therefore did not choose to act at all, I cannot tell, but so it is, that they have not yet publicly declared their sentiments for, nor have done anything in favor of the proposed system: in this situation Pennsylvania hath adopted the system. It is a very serious question, whether supposing nine States had agreed to it in this manner, the system would be practicable, whether general confidence would not be necessary unless we had greater resources. In addition to Pennsylvania, Georgia, Delaware, New Jersey, and Connecticut, have also adopted the system; these States are not only small, but in a high degree delinquent, and there is no provision made in the new constitution to compel delinquent States or persons to make up their deficiencies. The convention of Massachusetts have adopted the system with a solemn disapprobation; they have pointed out amendments on the same parchment with the act of ratification, and have solemnly enjoined those who may be the first deputies in the new Congress, to exert their every endeavor to have these amendments made part of the constitution; and to add weight to them, they have officially requested Pennsylvania and the other states to concur in their propositions of amendment. The New Hampshire convention have, on motion of the friends of the system, adjourned until June, in order to prevent an immediate rejection, which otherwise was unavoidable: the adjournment was carried by only three voices. At present there is and will for some months be a solemn and serious pause, a time of deliberation, the result of which will fill an important page in the history of human society. For my own part, I think the heaviest clouds are dispersed, and the gloomy darkness admits the cheering rays of hope, which promise meridian splendor to the sun of liberty. Most of those who were from the best motives friends to the system, have penetrated the shade of mystery in which it was wrapped; they see the snares, and discover the delusions with which it is replete; they see that every other system of government, whether good or bad, is easy to be understood, but that this system excels all of the kind which hath come to their knowledge in darkness and ambiguity; they have been informed, too, that this mysterious veil was the fruit of deliberation and design.

Whilst posts are prevented from carrying intelligence, whilst newspapers are made the vehicles of deception, and dark intrigue employs the avaricious office-hunters who long to riot on the spoils of their country, the great body of the people are coolly watching the course of the times, and determining to preserve their liberties, and to judge for themselves by the principles of reason and common sense, and not by the weight of names.* A FARMER.

* Independent Gazetteer, Apr. 22, 1788.

A NEW FEDERAL SONG.

To the Tune of W——'s March.

I

A tavern-keeper spoke, a federal sign was made,
 Saints, conjurers, Cincinnati, lawyers, and men o' the blade,
With defaulters, deists, bankrupts, and office-hunters, just 39,
 Their faces, figures, and attitudes all painted quite fine.

2

This conclave being reared on the post near the inn door,
 Attracted the attention of every comer and goer;
Its beauties were admired for near half a long day,
 But how transient are the goods of this world, you will say!

3

Some mischievous *Anti's* seeing it cut such a dash,
 The next time they passed by, threw up a great splash.
The face of this most beauteous sign was now all over spotted,
 And the ears, mouths, and noses of these patriots much blotted.

4

The famed wisdom and virtue of the union here collected,
 Which had for such a length of time so much lustre reflected,
Was now on a sudden, when at its meridian glory,
 All besmeared with the tagh of Jamie the Rover.

5

As for 'Simons and the Caledonian, their eyes were turned green,
 And General Tommy, Benny and Bobby, were also unclean.
Bob seemed to hold guineas and Jamie to beg,
 But old Harry had hold of the man with one leg.

6

In short, the shape of most the figures were altered,
 And instead of masqued patriots, rose up rogues ready haltered.
All that was wanted to complete the black scene,
 Was a gallows that would hold at least ten or fifteen.*

THE FEDERALIST'S POLITICAL CREED.

Mr. Printer: Though religious creeds have long since been
deemed quite useless, or rather indeed extremely prejudicial
to the interests of virtue and true piety; yet I must at the
same time be of opinion that political creeds are of a very
different nature, and that no government, and least of all an

* Independent Gazetteer, Apr. 24, 1788.

arbitrary one, can be supported without some such summary of its *credenda*, or articles of faith. Our late C——n, sensible of the truth of this maxim, have taken care to draw up a very full and comprehensive creed for the use of their creatures and expectants, who are obliged to believe and maintain every article of it, right or wrong, on pain of political damnation. And to do those slavish expectants justice, there never was on earth a set of more firm and sincere believers, nor any who were willing to run greater risks in defence of their political dogmas.

This political creed, however, is no new invention: 'tis the old tory system revived by different hands. And the articles of it can be a secret to no one, who has the misfortune to converse with any of its advocates. But as such doctrines and maxims would better become the slave of a bashaw of three tails than the subject of a free republican government, I shall just take the liberty, by way of specimen, to mention a few of these articles for the sake of your more uninformed readers. And,

1. They maintain that the revolution and the Declaration of Independence, however important at those periods, are now to be considered as mere farces, and that nothing that was then done ought to be any bar in the way of establishing the proposed system of arbitrary power.

2. That as most of the European nations are in a state of vassalage and slavery, the Americans easily may be brought to a similar situation, and therefore ought to be reduced to the same abject condition.

3. That to compass this end, a large standing army should be kept up in time of peace, under the specious pretence of guarding us against foreign invasions and our frontiers against the savages; but in reality to overawe and enslave the people, who if provoked at the violation of their rights, should at any time dare to murmur or complaim, the military should be employed to bayonet them for their arrogance and presumption.

4. That to say the late convention was not authorized by the people at large to form an aristocratic, consolidated system

of government for them, but merely to recommend alterations and amendments of the good old articles of confederation, is downright treason and rebellion.

5. That to assert that it was a shameful departure from the principles of the revolution and republicanism, and a base violation of the trust reposed in them, is a crime of the deepest dye, and never to be forgiven.

6. That if any man in the course of his writings should happen to give offence to a haughty favorite of the junto, it should be an express condition in the admission of every person into the new administration, that he concur in the prosecution of the author, or printer (or both, if the name of the author can be extorted or discovered, no matter how vile and infamous the means), to the utmost rigor of the law, and even in contra-distinction to all law and justice.

7. That the trial by jury, whether in civil or criminal cases, ought to be entirely abolished, and that the judges only of the new federal court, appointed by the well-born in the ten-mile-square, should determine all matters of controversy between individuals.

8. That the trial by jury ought likewise to be abolished in the case of libels, and every one accused of writing or even publishing a libel, ought to be tried by informations, attachments, interrogatories, and the other arbitrary methods practiced in the court of star-chamber.

9. That a libel is whatever may happen to give offence to any great man, or old woman; and the more true the charge, the more virulent the libel.

10. That an unrestrained liberty of the press should be granted to those who write and publish against the liberties of the people, but be absolutely denied to such as write against unconstitutional measures, and the abominable strides of arbitrary power, which have recently been attempted by any of the rump conclaves or conventions.

11. That the people indeed have no rights and privileges, but what they enjoy at the mercy of the rich lordlings, who may, of right, deprive them of any or of all their liberties whenever they think proper.

12. That the freemen of America have no right to think for themselves, nor to choose their own officers of government, who ought to be named and appointed by the king elect, the half king and the senate; these being evidently much better judges of what is for the good of the people than the people themselves.

13. That a bill of rights and other explicit declarations in favor of the people, are old musty things, and ought to be destroyed; and that for any set of men to declare themselves in favor of a bill of rights, is a most daring insult offered to General Washington and Doctor Franklin, who, it must be allowed by the whole world, are absolutely infallible.

14. That those men are best qualified to conduct the affairs of a free people, who breathe nothing but a spirit of tyranny, and who, by their violent, illegal, and unconstitutional (consolidating, energetic, as they are pleased to style it) procedures, have well nigh reduced the good people of this great continent to the very eve of a civil war. And that as soon as nine States should accede to the new system of slavery, every one who would presume to lisp a syllable against it, ought to be taken up, imprisoned, and punished at the discretion of the judges of the supreme federal court.

Such are a few of the many articles of the political creed of the federal hacks, and how firmly they believe and diligently act up to them, is a matter of equal notoriety and grief to every real patriot in America.*

[While the Antifederalists were thus abusing the constitution, the men who framed, and the men who approved it, State after State continued to adopt it. No special demonstrations of joy were made by the Federalists, till they heard of the approval of Virginia and New York. Then, the new government being assured, they began to rejoice in earnest.]

The following account of the celebration, by the citizens of Pittsburgh and vicinity, of the adoption of the Constitution of the United States by Virginia, the ninth State, is taken from the *Pittsburgh Gazette*, of June 28th, 1788. The speech

*Independent Gazetteer, May 10, 1788.

of Mr. Brackenridge we omit for the present, but will probably find a place for it shortly.*

Pittsburgh, June 28.

On Friday last, the 20th instant, the news arrived at this
place of the adoption of the new constitution by Virginia,
making the ninth State. On Saturday evening following,
the inhabitants of this town and the adjacent country, to the
number of about fifteen hundred, assembled on Grant's Hill,
a beautiful rising mount to the east of the town, having the
two rivers, the Allegheny and Monongahela, and their junction forming the Ohio, in prospect. Occupying the verge of
the hill, they were addressed by Mr. Brackenridge. * * *

Three cheers were now given, and the hats thrown into
the air. Nine piles of wood were then lighted, representing
the nine States which had adopted the constitution. At intermediate distances, four piles were left uninflamed, representing those which had not adopted it. Fire was then
kindled in them, but oppressed by green leaves and heavy
boughs; in spite of all that could be done, the pile of New
Hampshire burst out, and gave a luminous splendor; that of
Rhode Island not having sent delegates to the general convention, or called a convention of their own, had brimstone,
tar and feathers thrown into it; yet still some boughs of wood
that were at the bottom, catching the flame, purged off the
noxious vapor and materials. That of New York and North
Carolina at length took fire, and exceeded even the other
piles. The whole thirteen now in one blaze began to burn.
The youths of the village danced around them on the green;
and the Indians who were present, the chiefs of several
nations, on the way to their treaty at Muskingum, stood in
amazement at the scene; concluding this to be the great council, seeing the thirteen fires kindled on the hill.

[On June 25th, 1788, Virginia ratified the constitution as
the tenth State. As the approval of nine was to put it in
force, all hope of defeating the new plan was now ended. So
many States, however, had accepted the constitution with re-

*Hazard's Register of Penna., Sep. 14, 1833.

luctance, and with long lists of proposed amendments, that the Antifederalists determined to make one more effort to have it sent to a new convention of the states for revision and amendment.

The earliest movement for such a convention began in the county of Cumberland, and was probably the work of Robert Whitehill. However this may be, representatives from the townships of Cumberland met towards the close of June, called for a conference of counties at Harrisburg, September 3d, elected delegates to represent it on that day, and sent a circular letter to prominent Antifederalists all over the state. The letter is as follows :]

East Pennsborough, Cumberland, July 3, 1788.

SIR: That ten states have already unexpectedly, without amending, ratified the constitution proposed for the government of these United States, cannot have escaped the notice of the friends of liberty. That the way is prepared for the full organization of the government, with all its foreseen and consequent dangers, is too evident, and unless prudent steps be taken to combine the friends to amendments in some plan in which they may confidently draw together, and exert their power in unison, the liberty of the American citizens must lie at the discretion of Congress, and most probably posterity become slaves to the officers of government.

The means adopted and proposed by a meeting of delegates from the townships of this county for preventing the alleged evils, and also the calamities of a civil war, are, as may be observed in perusing the proceedings of the said meeting herewith transmitted, to request such persons as shall be judged fit within the counties, respectively, to use their influence to obtain a meeting of delegates from each township, to take into consideration the necessity of amending the constitution of these United States, and for that purpose to nominate and appoint a number of delegates to represent the county in a general conference of the counties of this commonwealth, to be held at Harrisburg on the third day of September next, then and there to devise such amendments, and such mode of obtaining them, as in the wisdom of the delegates shall be judged most satisfactory and expedient.

A law will, no doubt, be soon enacted by the General Assembly for electing eight members to represent this state in the new Congress. It will, therefore, be expedient to have proper persons put in nomination by the delegates in conference, being the most likely method of directing the voices of the electors to the same object and of obtaining the desired end.

The society, of which you are chairman, is requested to call a meeting agreeable to the foregoing designs, and lay before the delegates the proceedings of this county, to the intent that the state may unite in casting off the yoke of slavery, and once more establish union and liberty.

By order of the meeting, I am with real esteem, sir,

Your most obedient servant,

BENJAMIN BLYTH, Chairman.

[This letter in time was followed by another, addressed to prominent men in each township of Bucks county, and is as follows:]

Newtown, August 15, 1788.

GENTLEMEN: The important crisis now approaching (confident I am you will think with me) demands the most serious attention of every friend of American liberty. The constitution of the United States is now adopted by eleven states in the Union, and no doubt the other two will follow their example; for, however just the sentiments of the opposition may be, I do conceive it would be the height of madness and folly, and in fact a crime of very detrimental consequence to our country, to refuse to acquiesce in a measure received in form by so great a majority of our country; not only to ourselves individually, but to the community at large—for the worst that we can expect from a bad form of government is anarchy and confusion, with all its common train of grievances—and by an opposition in the present situation of affairs we are sure of it. On the other hand, by a sullen and inactive conduct, it will give the promoters and warm advocates of the plan an opportunity (if any such design they have) to shackle us with those manacles, that we fear may be formed under color of law, and we be led to know it is constitutional, when it is too late to extricate ourselves and posterity from bondage.

To you it is not worth while to animadvert on the plain and pointed tendency the constitution has to this effect, and how easily it may be accomplished in power under its influence. That virtue is not the standard that has principally animated the adoption of the constitution in this state, I believe, is too true. Let us, therefore, as we wish to serve our country, and show the world that those only who have wished amendments were truly federal, adopt the conduct of our fellow-citizens in the back counties. Let us, as freemen, call a meeting of those citizens who wish for amendments, in a committee of the county, delegated from each township, for the purpose expressed in a copy of the (circular) inclosed. In promoting a scheme of this kind, I hope we shall not only have the satisfaction of seeing the minds and exertions of all who wish for amendments centre in this object, which will swallow others more injurious, but we will enjoy the supreme felicity of having assisted in snatching from slavery a once happy and worthy people.

I therefore hope you will undertake to call together your township, have delegates chosen to represent them in a committee to be held in the house of George Piper, on Monday, the 21st inst., at nine o'clock in the forenoon, for the purpose of appointing delegates to represent them in the state conference, and for giving them instructions, etc.

If you should apprehend the people will not call a town-meeting for the purpose, that you will, as we intend here, write or call on a few of the most respectable people of your township to attend at the general meeting, as they intend to do at Philadelphia, if they cannot accomplish their purpose in the other way.

Your usual public spirit on occasions of this kind, I am sure, needs no spur. We shall, therefore, rest assured that we will meet a representation of the township committed to your charge on the day appointed.

I am, with every sentiment of esteem,

(Signed.) Yours, &c., JAMES HANNA.

To John Vandegrift, Esq., Capt. Nathan Vansant, and Mr. Jacob Vandegrift, Bensalem.

[The meeting of townships thus called was held at Piper's tavern, Bedminster, and the following course of action taken:]

Bucks County, State of Pennsylvania, August 25, 1788.

The ratification of the federal constitution and its expected operation forming a new area in the American world, and giving cause of hope to some and fear to others, it has been thought proper that the freemen of the State, or delegates chosen by them, should meet together and deliberate on the subject. Accordingly it has been proposed that a meeting of deputies from the different counties be held at Harrisburg, the 3d day of September next. A circular letter bearing the above proposition was sent to this county, and in pursuance thereof, there met this day at Piper's tavern, in Bedminster township, the following gentlemen from the townships annexed to their names, respectively:

Newtown.—James Hanna, Esquire.

Warwick.—John Crawford, Hugh Ramsay, Capt. William Walker, Benjamin Snodgrass, Samuel Flack.

New Britain.—James Snodgrass, Thomas Stuart, David Thomas.

Bedminster.—Jacob Utt, Alexander Hughes, George Piper, Daniel Soliday.

Haycock.—Capt. Manus Yost, John Keller.

Rockhill.—Samuel Smith, Esquire.

Millford.—Henry Blilaz, Henry Hoover.

Springfield.—Colonel John Smith, Charles Fleming.

Durham.—Richard Backhouse, Esquire.

Tinicum.—John Thompson, Jacob Weaver, George Bennet.

Nockamixon.—Samuel Willson, George Vogle.

Richland.—Benjamin Seagle.

Plumstead.—Thomas Wright, Thomas Gibson, James Ruckman, Major John Shaw, James Farres, Thomas Henry, Moses Kelly, Henry Geddis.

Warrington.—Rev. Nathaniel Erwin, Captain William Walker.

Buckingham.—Captain Samuel Smith.

Solesbury.—Henry Seabring.

Hilltown.—Joseph Grier.

Samuel Smith, Esq., chosen Chairman, and James Hanna,

Esq., Secretary. After some time spent in discussing the business of the meeting,

Resolved, that the Reverend Nathaniel Erwin, Richard Backhouse, Samuel Smith, John Crawford, and James Hanna, Esquires, be a committee to draw up resolves expressive of the sense of this meeting on the subject before them.

In a short time thereafter the following were presented by the gentlemen appointed, and unanimously approved:

Resolved 1. That it is the opinion of this meeting, that the plan of government for the United States, formed by the general convention, having been adopted by eleven of the States, ought, in conformity to the resolves of said convention, to come into operation, and have force until altered in a constitutional way.

2. That as we mean to act the part of peaceable citizens ourselves, so we will support the said plan of government, and those who act under it, against all illegal violence.

3. That the said plan of government will admit of very considerable amendments, which ought to be made in the mode pointed out in the constitution itself.

4. That as few governments, once established, have ever been altered in favor of liberty without confusion and bloodshed, the requisite amendments in said constitution ought to be attempted as soon as possible.

5. That we will use our utmost endeavors in a pacific way to procure such alterations in the federal constitution as may be necessary to secure the rights and liberties of ourselves and posterity.

6. That we approve of a State meeting being held at Harrisburg, the third day of September next, on the subject of the above resolves.

7. That four persons ought to be delegated from this county to attend said meeting, and join with the deputies from other counties who may meet with them (in a recommendation to the citizens of this State) of a suitable set of men to represent them into the new Congress, and generally to acquiesce and assist in the promotion of such plan or plans as may be designed by the said State conferrees for the purpose of obtaining the necessary amendments of said consti-

tution, as far as is consistent with our views, expressed in the foregoing resolves.

Agreeably to the resolve last past, the Reverend Nathaniel Erwin, Richard Backhouse, John Crawford, and James Hanna, Esquires, or any two of them, were appointed to represent us in said conference to be held at Harrisburg.

Resolved, That James Hanna, Esquire, be requested to hand the foregoing proceedings to the press for publication.

SAMUEL SMITH, Chairman.

[Thus chosen, the delegates to Harrisburg assembled September 3d, and made Blair M'Clenachan, of Philadelphia, Chairman, and John A. Hannah, of Harrisburg, Secretary. Precisely what the proceedings were cannot now be known, but it is certain that in the course of debate Albert Gallatin, then unknown to fame, submitted the following resolutions:]

1st. "*Resolved*, That in order to prevent a dissolution of the Union, and to secure our liberties, and those of our posterity, it is necessary that a revision of the federal constitution be obtained in the most speedy manner.

2d. "That the safest manner to obtain such a revision will be, in conformity to the request of the State of New York, to use our endeavors to have a convention called as soon as possible;

"*Resolved*, therefore, that the assembly of this State be petitioned to take the earliest opportunity to make an application for that purpose to the new Congress.

3d. "That in order that the friends to amendments to the federal constitution who are inhabitants of this State may act in concert, it is necessary, and it is hereby recommended to the several counties in the State, to appoint committees, who may correspond one with another, and with such similar committees as may be formed in other States.

4th. "That the friends to amendment to the federal constitution in the several States be invited to meet in a general conference, to be held at —, on —, and — members elected by this conference, who, on any of them, shall meet at said place and time, in order to devise, in concert with such other delegates from the several States as may come under similar appointments, on such amendments to the federal constitution as to them may seem most necessary, and on the most likely way to carry them into effect.''

[The resolutions of Mr. Gallatin seem to have been too strong, and not specific enough, and were not accepted by the convention. Concerning the proceedings very little is known, and that little is contained in a summary which appeared in the newspapers. The document is as follows :]

Harrisburg, Dauphin County, State of Pennsylvania,
September 3, 1788.

Agreeably to a circular letter which originated in the county of Cumberland, inviting to a conference such of the citizens of this State, who conceive that a revision of the federal system, lately proposed for the government of these United States, is necessary, a number of gentlemen from the city of Philadelphia, and counties of Philadelphia, Bucks, Chester, Lancaster, Cumberland, Berks, Northumberland, Bedford, Fayette, Washington, Franklin, Dauphin, and Huntingdon, assembled at this place for the said purpose, viz:

Hon. George Bryan, Esq.,	William Petricken,
Charles Pettit,	Jonathan Hoge,
Blair M'Clenachan,	John Bishop,
Richard Backhouse,	Daniel Montgomery,
James Hanna,	John Lytle,
Joseph Gardner,	John Dickey,
James Mercer,	Honorable John Smiley,
Benjamin Blyth,	Albert Gallatin,
Robert Whitehill,	James Marshel,
John Jordan,	Benjamin Elliott,
William Sterrett,	Richard Bard,
William Rodgers,	James Crooks,
Adam Orth,	John A. Hannah,
John Rodgers,	Daniel Bradley,
Thomas Murray,	Robert Smith,
Robert M'Kee,	James Anderson,
John Kean.	

Blair M'Clenachan, Esq., was unanimously elected chairman, and John A. Hannah, Esq., secretary.

After free discussion and mature deliberation had upon the subject before them, the following resolutions and propositions were adopted.

The ratification of the federal constitution having formed a new era in the American world, highly interesting to all the citizens of the United States, it is not less the duty than the privilege of every citizen, to examine with attention the principles and probable effects of a system on which the happiness or misery of the present, as well as future generations, so much depends. In the course of such examination, many of the good citizens of the State of Pennsylvania have found their apprehensions excited that the constitution in its present form contains in it some principles which may be perverted to purposes injurious to the rights of free citizens, and some ambiguities which may probably lead to contentions incompatible with order and good government. In order to remedy these inconveniences, and to avert the apprehended dangers, it has been thought expedient that delegates, chosen by those who wish for early amendments in the said constitution, should meet together for the purpose of deliberating on the subject, and uniting in some constitutional plan for obtaining the amendments which they may deem necessary.

We the conferees assembled, for the purpose aforesaid, agree in opinion:

That a federal government only can preserve the liberties and secure the happiness of the inhabitants of a country so extensive as these United States; and experience having taught us that the ties of our union, under the articles of confederation, were so weak as to deprive us of some of the greatest advantages we had a right to expect from it, we are fully convinced that a more efficient government is indispensably necessary; but although the constitution proposed for the United States is likely to obviate most of the inconveniences we labored under, yet several parts of it appear so exceptionable to us, that we are clearly of opinion considerable amendments are essentially necessary. In full confidence however of obtaining a revision of such exceptionable parts by a general convention, and from a desire to harmonize with our fellow citizens, we are induced to acquiesce in the organization of the said constitution.

We are sensible that a large number of the citizens both in this and the other states, who gave their assent to its being carried into execution, previous to any amendments, were actuated more by the fear of the dangers that might arise from delays, than by a conviction of its being perfect; we therefore hope they will concur with us in pursuing every peaceable method of obtaining a speedy revision of the constitution in the mode therein provided; and when we reflect on the present circumstances of the union, we can entertain no doubt that motives of conciliation, and the dictates of policy and prudence, will conspire to induce every man of true federal principles to give his support to a measure which is not only calculated to recommend the new constitution to the approbation and support of every class of citizens, but even necessary to prevent the total defection of some members of the union.

Strongly impressed with these sentiments, we have agreed to the following resolutions:

1. *Resolved*, That it be recommended to the people of this State to acquiesce in the organization of the said government; but although we thus accord in its organization, we by no means lose sight of the grand object of obtaining very considerable amendments and alterations, which we consider essential to preserve the peace and harmony of the union, and those invaluable privileges for which so much blood and treasure have been recently expended.

2. *Resolved*, That it is necessary to obtain a speedy revision of said constitution by a general convention.

3. *Resolved*, That in order to effect this desirable end, a petition be presented to the legislature of this State, requesting that honorable body to take the earliest opportunity to make application for that purpose to the new Congress.

The petition proposed is as follows:

To the Honorable the Representatives of the Freemen of the Commonwealth of Pennsylvania, in General Assembly met, the Petition and Representation of the Subscribers humbly show :

That your petitioners possess sentiments completely federal; being convinced that a confederacy of republican States, and no other, can secure political liberty, happiness, and safety throughout a territory so extended as the United States of America. They are well apprised of the necessity of devolving extensive powers to Congress, and of vesting the supreme legislature with every power and resource of a general nature; and consequently they acquiesce in the general system of government framed by the late federal convention; in full confidence, however, that the same will be revised without delay: for however worthy of approbation the general principles and outlines of the said system may be, your petitioners conceive that amendments in some parts of the plan are essential, not only to the preservation of such rights and privileges as ought to be reserved in the respective States, and in the citizens thereof, but to the fair and unembarrassed operation of the government in its various departments. And as provision is made in the constitution itself for the making of such amendments as may be deemed necessary, and your petitioners are desirous of obtaining the amendments which occur to them as more immediately desirable and necessary, in the mode admitted by such provision, they pray that your honorable House, as the Representatives of the people in this Commonwealth, will, in the course of your present session, take such measures as you in your wisdom shall deem most effectual and proper, to obtain a revision and amendment of the constitution of the United States, in such parts and in such manner as have been or shall be pointed out by the conventions or assemblies of the respective States; and that such revision be by a general convention of representatives from the several States in the union.

Your petitioners consider the amendments pointed out in the propositions hereto subjoined as essentially necessary, and as such they suggest them to your notice, submitting to your wisdom the order in which they shall be presented to the consideration of the United States.

The amendments proposed are as follows, viz:

I. That Congress shall not exercise any powers whatsoever, but such as are expressly given to that body by the constitution of the United States; nor shall any authority, power or jurisdiction, be assumed or exercised by the executive or judiciary departments of the union under color or pretense of construction or fiction. But all the rights of sovereignty, which are not by the said constitution expressly and plainly vested in the Congress, shall be deemed to remain with, and shall be exercised, by the several states in union according to their respective constitutions. And that every reserve of the rights of individuals, made by the several constitutions of the states in union to the citizens and inhabitants of each State respectively, shall remain inviolate, except so far as they are expressly and manifestly yielded or narrowed by the national constitution.

Article 1, Section 2, Paragraph 3.

II. That the number of representatives be for the present one for every twenty thousand inhabitants, according to the present estimated number in the several states, and continue in that proportion till the whole number of representatives shall amount to two hundred; and then to be so proportioned and modified as not to exceed that number till the proportion of one representative for every thirty thousand inhabitants shall amount to the said number of two hundred.

Section 3.

III. That Senators, though chosen for six years, shall be liable to be recalled or superseded by other appointments, by the respective legislatures of the States, at any time.

Section 4.

IV. That Congress shall not have power to make or alter regulations concerning the time, place, and manner of electing Senators and Representatives, except in case of neglect or refusal by the State to make regulations for the purpose, and then only for such time as such neglect or refusal shall continue.

Section 8.

V. That when Congress shall require supplies, which are to be raised by direct taxes, they shall demand from the several States their respective quotas thereof, giving a reasonable time to each State to procure and pay the same; and if any State shall refuse, neglect, or omit to raise and pay the same within such limited time, then Congress shall have power to assess, levy, and collect the quota of such State, together with interest for the same from the time of such delinquency, upon the inhabitants and estates therein, in such manner as they shall by law direct, provided that no poll-tax be imposed.

Section 8.

VI. That no standing army of regular troops shall be raised or kept up in time of peace, without the consent of two-thirds of both Houses in Congress.

Section 8.

VII. That the clause respecting the exclusive legislation over a district not exceeding ten miles square, be qualified by a proviso that such right of legislation extend only to such regulations as respect the police and good order thereof.

Article 1, Section 8.

VIII. That each State respectively shall have power to provide for organizing, arming, and disciplining the militia thereof, whensoever Congress shall omit or neglect to provide for the same. That the militia shall not be subject to martial law, but when in actual service in time of war, invasion or rebellion; and when not in the actual service of the United States, shall be subject to such fines, penalties, and punishments only, as shall be directed or inflicted by the laws of its own State: nor shall the militia of any State be continued in actual service longer than two months under any call of Congress, without the consent of the legislature of such State, or, in their recess, the executive authority thereof.

Section 9.

IX. That the clause respecting vessels bound to or from any one of the States, be explained.

Article 3. Section 1.

X. That Congress establish no court other than the Supreme Court, except such as shall be necessary for determining causes of admiralty jurisdiction.

Section 2. Paragraph 2.

XI. That a proviso be added at the end of the second clause of the second section of the third article, to the following effect, viz.: Provided, That such appellate jurisdiction, in all cases of common law cognizance, be by writ of error, and confined to matters of law only; and that no such writ of error shall be admitted except in revenue cases, unless the matter in controversy exceed the value of three thousand dollars.

Article 6. Paragraph 2.

XII. That to article six, clause two, be added the following proviso, viz.: Provided always, That no treaty which shall hereafter be made, shall be deemed or construed to alter or affect any law of the United States, or of any particular State, until such treaty shall have been laid before and assented to by the House of Representatives in Congress.

Resolved, That the foregoing proceedings be committed to the chairman for publication.*

BLAIR M'CLENACHAN, Chairman.

Attest, JOHN A. HANNAH, Secretary.

* Independent Gazetteer, Sep. 15, 1788.

CHAPTER VII.

CENTINEL, No. I.*

MR. OSWALD: *As the Independent Gazetteer seems free for the discussion of all public matters, I expect you will give the following a place in your next.*

To the FREEMEN of PENNSYLVANIA. *Friends, Countrymen and Fellow Citizens.*

Permit one of yourselves to put you in mind of certain *liberties* and *privileges* secured to you by the constitution of this commonwealth, and to beg your serious attention to his uninterested opinion upon the plan of federal government submitted to your consideration, before you surrender these great and valuable privileges up forever. Your present frame of government secures to you a right to hold yourselves, houses, papers and possessions free from search and seizure, and therefore warrants granted without oaths or affirmations first made, affording sufficient foundations for them, whereby any officer or messenger may be commanded or required to search your houses or seize your persons or property not particularly described in such warrant, shall not be granted. Your constitution further provides "that in controversies respecting property, and in suits between man and man, the parties have a right *to trial by jury, which ought to be held sacred.*" It also provides and declares, "*that the people have a right of* FREEDOM OF SPEECH, *and of* WRITING *and* PUBLISHING *their sentiments*, therefore THE FREEDOM OF THE PRESS OUGHT NOT TO BE RESTRAINED." The constitution of Pennsylvania is *yet* in existence, *as yet* you have the right to *freedom of speech*, and of *publishing your sentiments.* How long those rights will appertain to you, you yourselves are called upon to say; whether your *houses* shall

*From "The Independent Gazetteer; or, The Chronicle of Freedom." Oct. 5, 1787.

(565)

continue to be your *castles*, whether your *papers*, your *persons* and your *property*, are to be held sacred and free from *general warrants*, you are now to determine. Whether the *trial by jury* is to continue as your birth-right, the freemen of Pennsylvania, nay, of all America, are now called upon to declare.

Without presuming upon my own judgment, I cannot think it an unwarrantable presumption to offer my private opinion, and call upon others for theirs; and if I use my pen with the boldness of a freeman, it is because I know that *the liberty of the press yet remains unviolated and juries yet are judges.*

The late Convention have submitted to your consideration a plan of a new federal government. The subject is highly interesting to your future welfare. Whether it be calculated to promote the great ends of civil society, viz., the happiness and prosperity of the community, it behoves you well to consider, uninfluenced by the authority of names. Instead of that frenzy of enthusiasm, that has actuated the citizens of Philadelphia, in their approbation of the proposed plan, before it was possible that it could be the result of a rational investigation into its principles, it ought to be dispassionately and deliberately examined on its own intrinsic merit, the only criterion of your patronage. If ever free and unbiased discussion was proper or necessary, it is on such an occasion. All the blessings of liberty and the dearest privileges of freemen are now at stake and dependent on your present conduct. Those who are competent to the task of developing the principles of government, ought to be encouraged to come forward, and thereby the better enable the people to make a proper judgment; for the science of government is so abstruse, that few are able to judge for themselves. Without such assistance the people are too apt to yield an implicit assent to the opinions of those characters whose abilities are held in the highest esteem, and to those in whose integrity and patriotism they can confide; not considering that the love of domination is generally in proportion to talents, abilities and superior requirements, and that the men of the greatest purity of intention may be made instruments of despotism in the hands of the *artful and designing*. If it were not for the stability and attachment which time and habit gives to forms of government, it would be in the power of the enlightened and aspiring few, if they should combine, at any time to destroy the best establishments, and even make the people the instruments of their own subjugation.

The late revolution having effaced in a great measure all former habits, and the present institutions are so recent, that there exists not that great reluctance to innovation, so remarkable in old communities, and which accords with reason, for the most comprehensive mind cannot foresee the full operation of material changes on civil polity; it is the genius of the common law to resist innovation.

The wealthy and ambitious, who in every community think they have a right to lord it over their fellow creatures, have availed themselves very successfully of this favorable disposition; for the people thus unsettled in their sentiments, have been prepared to accede to any extreme of government. All the distresses and difficulties they experience, proceeding from various causes, have been ascribed to the impotency of of the present confederation, and thence they have been led to expect full relief from the adoption of the proposed system of government; and in the other event, immediately ruin and annihilation as a nation. These characters flatter themselves that they have lulled all distrust and jealousy of their new plan, by gaining the concurrence of the two men in whom America has the highest confidence, and now triumphantly exult in the completion of their long meditated schemes of power and aggrandizement. I would be very far from insinuating that the two illustrious personages alluded to, have not the welfare of their country at heart; but that the unsuspecting goodness and zeal of the one has been imposed on, in a subject of which he must be necessarily inexperienced, from his other arduous engagements; and that the weakness and indecision attendant on old age, has been practiced on in the other.

I am fearful that the principles of government inculcated

in Mr. Adams' treatise, and enforced in the numerous essays and paragraphs in the newspapers, have misled some well designing members of the late Convention. But it will appear in the sequel, that the construction of the proposed plan of government is infinitely more extravagant.

I have been anxiously expecting that some enlightened patriot would, ere this, have taken up the pen to expose the futility, and counteract the baneful tendency of such principles. Mr. Adams' *sine qua non* of a good government is three balancing powers; whose repelling qualities are to produce an equilibrium of interests, and thereby promote the happiness of the whole community. He asserts that the administrators of every government, will ever be actuated by views of private interest and ambition, to the prejudice of the public good; that therefore the only effectual method to secure the rights of the people and promote their welfare, is to create an opposition of interests between the members of two distinct bodies, in the exercise of the powers of government, and balanced by those of a third. This hypothesis supposes human wisdom competent to the task of instituting three co-equal orders in government, and a corresponding weight in the community to enable them respectively to exercise their several parts, and whose views and interests should be so distinct as to prevent a coalition of any two of them for the destruction of the third. Mr. Adams, although he has traced the constitution of every form of government that ever existed, as far as history affords materials, has not been able to adduce a single instance of such a government; he indeed says that the British constitution is such in theory, but this is rather a confirmation that his principles are chimerical and not to be reduced to practice. If such an organization of power were practicable, how long would it continue? Not a day—for there is so great a disparity in the talents, wisdom and industry of mankind, that the scale would presently preponderate to one or the other body, and with every accession of power the means of further increase would be greatly extended. The state of society in England is much more favorable to such a scheme of government than that of

America. There they have a powerful hereditary nobility, and real distinctions of rank and interests; but even there, for want of that perfect equality of power and distinction of interests in the three orders of government, they exist but in name; the only operative and efficient check upon the conduct of administration, is the sense of the people at large.

Suppose a government could be formed and supported on such principles, would it answer the great purposes of civil society? If the administrators of every government are actuated by views of private interest and ambition, how is the welfare and happiness of the community to be the result of such jarring adverse interests?

Therefore, as different orders in government. will not produce the good of the whole, we must recur to other principles. I believe it will be found that the form of government, which holds those entrusted with power in the greatest responsibility to their constituents, the best calculated for freemen. A republican, or free government, can only exist where the body of the people are virtuous, and where property is pretty equally divided. In such a government the people are the sovereign and their sense or opinion is the criterion of every public measure; for when this ceases to be the case, the nature of the government is changed, and an aristocracy, monarchy or despotism will rise on its ruin. The highest responsibility is to be attained in a simple structure of government, for the great body of the people never steadily attend to the operations of government, and for want of due information are liable to be imposed on. If you complicate the plan by various orders, the people will be perplexed and divided in their sentiment about the source of abuses or misconduct; some will impute it to the senate, others to the house of representatives, and so on, that the interposition ot the people may be rendered imperfect or perhaps wholly abortive. But if, imitating the constitution of Pennsylvania, you vest all the legislative power in one body of men (separating the executive and judicial) elected for a short period, and necessarily excluded by rotation from permanency, and guarded from precipitancy and surprise by delays imposed on its proceedings, you will create the most perfect responsibility; for then, whenever the people feel a grievance, they cannot mistake the authors, and will apply the remedy with certainty and effect, discarding them at the next election. This tie of responsibility will obviate all the dangers apprehended from a single legislature, and will the best secure the rights of the people.

Having premised this much, I shall now proceed to the examination of the proposed plan of government, and I trust, shall make it appear to the meanest capacity, that it has none of the essential requisites of a free government; that it is neither founded on those balancing restraining powers, recommended by Mr. Adams and attempted in the British constitution, or possessed of that responsibility to its constituents, which, in my opinion, is the only effectual security for the liberties and happiness of the people; but on the contrary, that it is a most daring attempt to establish a despotic aristocracy among freemen, that the world has ever witnessed.

I shall previously consider the extent of the powers intended to be vested in Congress, before I examine the construction of the general government.

It will not be controverted that the legislative is the highest delegated power in government, and that all others are subordinate to it. The celebrated *Montesquieu* establishes it as a maxim, that legislation necessarily follows the power of taxation. By sect. 8, of the first article of the proposed plan of government, ''the Congress are to have power to lay and collect taxes, duties, imposts, and excises, to pay the debts and provide for the common defense and *general welfare* of the United States; but all duties, imposts and excises, shall be uniform throughout the United States.'' Now what can be more comprehensive than these words? Not content by other sections of this plan, to grant all the great executive powers of a confederation, and a STANDING ARMY IN TIME OF PEACE, that grand engine of oppression, and moreover the absolute control over the commerce of the United States and all external objects of revenue, such as unlimited imposts upon imports, etc., they are to be vested with every species of *internal* taxation; whatever taxes, duties and excises that they may deem requisite for the *general welfare*, may be imposed on the citizens of these states, levied by the officers of Congress, distributed through every district in America; and the collection would be enforced by the standing army, however grievous or improper they may be. The Congress may construe every purpose for which the State legislatures now lay taxes, to be for the *general welfare*, and thereby seize upon every object of revenue.

The judicial power by Article 3d sect. 1st shall extend to all cases, in law and equity, arising under this constitution, the laws of the United States, and treaties made or which shall be made under their authority; to all cases affecting ambassadors, other public ministers and consuls; to all cases of admiralty and maritime jurisdiction, to controversies to which the United States shall be a party, to controversies between two or more States, between a State and citizens of another State, between citizens of different States, between citizens of the same State claiming lands under grants of different States, and between a State, or the citizens thereof, and foreign States, citizens or subjects.

The judicial power to be vested in one Supreme Court, and in such inferior Courts as the Congress may from time to time ordain and establish.

The objects of jurisdiction recited above are so numerous, and the shades of distinction between civil causes are oftentimes so slight, that it is more than probable that the State judicatories would be wholly superseded; for in contests about jurisdiction, the federal court, as the most powerful, would ever prevail. Every person acquainted with the history of the courts in England, knows by what ingenious sophisms they have, at different periods, extended the sphere of their jurisdiction over objects out of the line of their institution, and contrary to their very nature; courts of a criminal jurisdiction obtaining cognizance in civil causes.

To put the omnipotency of Congress over the State government and judicatories out of all doubt, the 6th article ordains that "this constitution and the laws of the United States which shall be made in pursuance thereof, and all treaties made, or which shall be made under the authority of the United States, shall be the *supreme law of the land,* and the judges in every State shall be bound thereby, anything in the constitution or laws of any State to the contrary notwithstanding."

By these sections the all-prevailing power of taxation, and such extensive legislative and judicial powers are vested in the general government, as must in their operation necessarily absorb the State legislatures and judicatories; and that such was in the contemplation of the framers of it, will appear from the provision made for such event, in another part of it (but that, fearful of alarming the people by so great an innovation, they have suffered the forms of the separate governments to remain, as a blind). By Article 1st sect. 4th, "the times, places and manner of holding elections for senators and representatives, shall be prescribed in each State by the legislature thereof; *but the Congress may at any time, by law, make or alter such regulations, except as to the place of choosing senators.*" The plain construction of which is, that when the State legislatures drop out of sight, from the necessary operation of this government, then Congress are to provide for the election and appointment of representatives and senators.

If the foregoing be a just comment, if the United States are to be melted down into one empire, it becomes you to consider whether such a government, however constructed, would be eligible in so extended a territory; and whether it would be practicable, consistent with freedom? It is the opinion of the greatest writers, that a very extensive country cannot be governed on democratical principles, on any other plan than a confederation of a number of small republics, possessing all the powers of internal government, but united in the management of their foreign and general concerns.

It would not be difficult to prove, that anything short of despotism could not bind so great a country under one government; and that whatever plan you might, at the first setting out, establish, it would issue in a depotism.

If one general government could be instituted and maintained on principles of freedom, it would not be so competent to attend to the various local concerns and wants, of every particular district, as well as the peculiar governments, who are nearer the scene, and possessed of superior means of information; besides, if the business of the *whole* union is to be managed by one government, there would not be time. Do we not already see, that the inhabitants in a number of larger States, who are remote from the seat of government, are loudly complaining of the inconveniences and disadvantages they are subjected to on this account, and that, to enjoy the comforts of local government, they are separating into smaller divisions?

Having taken a review of the powers, I shall now examine the construction of the proposed general government.

Article 1st, sect. 1st. "All legislative powers herein granted shall be vested in a Congress of the United States, which shall consist of a senate and house of representatives." By another section, the President (the principal executive officer) has a conditional control over their proceedings.

Sect. 2d. "The house of representatives shall be composed of members chosen every second year, by the people of the several States. The number of representatives shall not exceed one for every 30,000 inhabitants."

The senate, the other constituent branch of the legislature, is formed by the legislature of each State appointing two senators, for the term of six years.

The executive power by Article 2d, sect. 1st, is to be vested in a President of the United States of America, elected for four years: Sec. 2 gives him "power, by and with the consent of the senate to make treaties, provided two-thirds of the senators present concur; and he shall nominate, and by and with the advice and consent of the senate, shall appoint ambassadors, other public ministers and consuls, judges of the Supreme Court, and all other officers of the United States, whose appointments are not herein otherwise provided for, and which shall be established by law, etc. And by another section he has the absolute power of granting reprieves and pardons for treason and all other high crimes and misdemeanors, except in case of impeachment.

The foregoing are the outlines of the plan.

Thus we see, the house of representatives are on the part of the people to balance the senate, who I suppose will be composed of the *better sort*, the *well born*, etc. The number of the representatives (being only one for every 30,000 inhabitants) appears to be too few, either to communicate the requisite information of the wants, local circumstances and sentiments of so extensive an empire, or to prevent corruption and undue influence, in the exercise of such great powers; the term for which they are to be chosen, too long to preserve a due dependence and accountability to their constituents; and the mode and places of their election not sufficiently ascertained, for as Congress have the control over both, they may govern the choice, by ordering the *representatives* of a *whole* State, to be *elected* in *one* place, and that too may be the most *inconvenient*.

The senate, the great efficient body in this plan of government, is constituted on the most unequal principles. The smallest State in the Union has equal weight with the great States of Virginia, Massachusetts or Pennsylvania. The senate, besides its legislative functions, has a very considerable share in the executive; none of the principal appointments to office can be made without its advice and consent. The term and mode of its appointment will lead to permanency; the members are chosen for six years, the mode is under the control of Congress, and as there is no exclusion by rotation, they may be continued for life, which, from their extensive means of influence, would follow of course. The President, who would be a mere pageant of State, unless he coincides with the views of the senate, would either become the head of the aristocratic junto in that body, or its minion; besides, their influence being the most predominant, could the best secure his re-election to office. And from his power of granting pardons, he might screen from punishment the most treasonable attempts on the liberties of the people, when instigated by the senate.

From this investigation into the organization of this government, it appears that it is devoid of all responsibility or accountability to the great body of the people, and that so far from being a regular balanced government, it would be in practice a *permanent* ARISTOCRACY.

The framers of it, actuated by the true spirit of such a government, which ever abominates and suppresses all free inquiry and discussion, have made no provision for the *liberty of the press*, that grand *palladium of freedom*, and *scourge of tyrants;* but observed a total silence on that head. It is the opinion of some great writers, that if the liberty of the press, by an institution of religion or otherwise, could be rendered *sacred*, even in *Turkey*, that despotism would fly before it. And it is worthy of remark that there is no declaration of personal rights, premised in most free constitutions; and that trial by *jury* in *civil* cases is taken away; for what other construction can be put on the following, viz: Article 3d, sect. 2d, "In all cases affecting ambassadors, other public ministers and consuls, and those in which a State shall be party, the Supreme Court shall have *original* jurisdiction. In all the other cases above mentioned, the Supreme Court shall have *appellate* jurisdiction, both as to *law and fact!* " It would be a novelty in jurisprudence, as well as evidently improper, to allow an appeal from the verdict of a jury, on the matter of fact; therefore it implies and allows of a dismission of the jury in civil cases, and especially when it is considered, that jury trial in criminal cases is expressly stipulated for, but not in civil cases.

But our situation is represented to be so *critically* dreadful, that, however reprehensible and exceptionable the proposed plan of government may be, there is no alternative between the adoption of it and absolute ruin. My fellow citizens, things are not at that crisis; it is the argument of tyrants; the present distracted state of Europe secures us from injury on that quarter, and as to domestic dissensions, we have not so much to fear from them, as to precipitate us into this form of government, without it is a safe and a proper one. For remember, of all *possible* evils, that of *despotism* is the *worst* and the most to be dreaded.

Besides, it cannot be supposed that the first essay on so
difficult a subject, is so well digested as it ought to be; if
the proposed plan, after a mature deliberation, should meet
the approbation of the respective States, the matter will end;
but if it should be found to be fraught with dangers and inconveniences, a future general Convention, being in possession
of the objections, will be the better enabled to plan a suitable
government.

> "Who's here so base, that would a bondman be?
> If any, speak; for him have I offended.
> Who's here so vile, that will not love his country?
> If any, speak; for him have I offended."
>
> CENTINEL.

Centinel, No. II.*

To the People of Pennsylvania. *Friends, Countrymen,
and Fellow Citizens.*

As long as the liberty of the press continues unviolated,
and the people have the right of expressing and publishing
their sentiments upon every public measure, it is next to impossible to enslave a free nation. The state of society must
be very corrupt and base indeed, when the people, in possession of such a monitor as the press, can be induced to exchange the heaven-born blessings of liberty for the galling
chains of despotism. Men of an aspiring and tyrannical disposition, sensible of this truth, have ever been inimical to
the press, and have considered the shackling of it as the
first step towards the accomplishment of their hateful domination, and the entire suppression of all liberty of public
discussion, as necessary to its support. For even a standing
army, that grand engine of oppression, if it were as numerous
as the abilities of any nation could maintain, would not be
equal to the purposes of despotism over an enlightened people.

The abolition of that grand palladium of freedom, the
liberty of the press, in the proposed plan of government, and
the conduct of its authors and patrons, is a striking exempli-
fication of these observations. The reason assigned for the

* From the *Freeman's Journal*, Oct., 24, 1787.

omission of a *bill of rights*, securing the *liberty of the press*, and *other invaluable personal rights*, is an insult on the understanding of the people.

The injunction of secrecy imposed on the members of the late Convention during their deliberations, was obviously dictated by the genius of Aristocracy; it was deemed impolitic to unfold the principles of the intended government to the people, as this would have frustrated the object in view.

The projectors of the new plan, supposed that an ex parte discussion of the subject, was more likely to obtain unanimity in the Convention; which would give it such a sanction in the public opinion, as to banish all distrust, and lead the people into an implicit adoption of it without examination.

The greatest minds are forcibly impressed by the immediate circumstances with which they are connected; the particular sphere men move in, the prevailing sentiments of those they converse with, have an insensible and irresistible influence on the wisest and best of mankind; so that when we consider the abilities, talents, ingenuity and consummate address of a number of the members of the late Convention, whose principles are despotic, can we be surprised that men of the best intentions have been misled in the difficult science of government? Is it derogating from the character of the *illustrious and highly revered* WASHINGTON, to suppose him fallible on a subject that must be in a great measure novel to him? As a patriotic hero, he stands unequalled in the annals of time.

The new plan was accordingly ushered to the public with such a splendor of names, as inspired the most unlimited confidence; the people were disposed to receive upon trust, without any examination on their part, what would have proved either a *blessing* or a *curse* to them and their posterity. What astonishing infatuation! to stake their happiness on the wisdom and integrity of any set of men! In matters of infinitely smaller concern, the dictates of prudence are not disregarded! The celebrated *Montesquieu*, in his Spirit of Laws, says, that "slavery is ever preceded by sleep." And again, in his account of the rise and fall of the Roman Empire, page 97, "That it may be advanced as a general rule, that in a free State, whenever a perfect calm is visible, the spirit of liberty no longer subsists." And Mr. *Dickinson*, in his Farmer's Letters, No. XI., lays it down as a maxim, that "A perpetual jealousy respecting liberty is absolutely requisite in all free States."

"Happy are the men, and happy the people, who grow wise by the misfortunes of others. Earnestly, my dear countrymen, do I beseech the author of all good gifts, that you may grow wise in this manner, and I beg leave to recommend to you in general, as the best method of obtaining this wisdom, diligently to study the histories of other countries. You will there find all the arts, that can possibly be practised by cunning rulers, or false patriots among yourselves, so fully delineated, that changing names, the account would serve for your own times."

A *few* citizens of Philadelphia (too few, for the honor of human nature) who had the wisdom to think *consideration* ought to precede *approbation*, and the fortitude to avow that they would take time to judge for themselves on so momentous an occasion, were stigmatized as enemies to their country; as monsters, whose existence ought not to be suffered, and the destruction of them and their houses recommended, as meritorious. The authors of the new plan, conscious that it would not stand the test of enlightened patriotism, tyrannically endeavored to preclude all investigation. If their views were laudable, if they were honest, the contrary would have been their conduct, they would have invited the freest discussion. Whatever specious reasons may be assigned for secrecy during the framing of the plan, no good one can exist for leading the people blindfolded into the implicit adoption of it. Such an attempt does not augur the public good—it carries on the face of it an intention to juggle the people out of their liberties.

The virtuous and spirited exertions of a few patriots have at length roused the people from their fatal infatuation to a due sense of the importance of the measure before them. The glare and fascination of names is rapidly abating, and the subject begins to be canvassed on its own merits; and so serious and general has been the impression of the objection urged against the new plan, on the minds of the people, that its advocates, finding mere declamation and scurrility will no longer avail, are reluctantly driven to defend it on the ground of argument. Mr. *Wilson*, one of the deputies of this State in the late Convention, has found it necessary to come forward.* From so able a lawyer, and so profound a politician, what might not be expected, if this act of Convention be the heavenly dispensation which some represent it? Its divinity would certainly be illustrated by one of the principal instruments of the Revelation; for this gentleman has that transcendent merit! But if, on the other hand, this able advocate has failed to vindicate it from the objections of its adversaries, must we not consider it as the production of *frail* and *interested* men.

Mr. *Wilson* has recourse to the most flimsy sophistry in his attempt to refute the charge that the new plan of general government will supersede and render powerless the state governments. His quibble upon the term *Corporation*, as sometimes equivalent to communities which possess sovereignty, is unworthy of him. The same comparison in the case of the British parliament assuming to tax the colonies, is made in the Xth of the Farmer's Letters, and was not misunderstood in 1768 by any. He says that the existence of the proposed federal plan depends on the existence of the State governments, as the senators are to be appointed by the several legislatures, who are also to nominate the electors who choose the President of the United States; and that hence all fears of the several States being melted down into one empire, are groundless and imaginary. But who is so dull as not to comprehend, that the *semblance* and *forms* of an ancient establishment may remain, after the *reality* is gone. *Augustus*, by the aid of a great army, assumed despotic power, and notwithstanding this, we find even under Tiberius, Caligula and Nero, princes who disgraced human nature by their excesses, the shadows of the ancient consti-

* See speech of James Wilson, Oct. 6, 1787.—EDITOR.

tution held up to amuse the people. The senate sat as formerly; consuls, tribunes of the people, censors and other officers were annually chosen as before, and the forms of republican government continued. Yet all this was in *appearance* only.—Every *senatus consultum* was dictated by him or his ministers, and every Roman found himself constrained to submit in all things to the despot.

Mr. *Wilson* asks, "What control can proceed from the federal government to shackle or destroy that *sacred palladium* of natural freedom, the *liberty of the press?*" What! Cannot Congress, when possessed of the immense authority proposed to be devolved, restrain the printers, and put them under regulation? Recollect that the omnipotence of the federal legislature over the State establishments, is recognized by a special article, viz.,—"that this Constitution, and the laws of the United States which shall be made in pursuance thereof, and all treaties made, or which shall be made, under the authority of the United States, shall be the *supreme law* of the land; and the judges in every State shall be bound thereby, any thing in the *Constitutions* or laws of any State to the contrary notwithstanding." After such a declaration, what security do the *Constitutions* of the several States afford for the *liberty of the press and other invaluable personal rights*, not provided for by the new plan? Does not this sweeping clause subject everything to the control of Congress?

In the plan of Confederation of 1778, now existing, it was thought proper by Article the 2d, to declare that "each State retains its sovereignty, freedom and independence, and every power, jurisdiction and right, which is not by this Confederation expressly delegated to the United States in Congress assembled." *Positive* grant was not *then* thought sufficiently descriptive and restraining upon Congress, and the omission of such a declaration *now*, when such great devolutions of power are proposed, manifests the design of reducing the several States to shadows. But Mr. Wilson tells you, that every right and power not specially granted to Congress is considered as withheld. How does this appear? Is this principle established by the proper authority? Has the Convention made such a stipulation? By no means. Quite the reverse; the *laws* of Congress are to be "the *supreme law* of the land, any thing in the *Constitutions* or laws of any State to the contrary notwithstanding;" and consequently, would be *paramount* to all *State* authorities. The lust of power is so universal, that a speculative unascertained rule of construction would be a *poor* security for the liberties of the people.

Such a body as the intended Congress, unless particularly inhibited and restrained, must grasp at omnipotence, and before long swallow up the legislative, the executive, and the judicial powers of the several States.

In addition to the respectable authorities quoted in my first number, to show that the right of *taxation* includes all the powers of government, I beg leave to adduce the Farmer's Letters, see particularly letter 9th, in which Mr. Dickinson has clearly proved, that if the British Parliament assumed the power of taxing the colonies, *internally*, as well as *externally*, and it should be submitted to, the several colony legislatures would soon become contemptible, and before long fall into disuse. Nothing, says he, would be left for them to do, higher than to frame by-laws for empounding of cattle or the yoking of hogs.

By the proposed plan, there are divers cases of judicial authority to be given to the courts of the United States, besides the two mentioned by Mr. *Wilson.* In maritime causes about property, jury trial has not been usual; but in suits in *equity*, with all due deference to Mr. *Wilson's* professional abilities, (which he calls to his aid) jury trial, as to facts, is in full exercise. Will this jurisperitus say that if the question in equity should be, did *John Doe* make a will, that the chancellor of England would decide upon it? He well knows that in this case, there being no mode of jury trial before the chancellor, the question would be referred to the court of king's bench for discussion according to the common law, and when the judge in equity should receive the *verdict*, the fact so established could never be re-examined or controverted. Maritime causes and those appertaining to a court of equity, are, however, but *two* of the many and extensive subjects of federal cognizance mentioned in the plan. This jurisdiction will embrace all suits arising under the laws of impost, excise and other revenue of the United States. In England if goods be seized, if a ship be prosecuted for non-compliance with, or breach of the laws of the customs, or those for regulating trade, in the courts of exchequer, the claimant is secured of the transcedent privilege of Englishmen, *trial by a jury of his peers.* Why not in the United States of America? This jurisdiction also goes to all cases under the laws of the United States, that is to say, under all statutes and ordinances of Congress. How far this may extend, it is easy to forsee; for upon the decay of the state powers of legislation, in consequence of the loss of the *purse-strings*, it will be found necessary for the federal legislature to make laws upon every subject of legislation. Hence the state courts of justice, like the barony and hundred courts of England, will be eclipsed and gradually fall into disuse.

The jurisdiction of the federal court goes, likewise, to the laws to be created by treaties, made by the President and Senate (a species of legislation) with other nations; "to all cases affecting foreign ministers and consuls; to controversies wherein the United States shall be a party; to controversies between citizens of different states," as when an inhabitant of *New York* has a demand on an inhabitant of *New Jersey.* This last is a very invidious jurisdiction, implying an improper distrust of the impartiality and justice of the tribunals of the states. It will include all legal debates between foreigners in Britain, or elsewhere, and the people of this country. A reason hath been assigned for it, viz: "That large tracts of land, in neighboring states, are claimed under royal or other grants, disputed by the states where the lands lie, so that justice cannot be expected from the state tribunals." Suppose it were proper indeed to provide for such cases, why include all cases, and for all time to come? Demands as to land for 21 years would have satisfied this. A London merchant shall come to America, and sue for his supposed debt, and the citizen of this country shall be deprived of jury trial, and subjected to an appeal (tho' nothing but the *fact* is disputed) to a court 500 or 1000 miles from home; when if this American has a claim upon an inhabitant of England, his adversary is secured of the privilege of jury trial. This jurisdiction goes also to controversies between any state and its citizens; which, though *probably* not intended, may hereafter be set up as a ground to divest the states, severally, of the trial of criminals; inasmuch as every charge of felony or misdemeanor, is a controversy between the state and a citizen of the same: that is to say, the state is plaintiff and the party accused is defendant in the prosecution. In all doubts about jurisprudence, as was observed before, the paramount courts of Congress will decide, and the judges of the state, being *sub graviore lege*, under the paramount law, must acquiesce.

Mr. *Wilson* says that it would have been impracticable to have made a general rule for jury trial in the civil cases assigned to the federal judiciary, because of the want of uniformity in the mode of jury trial, as practiced by the several states. This objection proves too much, and therefore amounts to nothing. If it precludes the mode of common law in civil cases, it certainly does in criminal. Yet in these we are told "the oppression of government is effectually barred by declaring that in all criminal cases *trial by jury* shall be preserved." Astonishing that provision could not be made for a jury in civil controversies of twelve men, whose verdict should be unanimous, *to be taken from the vicinage;* a precaution which is omitted as to trial of crimes, which may be anywhere in the State within which they have been committed. So that an inhabitant of *Kentucky* may be tried for treason at *Richmond.*

The abolition of jury trial in civil cases, is the more considerable, as at length the courts of Congress will supersede the state courts, when such mode of trial will fall into disuse among the people of the United States.

The northern nations of the European continent have all lost this invaluable privilege: *Sweden*, the last of them, by the artifices of the *aristocratic* senate, which depressed the king and reduced the house of commons to insignificance. But the nation a few years ago, preferring the absolute authority of a monarch to the *vexatious* domination of the *well-born* few, an end was suddenly put to their power.

"The policy of this right of juries, (says Judge Blackstone) to decide upon *fact*, is founded on this: That if the power of judging were entirely trusted with the magistrates, or any select body of men, named by the executive authority, their decisions, in spite of their own natural integrity, would have a bias towards those of their own rank and dignity; for it is not to be expected, that the *few* should be attentive to the rights of the *many*. This therefore preserves in the hands of the people, that share which they ought to have in the administration of justice, and prevents the encroachments of the more powerful and wealthy citizens."

The attempt of governor *Colden*, of New York, before the Revolution, to re-examine the *facts* and re-consider the *damages*, in the case of *Forsey* against *Cunningham*, produced about the year 1764 a flame of patriotic and successful opposition, that will not be easily forgotten.

To manage the various and extensive judicial authority, proposed to be vested in Congress, there will be one or more inferior courts immediately requisite in each State; and laws and regulations must be forthwith provided to direct the judges—here is a wide door for inconvenience to enter. Contracts made under the acts of the States respectively, will come before courts acting under new laws and new modes of proceedings, not thought of when they were entered into. An inhabitant of Pennsylvania residing at Pittsburgh, finds the goods of his debtor, who resides in Virginia, within the reach of his attachment; but no writ can be had to authorize the marshal, sheriff, or other officer of Congress, to seize the property, about to be removed, nearer than 200 miles: suppose that at Carlisle, for instance, such a writ may be had, meanwhile the object escapes. Or if an inferior court, whose judges have ample salaries, be established in every county, would not the expense be enormous? Every reader can extend in his imagination, the instances of difficulty which would proceed from this needless interference with the judicial rights of the separate States, and which as much as any other circumstance in the new plan, implies that the dissolution of their forms of government is designed.

Mr. *Wilson* skips very lightly over the danger apprehended from the standing army allowed by the new plan. This grand machine of power and oppression, may be made a fatal instrument to overturn the public liberties, especially as the funds to support the troops may be granted for *two* years, whereas in Britain, the grants ever since the revolution in 1688, have been *from year to year*. A standing army with regular provision of pay and contingencies, would afford a strong temptation to some ambitious man to step up into the throne, and to seize absolute power. The keeping on foot a hired military force *in time of peace*, ought not to be gone into, unless *two-thirds* of the members of the federal legislature agree to the necessity of the measure, and adjust the numbers employed. Surely Mr. *Wilson* is not serious when he adduces the instance of the troops now stationed on the Ohio, as a proof of the propriety of a standing army. They are a mere occasional armament for the purpose of restraining divers hostile tribes of savages. It is contended that under the present confederation, Congress possess the power of raising armies at pleasure; but the opportunity which the States severally have of withholding the supplies necessary to keep these armies on foot, is a sufficient check on the *present* Congress.

Mr. *Wilson* asserts, that never was charge made with less reason, that that which predicts the institution of a *baneful aristocracy* in the federal Senate. In my first number, I stated that this body would be a very unequal representation of the several States, that the members being appointed for the long term of six years, and there being no exclusion by rotation, they might be continued for life, which would follow of course from their extensive means of influence, and that possessing a considerable share in the *executive* as well as *legislative*, it would become a *permanent aristocracy*, and swallow up the other orders in the government.

That these fears are not imaginary, a knowledge of the history of other nations, where the powers of government have been injudiciously placed, will fully demonstrate. Mr. *Wilson* says, "the senate branches into two characters; the one legislative and the other executive. In its legislative character it can effect no purpose, without the co-operation of the house of representatives, and in its executive character it can accomplish no object without the concurrence of the president. Thus fettered, I do not know any act which the senate can of itself perform, and such dependence necessarily precludes every idea of influence and superiority." This I confess is very specious, but experience demonstrates that checks in government, unless accompanied with *adequate* power and *independently* placed, prove *merely nominal*, and will be *inoperative*. Is it probable, that the President of the United States, limited as he is in power, and dependent on the will of the senate, in appointments to office, will either have the *firmness* or *inclination* to exercise his prerogative of a conditional control upon the proceedings of that body, however injurious they may be to the public welfare? It will be his interest to coincide with the views of the senate, and thus become the head of the aristocratic junto. The king of England is a constitutent part in the legislature, but although an hereditary monarch, in possession of the whole executive power, including the unrestrained appointment to offices, and an immense revenue, enjoys but in *name* the prerogative of a negative upon the parliament. Even the king of England, circumstanced as he is, has not dared to exercise it for near a century past. The check of the house of representatives upon the senate will likewise be rendered nugatory for want of due weight in the democratic branch, and from their constitution *they* may become so *independent* of the *people* as to be indifferent of its interests: nay, as Congress would have the control over the mode and place of their election, by ordering the representatives of a *whole* state to be elected at *one* place, and that too the most *inconvenient*, the ruling powers may govern the *choice*, and thus the house of representatives may be composed of the *creatures* of the senate. Still the *semblance* of checks may remain, but without *operation*.

This mixture of the legislative and executive moreover highly tends to corruption. The chief improvement in government, in modern times, has been the complete separation of the great distinctions of power; placing the *legislative* in different hands from those which hold the *executive;* and again severing the *judicial* part from the ordinary *administrative.* "When the legislative and executive powers (says Montesquieu) are united in the same person, or in the same body of magistrates, there can be no liberty."

Mr. *Wilson* confesses himself not satisfied with the organization of the federal senate, and apologizes for it, by alleging a sort of compromise. It is well known that some members of convention, apprized of the mischiefs of such a compound of authority, proposed to assign the supreme executive powers to the president and a small council, made personally responsible for every appointment to office, or other act, by having their opinions recorded; and that without the concurrence of the majority of the quorum of this council, the president should not be capable of taking any step. Such a check upon the chief magistrate would admirably secure the power of pardoning, now proposed to be exercised by the president alone, from abuse. For as it is placed he may shelter the traitors whom he himself or his coadjutors in the senate have excited to plot against the liberties of the nation.

The delegation of the power of taxation to Congress, as far as duties on imported commodities, has not been objected to. But to extend this to excises, and every species of internal taxation, would necessarily require so many ordinances of Congress, affecting the body of the people, as would perpetually interfere with the State laws and personal concerns of the people. This alone would directly tend to annihilate the particular governments; for the people fatigued with the operation of two masters would be apt to rid themselves of the weaker. But we are cautioned against being alarmed with imaginary evils, for Mr. *Wilson* has predicted that the great revenue of the United States will be raised by impost. Is there any ground for this? Will the impost supply the sums necessary to pay the interest and principal of the foreign

loan, to defray the great additional expense of the new constitution; for the policy of the new government will lead it
to institute numerous and lucrative civil offices, to extend its
influence and provide for the swarms of expectants (the
people having in fact no control upon its disbursements), and
to afford pay and support for the proposed standing army,
that darling and long-wished for object of the *well-born* of
America; and which, if we may judge from the principles of
the intended government, will be no trifling establishment,
for cantonments of troops in every district of America will
be necessary to compel the submission of the people to the
arbitary dictates of the ruling powers? I say, will the impost
be adequate? By no means. To answer these there must be
excises and other indirect duties imposed, and as land taxes
will operate too equally to be agreeable to the wealthy aristocracy in the senate who will be possessed of the government,
poll taxes will be substituted, as provided for in the new plan;
for the doctrine then will be *that slaves ought to pay for
wearing their heads.*

As the taxes necessary for these purposes will drain your
pockets of every penny, what is to become of that virtuous
and meritorious class of citizens, the public creditors? However well disposed the people of the United States may be to
do them justice, it would not be in their power; and, *after
waiting year after year*, without prospect of the payment of
the interest or principal of the debt, they will be constrained
to sacrifice their certificates in the purchase of waste lands in
the far distant wilds of the western territory.

From the foregoing illustration of the powers proposed to
be devolved to Congress, it is evident that the general
government would necessarily annihilate the particular governments, and that the security of the personal rights of the
people by the state constitutions is superseded and destroyed;
hence results the necessity of such security being provided
for by a bill of rights to be inserted in the new plan of federal
government. What excuse can we then make for the omission of this grand palladium, this barrier between *liberty* and
oppression? For universal experience demonstrates the

necessity of the most express declarations and restrictions, to protect the rights and liberties of mankind from the silent, powerful and ever-active conspiracy of those who govern.

The new plan, it is true, does propose to secure the people of the benefit of personal liberty by the *habeas corpus*, and trial by jury for all crimes, except in case of impeachment: but there is no declaration, that all men have a natural and unalienable right to worship Almighty God, according to the dictates of their own consciences and understanding; and that no man ought, or of right can be compelled to attend any religious worship, or erect or support any place of worship, or maintain any ministry, contrary to, or against his own free will and consent; and that no authority can or ought to be vested in, or assumed by any power whatever, that shall in any case interfere with, or in any manner control, the right of conscience in the free exercise of religious worship: that the trial by jury in civil causes as well as criminal, and the modes perscribed by the common law for safety of life in criminal prosecutions, shall be held sacred; that the requiring of excessive bail, imposing of excessive fines and cruel and unusual punishments be forbidden; that monoplies in trade or arts, other than to authors of books or inventors of useful arts for a reasonable time, ought not to be suffered; that the right of the people to assemble peaceably for the purpose of consulting about public matters, and petitioning or remonstrating to the federal legislature, ought not to be prevented; that *the liberty of the press be held sacred;* that the people have a right to hold themselves, their houses, papers and possessions free from search or seizure; and that therefore warrants without oaths or affirmations first made affording a sufficient foundation for them, and whereby any officer or messenger may be commanded or required to search suspected places, or to seize any person or his property, not particularly described, are contrary to that right and ought not to be granted; and that standing armies in time of peace are dangerous to liberty, and ought not to be permitted but when absolutely necessary; all which is omitted to be done in the proposed government.

But Mr. *Wilson* says, the new plan does not arrogate perfection, for it provides a mode of alteration and correction, if found necessary. This is one among the numerous deceptions attempted on this occasion. True, there is a mode prescribed for this purpose. But it is barely possible that amendments may be made. The fascination of power must first cease, the nature of mankind undergo a revolution, that is not to be expected on this side of eternity. For to effect this (Art. 6) it is provided, that if *two-thirds* of both houses of the federal legislature shall propose them, or when two thirds of the several States by their legislatures shall apply for them, the federal assembly shall call a convention for proposing amendments, which when ratified by three-fourths of the State legislatures, or conventions, as Congress shall see best, shall control and alter the proposed confederation. Does history abound with examples of a voluntary relinquishment of power, however injurious to the community? No; it would require a general and successful rising of the people to effect anything of this nature. The provision therefore is mere sound.

The opposition to the new plan (says Mr. Wilson) proceeds from interested men, *viz.*, the officers of the state governments. He had before denied that the proposed transfer of powers to Congress would annihilate the state governments. But he here lays aside the masque, and avows the fact. For, the truth of the charge against *them* must entirely rest on such consequence of the new plan. For if the state establishments are to remain unimpaired, why should officers peculiarly connected with them, be interested to oppose the adoption of the new plan? Except the collector of the impost, judge of the admiralty, and the collectors of excise, (none of whom have been reckoned of the opposition) they would otherwise have nothing to apprehend. But the charge is unworthy and may with more propriety be retorted on the expectants of office and emolument under the intended government.

The opposition is not so partial and interested as Mr. *Wilson* asserts. It consists of a respectable yeomanry throughout the union, of characters far removed above the reach of his unsupported assertions. It comprises many worthy members of the late convention, and a majority of the present Congress, for a motion made in that honorable body, for their *approbation* and *recommendation* of the new plan, was after two days' animated discussion, prudently withdrawn by its advocates, and a simple *transmission** of the plan to the several states could only be obtained; yet this has been palmed upon the people as the approbation of Congress; and to strengthen the deception, the bells of the city of Philadelphia were rung for a whole day.

Are Mr. *W*——*n*, and many of his coadjutors in the late C———n, the disinterested patriots they would have us believe? Is their conduct any recommendation of their plan of government? View them the foremost and loudest on the floor of Congress, in our assembly, at town meetings, in sounding its eulogiums:—view them preventing investigation and discussion, and in the most despotic manner endeavoring to compel its adoption by the people, with such precipitancy as to preclude the possibility of a due consideration, and then say whether the motives of these men can be pure.

My fellow citizens, such false detestable *patriots* in every nation, have led their blind confiding country, shouting their applauses, into the jaws of *despotism* and *ruin*. May the wisdom and virtue of the people of America save them from the usual fate of nations.   CENTINEL.

---

* Upon the last motion being made, those who had strenuously and successfully opposed Congress giving any countenance of approbation or recommendation to this system of oppression, said: "We have no objection to transmit the new plan of government to the several states, that they may have an opportunity of judging for themselves on so momentous a subject." Whereupon it was unanimously agreed to, in the following words, viz: Congress having received the report of the Convention latety assembled in Philadelphia, resolved unanimously, that the said report, with the resolutions and letter accompanying the same, be transmitted to the several legislatures, in order to be submitted to a convention of delegates, chosen in each state by the people thereof, in conformity to the resolves of the Convention, made and provided in that case."

CENTINEL No. III. *

To the PEOPLE OF PENNSYLVANIA.

John 3d, verse 20th.—"*For every one that doeth evil, hateth the light, neither cometh to the light, lest his deeds should be reproved.*" But "*there is nothing covered that shall not be revealed; neither hid that shall not be known. Therefore whatever ye have spoken in darkness, shall be heard in the light: and that which ye have spoken in the ear in closets, shall be proclaimed on the housetops.*"—St. Luke, chap. xii, 2d and 3d verses.

Friends, Countrymen, and Fellow Citizens!

The formation of a good government is the greatest effort of human wisdom, actuated by disinterested patriotism; but such is the cursed nature of ambition, so prevalent among men, that it would sacrifice everything to its selfish gratification; hence the fairest opportunities of advancing the happiness of humanity, are so far from being properly improved, that they are too often converted by the votaries of power and domination, into the means of obtaining their nefarious ends. It will be the misfortune of America of adding to the number of examples of this kind, if the proposed plan of government should be adopted; but I trust, short as the time allowed you for consideration is, you will be so fully convinced of the truth of this, as to escape the impending danger; it is only necessary to strip the monster of its assumed garb, and to exhibit it in its native colours, to excite the universal abhorrence and rejection of every virtuous and patriotic mind.

For the sake of my dear country, for the honor of human nature, I hope and am persuaded that the good sense of the people will enable them to rise superior to the most formidable conspiracy against the liberties of a free and enlightened nation, that the world has ever witnessed. How glorious would be the triumph! How it would immortalize the present generation in the annals of freedom!

The establishment of a government, is a subject of such momentous and lasting concern, that it should not be gone into without the clearest conviction of its propriety, which can only be the result of the fullest discussion, the most

* From "The Independent Gazetteer, or, The Chronicle of Freedom," Nov. 8, 1787.

thorough investigation and dispassionate consideration of its nature, principles and construction. You are now called upon to make this decision, which involves in it not only your fate, but that of your posterity for ages to come. Your determination will either ensure the possession of those blessings which render life desirable, or entail those evils which make existence a curse: that such are the consequences of a wise or improper organization of government, the history of mankind abundantly testifies. If you viewed the magnitude of the object in its true light, you would join with me in sentiment, that the new government ought not to be implicitly admitted. Consider then duly before you leap, for after the Rubicon is once passed, there will be no retreat.

If you were even well assured that the utmost purity of intention predominated in the production of the proposed government, such is the imperfection of human reason and knowledge, that it would not be wise in you to adopt it with precipitation in toto, for all former experience must teach you the propriety of a revision on such occasions, to correct the errors, and supply the deficiencies that may appear necessary. In every government whose object is the public welfare, the laws are subjected to repeated revisions, in some by different orders in the governments, in others by an appeal to the judgment of the people and deliberative forms of procedure. A knowledge of this, as well as of other states, will show that in every instance where a law has been passed without the usual precautions, it has been productive of great inconvenience and evils, and frequently has not answered the end in view, a supplement becoming necessary to supply its deficiencies.

What then are we to think of the motives and designs of those men who are urging the implicit and immediate adoption of the proposed government; are they fearful, that if you exercise your good sense and discernment, you will discover the masqued aristocracy, that they are attempting to smuggle upon you under the suspicious garb of republicanism? When we find that the principal agents in this business are the very men who fabricated the form of government, it certainly ought to be conclusive evidence of their invidious design to deprive us of our liberties. The circumstances attending this matter, are such as should in a peculiar manner excite your suspicion; it might not be useless to take a review of some of them.

In many of the states, particularly in this and the northern states, there are aristocratic juntos of the *well-born few*, who had been zealously endeavoring since the establishment of their constitutions, to humble that offensive *upstart, equal liberty;* but all their efforts were unavailing, the *ill-bred churl* obstinately kept his assumed station.

However, that which could not be accomplished in the several states, is now attempting through the medium of the future Congress. Experience having shown great defects in the present confederation, particularly in the regulation of commerce and maritime affairs; it became the universal wish of America to grant further powers, so as to make the federal government adequate to the ends of its institution. The anxiety on this head was greatly increased, from the impoverishment and distress occasioned by the excessive importations of foreign merchandise and luxuries and consequent drain of specie, since the peace: thus the people were in the disposition of a drowning man; eager to catch at anything that promised relief, however delusory. Such an opportunity for the acquisition of *undue* power has never been viewed with indifference by the ambitious and designing in any age or nation, and it has accordingly been too successfully improved by such men among us. The deputies from this state (with the exception of two) and most of those from the other states in the union, were unfortunately of this complexion, and many of them of such superior endowments, that in an *ex parte* disussion of the subject by specious glosses, they have gained the concurrence of some well disposed men, in whom their country has great confidence, which has given a great sanction to their scheme of power.

A comparison of the authority under which the convention acted, and their form of government, will show that they have despised their delegated power, and assumed sove-

reignty; that they have entirely annihilated the old confederation, and the particular governments of the several States,
and instead thereof have established one general government
that is to pervade the union; constituted on the most *unequal* principles, destitute of accountability to its constituents,
and as despotic in its nature, as the Venetian aristocracy; a
government that will give full scope to the magnificent
designs of the *well-born*, a government where tyranny may
glut its vengeance on the *low-born*, unchecked by *an odious
bill of rights*, as has been fully illustrated in my two preceding numbers; and yet as a blind upon the understandings of
the people, they have continued the forms of the particular
governments, and termed the whole a confederation of the
United States, pursuant to the sentiments of that profound,
but corrupt politician Machiavel, who advises any one who
would change the constitution of a State to keep as much as
possible to the old forms; for then the people seeing the
same officers, the same formalities, courts of justice and other
outward appearances, are insensible of the alteration, and believe themselves in possession of their old government.
Thus Cæsar, when he seized the Roman liberties, caused
himself to be chosen dictator (which was an ancient office)
continued the senate, the consuls, the tribunes, the censors,
and all other offices and forms of the commonwealth; and
yet changed Rome from the most free, to the most tyrannical
government in the world.

The convention, after vesting all the great and efficient
powers of sovereignty in the general government, insidiously
declare by section 4th of article 4th, "that the United States
shall guarantee to every State in this union, a republican
form of government;" but of what avail will be the *form*,
without the *reality* of freedom?

The late convention, in the majesty of its assumed omnipotence, have not even condescended to submit the plan of the
new government to the confederation of the people, the true
source of authority; but have called upon them by their several constitutions, to 'assent to and ratify'* in toto, what

* See resolution of Convention accompanying the instrument of the proposed government.

they have been pleased to decree; just as the grand monarque of France requires the parliament of Paris to register his edicts without revision or alteration, which is necessary previous to their execution.

The authors and advocates of the new plan, conscious that its establishment can only be obtained from the ignorance of the people of its true nature, and their unbounded confidence in some of the men concurring, have hurried on its adoption with a precipitation that betrays their design; before many had seen the new plan, and before any had time to examine it, they by their ready minions, attended by some well-disposed but mistaken persons, obtained the subscriptions of the people to papers expressing their entire approbation of, and their wish to have it established; thus precluding them from any consideration; but lest the people should discover the juggle, the elections of the State conventions are urged on at very early days: the proposition of electing the convention for this State in nine days after the date of the resolution for all counties east of Bedford, and supported by three or four of the deputies of the convention, and who were also members of the then assembly, is one of the most extravagant instances of this kind; and even this was only prevented by the secession of nineteen virtuous and enlightened members.*

*The message of the President and Council, sent into the present General Assembly on the 27th of October last, discloses another imposition. The Board sent to the House the official transmission of the proposed constitution of the United States, inclosed in a letter from the President of Congress, which proves that the paper produced to the last House on the day before the final rising of the same, was a surreptitious copy of the vote of Congress, obtained for the purpose of deluding the Legislature into the extravagance of directing an election of Convention within *nine* days.

The provision made by the Convention of Pennsylvania, which sat in 1776 for amending the constitution, is guarded with admirable wisdom and caution. A Council of Censors is to be holden every seven years, which shall have power (two-thirds of the whole number elected agreeing) to propose amendments of the same government, and to call a Convention to adopt and establish these propositions; but the alterations must be "promulgated *at least* six months before the day appointed for the *election* of such Convention, for the *previous consideration* of the people, that they may have an opportunity of instructing their delegates on the subject." The present measures explain the conduct of a certain party of the Censors, who sat in

In order to put the matter beyond all recall, they have proceeded a step further; they have made the deputies nominated for the state convention for this city and elsewhere, pledge their sacred honor, previous to their election, that they would implicitly adopt the proposed government in toto. Thus, short as the period is before the final fiat is to be given, consideration is rendered nugatory, and conviction of its dangers or impropriety unavailable. A good cause does not stand in need of such means; it scorns all indirect advantages and borrowed helps, and trusts alone to its own native merit and intrinsic strength: the lion is never known to make use of cunning, nor can a good cause suffer by a free and thorough examination—it is knavery that seeks disguise. Actors do not care that any one should look into the tiring room, nor jugglers or sharpers into their hands or boxes.

Every exertion has been made to suppress discussion by shackling the press; but as this could not be effected in *this* state, the people were warned not to listen to the adversaries of the proposed plan, lest they should impose upon them, and thereby prevent the adoption of this blessed government. What figure would a lawyer make in a court of justice, if he should desire the judges not to hear the counsel of the other side, lest they should perplex the cause and mislead the court? Would not every bystander take it for granted, that he was conscious of the weakness of his client's cause, and that it could not otherwise be defended than by not being understood?

All who are friends to liberty are friends to reason, the champions of liberty; and none are foes to liberty but those who have truth and reason for their foes. He who has dark purposes to serve, must use dark means: light would discover him, and reason expose him: he must endeavor to shut out both, and make them look frightful by giving them ill names.

Liberty only flourishes where reason and knowledge are

1784 (much fewer than two-thirds of the whole), that proposed to abolish the 47th article of the constitution, whereby the manner of amending the same was regulated.

encouraged: and whenever the latter are stifled, the former is extinguished. In Turkey printing is forbid, enquiry is dangerous, and free speaking is capital; because they are all inconsistent with the nature of the government. Hence it is that the Turks are all stupidly ignorant and are all slaves.

I shall now proceed in the consideration of the construction of the proposed plan of government. By section 4th of article 1st of the proposed government it is declared, "that the times, places, and manner of holding elections for senators and representatives shall be prescribed in each State by the legislature thereof; *but the Congress may at any time by law make or alter such regulations except as to the place of choosing senators.*" Will not this section put it in the power of the future Congress to abolish the suffrage by ballot, so indispensable in a free government? Montesquieu in his Spirit of Laws, vol. 1, page 12, says "that in a democracy there can be no exercise of sovereignty, but by the suffrages of the people, which are their will; now the sovereign's will is the sovereign himself. The laws therefore which establish the right of suffrage, are fundamental to this government. In fact it is as important to regulate in a republic, in what manner, by whom, and concerning what, suffrages are to be given, as it is in a monarchy to know who is the Prince and after what manner he ought to govern." This valuable privilege of voting by ballot ought not to rest on the discretion of the government, but be irrevocably established in the constitution.

Will not the above quoted section also authorize the future Congress to lengthen the terms for which the senators and representatives are to be elected, from 6 and 2 years respectively, to any period, even for life?—as the parliament of England voted themselves from triennial to septinnial; and as the long parliament under Charles the 1st became perpetual?

Section 8th of article 1st, vests Congress with power " to provide for calling forth the militia to execute the laws of the union, suppress insurrections and repel invasions; to provide for organizing, arming, and disciplining the militia, and for

governing such part of them as may be employed in the service of the United States, reserving to the States respectively,
the appointment of the officers, and the authority of training
the militia according to the discipline prescribed by Congress." This section will subject the citizens of these States
to the most arbitary military discipline: even death may be
inflicted on the disobedient; in the character of militia, you
may be dragged from your families and homes to any part of
the continent and for any length of time, at the discretion of
the future Congress; and as militia you may be made the
unwilling instruments of oppression, under the direction of
government; there is no exemption upon account of conscientious scruples of bearing arms, no equivalent to be received in lieu of personal services. The militia of Pennsylvania may be marched to Georgia or New Hampshire, however incompatible with their interests or consciences; in short,
they may be made as mere machines as Prussian soldiers.

Section the 9th begins thus:—"The migration or importation of such persons as any of the states, now existing, shall
think proper to admit, shall not be prohibited by Congress,
prior to the year 1808, but a duty or tax may be imposed on
such importation, not exceeding ten dollars for each person."
And by the fifth article this restraint is not to be removed by
any future convention. We are told that the objects of this
article are slaves, and that it is inserted to secure to the
southern states the right of introducing negroes for twenty-
one years to come, against the declared sense of the other
states to put an end to an odious traffic in the human species,
which is especially scandalous and inconsistent in a people,
who have asserted their own liberty by the sword, and which
dangerously enfeebles the districts wherein the laborers are
bondsmen. The words, dark and ambiguous, such as no
plain man of common sense would have used, are evidently
chosen to conceal from Europe, that in this enlightened
country, the practice of slavery has its advocates among men
in the highest stations. When it is recollected that no poll
tax can be imposed on *five* negroes, above what *three* whites
shall be charged; when it is considered, that the imposts on

the consumption of Carolina field negroes must be trifling, and the excise nothing, it is plain that the proportion of contributions, which can be expected from the southern states under the new constitution, will be unequal, and yet they are to be allowed to enfeeble themselves by the further importation of negroes till the year 1808.   Has not the concurrence of the five southern states (in the convention) to the new system, been purchased too dearly by the rest, who have undertaken to make good their deficiences of revenue, occasioned by their wilful incapacity, without an equivalent?

The general acquiescence of one description of citizens in the proposed government, surprises me much; if so many of the Quakers have become indifferent to the sacred rights of conscience, so amply secured by the constitution of this commonwealth; if they are satisfied to rest this inestimable privilege on the discretion of the future government; yet in a political light they are not acting wisely: in the state of Pennsylvania, they form so considerable a portion of the community, as must ensure them great weight in the government; but in the scale of general empire, they will be lost in the balance.

I intended in this number to have shown from the nature of things, from the opinions of the greatest writers and from the peculiar circumstances of the United States, the impracticability of establishing and maintaining one government on the principles of freedom in so extensive a territory; to have shown, if practicable, the inadequacy of such government to provide for its many and various concerns; and also to have shown that a confederation of small republics, possessing all the powers of internal government, and united in the management of their general and foreign concerns, is the only system of government by which so extensive a country can be governed consistent with freedom: but a writer under the signature of Brutus, in the New York paper, which has been re-published by Messrs. Dunlap and Claypoole, has done this in so masterly a manner, that it would be superfluous in me to add anything on this subject.

My fellow citizens, as a lover of my country, as the friend

to mankind, whilst it is yet safe to write, and whilst it is yet in your power to avoid it, I warn you of the impending danger. To this remote quarter of the world has liberty fled. Other countries now subject to slavery, were once as free as we yet are; therefore for your own sakes, for the sake of your posterity, as well as for that of the oppressed of all nations, cherish this remaining asylum of liberty.

CENTINEL.

Philadelphia, November 5th, 1787.

CENTINEL No. IV.*

To the PEOPLE of PENNSYLVANIA. *Friends, Countrymen and Fellow Citizens,*

That the present confederation is inadequate to the objects of the union, seems to be universally allowed. The only question is, what additional powers are wanting to give due energy to the federal government? We should, however, be careful, in forming our opinion on this subject, not to impute the temporary and extraordinary difficulties that have hitherto impeded the execution of the confederation, to defects in the system itself. Taxation is in every government a very delicate and difficult subject; hence it has been the policy of all wise statesmen, as far as circumstances permitted, to lead the people by small beginnings and almost imperceptible degrees, into the habits of taxation; where the contrary conduct has been pursued, it has ever failed of full success, not unfrequently proving the ruin of the projectors. The imposing of a burdensome tax at once on a people, without the usual gradations, is the severest test that any government can be put to; despotism itself has often proved unequal to the attempt. Under this conviction, let us take a review of our situation before and since the revolution. From the first settlement of this country until the commencement of the late war, the taxes were so light and trivial as to be scarcely felt by the people; when we engaged in the expensive contest with Great Britain, the Congress, sensible of the difficulty of levy-

* From "The Independent Gazetteer; or, The Chronicle of Freedom." Nov. 30, 1787.

ing the moneys necessary to its support, by *direct* taxation, had resource to an anticipation of the public resources, by emitting bills of credit, and thus postponed the necessity of taxation for several years; this means was pursued to a most ruinous length; but about the year 80 or 81, it was wholly exhausted, the bills of credit had suffered such a depreciation from the excessive quantities in circulation, that they ceased to be useful as a medium. The country at this period was very much impoverished and exhausted; commerce had been suspended for near six years; the husbandman, for want of a market, limited his crops to his own subsistence; the frequent calls of the militia and long continuance in actual service, the devastations of the enemy, the subsistence of our own armies, the evils of the depreciation of the paper money, which fell chiefly upon the patriotic and virtuous part of the community, had all concurred to produce great distress throughout America. In this situation of affairs, we still had the same powerful enemy to contend with, who had even more numerous and better appointed armies in the field than at any former time. Our allies were applied to in this exigence, but the pecuniary assistance that we could procure from them was soon exhausted; the only resource now remaining was to obtain by direct taxation, the moneys necessary for our defence. The history of mankind does not furnish a similar instance of an attempt to levy such enormous taxes at once, of a people so wholly unprepared and uninured to them—the lamp of sacred liberty must indeed have burned with unsullied lustre, every sordid principle of the mind must have been then extinct, when the people not only submitted to the grievous impositions, but cheerfully exerted themselves to comply with the calls of their country; their abilities, however, were not equal to furnish the necessary sums—indeed the requisition of the year 1782, amounted to the whole income of their farms and other property, including the means of their subsistence; perhaps the strained exertions of *two* years, would not have sufficed to the discharge of this requisition; how then can we impute the difficulties of the people to a due compliance with the requisitions of Congress, to a defect in the confederation? for any government, however energetic, in similar circumstances, would have experienced the same fate. If we review the proceedings of the States, we shall find that they gave every sanction and authority to the requisitions of Congress that their laws could confer, that they attempted to collect the sums called for in the same manner as is proposed to be done in future by the general government, instead of the State legislatures.

It is a maxim that a government ought to be cautious not to govern over much, for when the cord of power is drawn too tight, it generally proves its destruction. The impracticability of complying with the requisitions of Congress has lessened the sense of obligation and duty in the people, and thus weakened the ties of the union; the opinion of power in a free government is much more efficacious than the exercise of it; it requires the maturity of time and repeated practice to give due energy and certainty to the operations of government, especially to such as affect the purses of the people.

The thirteen Swiss Cantons, confederated by more general and weaker ties than these United States are by the present articles of confederation, have not experienced the necessity of strengthening their union by vesting their general diet with further or greater powers; this national body has only the management of their foreign concerns, and in case of a war can only call by requisition on the several Cantons for the necessary supplies, who are sovereign and independent in every internal and local exercise of government—and yet this rope of sand, as our confederation has been termed, which is so similar to that, has held together for ages without any apparent chasm.

I am persuaded that a due consideration will evince, that the present inefficacy of the requisitions of Congress is not owing to a defect in the confederation, but the peculiar circumstances of the times.

The wheels of the general government having been thus clogged, and the arrearages of taxes still accumulating, it may be asked what prospect is there of the government resuming its proper tone, unless more compulsory powers are granted? To this it may be answered, that the produce of imposts on commerce, which all agree to vest in Congress, together with the immense tracts of land at their disposal, will rapidly lessen and eventually discharge the present incumbrances; when this takes place, the mode by requisition will be found perfectly adequate to the extraordinary exigencies of the union. Congress have lately sold land to the amount of eight millions of dollars, which is a considerable portion of the whole debt.

It is to be lamented that the interested and designing have availed themselves so successfully of the present crisis, and under the specious pretence of having discovered a panacea for all the ills of the people, they are about establishing a system of government, that will prove more destructive to them than the wooden horse filled with soldiers did in ancient times to the city of Troy: this horse was introduced by their hostile enemy the Grecians, by a prostitution of the sacred rites of their religion; in like manner, my fellow citizens, are aspiring despots among yourselves prostituting the name of a Washington to cloak their designs upon your liberties.

I would ask how is the proposed government to shower down those treasures upon every class of citizens, as is so industriously inculcated and so fondly believed? Is it by the addition of numerous and expensive establishments? Is it by doubling our judiciaries, instituting federal courts in every county of every State? Is it by a superb presidential court? Is it by a large standing army? In short, is it by putting it in the power of the future government to levy money at pleasure, and placing this government so independent of the people as to enable the administration to gratify every corrupt passion of the mind, to riot on your spoils, without check or control?

A transfer to Congress of the power of imposing imposts on commerce and the unlimited regulation of trade, I believe is all that is wanting to render America as prosperous as it is in the power of any form of government to render her; this properly understood would meet the views of all the honest and well-meaning.

What gave birth to the late Continental Convention? Was it not the situation of our commerce, which lay at the mercy of every foreign power, who from motives of interest or enmity could restrict and control it, without risking a retaliation on the part of America, as Congress was impotent on this subject? Such indeed was the case with respect to Britain, whose hostile regulations gave such a stab to our navigation as to threaten its annihilation: it became the interest of even the American merchant to give a preference to foreign bottoms; hence the distress of our seamen, shipwrights, and every mechanic art dependent on navigation.

By these regulations too we were limited in markets for our produce; our vessels were excluded from their West India Islands, many of our staple commodities were denied entrance in Britain; hence the husbandmen were distressed by the demand for their crops being lessened and their prices reduced. This is the source to which may be traced every evil we experience, that can be relieved by a more energetic government. Recollect the language of complaint for years past, compare the recommendations of Congress founded on such complaints, pointing out the remedy, examine the reasons assigned by the different States for appointing delegates to the late Convention, view the powers vested in that body; they all harmonize in one sentiment, that the due regulation of trade and navigation was the anxious wish of every class of citizens, was the great object of calling the Convention.

This object being provided for by the proposed Constitution, the people overlook and are not sensible of the needless sacrifice they are making for it. Of what avail will be a prosperous state of commerce, when the produce of it will be at the absolute disposal of an arbitrary and unchecked government, who may levy at pleasure the most oppressive taxes; who may destroy every principle of freedom; and may even destroy the privilege of complaining.

If you are in doubt about the nature and principles of the proposed government, view the conduct of its authors and patrons: that affords the best explanation, the most striking comment.

The evil genius of darkness presided at its birth, it came forth under the veil of mystery, its true features being carefully concealed, and every deceptive art has been and is practising to have this spurious brat received as the genuine offspring of heaven-born liberty. So fearful are its patrons that you should discern the imposition, that they have hurried on its adoption, with the greatest precipitation; they have endeavored also to preclude all investigation, they have endeavored to intimidate all opposition; by such means as these, have they surreptitiously procured a Convention in this State, favorable to their views; and here again investigation and discussion are abridged, the final question is moved before the subject has been under consideration, an appeal to the people is precluded even in the last resort, lest their eyes should be opened; the Convention have denied the minority the privilege of entering the reasons of their dissent on its journals. Thus despotism is already triumphant, and the genius of liberty is on the eve of her exit, is about bidding an eternal adieu to this once happy people.

After so recent a triumph over British despots, after such torrents of blood and treasure have been spent, after involving ourselves in the distresses of an arduous war, and incurring such a debt for the express purpose of asserting the rights of humanity; it is truly astonishing that a set of men among ourselves should have the effrontery to attempt the destruction of our liberties. But in this enlightened age to hope to dupe the people by the arts they are practicing is still more extraordinary.

How do the advocates of the proposed government combat the objections urged against it? Not even by an attempt to disprove them, for that would the more fully confirm their truth; but by a species of reasoning that is very congenial to that contempt of the understandings of the people that they so eminently possess, and which policy cannot even prevent frequent ebullitions of. They seem to think that the oratory and fascination of great names and mere sound will suffice to ensure success; that the people may be diverted from a consideration of the merits of the plan by bold assertions and mere declamation. Some of their writers, for instance, paint the distresses of every class of citizens with all the glowing language of eloquence, as if this was a demonstration of the excellence, or even the safety of the new plan, which, notwithstanding the reality of this distress, may be a system of tyranny and oppression. Other writers tell you of the great men who composed the late convention, and give you a pompous display of their virtues instead of a justification of the plan of government; and others again urge the tyrant's plea, they endeavor to make it a case of necessity, now is the critical moment, they represent the adoption of this government as our only alternative, as the last opportunity we shall have of peaceably establishing a government; they assert it to be the best system that can be formed, and that if we reject it, we will have a worse one or none at all; nay, that if we presume to propose alterations, we shall get into a labyrinth of difficulties from which we cannot be extricated, as no two states will agree in amendments; that therefore it would involve us in irreconcilable discord. But they all sedulously avoid the fair field of argument, a rational investigation into the origination of the proposed government. I hope the good sense of the people will detect the fallacy of such conduct, will discover the base juggle, and with becoming resolution resent the imposition.

That the powers of Congress ought to be strengthened, all allow: but is this a conclusive proof of the necessity to adopt the proposed plan? is it a proof that because the late convention, in the first essay upon so arduous and difficult a subject, harmonized in their ideas, that a future convention will not, or that after a full investigation and mature consideration of the objections, they will not plan a better government and one more agreeable to the sentiments of America, or is it any proof that they can never again agree in any plan? The late convention must indeed have been inspired, as some of its advocates have asserted, to admit the truth of these positions, or even to admit the possibility of the proposed government being such a one as America ought to adopt; for this body went upon original ground, foreign from their intentions or powers; they must therefore have been wholly uninformed of the sentiments of their constituents in respect to this form of government, as it was not in their contemplation when the convention was appointed to erect a new government, but to strengthen the old one. Indeed, they seem to have been determined to monopolize the exclusive merit of the discovery, or rather as if darkness was essential to its success they precluded all communication with the people, by closing their doors; thus the well-disposed members, unassisted by public information and opinion, were induced by those arts that are now practicing on the people, to give their sanction to this system of despotism.

Is there any reason to presume that a new convention will not agree upon a better plan of government? Quite the contrary, for perhaps there never was such a coincidence on any occasion as on the present. The opponents to the proposed plan at the same time in every part of the continent, harmonized in the same objections; such an uniformity of opposition is without example, and affords the strongest demonstration of its solidity. Their objections too are not local, are not confined to the interests of any one particular State to the prejudice of the rest, but with a philanthropy and liberality that reflects lustre on humanity, that dignifies the character of America, they embrace the interests and happiness of the whole Union. They do not even condescend to minute blemishes, but show that the main pillars of the fabric are bad, that the essential principles of liberty and safety are not to be found in it, that despotism will be the necessary and inevitable consequence of its establishment. CENTINEL.

CENTINEL, No. V.*

To the PEOPLE of PENNSYLVANIA. *Friends, Countrymen, and Fellow Citizens.*

Mr. Wilson in a speech delivered in our Convention on Saturday the 24th instant, has conceded, nay forcibly proved, that one consolidated government will not answer

* From "The Independent Gazetteer, or The Chronicle of Freedom." Dec. 4, 1787.

for so extensive a territory as the United States includes, that slavery would be the necessary fate of the people under such a government. His words are so remarkable that I cannot forbear reciting them: they are as follows, viz., "The extent of country for which the new constitution was required, produced another difficulty in the business of the federal convention. It is the opinion of some celebrated writers, that to a small territory the democratical, to a middling territory (as Montesquieu has termed it) the monarchical, and to an extensive territory the despotic form of government, is best adapted. Regarding then, the wide and almost unbounded jurisdiction of the United States, at first view, the hand of despotism seemed necessary to control, connect, and protect it; and hence the chief embarrassment rose. For, we knew that, although our constituents would cheerfully submit to the legislative restraints of a free government, they would spurn at every attempt to shackle them with despotic power." See page 5* of the printed speech. And again in page 7,† he says "Is it probable that the dissolution of the State governments, and the establishment of one consolidated empire, would be eligible in its nature, and satisfactory to the people in its administration? I think not, as I have given reasons to show that so extensive a territory could not be governed, connected, and preserved, but by the supremacy of despotic power. All the exertions of the most potent emperors of Rome were not capable of keeping that empire together, which, in extent, was far inferior to the dominion of America."

This great point having been now confirmed by the concession of Mr. Wilson, though indeed it was self-evident before, and the writers against the proposed plan of government having proved to demonstration, that the powers proposed to be vested in Congress will necessarily annihilate and absorb the State Legislatures and judiciaries, and produce from their wreck one consolidated government, the question is determined. Every man therefore who has the welfare of

* See page 220 of this volume.
† Ibid.

his country at heart, every man who values his own liberty and happiness, in short, every description of persons, except those aspiring despots who hope to benefit by the misery and vassalage of their countrymen, must now concur in rejecting the proposed system of government, must now unite in branding its authors with the stigma of eternal infamy. The anniversary of this great escape from the fangs of despotism ought to be celebrated as long as liberty shall continue to be dear to the citizens of America.

I will repeat some of my principal arguments, and add some further remarks on the subject of consolidation:

The Legislature is the highest delegated power in government; all others are subordinate to it. The celebrated Montesquieu established it as a maxim, that legislation necessarily follows the power of taxation. By the 8th sect. of article the 1st, of the proposed government, "the Congress are to have power to lay and collect taxes, duties, imposts, and excises, to pay the debts and provide for the common defence and *general welfare* of the United States." Now what can be more comprehensive than these words? Every species of taxation, whether external or internal, is included. Whatever taxes, duties, and excises that the Congress may deem necessary to the *general welfare* may be imposed on the citizens of these states, and levied by their officers. The Congress are to be the absolute judges of the propriety of such taxes; in short, they may construe every purpose for which the state legislatures now lay taxes, to be for the *general welfare;* they may seize upon every source of taxation, and thus make it impracticable for the states to have the smallest revenue, and if a state should presume to impose a tax or excise that would interfere with a federal tax or excise, Congress may soon terminate the contention by repealing the state law, by virtue of the following section: "To make all laws which shall be necessary and proper for carrying into execution the foregoing powers and all other powers vested by this constitution in the government of the United States, or in any department thereof." Indeed, every law of the states may be controlled by this power. The legislative power granted for these sections is so unlimited in its nature, may be so comprehensive and boundless in its exercise, that this alone would be amply sufficient to carry the coup de grace to the state governments, to swallow them up in the grand vortex of general empire. But the legislative has an able auxiliary in the judicial department, for a reference to my second number will show that this may be made greatly instrumental in effecting a consolidation; as the federal judiciary would absorb all others. Lest the foregoing powers should not suffice to consolidate the United States into one empire, the Convention, as if determined to prevent the possibility of a doubt, as if to prevent all clashing by the opposition of state powers, as if to preclude all struggle for state importance, as if to level all obstacles to the supremacy of universal sway, which in so extensive a territory would be an iron-handed despotism, have ordained by article the 6th, "That this constitution, and the laws of the United States which shall be made in pursuance thereof, and all treaties made, or which shall be made, under the authority of the United States, shall be the *supreme law of the land; and the judges in every state shall be bound thereby, anything in the constitution or laws of any state to the contrary notwithstanding.*"

The words "pursuant to the constitution" will be no restriction to the authority of Congress; for the foregoing sections give them unlimited legislation; their unbounded power of taxation does alone include all others, as whoever has the purse-strings will have full dominion. But the convention has superadded another power, by which the Congress may stamp with the sanction of the constitution every possible law; it is contained in the following clause: "To make all laws which shall be necessary and proper for carrying into execution the foregoing powers, and all other powers vested by this constitution in the government of the United States, or in any department or officer thereof." Whatever law Congress may deem necessary and proper for carrying into execution any of the powers vested in them may be enacted; and by virtue of this clause, they may control and abrogate any and every of the laws of the State governments, on the allegation that they interfere with the execution of any of their powers, and yet these laws will "be made in pursuance of the constitution," and of course will "be the supreme law of the land, and the judges in every State shall be bound thereby, anything in the *constitution* or *laws* of any state to the contrary notwithstanding."

There is no reservation made in the whole of this plan in favor of the rights of the separate States. In the present plan of confederation, made in the year 1778, it was thought necessary by article the 2d to declare that "each State retains its sovereignty, freedom and independence, and every power, jurisdiction and right, which is not by this confederation *expressly* delegated to the United States in Congress assembled." *Positive* grant was not *then* thought sufficiently descriptive and restrictive upon Congress, and the omission of such a declaration *now*, when such great devolutions of power are proposed, manifests the design of consolidating the States.

What restriction does Mr. Wilson pretend there is in the new constitution to the supremacy of despotic sway over the United States? What barrier does he assign for the security of the State governments? Why truly, a mere cobweb of a limit! by interposing the shield of what will become mere *form*, to check the *reality* of power. He says, that the existence of the State governments is essential to the organization of Congress, that the former is made the necessary basis of the latter, for the federal senators and President are to be appointed by the State legislatures; and that hence all fears of a consolidation are groundless and imaginary. It must be confessed as reason and argument would have been foreign to the defence of the proposed plan of government, Mr. Wilson has displayed much ingenuity on this occasion; he has involved the subject in all the mazes of sophistry, and by subtil distinctions, he has established principles and positions, that exist only in his own fertile imagination. It is a solecism in politics for two co-ordinate sovereignties to exist together; you must separate the sphere of their jurisdiction or after running the race of dominion for some time, one would nec-

essarily triumph over the other, but in the meantime the
subject of it would be harassed with double impositions to
support the contention; however, the strife between Congress
and the States could not be of long continuance, for the
former has a decisive superiority in the outset, and has moreover the power by the very constitution itself to terminate it
when expedient.

As this necessary connection, as it has been termed, between
the State governments and the general government, has been
made a point of great magnitude by the advocates of the new
plan, as it is the only obstacle alleged by them against a consolidation, it ought to be well considered.   It is declared by
the proposed plan, that the federal senators and the electors
who choose the President of the United States, shall be appointed by the State legislatures for the long period of six
and four years respectively; how will this connection prevent
the State legislatures being divested of every important, every
efficient power? may not they, will not they, dwindle into
mere boards of appointment as has ever happened in other
nations to public bodies, who, in similar circumstances, have
been so weak as to part with the essentials of power?   Does
not history abound with such instances?   And this may be
the mighty amount of this inseparable connection which is
so much dwelt upon as the security of the State governments.
Yet even this shadow of a limit against consolidation may be
annihilated by the imperial fiat without any violation of even
the forms of the constitution.   Article 1st, section 4th, has
made a provision for this, when the people are sufficiently
fatigued with the useless expense of maintaining the *forms*
of departed power and security, and when they shall pray to
to be relieved from the imposition.   This section cannot be
too often repeated, as it gives such a latitude to the designing,
as it revokes every other part of the constitution that may be
tolerable, and as it may enable the administration under it,
to complete the system of despotism; it is in the following
words, viz: "The times, places and manner of holding elections for senators and representatives shall be prescribed in
each State by the legislature thereof; *but the Congress may at*

*any time by law make or alter such regulations, except as to
the place of choosing senators.*'' The only apparent restriction in this clause is as to the *place* of appointing senators,
but even this may be rendered of no avail, for as the Congress have the control over the time of appointment of both
senators and representatives, they may, under the pretence
of an apprehension of invasion, upon the pretence of the turbulence of what they may style a faction, and indeed pretences are never wanting to the designing, they may postpone
the time of the election of the senators and the representatives
from period to period to perpetuity; thus they may, and if
they may, they certainly will, from the lust of dominion, so
inherent in the mind of man, relieve the people from the
trouble of attending elections by condescending to create
themselves.   Has not Mr. Wilson avowed it in fact?   Has he
not said in the convention that it was necessary that Congress
should possess this power as the means of its own preservation?
Otherwise, says he, an invasion, a civil war, a faction, or a
secession of a minority of the assembly, might prevent the
representation of a State in Congress.

The advocates of the proposed government must be hard
driven when they represent that because the legislatures of
this and the other states have exceeded the due bounds of
power, notwithstanding every guard provided by their constitutions; that because the lust of arbitrary sway is so powerful as sometimes to get the better of every obstacle; that
therefore we should give full scope to it, for that all restriction to it would be useless and nugatory.   And further, when
they tell you that a good administration will atone for all the
defects in the government, which, say they, you must necessarily have, for how can it be otherwise? your rulers are to
be taken from among yourselves.   My fellow citizens, these
aspiring despots must indeed have a great contempt for your
understandings when they hope to gull you out of your liberties by such reasoning; for what is the primary object of
government, but to check and control the ambitious and designing?   How then can moderation and virtue be expected
from men who will be in possession of absolute sway, who will

have the United States at their disposal? They would be more than men, who could resist such temptation! their being taken from among the people would be no security; tyrants are of native growth in all countries, the greatest bashaw in Turkey has been one of the people, as Mr. Wilson tells you the president-general will be. What consolation would this be when you shall be suffering under his oppression?   CENTINEL.

Philadelphia, Nov. 30, 1787.

CENTINEL, No. VI.*

To the PEOPLE of PENNSYLVANIA.

"Man is the glory, jest, and riddle of the world."
POPE.

Incredible transition! the people who, seven years ago, deemed every earthly good, every other consideration, as worthless, when placed in competition with liberty, that heaven-born blessing, that zest of all others; the people, who, actuated by this noble ardor of patriotism, rose superior to every weakness of humanity, and shone with such dazzling lustre amidst the greatest difficulties; who, emulous of eclipsing each other in the glorious assertion of the dignity of human nature, courted every danger, and were ever ready, when necessary, to lay down their lives at the altar of liberty: I say the people, who exhibited so lately a spectacle that commanded the admiration, and drew the plaudits of the most distant nations, are now reversing the picture, are now lost to every noble principle, are about to sacrifice that inestimable jewel, liberty, to the genius of despotism. A *golden phantom* held out to them by the crafty and aspiring despots among themselves, is alluring them into the fangs of arbitrary power; and so great is their infatuation, that it seems as if nothing short of the reality of misery necessarily attendant on slavery, will rouse them from their false confidence, or convince them of the direful deception—but then alas! it

* From "The Independent Gazetteer; or, The Chronicle of Freedom," Dec. 26, 1787.

will be too late, the chains of depotism will be fast rivetted and all escape precluded.

For years past, the harpies of power have been industriously inculcating the idea that all our difficulties proceed from the impotency of Congress, and have at length succeeded to give to this sentiment almost universal currency and belief: the devastations, losses and burthens occasioned by the late war; the excessive importations of foreign merchandise and luxuries, which have drained the country of its specie and involved it in debt, are all overlooked, and the inadequacy of the powers of the present confederation is erroneously supposed to be the only cause of our difficulties; hence persons of every description are revelling in the anticipation of the halcyon days consequent on the establishment of the new constitution. What gross deception and fatal delusion! Although very considerable benefit might be derived from strengthening the hands of Congress, so as to enable them to regulate commerce, and counteract the adverse restrictions of other nations, which would meet with the comcurrence of all persons; yet this benefit is accompanied in the new constitution with the scourge of despotic power, that will render the citizens of America tenants at will of every species of property, of every enjoyment, and make them the mere drudges of government. The gilded bait conceals corrosives that will eat up their whole substance.

Since the late able discussion, all are now sensible of great defects in the new constitution, are sensible that power is thereby granted without limitations or restriction; yet such is the impatience of the people to reap the golden harvest of regulated commerce, that they will not take time to secure their liberty and happiness, nor even to secure the benefit of the expected wealth; but are weakly trusting their every concern to the discretionary disposal of their future rulers: are content to risk every abuse of power, because they are promised a good administration, because moderation and self-denial are the characteristic features of men in possession of absolute sway. What egregious folly! What superlative ignorance of the nature of power does such conduct discover!

History exhibits this melancholy truth, that slavery has been the lot of nearly the whole of mankind in all ages, and that the very small portion who have enjoyed the blessings of liberty, have soon been reduced to the common level of slavery and misery. The cause of this general vassalage may be traced to a principle of human nature, which is more powerful and operative than all the others combined; it is that lust of dominion that is inherent in every mind, in a greater or less degree; this is so universal and ever active a passion as to influence all our ancestors; the different situation and qualifications of men only modifies and varies the complexion and operation of it.

For this darling pre-eminence and superiority, the merchant, already possessed of a competency, adventures his all in the pursuit of greater wealth; it is for this that men of all descriptions, after having amassed fortunes, still persevere in the toils of labor; in short, this is the great principle of exertion in the votaries of riches, learning, and fame.

In a savage state, pre-eminence is the result of bodily strength and intrepidity, which compels submission from all such as have the misfortune to be less able; therefore the great end of civil government is to protect the weak from the oppression of the powerful, to put every man upon the level of equal liberty; but here again the same lust of dominion by different means frustrates almost always this salutary intention. In a polished state of society, wealth, talents, address and intrigue are the qualities that attain superiority in the great sphere of government.

The most striking illustration of the prevalence of this lust of dominion is, that the most strenuous assertors of liberty in all ages, after successfully triumphing over tyranny, have themselves become tyrants, when the unsuspicious confidence of an admiring people has entrusted them with unchecked power. Rare are the instances of self-denial, or consistency of conduct in the votaries of liberty when they have become possessed of the reins of authority; it has been the peculiar felicity of this country, that her *great Deliverer* did not prove a *Cromwell* nor a *Monk*.

Compare the declarations of the most zealous assertors of *religious* liberty, whilst under the lash of persecution, with their conduct when in power; you will find that even the benevolence and humility inculcated in the gospels, prove no restraint upon this love of domination. The mutual contentions of the several sects of religion in England some ages since, are sufficient evidence of this truth.

The annals of mankind demonstrate the precarious tenure of privileges and property dependent upon the will and pleasure of rulers; these illustrate the fatal danger of relying upon the moderation and self-denial of men exposed to the temptations that the Congress under the new constitution will be. The lust of power or dominion is of that nature as seeks to overcome every obstacle, and does not remit its exertions whilst any object of conquest remains; nothing short of the plenitude of dominion will satisfy this cursed demon. Therefore, liberty is only to be preserved by a due responsibility in the government, and by the constant attention of the people; whenever that responsibility has been lessened or this attention remitted, in the same degree has arbitrary sway prevaled.

The celebrated *Montesquieu* has warned mankind of the danger of an implicit reliance on rulers; he says that "a perpetual *jealousy* respecting liberty, is absolutely requisite in all free states," and again, "that slavery is ever preceded by sleep."

I shall conclude this number with an extract from a speech delivered by Lord *George Digby*, afterwards *Earl* of *Bristol*, in the *English* Parliament, on the triennial bill in the year 1641, viz: "It hath been a maxim among the wisest legislators that whoever means to settle good laws must proceed in them with a sinister opinion of all mankind; and suppose that whoever is not wicked, it is for want only of the opportunity. It is that opportunity of being ill, Mr. Speaker, that we must take away, if ever we mean to be happy, which can never be done but by *the frequency of parliaments*.

"No State can wisely be confident of any public minister's continuing good, longer than the rod is held over him.

"Let me appeal to all those that were present in this house at the agitation of the *petition of right*. And let them tell themselves truly of whose promotion to the management of public affairs do they think the generality would, at that time, have had better hopes than of Mr. *Noy* and Sir *Thomas Wentworth;* both having been at that time and in that business, as I have heard, most keen and active patriots, and the latter of them, to the eternal aggravation of his infamous treachery to the commonwealth be it spoken, the first mover and insister to have this clause added to the *petition of right,* viz:

"That for the comfort and safety of his subjects his Majesty would be pleased to declare his will and pleasure, that all his ministers should serve him according to the laws and statutes of the realm.

"And yet, Mr. Speaker, to whom now can all the inundations upon our *liberties*, under pretence of law, and the late shipwreck at once of all our property, be attributed more than to *Noy*, and all those other mischiefs whereby this monarchy hath been brought almost to the brink of destruction so much to any as to that *grand apostate* to the commonwealth, the now Lieutenant of Ireland, Sir Thomas Wentworth? Let every man but consider those men as once they were."— British Liberties, page 184 and 185.   CENTINEL.

Philadelphia, December 22, 1787.

CENTINEL No. VII.*

To the PEOPLE of PENNSYLVANIA. *Friends and Fellow Citizens:*

The admiring world lately beheld the sun of liberty risen to meridian splendor in this western hemisphere, whose cheering rays began to dispel the glooms of even trans-atlantic despotism; the patriotic mind, enraptured with the glowing scene, fondly anticipated an universal and eternal day to the orb of freedom; but the horizon is already darkened and the glooms of slavery threaten to fix their empire. How transitory

* From "The Independent Gazetteer; or, The Chronicle of Freedom," Dec. 29, 1787.

are the blessings of this life! Scarcely have four years elapsed since these United States, rescued from the domination of foreign despots by the unexampled heroism and perseverance of its citizens at such great expense of blood and treasure, when they are about to fall a prey to the machinations of a profligate junto at home, who seizing the favorable moment when the temporary and extraordinary difficulties of the people have thrown them off their guard and lulled that jealousy of power so essential to the preservation of freedom, have been too successful in the sacrilegious attempt; however I am confident that this formidable conspiracy will end in the confusion and infamy of its authors; that if necessary, the avenging sword of an abused people will humble these aspiring despots to the dust, and that their fate, like that of Charles the First of England, will deter such attempts in future, and prove the confirmation of the liberties of America until time shall be no more.

One would imagine by the insolent conduct of these harpies of power that they had already triumphed over the liberties of the people, that the chains were riveted and tyranny established. They tell us all further opposition will be vain, as this state has passed the Rubicon. Do they imagine the freemen of Pennsylvania will be thus trepanned out of their liberties, that they will submit without a struggle? They must indeed be inebriated with the lust of dominion to indulge such chimerical ideas. Will the act of one-sixth of the people and this too founded on deception and surprise bind the community? Is it thus that the altar of liberty, so recently crimsoned with the blood of our worthies, is to be prostrated and despotism reared on its ruins? Certainly not. The solemn mummery that has been acting in the name of the people of Pennsylvania will be treated with the deserved contempt; it has served indeed to expose the principles of the men concerned, and to draw a line of discrimination between the real and affected patriots.

Impressed with an high opinion of the understanding and spirit of my fellow citizens, I have in no stage of this business entertained a doubt of its eventual defeat; the momentary delusion, arising from an unreserved confidence placed in some of the characters whose names sanctioned this scheme of power, did not discourage me: I foresaw that this blind admiration would soon be succeeded by rational investigation, which, stripping the monster of its gilded covering, would discover its native deformity.

Already the enlightened pen of patriotism, aided by an able public discussion, has dispelled the mist of deception, and the great body of the people are awakened to a due sense of their danger, and are determined to assert their liberty, if necessary by the sword, but this mean need not be recurred to, for who are their enemies? A junto composed of the lordly and high-minded gentry of the profligate and the needy office-hunters; of men principally who in the late war skulked from the common danger. Would such characters dare to face the majesty of a free people? No. All the conflict would be between the offended justice and generosity of the people, whether these sacrilegious invaders of their dearest rights should suffer the merited punishment or escape with an infamous contempt?

However, as additional powers are necessary to Congress, the people will no doubt see the expediency of calling a convention for this purpose as soon as may be by applying to their representatives in assembly at their next session to appoint a suitable day for the election of such Convention.

Philadelphia, December 27, 1787.   CENTINEL.

CENTINEL, No. VIII.*

To the PEOPLE of PENNSYLVANIA. *Fellow Citizens.*

Under the benign influence of liberty, this country, so recently a rugged wilderness and the abode of savages and wild beasts, has attained to a degree of improvement and greatness, in less than two ages, of which history furnishes no parallel. It is here that human nature may be viewed in all its glory; man assumes the station designed him by the creation, a happy equality and independency pervades the community,

* From "The Independent Gazetteer; or, The Chronicle of Freedom," Jan. 2, 1788.

it is here the human mind, untrammeled by the restraints of arbitrary power, expands every faculty: as the field to fame and riches is open to all, it stimulates universal exertion, and exhibits a lively picture of emulation, industry and happiness. The unfortunate and oppressed of all nations, fly to this grand asylum, where liberty is ever protected, and industry crowned with success.

But as it is by comparison only that men estimate the value of any good, they are not sensible of the worth of those blessings they enjoy, until they are deprived of them; hence from ignorance of the horrors of slavery, nations, that have been in possession of that rarest of blessings, liberty, have so easily parted with it: when groaning under the yoke of tyranny what perils would they not encounter, what consideration would they not give to regain the inestimable jewel they had lost; but the jealously of despotism guards every avenue to freedom, and confirms its empire at the expense of the devoted people, whose property is made instrumental to their misery, for the rapacious hand of power seizes upon every thing; despair presently succeeds, and every noble faculty of the mind being depressed, and all motive to industry and exertion being removed, the people are adapted to the nature of the government, and drag out a listless existence.

If ever America should be enslaved it will be from this cause, that they are not sensible of their peculiar felicity, that they are not aware of the value of the heavenly boon, committed to their care and protection, and if the present conspiracy fails, as I have no doubt will be the case, it will be the triumph of reason and philosophy, as these United States have never felt the iron hand of power, nor experienced the wretchedness of slavery.

The conspirators against our liberties have presumed too much on the maxim that nations do not take the alarm, until they feel oppression; the enlightened citizens of America have on two memorable occasions convinced the tyrants of Europe that they are endued with the faculty of foresight, that they will jealously guard against the first introduction of tyranny, however speciously glossed over, or whatever appearance it may assume. It was not the mere amount of *the duty on stamps*, or *tea* that America opposed, they were considered as signals of approaching despotism, as precedents whereon the superstructure of arbitrary sway was to be reared.

Notwithstanding such illustrious evidence of the good sense and spirit of the people of these United States, and contrary to all former experience of mankind, which demonstrates that it is only by gradual and imperceptible degrees that nations have hitherto been enslaved, except in case of conquest by the sword, the authors of the present conspiracy are attempting to seize upon absolute power at one grasp; impatient of dominion they have adopted a decisive line of conduct, which, if successful, would obliterate every trace of liberty. I congratulate my fellow citizens that the infatuated confidence of their enemies has so blinded their ambition that their defeat must be certain and easy, if imitating the refined policy of successful despots, they had attacked the citadel of liberty by sap, and gradually undermined its outworks, they would have stood a fairer chance of effecting their design; but in this enlightened age thus rashly to attempt to carry the fortress by storm, is folly indeed. They have even exposed some of their batteries prematurely, and thereby unfolded every latent view, for the unlimited power of taxation would alone have been amply sufficient for every purpose; by a proper application of this, the will and pleasure of the rulers would of course have become the supreme law of the land; therefore there was no use in portraying the ultimate object by superadding the form to reality of supremacy in the following clause, viz: That which empowers the new Congress to make all laws that may be necessary and proper for carrying into execution any of their powers, by virtue of which every possible law will be constitutional, as they are to be the sole judges of the propriety of such laws, that which ordains that their acts shall be the supreme law of the land, anything in the laws or constitution of any State to the contrary notwithstanding; that which gives Congress the absolute control over the time and mode of its appointment and election, whereby, independent of any other means, they may establish hereditary despotism; that which authorizes them to keep on foot at all times a standing army; and that which subjects the militia to absolute command, and to accelerate the subjugation of the people, trial by jury in civil cases and the liberty of the press are abolished.

So flagrant, so audacious a conspiracy against the liberties of a free people is without precedent. Mankind in the darkest ages have never been so insulted; even then, tyrants found it necessary to pay some respect to the habits and feelings of the people, and nothing but the name of a Washington could have occasioned a moment's hesitation about the nature of the new plan, or saved its authors from the execration and vengeance of the people, which eventually will prove an aggravation of their treason; for America will resent the imposition practiced upon the unsuspicious zeal of her *illustrious deliverer*, and vindicate her character from the aspersions of these enemies of her happiness and fame.

The advocates of this plan have artfully attempted to veil over the true nature and principles of it with the names of those respectable characters that by consummate cunning and address they have prevailed upon to sign it, and what ought to convince the people of the deception and excite their apprehensions, is that with every advantage which education, the science of government and of law, the knowledge of history and superior talents and endowments, furnish the authors and advocates of this plan with, they have from its publication exerted all their .power and influence to prevent all discussion of the subject, and when this could not be prevented they have constantly avoided the ground of argument and recurred to declamation, sophistry and personal abuse, but principally relied upon the magic of names. Would this have been their conduct, if their cause had been a good one? No, they would have invited investigation and convinced the understandings of the people.

But such policy indicates great ignorance of the good sense and spirit of the people, for if the sanction of every convention throughout the union was obtained by the means these men are practising; yet their triumph would be momentary, the favorite object would still elude their grasp; for a good government founded on fraud and deception could not be maintained without an army sufficiently powerful to compel submission, which the *well-born* of America could not speedily accomplish. However the complexion of several of the more considerable States does not promise even this point of success. The Carolinas, Virginia, Maryland, New York and New Hampshire have by their wisdom in taking a longer time to deliberate, in all probability saved themselves from the disgrace of becoming the dupes of this gilded bait, as experience will evince that it need only be properly examined to be execrated and repulsed.

The merchant, immersed in schemes of wealth, seldom extends his views beyond the immediate object of gain; he blindly pursues his seeming interest, and sees not the latent mischief; therefore it is, that he is the last to take the alarm when public liberty is threatened. This may account for the infatuation of some of our merchants, who, elated with the imaginary prospect of an improved commerce under the new government, overlook all danger: they do not consider that commerce is the hand-maid of liberty, a plant of free growth that withers under the hand of despotism, that every concern of individuals will be sacrificed to the gratification of the men in power, who will institute injurious monopolies and shackle commerce with every device of avarice; and that property of every species will be held at the will and pleasure of rulers.

If the nature of the case did not give birth to these well founded apprehensions, the principles and characters of the authors and advocates of the measure ought. View the monopolizing spirit of the principal of them. See him converting a band, instituted for common benefit, to his own and creatures' emoluments, and by the aid thereof, controlling the credit of the state, and dictating the measures of government. View the vassalage of our merchants, the thraldom of the city of Philadelphia, and the extinction of that spirit of independency in most of its citizens so essential to freedom. View this Collosus attempting to grasp the commerce of

America and meeting with a sudden repulse—in the midst of his immense career, receiving a shock that threatens his very existence. View the desperate fortunes of many of his coadjutors and dependants, particularly the bankrupt situation of the principal instrument under the *great man* in promoting the new government, whose superlative arrogance, ambition and rapacity, would need the spoils of thousands to gratify; view his towering aspect—he would have no bowels of compassion for the oppressed, he would *overlook* all their sufferings. Recollect the strenuous and unremitted exertions of these men, for years past, to destroy our admirable Constitution, whose object is to secure equal liberty and advantages to all, and the great obstacle in the way of their ambitious schemes, and then answer whether these apprehensions are chimerical, whether such characters will be less ambitious, less avaricious, more moderate, when the privileges, property, and every concern of the people of the United States shall lie at their mercy, when they shall be in possession of absolute sway? - CENTINEL.

Philadelphia, December 29, 1787.

CENTINEL, NO. IX.*

To the PEOPLE of PENNSYLVANIA. *Fellow Citizens,*

You have the peculiar felicity of living under the most perfect system of local government in the world; prize then this invaluable blessing as it deserves. Suffer it not to be wrested from you, and the scourge of despotic power substituted in its place, under the specious pretence of vesting the general government of the United States with necessary power; that this would be the inevitable consequence of the establishment of the new constitution, the least consideration of its nature and tendency is sufficient to convince every unprejudiced mind. If you were sufficiently impressed with your present favored situation, I should have no doubt of a proper decision of the question in discussion.

The highest illustration of the excellence of the constitution

* From "The Independent Gazetteer; or, The Chronicle of Freedom." Jan. 8, 1788.

of this commonwealth, is, that from its first establishment, the ambitious and profligate have been united in a constant conspiracy to destroy it; so sensible are they that it is their great enemy, that it is the great palladium of equal liberty, and the property of the people from the rapacious hand of power. The annals of mankind do not furnish a more glorious instance of the triumph of patriotism over the lust of ambition aided by most of the wealth of the State. The few generally prevail over the many by uniformity of council, unremitted and persevering exertion, and superior information and address; but in Pennsylvania the reverse has happened; here the *well-born* have been baffled in all their efforts to prostrate the altar of liberty for the purpose of substituting their own insolent sway that would degrade the freemen of this State into servile dependence upon the *lordly* and *great*. However it is not the nature of ambition to be discouraged; it is ever ready to improve the first opportunity to rear its baneful head and with irritated fury to wreak its vengeance on the votaries of liberty. The present conspiracy is a continental exertion of the *well-born* of America to obtain that darling domination, which they have not been able to accomplish in their respective States. Of what complexion were the deputies of this State in the general convention? *Six* out of *eight* were the inveterate enemies of our inestimable constitution, and the principals of that faction that for ten years past have kept the people in continual alarm for their liberties. Who are the advocates of the new constitution in this State? They consist of the same faction, with the addition of a few deluded well-meaning men, but whose number is daily lessening.

These conspirators have come forward at a most favorable conjuncture, when the state of public affairs has lulled all jealousy of power: Emboldened by the sanction of the august name of a *Washington*, that they have prostituted to their purpose, they have presumed to overleap the usual gradations to absolute power, and have attempted to seize at once upon the supremacy of dominion. The new instrument of government does indeed make a fallacious parade of some remaining privileges, and insults the understandings of the people with the semblance of liberty in some of its artful and deceptive clauses, which form but a flimsy veil over the reality of tyranny, so weakly endeavored to be concealed from the eye of freedom. For, of what avail are the few inadequate stipulations in favor of the rights of the people, when they may be effectually counteracted and destroyed by virtue of other clauses, when these enable the rulers to renounce all dependence on their constituents, and render the latter tenants at will of every concern? The new constitution is in fact a *carte blanche*, a surrender at discretion to the will and pleasure of our rulers: as this has been demonstrated to be the case, by the investigation and discussion that have taken place, I trust the same good sense and spirit which have hitherto enabled the people to triumph over the wiles of ambition, will be again exerted for their salvation. The accounts from various parts of the country correspond with my warmest hopes, and justify my early predictions of the eventual defeat of this scheme of power and office making.

The genius of liberty has sounded the alarm, and the dormant spirit of her votaries is reviving with enthusiastic ardor; the like unanimity which formerly distinguished them in their conflict with foreign despots, promises to crown their virtuous opposition on the present occasions, with signal success. The structure of despotism that has been reared in this state, upon deception and surprise, will vanish like the baseless fabric of a dream and leave not a trace behind.

The parasites and tools of power in Northampton County ought to take warning from the fate of the Carlisle junto, lest like them, they experience the resentment of an injured people. I would advise them not to repeat the imposition of a set of fallacious resolutions as the sense of that county, when in fact, it was the act of a despicable few, with Alexander Paterson at their head, whose achievements at Wyoming, as the meaner instrument of unfeeling avarice, have rendered infamously notorious; but yet, like the election of a Mr. Sedgwick for the little town of Stockbridge, which has been adduced as evidence of the unanimity of the western counties of Massachusetts State in favor of the new Constitution, when the fact is far otherwise, this act of a few individuals will be sounded forth over the continent as a testimony of the zealous attachment of the county of Northampton to the new Constitution. By such wretched and momentary deceptions do these harpies of power endeavor to give the complexion of strength to their cause. To prevent the detection of such impositions, to prevent the reflection of the rays of light from State to State, which, producing general illumination, would dissipate the mist of deception, and thereby prove fatal to the new Constitution, all intercourse between the patriots of America is as far as possible cut off; whilst on the other hand, the conspirators have the most exact information, a common concert is everywhere evident; they move in unison. There is so much mystery in the conduct of these men, such systematic deception and fraud characterizes all their measures, such extraordinary solicitude shown by them to precipitate and surprise the people into a blind and implicit adoption of this government, that it ought to excite the most alarming apprehensions in the minds of all those who think their privileges, property, and welfare worth securing.

It is a fact that can be established, that during almost the whole of the time that the late convention of this State was assembled, the newspapers published in New York by Mr. Greenleaf, which contains the essays written there against the new government, such as the patriotic ones of Brutus, Cincinnatus, Cato, etc., sent as usual by the printer of that place to the printers of this city, miscarried in their conveyance, which prevented the republication in this State of many of these pieces; and since that period great irregularity prevails, and I stand informed that the printers in New York complain that the free and independent newspapers of this city do not come to hand; whilst on the contrary we find the devoted vehicles of despotism pass uninterrupted. I would ask what is the meaning of the new arrangement at the post-office which abridges the circulation of newspapers at this momentous crisis, when our every concern is dependent upon a proper decision of the subject in discussion. No trivial excuse will be admitted; the Centinel will, as from the first approach of despotism, warn his countrymen of the insidious and base strategems that are practicing to hoodwink them out of their liberties.

The more I consider the manœuvres that are practicing, the more am I alarmed—foreseeing that the juggle cannot long be concealed, and that the spirit of the people will not brook the imposition, they have guarded as they suppose against any danger arising from the opposition of the people and rendered their struggles for liberty impotent and ridiculous. What otherwise is the meaning of disarming the militia, for the purpose as it is said of repairing their muskets at such a particular period? Does not the timing of the measure determine the intention? I was ever jealous of the select militia, consisting of infantry and troops of horse, instituted in this city and in some of the counties, without the sanction of law, and officered principally by the devoted instruments of the *well born*, although the illustrious patriotism of one of them has not corresponded with the intention of appointing him. Are not these corps provided to suppress the first efforts of freedom, and to check the spirit of the people until a regular and sufficiently powerful military force shall be embodied to rivet the chains of slavery on a deluded nation? What confirms these apprehensions is the declaration of a certain major, an active instrument in this business, and the echo of the principal conspirators, who has said he should deem the cutting off of five thousand men, as a small sacrifice, a cheap purchase for the establishment of the new Constitution.

Philadelphia, January 5, 1788.   CETINEL.

CENTINEL No. X.*

To the PEOPLE of PENNSYLVANIA. *Fellow Citizens.*

What illustrious evidence and striking demonstration does the present momentous discussion afford of the inestimable value of the liberty of the press? No doubt now remains, but that it will prove the rock of our political salvation.

* From "The Independent Gazetteer; or, The Chronicle of Freedom," Jan. 12, 1788.

Despotism, with its innumerable host of evils, by gliding through the mist of deception, had gained some of the principal works, had made a lodgment in the very citadel of liberty before it was discovered, and was near carrying the fortress by surprise; at this imminent alarming crisis the centries from the watch-towers sounded the alarm, and aroused the dormant votaries of liberty to a due sense of their danger; who, with an alacrity and spirit suited to the exigence, answered to the call, repulsed the enemy, dislodged it from most of its acquisitions, and nothing is now wanting to a total rout and complete defeat, but a general discharge from the artillery of freedom. As the shades of night fly before the approach of the radiant sun, so does despotism before the majesty of enlightened truth; wherever free discussion is allowed, this is invariably the consequence. Since the press has been unshackled in Pennsylvania, what an astonishing transition appears in the sentiments of the people! Infatuation is at an end, execration and indignation have succeeded to blind admiration and mistaken enthusiasm. The rampant insolence of the conspirators is prostrated, black despair has taken possession of many of them, their countenances proclaim their defeat, and express serious apprehension for their personal safety from the rising resentment of injured freemen.

James, the Caledonian, lieutenant general of the myrmidons of power, under Robert, the cofferer, who, with his aid-de-camp, *Gouvero*, the cunning man, has taken the field in Virginia. I say James, in this exigence summonses a grand council of his partisans in this city and represents in the most pathetic moving language, the deplorable situation of affairs, stimulates them to make a vigorous effort to recover the ground they have lost and establish their empire; that for this purpose a generous contribution must be made by all those who expect to taste the sweets of power, or share in the fruits of dominion, in order to form a fund adequate to the great design, that may put them in possession of the darling object; then recommends that a committee be appointed of those who are gifted with Machiavelian talents of those who excel in ingenuity, artifice, sophistry and the refinements of falsehood, who can assume the pleasing appearance of truth and bewilder the people in all the mazes of error; and as the talk will be arduous, and requires various abilities and talents, the business ought to be distributed, and different parts assigned to the members of the committee, as they may be respectively qualified; some by ingenious sophisms to explain away and counteract those essays of patriotism that have struck such general convictions; some to manufacture extracts of letters and notes from correspondents, to give the complexion of strength to their cause, by representing the unanimity of all corners of America in favor of the new constitution; and others to write reams of letters to their tools in every direction, furnishing them with the materials of propagating error and deception; in short, that this committee ought to make the press groan and the whole country reverberate with their productions; thus to overpower truth and liberty by the din of empty sound and the delusion of falsehood.

The conspirators, deceived by their first success, grounded on the unreserved confidence of the people, do not consider that with the detection of their views all chance of success is over; that suspicion once awakened is not so soon to be lulled, but with eagle eye will penetrate all their wiles, and detect their every scheme, however deeply laid or speciously glossed. The labors of their committee will be unavailing: the point of deception is passed, the rays of enlightened patriotism have diffused general illumination. However, this new effort will serve to show the perseverance of ambition and the necessity of constant vigilance in the people for the preservation of their liberty.

Already we recognize the ingenuity and industry of this committee; the papers teem with paragraphs, correspondents, etc., that exhibit a picture which bears no resemblance to the original. If we view this mirror for the representation of the sentiments of the people, a perfect harmony seems to prevail: every body in every place is charmed with the new Constitution—considers it as a gift from heaven, as their only salvation, etc., etc., etc., and I am informed expresses are employing to waft the delusion to the remotest corners. Such a scene of bustle, lying, and activity, was never exhibited since the days of Adam. The contributions to the grand fund are so great, that it is whispered a magazine of all the apparatus of war is to be immediately provided, and if all other means fail, force is to be recurred to, which they hope will successfully terminate the disagreeable discussion of the rights of mankind, of equal liberty, etc., and thus establish a due subordination to the *well born few.*

CENTINEL.

CENTINEL No. XI.*

To the PEOPLE of PENNSYLVANIA. *Fellow Citizens.*

The arguments upon which the advocates of the new constitution the most dwell, are the distresses of the community, the evils of anarchy, and the horrible consequences that would ensue from the dissolution of the union of the States, and the institution of separate confederacies or republics: The unanimity of the federal convention, and the sanction of great names, can be no further urged as an argument after the exposition made by the attorney-general of Maryland,† who was a member of that convention; he has opened such a scene of discord and accommodation of republicanism to despotism as must excite the most serious apprehensions in every patriotic mind. The first argument has been noticed in the preceding essays; wherein it is shown that this is not the criterion whereby to determine the merits of the new constitution; that notwithstanding the reality of the distresses of the people, the new constitution may not only be inadequate as a remedy, but destructive of liberty, and the completion of misery. The remaining two arguments will be discussed in this number; their futility elucidated; and thus the medium of deception being dissipated, the public attention, with undirected, undiminished force, will be directed to the proper object, will be confined to the consideration of the

---

* From "The Independent Gazetteer; or, The Chronicle of Freedom," Jan. 16, 1788.

† Luther Martin. See his Genuine Information for the people of Maryland, etc., etc.

nature and construction of the plan of government itself, the question will then be, whether this plan be calculated for our welfare, or misery; whether it is the temple of liberty, or the structure of despotism? and as the former, or the latter, shall appear to be the case, to adopt or reject it accordingly, otherwise to banish the demon of domination by suitable amendments and qualifications.

The evils of anarchy have been portrayed with all the imagery of language in the glowing colors of eloquence; the affrighted mind is thence led to clasp the new Constitution as the instrument of deliverance, as the only avenue to safety and happiness. To avoid the possible and transitory evils of one extreme, it is seduced into the certain and permanent misery necessarily attendant on the other. A state of anarchy from its very nature can never be of long continuance; the greater its violence the shorter the duration; order and security are immediately sought by the distracted people beneath the shelter of equal laws and the salutary restraints of regular government, and if this be not attainable absolute power is assumed by the *one*, or a *few*, who shall be the most enterprising and successful. If anarchy, therefore, were the inevitable consequence of rejecting the new Constitution, it would be infinitely better to incur it, for even then there would be at least the chance of a good government rising out of licentiousness; but to rush at once into despotism because there is a bare possibility of anarchy ensuing from the rejection, or from what is yet more visionary, the small delay that would be occasioned by a revision and correction of the proposed system of government is so superlatively weak, so fatally blind, that it is astonishing any person of common understanding should suffer such an imposition to have the least influence on his judgment; still more astonishing that so flimsy and deceptive a doctrine should make converts among the enlightened freemen of America, who have so long enjoyed the blessings of liberty; but when I view among such converts men otherwise *pre-eminent* it raises a blush for the weakness of humanity that these, her brightest ornaments, should be so dimsighted to what is self-evident to most men, that such imbecility of judgment should appear where so much perfection was looked for; this ought to teach us to depend more on our own judgment and the nature of the case than upon the opinions of the greatest and best of men, who, from *constitutional* infirmities or *particular* situations, may sometimes view an object through a delusive medium, but the opinions of great men are more frequently the dictates of ambition or private interest.

The source of the apprehensions of this so much dreaded anarchy would upon investigation be found to arise from the artful suggestions of designing men, and not from a rational probability grounded on the actual state of affairs; the least reflection is sufficient to detect the fallacy to show that there is no one circumstance to justify the prediction of such an event. On the contrary a short time will evince, to the utter dismay and confusion of the conspirators, that a perseverance in cramming down their scheme of power upon the freemen of this State will inevitably produce *an anarchy* destructive of their darling domination, and *may* kindle a flame prejudicial to their safety; they should be cautious not to trespass too far on the forbearance of freemen when wresting their dearest concerns, but prudently retreat from the gathering storm.

The other specter that has been raised to terrify and alarm the people out of the exercise of their judgment on this great occasion, is the dread of our splitting into separate confederacies or republics, that might become rival powers and consequently liable to mutual wars from the usual motives of contention. This is an event still more improbable than the foregoing; it is a presumption unwarranted, either by the situation of affairs, or the sentiments of the people; no disposition leading to it exists; the advocates of the new constitution seem to view such a separation with horror, and its opponents are strenuously contending for a confederation that shall embrace all America under its comprehensive and salutary protection. This hobgoblin appears to have sprung from the deranged brain of *Publius*,* a New York writer, who,

* The signature under which Hamilton, Jay and Madison issued the Essays that form The Federalist.

mistaking sound for argument, has with Herculean labor accumulated myriads of unmeaning sentences, and *mechanically*
endeavored to force conviction by a torrent of misplaced
words; he might have spared his readers the fatigue of wad-
ing through his long-winded disquisitions on the direful
effects of the contentions of inimical states, as totally inapplicable to the subject he was *professedly* treating; this
writer has devoted much time, and wasted more paper in
combating chimeras of his own creation.   However, for the
sake of argument, I will admit that the necessary consequence of rejecting or delaying the establishment of the new
constitution, would be the dissolution of the union, and the
institution of even rival and inimical republics; yet ought
such an apprehension, if well founded, to drive us into the
fangs of despotism? Infinitely preferable would be occasional
wars to such an event; the former, although a severe scourge,
is transient in its continuance, and in its operation partial,
but a small proportion of the community are exposed to
its greatest horrors, and yet fewer experience its greatest
evils; the latter is permanent and universal misery, without
remission or exemption: as passing clouds obscure for a time
the splendor of the sun, so do wars interrupt the welfare of
mankind; but despotism is a settled gloom that totally ex-
tinguishes happiness, not a ray of comfort can penetrate to
cheer the dejected mind; the goad of power with unabating
rigor insists upon the utmost exaction, like a merciless task-
master, is continually inflicting the lash, and is never satiated
with the feast of unfeeling domination, or the most abject
servility.

The celebrated Lord Kaims, whose disquisitions on human
nature evidence extraordinary strength of judgment and depth
of investigation, says that a continual *civil* war, which is the
most destructive and horrible scene of human discord, is preferable to the uniformity of wretchedness and misery attendant upon despotism; of all *possible* evils, as I observed in my
first number, *this* is the worst and the most to be *dreaded*.

I congratulate my fellow citizens that a good government,
the greatest earthly blessing, may be so easily obtained, that

our circumstances are so favorable, that nothing but the folly of the conspirators can produce anarchy or civil war, which would presently terminate in their destruction and the permanent harmony of the state, alone interrupted by their ambitious machinations.

In a former number I stated a charge of a very heinous nature, and highly prejudicial to the public welfare, and at this great crisis peculiarly alarming and threatening to liberty. I mean the suppression of the circulation of the newspapers from State to State by the of—c—rs of the P—t O—ce, who in violation of their duty and integrity, have prostituted their of—ces to forward the nefarious design of enslaving their countrymen, by thus cutting off all communication by the usual vehicle between the patriots of America; I find that notwithstanding that public appeal, they persevere in this villainous and daring practice. The newspapers of the other States that contain any useful information are still withheld from the printers of this State, and I see by the annunciation of the editor of Mr. Greenleaf's patriotic New York paper, that the printers of that place are still treated in like manner. This informs his readers that but two southern papers have come to hand, and that they contain no information, which he affects to ascribe to the negligence of the p—t boy, not caring to quarrel with the p—t m—t—r g—l.

CENTINEL.

Philadelphia, January 12, 1788.

CENTINEL No. XII. *

To the PEOPLE of PENNSYLVANIA. *Fellow Citizens.*

Conscious guilt has taken the alarm, thrown out the signal of distress, and even appealed to the generosity of patriotism. The authors and abettors of the new Constitution shudder at the term *conspirators* being applied to them, as it designates their true character, and seems prophetic of the catastrophe; they read their fate in the epithet.

In despair they are weakly endeavoring to screen their

* From "The Independent Gazetter, or The Chronicle of Freedom," Jan. 23, 1788.

criminality by interposing the shield of the virtues of a Washington, in representing his concurrence in the proposed system of government as evidence of the purity of their intentions; but this impotent attempt to degrade the brightest ornament of his country to a base level with themselves will be considered as an aggravation of their treason, and an insult on the good sense of the people, who have too much discernment not to make a just discrimination between the honest mistaken zeal of the patriot and the flagitious machinations of an ambitious junto, and will resent the imposition that Machiavelian arts and consummate cunning have practiced upon our *illustrious chief.*

The term *conspirators* was not, as has been alleged, rashly or inconsiderately adopted; it is the language of dispassionate and deliberate reason, influenced by the purest patriotism; the consideration of the nature and construction of the new Constitution naturally suggests the epithet; its justness is strikingly illustrated by the conduct of the patrons of this plan of government, but if any doubt had remained whether this epithet is merited, it is now removed by the very uneasiness it occasions; this is a confirmation of its propriety. Innocence would have nothing to dread from such a stigma, but would triumph over the shafts of malice.

The conduct of men is the best clue to their principles. The system of deception that has been practiced; the constant solicitude shown to prevent information diffusing its salutary light are evidence of a conspiracy beyond the arts of sophistry to palliate, or the ingenuity of falsehood to invalidate; the means practiced to establish the new Constitution are demonstrative of the principles and designs of its authors and abettors.

At the time, says Mr. Martin (deputy from the State of Maryland in the general convention), when the public prints were announcing our perfect unanimity, discord prevailed to such a degree that the minority were upon the point of appealing to the public against the machinations of ambition. By such a base imposition, repeated in every newspaper and reverberated from one end of the union to the other, was the people lulled into a false confidence, into an implicit reliance upon the wisdom and patriotism of the convention; and when ambition, by her deceptive wiles, had succeeded to usher forth the new system of government with apparent unanimity of sentiment, the public delusion was complete. The most extravagant fictions were palmed upon the people, the seal of divinity was even ascribed to the new Constitution; a felicity more than human was to ensue from its establishment; overlooking the real cause of our difficulties and burthens, which have their proper remedy, the people were taught that the new Constitution would prove a mine of wealth and prosperity equal to every want, or the most sanguine desire; that it would effect what can only be produced by the exertion of industry and the practice of economy.

The conspirators, aware of the danger of delay, that allowing time for a rational investigation would prove fatal to their designs, precipitated the establishment of the new Constitution with all possible celerity; in Massachusetts the deputies of that convention, who are to give the final fiat in behalf of that great State to a measure upon which their dearest concerns depend, were elected by express in the first moments of blind enthusiasm; similar conduct has prevailed in the other States as far as circumstances permitted.

If the foregoing circumstances did not prove a conspiracy, there are others that must strike conviction in the most unsuspicious. Attempts to prevent discussion by shackling the press ought ever to be a signal of alarm to freemen, and considered as an annunciation of meditated tyranny; this is a truth that the uniform experience of mankind has established beyond the possibility of doubt. Bring the conduct of the authors and abettors of the new constitution to this test, let this be the criterion of their criminality, and every patriotic mind must unite in branding them with the stigma of conspirators against the public liberties. No stage of this business but what has been marked with every exertion of influence and device of ambition to suppress information and intimidate public discussion; the virtue and firmness of some of the printers rose superior to the menaces of violence and the lucre of private interest; when every means failed to shackle the press, the free and independent papers were attempted to be demolished by withdrawing all the subscriptions to them within the sphere of the influence of the conspirators; fortunately for the cause of liberty and truth, these daring high-handed attempts have failed except in one instance, where, from a peculiarity of circumstances, ambition has triumphed. Under the flimsy pretense of vindicating the character of a contemptible drudge of party, rendered ridiculous by his superlative folly in the late convention, of which the statement given in the Pennsylvania Herald was confessedly a faithful representation, this newspaper has been silenced * by some hundreds of its subscribers (who it seems are generally among the devoted tools of party, or those who are obliged from their thraldom to yield implicit assent to the mandates of the junto) withdrawing their support from it; by this stroke the conspirators have suppressed the publication of the most valuable debates of the late convention, which would have been given in course by the editor of that paper, whose stipend now ceasing, he cannot afford without compensation the time and attention necessary to this business.

Every patriotic person who had an opportunity to hearing that illustrations advocate of liberty and his country, Mr. Findley, must sensibly regret that his powerful arguments are not to extend beyond the confined walls of the State-House, where they could have so limited an effect; that the United States could not have been his auditory through the medium of the press. I anticipate the answer of the conspirators; they will tell you that this could not be their motive for silencing this paper, as the whole of the debates were taken down in short-hand by another person and published, but the public are not to be so easily duped, they will not receive a spurious as an equivalent for a genuine production; equal solicitude was expressed for the publication of the former as for the suppression of the latter—the public will judge of the motives.

* *The Herald it is said is to be discontinued the 23d instant (the editor is already dismissed).*

That investigation into the nature and construction of the new constitution, which the conspirators have so long and zealously struggled against, has, notwithstanding their partial success, so far taken place as to ascertain the enormity of their criminality. That system which was pompously displayed as the perfection of government, proves upon examition to be the most odious system of tyranny that was ever projected, a many-headed hydra of despotism, whose complicated and various evils would be infinitely more oppressive and afflictive than the scourge of any single tyrant: the objects of dominion would be tortured to gratify the calls of ambition and the cravings of power of rival despots contending for the sceptre of superiority; the devoted people would experience a distraction of misery.

No wonder then that such a discovery should excite uneasy apprehensions in the minds of the conspirators, for such an attempt against the public liberties is unprecedented in history; it is a crime of the blackest dye, as it strikes at the happiness of millions and the dignity of human nature, as it was intended to deprive the inhabitants of so large a portion of the globe of the choicest blessings of life and the oppressed of all nations of an asylum.

The explicit language of the Centinel during the empire of delusion was not congenial to the feelings of the people, but truth when it has free scope is all powerful, it enforces conviction in the most prejudiced mind; he foresaw the consequences of an exertion of the good sense and understanding of the people, and predicted the defeat of the measure he ventured to attack, when it was deemed sacred by most men and the certain ruin of any who should dare to lisp a word against it: he has persevered through every discouraging appearance, and has now the satisfaction to find his countrymen are aware of their danger and are taking measures for their security.

Since writing the foregoing. I am informed that the printer of the Pennsylvania Herald is not quite decided whether he will drop his paper; he wishes, and perhaps will be enabled, to perseverve; however, the conspirators have effected their purpose; the editor is dismissed and the debates of the convention thereby suppressed.

CENTINEL.

CENTINEL, No. XIII.*

To the PEOPLE of PENNSYLVANIA. *Fellow Citizens.*

The conspirators are putting your good sense, patriotism and spirit to the severest test. So bold a game of deception, so decisive a stroke for despotic power, was never before attempted among enlightened freemen. Can there be apathy so indifferent as not to be roused into indignation, or prejudice so blind as not to yield to the glaring evidence of a flagitious conspiracy against the public liberties? The audacious and high-handed measures practiced to suppress information, and intimidate discussion, would in any other circumstances than the present, have kindled a flame fatal to such daring invaders of our dearest privileges.

The conspirators having been severely galled and checked in their career by the artillery of freedom, have made more vigorous and successful efforts to silence her batteries, while falsehood with all her delusions is making new and greater exertions in favor of ambition. On the one hand, every avenue to information is as far as possible cut off; the usual communication between the states, through the medium of the press, is in a great measure destroyed by a new arrangement at the Post Office—scarcely a newspaper is suffered to pass† by this conveyance, and the arguments of a Findley, a Whitehill and a Smilie, that bright constellation of patriots, are suppressed, and a spurious publication substituted; and on the other hand the select committee are assiduously employed in manufacturing deception in all its ensnaring colors, and having an adequate fund at their command, they are deluging the country with their productions. The only newspaper that circulates extensively out of the city is kept running over with deceptive inventions. Doctor Puff, the paragraphist,

* From "The Independent Gazetteer; or, The Chronicle of Freedom," Jan. 30, 1788.

† For the truth of this charge I appeal to the printers.

has scarcely slept since his appointment, having received orders to work double tides; beneath his creative pen thousands of correspondents rise into view, who all harmonize in their sentiments and information about the new constitution; but the chief reliance is on James the Caledonian, who can to appearance destroy all distinction between liberty and despotism, and make the latter pass for the former, who can bewilder truth in all the mazes of sophistry, and render the plainest propositions problematical. He, chameleon-like, can vary his appearance at pleasure, and assume any character for the purposes of deception. In the guise of a *Conciliator*, in the Independent Gazetteer, he professes great candor and moderation, admits some of the principal objections to the new constitution to be well founded and insidiously proposes a method to remove them, which is to consider the first Congress under the new constitution as a convention, competent to supply all defects in the system of government. This is really a discovery that does honor to his invention. What! a legislative declaration or law a basis upon which to rest our dearest liberties? Does he suppose the people have so little penetration as not to see through so flimsy a delusion, that such a security would amount to no more than the will and pleasure of their rulers, who might repeat this *fundamental* sanction whenever ambition stimulated? In the feigned *character* of *A Freeman*, he combats the weighty arguments of the minority of the late convention, by a mere play upon words, carefully avoiding the real merits of the question; and we moreover trace him in a variety of miscellaneous productions in every shape and form; he occasionally assists Doctor Puff in the fabrication of extracts of letters, paragraphs, correspondents, etc., etc.

So gifted and with such a claim of merit from his extraordinary and unwearied exertions in the cause of despotism, who so suitable or deserving of the office of Chief Justice of the United States? How congenial would such a post be to the principles and dispositions of James! Here he would be both judge and jury, sovereign arbiter in law and equity. In this capacity he may satiate his vengeance on patriotism for the opposition given to his projects of dominion. Here he may gratify his superlative arrogance and contempt of mankind, by trampling upon his fellow creatures with impunity, here he may give the finishing stroke to liberty, and silence the offensive complaints of violated justice and innocence, by adding the sanction of his office to the rapacity of power and the wantonness of oppression; there will be no intervening jury to shield the innocent, or procure redress to the injured.

Fellow citizens, although the conspirators and their abettors are not sufficiently numerous to endanger our liberties by an open and forcible attack on them, yet when the characters of which they are composed and the methods they are practicing are considered, it ought to occasion the most serious alarm, and stimulate to an immediate, vigorous, and united exertion of the patriotic part of the community for the security of their rights and privileges. Societies ought to be instituted in every county, and a reciprocity of sentiments and information maintained between such societies, whereby the patriots throughout Pennsylvania, being mutually enlightened and invigorated, would form an invincible bulwark to liberty, and by unity of counsel and exertion might the better procure and secure to themselves and to unborn ages the blessings of a good federal government. Nothing but such a system of conduct can frustrate the machinations of an ambitious junto, who, versed in Machiavellian arts, can varnish over with the semblance of freedom the most despotic instrument of government ever projected; who cannot only veil over their own ambitious purposes, but raise an outcry against the real patriots for interested views, when they are advocating the cause of liberty and of their country by opposing a scheme of arbitrary power and office making; who can give the appearance of economy to the introduction of a numerous and permanent standing army, and the institution of lucrative, needless offices to provide for the swarms of gaping, almost famished expectants, who have been campaigning it for ten years without success against our inestimable State Constitution, as a reward for their persevering toils, but particularly for their zeal on the present occasion, and also as a phalanx to tyranny;

and who, notwithstanding the testimony of uniform experience, evinces the necessity of restrictions on those entrusted with power, and a due dependence of the deputy on the constituent being maintained to ensure the public welfare; who, notwithstanding the fate that liberty has ever met from the remissness of the people and the persevering nature of ambition, who, ever on the watch, grasps at every avenue to supremacy. I say, notwithstanding such evidence before them of the folly of mankind, so often duped by similar arts, the conspirators have had the address to inculcate the opinion that forms of government are no security for the public liberties; that the administration is everything; that, although there would be no responsibility under the new Constitution —no restriction on the powers of the government, whose will and pleasure would be literally the law of the land, yet that we should be perfectly safe and happy. That as our rules would be made of the same corrupt materials as ourselves, they certainly could not abuse the trust reposed in them, but would be the most self-denying order of beings ever created; with your purses at their absolute disposal, and your liberties at their discretion, they would be proof against the charms of money and the allurements of power. However, if such Utopian ideas should prove chimerical, and the people should find the yoke too heavy, they might at pleasure alleviate or even throw it off. In short, the conspirators have displayed so much ingenuity on this occasion, that if it had not been for the patriotism and firmness of some of the printers, which gave an opportunity to enlightened truth to come forward, and by her invincible powers to detect the sophistry and expose the fallacy of such impositions, liberty must have been overcome by the wiles of ambition, and this land of freemen have become the miserable abode of slaves.

CENTINEL.

Philadelphia, January 26, 1788.

CENTINEL, No. XIV.*

To the PEOPLE of PENNSYLVANIA. *Fellow Citizens.*

I am happy to find the comment that I have made upon the nature and tendency of the new constitution, and my suspicions of the principles and designs of its authors, are fully confirmed by the evidence of the Honorable LUTHER MARTIN, esquire, late deputy in the general convention. He has laid open the conclave, exposed the dark scene within, developed the mystery of the proceedings, and illustrated the machinations of ambition. His public spirit has drawn upon him the rage of the conspirators, for daring to remove the veil of secrecy, and announcing to the public the meditated, gilded mischief: all their powers are exerting for his destruction, the mint of calumny is assiduously engaged in coining scandal to blacken his character, and thereby to invalidate his testimony; but this illustrious patriot will rise superior to all their low arts, and be the better confirmed in the good opinion and esteem of his fellow-citizens, upon whose gratitude he has an additional claim by standing forth their champion at a crisis when most men would have shrunk from such a duty. Mr. Martin has appealed to general Washington for the truth of what he has advanced, and undaunted by the threats of his and his country's enemies, is nobly persevering in the cause of liberty and mankind. I would earnestly recommend it to all well meaning persons to read his communication, as the most satisfactory and certain method of forming a just opinion on the present momentous question, particularly the three or four last continuances, as they go more upon the general principles and tendency of the new constitution. I have in former numbers alluded to some passages in this publication; I shall in this number quote some few others, referring to the work itself for a more lengthy detail. The following paragraphs are extracted from the continuances republished in the "Independent Gazetteer" of the 25th January, and the "Pennsylvania Packet" of the 1st February instant, viz.

* From "The Independent Gazetteer; or, The Chronicle of Freedom," Feb. 5, 1788.

" By the eighth section of this article, Congress is to have power to lay and collect taxes, duties, imposts, and excises. When we met in convention after our adjournment, to receive the report of the committee of detail, the members of that committee were requested to inform us what powers were meant to be vested in Congress by the word duties in this section, since the word imposts extended to duties on goods imported, and by another part of the system no duties on exports were to be laid. In answer to this inquiry we were informed, that it was meant to give the general government the power of laying stamp duties on paper, parchment and vellum. We then proposed to have the power inserted in express words, lest disputes hereafter might arise on the subject, and that the meaning might be understood by all who were to be affected by it; but to this it was objected, because it was said that the word stamp would probably sound odiously in the ears of many of the inhabitants, and be a cause of objection. By the power of imposing stamp duties the Congress will have a right to declare that no wills, deeds, or other instruments of writing, shall be good and valid, without being stamped—that without being reduced to writing and being stamped, no bargain, sale, transfer of property or contract of any kind or nature whatsoever shall be binding; and also that no exemplifications of records, depositions, or probates of any kind shall be received in evidence, unless they have the same solemnity. They may likewise oblige all proceedings of a judicial nature to be stamped to give them effect—those stamp duties may be imposed to any amount they please—and under the pretense of securing the collection of these duties, and to prevent the laws which imposed them from being evaded, the Congress may bring the decision of all questions relating to the conveyance, disposition and rights of property, and every question relating to contracts between man and man, into the courts of the general government—their inferior courts in the first instance and the superior court by appeal. By the power to lay and collect imposts, they may impose duties on any or every article of commerce imported into these states, to what amount they

please. By the power to lay excises, a power very odious in
its nature, since it authorizes officers to go into your houses,
your kitchens, your cellars, and to examine into your private
concerns, the Congress may impose duties on every article of
use or consumption; on the food that we eat—on the liquors
we drink—on the clothes we wear—on the glass which en-
lightens our houses—on the hearths necessary for our warmth
and comfort. By the power to lay and collect taxes, they
may proceed to direct taxation on every individual, either by
a capitation tax on their heads, or an assessment on their
property. By this part of the section, therefore, the government has a power to lay what duties they please on goods imported—to lay what duties they please afterwards on whatever we use or consume—to impose stamp duties to what
amount they please, and in whatever cases they please—
afterwards to impose on the people direct taxes, by capitation
tax, or by assessment, to what amount they choose, and thus
to sluice them at every vein as long as they have a drop of
blood, without any control, limitation or restraint—while all
the officers for collecting these taxes, stamp duties, imposts
and excises, are to be appointed by the general government,
under its direction, not accountable to the states; nor is there
even a security that they shall be citizens of the respective
states, in which they are to exercise their offices; at the same
time the construction of every law imposing any and all
these taxes and duties, and directing the collection of them,
and every question arising thereon, and on the conduct of the
officers appointed to execute these laws, and to collect these
taxes and duties so various in their kinds, are taken away
from the courts of justice of the different states, and confined
to the courts of the general government, there to be heard
and determined by judges holding their offices under the appointment, not of the states, but of the general government.

"Many of the members, and myself in the number, thought
that the states were much better judges of the circumstances
of their citizens, and what sum of money could be collected
from them by direct taxation, and of the manner in which it
could be raised with the greatest ease and convenience to

their citizens, than the general government could be; and
that the general government ought not in any case to have
the power of laying direct taxes, but in that of the delinquency of a state. Agreeable to this sentiment, I brought in
a proposition on which a vote of the convention was taken.
The proposition was as follows: 'And whenever the legislature
of the United States shall find it necessary that revenue should
be raised by direct taxation, having appointed the same by
the above rule, requisitions shall be made of the respective
states to pay into the continental treasury their respective
quotas within a time in the said requisition to be specified,
and in case of any of the states failing to comply with such
requisition, then and then only, to have power to devise and
pass acts directing the mode and authorizing the collection of
the same.' Had this proposition been acceded to, the dangerous and oppressive power in the general government of
imposing direct taxes on the inhabitants, which it now enjoys
in all cases, would have been only vested in it in case of the
non-compliance of a state, as a punishment for its delinquency, and would have ceased that moment that the state
complied with the requisition. But the proposition was rejected by a majority, consistent with their aim and desire of
increasing the power of the general government as far as possible, and destroying the powers and influence of the states.
And though there is a provision that all duties, imposts and
excises shall be uniform, that is, to be laid to the same
amount on the same articles in each state, yet this will not
prevent Congress from having it in their power to cause them
to fall very unequal and much heavier on some states than on
others, because these duties may be laid on articles but little
or not at all used in some states, and of absolute necessity for
the use and consumption of others, in which case the first
would pay little or no part of the revenue arising therefrom,
while the whole or nearly the whole of it would be paid by
the last, to wit: The states which use and consume the articles on which the imposts and excises are laid."

Another extract, viz:

"But even this provision, apparently for the security of

the State governments, inadequate as it is, is entirely left at the mercy of the general government, for by the fourth section of the first article, it is expressly provided, that the Congress shall have a power to make and alter all regulations concerning the time and manner of holding elections for senators—a provision expressly looking forward to, and I have no doubt designed for the utter extinction and abolition of all State governments. Nor will this, I believe, be doubted by any person, when I inform you that some of the warm advocates and patrons of the system in convention, strenuously opposed the choice of the senators by the State legislatures, insisting that the State governments ought not to be introduced in any manner so as to be component parts of, or instruments for, carrying into execution the general government. Nay, so far were the friends of the system from pretending that they meant it or considered it as a federal system, that on the question being proposed, 'that a union of the States merely federal ought to be the sole object of the exercise of the powers vested in the convention,' it was negatived by a majority of the members, and it was resolved 'that a national government ought to be formed.' Afterwards the word 'national' was struck out by them, because they thought the word might tend to alarm; and although now they who advocate the system pretend to call themselves federalists, in convention the distinction was just the reverse: those who opposed the system, were there considered and styled the federal party; those who advocated it, the anti-federal.

"Viewing it as a national, not a federal government; as calculated and designed not to protect and preserve, but to abolish and annihilate the State governments, it was opposed for the following reasons:—It was said that this continent was much too extensive for one national government, which should have sufficient power and energy to pervade and hold in obedience and subjection all its parts, consistent with the enjoyment and preservation of liberty; that the genius and habits of the people of America were opposed to such a government; that during their connection with Great Britain, they had been accustomed to have all their concerns transacted within a narrow circle—their colonial districts; they had been accustomed to have their seats of government near them, to which they might have access without much inconvenience, when their business should require it; that at this time we find if a county is rather large, the people complain of the inconvenience, and clamor for a division of their county, or for a removal of the place where their courts are held, so as to render it more central and convenient; that in those States, the territory of which is extensive, as soon as the population increases remote from the seat of government, the inhabitants are urgent for a removal of the seat of their government, or to be erected into a new State. As a proof of this, the inhabitants of the western parts of Virginia and North Carolina, of Vermont and the province of Maine, were instances; even the inhabitants of the western parts of Pennsylvania, who it was said already seriously look forward to the time when they shall either be erected into a new State, or have their seat of government removed to the Susquehanna. If the inhabitants of the different States consider it as a grievance to attend a county court, or the seat of their own government, when a little inconvenient, can it be supposed they would ever submit to have a national government established, the seat of which would be more than a thousand miles removed from some of them? It was insisted that governments of a republican nature are those best calculated to preserve the freedom and happiness of the citizen; that governments of this kind are only calculated for a territory but small in its extent; that the only method by which an extensive continent like America could be connected and united together consistent with the principles of freedom, must be by having a number of strong and energetic State governments for securing and protecting the rights of the individuals forming those governments, and for regulating all their concerns, and a strong, energetic federal government over those States for the protection and preservation, and for regulating the common concerns of the States; it was further insisted, that even if it was possible to effect a total abolition of the State governments at this time, and to establish one general government over the people of America, it could not long subsist, but in a little time would again be broken into a variety of governments of a smaller extent, similar in some manner to the present situation of this continent: the principal difference in all probability would be that the governments, so established, being effected by some violent convulsions, might not be formed on principles so favorable to liberty as those of our present State governments; that this ought to be an important consideration to such of the states who had excellent governments, which was the case with Maryland and most others, whatever it might be to persons who, disapproving of their particular State government, would be willing to hazard everything to overturn and destroy it. These reasons, sir, influenced me to vote against two branches in the legislature, and against every part of the system which was repugnant to the principles of a federal government. Nor was there a single argument urged, or reason assigned, which to my mind was satisfactory, to prove that a good government on federal principles was unattainable—the whole of their arguments only proving, what none of us controverted, that our federal government as originally formed was defective, and wanted amendment. However, a majority of the convention hastily and inconsiderately, without condescending to make a fair trial, in their great wisdom, decided that a kind of government which a Montesquieu and a Price have declared the best calculated of any to preserve internal liberty, and to enjoy external strength and security, and the only one by which a large continent can be connected and united consistent with the principles of liberty, was totally impracticable, and they acted accordingly."

After such information, what are we to think of the declarations of Mr. Wilson, who assured our state convention that it was neither the intention of the authors of the new constitution, nor its tendency, to establish a consolidated or national government, founded upon the destruction of the State governments, that such could not have been the design of the general convention he said was certain, because the testimony of experience, the opinions of the most celebrated writers, and the nature of the case demonstrated in the clearest manner that so extensive a territory as these United States include could not be governed by any other mode than a confederacy of republics consistent with the principles of freedom, and that their own conviction was that nothing short of the supremacy of despotism could connect and bind together this country under ONE GOVERNMENT? Has any one a doubt now remaining of the guilt of the conspirators!

The O——rs of the P—t O——ce, fearful of the consequences of their conduct, are taking measures to invalidate the charge made against them. As this is a matter of the highest importance to the public, it will be necessary to state the charge and the evidence. In two of my former numbers, I asserted that the patriotic newspapers of this city and that of New York miscarried in their passage, whilst the vehicles of despotism, meaning those newspapers in favor of the new constitution, passed as usual; and it was particularly asserted that the patriotic essays of Brutus, Cincinnatus, Cato, etc., published at New York, were withheld during the greatest part of the time that our state convention sat; and in a late number, I further asserted that since the late arrangement at the P—t O——ce, scarcely a newspaper was suffered to pass by the usual conveyance, and for the truth of this last charge I appealed to the printers; however, I understand this last is not denied or controverted. When the dependence of the printers on the P—t O——ce is considered, the injury they may sustain by incurring the displeasure of these of—rs, and when to this is added that of the complexion of the printers in respect to the new constitution, that most of them are zealous in prompting its advancement, it can scarcely be expected that they would volunteer it against the P—t O—rs, or refuse their names to a certificate exculpating the o—rs; accordingly we find that most of the printers have signed a certificate that the newspapers arrived as usual prior to the first of January, when the new arrangement took place; however, the printer of the Freeman's Journal when applied to, had the spirit to refuse his name to the establishment of a falsehood, and upon being called upon to specify the missing papers, particularly during the sitting of the State convention, he pointed out and offered to give a list of a considerable number, instancing no less than seven successive Greenleaf's patriotic New York papers, besides others occasionally withheld from him; Colonel Oswald was out of town when his family was applied to, or, I have no doubt, he would have observed a similar conduct. But there is a fact that will invalidate any certificate that can be procured on this occasion, and is alone demonstrative of the suppression of the patriotic newspapers. The opponents to the new constitution in this state were anxious to avail themselves of the well-written essays of the New York patriots, such as Brutus, Cincinnatus, Cato, etc., and with that view were attentive to have them republished here as soon as they came to hand, and especially during the sitting of our state convention, when they would have been the most useful to the cause of liberty by operating on the members of that convention; a recurrence to the free papers of this city at that period, will show a great chasm in these republications, owing to the miscarriage of Greenleaf's New York papers. Agreeable to my assertions it will appear that for the greatest part of the time that our state convention sat, scarcely any of the number of Brutus, Cincinnatus, Cato, etc., were republished in this city; the fifth number of Cincinnatus, that contained very material information about the finances of the union, which strikes at some of the principal arguments in favor of the new constitution, which was published at New York the 29th November, was not republished here until the 15th December following, two or three days after the convention rose, and so of most of the other numbers of this and the other signatures; so great was the desire of the opponents here to republish them, that the fourth number of Cincinnatus was republished so lately as in Mr. Bailey's last paper, which with other missing numbers were procured by private hands from New York, and in two or three instances, irregular numbers were republished. The new arrangement at the P—t O—ce, novel in its nature, and peculiarly injurious by the suppression of information at this great crisis of public affairs, is a circumstance highly presumptive of the truth of the other charge.   Centinel.

CENTINEL, No. XV.*

To the PEOPLE of PENNSYLVANIA. *Fellow Citizens.*

There are few of the maxims or opinions we hold, that are the result of our own investigation or observation, and even those we adopt from others are seldom on a conviction of their truth or propriety, but from the fascination of example and the influence of what is or appears to be the general sentiment. The science of government being the most abstruse and unobvious of all others, mankind are more liable to be imposed upon by the artful and designing in systems and regulations of government, than on any other subject: hence a jealousy of innovation confirmed by uniform experience prevails in most communities; this reluctance to change has been found to be the greatest security of free governments, and the principal bulwark of liberty; for the aspiring and ever-restless spirit of ambition would otherwise, by her deceptive wiles and ensnaring glosses, triumph over the freest and most enlightened people. It is the peculiar misfortune of the people of these United States, at this awful crisis of public affairs, to have lost this useful, this absolutely necessary jealousy of innovation in government, and thereby to lie at the mercy and be exposed to all the artifices of ambition, without this usual shield to protect them from imposition. The conspirators, well aware of their advantage, have seized the favorable moment, and by the most unparalleled arts of deception, have obtained the sanction of the conventions of several states to the most tyrannic system of government ever projected.

The magic of great names, the delusion of falsehood, the suppression of information, precipitation and fraud have been the instruments of this partial success, the pillars whereon the structure of tyranny has been so far raised. Those influential vehicles, the newspapers, with few exceptions, have been devoted to the cause of despotism, and by the subserviency of the P—— O——, the usefulness of the patriotic

* From "The Independent Gazetteer; or, The Chronicle of Freedom," Feb. 22, 1788.

newspapers has been confined to the places of their publication, whilst falsehood and deception have had universal circulation, without the opportunity of refutation. The feigned unanimity of one part of America, has been represented to produce the acquiescence of another, and so mutally to impose upon the whole by the force of example.

The adoption of the new constitution by the convention of the state of Massachusetts, by a majority of nineteen out of near four hundred members, and that too qualified by a number of propositions of amendment, cannot afford the conspirators much cause for triumph, and especially when all the circumstances under which it has been obtained are considered. The late alarming disorders which distracted that state, and even threatened subversion of all order and government, and were with difficulty suppressed, occasioned the greatest consternation among all men of property and rank. In this disposition even the most high-toned and arbitrary government became desirable as a security against licentiousness and agrarian laws; consequently the new constitution was embraced with eagerness by men of these descriptions, who in every community form a powerful interest, and, added to the conspirators, office hunters, etc., etc., made a formidable and numerous party in favor of the new constitution. The elections of the members of convention were, moreover, made in the first moments of blind enthusiasm, when every artifice was practiced to prejudice the people against all those who had the enlightened patriotism to oppose this system of tyranny. Thus was almost every man of real ability, who was in opposition, excluded from a seat in this convention. Consequently the contest was very unequal: well-meaning though uninformed men were opposed to great learning, eloquence, and sophistry, in the shape of lawyers, doctors, and divines, who were capable and seemed disposed to delude by deceptive glosses and specious reasoning. Indeed, from the specimens we have seen of the discussion on this occasion, every enlightened patriot must regret that the cause of liberty has been so weakly although zealously advocated—that its champions were so little illuminated. In addition to these numerous advantages in the convention, the friends of the new constitution had the weight and influence of the town of Boston to second their endeavors, and yet, notwithstanding all this, were near losing the question, although delusively qualified. Is this any evidence of the excellency of the new constitution? Certainly not. Nor can it have any influence in inducing the remaining states to accede. They will examine and judge for themselves, and from their wisdom in taking due time for deliberation, I have no doubt will prove the salvation of the liberties of the United States.

CENTINEL.

Philadelphia, February 20th, 1788.

CENTINEL, No. XVI.*

To the PEOPLE of PENNSYLVANIA. *Fellow Citizens.*

The new constitution, instead of being the panacea or cure of every grievance so delusively represented by its advocates, will be found upon examination like Pandora's box, replete with every evil. The most specious clauses of this system of ambition and iniquity contain latent mischief, and premeditated villainy. By section 9th of the 1st article, "No *ex post facto* law shall be passed." This sounds very well upon a superficial consideration, and I dare say has been read by most people with approbation. Government undoubtedly ought to avoid retrospective laws as far as may be, as they are generally injurious and fraudulent: yet there are occasions when such laws are not only just but highly requisite. An ex post facto law is a law made after the fact, so that the Congress under the new constitution are precluded from all control over transactions prior to its establishment. This prohibition would screen the numerous public defaulters, as no measure could be constitutionally taken to compel them to render an account and restore the public moneys; the unaccounted millions lying in their hands would become their private property. Hitherto these characters from their great weight and numbers have had the influence to prevent an in-

---

* From "The Independent Gazetteer; or, The Chronicle of Freedom," Feb. 26, 1788.

vestigation of their accounts; but if this constitution be established, they may set the public at defiance, as they would be completely exonerated of all demands of the United States against them. This is not a strained construction of this section, but the proper evident meaning of the words, which not even the ingenuity or sophistry of the *Caledonian* can disguise from the meanest capacity. However if this matter admitted of any doubt, it would be removed by the following consideration, viz., that the new constitution is founded upon a dissolution of the present articles of confederation and is an original compact between those states, or rather those individuals, who accede to it; consequently all contracts, debts and engagements in favor or against the United States, under the *old* government, are cancelled unless they are provided for in the *new* constitution. The framers of this constitution appear to have been aware of such consequence by stipulating in article 6th, that all debts contracted, and engagements entered into before the adoption of this constitution shall be valid *against* the United States under the new constitution, but there is no provision that the debts, etc., due *to* the United States, shall be valid or recoverable. This is a striking omission, and must have been designed, as debts of the latter description would naturally occur and claim equal attention with the former. This article implied, cancels all debts due to the United States prior to the establishment of the new constitution. If equal provision had been made for the debts due *to* the United States, as *against* the United States, the ex post facto clause would not have so pernicious an operation.

The immaculate convention that is said to have possessed the fullness of patriotism, wisdom and virtue, contained a number of the principal public defaulters; and these were the most influential members and chiefly instrumental in the framing of the new constitution. There were several of this description in the deputation from the state of Pennsylvania, who have long standing and immense accounts to settle, and MILLIONS perhaps to refund. The late Financier alone, in the capacity of chairman of the commercial committee of

Congress, early in the late war, was entrusted with millions of public money, which to this day remain unaccounted for, nor has he settled his accounts as Financier. The others may also find it a convenient method to balance accounts with the public; they are sufficiently known and therefore need not be designated. This will account for the zealous attachment of such characters to the new constitution and their dread of investigation and discussion. It may be said that the new Congress would rather break through the constitution than suffer the public to be defrauded of so much treasure, when the burthens and distresses of the people are so very great; but this is not to be expected from the characters of which that Congress would in all probability be composed, if we may judge from the predominant influence and interest these defaulters now possess in many of the states. Besides, should Congress be disposed to violate the fundamental articles of the constitution for the sake of public justice, they would be prevented in so doing by their oaths,* but even if this should not prove an obstacle, if it can be supposed that any set of men would perjure themselves for the public good, and combat an host of enemies on such terms, still it would be of no avail, as there is a further barrier interposed between the public and these defaulters, namely, the supreme court of the union, whose province it would be to determine the constitutionality of any law that may be controverted; and supposing no bribery or corrupt influence practiced on the bench of judges, it would be their sworn duty to refuse their sanction to laws made in the face and contrary to the letter and spirit of the constitution, as any law to compel the settlement of accounts and payment of moneys depending and due under the old confederation would be. The 1st section of 3d article gives the

---

* Article VI. "The senators and representatives before mentioned and the members of the several state legislatures, and all executive and judicial officers, both of the United States and of the several states, shall be bound by oath to support this constitution." Were ever public defaulters so effectually screened! Not only the administrators of the general government, but also of the state governments, are prevented by oath from doing justice to the public; and the legislature of Pennsylvania could not without perjury insist upon the delinquent states discharging their arrears.

supreme court cognizance of not only the laws, but of all cases arising under the constitution, which empowers this tribunal to decide upon the construction of the constitution itself in the last resort. This is so extraordinary, so unprecedented an authority that the intention in vesting of it must have been to put it out of the power of Congress, even by breaking through the constitution, to compel these defaulters to restore the public treasure.

In the present circumstances these sections of the new constitution would be also productive of great injustice between the respective states; the delinquent states would be exonerated from all existing demands against them on account of the great arrearages of former requisitions, as they could not be constitutionally compelled to discharge them. And as the majority of the states are in this predicament, and have an equal voice in the senate, it would be their interest, and in their power by not only the constitution, but by a superiority of votes, to prevent the levying of such arrearages. Besides the constitution, moreover, declares that all taxes, etc., shall be uniform throughout the United States, which is an additional obstacle against noticing them.

The state of Pennsylvania in such cases would have no credit for her extraordinary exertions and punctuality heretofore; but would be taxed equally with those states which for years past have not contributed anything to the common expenses of the union; indeed, some of the states have paid nothing since the revolution.   CENTINEL.

Philadelphia, 23d February, 1788.

CENTINEL, No. XVII.*

To the PEOPLE of PENNSYLVANIA. *Fellow Citizens.*

In my last number I exposed the villainous intention of the framers of the new constitution, to defraud the public out of the millions lying in the hands of individuals by the construction of this system, which would, if established, cancel

* From "The Independent Gazetteer; or, The Chronicle of Freedom," March 24, 1788.

all debts now due to the United States. I also showed that thereby the delinquent states would be exonerated of all arrearages due by them on former requisitions of Congress; and to prove that the cancelling of all public dues was premeditated in regard to individuals, I stated that the general convention contained a number of the principal public defaulters, and that these were the most influential members, and chiefly instrumental in framing the new constitution: in answer to which, the conspirators have, by bold assertions, spurious vouchers, and insufficient certificates, endeavored to exculpate one member, and to alleviate the weight of the charge of delinquency against another. In the face of a resolution of Congress of the 20th June, 1785, declaring their intention of appointing three commissioners, to settle and adjust the receipts and expenditures of the late financier, the conspirators have asserted that his accounts were finally settled in November, 1784, for which they pretend to have vouchers, and by a pompous display of certain resolutions of Congress, respecting a particular charge of fraud against him, as commercial agent to the United States, they vainly hope to divert the public attention from his great delinquency, in never accounting for the millions of public money entrusted to him in that line. When we consider the immense sums of money taken up by Mr. M——s,* as commercial agent, to import military supplies, and even to trade in behalf of the United States, at a time when the risk was so great, that individuals would not venture their property; that all these transactions were conducted under the private firm of W——g and M——, which afforded unrestrained scope to peculation and embezzlement of the public property, by enabling Mr. M——s to throw the loss of all captures by the enemy, at that hazardous period, on the public, and converting most of the safe arrivals (which were consequently very valuable) into his private property; and when we add to these considerations the principles of the MAN, his bankrupt situation at the commencement of the late war, and the immense wealth he has dazzled the world with since, can it be thought unreasonable to conclude, that the principal source of his affluence

* See Append'x.

was the commercial agency of the United States, during the war?—not that I would derogate from his successful ingenuity in his numerous speculations in the paper moneys, Havannah monopoly and job, or in the sphere of financiering.*

The certificate published in behalf of general M–ffl–n, the quartermaster gen—l, will not satisfy a discerning public, or acquit him of the charge of delinquency, as this certificate was procured to serve an electionering purpose, upon a superficial and hasty inspection of his general account, unchecked by the accounts of his deputies, whose receipts and expenditures had not been examined, and consequently, by errors, collusion between him and them, or otherwise g———l M–ffl–n may retain a large balance in his hands; in such case a *quietus* may have been thought expedient to coutinue his affluence.

For the honor of human nature, I wish to draw a veil over the situation and conduct of another weighty character, whose name has given a false lustre to the new constitution, and been the occasion of sullying the laurels of a *Washington*, by inducing him to acquiesce in a system of despotism and villainy, at which enlightened patriotism shudders.

The discovery of the intended fraud, which for magnitude and audacity is unparalleled, must open the eyes of the deluded to the true character and principles of the men who had assumed the garb of patriotism with an insidious design of enslaving and robbing their fellow citizens, of establishing those odious distinctions between the well-born and the great body of the people, of degrading the latter to the level of slaves and elevating the former to the rank of nobility.

The citizens of this state, which is in advance in its payments to the federal treasury, whilst some of the others have not paid a farthing since the war, ought in a peculiar manner to resent the intended imposition and make its authors experience their just resentment; it is incumbent upon them in a particular manner to exert themselves to frustrate the measures of the conspirators, and set an example to those parts of the union who have not enjoyed the blessing of a free press on this occasion, but are still enveloped in the darkness of delusion, and enthralled by the fascination of names.

* See Appendix.

Could it have been supposed seven years ago, that, before the wounds received in the late conflict for liberty were scarcely healed, a postmaster-general and his deputies would have had the daring presumption to convert an establishment intended to promote and secure the public welfare into an engine of despotism, by suppressing all those newspapers that contain the essays of patriotism and real intelligence, and propagating instead thereof falsehoods and delusion? Such a supposition at that time would have been treated as chimerical; but how must our indignation rise when we find this flagitious practice is persevered in, after being publicly detected! Must not the bribe from the conspirators be very great to compensate the postmaster-general and his deputies for the loss of character and infamy consequent upon such conduct, and for the danger they incur of being impeached and turned out of office?

The scurrilous attack of the *little Fiddler* upon Mr. Workman of the university, on a suspicion, perhaps unfounded, of his being the author of a series of essays under the signature of *Philadelphiensis*, is characteristic of the man. He has ever been the base parasite and tool of the wealthy and great, at the expense of truth, honor, friendship, treachery to benefactors—nay, to the nearest relatives: all have been sacrificed by him at the shrine of the great. He ought, however, to have avoided a contrast with so worthy and highly respected a character as Mr. Workman, who had an equal right with himself to offer his sentiments on the new constitution; and if he viewed it as a system of despotism, and had talents to unfold its nature and tendency, he deserves the thanks of every patriotic American, if he has exerted them under the character of Philadelphiensis. His not being above four years in the country can be no objection. The celebrated Thomas Paine wrote his Common Sense before he had been two years in America, which was not the less useful or acceptable upon that account. The public have nothing to do with the author of a piece: it is the merits of the writing that are alone to be considered. Mr. Workman, prior to his coming to America, was a professor in an eminent academy in

Dublin. Little Francis should have been cautious in giving provocation, for insignificance alone could have preserved him the smallest remnant of character. I hope he will take the hint, or such a scene will be laid open as will disgrace even his patrons: the suit of clothes, and the quarter cask of wine, will not be forgot.   Centinel.

Philadelphia, March 19th, 1788.

Centinel, No. XVIII.*

To the People of Pennsylvania. *Fellow Citizens.*

The measures that are pursuing to effect the establishment of the new constitution, are so repugnant to truth, honor, and the well-being of society, as would disgrace any cause. If the nature and tendency of this system were to be judged of by the conduct of its framers and patrons, what a picture of ambition and villainy would present itself to our view! From the specimens they have already given, anticipation may easily realize the consequences that would flow from the new constitution, if established; we may bid adieu to all the blessings of liberty, to all the fruits of the late glorious assertion of the rights of human nature, made at the expense of so much blood and treasure. Yet such is the infatuation of many well meaning persons, that they view with indifference the atrocious villainy which characterizes the proceedings of the advocates of the new system. The daring, and in most parts of the United States, the successful methods practised to shackle the press, and destroy the freedom of discussion, the silencing the Pennsylvania Herald, to prevent the publication of the invaluable debates of the late convention of this state; the total suppression of real intelligence, and of the illuminations of patriotism, through the medium of the post-office; the systematic fraud and deception that pervade the union; the stigmatizing, and by every art which ambition and malice can suggest, laboring to villify, intimidate and trample under foot every disinterested patriot who, per-

* From "The Independent Gazetteer; or, The Chronicle of Freedom," April 9, 1788.

ferring his country's good to every other consideration, has the courage to stand forth the champion of liberty and the people; and the intercepting of private confidential letters passing from man to man, violating the sacredness of a seal, and thus infringing one of the first privileges of freemen— that of communicating with each other: I say all these are overlooked by the infatuated admirers of the new system, who, deluded by the *phantom* of wealth and prosperity, profit not by the admonitory lesson which such proceedings afford, are deaf to the calls of patriotism, and would rush blindly into the noose of ambition.

However, to the honor of Pennsylvania, a very large majority of her citizens view the subject in its true light, and spurn the shackles prepared for them. They will in due time convince the aspiring despots and avaricious office-hunters, that their dark intrigues, and deep concerted schemes of power and aggrandizement, are ineffectual; that they are neither to be duped nor dragooned out of their liberties. The conspirators, I know, insolently boast that their strength in the other states will enable them to crush the opposition in this; but let them not build upon that which is in its nature precarious and transient, which must fail them the moment the delusion is dispelled. Their success in the other states is the fruit of deceptions that cannot be long supported. Indeed, the audacity and villainy of the conspirators on the one hand, and the frantic enthusiasm and easy credulity of the people on the other, in some of the states, however well attested and recorded in the faithful page of history, will be treated by posterity as fabulous.

The great artifice that is played off on this occasion, is the persuading the people of one place, that the people everywhere else are nearly unanimous in favor of the new system, and thus endeavoring by the fascination of example and force of general opinion to prevail upon the people every where to acquiesce in what is represented to them as the general sentiment.

Thus as one means of deception has failed them, they have adopted another, always avoiding rational discussion. When the glare of great names, the dread of annihilation if the new system was rejected or the adoption of it even delayed, were dissipated by the artillery of truth and reason; they have recurred to the one now practising, the intimidating and imposing influence of. imaginary numbers and unanimity that are continually reverberated from every part of the union, by the tools and vehicles of the would-be despots; and in which they have had astonishing success. The people in the Eastern States have been taught to believe that it is all harmony to the Southward; and in the Southern States they are discouraged from opposition by the unanimity of the Eastern and Northern States; nay, what will appear incredible, considering the distance, a gentleman of veracity just returned from New York, assures that the conspirators have had the address to inculcate an opinion there that all opposition had ceased in this state, notwithstanding the evidence of the contrary is so glaring here; this gentleman further informs, that so entirely devoted is the post-office, that not a single newspaper is received by the printers of that place from this city or elsewhere; and a Boston newspaper, come by private hand, announces to the public, that for some months past, the printers there have received no newspapers to the Southward of New Haven, in Connecticut, where the press is muzzled, and consequently cannot injure the cause; that all intelligence of the occurrences in the other States is withheld from them; and that they know more of the state of Europe, than of their own country.

Notwithstanding many thousand copies of the Reasons of Dissent of the minority of the late convention of this state were printed and forwarded in every direction, and by various conveyances, scarcely any of these got beyond the limits of this state, and most of them not until a long time after their publication. The printer of these Reasons, by particular desire, addressed a copy of them to every printer in the union, which he sent to the Post Office to be conveyed in the mail as usual, long before the *new arrangement*, as it is called, took place; and yet we since find that none of them reached the place of their destination. This is a full demonstration of the subserviency of the Post Office, and a striking evidence of the vigilance that has been exerted to suppress information. It is greatly to be regretted that the opposition in Massachusetts were denied the benefits of our discussion that the unanswerable dissent of our minority did not reach Boston in time to influence the decision of the great question by their convention as it would in all probability have enabled patriotism to triumph; not that I would derogate from the good sense and public spirit of that state, which I have no doubt would in common circumstances have shone with equal splendor, but this was far from being the case; the new constitution was viewed in Massachusetts through the medium of a SHAYS, the terrors of HIS insurrection had not subsided; a government that would have been execrated at another time was embraced by many as a refuge from anarchy, and thus liberty deformed by mad riot and dissention, lost her ablest advocates.

As the liberties of all the states in the union are struck at in common with those of Pennsylvania, by the conduct of the Post Master General and deputies, I trust that the example which her Legislature* has set by instructing her delegates in Congress on this subject, will be followed by the others, that with one accord they will hurl their vengeance on the venal instruments of ambition, who have presumed to prostrate one of the principal bulwarks of liberty. In a confederated government of such extent as the United States, the freest communication of sentiment and information should be maintained, as the liberties, happiness and welfare of the union depend upon a concert of counsels; the signals of alarm whenever ambition should rear its baneful head, ought to be uniform. Without this communication between the members of the confederacy the freedom of the press, if it could be maintained in so severed a situation, would cease to be a security against the encroachments of tyranny. The truth of the foregoing position is strikingly illustrated on the present occasion; for want of this intercommunity of sentiment and information, the liberties of this country are brought to an

---

* The application to Congress from our Legislature was made upon the complaint of all the printers of newspapers in the city of Philadelphia.

awful crisis; ambition has made a great stride towards dominion, has succeeded through the medium of muzzled presses
to delude a great body of the people in the other states, and
threatens to overwhelm the enlightened opposition in this by
external force. Here, indeed, notwithstanding every nerve
was strained by the conspirators, to muzzle or demolish every
newspaper that allowed free discussion, two printers have
asserted the independency of the press, whereby the arts of
ambition have been detected, and the new system has been
portrayed in its native villainy; its advocates have long since
abandoned the field of argument, relinquished the unequal
contest, and truth and patriotism reign triumphant in this
state; but the conspirators trust to their success in the other
states for the attainment of their darling object, and therefore
all their vigilance is exerted to prevent the infectious spirit
of freedom and enlightened patriotism communicating to the
rest of the union—all intercourse is as far as possible cut off.

To rectify the erroneous representation made in the other
states of the sentiments of the people in this respecting the
new constitution, I think it my duty to state the fact as it
really is.—Those who favor this system of tyranny are most
numerous in the city of Philadelphia, where perhaps they
may be a considerable majority. In the most eastern counties they compose about one-fourth of the people, but in the
middle, northern and western counties not above a twentieth
part, so that upon the whole the friends to the new constitution in this state are about one-sixth of the people. The following circumstance is an evidence of the spirit and decision
of the opposition.—An individual, unadvisedly and without
concert, and contrary to the system of conduct generally
agreed upon, went to the expense of printing and circulating
an address to the legislature, reprobating in the strongest
terms the new constitution, and praying that the deputies of
this state in the federal convention, who in violation of their
duty acceded to the new constitution, be called to account
for their daring procedure. This address, or petition, was
signed by upwards of four thousand citizens in only two
counties, viz., Franklin and Cumberland; and if the time

had admitted, prior to the adjournment of the legislature, there is reason to believe that this high-toned application would have been subscribed by five-sixth of the freemen of this state. The advocates of the new constitution, availing themselves of this partial measure of two counties, have asserted it to be the result of a general exertion, which is so evidently false that it can only deceive people at a distance from us, for the counties over the mountain are nearly unanimous in the opposition. In Fayette at a numerous county meeting, there appeared to be but two persons in favor of the constitution; in Bedford county, in the mountains, there are not above twenty; in Huntingdon adjoining, about 30; in Dauphin, in the middle country, not 100; in Berks, a large eastern county that has near 5,000 taxable inhabitants, not more than 50, and so of several others, and yet no petitions were circulated or signed in these counties. The system of conduct alluded to is the forming societies in every county in the state, who have committees of correspondence. These are now engaged in planning a uniform exertion to emancipate this state from the thraldom of despotism. A convention of deputies from every district will in all probability be agreed upon as the most eligible mode of combining the strength of the opposition, which is increasing daily both in numbers and spirit.

The Centinel, supported by the dignity of the cause he advocates, and sensible that his well-meant endeavors have met the approbation of the community, views with ineffable contempt the impotent efforts of disappointed ambition to depreciate his merit and stigmatize his performances, and without pretending to the spirit of divination, he thinks he may predict that the period is not far distant when the authors and *wilful* abettors of the new constitution will be viewed with detestation by every good man, whilst the Centinels of the present day will be honored with the esteem and confidence of a grateful people.

Great pains have been taken to discover the author of these papers, with a view, no doubt, to villify his private character, and thereby lessen the usefulness of his writings, and many suppose they have made the discovery, but in this they are mistaken. The Centinel submits his performances to the public judgment, and challenges fair argumentation; the information he has given from time to time, has stood the test of the severest scrutiny, and thus his reputation as a writer, is established beyond the injury of his enemies. If it were in the least material to the argument or answered any one good purpose, he would not hesitate a moment in using his own signature; as it would not, but on the contrary, point where the shafts of malice could be levelled with most effect, and thus divert the public attention from the proper object, to a personal altercation, he from the first determined that the prying eye of party or curiosity should never be gratified with his real name, and to that end to be the sole depository of the secret. He has been thus explicit to prevent the repetition of the weakness of declaring off, when charged with being the author, and to put the matter upon its true footing; however, it may flatter his vanity, that these papers should be ascribed to an illustrious patriot, whose public spirit and undaunted firmness of mind, eclipse the most shining ornaments of the Roman commonwealth, in its greatest purity and glory whose persevering exertions for the public welfare, have endeared him to his country, whilst it has made every knave and aspiring despot, his inveterate enemy, and who has never condescended to deny any writings that have been ascribed to him, or to notice the railings of party.

CENTINEL.

Philadelphia, April 5th, 1788.

CENTINEL No. XIX.*

To the PEOPLE of PENNSYLVANIA. *Friends, Countrymen and Fellow Citizens.*

When I last addressed you on the subject of the new constitution, I had not a doubt of its rejection. The baneful nature and tendency of this system of ambition had been so fully exposed that its most zealous advocates were constrained

* "Independent Gazetteer; or, The Chronicle of Freedom;' Oct. 7, 1788.

to acknowledge many imperfections and dangers, and *seemingly* to acquiesce in the necessity of amendments. However, by the time this general conviction had taken place in the minds of the people, so many states had adopted the constitution and the public anxiety was so great to have an efficient government that the votaries of power and ambition were enabled by adapting their language and conduct to the temper of the times, to prevail upon a competent number of the states to establish the constitution without previous alteration upon the implied condition of subsequent amendments, which they assured would certainly be made, as every body was agreed in their propriety.

My knowledge of the principles and conduct of these men for many years past left me no room to doubt of their insincerity on this occasion. I was persuaded that all their professions of moderation and assurance of future amendments, were founded in deception, that they were but the blind of the moment, the covered way to dominion and empire. Like a barrel thrown to the whale, the people were to be amused with fancied amendments until the harpoon of power should secure its prey and render resistance ineffectual. Already the masque of ambition begins to be removed and its latent features to appear in their genuine hue, disdaining any further veil from policy; the *well-born*, inebriated with success, and despising the people for their easy credulity, think it unnecessary to dissemble any longer; almost every newspaper ridicules the idea of amendments and triumphs over the deluded people. Ye patriots of America, arouse from the dangerous infatuation in which ye are lulled, and while it is yet time, strain every nerve to rescue your country from the servile yoke of bondage and to preserve that liberty which has been so recently vindicated at the expense of so much blood and treasure. Upon the improvement of the present moment depends the fate of your country; you have now a constitutional opportunity afforded you to obtain a safe and a good government by making choice of such persons to represent you in the new congress, as have congenial sentiments with yourselves. Suffer not, ye freemen of America, the *well-born*, or their *servile minions*, to usurp the sacred trust—to impose themselves upon you as your guardians; for whatever professions they may make, or assurances they may give you, depend upon it they will deceive you: like the wolf in sheep's clothing, they will make you their prey. Treat with contempt the slanderous arts of the well-born to prejudice you against your true friends, and convince them on this great occasion, by your good sense, union and vigor, that you are not to be duped out of your liberties by all the refinements of *Machiavellian* policy. The future government of these United States will take its tone from the complexion of the first congress; upon this will greatly depend whether despotic sway, or the salutary influence of a well-regulated government shall hereafter rule this once happy land. As the legislature of this state have appointed the last Wednesday in November next for the election of the eight representatives from this state in the new congress, you ought to be prepared for that *all-important* day; and as success is only to be ensured by unanimity among the friends of equal liberty, local and personal predilections and dislikes should give place to the general sentiment. Whatever ticket may be agreed to by the majority of the opposition to the new constitution in its present shape ought to be supported by all those who are sincere in wishing for amendments. I trust that all prejudices and antipathies arising from the late war, or from difference of religion, will be sacrificed to the great object of the public welfare, and that all good and well-meaning men of whatever description will harmonize on this occasion. For among the various practices and stratagems of the well-born, the principal one, and upon which they will the most rely for success, will be the endeavor to divide you, and thus by scattering your suffrages between various candidates, to frustrate your object.

From the mode of appointment, the Senate of the general government will be chiefly composed of the *well-born*, or their minions, and when we consider the great and various powers which they will possess, and their permanency, it ought to operate as an additional stimulus with you to obtain faithful representatives in the other branch of legislature, to shield your privileges and property from the machinations of ambition and the rapacity of power. The Senate, besides their proper share in the Legislature, have great executive and judicial powers—their concurrence is made necessary to all the principal appointments in government. What a fruitful source of corruption does not this present! in the capacity of Legislators they will have the irresistible temptation to institute lucrative and needless offices, as they will in fact, have the appointment of the *officers*.

When I consider the nature of power and ambition, when I view the numerous swarm of hungry office-hunters, and their splendid expectations, anticipation exhibits such a scene of rapacity and oppression, such burthensome establishments to pamper the pride and luxury of a useless herd of officers, such dissipation and profusion of the public treasure, such consequent impoverishment and misery of the people that I tremble for my country.

Such evils are only to be averted by a vigorous exertion of the freemen of America, to procure a virtuous, disinterested, and patriotic House of Representatives. That you may all view the importance of this election in its true light, and improve the only means which the constitution affords you for your preservation, is the fervent wish of

CENTINEL.

Philadelphia, October 3d, 1788.

CENTINEL No. XX.*

To the CITIZENS of PHILADELPHIA.

I congratulate my fellow citizens on the dawn of returning independence of sentiment evinced at the last election; may its ennobling influence stimulate to further and more effectual exertions; may the dictates of the *well-born junto* be treated on every occasion, with the contempt they experienced in regard to the late choice of councillor for this city.

Blinded by prejudice industriously fomented, influenced by

---

* From "The Independent Gazetteer; or, The Chronicle of Freedom," Nov. 13, 1788.

sordid motives of private interest, or intimidated by apprehensions of being ruined in their professions, a great majority of the citizens of Philadelphia have suffered themselves to be made the scaffold upon which the *well-born junto* have ascended to the government of this state, and thereby to a predominancy in that of the United States. For several years past the essential privilege of freemen, that of electing their legislators has been reduced to unsubstantial form, to a mere farce, the appointment being really made by the *junto*, previous to the legal election. The situation of this city has been similar to that of Rome, under the *emperors*, who artfully gratified the people with the forms of that liberty which they had enjoyed under the republic; continuing their ostensible representatives and officers, although in fact they were the creatures of the emperors and entirely subservient to them. Thus you have been amused with the show of annual elections, and the *name* of representatives without the reality.

It may be useful to take a retrospect of the means by which this *well-born junto*, who ten years ago could not muster more than eighty-two devoted adherents in the state of Pennsylvania, have now become so formidable as to threaten the liberties of all America.

The first consideration that this review presents is, the policy by which the *junto* have attached to their party the weighty interest of the Quakers and Tories. In the late arduous contest with Great Britain, wherein the lives and fortunes of the Whigs were dependent upon the uncertain issue of the war, and in the course of which so much barbarity and devastation were committed by the British; it is not to be wondered at that those persons who were disaffected to the common cause, who refused to share the dangers or contribute to the expenses of the war, and on the contrary were justly suspected to be aiding and assisting a cruel and vindictive foe, should in consequence thereof, incur the resentment of the Whigs and be treated rather as enemies to their country than as fellow citizens. Hence the *test-law*, which was made to draw the line of discrimination, and to exclude from our councils those who were inimical to our cause:

hence too the violence and severity with which the disaffected were treated; which has laid the foundation of the most implacable resentments and lasting prejudices.

The *junto*, considering that persons so situated and under the influence of such feelings, would make zealous adherents if they could be flattered with hopes of protection from what they deemed oppression and persecution, and still more so if they could be flattered with the pleasing prospect of a repeal of the test-law, and thereby having it in their power to assert their rights and vindicate their sufferings; the *junto* accordingly made the most liberal offers of their services to the disaffected, and as their dislike and dread of the Whigs was the cement of union, the basis upon which the *well-born* meant to build their meditated schemes of profit and aggrandisement, *Galen*, and such minions were employed to aggravate the feelings and confirm the resentments of the disaffected by such misrepresentations of the principles and designs of the Whigs as to keep the former under continual apprehension of violence and rapine;* this persuasion had the

* It is astonishing to think how successful this artifice has been. The disaffected were too highly prejudiced against the constitutional Whigs by the odious light in which they were continually represented by the well-born and their minions, as they were brought to consider them as the most violent, unprincipled, and abandoned of men, who were conspiring against the lives, property, and happiness of all other classes of people. Under such impressions two very worthy quakers, Robert Smith and Jonathan Morris, were, after the repeal of the test-law, elected members of the legislature for Chester county. But what was the astonishment of these honest men, when, in pursuing the dictates of their conscience and judgment, they found that in almost every vote they harmonized with the constitutionalists, and differed with those men they had been so highly prejudiced in favor of, whose corrupt principles and views they had now a demonstration of. Often have I heard them express their ardent wish, that all those of their constituents who were under the same delusion that they had been, might have the same opportunity of seeing and judging for themselves. But the upright conduct of these men was so highly displeasing to the junto, that at the next election they were turned out. Indeed, during the course of the year that they were in the assembly, they were continually warned of the consequences of daring to exercise their judgment, and voting against the measures of the well-born; but they virtuously answered that they would not purchase a seat in the legislature at the expense of their integrity and the duty they owed their country.

desited effect, it riveted the disaffected so closely to the interests of the *junto* that they zealously and implicitly supported all their measures without attending to their nature or consequences.   At length the liberal Whigs seeing the imposition that was practicing on the disaffected, that they were made the dupes of a set of interested designing men, resolved to convince them that their apprehensions were groundless by repealing the test-law, which excluded so many of them from the right of suffrage, and thereby putting them in a situation to judge and act for themselves; the junto who had gained so much by the subordinate situation of the disaffected, were alarmed at the proposition and accordingly opposed it, which so incensed their allies that, at an election which took place soon after for a censer in the room of Col. Miles, resigned, not one of them could be persuaded to vote, and of course the constitutionalists carried the election; however the junto retrieved this *faux pas* afterwards, by the zeal they showed in procuring the repeal of the test-law.

I was always against the policy of continuing the test-law one hour longer than was absolutely necessary for the preservation of the country from a threatening enemy, as the history of other nations had taught me the injurious consequences of depriving a large proportion of the community of the important privileges of citizenship.   I was aware that ambition always availed itself of such distinctions among the people to accomplish their common ruin; that the grievous oppression and misery which the Irish nation have experienced for some centuries past, have arisen from the unequal situation of the people in respect to the government—from the depressed subordinate state in which the Roman Catholics have been held, who, not having a common interest in and attachment to the government, but on the contrary highly embittered by the odious light in which they were regarded, and the severity with which they were treated, occasioned continual apprehensions to the Protestants for their safety.   And this alienated state of the people, and their reciprocal enmities and suspicions, put it in the power of the English ministry, by playing one party off against the other, to keep the whole under the most submissive subjection. However, the situation of the Irish nation is much improved since the liberality and harmony of sentiment that the late war gave birth to: their common danger from foreign invasion evinced the folly of their prejudices, and the necessity of union. The Irish now act in a great measure as one people, and in consequence thereof their affairs have assumed a different aspect. England has been obliged to relinquish many of her injurious monopolies and partial restrictions on the Irish commerce, and oppressive arrangements in their government. Tyranny has fled before the united voice of that people who were so lately enslaved by their internal divisions.

Another great engine of influence has been the *Bank*, which having the power of controlling the credit of every person concerned in trade, of course governed the mercantile interest, and made it entirely subservient to the views of *the well-born junto.*

It has been, moreover, the policy of the junto from the beginning to ruin, by every device of calumny and exertion of influence, the character and circumstances of every leading patriot—well knowing that the people are only important and powerful when united under confidential leaders; and as this policy was supported by a numerous and weighty party, and pursued with unremitted perseverance, the ablest and most influential patrons of the people fell victims to it. Character after character was successively attacked and hunted down by the dogs of party, with the most unfeeling rancour; even the death of the victim did not assuage their gall. In this barbarous game of policy, *Galen* bore away the palm, and shone conspicuous beyond all the imps of the *well-born.* He boasted that the superior malignity of his pen had deprived the illustrious and patriotic Reed of his existence, and in his fate had made a signal example to deter others from emulating his virtues, and standing forth the advocates of the privileges of the people, which is so highly criminal in the eyes of the *well-born.*

By such means have the *well-born* attained to their present power and importance, to a situation which has enabled them to dictate and procure the establishment of a form of government for the United States, which, if not amended, will put the finishing stroke to popular liberty and confirm the sway of the *well-born*. Whilst the fate of the new constitution was doubtful, great was the assumed moderation, specious were the promises of its advocate. The despotic principles and tendency of this system of government were so powerfully demonstrated as to strike conviction in almost every breast, but this was artfully obviated by urging the pressing necessity of having an energetic government and assurance of subsequent amendments. The people were moreover told, "you will have the means in your own power to prevent the oppression of government, viz: the choice of your representatives to the federal legislature, who will be the guardians of your rights and property, your shield against the machinations of the *well-born*."

But how changed the language, how different the conduct of these men since its establishment!—they are taking effectual measures as far as in their power to realize the worst predictions of the opponents to the new constitution.—Having secured the avenue to offices under the new congress by the appointment of the senators, they are now exerting all their influence to carry the election of the representatives in the federal legislature, and thereby get the absolute command of the *purse-strings* to confirm their domination; every artifice is practicing to delude the people on this great occasion, which in all probability will be the last opportunity they will have to preserve their liberties, as the new congress will have it in their power to establish despotism without violating the principles of the constitution. The proposed meeting at Lancaster is a high game of deception; under the appearance of giving the people an opportunity to nominate their representatives, the minions of ambition are to be palmed upon them. Ostensible deputies are to be sent from every county for this purpose, who, if we may judge from those already appointed, will take especial care to prevent the nomination of men who have congenial feelings with the people, as such would prove troublesome obstacles in the way of ambition;

the intention is to monopolize both branches of the legislature and make the government harmonize with the aggrandizement of the *well-born* and their minions.

The deputies appointed to go from this city characterize the juggle and designate the intention more strikingly than is in the power of language to express or the ingenuity of artifice to conceal; the man who confessedly has had a principal share in the framing of a constitution that is universally allowed to be dangerously despotic, and therefore to require great amendments; the man who in every stage of its adoption has been its greatest advocate; whose views of aggrandizement are founded upon the unqualified execution of this government, whose aristocratic principles, aspiring ambition, and contempt of the common people have long distinguished him; I say this man is now selected as one of that body who are to dictate the choice of the people—to point out *faithful* representatives who are to check ambition and defend their rights and privileges.   If the people suffer themselves to be thus fooled upon so momentous an occasion, they will deserve their fate.   But I am persuaded they will discern the fraud and act becoming freemen, that they will give their suffrages to real patriots and genuine representatives.

Philadelphia, October 22d, 1788.   CENTINEL.

CENTINEL, No. XXI.*

To the PEOPLE of PENNSYLVANIA.   *Friends and Countrymen.*

France exhibits at this moment one of the most interesting scenes to human nature, and peculiarly instructive to the citizens of the United States;—a people who for many centuries had been accustomed to yield implicit obedience to the mandates of royalty, who never presumed to judge of the propriety of any measure of government, but whose highest glory was to recommend itself to the idol on the throne by the most obsequious services, to sacrifice every manly feeling, every consideration whether of self or country, at the shrine

* From "The Independent Gazetteer; or, The Chronicle of Freedom," Nov. 8, 1788.

of his grandeur; I say this people, so long obsequious and subservient to the will and pleasure of a despot, seem to have imbibed a new nature, to be animated with the noblest, most enlightened sentiments of patriotism, and in opposition to a court supported by a standing army of 200,000 mercenaries, is asserting its rights and privileges. Various causes have concurred to produce this astonishing revolution of sentiments and conduct in the people of France: perhaps the divine writings of a *Montesquieu* laid the foundation, and doubtless the able, animated discussion of the native rights of mankind occasioned by the late contest between America and Britain, must have been very instrumental in effecting this general illumination and inspiring this ardent love of liberty in France. But it is probable from the strength which arbitrary power had acquired by custom and long-established habits of obedience, that it might have continued in uninterrupted exercise for a long time to come, if the French court had not precipitated its destruction by an extraordinary stretch of power, which struck at all the remaining privileges of the people, and aimed at the unqualified establishment of despotism.

The French, enlightened to their native rights had availed themselves of institutions and provincial privileges, hitherto enjoyed but in name, to check the despotism of power, which, insensible of the great change of sentiment that had taken place in France, was so rash as to attempt the enforcement of new arrangements and impositions, itstead of adhering to the old establisments that time and custom had sanctioned. The French nation, already prepared, wanted but a suitable occasion to vindicate their rights: this was now afforded by the indiscretion of the court, and they embraced it by reviving the exercise of the long-dormant privilege of their parliaments to negative the arrets of the court, by refusing to register such of them as they disapproved, without which they could not be legally executed.

The French court, finding their projects of power and dominion frustrated by the patriotism of these local parliaments, who, from their vicinity and near connection with the people, were greatly influenced by the common feelings and interest, came to the bold resolution of annihilating them at one stroke, and substituting in lieu of them one general parliament, or *court pleniere*, under the specious pretence of reinstating the public finances and credit, deranged and prostrated by the late expensive war and the peculations of the ministers of state.

But the French nation had too much discernment to be thus imposed on: they saw the object and tendency of the new constitution, or *court pleniere;* they were sensible that a parliament so remote from the people would be wholly subservient to the views of the court, however despotic they might be; they had experienced the fidelity, the patriotism, and the fellow-feeling of their provincial parliaments too much to acquiesce in their annihilation; and accordingly they opposed this decisive step of the court with a spirit and unanimity that has appalled its despotic spirit, and suspended, if not frustrated, the intended innovation.

What a surprising familarity there is in this project of the French court and that of our *would-be despots!* The Cæsars of this country, having been baffled in all their attempts upon the liberties of the separate states, by the patriotism and vigilance of the representatives of the people in the state legislatures, they have availed themselves a peculiar crisis of trade and public affairs, of the universal wish to vest Congress with competent powers, to procure the establishment of a general government, or *court pleniere*, that will from its constitution grasp all powers and silently abrogate the state governments.

In the conduct and example of the French provincial parliaments we have a striking illustration of the great utility and indeed necessity of local or provincial governments being vested with competent power to prevent the oppression of the general government, who being so far removed from the people, would possess neither the means or the disposition to consult and promote their interests and felicity. The provincial parliaments of France, although infinitely inferior in their constitution and independency to our state legislatures, have proved an efficient obstacle to the extension of arbitrary power, and in all probability will be the instruments of procuring a constitution of government that will secure the enjoyment of the inestimable blessings of liberty to every citizen of France.

Our *grandees*, apprehensive that the opposition making by the French nation to the abolition of their provincial parliaments, and against the establishment of the new constitution, or *court pleniere*, might from similarity of principles and circumstances, open the eyes of the Americans to the despotism aimed at in our new constitution or *court pleniere*, has endeavored to conceal the true nature of the convulsions by which France is at present agitated; and in this view, in contradiction to the most authentic information both public and private, they have industriously circulated the idea that the designs of the French court are patriotic and in favor of the people, and that the opposition to their measures proceeds from a set of interested men, who wish to exempt themselves from the common burthens; but where is the American patriot who credits this representation, when he sees a *Fayette*, an *Armand*, among the foremost in this opposition, when he beholds the magnanimity and heroism displayed by this opposition who, fearless of the frowns and persecution of the court, presevere in the defense of their rights, esteeming banishment, imprisonment, loss of offices and emoluments, highly honorable when incurred in such a cause?

Galen, who in common with those of his party, had experienced the galling mortification of being defeated in every attempt to overthrow our invaluable state constitution, declared in the Convention, "that he rejoiced at the prospect which the establishment of the new constitution afforded of the state governments being laid at the feet of Congress." This sentiment, which the Doctor had indiscreetly suffered to escape from him in the hour of insolence and triumph, was afterwards ingeniously explained away, lest the people should be apprised of the real object in view by this premature discovery; for James the Caledonian, the principal framer and advocate of the new constitution, had been obliged to confess, that so extensive a country as the United States include, could not be governed on the principles of freedom by one consolidated government, but that such a one must necessarily be supremely despotic.

My next number will be on the subject of the immense sums of public money unaccounted for, now ascertained by a late investigation of Congress, which perhaps will be the most effectual method of elucidating the principles of a number of the great advocates of the new constitution, and enable the public to form a better judgment of one of the men lately appointed by the legislature of this State to a seat in the Federal Senate and of some of the men proposed as Federal representatives, who will be found to be but puppets to this great public defaulter.   CENTINEL.

Philadelphia, November 6, 1788.

CENTINEL, No. XXII.*

To the PEOPLE of PENNSYLVANIA. *Friends and Fellow Citizens.*

It was my intention to appropriate this number to the consideration of the enormous sums of public money unaccounted for by individuals, now ascertained by a late investigation of Congress; but accidentally meeting with an address to the freemen of Pennsylvania, signed *Lucullus*, published in the *Federal Gazette* of November 6th, I thought no time should be lost in detecting the atrocious falsehoods, and counteracting the baneful poison contained in that address. In a former number I noticed the base policy practised by the *Republicans*, as they styled themselves, of imitating and prejudicing that part of the community who were disaffected to our cause in the late war against the constitutional Whigs, by the grossest calumny and misrepresentation of their conduct and principles, and thereby duping the disaffected into the support of measures, which their dispassionate judgment would have reprobated as highly injurious to the common welfare. That address is a continuation of the same policy, and from characteristic features, is known to be the production of *Galen*, who has done more to destroy the harmony of

* From "The Independent Gazetteer; or, The Chronicle of Freedom," Nov. 14, 1788.

Pennsylvania, and forward the vassalage of her citizens to the *rich and aspiring* than all the other firebrands of party and instruments of ambition.

We are now hastening to a crisis that will determine the fate of this great country—that will decide whether the United States is to be ruled by a free government, or subjected to the supremacy of a *lordly and profligate few.* Hitherto the gratification of party spirit and prejudice was attended with the ruin of the honest Whigs and the emolument and aggrandizement of the *Republicans* at the common expense; but now it would be attended with the loss of all liberty and the establishment of a general thraldom—men of all descriptions, except our rulers, would equally wear the fetters, and experience the evils of despotism; it therefore behooves every man who has any regard for the welfare and happiness of his country, of himself, or his posterity, to endeavor to divest himself of all prejudices that may bias or blind his judgment on this great occasion. In confidence of a dispassionate perusal and consideration, I will now take up the address and expose its fallacy. It begins, "You will be called upon on the last Wednesday of the present month to give your votes for *eight* persons to represent you in the Legislature of the United States. You never were called upon to exercise the privilege of electing rulers upon a more important occasion. Two tickets will be offered you. The one will contain men who will support the new constitution *in its present form:* the other ticket will contain men who will overset the government under the specious pretext of amending it." Here is a plain, explicit avowal that the new constitution is to be supported in its *present form*; I hope this declaration will open the eyes of those people who have been deluded by the deceitful promises of amendments, and that being thereby convinced of the fallacy of the reiterated assurances of amendments, they will now embrace the only method left of obtaining them, by giving their suffrages and influence to the other ticket. The bugbear raised to intimidate the people from voting for this ticket, viz: "that the design is to destroy the government under the specious pretext of amending it," I trust will be treated with the deserved contempt, and that this low device will only confirm the people the more in their determination to support men favorable to amendments. The address proceeds, "To give you just ideas of the anti-federal ticket, I shall only add that it was composed and will be supported by persons who violated the rights of conscience by imposing a wicked and tyrannical *test-law* upon the Quakers, Mennonists, and other sects of Christians who hold war to be unlawful." In regard to the *test-law*, I shall only observe that the circumstances of the times justified, nay, made it indispensably necessary; that it was a dictate of common sense and agreeable to the great law of self-preservation to draw a line of discrimination, and exclude from our councils and places of power and trust those persons who were inimical to our cause; and that such has been, and must ever be, from the nature of things, the practice of all nations when engaged in civil war. However, I am clearly of opinion that sound policy dictates the repeal of such laws as soon as it can be done consistent with the public safety, to prevent men of such principles and views of *Galen* and his party from availing themselves of the irritated feelings of the non-jurors and their friends, to compass designs prejudicial to the public liberties and welfare.

The *tender law* stands next in the catalogue of crimes. "Who ruined half the widows, orphans and aged citizens in the State, by an unjust and cruel tender law?" In order to form a judgment of the propriety of this law, we must recur to the occasion of making it. When the thirteen late provinces, now States of America, in Congress assembled, came to the resolution of supporting their liberty and independence by the sword, they found it necessary to anticipate the resources of the country by emitting bills of credit; and as the value and efficiency of this means depended on their being received in all transactions equal to gold and silver money of like denominations, a legal compulsion to ensure this currency to them was *then* deemed essentially necessary, and accordingly Congress recommended the measure to the several States, who, in compliance therewith, passed laws making the continental money a legal tender. This paper money was the sinew of the war, and as such was to be cherished—upon its credit depended our political salvation. However, it is my decided opinion that Congress was mistaken in supposing that the credit of paper money could be supported by making it a legal tender: it is adequate funds of redemption being provided, and public confidence only that can stamp the value of money on paper.

But why censure the Government of Pennsylvania for laws that were made ministerially, in compliance with the recommendation of Congress? May not every government in the union be stigmatized on the same principle, as they all passed similar laws? Moreover, with what consistency can the *Republicans* adduce the tender laws as a crime against the *Constitutionalists*, when the former were the authors of the most oppressive of them, when they renewed these laws after they had been suspended by the Constitutionalists? A recurrents to the minutes of the assembly and the laws of the State will fully establish this fact. It will thereby appear that the assembly elected in October 1779, who were to a man Constitutionalists, suspended the operation of the laws making the continental money a legal tender for three months, by their act passed on the 31st May, 1780, which was further continued by their act of the 22d of September following; and by the succeeding assembly, which were *Republicans*, it was continued without limitation. Thus the legal tender of the continental money was first suspended by the Constitutionalists; and this same assembly passed a law, on the 25th March, 1780, for emitting £100,000 in bills of credit, founded on the City Lots and Province Island, without mading them a legal tender.

It will also appear by the minutes of Assembly and laws, that the Republicans afterwards, viz., on the 9th of April, 1781, emitted the enormous sum of £500,000 in bills of credit, at a time when the public exigencies did not require or justify this oppressive emission of paper money, and could only be accounted for by the scene of profitable speculation that was made on this money by the *Cofferer* and his friends; and this paper the Republicans made a legal tender, with heavy forfeitures and penalties in case of refusal.

The Republicans moreover made the £100,000 island money emitted by the Constitutionalists a legal tender, although the fund of redemption was so abundantly adequate, the consequence of which was a greater depreciation. And these tender laws were not made in pursuance of recommendations of Congress, but were the original acts of the Republicans.

If the *tender laws* have been so cruel and wicked, so destructive as "to ruin half the widows, orphans, and aged citizens in the state," how came the immaculate Republicans to renew them at so late a period in the war, when they must have been fully informed of their operation, and when they had not so good a plea to justify them? What unparalleled impudence to charge the *Constitutionalists* with the hardships and evils of laws that they, the Republicans, were instrumental in reviving and continuing! And yet as extravagant and inconsistent as this charge is, the prejudice and credulity of party spirit has implicitly believed it. Although the Republican party devised and made the last *tender laws* for their private emolument, although *they* reaped the rich harvest of speculations on the public credit by means of these laws, yet the Constitutionalists must bear all the odium of *them*.

The *Doctor* has exhibited a most exaggerated picture of the grievous consequences of the *militia law;* he says "that wagons have been sold for 3s. 9d, cows for 9d, etc. Whoever reprobates the militia law, must on the same principle reprobate the late glorious contest for liberty; for any person the least acquainted with the transactions of the war, must know that the militia were very instrumental to our success; a law was therefore necessary to form and call forth this militia when requisite. If, in the execution of a general system, hardships have happened to individuals, they are to be considered as private misfortunes, not public oppressions; or if collectors and other officers have prostituted this law to private gain, they are to be stigmatized, not the law or its framers.

The address continues, "who have pocketed, or squandered away as much confiscated property as would have paid, if it had been properly disposed of, half the debt of the state!" This is a charge easily made, but until the mere assertion of an anonymous writer is deemed sufficient to substantiate the fact, the public will expect better evidence. I call upon the doctor to name the instances, point out the persons, and produce the proof of this peculation on the confiscated property; and in answer to the other part of the charge, viz: "that it was squandered," I will say it is equally groundless, whether as to the appropriation that was made of this property, or as to the premature disposition of it; for if we may judge from the temper and conduct of succeeding houses of assembly, it is evident that had the sales of this property been postponed, they would never have taken place, as it would have been restored to the original owners.

The address proceeds, "who have banished specie and credit from the state, by their last emission of paper money. Who have nearly ruined the state by assuming and funding the debts of the United States, whereby they have checked our agriculture, commerce and manufactures, and driven many thousands of farmers and mechanics to Kentucky and Niagara." If an honest, just compliance with public engagements, if the support of public credit, so prized by every wise nation and inviolably maintained by the enlightened government of *Great Britain*, as its great resource in time of need, is considered criminal in *Pennsylvania*, the funding law and the last emission of paper money cannot be vindicated; but I am persuaded the people of this state have too high a sense of justice and too much discernment to their permanent interests for this doctrine to become popular.

"Who have burdened the state with expensive establishments and salaries, thereby encouraging idleness, dependence and servility among our citizens." This is a groundless assertion and base calumny.

"Who have violated the constitution of the state by sacrilegiously robbing an institution of learning and charity of its charter and funds." I refer my readers to the reasons of the majority of the council of censors, for a complete refutation of this charge.

"Who by the number and weight of their taxes, have reduced landed property to one fourth of its former value, and thereby forced many ancient and respectable farmers and merchants, possessed of large visible estates, to submit to the operations of laws which have reduced them from well-earned affluence or independence to poverty and misery.'' How lost to all sense of truth and decency must the Doctor be to ascribe the evils of the oppressive taxes to the *Constitutionalists*, when he knows his party were the authors of them? Does he forget the enormous tax of 1782, imposed by his friend Mr. *Morris*, which vastly exceeded the ability of the people to pay, amounting to £425,000 in specie besides the paper money?—a tax that has been productive of more distress and mischief than the aggregate of all the previous and subsequent taxes, and is the efficient cause of our present difficulties in taxation; and does the Doctor forget the other numerous taxes imposed by the same party, some of them to favor their speculations in the paper moneys?

"Who have opposed the adoption of the Federal government by the grossest falsehoods, by the abuse of the best characters in the United States, and by an attempt to excite a civil war." A review of the discussion of the new constitution will expose the fallacy of this charge; whilst sound reason and well-supported arguments were made use of by the opposition, scurrility and abuse of every person who dared to object to the new constitution, were lavished by the *Federalists*, and if there was any danger of a civil war, it arose from their violence and precipitance in forcing down the government without glving the people time or opportunity to examine or judge for themselves.

"Who aim at nothing but power or office—who have nothing to lose, and everything to hope, from a general convulsion." This comes very consistently from a party which abounds in needy office hunters, whose staunch federalism and obsequious services are founded on, and stimulated by, the ravishing prospect of sharing in the great loaves and fishes of the United States, under the new constitution.

"Whose private characters are as profligate as their public conduct has been oppresive, dishonest, and selfish, and who, instead of aiming to share in the honors of the new government, should retire in silent gratitude for having escaped those punishments to which their numerous frauds, oppressions and other crimes, have justly exposed them." If I was disposed to recriminate—there is an ample field—I would begin with the *cofferer*, the head of the other party, and trace his character through the numerous speculations on the public, from his appointment to the c——l a——y of the United States, to his resignation as f——r; I would delineate the corrupt principles and conduct of the rest of the party down to the herd of base parasites and minions, the Doctor included, who would make a conspicuous figure in the black picture. On the other hand, I challenge the Doctor or his associates to sully the integrity, the disinterested conduct of the leaders of the constitutional party, by any colorable charge of peculation or abuse of the public trusts so often confided to them. Like the virtuous *Fabricius*, they retired from offices of the highest eminence and opportunities of embezzling the public treasure, with unpolluted hands and native integrity; so far from growing rich in the public service, they have impaired their own fortunes by their zeal and contributions for the public welfare; and instead of receiving applause for their patriotism, they are loaded with obloquy, are vilified and stigmatized with that poverty which is their greatest glory, and by the very men too who charge them with peculating on the public. How ungenerous and inconsistent! At the same time I must confess, that there have been villains of the constitutional party, for perfection is not to be expected on this side eternity. But it has been the good fortune of this party, that the instances have been rare and of an inferior kind; they did not ascend to the principals of the party, to the great influential leading characters, who gave the complexion and tone to the measures of government.

The foregoing remarks upon the first part of the address apply equally to the remainder, and prove the fallacy and turpitude of the whole of it.   CENTINEL.

Philadelphia, November 12th, 1788.

CENTINEL, NO. XXIII.*

To the PEOPLE of PENNSYLVANIA. *Friends and Fellow Citizens.*

I have promised a number on the subject of the enormous sums of public moneys unaccounted for by individuals, now ascertained by a late investigation of Congress, but find so extensive a field opened, as to require many numbers to treat of the several parts in a proper manner; I shall, therefore, confine my remarks at present to one paragraph of it. This investigation, after being long suppressed, has at length reached the public eye, and is of such magnitude and exhibits such immense peculations on the public treasure by men who now assume the lead in this and some other of the state governments, and are among the most distinguished patrons of the new constitution, as to demand the serious attention of the citizens of the United States at this peculiar crisis of public affairs.

Unawed by that power and influence, that false glare of reputation and by that clamor and partiality of party spirit, which for many years had rendered the characters of the great public defaulters sacred and impervious to public scrutiny, the *Centinel*, regardless of consequences in such a cause, impeached them at the bar of the public; he charged them with the receipt of millions of public money, for which they had not accounted; and notwithstanding he produced sufficient documents to substantiate the charge—such was the shameless effrontery of these men and their minions on the one hand, and the confirmed prejudice and partiality of the public on the other hand, that the Centinel was deemed a *libeller*, a *calumniator* of some of the best and most illustrious characters in the United States. So immaculate was the *Cofferer* considered, that the epithets of rascal, villian etc., were lavished upon every person who dared to assert anything to his prejudice, and the cry of a cruel persecution was raised against the Centinel and others for endeavoring to compel him to disgorge the public treasure.

*From "The Independent Gazetteer; or, The Chronicle of Freedom," Nov. 20, 1788.

Congress have now confirmed the charges adduced by the Centinel against Mr. *Robert Morris* and the other great public defaulters, so that if any person hereafter advocates the principles and measures of these men, he will thereby acknowledge congenial sentiments and proclaim his own character—the public will be equally aware of the one as of the other.

In my seventeenth number, there is the following paragraph: "When we consider the immense sums of public money taken up by Mr. Morris, as commercial agent, to import military supplies, and even to trade in behalf of the United States, at a time when the risk was so great that individuals would not venture their property; that all these transactions were conducted under the private firm of *Willing* and *Morris*, which afforded unrestrained scope to peculation and embezzlement of the public property, by enabling Mr. Morris to throw the loss of all captures by the enemy at that hazardous period on the public, and converting most of the safe arrivals (which were consequently very valuable) into his private property; and when we add to these considerations, the principles of the *man*, his bankrupt situation at the commencement or the war, and the immense wealth he has dazzled the world with since, can it be thought unreasonable to conclude that the principal source of his wealth was the commercial agency of the United States during the war?—not that I would derogate from his successful ingenuity in his numerous speculations in the paper moneys, Havannah monopoly and job, or in the sphere of financiering."

And in a piece which I wrote under the signature of "*One of the People*," published in the *Independent Gazetteer* of April 17th last, I referred to a report of a committee of Congress of the 11th of February, 1779, to prove that Mr. Morris was a member of the secret or commercial committee, and that this committee had authorized and entrusted him *solely* with the purchasing of produce in the different states, and exporting the same on the public account, and that all such contracts were made by him under the private firm of *Willing* and *Morris*.

Mr. Morris, being absent in Virginia when the Centinel made the foregoing charge against him, his friends and minions undertook the vindication of his character; they asserted that he had rendered his accounts as commercial agent, and that they were settled; but Mr. Morris, sensible that the ground which his advocates had taken for his justification was not tenable, and that their officious zeal had led them to make assertions that could easily be disproved, was obliged to confess that he had not settled, nor even rendered his accounts as commercial agent, at the distant period of ten years after his transactions in that capacity; but with his usual ingenuity endeavored to apologize for not doing it, as will appear by a recurrence to his address to the public, dated Richmond, March 21st, and published in the *Independent Gazetteer* of April 8th last.

I will make an extract of this address containing Mr. Morris's acknowledgment of receiving the public money and his not settling his accounts. It is as follows, viz.: "At an early period of the revolution, I contracted with the committees to import arms, ammunition and clothing, and was employed to export American produce, and make remittances on account of the United States, for the purpose of lodging funds in Europe. To effect these objects, I received considerable sums of money. The business has been performed, but the accounts are not yet settled."

Having stated the charge formerly made against Mr. Morris and the evidence that was then in my power to establish it, I will now add a quotation from the late investigation made by Congress, extracted from their journals of the 30th September last, viz.: "Your committee turning their attention to an act of Congress on the 22d of May last, directing the board of treasury to call upon all such persons as had been entrusted with public money, and had neglected to account for the same, and such other persons as had made partial or vague settlements, without producing proper vouchers, were desirous to obtain a particular statement of the accounts which are in the above predicament; but they are sorry to find that such a detail is too lengthy to be here inserted.

Some of those accounts are stated in the file of papers marked *papers respecting unsettled acccunts*, which is herewith submitted. From the general aspect of those accounts, your committee are constrained to observe, that there are many strong marks of the want of responsibility or attention in the former trasactions respecting the public treasures. No less a sum than 2,122,600 dollars has been advanced to the secret committee of Congress, before August 2d, 1777, and a considerable part of this money remains to be accounted for otherwise than by contracts made with individuals of their *own* body, while those individuals neglect to account.''

Thus it appears that a considerable part of the enormous sum of two millions, one hundred twenty-two thousand and six hundred dollars, nearly equal to specie, which was advanced to the secret committee of Congress, remains unaccounted for, otherwise than by contracts made with individuals of their *own* body, *while those individuals neglected to account.* And who those individuals are is evident from the report of the committee of Congress on the 11th of February, 1779, before quoted, and from other records of Congress. By them it appears, that after the death of Mr. *Ward*, who was the first chairman and agent of the *secret* committee, which happened very early, before this committee had transacted much business, that Mr. Robert Morris was solely entrusted by the secret committee with the disposition of the public money advanced to them, and that all his transactions as commercial agent, were conducted by him under the private firm of Willing and Morris.

Eleven years have now elapsed since Mr. Morris was entrusted with the disposition of near two millions of specie dollars, and no account of this immense sum has yet been rendered by him. What conclusion must every dispassionate person make of this delinquency? Is it not more than probable that he has converted the public money to his own property, and that, fearful of detection, and reluctant to refund, he has, and will, as long as he is able, avoid an investigation and settlement of these long standing accounts?

I will ask, did the majority of the late assembly evince

either wisdom or virtue, when they appointed this man to a seat in the *federal senate*, or will the people evidence any regard to their own interests if they give their suffrages to his creatures, who are now proposed as federal representatives? Under the administration of such men, is it rational to expect that public defaulters will be called to account, or that future peculation and pocketing of the public money will be discouraged or detected?

I intend in future numbers to notice the other numerous instances of public defaulters, and to show that if it had not been for the immense peculations and pocketing of the public moneys by individuals, and those among our most distinguished *Federalists*, that the people would not have been burdened with above one-third of the present national debt and consequent taxes.

The following article of the last report of the committee of congress on the finances, will be the subject of my next number, viz.: "Your committee were desirous to discover in what manner the large sums of money received in France have been accounted for, but the subject of this inquiry seems to be involved in darkness.

	Livres	s.	d.
The amount of the several receipts is	47,111,859	12	8
Of this sum there has been sent over or drawn for and expended in America 26,246,727 5 5			
Salaries of foreign ministers 1,160,183			
	27,406,910	5	5
There remains	19,704,949	7	3

"The documents for the expenditures of this balance have never been produced at the treasury. They must be in France if there are any such papers. A full inquiry into the premises now claims the attention of the board of treasury. Some time must be expended in making the necessary investigation, but the result may be of important service to the United States."

In the investigation of this article, which informs us of a deficiency of upwards of nineteen millions of livres specie, however it may offend, I must expose the names of the men who have received this money. CENTINEL.

Philadelphia, November 17, 1788.

To the PEOPLE of PENNSYLVANIA. *Friends and Fellow Citizens.*

This number was appropriated to the investigation of that article of the last report of a committee of Congress, which informs us of a deficiency of NINETEEN MILLIONS of livres SPECIE, in the moneys entrusted to our *Commissioners* in *France*, the principal of whom was the Honorable BEN-JAMIN FRANKLIN the sanction of whose name has given such weight and success to the new constitution; but I shall be obliged to postpone the discussion of this subject in order to notice Mr. *Morris's* answer published in the *Independent Gazetteer* of this morning to my last number.

Mr. Morris, presuming upon the strength and continuance of those prejudices which his ingenuity and address had so successfully raised, and which for many years had blinded the public to his real principles and conduct, and enabled him to prosecute his schemes of profit and aggrandizement to an immense extent, without detection or jealousy, has now the effrontery to treat the serious, well founded charges of the CENTINEL, and a report of a committee of Congress, with supercilious contempt, and to suppose that his unsup-ported assertions in a matter where he is so deeply interested, will be implicitly believed by that public whose property, to the amount of millions, he was entrusted with above eleven years ago, and for which he has not yet accounted.

Mr. Morris says, "On the repeated slanders of my enemies, so far as they can affect myself, I look down with silent con-tempt; but as I have been lately honored with a high trust in the federal government, and as an attempt is made to wound the federal cause by attacks on my reputation and the con-duct of those who appointed me to a seat in the senate, *my attachment to that cause*, and my respect for my fellow citizens, lead me to inform them that I have lately been at New York for the purpose of bringing forward a settlement of my ac-counts with the United States, and they are now in a *train*

* From Independent Gazetteer, Nov. 24, 1788.

of investigation, and that I shall do everything in my power
to obtain a final settlement of them before the meeting of
Congress under the new constitution.''

Is it slander to call upon a public officer to account for the
disposition of millions of public money entrusted to him
above eleven years ago? Or is it slander to denominate such
a man a public defaulter? Can any reasonable or honest obstacle have so long delayed the settlement of his accounts,
especially when we consider the abilities and accuracy of this
man in accounts, and his persevering diligence and assiduity
to business? Is it now probable that he really means to
render his accounts, when we advert to the unsuccessful exertions of a series of the greatest characters in Congress to
compel him to account, and who for more than eleven years
have been baffled in all their virtuous and patriotic attempts
by the predominant influence and the machinations of this
man and his minions? What have become of the labors of
Manheim, where Mr. Morris retired at a gloomy and doubtful crisis of public affairs under the avowed pretence of preparing these very accounts for settlement? Where is the
man besides Mr. Morris, who can thus act and preserve any
character or confidence, or who with so serious and weighty
a charge against him would continue to be preferred to the
highest honors and trusts of his country, with the power of
screening past delinquencies, and the opportunity of further
speculations; or who would be supported and justified by so
numerous and powerful a party?

As an instance of Mr. Morris's dangerous influence, and
also of his reluctance to have his accounts, even as superintendent of finance, investigated, it may be observed that the
public spirited men in Congress on the 21st of June, 1785,
procured, with great difficulty, against the strenuous opposition and low subterfuges of Mr. Morris's friends and minions,
a resolution of that honorable body to this effect, that three
commissioners be appointed to examine the receipts and expenditures of the late superintendent of finance; but this resolution was the only consequence of this virtuous effort, for
Mr. Morris has been able to prevent any Commissioners being

appointed in pursuance of this resolution entered into above three years since.   It is true that very lately the disinterested part of Congress, strengthened by the attacks made by the Centinel and others upon the great public defaulters, and the consequent clamor of the people, have, against the secret inclination of a majority of Congress, obtained resolutions and appointments of officers to compel the public defaulters to account and restore the public moneys; but the efficacy of these resolutions and appointments entirely depends on the complexion of the Congress under the new constitution; for if the great public defaulters and their minions be elected, it would be ridiculous to suppose that they would countenance scrutiny into the conduct of themselves and patrons.   Mr. Morris, sensible that if he can carry his creatures who are proposed as representatives in the new Congress, he may laugh at and *really* contemn any future attempts to call him to account, has, therefore, at the eve of the approaching decisive election promised to settle and account for the immense sums of public money that he received above eleven years ago, and even assures that he has been at New York lately on this business and that his accounts are in a *train* of investigation. But like the Manheim investigation promised as seriously eight or nine years ago, the present will prove to have no other existence than in the deception of the moment, and this *train* will be found delusive and without end.

My fellow citizens, suffer not yourselves to be thus continually imposed on by a man whose whole career in public life has been marked by delinquencies in money concerns; but make choice of such men to represent you as will secure your liberties and property.   And as you are now well acquainted with the principles and views of Mr. Morris, you are enabled to form a proper opinion of Messrs. *Fitzsimons*, *Clymer*, etc., who for ten years past have been the devoted instruments and partisans of Mr. Morris, and participators in his numerous speculations.   CENTINEL.

Philadelphia, Saturday Noon, November 22d, 1788.

CHAPTER VIII.

SKETCHES OF THE PENNSYLVANIA MEMBERS OF THE FEDERAL CONVENTION.

PENNSYLVANIA was represented in the federal convention by a larger delegation than any of the other states. This was no doubt owing to the fact that Philadelphia had been chosen as the place where the sessions of the convention were to be held, and it imposed no hardship or expense on her citizens to attend. Travelling in those days on horseback or by stage wagon was attended by fatigue and expense, and so closely were expenses watched that when the Pennsylvania Assembly declined to provide compensation for its delegates, representatives from the rural districts declined to serve.

Not only was the delegation the largest in the convention, but it was one of the most distinguished. Of the fifty-six men who signed the Declaration of Independence but six signed the constitution, and of these four were from Pennsylvania. Gouverneur Morris and James Wilson led the debate in the convention. The former spoke one hundred and seventy-three times, the latter one hundred and sixty-eight times. But Wilson must be regarded as the father of the constitution in Pennsylvania. His advocacy of it before the people, his clear and forcible explanation of its meaning in the state convention, clearly entitle him to this. The attacks made upon him in the public press show how he was recognized as its chief advocate by those who opposed it. For months his time was entirely devoted to the work, and it is doubtful if without his earnest effort, the constitution would have been ratified by Pennsylvania.

We print the sketches of the Pennsylvania members in the order in which they signed the constitution.

BENJAMIN FRANKLIN was the oldest member of the convention, being at that time eighty-one years of age. A philosopher whose wisdom was world-renowned, he exceeded in practical knowledge every one of his associates. With no pretensions as a speaker, he disposed of every question with extraordinary brevity, sometimes by a happy allegory, sometimes by a single sentence. No man in the convention, save Washington, was more revered. No man could boast of such a remarkable career. To give more than a bare outline of this here would be the work of supererogation.

He was the son of Josiah Franklin and Mary Folger; was born at Boston, Mass., January 17, 1706. Apprenticed to his brother James as a printer, after a few years, owing to a disagreement, he left home and established himself in Philadelphia. He worked as a journeyman printer in London in 1725, but returned the next year to Pennsylvania, subsequently becoming editor and proprietor of the *Pennsylvania Gazette*, and publisher of Poor Richard's Almanac. In 1731 he assisted in founding the Philadelphia Library; became clerk to the Assembly in 1736; postmaster of Philadelphia in 1737; and in 1753 was deputy postmaster-general of the British Colonies. On October 4, 1748, he was chosen one of the Common Councilmen of the city of Philadelphia; and on October 1, 1751, alderman. In 1752 he made the discovery of the identity of lightning with the electric fluid. In 1754, as a commissioner from Pennsylvania to the Albany Congress, he prepared the plan of union for the common defence adopted by that body. During the French and Indian wars he was commissioned a Colonel in the provincial service, and in 1755 superintended the furnishing of transportation for the supplies of Braddock's army. He served as a member of the Assembly from 1751 to 1763, the latter year being speaker; from 1757 to 1762, and again from 1765 to 1775, he was the agent of the province to Great Britain, spending most of his time in England, and while there aided in securing the repeal of the obnoxious stamp act. In 1762 the Universities of Oxford and Edinburgh conferred on him for his scientific discoveries the degree of LL. D., he having been previously honored with a membership in the Royal Society, and by being the recipient of the Copley gold medal. From 1773 to

1775 he was again elected to the Assembly. Returning to Philadelphia in the spring of 1775, he was chosen a member of the continental Congress. He was a member of the provincial conference at Carpenters' Hall, June 18, 1775, and of the Committee of Safety from June 30, 1775, to July 22, 1776. While in Congress he was one of the committee to prepare, as he was also a signer of the Declaration of Independence. He was a member of the constitutional convention of July 15, 1776, and chosen its President. From the close of 1776 to September, 1785, he was the American Ambassador to France, and secured the treaty of alliance with that country, signed February 6, 1778, which greatly assisted in securing the independence of the colonies. He took a prominent part in negotiating the preliminary treaty of peace with England, which was signed at Paris, November 30, 1782, and with Adams and Jay signed that at Ghent, September 3, 1783. He was President of Pennsylvania from October 17, 1785, to November 5, 1788, declining on account of his advanced years to continue in office. In May, 1787, he was a delegate to the convention which framed the constitution of the United States. He died in the city of Philadelphia; April 17, 1790.

THOMAS MIFFLIN was born in Philadelphia in 1744. It was the intention of his father that he should be a merchant, and after he had graduated at the College of Philadelphia he was placed in the counting-house of William Coleman. When he was 21 years of age he visited Europe to improve his knowledge of commercial affairs and after his return home entered into business with his brother, the connection continuing until after the commencement of the Revolution. His interest in public affairs began while he was quite a young man, and in 1765 he signed the famous non-importation agreement, opposing the stamp act. In 1772 he was chosen one of the two representatives of Philadelphia in the Assembly, and was so continued until 1776. He was a delegate to the Congress of 1774, that met in Carpenters' Hall. In 1775 he was Colonel and Adjutant-General of the continental army, Brigadier General in 1776, Major General in

1777. In the latter part of that year he resigned his position and was chosen a member of the Board of War. In 1780 he was again engaged in mercantile pursuits. He was a member of the continental Congress in 1782 and 1783, serving as President during the latter year. He was Speaker of the Assembly in 1785–88; member of the Federal Convention 1787; President of the Supreme Executive Council 1788–90; President of the constitutional Convention of Pennsylvania in 1790; Governor of Pennsylvania from 1790–9; member of the Legislature 1799–1800, dying in January of the latter year.

Mifflin was a fluent speaker, and used his powers to the utmost in organizing an opposition to the Boston Port Bill and similar measures. In the darkest days of the Revolution, when Washington's army reduced to a handful was retreating through Jersey, Mifflin, at the request of Congress, went through the State, addressing the people at all the principal points, urging them to join Washington with as little delay as possible. So successful was he that some of the militia reached the army before it had crossed the Delaware, and the thousands that soon poured into camp, made the advance that resulted in the victory at Princeton a necessity. Unfortunately for the reputation of Mifflin, he afterwards associated with Gates and Conway, and his name has come down in history as one who sought to remove Washington from command of the army. While he left on record a solemn protest that his action was dictated by the purest patriotism, it is impossible not to believe that his judgment was warped by jealousy excited by the preference Washington showed for others. While Mifflin was President of Congress the war closed and Washington resigned his commission. It was tendered personally to Mifflin, whose reply to the few words uttered by Washington were dignified and eloquent. "We join you," he said, "in commending the interests of our dearest country to the protection of Almighty God, beseeching Him to dispose the hearts and minds of its citizens to improve the opportunity afforded them to become a happy and respectable nation. And for you we address to

Him our earnest prayers that a life so beloved may be fostered with all His care; that your days may be as happy as they have been illustrious; and that He will finally give you that reward which this world cannot give."

Whatever Mifflin's sentiments were at one time regarding Washington, the latter harbored no ill feelings in return, and on several subsequent occasions was Mifflin's guest. Although a warm advocate of the adoption of the constitution, Mifflin subsequently belonged to the republican or anti-federal party, but this did not prevent him from supporting the general government in the suppression of the Whisky Insurrection. The elder Rawle, who knew him personally, says: "In person he was remarkably handsome, though his stature did not exceed five feet eight inches. His frame was athletic, and seemed capable of bearing much fatigue."

ROBERT MORRIS, the financier of the American Revolution, was born in Liverpool on the 31st of January, 1734. Prior to 1740 he came with his father, also Robert Morris, to America, and settled in Oxford county, Maryland. While quite young, Robert, the son, was sent to Philadelphia, and entered the counting house of Charles Willing, and in 1754 formed a partnership with his son, Thomas Willing, which lasted until 1793. In 1765 he vigorously opposed the Stamp Act, and signed the non-importation agreement. Upon the formation of the Committee of Safety in 1775, he was made its Vice-President, and continued in that office until its dissolution in 1776. He was a member of the second continental Congress that met in Philadelphia in 1775, and served on committees for furnishing the colonies with a naval armament and for procuring money for Congress. When the question of Independence came up for final action on July 2, 1776, Morris voted against it, and on the FOURTH, when the Declaration was submitted for approval, absented himself from Congress, as in his opinion it was "an improper time" for such a measure. He subsequently, however, signed the engrossed Declaration.

In December, 1776, when the Congress retired to Baltimore, he was one of the committee left behind to attend to public business, and it was at that time on his personal credit he raised the money that kept the army together and enabled Washington to follow up his advantage at Trenton with his victory at Princeton. On July 9, 1778, he signed the Articles of Confederation, and in 1780 organized the Bank of Pennsylvania to supply the army with provisions for two months, to which he subscribed £10,000. On May 14, 1781, he accepted the office of Superintendent of Finance, a position he held until November 1, 1784. His success in bringing order out of the chaotic state into which the finances of the country had fallen is too well known to require more than mention. "The Bank of North America," the first incorporated bank in the United States, was organized by him to aid him in the work, and his own fortune was frequently risked for the cause of his adopted country.

In accepting the position of financier he wrote: "The United States may command everything I have except my integrity, and the loss of that would effectually disable me from serving them more."

As a member of the federal convention, Mr. Morris urged that Senators should be chosen for life, and that they should be "men of great and established property." Entertaining such views, he had naturally many opponents, and in the discussions of the day he was vigorously attacked. He was one of the first senators from Pennsylvania under the constitution. After his retiring from public life he entered into vast speculations in unimproved lands, that eventually wrecked his immense fortune, and for a period of over three years and a half he was an inmate of a debtors' prison. He was released on the 16th of February, 1798, and died on May 7, 1806, in his seventy-third year.

GEORGE CLYMER was the son of Christopher and Deborah Clymer. He was born in Philadelphia June 1, 1739. His parents died in 1740, and he was adopted by his uncle, William Coleman, a prominent merchant of Philadelphia. He was educated at the College of Philadelphia, but not formally graduated, and entered the counting house of his uncle, where he obtained an extensive knowledge of mercantile affairs. In

1765 he opposed the stamp act and signed the non-importation agreement. After having occupied a number of positions of honor and trust of a public character, and having served on many of the committees appointed at the outbreak of the Revolution, Mr. Clymer, on July 20, 1775, was chosen one of the treasurers of the Continental Congress, his colleague being Michael Hillegas. From October 20, 1775, until July 22, 1776, Mr. Clymer was a member of the Committee of Safety, and was also a delegate to the constitutional convention of 1776. By that body he was chosen a delegate to the continental Congress, and on August 2d signed the engrossed copy of the Declaration of Independence. He was also elected to Congress in 1778, 80 and 81, and was repeatedly chosen a member of the Assembly of Pennsylvania.

Few men served the public more faithfully or in more diversified ways. Well educated, with refined tastes, and ample fortune to indulge them, he shrank from no responsibility laid upon him, although at utter variance with his retiring disposition. As captain of a company of militia he took part in several campaigns. As a member of a Committee of Congress when that body fled in panic to Baltimore, he remained in Philadelphia with Robert Morris to attend public business. He visited Fort Pitt to pacify the savages in that quarter during the Revolution, and after the adoption of the constitution assisted in forming a treaty with the Creeks and Cherokees in Georgia. He was active in organizing the temporary Bank of Pennsylvania in 1780, and subscribed £5,000 to its capital. He was one of the first directors of the Bank of North America, and subsequently president of the Philadelphia Bank. When it is remembered how the need of a Federal government was made manifest through the disordered condition of the finances of the country, it is not surprising that a person so versed in monetary affairs as Mr. Clymer, should have been selected as a delegate to the general convention. In that body he bore a conspicuous part, and when the constitution was submitted to the States it was he who, in the assembly, moved the calling of a convention for its consideration, thus securing the

early support of Pennsylvania, the first large State that ratified the constitution, and second only in point of time to
Delaware. Under the constitution Mr. Clymer served as a
representative from Pennsylvania during the first Congress.
In the Legislature of the State he urged a revision of the
penal code, and a lessening of its rigorous measures, contending successfully that capital punishment should only be inflicted in extreme cases. He was the first president of the
Academy of the Fine Arts; Vice-President of the American
Philosophical Society and of the Philadelphia Agricultural
Society. He died at the residence of his son, near Morris-
ville, Bucks county, June 24, 1813, in the seventy-fourth
year of his age.

THOMAS FITZSIMONS was born in Ireland in 1741. The
victim of oppression, he came to this country between the
years 1762 and 1765 and settled in Philadelphia, where he engaged in mercantile pursuits. Not long after, he married the
daughter of Mr. Robert Meade, the great-grandfather of the
late Gen. George G. Meade, and formed a partnership with his
brother-in-law, who was one of the prominent merchants and
ship-owners of Philadelphia. He warmly espoused the cause
of the Colonies in their contest with the mother country, and
raised and commanded a military company. He was with
General Cadwalader at Bristol and Burlington, in the move-
ments contemporary with the battles of Trenton and Princeton, and was also a member of the Council of Safety, and of
the Navy Board. His house subscribed, in 1780, £5,000 to
supply the necessities of the army. In 1782, he was elected a
member of the continental Congress, and took a leading part
in the debates on the financial situation. After the peace he
was for several years a member of the General Assembly of
Pennsylvania, and in 1787 he became a member of the Federal
Convention. He opposed universal suffrage and contended
that the privilege of voting should be restricted to freeholders.
He favored giving Congress the power to tax exports as well
as imports, and argued that the House of Representatives
should be united with the President, as well as the Senate, in
making treaties. In the great federal procession in Phila-

delphia, July 4th, 1788, by which the ratification of the constitution by ten States was celebrated, Mr. Fitzsimons appeared, representing the French alliance, mounted on a horse formerly owned by Count Rochambeau, and carrying a flag of white silk, emblazoned with the ensigns of France and the United States. When the National Government was organized, Mr. Fitzsimons was elected by the city of Philadelphia a member of Congress, and remained so until 1795. His views upon all questions of commerce, finance and exchange were highly valued. He also was a conspicuous advocate of a protective tariff. In 1794, he failed of a re-election, that year proving disastrous to the Federalists. With his retirement from Congress, his political career closed. He was a trustee of the University of Pennsylvania; a founder and director of the Bank of North America; a director and subsequently President of the Insurance Company of North America. He was a member of the Catholic church. He is described as a man of commanding figure, and of agreeable, though stately and reserved manners. He died August 26th, 1811.

JARED INGERSOLL* was the only child of Jared Ingersoll, of Connecticut, who represented that colony as commissioner in England when Franklin resided there in a similar capacity for Pensylvania. The family was altogether and exclusively English, without Scotch, Irish, German, Swiss, French, Spanish, or any others of the foreign lineage common in so many other Americans, and had been Americanized by more than a century's descent in New England, when Jared Ingersoll, the second, was born. In 1761–2, his father returned from England with the obnoxious appointment, which his friend Franklin there induced him to undertake, of Stamp-Master General for the New England Colonies. Compelled by a tumultuous assemblage of his fellow colonists forcibly to relinquish that place, Jared Ingersoll the elder was then appointed Admiralty Judge for the colony of Pennsylvania, whereupon he removed to Philadelphia, where he resided till the Revolution.

* By Charles J. Ingersoll in Lives of Eminent Philadelphians

His son Jared, after graduating at Yale College, chose Philadelphia for his residence and the Bar for his profession. Repairing to England to accomplish his professional education, he was entered of the Middle Temple; and during five years, passed in London, diligently studied the science of law, and attended its practice in the courts. Mansfield, Blackstone, Chatham, Garrick and other luminaries of that period were objects of his constant attention, and of his correspondence, and ever after among the pleasures of his memory. Literature, as well as law, was his study; polite society his enjoyment. He formed acquaintances with the distinguished lawyers and members of Parliament.

Soon after the American Revolution was completely pronounced he espoused its cause with the considerate preference of youthful patriotism. Although the only child of a loyalist, he did not hesitate, without filial offence, to side with his own against the mother country, where he had for several years resided.

Taking, therefore, his departure from a country to which he disclaimed allegiance, he passed over to France, and spent a year and a half in Paris. There he added the French language to his acquirements. His father's friend, Franklin, living at Passy, as Minister of the United States, kindly welcomed Mr. Ingersoll there. With Ralph Izard, appointed Minister to Italy, but staying in Paris, John Julius Pringle, of South Carolina, and other afterwards distinguished Americans, Mr. Ingersoll likewise formed intimacies in Paris, which subsisted during life. These southern associations, without diminishing his native eastern attachments, liberalized his patriotism, freed him from local and sectional prejudices, and imbued his politics with that spirit of enlarged nationality in which, following Washington, he always abided.

Returning by a winter-passage in a small schooner, he escaped the perils of the sea and hostile capture, and attained as a superior lawyer, the place he ever after occupied at the Bar of Philadelphia. Philadelphia was then the seat of Government, both Federal and State. The Supreme Court of the United States and of the State held their sessions there, where the most elevated jurisprudence in every branch of law was dispensed. In these courts Jared Ingersoll soon rose to the first rank. His practice was larger than that of any others. His opinions were taken on all important controversies, his services engaged in every great litigation.

In 1787 he was chosen one of the Pennsylvania delegates to assist in forming the constitution of the United States. Twice Attorney General of the State at different periods, for a short time District Attorney of the United States for Pennsylvania, and offered the Chief Judgeship of the Federal Court created in 1801, his large practice prompted him to decline all these eminent stations. During a long career he had no superior at the Bar. Eminent for wisdom and eloquence, he was equally so for probity and honor. Contributing liberally to every improvement introduced for the city of Philadelphia and the State of Pennsylvania, he ended his useful and exemplary life as President Judge of the District Court of Philadelphia, October 31st, 1822, in the seventy-third year of his age.

JAMES WILSON.—For a sketch of James Wilson see page 757.

GOUVERNEUR MORRIS was a grandson of Richard Morris, the first of the family to come to America, and who purchased a large estate in West Chester county, New York, invested with manorial privileges, which he called Morris-ania. He was the youngest son, by a second marriage, of Lewis Morris, for some time Governor of New Jersey, and was born 31st January, 1752.ˈ Graduating from Kings, now Columbia College, in 1768, he began to read law under William Smith, Esq., who was subsequently Chief Justice of the Province of New York, and in October of 1771 was admitted to practice, being not quite twenty years of age.

From the beginning of his career, Gouverneur Morris took a lively interest in public affairs, and in 1775 he was elected a delegate to represent the county of West Chester in the congress convened on 22d May in the city of New York. He continued almost without interruption a member of this body under its different names of congress, convention and Committee of Safety; was a member of the committee which drafted the State constitution of 1776; and when the resolution of the continental Congress recommending a new form of government came up for consideration, he spoke with force and ability. "Sir," said he, "these and ten thousand other reasons will serve to convince me that to make a solid and lasting peace, with liberty and security, is utterly impracticable. My argument, therefore, stands thus: As a connection with Great Britain cannot again exist without enslaving America, an independence is absolutely necessary. I cannot balance between the two. We run a hazard in one path, I confess; but then we are infallibly ruined if we pursue the other."

New York was the last State to sign the Declaration of Independence, her delegates to Congress not being empowered to act independently of the New York convention. But no time was lost. The convention met on the 9th of July, and on that day a copy of the act was received and a resolution of approval passed. To Mr. Morris was entrusted the drafting of the reply to the delegates from New York in the continental Congress. It should also be noted, that he endeavored to introduce an article recommending the future Legislature to take measures for the abolishment of domestic slavery.

In 1778, Gouverneur Morris was sent to the continental Congress, then seated at York, Pennsylvania, and on the day his credentials were approved, he was appointed a member of the committee to investigate the condition of the army at Valley Forge. From this date began the friendship with Washington, which continued through life. He also served on many standing and special committees, and was chairman of three. His ardent interest in the cause of the Colonies did not meet with the approbation of his mother and other members of the family, and he also incurred the displeasure of his early friend and adviser, Judge William Smith. Not being returned to Congress, after a service of five years, Gouverneur Morris began the practice of his profession in Philadelphia, and became a citizen of Pennsylvania. In May of 1780, by a fall from his carriage, Mr. Morris received an injury that resulted in the loss of a leg. Robert Morris—to whom he was not related—appointed him, in 1781, Assistant Superintendent of the Finances, in which position he served with ability for three years and a half. General Washington appointed Morris and Gen. Knox, on behalf of the United States, to consult with the British Commissioners with regard to the exchange of prisoners, the first meeting taking place in March of 1782. Gouverneur Morris was a delegate from Pennsylvania to the convention called for framing the constitution of the United States, which met in Philadelphia in May of 1787, and to his pen is due the clear and forcible language in which the constitution is expressed. Although dissenting from the majority of his colleagues on many important points, when the Constitution was adopted he signed it with entire willingness.

In December of 1788, Mr. Morris sailed for Europe, with confidential letters from Washington, and while abroad was appointed Minister Plenipotentiary to the Court of France. On the recall, in 1793, of M. Genet, the Minister of France, being demanded by the United States, that of Mr. Morris was requested by France, and in 1794 he was succeeded by James Monroe. On his return to America, he established himself at Morrisania, intending never again to enter upon public life, but in 1800 he was chosen to the Senate of the United States to fill a vacancy, and served three years. In politics he was a federalist, but during the "Tie Controversy," he differed with his party and approved the choice of Jefferson.

Gouverneur Morris was a man of strong convictions. In political life he was too independent to be trammelled by the dictates of party, and in private life his integrity was above suspicion; in neither was he influenced by low aims or selfish ambitions. He lived not for fame, but for duty; not for self, but for his country. He died 6th November, 1816.

CHAPTER IX.

BY W. H. EGLE, M. D.

ALLISON, JOHN, of Franklin county, was born in Antrim township, that county, December 23, 1738. His father, William Allison, was a native of the north of Ireland, where he was born on the 12th of November, 1693; came to America about 1730, and located in the Cumberland Valley, where he died on the 14th of December, 1778. John, the second son, received a thorough English and classical education, chiefly under the care of the Scotch-Irish Presbyterian ministers of the locality. As early as October, 1764, he was appointed one of the provincial magistrates for Cumberland county, and reappointed in 1769. At a meeting of the citizens of that county, held at Carlisle on July 12, 1774, he was appointed on the Committee of Observation for Cumberland, and became quite active in the struggle for independence. He was a member of the provincial conference held at Carpenters' Hall, 18th of June, 1776, and appointed by that body one of the judges of the election of members to the first Constitutional Convention for the second division of the county, at Chambersburg. He was in command of one of the Associated battalions of Cumberland county during the Jersey campaigns of 1776 and 1777, and a member of the General Assembly in 1778, 1780, and 1781. In the latter year he laid out the town of Greencastle, which has grown to be one of the most flourishing towns in the Cumberland Valley. In 1787 he was chosen a delegate to the Pennsylvania convention to ratify the federal constitution, and in that body seconded the motion of Thomas McKean to assent to and ratify it. At the first federal conference, held at Lancaster in 1788,

(712)

he was nominated for Congress, but defeated at the election that year. Colonel Allison died June 14, 1795.

ARNDT, JOHN, of Northampton county, son of Jacob Arndt, was born 3d of June, 1748, in Bucks county, province of Pennsylvania. His father removed to Northampton county in 1760, where he erected what was long known as Arndt's mill, on the Bushkill, and here most of his life was spent. At the outset of the war of the Revolution he became one of the leading spirits in that struggle. He was captain of a company in Colonel Baxter's battalion of Northampton county of the "Flying Camp," and in the battle of Long Island was wounded and taken prisoner. He was soon after exchanged, and on the 25th of March, 1777, was commissioned register of wills; and justice of the peace, June, 1777. He was appointed one of the commissioners to take subscriptions for the continental loan, December 16, 1777; and commissary of purchases in Pennsylvania, February 9, 1778. While filling this latter position he advanced large sums of money to the government, most of which was refunded to him. He served on the Committee of Safety for the county, was one of its most efficient members, and earnestly devoted to the patriot cause; was appointed by the General Assembly one of the commissioners to settle the accounts of the County Lieutenants, December 4, 1778; and one of the Commissioners of Exchange, April 5, 1779. He was elected a member of the Council of Censors, 1783–84; delegate to the Pennsylvania convention to ratify the federal constitution, 1787; and chosen an elector at the first presidential election following. In 1783, when Dickinson College was incorporated, he was named one of the original trustees. He served several years as county treasurer, was appointed recorder of deeds and clerk of the Orphans' Court, May 22, 1788, and continued in office under the constitution of 1790 until the election of Governor McKean, when he was removed. Under the act of 1796 the county records were required to be kept at the county seat, when Mr. Arndt took up his residence at Easton, where, after going out of office, he devoted the balance of his life to mercantile pursuits. In 1796 he was nominated for Congress, but defeated by ninety votes.   During the so-called Fries Insurrection of 1798 his utmost exertions were given to the preservation of law and order, and his wise and judicious counsels were heeded by many of the rebellious.   Henry says that Mr. Arndt "as mineralogist and botanist held no mean rank; and his correspondence with Rev. Mr. Gross and other clergymen shows that he was a pious man."   Captain Arndt died on the 6th of May, 1814.

ASHMEAD, SAMUEL, of the county of Philadelphia, the son of John Ashmead, was born in 1731.   Little is known of his early history, save that he received a good education and was brought up to mercantile pursuits.   Early in life he was commissioned one of the provincial magistrates; on January 16, 1767, appointed an associate justice of the Court of Common Pleas, and recommissioned April 27, 1772; and in 1773-74 became presiding justice of the courts.   He was a delegate to the provincial convention held at Philadelphia, January 23, 1775, and served in the General Assembly in 1782, 1783 and 1789.   In 1787 he represented his county in the convention to ratify the federal constitution.   Mr. Ashmead died at his residence in the Northern Liberties on the 19th of March, 1794, and was interred on the 21st in the Baptist Church burial-place.

BAIRD, JOHN, of Westmoreland county, was born about 1740, in Lancaster, now Dauphin county.   He removed to Westmoreland county about 1770, in company with some Scotch-Irish neighbors, and took up land in what was afterwards Huntingdon township.   He appears to have been a man of mark west of the Alleghenies, but in all the histories recently published no mention is made of him.   He served as one of the overseers of the poor in 1773; was appointed by the constitutional convention of 1776 one of the board of commissioners for Westmoreland county, and commissioned a justice of the peace June 11, 1777.   During the war of the Revolution, and in the border wars of his section, he was very efficient in recruiting the military forces.   He was a member of the Supreme Executive Council from November 18, 1786, to November 25, 1789; and a delegate to the Pennsylvania convention to ratify the federal constitution in 1787, but his name was not signed to the ratification. He was one of the members of the anti-constitution party who were mobbed in the city of Philadelphia on the 6th of November, 1787. He was a member of the General Assembly in 1789-'90, and of the House of Representatives in 1790 and 1791. Under the constitution of 1790, he was commissioned one of the associate judges of the county, August 17, 1791. Mr. Baird, we are inclined to believe, died about the beginning of the present century.

BAKER, HILARY, of the city of Philadelphia, was born in Germantown about 1750. He was the son of Hilarius Becker, or Baker, who in 1761 was elected teacher of the Germantown Academy, he having "for some time past kept a German school in Germantown." It is naturally to be supposed that the son received a good classical education, which he did; entered mercantile life, became an iron merchant, which business he carried on for some years. He was commissioned clerk of the Court of Quarter Sessions for the county of Philadelphia, August 19, 1777, which position he filled several years; was appointed interpreter of English and German resident at Philadelphia, February 4, 1779, and the same day notary public for the State. On the 11th of March, 1789, by act of the General Assembly, he was appointed an alderman of the city, and reappointed under the act of April 4, 1796. He was chosen a delegate to the State convention of 1787 on the Republican ticket, and served as a member of the State constitutional convention of 1789–90. He was elected mayor of Philadelphia in April, 1796, re-elected in October that year, and again in October, 1797. He died while filling that position on the 25th of September, 1798, of yellow fever. In the war for independence he was a firm patriot, and in every official position he proved a faithful citizen.

BALLIET, STEPHEN, of Northampton county, was born in 1753, in Whitehall township, that county. His father, Paul Balliet, was of Huguenot ancestry, and a native of Alsace, who came to Pennsylvania in 1738. His mother was Maria Magdalena Watring, a native of Lorraine. Stephen acquired a very limited education, and was brought up to mercantile life under his father. During the war of the Revolution he commanded one of the battalions of Northampton Associators in 1777 and 1778, and was in active service at the battle of Brandywine. He was appointed agent for forfeited estates in Northampton county, May 6, 1778; was a member of the Supreme Executive Council from October 20, 1783, to October 23, 1786, and member of the Pennsylvania convention to ratify the federal constitution in 1787. He was appointed one of the commissioners to superintend the drawing of the Donation Land Lottery, October 2, 1786, and also in relation to the Wyoming controversy, June 1, 1787. He served as a member of the General Assembly from 1788 to 1790, and of the House of Representatives from 1794 to 1797. For several years, under a commission dated October 25, 1797, he filled the office of revenue collector of the second district of Pennsylvania for the United States direct tax. Scattered. through the Provincial and State records are various references to him, going to show that he was an active and efficient officer. During the so-called Fries Rebellion, Mr. Burkhalter, a collector, was beaten, and the blame thrown upon the insurrectionists; but a circular, signed by Jonas Hartzel, Nicholas Kern, and A. Thorn, stated "that the beating Mr. Burkhalter received was from his own brother-in-law, Stephen Balliet, and that it was a *family* difference which gave rise to the flagellation." Colonel Balliet died August 4, 1821.

BARCLAY, JOHN, of Bucks county, was born in 1749 in that county. He was the son of Alexander Barclay, an officer of the Crown under the proprietary government, and received a classical education. At the outset of the Revolution he entered the service, and was commissioned, January 8, 1776, an ensign in the fourth battalion, Colonel Anthony Wayne; promoted second lieutenant October 1, 1776; commissioned first lieutenant in the fifth regiment of the Pennsylvania Line January 1, 1777; promoted captain-lieutenant June 13, 1777; and retired the service January 1, 1781, with the brevet rank of captain. He was appointed justice of the peace

December 23, 1782; one of the justices of the Court of Quarter Sessions, August 14, 1788; and presiding justice of the Court of Common Pleas, February 27, 1790. In 1787 he was chosen one of the delegates to the Pennsylvania convention to ratify the federal constitution, and served as a member of the State constitutional convention of 1789–90, under which he was appointed an associate judge of the courts of Bucks county, serving from August 17, 1791, to January 2, 1803. He also represented the district comprising his own and a portion of Philadelphia county in the State Senate. Captain Barclay afterwards removed to the Northern Liberties, Philadelphia, where he continued to reside until his death, filling for some time the presidency of the Bank of the Northern Liberties of that district. He was a member of the Pennsylvania Society of the Cincinnati, and was succeeded by his son, John Louis Barclay, in 1832. He died September 15, 1824, at the age of seventy-five years.

BARD, RICHARD, of Franklin county, was born in 1735. His father, Bernard Bard, was an early settler on "Carroll's tract," York, now Adams county, where he established what was for years known as "Bard's mill," and subsequently "Marshall's." Here, on the morning of 13th of April, 1758, the house was invested by a party of nineteen Indians, and Richard Bard and his wife were made prisoners by the Indians. An account of their captivity was prepared by their son, Archibald Bard, and published in Pritt's "Border Life." Subsequently they removed near Thomas Poe's, in now Franklin county, Mrs. Bard being his daughter. He erected a stone house near Mercersburg, which is still standing. During the war of the Revolution Mr. Bard greatly assisted in organizing the troops, and commanded a company of rangers on the frontiers of Cumberland county to protect the settlers in gathering their crops. He was appointed a justice of the peace March 14, 1786, and was a delegate to the Pennsylvania convention to ratify the federal constitution, but did not sign the ratification. He was one of the delegates to the Harrisburg conference of September, 1788, in opposition to that instrument. He was a gentleman of considerable ability, but his hostility to the federal constitution placed him in the background.

BISHOP, JOHN, of Berks county, was born March 4, 1740, in Exeter township, that county, his father, John Bishop, coming to Pennsylvania with the Boones and Lincolns. He was brought up as a farmer, an occupation he was engaged in all his life, although other enterprises engrossed much of his attention. He had extensive business connections, and became an ironmaster. He was a large landholder, not only in Berks county, but in the Valley of Virginia. As a consequence, he was more or less prominent and influential in public affairs. During the Revolution he greatly aided the county lieutenants in organizing the Associators and militia, by advancing large sums of money in emergencies. He was elected to the General Assembly, serving from 1781 to 1784, and chosen a delegate to the Pennsylvania convention to ratify the federal constitution in 1787. He did not sign the ratification, and the year following was a member of the Harrisburg conference which protested so loudly against that instrument. He filled the office of county auditor in 1797-98, and represented Berks in the State legislature in 1805-06. He died at his residence in Exeter township the 3d of September, 1812, aged seventy-two years.

BLACK, JOHN, of York county, was born in that county about the year 1750. His father, Robert Black, was an early settler in that section, but in the great Scotch-Irish immigration to the southward removed to North Carolina when his son John was an infant. Hence the statement of his being born there. He entered Nassau Hall in the junior year, 1769, graduating in 1771. He was licensed by Donegal Presbytery, October 14, 1773, and was ordained and installed pastor of Upper Marsh Creek Congregation, York county, August 15, 1775. For almost nineteen years he served that congregation. During that period the old log church was replaced by a stone structure. As a preacher he possessed a high order of talent, and was undoubtedly a strong man. He was quite prominent in public affairs, but lost much of his hold upon the community and the church by his vigorous measures in the cause of temperance. In this he was bold and outspoken. In a Scotch-Irish neighborhood this was not wisdom. As a result, owing to this fact, as also to the exodus of many of his congregation westward at the close of the Revolution, the Presbytery relieved him from his charge at his own request, April 10, 1794. The only secular office he ever held was delegate to the Pennsylvania convention to ratify the federal constitution in 1787. The Rev. Mr. Black remained several years in the neighborhood of his flock, ministering occasionally to the remnants of a Reformed Dutch church near by. He afterwards received a call from the churches of Unity and Greensburg, in Westmoreland county, Pennsylvania, accepted it, became a member of the Presbytery of Redstone, and was installed October 23, 1800. He died there on the 16th of August, 1802. He published several pamphlets, the titles of only two being preserved to us,—" The Duty of Christians in Singing the Praise of God Explained, a Sermon preached at Upper Marsh Creek on the 14th and 21st of September, 1788," and " A Discourse on Psalmody, in reply to Rev. Dr. John Anderson, of the Associate Church." These attracted considerable attention in their day.

BOYD, JOHN, of Northumberland county, was born the 22d of February, 1750, in Lancaster county, of Scotch-Irish ancestry. Of his early occupation and education we have little knowledge. When the war for independence came he entered the service, and was commissioned second lieutenant in the twelfth regiment of the Pennsylvania Line, Colonel William Cooke, October 16, 1776. He was promoted first lieutenant and transferred to the third Pennsylvania regiment as captain-lieutenant. Under the rearrangement of January 1, 1781, he was retired the service, but afterwards appointed captain of a company of rangers on the frontiers, and was an excellent partisan officer. According to C. Biddle (see Autobiography, p. 204), " During the war he was wounded and taken prisoner by the Indians. Having killed a number of them before he was taken, they were determined to burn him. For this purpose he was stripped naked and tied to a stake, and expected every

moment to suffer death, when he was released by the inter-
cession of one of the squaws, who had her husband killed
in the engagement with Boyd. His life was probably saved
in consequence of his being a stout, well-made man." During the war he served one year as collector of the excise
for Northumberland county. After the restoration of peace,
in partnership with Colonel William Wilson, he entered into
merchandising at the town of Northumberland, and in a
mill at the mouth of Chillisquaqua Creek. They manufact-
ured large quantities of potash, which they shipped to Philadelphia, where it met with a ready sale; but the difficulties
of transportation compelled them to relinquish this enterprise.
He served as a member of the Supreme Executive Council of
the State from November 22, 1783, to November 23, 1786.
On the 2d of October, the latter year, he was appointed by
the General Assembly one of the commissioners for superintending the drawing of the Donation Land Lottery. He
was a member of the House of Representatives from 1790 to
1792, and a presidential elector at the second election. He
served as a justice of the peace many years. Was one of the
original members of the Pennsylvania Society of the Cincinnati. He died at Northumberland on the 13th of February,
1832, aged eighty-two years.

BREADING, NATHANIEL, of Fayette county, was born in
Little Britain township, Lancaster county, March 16, 1751.
His grandfather, David Breading, came to Pennsylvania from
near Coleraine, county Londonderry, Ireland, about 1728.
His son James married Ann Ewing, and they were the
parents of the subject of this sketch. Nathaniel received a
classical education, afterwards took charge of the Newark
Academy, Delaware, and also taught school in Prince Edward
county, Virginia. At the outset of the Revolution he returned to Pennsylvania, and was acting commissary under
General James Ewing, who was in command of a portion of
the Associated battalions during the years 1777 and 1778. In
1784 he removed to Luzerne township, Fayette county, and
shortly after was appointed a justice of the peace, and, November 6, 1785, one of the judges of the Court of Common

Pleas. On the 5th of March, 1785, he was appointed by the Assembly one of the commissioners to survey the lands recently purchased from the Indians north and west of the Ohio and Allegheny Rivers to Lake Erie, as also to assist in running the boundary-lines between Pennsylvania and Virginia. He was a delegate to the Pennsylvania convention to ratify the federal constitution, but in deference to his constituents did not sign the ratification. He served as a member of the Supreme Executive Council from November 19, 1789, until the dissolution of that body by the adoption of the constitution of 1790. He was commissioned one of the associate judges of Fayette county, August 17, 1791, and served continuously during the several changes of administration until his death, a period of thirty years, perchance the longest term of any who filled that honorable position. During the excitement in Western Pennsylvania consequent upon the enforcement of the excise laws, Judge Breading, although these were obnoxious to him, took a bold stand in the maintenance of law and order. As the result, much of his property was burned by the insurgents. He was one of the delegates from the county to the conference held at Pittsburgh, September 7, 1791, to take measures toward suppressing the threatened insurrection. Apart from the public positions Judge Breading filled so faithfully and honorably, he was engaged in various enterprises looking to the development of the Western country. He died on the 21st of April, 1821.

BROWN, WILLIAM, of Dauphin county, was born in 1733, on the Swatara, in Lancaster county, Pennsylvania. His grandfather, James Brown, came with his brother John from the north of Ireland to Pennsylvania in 1720, and, while he settled on the Swatara, subsequently Hanover township, the latter located in Paxtang township, in Lancaster county. John Brown was the father of another William Brown, no less eminent than his distinguished cousin. The former was designated as "William Brown, of Paxtang," while the subject of our sketch as "Captain William Brown." He was educated at the school of Rev. John Blair, became quite prominent on the frontiers, and was an officer in Rev. Colonel

Elder's battalion of rangers during the French and Indian war. He was one of the prime movers at the Hanover meeting of June 4, 1774, and probably the author of the celebrated resolutions there passed. He recruited a company of Associators, and was in active service during the Jersey campaign of 1776, as well in and around Philadelphia in 1777 and 1778. In 1779 he commanded a company of rangers in the expedition to the West Branch against the Indians and Tories, who were threatening the exposed frontiers. He was a delegate to the Pennsylvania convention to ratify the federal constitution of 1787, but did not sign the ratification. He was a member of the State constitutional convention of 1789–90, and under that instrument represented his county in the Legislature in 1792 and 1793. He was chosen one of the Presidential electors in 1797, voting for Mr. Jefferson. Captain Brown died July 20, 1808, at the age of seventy-five.

BULL, THOMAS, of Chester county, was born June 9, 1744, the son of William Bull, an early settler in that county. He received the meagre education afforded in his day, and learned the trade of a stone-mason. Prior to the Revolution he was the manager of Warwick Furnace. When that struggle came he entered heartily into the contest, and assisted in organizing the Chester county battalion of Associators of the "Flying Camp," commanded by Colonel William Montgomery, of which he was commissioned lieutenant-colonel. He was taken prisoner at Fort Washington in November, 1776, and confined on the Jersey prison-ship. After several months he was properly exchanged. He subsequently returned to his position as manager of Warwick Furnace, where he remained several years. In 1780 he was appointed by act of the General Assembly one of the commissioners for the for the removal of the county seat. He was elected a delegate to the Pennsylvania convention to ratify the federal constitution in 1787, and served as a member of the State constitutional convention of 1789–90. He was chosen a presidential elector in 1792, and from 1795 to 1801 represented Chester county in the Legislature of the State. He died on the 13th of July, 1837, aged ninety-three years.

CAMPBELL, THOMAS, of York county, the son of John Campbell, was born about 1750 in Chanceford township, that county. His father took up a tract of land at an early day, situated on the "Great Road leading from York to Nelson's Ferry." He was of Scotch-Irish descent, and received the education accorded that sturdy race. He was a farmer by occupation. When the Revolutionary struggle began, he enlisted as a private in Captain Michael Doudel's company, attached to Colonel William Thompson's battalion of riflemen, in July, 1775. He served through the New England campaign, and was commissioned first lieutenant in the fourth regiment of the Pennsylvania Line, January 3, 1777. He was severely wounded at Germantown, was promoted captain-lieutenant January 1, 1781, and retired the service January 1, 1783. He was one of the original members of the Pennsylvania Society of the Cincinnati. Captain Campbell was chosen a delegate to the State convention to ratify the federal constitution in 1787; served as a member of the Pennsylvania House of Representatives from 1797 to 1800, and of the Senate from the York and Adams district from 1805 to 1808. He died at his residence in Monaghan township, York county, January 19, 1815.

CHAMBERS, STEPHEN, of Lancaster county, was a native of the north of Ireland, where he was born about 1750. He came to Pennsylvania prior to the Revolution. Fithian, in his Journal of date July 20, 1775, met him at Sunbury, "a lawyer, . . . serious, civil, and sociable." At the outset of the war he entered the service, was appointed first lieutenant of the twelfth regiment of the Line, October 16, 1776, and promoted captain in 1777. He was chosen to the General Assembly from the county of Northumberland in 1778, and while in attendance thereon was admitted to the Philadelphia bar, March 6, 1779. He was admitted to the Lancaster bar in 1780, removing there the same year, and to that of York, April 23, 1781. In 1779 he was a member of the Republican Society of Philadelphia, whose object was the revision of the constitution of 1776. He was also one of the original members of the Pennsylvania Society of the Cincinnati. He represented Lancaster county in the Council of Censors, 1783–84, and was a delegate to the convention of November 20, 1787, to ratify the federal constitution. At the constituting of Lodge 22, Ancient York Masons, at Sunbury, December 27, 1779, he became its first Worshipful Master, and the warrant for that body was produced and presented by him at "his own proper cost and charges." In May, 1789, he was challenged by Dr. Reiger, of Lancaster, for some offence said to have been given at Stake's tavern in that town. The duel took place on Monday, May 11, 1789, and Mr. Chambers was seriously wounded, dying on Saturday following, the 16th.

CHEYNEY, THOMAS, of Chester county, son of John Cheyney, Jr., and Ann Hickman, was born in Thornbury township, that county, December 12, 1731. His grandfather, John Cheyney, Sr., came to Pennsylvania about the close of the century, located in Middletown township, Chester county, where he died in 1722, leaving two sons, John and Thomas. They became possessed of a large tract of land in Thornbury in 1724, and here it was that the subject of this sketch lived all his fourscore years, an intelligent and progressive farmer. At the commencement of the Revolution he was an earnest Whig. He was appointed by the Assembly, December 16, 1777, to take subscriptions for the continental loan; one of the agents for forfeited estates under the Act of Attainder, May 6, 1778; and sub-lieutenant of Chester county, March 30, 1780. He was commissioned one of the justices in 1779, and again in 1784. Under the constitution of 1790 he was continued by Governor Mifflin, his commission bearing date August 26, 1791. He served as one of the delegates to the Pennsylvania convention to ratify the federal constitution in 1787, and signed the ratification. Squire Cheyney died January 12, 1811.

COLEMAN, ROBERT, of Lancaster county, was born November 4, 1748, near Castle-Finn, Donaghmore, county Donegal, Ireland. At the age of sixteen he came to America with letters to Blair McClenaghan and the Messrs. Biddle, of Philadelphia. Through them he secured a position with Mr. Read, prothonotary at Reading, in whose employ he remained two years, at the expiration of which he accepted a situation as clerk with Peter Grubb at Hopewell Forge. At the end of six months he entered the employ of James Old at Quittopehille Forge, near Lebanon. Mr. Old, some time after, removing from Speedwell Forge to Reading, took Mr. Coleman with him. In 1773 he rented Salford Forge, near Norristown, where he remained three years. In 1776 he moved to Elizabeth Furnace, in Lancaster county, which he first rented, and afterwards bought out gradually the different shares from the firm who owned it, namely, Stiegel, Stedman, and Benezet. By his energy and indomitable perseverance Mr. Coleman became the most enterprising and successful iron-master in Pennsylvania. Mr. Coleman served as a member of the General Assembly in 1783–84, as delegate to the convention to ratify the federal constitution in 1787, and as a member of the constitutional convention of 1789–90. Under that organic law he was commissioned, August 17, 1791, one of the associate judges for Lancaster county, an office he held twenty years. He was chosen a presidential elector in 1792, and again in 1796. In 1809 Mr. Coleman removed to Lancaster, where he died August 14, 1825.

DESHLER, DAVID, of Northampton county, was born at Egypta, in the upper part of North Whitehall township, in 1733, where his father, Adam Deshler, was among the first settlers. The latter operated a mill on the Little Lehigh, of which the son subsequently became owner. He was quite prominent in the French and Indian war, and was active in the adoption of measures in defending the frontiers; and his house, a large stone structure, became a place of refuge for the people of the vicinity in case of an Indian alarm. In 1764 he was a shopkeeper in Allentown, but two years afterwards sold out and removed to his grist and saw-mills, which he continued to operate until almost the close of his life. During the Revolutionary war he became one of the most influential personages in Northampton county; acted as commissary of supplies, and, with his colleague and neighbor, Captain John Arndt, advanced money out of his private means at a time when not only the United States treasury but also that of Pennsylvania was empty. He was a member of the provincial conference which met at Carpenters' Hall June 18, 1776, and appointed by that body one of the judges of the election for the second division of the county, held at Allentown. He was a delegate to the convention to ratify the federal constitution in 1787, and filled other positions of public trust. Mr. Deshler died at his residence at Biery's Bridge, now Catasauqua, in December, 1796.

DOWNING, RICHARD, of Chester county, son of Richard Downing and his wife, Mary Edge, was born May 4, 1750, in Caln township, that county. His father operated a fulling, grist and saw-mill, and the son was brought up in that occupation. During the struggle for independence he was a Non-Associator. He was a delegate to the Pennsylvania convention to ratify the federal constitution in 1787; served in the General Assembly from 1788 to 1790, and was one of the representatives of his county in the Legislature from 1790 to 1792. During the local excitement caused by changing the county-seat, when it was not only proposed but really attempted to locate it at Milltown, now Downingtown, he was one of the leading spirits in opposing it. He died January 5, 1820, in his seventieth year.

EDGAR, JAMES, of Washington county, the son of James Edgar, was born November 15, 1744, in Fawn township, York county. He was a member of the convention to ratify the federal constitution in 1787, but did not sign the ratification. He died on his farm on the 8th of June, 1814, in the seventy-first year of his age.

EDWARDS, ENOCH, of the county of Philadelphia, the son of Alexander Edwards, was born in 1751, in Lower Dublin, that county. He received a classical education, studied medicine, and was in the active practice of his profession when the Revolutionary war began, and in which he became an earnest participant. He was a member of the provincial conference held at Carpenters' Hall, June 18, 1776, and the same year served as surgeon in the Philadelphia Battalion of the "Flying Camp." He afterwards served as an aide on the staff of General Lord Stirling. He was commissioned one of the justices of the peace for the county of Philadelphia, June 6, 1777, and continued in office August 16, 1789. He was a delegate to the convention to ratify the federal constitution of 1787, and a member of the Pennsylvania constitutional convention of 1789–90. He was appointed by Governor Mifflin, August 17, 1791, one of the associate judges, and continued in office by Governor McKean until his death at Frankford on the 25th of April, 1802, aged fifty years.

ELLIOTT, BENJAMIN, of Huntingdon county, eldest son of Robert and Martha Elliott, was born in 1752 in Peters township, Cumberland, now Franklin, county, and settled at the town of Huntingdon prior to the Revolution. He was chosen a member of the convention of July 15, 1776, and served as a member of the Assembly during that and the following year as one of the representatives of Bedford county. He was commissioned Sheriff of that county, October 31, 1785, and of Huntingdon, October 22, 1787, after its erection from Bedford; member of the convention of Pennsylvania to consider the federal constitution, November 20, 1787; appointed county lieutenant on the 23d of the same month, and in April, 1789, in conjunction with Matthew Taylor, of Bedford, and James Harris, of Cumberland, appointed to run and mark the boundary lines of Huntingdon county. He served as treasurer of the county in 1789, and again in 1799; was admitted a member of the Supreme Executive Council, December 29, 1789, and member of the Board of Property, August 3, 1790. On the 17th of August, 1791, he was commissioned one of the associate judges for Huntingdon county. He had previously held the office of justice of the Court of Common Pleas under the constitution of 1776. He was the first chief burgess elected in the borough of Huntingdon after its incorporation in 1796. He was appointed brigadier-general of the militia, 1797, and in 1800 elected county commissioner. He died at Huntingdon, March 13, 1835, aged 83 years. Judge Elliott was what was then termed a Republican in politics. He signed the ratification.

FINDLEY, WILLIAM, of Westmoreland county, was born in 1741, near Londonderry, province of Ulster, Ireland. His grandfather was a native of Scotland, but settled early in life in the north of Ireland, and was one of the brave men who assisted in the heroic defence of Derry. The grandson received a fair English education, and came to Pennsylvania in 1763. Owing to the Indian troubles on the frontiers he remained within the settlements, where he taught school. At the beginning of the Revolution he was in the Cumberland valley. He served as a captain in the militia in the years 1776 and 1777 under Colonel John Findlay, the period of the invasion into Pennsylvania, and was at the battle of the Crooked Billet. Towards the close of the war he removed with his family to Western Pennsylvania and took up a tract of land in Westmoreland county, on which he resided until his death. Here he became prominent in political affairs, his first entry upon the scene being in the character of a member of the Council of Censors. In this body he voted invariably against the party which professed Federalism. He served in the General Assembly from 1784 to 1788; was a delegate to the convention to ratify the federal constitution in 1787, one of its bitterest opponents, and did not sign the ratification. He was one of the members of the anti-constitution party who were mobbed in Philadelphia on the evening of the 6th of November that year. At the Harrisburg conference in September, 1788, with Smilie and Gallatin, he was a leading spirit, and this trio almost accomplished the total defeat of the constitutionalist ticket, electing two of the eight Congressmen, the parties being evenly balanced. He served as a member of the Supreme Executive Council from November 25, 1789, until the constitution of 1790, of the convention to form which he was a member, went into effect. He was elected a member of the Pennsylvania House of Representatives in 1790, at the same time a member of the Second Congress. He was re-elected to the third, fourth, fifth, and sixth Congresses, and then, after an interval of two terms, during which period he served in the State Senate, to the eighth, ninth, tenth, eleventh, twelfth, thirteenth, and fourteenth Congresses, serving a longer time in that representative body than any other person from Pennsylvania. During the so-called Whisky Insurrection of 1794 he took a decided part, and as an apology for his share in it we are indebted to him for one of the most impartial histories of that transaction. He was as forcible a writer as a speaker, and the newspapers of the day contained many political articles from his pen. He was a shrewd politician without being a demagogue, and no man in Western Pennsylvania had as strong hold upon the people or was more popular than William Findley. He was a statesman of whom Pennsylvania should be proud. Mr. Findley died at his residence in Unity township, Westmoreland county, on the 5th of April, 1821, in the eightieth year of his age.

GIBBONS, WILLIAM, of Chester county, the son of James Gibbons and Jane Sheward, was born in 1737 in the township of Westtown, that county. The parents were prominent members of the Society of Friends, the mother being a minister thereof. After his marriage he resided in Philadelphia, subsequently, in 1766, removing to Thornbury township, and in 1769 to West Nantmeal, on a fine farm left him by his parents. For the active part he took in the struggle for independence he was disowned by the Society. He served as lieutenant-colonel of one of the Chester county battalions of Associators, was appointed justice of the peace March 31, 1777, and directed by the Supreme Executive Council, October 21, 1777, to collect blankets, arms, etc., from those not taking the oath of allegiance. Towards the close of the war he removed to Paxtang township, in Lancaster county, where he resided a year or two, for what purpose it is not known. In 1783 he was elected sheriff of Chester county, and it was during his time of service the seat of justice was removed from Chester to West Chester. He served as a delegate to the convention to ratify the federal constitution in 1787, and as a member of the constitutional convention of 1789–90. Governor Mifflin commissioned him prothonotary of the county August 17, 1791, in which he served nine years. During the Whiskey Insurrection, in 1794, he volunteered under Captain Joseph McClellan for the expedition westward, performing that tour of military duty. He was elected a member of the House of Representatives in 1801, and served one term. Colonel Gibbons died October 30, 1803.

GRAFF, SEBASTIAN, of Lancaster county, was the grandson of Sebastian Graff, a member of the Moravian Church, who emigrated with his family from Germany in 1731 or 1732, and settled in the town of Lancaster, where he was a "shop-keeper" in 1734. The Sebastian of the third generation was born at Lancaster about 1750, and was in active business when the war for independence began. He took a prominent part, and was on the Committee of Observation for the county of Lancaster. He was a delegate to the provincial convention of January 23, 1775, and to the convention to ratify the federal constitution of 1787, signing the ratification. He was a member of the convention which framed the constitution of 1789–'90, and under that form of government was chosen to the State Senate in 1790. He died in July, 1792.

GRAY, GEORGE, of the county of Philadelphia, the fifth of that name in the line of descent from George Gray, of Barbadoes, a wealthy member of the Society of Friends, was born at Gray's Ferry, that county. He took an early and active part in the affairs of the province, and was elected a member of the Assembly in 1772, and annually until the commencement of the Revolutionary struggle. He was the author of the celebrated "Treason Resolutions" reported by the committee of which he was chairman. For the part he took in this and other warlike measures he was "turned out of meeting." He was a delegate to the provincial conference of July 15, 1774, and a member of the provincial convention of January 23, 1775. He was a member of the General Committee of Safety in 1776 and 1777, and of the Pennsylvania Board of War during its existence in 1777, serving a portion of the time as its chairman. He was one of the signers of the bills of credit in 1775, and a member of the Assembly in 1776. Under the constitution of the latter year he served in the General Assembly from 1780 to 1787, being Speaker of that body in 1783–84. He was a delegate to the convention to ratify the federal constitution in 1787, and a member of the Pennsylvania constitutional convention of 1789–90.

During the entire period of the Revolution he was conspicuous by his patriotism. He died in the year 1800.

GRIER, DAVID, of York county, son of William Grier, was born in Mount Pleasant township, that county, in 1742. He received a classical education, studied law with James Smith, and was admitted to the York county bar April 23, 1771. Having served in the French and Indian war as a subaltern officer, when the war for independence commenced he became a prominent participant. He was commissioned captain of the sixth battalion of the Line, Colonel William Irvine, January 9, 1776, served in the campaign against Canada, and was promoted to major October 25, 1776. He was subsequently promoted to lieutenant-colonel of the seventh regiment Pennsylvania Line, ranking from October 2, 1776. He was wounded in the side by a bayonet at the Paoli massacre in September, 1777. He continued in the service until, under the new arrangement of January 1, 1781, he was retired at that date. At the close of the war he resumed his profession at York, was elected to the General Assembly in 1783, served as a delegate to the convention to ratify the federal constitution in 1787, and was chosen by the constitutionalists one of the first presidential electors. Colonel Grier died at York, June 3, 1790, aged forty-eight years.

HANNA, JOHN ANDRÉ, son of Rev. John Hanna and Mary McCrea, was born about 1761, at Flemington, N. J. He received a good classical education under his father, who was a most excellent tutor. He served in the war of the Revolution, towards its close came to Pennsylvania, and studied law with Stephen Chambers, of Lancaster, whose acquaintance he had made in the army, and was admitted to the bar of Lancaster county at November session, 1783. He located at Harrisburg upon the formation of the county of Dauphin, and was among the first lawyers admitted there. He took a deep interest in early municipal affairs, and there was little transpiring looking to the welfare and development of the new town in which Mr. Hanna did not take part. His marriage with a daughter of John Harris, the founder, brought him into unusual prominence. He represented the county in the

Legislature, and in 1795 was elected to the United States Congress, a position he filled up to the time of his death by successive re-election. During the Whisky Insurrection he was a brigadier-general of the Pennsylvania troops, in command of the second brigade, second division. In 1800 Governor McKean commissioned him a major-general of the third division of the militia forces of the State. He died at Harrisburg, on the 13th of July, 1805, aged forty-four years.

HANNUM, JOHN, of Chester county, was born in 1742, in Concord, that county. He was the son of John Hannum, Jr., and his wife, Jane Neild. Arriving at maturity, he settled on a large farm in East Bradford township. He was commissioned early in life one of the provincial justices of the peace, and continued in commission by the constitutional convention of 1776. At the outset of the struggle with the mother-country he became an ardent Whig, and was appointed one of the Committee of Observation for the county of Chester the 20th of December, 1774. In 1777 he was chosen to the command of one of the Associated Battalions, and became an active participant in the Revolutionary contest. He was with Wayne at the Paoli. Subsequently he was captured at his own residence by a squad of British lighthorse, led thither by a Tory neighbor, and taken to Philadelphia, then occupied by the enemy. He soon after escaped, and was more energetic than ever in the cause of his country. He was appointed one of the commissioners of purchases, June 27, 1780, one of the auditors of depreciation accounts, March 3, 1781, and on the 8th of November, the latter year, one of the agents for forfeited estates. He was chosen to the General Assembly in 1781, serving until 1785. While a member of this body, independence having been established, he was largely instrumental in securing the repeal of the "Test Law," then no longer necessary as a war measure. He was a delegate to the Pennsylvania convention to ratify the federal constitution in 1787, and signed the ratification. He was re-commissioned one of the justices for the county in 1788, serving until his appointment by Governor Mifflin of register and recorder, December 13, 1793, which office he held until the 6th of December, 1798, when he was succeeded by his son, Richard Montgomery Hannum. He had previously served in the House of Representatives, 1792 –93. Colonel Hannum died the 7th of February, 1799, and was interred at Bradford Meeting-house, Marshallton.

HARRIS, JOHN, of Cumberland county, was born in county Donegal, Ireland, in 1723. He was related to Harris of Harris's Ferry, to the family in Buffalo Valley, and has frequently been confounded with others of the same name. In 1753 he was located on the Swatara, Lancaster county, as his autograph to a road petition is a counterpart of that of twenty years later. He was one of the most prominent men in the Cumberland Valley. He was a delegate to the Pennsylvania convention to ratify the federal constitution of 1787, and voted against the ratification. He died at Mifflintown, which he laid out, February 24, 1794.

HARTLEY, THOMAS, of York County, was born in Colebrookdale township, Berks county, Pennsylvania, on the 7th of September, 1748. His father, George Hartley, was an early settler in Pennsylvania and a well-to-do farmer. The son received a good classical education at Reading, and at the age of eighteen began the study of law at York with Samuel Johnston, a distinguished lawyer and a relative on his mother's side. He was admitted to the bar of York county July 25, 1769, and to that of Philadelphia on the 10th of August following. He soon rose rapidly to legal distinction, and was in a successful career when the war of the Revolution opened. In 1774 he was vice-president of the Committee of Observation for York county, and again in November, 1775. He was chosen a deputy to the provincial conference held at Philadelphia, July 15, 1774, and a delegate to the provincial convention of January 23, 1775. In December, 1774, he was first lieutenant of Captain James Smith's company of Associators, and in December, 1775, chosen lieutenant-colonel of the first battalion of York county. On the 10th of January, 1776, Congress elected him lieutenant-colonel of the sixth battalion of the Pennsylvania Line, and he served in the Canada campaign of that year. On the 27th of December, the same year, General Washington, by authority of the Congress, issued commissions and authority to raise two "additional regiments in Pennsylvania," the command of one being given to Colonel Hartley. He commanded the first Pennsylvania brigade, Wayne's division, in the battles of Brandywine and Germantown. In 1778 he was in command of the troops on the West Branch, upon which the Indians and Tories from New York had made inroads. By a resolution of Congress of 16th December, 1778, the remains of Patton's and Hartley's regiments, with several detached companies, were organized into what was termed the "new eleventh" regiment of the Pennsylvania Line, to which he was transferred on the 13th of January, 1779, but resigned the month following, having been chosen to the General Assembly. In accepting his resignation Congress, deeming his reasons satisfactory, bore testimony of their "high sense of Colonel Hartley's merit and services." He served as a member of the Council of Censors, 1783–84, and as a delegate to the Pennsylvania convention to ratify the federal constitution in 1787. He was elected by the constitutionalists on the general ticket for members of Congress in 1788, and continued in that high official position for a period of twelve years. He was one of the original members of the Society of the Cincinnati, and a trustee of Dickinson College at the beginning of its educational career. In 1799 he laid out the town of Hartleton in the Buffalo Valley, on a tract of one thousand acres purchased by him during the Revolution. Governor McKean commissioned him, April 28, 1800, a major-general in the Pennsylvania militia. General Hartley died at his residence in York, December 21, 1800.

HIESTER, JOSEPH, of Berks county, was born November 18, 1752, in Bern township, Berks county, Pennsylvania. He was the son of John Hiester, a native of Elsoff, in the province of Westphalia, Germany. The son acquired the rudiments of a good English and German education under the supervision of the pastor of Bern Church. Until near age he worked upon his father's farm, when he went to Reading and learned merchandising. He was a member of the provincial conference held at Carpenters' Hall, June 18, 1776, which called the convention of July following. The war of the Revolution breaking out, he raised a company of Associators for the Flying Camp, which participated in the battle of Long Island, where he was taken prisoner. After several months' imprisonment, he was exchanged, and returned in time to take part in the battle of Germantown, where he was wounded. He was appointed by the Supreme Executive Council one of the commissioners of exchange, April 5, 1779, and on the 21st of October following one of the committee to seize the personal effects of traitors. He was chosen to the General Assembly in 1780, and served almost continuously from that date until 1790. He was a delegate to the Pennsylvania convention to ratify the federal constitution in 1787, but did not sign the ratification. He was a member of the State constitutional convention of 1789–90, and under that instrument was elected to the first Senate, serving a full term. He was chosen a presidential elector in 1792, and again in 1796. He served in the fifth, sixth, seventh, and eighth Congresses, and again in the fourteenth, fifteenth, and sixteenth Congresses. It was during his last term that he was elected Governor of Pennsylvania by the Federalists, in a campaign which for personal vituperation has never been equalled in Pennsylvania. His administration, however, of the affairs of State was a successful one, but he would not allow himself to be nominated for a second term. Returning to Reading, he retired to private life, and died there on the 10th of June, 1832.

HOGE, JONATHAN, of Cumberland county, son of John Hoge and his wife, Gwenthleen Bowen Davis, was born July 23, 1725. His parents residing about that date in the Three Lower Counties of Penn's Province, it is certain he was born there, and not in Ireland. He was a delegate to the Pennsylvania convention to ratify the federal constitution, but opposed the ratification. He died April 19, 1800.

HORSFIELD, JOSEPH, of Northampton county, was born at Bethlehem, Pennsylvania, November 24, 1750. His father, Timothy Horsfield, was an early Moravian settler, at Bethlehem, and quite prominent in the history of that settlement. But little is known of the son's early history save that he was a man of good education and of influence in the community. He was chosen a delegate to the Pennsylvania convention to ratify the federal constitution in 1787, and signed the ratification. He was appointed by President Washington, June 12, 1792, the first postmaster at Bethlehem, an office he held until the 13th of February, 1802. He died at Bethlehem on the 9th of September, 1834, at the age of eighty-three years.

HUBLEY, JOHN, of Lancaster county, the son of Michael Hubley and Rosina Strumpf, was born in the town of Lancaster the 25th of December, 1747. He was a member of the convention of 1776, and also of that of 1789–90. He was a constitutionalist, and signed the ratification of the federal constitution in the Pennsylvania convention of 1787. He also served in the Supreme Executive Council in 1777, and was chosen a presidential elector in 1801. A lawyer by profession, although by no means a brilliant one, yet there was a magnetism about him which, next to Judge Yeates, made him the most popular attorney at the Lancaster bar, always justly celebrated for its great legal minds. He died January 21, 1821, aged seventy-three years.

HUNN, JOHN, of the county of Philadelphia, was born in 1746, in Kent county, Delaware. His grandfather, Nathaniel Hunn, was an early settler on the Delaware. John, the subject of our sketch, was brought up to a sea-faring life, and was a captain in the merchant service at the breaking out of the War for Independence. He was an ardent patriot, and was intrusted with very important duties. In July, 1776, he was in command of the privateer "Security;" while in the following summer, when it was momentarily expected that the British fleet would attempt to pass up the Delaware, at the request of General Washington he was sent by the Council of Pennsylvania to the Capes to give the earliest possible notice of the appearance of the enemy's vessels. In the campaign in and around Philadelphia he seems to have been in active military service. In the subsequent events he was not an idle spectator, his energies being principally devoted to perfect plans to destroy the power of the enemy at sea. When the war closed he retired to private life, only coming to the front in times of great political excitement. As a constitutionalist he was chosen to the Pennsylvania convention in 1787, and signed the ratification. He took a prominent part at the meeting held in Philadelphia, June 22, 1795, in opposition to the Jay Treaty, and was appointed one of the committee to prepare a memorial to the President. Captain Hunn died at Wilmington, Delaware, April 22, 1810, while on a visit to his daughter, Mrs. Rodney.

LATIMER, GEORGE, of the city of Philadelphia, was born there in 1750. He was educated at the College of Philadelphia, and entered upon a mercantile life. In the Revolutionary war he was active and influential, and was in military service prior to the occupation of Philadelphia by the British in 1777. He was a delegate to the Pennsylvania convention to ratify the federal constitution in 1787. He represented his native city in the Pennsylvania House of Representatives from 1792 to 1799, being Speaker of that body five years. He was a presidential elector in 1792, and from 1798 to 1804 was collector of the customs by appointment of the President. In politics he was a Federalist. During the war of 1812–14 he was a member of the Committee of Defence for the city of Philadelphia and treasurer of that body. He was an enterprising citizen, being a director of the old Bank of North America from the 9th of January, 1792, until his death, and also president of the Union Insurance Company. He was appointed April 5, 1786, one of the five commissioners from Pennsylvania to confer with those from Maryland and Delaware on the navigation of the river Susquehanna. In 1814 he was an independent candidate for Governor of Pennsylvania, receiving nine hundred and ten votes in the canvass which elected Simon Snyder for the third term by a majority of twenty-two thousand in a poll of seventy thousand. Mr. Latimer died at Philadelphia on Sunday evening, 12th of June, 1825, in his seventy-fifth year.

LINCOLN, ABRAHAM, of Berks county, the son of Mordecai

and Mary Lincoln, was born in 1736 in Amity township, Philadelphia, subsequently Berks county, Pennsylvania. His father, who died in May of that year, a few months before the birth of Abraham, was the ancestor of President Lincoln. The subject of our sketch was brought up on the paternal farm. He received a fair education, and became quite prominent in the affairs of his native county. Prior to the Revolution he served as county commissioner, continuing in office during the greater part of the struggle for independence. He was an active patriot, and was appointed one of the sub-lieutenants of the county March 21, 1777. He served in the General Assembly from 1782 to 1786, and was a delegate to the Pennsylvania convention to ratify the federal constitution in 1787. He did not sign the ratification. Under the act of the 14th of March, 1784, he was appointed one of the Commissioners of Fisheries. He was a member of the State constitutional convention of 1789–90, and appears to have been a man of much influence in that body. He died at his residence in Exeter township, January 31, 1806, in his seventieth year. He married, in 1761, Anne Boone, daughter of James Boone and Mary Foulke. She was a full cousin of Colonel Daniel Boone, of Kentucky. The Boones were Quakers, the Lincolns were Congregationalists. Hence it appears by the records of Exeter Meeting, October 27, 1761, that Anne Boone "condones" her marriage for marrying one not a member of the Society.

LUDWIG, JOHN, of Berks county, was a native of the county. But little is known of his early history. He became, however, a substantial farmer, and at the opening of the Revolutionary war was a man of prominence in the county. He served as a captain in the third battalion of Associators, and was in service at Trenton and Princeton. He was commissioned a justice of the peace in 1777, and re-commissioned in 1784. He was a delegate to the Pennsylvania convention to ratify the federal constitution in 1787, but with his colleagues, did not sign the ratification. He served in the General Assembly in 1782–83, and again in 1788–90. In 1789 he voted against calling the convention to alter the State constitution of 1776. He was a member of the Pennsylvania House of Representatives from 1790 to 1793. Governor Mifflin appointed him a justice of the peace April 17, 1795, and he was yet in commission at the time of his death, which occurred in July, 1802.

LUTZ, or LOTZ, NICHOLAS, of Berks county, was born in the Palatinate, Germany, February 20, 1740, coming to America when a young man. He located in Berks county, was a millwright by occupation, establishing a mill near Reading, at the mouth of the Wyomessing Creek. He became early identified with the cause of independence, and was a member of the provincial conference which met at Carpenters' Hall, June 18, 1776. He was in command of a batallion of Associators at the battle of Long Island, where he was taken prisoner, and confined until April 16, 1777, when he was admitted to a parol, but not exchanged until the 10th of September, 1779. He was appointed commissary of purchases April 3, 1780, and served in the General Assembly almost continuously from 1783 to 1790. He was a delegate to the Pennsylvania convention to ratify the federal constitution in 1787, but did not sign the ratification. Under the constitution of 1789–90 he served as a member of the House of Representatives from 1790 to 1794. He was appointed by Governor Mifflin one of the associate judges of Berks county, February 6, 1795, serving until a short time before his death. He died at Reading on the 28th of November, 1807, aged sixty-seven years.

McKEAN, THOMAS, of the city of Philadelphia, son of William McKean, of Scotch-Irish ancestry, was born in Chester county, Pennsylvania, March 19, 1734. He was educated at the academy of Rev. Francis Alison, and entered the office of David Finney, a lawyer of New Castle, Delaware. He was appointed deputy prothonotary there, and afterwards admitted to the bar, and in May, 1755, to that of Chester county. He afterwards went to England, and studied at the Middle Temple, London, being admitted May 9, 1758. In 1762 he was elected a member of the Assembly from New Castle county, and was annually returned until the Revolution, although for a portion of the time a resident of Philadelphia. In 1765 he assisted in framing the address of the Colonies to the British House of Commons. In 1771 he was appointed collector of the port of New Castle; was a member of the Continental Congress in 1774, and annually re-elected until February, 1783, serving in that body during a period of eight and a half years, representing the State of Delaware. During this period he was not only President of that State (1781), but from July 28, 1777, to December, 1799, held the office and also executed the duties of chief justice of Pennsylvania. He was a member in 1778 of the convention which framed the Articles of Confederation, President of Congress (1781), and a promoter of and signer of the Declaration of Independence. He commanded a battalion which served in the Jersey campaigns of 1776-77. He was a delegate to the Pennsylvania convention to ratify the federal constitution in 1787, and, next to Wilson, one of the most fearless advocates for its adoption. He was a member of the Pennsylvania constitutional convention of 1789-90, and under it became its second executive, filling the gubernatorial office three terms, from December 17, 1799, to December 20, 1808. He was a trustee of the University of Pennsylvania, one of the founders of the Hibernian Society, and a member of the Society of the Cincinnati. The College of New Jersey conferred upon him the degree of LL.D., as did also Dartmouth College. He died at Philadelphia on the 24th of June, 1817.

MACPHERSON, WILLIAM, of the county of Philadelphia, was born in Philadelphia in 1756. He was the son of John Macpherson and Margaret Rodgers. The father was a noted privateersman during the French and Spanish wars, while his mother was a sister of the Rev. John Rodgers, D. D., both natives of Londonderry, Ireland. The son was educated partly in Philadelphia and at the College of New Jersey. At the age of thirteen he was appointed a cadet in the British army, and in his eighteenth year, by purchase, he was commissioned a lieutenant in the sixteenth British regiment. When the Revolutionary war began, his sympathies were with his countrymen, although his allegiance to his sovereign retained him in the British service. The death of his brother, Major John Macpherson, in front of Quebec, who had espoused the cause of his country, completely changed his feelings. Tendering his resignation, he found his way into the patriot lines in 1778, and was, on the recommendation of the Supreme Executive Council of Pennsylvania, commissioned by Congress a major by brevet in the Continental Line. He served as aid on the staff of Lafayette, and also on that of St. Clair, with distinction. He was one of the original members of the Society of the Cincinnati, served as a delegate to the Pennsylvania convention to ratify the federal constitution in 1787, and was a member of the General Assembly, 1788–89. He was appointed, September 19, 1789, by President Washington, surveyor of the customs at Philadelphia; inspector of the revenue, March 8, 1792; and on the 28th of November, 1793, naval officer, which latter position he held until his death. During the Whiskey Insurrection, in 1794, he commanded the Philadelphia battalion, which went by the name of "Macpherson Blues." President Adams commissioned him, March 11, 1799, one of the brigadier-generals of the provisional army, and in the so-called Fries Insurrection he was in command of the few volunteers called into that service. He died at his residence near Philadelphia, November 5, 1813, in his fifty-eighth year.

MARSHEL, JAMES, of Washington county, was born February 20, 1753, in Lancaster county. He moved to the western country some three years prior to the Revolution, and settled in what is now Cross Creek township, Washington (then Westmoreland) county. He was on the Committee of Observation for the latter county at the outset of the Revolution, and captain in the militia for the protection of the frontiers. He was appointed a justice of the peace June 11, 1777, and, when the county of Washington was organized, commissioned one of its presiding justices. Under the constitution of 1776 he held the office of register and recorder from April 4, 1781, to November 19, 1784, and also served as county lieutenant. Governor Mifflin reappointed him register and recorder August 17, 1791, continuing in office to March

6, 1795. In the mean time he filled the position of sheriff from November 3, 1784, to November 21, 1787; was a delegate to the Pennsylvania convention to ratify the federal constitution in 1787, of which he was a stern opponent; and was a member of the General Assembly, session of 1789–90. Biddle, in his autobiography, states that he was one of the principal promoters of the disturbance in 1794, but this arose from the fact that he was present when the mail was taken possession of by Bradford. The fact is, interference at such a time was useless. He was no doubt a man of considerable influence in the community, but far from being in league with the insurgents. Captain Marshall died March 17, 1829, at Wellsburg, West Virginia, whither he removed towards the close of the century.

MARTIN, JAMES, of Bedford county, was born in the Cumberland Valley, about the year 1750. In 1772 he resided in what was then Colerain township. In the campaign of 1776 he commanded a company of Associators, and during the Revolutionary era he was in active military service, chiefly stationed on the frontiers to protect the farmers in sowing and gathering their crops. He was one of the sub-lieutenants for the county September 12, 1777, and a justice of the peace for some years. On the 26th of February, 1785, he became one of the judges of the Court of Common Pleas, and in 1787 a delegate to the Pennsylvania convention to ratify the federal constitution. He did not sign the ratification. He was chosen a Councillor in 1789, and served in that capacity from November 12, 1789, until the constitution of 1790 dissolved that body. He was elected sergeant-at-arms of the House of Representatives in December, 1790, serving that session. On the 17th of August, 1791, Governor Mifflin commissioned him an associate judge, an office he filled acceptably up to the time of his death.

MORRIS, JAMES, of Montgomery county, son of Joseph Morris, was born in 1753. His father was a son of Anthony Morris, who was fourth son of Anthony Morris, an only child of Anthony Morris, born at St. Dunstan's, Stepney, London, August 23, 1654. In 1771, Joseph Morris, the father, bought a house and grist-mill, and ninety-four acres of land, on the now Morris Road and Butler Pike, in Upper Dublin township, Montgomery county, and located his son there. James Morris was elected to the General Assembly from Philadelphia county in 1782, and again in 1783. When the county of Montgomery was formed, he was commissioned one of its first justices of the peace, and judge of the Court of Common Pleas in 1785. He was a delegate to the Pennsylvania convention to ratify the federal constitution in 1787, and a member of the State constitutional convention of 1789–90. Under this latter instrument, Governor Mifflin appointed him register and recorder of the county, serving until March 5, 1799. He was chosen a presidential elector in 1792, and in 1793 commissioned a brigadier-general of the militia, having served in the military during and subsequent to the Revolution. He was on the Western Expedition of 1794. General Morris died the following year (1795), at the age of forty-two years.

MUHLENBERG, FREDERICK AUGUSTUS, of Montgomery county, was born at the Trappe, that county, June 2, 1750. His father was the eminent patriarch of the Lutheran Church in America, the Rev. Henry Melchoir Muhlenberg, while his mother was Anna Maria Weiser, daughter of the no less celebrated Conrad Weiser. At the age of thirteen, in company with his elder brother Peter, he entered the University of Halle, Germany. He was ordained to the work of the ministry, and from 1773 to 1775 was in charge of the church at Lebanon, Pennsylvania, removing the latter year to the city of New York, where he continued until the occupation of that city by the British. He officiated at New Hanover, Montgomery county, until called into political life, as did his brother Peter, when he laid aside the gown and the duties of the ministry. He was chosen to the Continental Congress in 1779, serving one term, the year following being elected to the General Assembly, and was Speaker of that body, 1781–82. He was a member of the Council of Censors, 1783–84, over which body he presided. Upon the organization of the county of Montgomery he was commissioned one of the justices of the first courts, October 4, 1784, as also register of wills and recorder of deeds, September 21, 1784. He was a delegate to the Pennsylvania convention to ratify the federal constitution in 1787, being President thereof, and at the first election for members of Congress was chosen on the so-called anti-federal ticket, his brother, General Peter Muhlenberg, being on the federal ticket and also elected. Of that distinguished body he was Speaker. He was chosen to the second, third, and fourth Congresses. Governor McKean appointed him, January 8, 1800, receiver-general of the Pennsylvania Land Office. He died at Lancaster, the seat of State government, June 4, 1801. In 1792, when nominated for the third Congress, the "address" contained the following: "Descended from an amiable, enlightened, and revered German clergyman, Mr. Muhlenberg was naturally regarded with a favorable eye by our fellow-citizens of that nation; and it is certainly a fortunate circumstance that the object to whom the attention of so important a part of the community was directed has proved himself capable to serve the public, and deserving of the confidence of his country. In the year 1779, when Whig principles warmed the hearts of the people and Whig politics controlled the operations of the government, he was elected a member of Congress; and at the expiration of that service he was chosen Speaker of the General Assembly of Pennsylvania. The contest by which he was placed in a situation to be Speaker of the House of Representatives in Congress will be commemorated for the honor of America as long as the Union lasts; and for Mr. Muhlenberg's honor the conduct which he observed in that arduous and important office ought never to be forgotten."

NEVILLE, JOHN, of Washington county, son of Richard Neville and Ann Burroughs, was born July 26, 1731, on the head-waters of Occoquan River, Virginia. He served with Washington in the Braddock expedition of 1755, held the office of sheriff of Frederick county, Virginia, and participated in the Dunmore expedition of 1774. Prior to this he had taken up, by purchase and entry, large tracts of land on Chartiers Creek, in Western Pennsylvania, and was elected a delegate from Augusta county to the provincial convention of Virginia, which body, on the 7th of August, 1775, ordered him to march with his company and take possession of Fort Pitt. On the 23d of December, 1776, he was commissioned a justice of the peace for Yohogania county, but declined the appointment owing to the boundary dispute, as well as being commandant at Fort Pitt. He was colonel of the fourth regiment of the Virginia line, and one of the original members of the Virginia Society of the Cincinnati. He served as a member of the Pennsylvania Supreme Executive Council from November 11, 1783, to November 20, 1786, and as a delegate to the Pennsylvania convention to ratify the federal constitution in 1787, signing the ratification. He was elected to the General Assembly in 1788 and the year following, while under the constitution of 1789–90, he was chosen to the House of Representatives, session of 1790–91. The latter year, at the urgent solicitation of the President and the Secretary of the Treasury, he accepted the appointment of inspector of the revenue in the Fourth Survey of the District of Pennsylvania, which he held until after the suppression of the Whiskey Insurrection and establishment of the supremacy of the laws of the United States. He was commissioned by Governor Mifflin brigade inspector, and was of great service in securing the defence of the frontiers of Western Pennsylvania. Under the act of Congress of May 18, 1796, he was appointed the agent at Pittsburgh for the sale of lands in the territory northwest of the Ohio. He died at his seat on Montour's Island (now Neville township), Allegheny county, Pennsylvania, Friday, July 29, 1803.

ORTH, ADAM, of Dauphin county, son of Balthaser (died October, 1788) and Gertrude Catharine Orth, was born March 10, 1733, in Lebanon township, Lancaster (now Lebanon) county. His parents came to America in 1729, and he was thus brought up amid the dangers and struggles of Pennsylvania pioneer life. He received the limited education of the "back settlements," and yet, by self-culture and reading, became a man well informed and of more than ordinary intelligence. During the French and Indian war he commanded the Lebanon township company in Rev. John Elder's ranging battalion. In 1769 he was one of the commissioners of the county of Lancaster. During the Revolution he was early identified with the movement, and, although well advanced in years, assisted in the organization of the associated battalions, and was appointed a sub-lieutenant of the county March 12, 1777. Upon the formation of the county of Dauphin, he served as a Representative in the General Assembly in 1789 and 1790. He was a delegate to the Pennsylvania convention of 1787, but opposed the adoption of the federal constitution, and took an active part in the Harrisburg conference of 1788. For a long period he operated and owned New Market Forge, which at his death he bequeathed to his son Henry. He was one of the pioneers in the manufacture of iron in Lebanon county, a man of energy and indomitable perseverance. He died November 15, 1794.

PEDAN, BENJAMIN, of York county, son of John Pedan, was born about 1740. His father in 1733 settled in Hempfield township, Lancaster county, along Big Chickies Creek, half a mile below where the Pennsylvania Railroad crosses. It is not known when the son removed west of the Susquehanna and took up his residence in what is now Lower Chanceford township, York county. When the struggle for independence came on he took an active part, and was on the Committee of Observation for the county. When supplies were asked for the people of Boston, personally and unaided he secured grain and flour, which he took to Baltimore for shipment. He was appointed by the constitutional convention of 1776 one of the Board of Commissioners for York county, and on June 10, 1777, commissioned a justice of the peace. He was a delegate to the Pennsylvania convention to ratify the federal constitution in 1787, which he signed, although he eventually became a prominent anti-federalist. He was a member of the constitutional convention of 1789–90, and represented his county in the Legislature of the State, session of 1805–6. He died at his residence in Lower Chanceford township, York county, in October, 1813.

PICKERING, TIMOTHY, of Luzerne county, son of Deacon Timothy Pickering, was born at Salem, Massachusetts, on the 17th of July, 1745. He graduated at Harvard University in 1763, studied law, and was admitted to the bar in 1768. At the outset of the Revolution he was on the Committee of Correspondence, and was the author of the address of the people of Salem to the British general, Gage, on the occasion of the Boston Port Bill. He first opposed an armed resistance to the British troops, when, on the 26th of February, 1775, he, while a colonel of militia, prevented their crossing at a drawbridge to seize some military stores. In the fall of 1776 he joined Washington's army in the Jerseys, was subsequently (1777) made his adjutant-general, and present at the battles of Brandywine and Germantown. On the 5th of August, 1780, he succeeded General Greene as quartermaster-general. He was a member of the Pennsylvania Society of the Cincinnati. After the war he took up his residence in Philadelphia, and in 1786 was sent by the government to assist in adjusting the claims of the Connecticut settlers in Wyoming. For an account of his adventures in that section, see "Hazard's Register," Vol. VII. In 1787 he represented the county of Luzerne in the Pennsylvania convention to ratify the federal constitution, but did not sign the ratification. At that period he held the offices of prothonotary, clerk of the courts, etc., for that county, and was subsequently a member of the Pennsylvania convention of 1789-90. He opposed Governor Mifflin's election to the gubernatorial office, but, nevertheless, continued to hold his positions under him. President Washington appointed him Postmaster-General, November 7, 1791, which he held until the 2d of January, 1795: filled the office of Secretary of State from December 10, 1795, to the 12th of May, 1800. Leaving office poor, he settled on a tract of land he possessed in Pennsylvania. He returned to Salem, Massachusetts, the year following, afterwards filling the various offices of judge of the courts, United States Senator, 1803-11, and member of the Massachusetts Board of War, 1812-14, and member of Congress, 1815-17. He wrote quite a number of political pamphlets during his brilliant political career, and was one of the leaders of the federal party. He died at Salem, Massachusetts, on the 29th of January, 1829.

POWELL, JOSEPH, of Bedford county, born about 1750, in Bethlehem township, Northampton county, Pennsylvania, son of Joseph Powell, a Moravian clergyman from White Church, Shropshire, England. He studied for the ministry, was settled in Bedford county, and during the Revolutionary period became quite prominent in political affairs. He was a member of the Pennsylvania convention to ratify the federal constitution in 1787, but united with his colleagues in opposing the ratification. As stated in the sketch referred to, he was a member of the State constitutional convention of 1776, and also of 1789–90. He died in November, 1804, in Bedford county.

REYNOLDS, JOHN, of Cumberland county, was born in 1749, near Shippensburg, that county. His father, John Reynolds, came from the north of Ireland and settled in the valley at an early period. Although there were three John Reynolds in that settlement during the Revolutionary period, the subject of our sketch appears to have been the more prominent one, "Justice Rannels," as he is generally noted. He was commissioned a justice of the peace prior to the Revolution, and during the struggle for independence was an active partisan. He was continued in commission of the peace by the Supreme Executive Council, June 9, 1777, and by virtue of seniority became one of the judges of the Court of Common Pleas. He was a member of the Pennsylvania convention to ratify the federal constitution in 1787, but voted against the ratification. He was an elder, as also was his father, of Middle Spring Presbyterian Church. He died the 20th of October, 1789, aged forty years.

RICHARDS, JOHN, of Montgomery county, son of Matthias and Margaret (Hillegas) Richards, was born April 17, 1753, in new New Hanover township, that county. His grandfather, John Frederick Richards, came from Würtemberg, Germany, to Pennsylvania prior to 1720, his warrant for a tract of land bearing that date. He died in 1748, and his son John in March, 1775, at the age of fifty-six years. The life of the subject of this sketch was an eventful and busy one,— with a fine estate, he was a progressive farmer, store-keeper, and iron-master. Having been appointed one of the justices of the peace for Philadelphia county, June 6, 1777, he was continued in commission, and upon the organization of the county of Montgomery, became one of the judges of the Court of Common Pleas, November 1, 1784. He was elected to the fourth Congress, 1796–97, and from 1801 to 1807 served in the State Senate. He died November 13, 1822, at the age of sixty-nine years.

ROBERTS, JONATHAN, of Montgomery county, eldest son of Matthew Roberts and Sarah Walter, was born in 1731. His grandfather, John Roberts, a native of Pennychland, Denbighshire, North Wales, came to America about the year 1682, and settled in Lower Merion, now Montgomery county. Jonathan was brought up as a farmer. From 1771 to 1775 he served in the provincial Assembly. When the Revolutionary struggle came on, belonging to the Society of Friends, he took the position of "a non-militant Whig,"—that is, he aided the patriot cause secretly, but did not bear arms. At the close of the struggle, when measures were taken to divide the county of Philadelphia, he became quite prominent in the formation of the county of Montgomery in 1784. He was one of the commissioners named in the act, and chiefly through his efforts was the county-seat located at Norristown. This injured him more or less politically, but he was a man always above reproach, and the bitterness of feeling soon subsided. He was elected a delegate to the Pennsylvania convention to ratify the federal constitution in 1787, and gave his vote for ratification, although he thought the outlines of that instrument were perhaps a too faithful copy of the British theory of government. From 1788 to 1790 he served in the General Assembly, and was a member of the House of Representatives, sessions of 1790–91 and 1799–1800. Mr. Roberts died in 1812, at the age of eighty-two years.

RUSH, BENJAMIN, of the City of Philadelphia, was born December 24, 1745, in Byberry township, county of Philadelphia. He was educated at the College of New Jersey, from whence he graduated in 1760. He studied medicine under Dr. John Redman, a famous physician in his day, went to Edinburgh, and graduated from the university there as Doctor of Medicine in 1768. Passing some time in the London hospitals, he returned to Pennsylvania, and in 1769 was elected Professor of Chemistry in the College of Philadelphia. He was in the successful practice of his profession when the war of the Revolution commenced. His native State establishing a navy for the protection of the Delaware, he was commissioned, September 27, 1775, fleet-surgeon thereof, only resigning, July, 1776, when he was elected by the General Assembly to the Continental Congress. He was one of the after-signers of the Declaration of Independence. He was on the commission to establish and superintend a saltpetre factory in Philadelphia in 1775, and was a member of the provincial conference held at Carpenters' Hall, June 18, 1776. In 1777 he was appointed physician-general to the hospital of the Middle Department, and served with great usefulness. In 1779 he assisted in organizing the Republican Society, which had for its object the revision of the Pennsylvania constitution of 1776. Towards the close of the war he was active in the cause for the abolition of slavery, and for a long time was secretary of the Pennsylvania Society. He was an intimate friend of the author of "Common Sense," and a pamphleteer of considerable prominence. In 1787 he was elected a delegate to the Pennsylvania convention to ratify the federal constitution, of which he was an earnest advocate. On the death of Dr. John Morgan, in 1789, he succeeded to the chair of the Theory and Practice of Medicine, and when, in 1791, the College of Philadelphia was transformed into the University of Pennsylvania, he became professor of the Institutes and Practice of Medicine and Clinical Practice, afterwards that of the Practice of Physic being added. Until the end of his life he filled these positions with distinguished ability. From 1790 to 1795 he was resident port-physician of the City of Philadelphia; was cashier of the United States Mint; and, upon the incorporation of Dickinson College, Carlisle, one of its original trustees. During the yellow-fever epidemic in Philadelphia in 1793 he remained at his post and battled with the fearful scourge, saying to those who counselled him to regard his personal safety, "I will remain if I remain alive." He died in Philadelphia, April 19, 1813, leaving a reputation in his professional life only equalled by his sterling patriotism and his great philanthropy.

SCOTT, THOMAS, of Washington county, was born February 28, 1739, in Donegal township, Lancaster county. In 1770 he removed with his family to Western Pennsylvania, and settled on Dunlap's Creek, near the Monongahela. Shortly after the erection of Westmoreland county, January 11, 1774, he was appointed a justice of the peace, and in that capacity was a warm and able supporter of the Pennsylvania jurisdiction, and drew on himself the particular resentment of the partisans of Virginia. When this contest sunk in the great cause of the Revolution, he was elected, in 1776, to the first Assembly under the constitution of the State passed that year. He was a member of the Council of Safety from Westmoreland county in 1777, and elected to the Supreme Executive Council, in which body he served three years. When the county of Washington was organized in 1781, he was appointed prothonotary April 2, 1781, serving until March 28, 1789. He was a delegate to the Pennsylvania convention to ratify the federal constitution in 1787, and in 1788 elected a member of the first Congress under that instrument, which he so zealously supported against the protests of his constituents and the contrary action of his colleagues. As the change of the constitution of Pennsylvania occasioned a new appointment of State officers in 1791, he declined being considered as a candidate for a seat in the second Congress, with a view to retain his office as clerk of the courts in Washington county. Governor Mifflin thought proper to supersede him. At the election, however, a few weeks after, he was chosen a member of the Assembly, and in 1792 a member of the third Congress. With only such opportunities of study as his residence in Philadelphia while in Council afforded him, and unaided by a liberal or professional education, he was admitted to the Washington county bar at the September term, 1791, afterwards to other of the western counties, and was a successful advocate. And it may be here stated that his arguments were natural and judicious, his language nervous, and his elocution remarkably emphatic. Mr. Scott died at his residence in the town of Washington, whither he removed upon the organization of the county, on Wednesday, March 2, 1796, a few days after he had completed his fifty-seventh year.

SLAGLE, HENRY, of York county, son of Christopher Slagle, an emigrant from Saxony, was born in 1735 in Lancaster county, Pennsylvania. He was commissioned one of the provincial magistrates, in October, 1764, and was continued in the office by the convention of 1776. In December, 1774, he served on the committee of inspection for York county; commanded a battalion of Associators in 1776; was a member of the provincial conference of June 18, 1776; and of the subsequent convention of the 15th of July. He was appointed by the Assembly, December 16, 1777, to take subscriptions for the continental loan; and November 22, 1777, acted as one of the commissioners who met at New Haven, Connecticut, to regulate the price of commodies in the colonies. He represented York county in the General Assembly from 1777 to 1779; was appointed sub-lieutenant of the county, March 30, 1780; one of the auditors of depreciation accounts for York county, March 3, 1781; delegate to the Pennsylvania convention to ratify the federal constitution in 1787, and member of the constitutional convention of 1789–90. He was commissioned by Governor Mifflin one of the associate judges of York county, August 17, 1791, and continued as such, on the organization of Adams county, and represented the latter county in the legislature, session of 1801–2. He served as one of the original trustees of Dickinson College, and was a zealous supporter of the system of public education, which he did not live to see adopted. He died at his residence in Adams county.

SMILIE, JOHN, of Fayette county, son of Thomas Smilie, was born September 16, 1742, in county Down, Ireland. His father came to Pennsylvania at an early period and settled in Lancaster county. The son early espoused the patriot cause, and at once took sides, being a member of the County Committee, of the provincial conference held at Carpenters' Hall June 18, 1775, and that of June 18, 1776. In the latter year, and that of 1777, he served as a private in the Associators, and continued in that situation during the most critical periods of the war. In 1778, and again in 1779, he was elected to the General Assembly from Lancaster county, and became an ardent promoter of the act of 1780, providing for the gradual abolition of slavery in Pennsylvania. In 1781, he removed with his family to then Westmoreland county, and was chosen a member of the Council of Censors, 1783–84, from that county. When the county of Fayette was organized in 1784, he was chosen its first Representative in the General Assembly, re-elected in 1785, and served in the Supreme Executive Council from November 2, 1786, to November 19, 1789. He was a delegate to the Pennsylvania convention to ratify the federal constitution in 1787—opposed the ratification—and was one of the anti-constitutional party who were mobbed in Philadelphia on the evening of the 6th of November, that year. With Gallatin, he represented Fayette in the State constitutional convention of 1789–90. In 1790 he was elected to the State Senate, but in 1792, having been elected to the third Congress, he resigned the last year of his senatorial term. He was sent to the Pennsylvania House of Representatives in 1795, '96, and '97, and was a presidential elector in 1796. In 1798 he was again chosen to Congress, the sixth, and re-elected to the succeeding Congresses up to and including the thirteenth. He died at the city of Washington on the 29th of December, 1813, aged seventy-one years.

STOUT, ABRAHAM, of Bucks county, was born in Rockhill township, Bucks county, in 1740. His father, Jacob Stout, in 1735, came from Germany and purchased a tract of land in the Proprietaries' manor of Perkasie, now covering the village of Perkasie. The son seems to have been an influential farmer; was chosen a delegate to the Pennsylvania convention to ratify the federal constitution in 1787, and also a member of the constitutional convention of 1789–90. He held the office of justice of the peace from August 27, 1791, to January 20, 1795. He died in June, 1812.

Todd, William, of Westmoreland county, was born about 1739, at the Trappe (now Montgomery county), Pennsylvania. His father was Robert Todd, a native of County Down, Ireland, who came to Pennsylvania in 1737, and located in then Philadelphia county, where he died in 1775. He was the ancestor of the Todd family of Kentucky, from whom descended the wife of President Lincoln. William Todd went to Western Pennsylvania about 1765, locating at first within the limits of Bedford county. He was a man of more than ordinary prominence, was appointed by the provincial conference held at Carpenters' Hall, Philadelphia, in June, 1776, one of the judges of the election in the western part of Bedford county for members of the first constitutional convention, by which latter body he was appointed one of the commissioners of that county, and also a justice of the peace. Shortly after he removed to Westmoreland county, where he settled upon land subsequently warranted to him, located "on both sides of the road leading from Cherry's Mill to Bud's Ferry, Youghiogheny River, Mount Pleasant township." He served in the General Assembly from 1783 to 1789, and opposed the calling of the convention of 1789–90. He was chosen a delegate to the Pennsylvania convention of 1787, voting against its ratification; and was also a member of the constitutional convention of 1789–90. He was an associate judge from August 17, 1791, to December 3, 1794, when he resigned to take his seat in the State Senate, serving one term, 1794 to 1796. He died in October, 1810.

Wayne, Anthony, of Chester county, son of Isaac Wayne, was born January 1, 1745, in that county. His grandfather, Anthony Wayne, who commanded a squadron of dragoons at the battle of the Boyne, came to Pennsylvania in 1722. The father was prominent in local affairs, and was a member of the provincial Assembly, 1757 to 1764. The son was a farmer and surveyor. In 1774 he was chosen to the General Assembly, was a deputy to the provincial conference of July 15, 1774, and a delegate to the provincial convention, January 23, 1775. He was on the Committee of Safety from June 30, 1775, resigning when he was commissioned colonel of the fourth battalion of the Pennsylvania Line, January 3, 1776. He was in the Canada campaign of that year, and wounded at Three Rivers. On the 23d of November, General Schuyler assigned him to the command of the fortress of Ticonderoga and garrison, composed of Wood's, Dayton's, Irvine's, Russell's, Whitcomb's, and his own battalion. He was promoted brigadier-general February 21, 1777. In May following, at his own earnest solicitation, he was called to the main army, where he arrived on the 15th of that month, and was placed in command of a brigade. He was with Washington at the battle of Brandywine, September 11, 1777, and held his ground against Knyphausen until the right of the American army was turned. He was surprised at the Paoli on the night of the 20th of September, and demanding a court of inquiry, was honorably acquitted. He was wounded at Germantown, and greatly distinguished himself at Monmouth. For his conduct at the storming of Stony Point, one of the most gallant achievements of the struggle for independence, on the night of July 15, 1779, Congress gave him a vote of thanks and a gold medal. His conduct during the revolt of the Pennsylvania Line, and his subsequent brilliant career in the South until the close of the Revolution, render the name of Wayne illustrious. Returning home, the well-scarred veteran was the recipient of many honors. Chester county elected him a member of the Council of Censors, 1783–84, and from 1784 to 1786 he represented her in the General Assembly of the State. He was a delegate to the Pennsylvania convention to ratify the federal constitution of 1787, and espoused the cause of its adoption. The defeat of St. Clair on the Maumee, in November, 1791, required a change of commanders, and the eyes and hopes of the people were turned to the discreet and cautious Wayne. He was appointed by President Washington, April 3, 1792, general-in-chief of the army, and on the 20th of August following, by the admirable discipline, courage, and bravery of his troops, he gained the battle of "Fallen Timbers," and dictated terms to the savages at Greenville. On the 14th of December, 1796, General Wayne suddenly closed his military career at Presqu' Isle, and was buried on the shores of Lake Erie. His remains were removed to Chester county in 1809, and in 1811 the Society of the Cincinnati, of which he was an original member, erected over them a plain, substantial monument.

WHITEHILL, JOHN, of Lancaster county, was born December 1, 1729, in Salisbury township, that county. His father, James Whitehill, a native of the north of Ireland, settled on Pequea Creek, in 1723. John received a good education. He was an ardent patriot, and came into prominence at the beginning of the Revolution. The Supreme Executive Council appointed him, March 31, 1777, one of the justices of the Common Pleas for Lancaster, and in the years 1778 to 1782 he represented the county in the General Assembly. He served as a member of the Council of Censors, 1783–84, and was a delegate to the Pennsylvania convention to ratify the federal constitution of 1787, but did not sign the ratification. From December 22, 1784, to December 16, 1787, he was a member of the Supreme Executive Council. Under the constitution of 1790 he was appointed by Governor Mifflin an associate judge of the county of Lancaster, August 17, 1791. He was a presidential elector in 1796, and elected to the eighth and ninth Congresses, serving with distinguished ability. A rigid Presbyterian, he was a trustee and elder of the church at Pequea. He died at his residence, Salisbury, in 1815. He left a large landed estate. Brought to the front by the Revolutionary war, he proved to be, like his compeers, a person of indomitable courage and vigor of intellect, and was ever tenacious of republican principles. He belonged to the Jeffersonian school of statesmen.

WHITEHILL, ROBERT, of Cumberland county, was born July 24, 1735, in Salisbury township, Lancaster county, Pennsylvania. He was the son of James Whitehill and his wife, Rachel Cresswell, and younger brother of the subject of the preceding sketch. He was educated in the school of the Rev. Francis Allison. In the spring of 1771 he removed to Cumberland county, locating on a farm two miles west of

Harrisburg. His entire public life was a successful and brilliant one. He was a member of the County Committee of 1774–75; of the convention of July 15, 1776; of the Assembly, 1776–8; Council of Safety from October to December, 1777; member of the Supreme Executive Council, December 28, 1779 to November, 30, 1781; of the Assembly, 1784–7; under the constitution of 1790, member of the House of Representatives from 1797 to 1801, and of the Senate from 1801 to 1804. During his term as Senator he was speaker of that body, and presided at the celebrated impeachment of the Supreme Court of Pennsylvania. In 1805 he was elected to Congress, and continued to be a member thereof until his death. From 1774 to the time of his death he filled almost every position in the gift of the people. In the Pennsylvania convention to ratify the federal constitution of 1787 he was one of the leaders in opposing the ratification, and it is to be regretted that his remarks were not fully reported. He died at his residence in Cumberland county, two miles west of the Susquehanna, on the 7th of April, 1813, while a member of Congress.

WILSON, JAMES, of the city of Philadelphia, was born September 14, 1742, in the Lowlands, near St. Andrew's, Scotland. His studies were pursued at Glasgow, St. Andrew's, and Edinburgh, emigrating to Pennsylvania in 1766, where he became a tutor in the College of Philadelphia. He at once began the study of the law with John Dickinson, one of the ablest legal minds in America, and was admitted to the bar November, 1767. He shortly after took up his residence at Carlisle, where he was in the enjoyment of a good practice when the war of the Revolution began. He early espoused the patriot cause, and was chosen a delegate from Cumberland county to the provincial convention held at Philadelphia, January 23, 1775. On May 6, 1775, the Assemby elected him one of the deputies to the Continental Congress, and on the 10th he took his seat in that body. He was re-elected by the Assembly, November 4, 1775, and voted for the Declaration of Independence, to which he had the honor of affixing his signature. The State constitutional convention, on July 20, 1776, chose him to the same position, and on March 10, 1777, he was elected by the Assembly. In 1782-83, and again in 1785-86, he served in that body. On May 23, 1782, he was appointed brigadier-general of the Pennsylvania militia. During the closing years of the Revolution he acted as the advocate-general of France in America, and for this service was handsomely rewarded by that government. In 1779 he was one of the active members of the Republican Society formed for the purpose of urging the revision of the State constitution of 1776. He was appointed by the Supreme Executive Council and the Assembly, February 14, 1784, one of the counsellors on the cause between Pennsylvania and Connecticut, a case which he conducted with great legal ability. He was a member of the convention which framed the federal constitution of 1787, and also of the Pennsylvania convention called to ratify that instrument, being its foremost defender. It may with truth be said that to him is due the honor of its ratification by that body. President Washington appointed him, in September, 1789, a judge of the United States Supreme Court. He was also a member of the constitutional convention of 1789-90. In addition to these duties he accepted the appointment in 1790 of law professor in the University of Pennsylvania. His course of lectures are published in his works, edited by his son. In 1792 he published, in connection with Chief Justice McKean, of Pennsylvania, "Commentaries on the United States Constitution." During the Revolutionary period he published several pamphlets relating to the contest with the mother-country. Judge Wilson died at Edenton, North Carolina, August 28, 1798, while on his judicial circuit, and was there buried. He was a profound thinker, and thoroughly learned in the law. His scientific attainments were of a high order, and the degree of Doctor of Laws was conferred upon him. Graydon, in his "Memoirs," says of Wilson, referring to the Pennsylvania convention: "He never failed to throw the strongest lights on his subject, and thence rather to flash than elicit conviction syllogistically. . . . He produced greater orations than any other man I have heard;

and I doubt much whether the ablest of those who sneer at his occasional simplicities and 'brilliant conceits' would not have found him a truly formidable antagonist."

WILSON, WILLIAM, of Northumberland county, emigrated from the north of Ireland when quite young. Upon the breaking out of the Revolution he was commissioned ensign of Captain John Lowdon's company, Colonel William Thompson's battalion, June 25, 1775, and marched to Cambridge, Massachusetts. He was promoted second lieutenant January 4, 1776. His regiment re-enlisting for the war, under General Edward Hand, became the first Pennsylvania regiment of the Continental Line. He was promoted first lieutenant September 25, 1776, and to captain March 2, 1777. His regiment, in Wayne's division, took a very prominent part in the action at Monmouth, June 22, 1778, where the Royal Grenadiers under Colonel Monckton undertook to break the centre occupied by Wayne and the Pennsylvania Line. Colonel Monckton was killed, and in a hand-to-hand fight over the colors of the Grenadiers they were secured by Captain Wilson, and are in possession of his descendants at Bellefonte. He was mustered out November 3, 1783, and settled in the mercantile business in Northumberland, Pennsylvania. On the death of Colonel Samuel Hunter, he succeeded him as county lieutenant, commission dating May 20, 1784. In the fall of 1787, Colonel Wilson and his partner in business, Captain John Boyd, were elected delegates to the Pennsylvania convention to ratify the federal constitution. There were parties in politics even at that time, and the ruling party in Northumberland county were opposed to the proposed constitution; but the old officers of the army rallied to its support, and selected two of their own number for delegates. In 1789 he became a member of the Supreme Executive Council, serving one year. In connection with his partner, Captain Boyd, he built Chillisquaque Mills, at the mouth of that creek, four miles above Northumberland. He was appointed an associate judge January 13, 1792. In September, 1794, he took a prominent part in favor of the government in suppressing liberty-poles and demonstrations on the part of those who sympathized in the Whiskey Insurrection. In 1798, when war was threatened with the French Directory and a provisional army was authorized, Washington selected Colonel Wilson for one of his division commanders. Happily, there was no necessity to bring that army into the field. He died in 1813.

WYNKOOP, HENRY, of Bucks county, son of Nicholas Wynkoop, was born in Northampton township, that county, March 2, 1737. His great-grandfather, Gerardus Wynkoop, settled in Moreland township, then Philadelphia county, in 1717. Henry Wynkoop, who received a collegiate education, came into active prominence at the outset of the Revolutionary struggle. He was on the County Committee of Observation in 1774, a deputy to the provincial conference of July 15, that year, and a member of the provincial conference which met at Carpenters' Hall on the 18th of June, 1775. He was chosen major of one of the Associated battalions, and was an efficient officer. He was on the General Committee of Safety from July, 1776, to July, 1777. The General Assembly appointed him one of the commissioners to settle the accounts of county lieutenants, December 4, 1778, and on March 3, 1779, when Edward Biddle resigned his seat in Congress, Major Wynkoop was chosen by that body to fill the position, being re-elected November 24, 1780, and November 22, 1781. He was commissioned one of the justices of the Court of Common Pleas and Orphans' Court, November 18, 1780, but resigned June 27, 1789, having been elected to the first Congress, 1789-91. On the expiration of his Congressional term he was appointed by Governor Mifflin an associate judge of Bucks county, August 17, 1791, filling that honorable station until his death, October 24, 1812.

YARDLEY, THOMAS, of Bucks county, was a native of Lower Makefield township, that county. He was descended from William Yardley (1632-93) and his wife Jane, of Banselough, near Leek, in Staffordshire, England, who, with their children, Thomas and William, arrived at the Falls September 28, 1682, and settled in Lower Makefield township, taking up a large tract of land, covering the site of Yardleyville.

He was a delegate to the Pennsylvania convention to ratify the federal constitution of 1787, and voted for the ratification. Governor Mifflin appointed him a justice of the peace August 27, 1791, which office he held until February 21, 1794, which, we presume, was the date of his death.

YEATES, JASPER, of Lancaster county, the son of John Yeates and his wife, Elizabeth Sidbotham, was born April 9, 1745, in the City of Philadelphia. He was educated at the College of Philadelphia, studied law, and was admitted to the bar October 5, 1765. Shortly after he located at Lancaster. When the war of the Revolution opened he took an active part, and was chairman of the Committee of Observation for Lancaster county. In 1776 he was one of the commissioners appointed to hold a conference with the Indians at Fort Pitt. Throughout the war for independence he occupied a conspicuous position in every patriotic effort. He was a member of the Pennsylvania convention to ratify the federal constitution, and one of the committee which reported the form of ratification. He was a strong federalist. Under the State constitution of 1789–91 he was commissioned by Governor Mifflin, March 21, 1791, a justice of the Supreme Court of Pennsylvania. President Washington appointed him one of the commissioners to confer with the insurgents in the so-called Whiskey Rebellion of 1794. In 1805, when politics ran exceedingly high in the State, he, with Chief Justice Shippen and Judge Thomas Smith, was impeached, tried, and acquitted, upon one of the most trivial charges which ever engaged the attention of a legislative body. He remained in office until his death, at Lancaster, March 14, 1817. Judge Yeates was the author of four volumes of "Reports of Cases in the Supreme Court of Pennsylvania," published after his death.

APPENDIX.

NOTES OF THE DEBATE

PENNSYLVANIA CONVENTION

TAKEN BY

JAMES WILSON.

FROM THE ORIGINAL MANUSCRIPT IN THE HISTORICAL SOCIETY OF
PENNSYLVANIA.

[The foot-notes to this appendix are given as marginal notes in the original manuscript
of James Wilson, and appear to be brief memorandums for a reply].

In Convention
Monday, 26th Nov., 1787, P. M.

* Mr. McKean—There can be only one Question before us. The Question
on separate Paragraphs would preclude A Vote of Approbation on the whole
system. Each Paragraph may be discussed; but without taking a Question
on the whole. A House convenient on the whole, may be defective in some
of its Apartments. We come not to compose a new Book.

Moved and seconded that the tenth Rule be repealed.

Mr. Smilie—It would be more proper to go into a Committee on the whole
than to repeal the Rule.—By going into a Committee there will be a double
Investigation.

† Mr. R. Whitehill—We are not precluded from proposing Amendments—
We are going to examine the Foundations of the Building. By proposing
Amendments we can hear what they say in the other States, and then can
accommodate.

Mr. Smilie—In a *legal* Discussion I am inferior to (Mr. McKean.).—The
mode proposed by him is contrary to every Idea of Order.—The Mode that
will give the *longest* Time to consider should be preferred.

In convention we can consider only each part *once.*—The People of Penna.

---

* The Matters of Form reduced to sound sense.
The Repeal of the Rule on Step to obtain the same free Debate as in Committee.
We have another Advantage as every Thing will appear on the Minutes.
We must take the System on the whole and, as the Result of the whole, ratify or not
ratify.
The gen'l Convention took allowances of Power, and were not appointed by the People.
† To whom shall we propose Amendments?
Do we know they will be agreeable to our Constcy as much in this as
Time in the other States.

will be taxed by the Representatives of U. S.—The Freemen of Penna. will *think* and *act.*

Mr. Scott—We are come to stamp the System with the Authority of the People, or to refuse it that Stamp.

Tuesday, 27th Nov., 1787, A. M.

Mr. Whitehill—Moves that Reasons for Yeas and Nays may be entered on the Journals.

Mr. McKean—A Speech to promote Candour and mutual Forbearance.— No two Govts. exactly alike.

Division of the legislative Power, into two Branches, with a qualified Negative highly proper—these should be Permanency in the Magistracies, and Stability in the Laws.

* The Constitution opens with a solemn and practical Declaration—that the Supreme Power resides in the People. It is announced in their Name. They ordain and establish. They can repeal and annul.

There should be more than one Branch.

† I. In order to secure Liberty and the Constitution, it is absolutely necessary that the Legislature should be restrained.

It may be restrained in several Ways:

1. By the Judges deciding agst. the Legislature in Favor of the Constn.

2. By Elections at proper Intervals of Time.

3. By the Interposition of the Supreme Power of the People on necessary Occasions.

4. *Principally* by a Division of the legislative Authority into more Bodies than one.

State the Necessity and Operation of this Division.

II. There will be more Caution—more Precision—more Stability in the Laws.

III. On the Principles of the Constitution, the *States* should be represented and possess the Powers of self-preservation.

‡ This power is so strongly guarded, that it never can be lost to any State, without its *own* Consent.

Ill-founded is the Objection of annihilating the State Governments.

‖ The Usefulness of the qualified Negative.

1. It enlarges the Field of Deliberation and Debate.

2. It provides the materials of a practical History of Legislation.

3. It secures an additional Degree of Deliberation in passing the Law.

§ 4. It gives an additional Independency and *Security* to the Powers delegated to the executive Department.

¶ The importance of the Right of Suffrage.

* Preamble.—Contrast this with the Principle of *Magna Charta.*

† Art. 1, s. 1.

‡ Last Proviso in Art. 5.

‖ The objections of the Presids. will be assisted by the Knowledge and Experience of the Heads of Departments. Art. 2, s. 2.

§ The Judges possess their power of Independence and Self-Preservation by their Decisions.

¶ Art. 1, s. 2.

Mont. 6. 2, c. 2.

In Convention. 28th Sept., [sic.] 1787.

Mr. Smilie—There is no *Security* for our Rights in this Constn.

Preamble to Declr. of Independence.

Why did they omit a Bill of Rights?

With Respect to Trial by Jury and Hab. Cor. there is a Bill of Rights.

Without one we cannot know when Congress exceed their Powers.—There is no Check but the People—no Security for the Rights of Conscience 6th Article of the Constu.

This sweeping Clause levels all the Bills of Rights of the several States and their Governments are not confirmed.

Mr. Whitehill—If we were sure that the general Government would not infringe on the State Govts. we would be satisfied. Power is of an increasing Nature.—We are not bound by Forms or Examples of other Countries. We should improve on them.

"We the People"—changes the Principles of *Confederation* and introduces a *consolidating* and *absorbing* Government.

Does not this System violate the Confedn? 9 States are sufficient here, 13 were necessary before—may not the other 4 still insist on the Confedn?

The Business was intended to give *more* Powers to Congress—the Powers of the Delegates of this State in the Convention.

A genl. Govt. was not thought of. Nor to unhinge the State Govts.—The Convention have made a Plan of their own—they have *assumed* the Power of *proposing.*—Alterations in Governmt. should proceed from the People.— The Assembly of Penna. are limited in their Powers: And the Business should have been left to the People.

This is a Mode of Amendment in the present Confedn.

Art 1, s. 1. Power unbounded.

Who are to be Judges of what is *necessary* and *proper.*

S. 2. *Annual* Parlts. and Assemblies necessary.—Br. Parl. *took* 7 years.— Present Delegates in Congress may be *recalled.*—6 years too long.

S. 4. Times and Places of Election. The Members of the Senate may enrich themselves: For they have a Power to Tax: Their Powers pervade every Thing. It forms one genl. consolidating Government.

Power of borrowing Money—raising Armies.

If we give the Power, we are wrong; tho' the Legislature are of our own Election.

Could any State oppose the genl. Govt? All are to be sworn to observe it.

A Bill of Rights may be dangerous to the Governours.

Ar. 1, 6. This Article *eradicates* every Vestige of State Govt.—And was *intended* so, for it was deliberated.

Art. 1. s. 4. This is intended to carry on the Business when the State Govts. are destroyed.

Can we give away the rights of Conscience? There is no *Reserve* of *it*, tho' these Reservations as to *ex post facto* Laws. Art. 1, s. 9.

Let us *secure* our Liberties, and not quarrel about the Bill of Rights.— They are not secured except as to Hab. Cor.

Mr Wilson.

Mr. Smilie—This Constn. goes too far in Favour of Tyranny.—We admit that the *Form* of the State Govnt. must subsist: But their *Efficiency* and *Power* must be destroyed by the superabundant Power of the general Govt.

It is not a federal Govt., not a Confederation.

It is a complete Govt.—Legislative—Judicial—Executive.

Its Powers extend to ——— legislation ———to Taxes; and leave only to the States what they please.

Art. 1, s. 8. "Collect Taxes."—"To make all Laws necessary," etc.

Who are to be the Judges of what is necessary for the Welfare of the U. S.

The State Govt. cannot make that agt. the genl. Government.

Power will not *lessen.*

A power appropriating Money—raising Armies, and commanding the Militia.—Could the State Govts. oppose this.

There would be a Rivalship between the Genl. and St. Govts.—On each Side they will endeavor to increase their Power.

Oaths to be taken to the Genl. Govt.

The State Govts. will lose the Attacht. of their citizens by losing their Power.

The People will not support them; but will suffer them to dwindle to Nothing.

The *Forms* of Govt. may subsist after the *substance* is gone—as in the Senate of Rome.

The State Elections will be ill attended.

The State Govts. will be *mere* Electors.

Will *one* consolidated Govt. be a proper one for the United States?

Mr. McKean—There has been no objection to *two* Branches in the Legislature—nor to the Mode of choosing them or the President.

The Powers are well defined and necessary.

The great guard agt. excessive Taxation, is that he that *lays, pays,* and frequent Election.

To prevent Mischief we will not give the Power of doing good.

Who are to [be] the Judges?—those who are chosen because they are capable of being so.

Admn. of Govt. is of as much *practical* Importance as its *Nature.*

In Convention. 30th Nov., 1787.

Mr. Whitehill—The genl. Govt. may subsist after the *Abolition* of the State Govt.

The Powers of Congress are unlimited and undefined.

The Senators may hold their Places as long as they live; and there is no Power to prevent them.

Art. 1, s. 8., last Clause gives the Power of self-preservation *independent* of the several States; for in case of their Abolition, it will be alleged in Favour of the genl. Govt. that self-preservation is the first Law.

The "Time" of Election is in their Power and therefore they may make it as long as they please.

There are *some Reservations* in this Govt.—Why not more?

It was systematically intended to abolish the State Goverts.

Mr. Hartley—England became enslaved at the Time of the Conquest.

The Power of *collecting* Taxes is necessary.

Recommendations have been insufficient.

Our Representatives have this Power.

In the Time of the Emperors, *they* appointed the Senate.

Dr. Rush—All Bills of Rights have been broken. There is no security for Liberty but in *two* Things—just *Representation* and Cheqks.

The Citizens of the U. S. have the *Preoccupancy* of Liberty; shall they make a Deed of Confiscation to themselves.

Mr. Yeates—Objections reducible to 2 Heads—the Want of Bill of Rights—Abolition of State Govt.

4 Art., 4 s. Guarantee of Repub. Government.

Power *must* be given. All power *may* be abused.

The Restrictions in Art. 1, s. 10, will revive our Commerce, restore public Credit, lessen Taxes.

Mr. Findlay—The Observations made relate to what is, and what is not in the System.

I confine myself to answering the Remarks that have been made this Forenoon.

The natural Course of Power is to make the many Slaves to the few.

This is verified by universal Experience.

England had always the Com. Law: Its Charter will not apply to us. Bills of Rights were great Improvements then.

Government will construe its own Powers so as to suit its own *Wishes*, which it will call *Necessities*.

Because *all* Securities are broken, shall we have *none*.

It is not a new Doctrine that, because a good Govt. ill-administered, produces Mischief, therefore we ought to be indifferent about it.

Powers *given*—Powers reserved—ought to be *all* enumerated.

Let us add a Bill of Rights to our other Securities.

In Britain the Appropriations are *annual*.

Annual Elections are absolutely necessary in the Govt. that is not merely federal.

The Senate, the principal Branch, is elected for 6 years, and removes Responsibility far.

Number of Representatives too small.—There should be more in this new and thinly settled Country, than in one old and populous.

Pennsylva. would not have any Representatives far from Philada.

This is not a *confederate* but a *consolidating* Government.

We ought to suppose that Congress will *abuse* its Powers.

The Powers of the genl. Govt. extend to *State* and *internal* Purposes.

Dr. Rush—Our Rights are not yet all known, why should we attempt to enumerate them?

Mr. Smilie—In the Remembrancer there is a Bill of Rights of Virginia.

Mr. McKean—I wish to see what kind of Bill of Rights those Gentlemen would propose.

Mr. Smilie—We will exhibit a Bill of Rights if the Convention will receive it.

1. Great Point.—Is a Bill of Rights necessary.

2. Does this System abolish the State Governments.

Direct Taxation—poll Tax—standing Army are Objections.

Freedom almost unknown in the old World.—Are we to go there for Precedents of Liberty?

Bill of Rights necessary as the Instrument of *original Compact*—and to mention the Rights reserved.—The Sovereignty and Independence of the States should be reserved.

There must be a People before there is a King; and the People, in the first Instance, have inherent and inalienable Rights.

We ought to know what Rights we *surrender*, and what we *retain*.

Suppose Congress to pass an Act for the Punishment of Libels and restrain the Liberty of the Press—for they are warranted to do this—what Security would a Printer have tried in one of their Courts?

An aristocratical Govt. cannot bear the Liberty of the Press.

The Senate will swallow up any Thing.

What Harm from a Bill of Rights?

In Convention, Dec. 1st, 1787.

Mr. Pickering—Our principal Debate during the many Days we have met has been whether the House would have a Porch. Let us first take a Survey of the Mansion and see whether a Porch is necessary.

Mr. Chambers—The Manner of Debate is been very irregular and desultory.

"All Legislative Powers *herein* granted."

Art. 1, s. 1.

Mr. Findlay—It has been the Endeavour of many to paint our Necessities highly, like persuading a Man in Health that [he] is sick. Our Situation is such that we are not hastened in Point of Time and Necessity. We are enjoying Liberty and Happiness to a very great Degree.

Our Difficulties arose from the Requisition and heavy Taxes laid in 1782.

This system not suitable to our Necessities or Expectations.

Necessities.—We could not enforce Treaties—regulate Commerce—and draw a Revenue from it.

This System goes to raise internal Taxes—Capitation—Excises—to an Extension of the Judiciary Power even to Capital Cases—a Dependence of the State officers in the genl. Govt.

This system is not such as was expected by me, by the People, by the Legislatures, nor within these Powers.

It is a *consolidating Government* and will abolish the State Govts. or reduce them to a Shadow of Power.

1. from its Organization.

* "We the People," not "We the States."

From this we could not find out that we were *United States*.

† The Sovereignty of the States not held forth nor represented.

"Each Senator shall have one Vote."—Under the present Confederation the State Sovereignty is represented.—In Congress they vote by *States*.—A State can speak but one Voice.

* " For the United States."

† " Sovereignty in the People."

2. From its Powers.

The[y] who can tax, possess all other Sovereign Powers. There cannot be two Sovereign Powers.

A *subordinate* Sovereignty is no Sovereignty.

Will the People submit to two taxing Powers

The Power of our Elections gives absolute Sovereignty.—So of judging Elections.

The Judicial Powers are coextensive with the Legislative Powers.

Oath of Allegiance shews it to be a Consolidating Govt.

The Wages paid out of the public Treasury a Proof of consolid Govt.

Mr. Smilie—Congress have Authority to declare what is a Libel. Art. 1, s. 8.

A Jury may be packed.

Mr. Findlay—That the Supreme Power is of Right in the People is true in all Countries.

Cajole the People.

Mr. Whitehill—Tho' it is not declared that Congress have a Power to destroy the Liberty of the Press; yet in Effect they will have it : For they will have the Powers of self-preservation.

They have a Power to secure to Authors the Right of their Writings.— Under this they may license the Press no Doubt—and under licensing the Press they may suppress it.

Art. 1, s. 6. The Press is by this clause restrained, because the Members shall not be questioned for Speeches in *any other Place.*

Admendts. may be laid before Congress.

Mr. Smilie—In the Construction of a complete Government all the necessary Powers are given that are not restrained.

The Supreme Court shall have Jurisdiction in Cases where a State is a Party.

Crimes shall be tried by Jury, erg. they have Power to declare.

Mr. Findlay—No Opposition on *local* Principles.

This Plan is *inimical* to our Liberties.

In Convention, Monday, 3d Dec., 1787, P. M.

Dr. Rush.—We sit here as Representatives of *the People*—we were not appointed by the Legislature.

A Passion for State Sovereignty despoiled the Union of Greece.

Britain–France—enjoyed more Advantages *united* than *separate.*

A. Plurality of Sovereigns is Political Idolatry.

The Sovereignty of Penna. is ceded to U. S.

1. I have now a Vote for Members of Congress.

2. I am a Citizen of every State.

3. I have more security for my ppty.—The Weakness of Penna. in the Wyoming Business.—The Insurgents are Antifederal.

4. No Corruption of Blood—or Forfeiture except.

5. No Paper Money or Tender Laws.

6. No religious Test.

7. Commerce—its Influence on Agriculture.

8. Ship building—Iron Mines.

9. Hemp.

10. Produce to load our Vessels built.—*One only* exists in the Southern—the *other only* in the Eastern States.

11. The Communication of the Mississippi with the Atlantic will be opened under the new Constitution.

The Members in Virginia from Kentucky are enthusiasts for this system.

By adopting the fundary System, we have assumed a great Disproportion of the public Debt. It must be thrown back on Congress.

Distress general thro' the Country.

Mr. Smilie.—

1. It is admitted that the State sovereignty is given up.

2. I never heard any Thing so ridiculous except a former [unintelligible] of the same Gent.

3. Our preposterous Commerce has been the Source of our Distress—together with our Extravagance.

4. We wish alterations made in the Confedn. But we wish not to sacrifice the Rights of Men to obtain them.

5. Rights of Conscience should be secured.—They are so in the Bill of Rights of Penna.

Mr. Findlay.—

6. A Confederation and good Government would be more to me and my family than Wealth, Honour and Offices.

7. This is a Govt. of Individuals, and not a Confederation of States.

8. Sovereignty is in the States and not in the People—in its Exercise.

9. Vattell's description of Sovereignty—it belonged originally to the Body of the Society. Vat. page 9 of the Sovereign.

10. Vattel's Description of a federal Republic. If I am wrong, Vattel and Montesquieu are wrong. Vat. p. 11, s. 10.

11. 1. Investigate the Nature and Principles of the Government.

12. 2. How will it apply to our Security and Interests.

13. Gentlemen should first explain its Principles.

14. General Interests are well secured.

15. A single Branch I will concede.

16. I wish not to destroy this system: Its Outlines are well laid. By amendments it may answer all our Wishes.

17. Notwithstand. the legislative Power in Art. 1, s. 1.

The Power of Treaties is given to the Presd. and Senate. This is Branch of legislative Power.

18. Dark Conclave.

Mr. Pickering—According to common Acceptation of Words—Treaties are not Part of the legislative Power. The King of Gr. Britain.

19. Mr. Findlay—The King of Gr. Britain makes laws *ministerially.*—And the Legislature confirms them.

20. Ministers impeached for the Partitior Treaty.

21. Mr. Smilie—If the Ministers of Gr. Br. make an inglorious Conduct, they may be impeached and punished.—But can you impeach the Senate before itself

22. If it is *ministerial,* the Senate are here not a Legislature.

23. Supreme Laws cannot be made ministerially, but legislatively.

Mr. Pickering—In Gr. Br. Treaties are obligatory.

24. Mr. Smilie. In Gr. Br. a Law is frequently necessary for the Execution of a Treaty.

25. Mr. Whitehill—When a Treaty is made in G. B. it binds not the People if unreasonable. Treaties are binding by Acts of Parlt. and the Consent of the People.

26. Mr. Findlay—The President has a qualified Negative: This is *another* Inconsistency.

27. Mr. Smilie—If the K. of G. Br. makes a treaty contrary to Act of Parlt. it cannot be executed till the Law is repealed. We have not the same security here.

28. If the Senate could be impeached as the British Ministers may be, we would have more security.

29. Mr. Findlay—The manner of numbering the Inhabitants is dark, "other Persons." Art. I, s, 2.

30. Art. I, s. 9. 1st clause—Migration, etc., is unintelligible: It is unfortunate if this guaranties the Importation of Slaves—or if it lays a Duty on the Importation of other Persons.

31. This is a Reservation; and yet the Power of preventing Importation is no where given.

In Convention, 4th Dec., 1787, A. M.

32. Mr. Smilie—As the greatest Part of the States have compound Legislatures, I shall give up that Point.

33. I shall not object to the President's negative, for he will never be able to execute it. The King of Gr. B. does not execute.

34. Tho' there be no separate Orders, there is a natural Aristocracy: The Senate will represent it. House of Reps. will represent the common Mass of the People.

35. Are the Rights of the People secured? Is the Balance preserved? A Comparison between the Powers of the two Houses.

36. The Number of the House of Reps. too small.

37. They will not have the Confidence of the People, because the People will not be known by them, as to their Characters, etc. Only 8 for Penna.—the Districts will be very large.

38. The greatest Part of the Members even in this House will be attached to the natural Aristocracy.

39. This Body will be subject to Corruption, and the Means of Corruption will be in the Senate; for they have a Share in the Appointment of all officers.

40. There will be People willing to receive Bribes. The lower House may be corrupted with offices by the Senate; as the House of Commons are. There will be Judges—Tax gatherers, Land Waiters—Tide Waters—Excise officers.

41. To the Legislative Power of the Senate are added some Judicial Power—and an alarming share of the Executive. They are to concur with the Presidt. in making Treaties, which are to be the Supreme *Law of the Land.*

42. *In G. B. if Treaties interfere with subsisting Laws, they must be conformed. Treaty of Com. between France and England, Art. 14.

43. The Senate may be bribed: Ought they not to be brought to Punishment? Will their Colleagues convict him on Impeachment?

44. If it was not for such Things as these, we would not contend agt. this Constitution.

45. The Senate may for ever prevent the Addition of a single member to the Lower House; while their own Representation may be increased.

46. This Constitution contradicts the leading Principles of Govt. Mont. 6, 11, is 6 p., 199.

47. We have not every Security from the judicial Department.—The Judges for disobeying a Law may be impeached by one House and tried by the other.

In Convention, 5th Dec., 1787, A. M.

48. Mr. Findlay—The States made Bills of Rights not because they were known in Britain; but because they were proper.

49. A Majority of the States have them.

50. M. 6, 202. "The People in whom the Supreme Power resides."

51. Vat. 6. 1, s. 1, 2. "Sovereignty."

52. The Sovereignty is essentially in the People; but is vested in a Senate or a Monarch.

53. Vat. 6. 1, s. *11, 10.*

54. If all the Powers of Sovereignty are vested in one *Man* or *Body*, it is Tyranny.

55. The States have already parted with a Portion of their Sovereignty: It is now proposed to give more: But the People did not mean that the whole should be given up to the general Government.

56. The State Governments are not subordinate to the genl. Government as to *internal Taxes* and other *internal* Purposes.

57. Congress may with safety raise a Revenue from Commerce.

58. The general Government is farther removed from the People than the State Governments.

59. There cannot be two taxing Powers on the same Subject.—Taxation draws Legislation with it. There will [be] no Sovereignty in the States with Regard to Taxation.

60. There is no Sovereignty left in the State Governments—the only one is in the general Government.

61. The general Interests of Pennsylvania were not represented in the Convention.

62. Sovereignty essentially resides in the People, but they have *vested* certain Parts of it in the State Governments and other Parts in the present Congress.

63. We never said that the People were made for the States.

64. Who denied that Sovereignty was *inalienably* in the People?

65. There is a Declaration in the Bill of Rights of Penna. that the People

* Bl. 252, 257.

may change the Constitution—and they only add a Constitutional Right—which is also done in the system before us.—The same Thing has also been done in some of the other States.

66. The Checks on the Senate are not *sufficient*.

67. We ought to draw Instruction from the State Constitutions. Many of them—Virginia in particular—declare that the legislative, executive and judicial Departments should be kept distinct and independent.

68. What can be a greater source of Corruption than for the Legislature to appoint Officers and fix Salaries?

69. I would be at any Expense rather than submit to the Beginnings of Corruption—such as this.

70. There can be no Legislation without Taxation.—The States will not be able to raise a civil List.

71. I mean by a consolidating Govt. that which puts all the thirteen States into one.

72. This is a consolidating Govermt. as to all useful Purposes of Sovereignty.

73. In the Senate a Citizen of Delaware enjoys ten Votes for one that a Citizen of Penna. enjoys.

74. It is all one for a Citizen of Penna. to be taxed by a Representative from Georgia as for by his own Representative.

75. The smaller States have a Majority in the Senate; and they may lay Taxes on the larger States.

76. Congress may make the Number of Representatives as few as they please.

77. In Penna. before the Revolution the new Counties were unequally represented.

78. Penna. is unequally represented in the House of Representatives.

79. 100 Members are enough for a deliberative Body: And, on the present Plan, the *Number* will be either too large or the Representation too small. To avoid this let us have a *federal* Government.—Internal Power in a federal Govt. is *inadmissible* See next page but one.

80. To state the Danger of refusing this plan is improper. It is the Tyrant's Plea: Take this or Nothing.

In Convention, 5th Dec., 1787, P. M.

81. Mr. Findlay. The partial Negative of the President is a Part of legislative Authority, as no Bill can become a Law without his Revision.

82. Mr. Adams defines a natural Aristocracy "Such as have a separate Interest from the Community." "Those that in most Countries are called the Nobles."

83. The larger the Districts, the purer the Elections—is a novel Doctrine to us, and opposed to the very End of Elections.

84. Adams' Def. Pref.; p. 3.

85. The Voice of the People is the Law of the Land.*

86. Are 8 Members a better Representation of Penna. than what they now enjoy?

* But not the Voice of *Districts*.

87. While the *Forms* of State Govts. continue, all their Apparatus of Offices continue.

88. We all mean the same Theory about the Sovereignty of the People.— Sovereignty remains *essentially* in them.

89. Annual Elections are an annual Recognition of the Sovereignty of the People.

90. *Are the State Governments a Snare? They are not wrapt in Mystery and Darkness.

91. I believe that there are Govts. that keep the several Powers more distinct than the System before us.

92. We are agreed as to the Independence of the Judges.

93. The present System has increased the Difficulty of drawing the Line between Genl. and State Governments by encroaching into *internal* objects.

94. The President may aid the aristocratical Senate—and must aid it.

95. Internal Powers in a federal Governt. are inadmissible.

96. There is no Guard against Congress making Paper Money.

97. The States have redeemed their Paper Money better than Congress have done.

98. Amendments will always take more Power from the People, and give more to the Government.

99. There is no Security for such Amendments as we want : If we don't obtain them now, we shall probably never procure them.

100. The System ought to speak for itself, and not need Explanations.

Mr. Chambers—From the Silence on the other Side, I conclude they have no more to say against the first Article ; I move to proceed to the Consideration of the second Article.

Mr. Wayne—I second the Motion : I hope the Reasons in Favour of the proposed Constitution will induce many of the Opposition to come over.

101. Mr. Whitehill—If we go to the 2d Article shall we be permitted to draw our Objection from the first—to show that this is a consolidating Govt. and will annihilate the States.

102. Art. 1, s. 3. How shall the Seats of the &c first Class of the Senators be vacated? This must be made by Law of the Senators and Representatives : But they may make or not make this Law at their Pleasure.

103. The present Congress or some other Body should have decided this Matter.

104. The Senate may be enlarged under the 5th Article. " Its equal Suffrage " may mean a Suffrage in Proportion to Numbers, and consequently would increase the Numbers and Influeuce of the Senate.

105. Such Members may be chosen as the City of Philada. shall please.— Men of Wealth, etc.

106. Art. 5. To whom are Congress to propose Amendments? to a few Men of the different States if they please.

107. Congress, when they propose Amendments, will have it in their Power to regulate the Elections of Conventions ; or may order one Election and one Convention for the whole Union.

---

*An Attempt was made to trap the People of Penn. at the Time of forming its Constitution.

108. As long as the World stands, there never will be another Amendment, if the present System be confirmed.

109. Even Post-Roads are in the Power of Congress.

110. A Citizen of one State may sue a Citizen of another State for an Inheritance of Land, claimed by Will under the Law of the State where the Land is.

111. They may establish the Rights of Primogeniture.

112. Mr. Smilie.—Has not this Day been pretty closely occupied by us in the Opposition?

In Convention, 6th Dec., 1787, A. M.

113. Mr. Smilie—I object to the Power of Congress over the Militia, and to keep a standing Army.

114. What I mean by a consolidating Govt. is one that will transfer the Sovereignty from the State Govts. to the genl. Govt.

115. It is properly an aristocracy.

116. Because the Representatives are too few, and will be elected only by a few Tools in very large Districts.

117. In Penna. before the Revolution, the little Country Towns governed the Elections.

118. The People will not attend the Election; only the Tools of the Government will attend.

119. If Congress exercise their Powers over the Times, Places and Manner of Elections, where are we? 8 Men may be elected in one Ticket and at one Place. Should any Body have this Power?

120. The Balance of Power is in the Senate. Their Share in the Executive Department will corrupt the Legislature and detract from the proper Power of the President, and will make the President merely a Tool to the Senate.

121. The President should have had the Appointment of all the Officers, with the Advice of a Council.

122. The Senate will overset the Balance of Government by having the Purse and the Sword: The President will act in Concord with them.

123. In a free Govt. there never will be Need of standing Armies, for it depends on the Confidence of the People. If it does not so depend, it is not free.

124. The Convention, in framing this Govt., knew it was not a free one; otherwise they would not have asked the Power of the Purse and the Sword.

125. The last Resource of a free People is taken away, for Congress are to have the Command of the Militia.

126. The Laws of Penna. have hitherto been executed without the aid of the Militia.

127. The Governour of each State will be only the drill Sergt. of Congress.

128. The Militia officers will be obliged by Oath to support the genl. Govt. agt. that of their own State.

129. Congress may give us a select Militia which will, in Fact, be a standing Army—or Congress, afraid of a general Militia, may say there shall be no Militia at all.

130. When a select Militia is formed, the People in general may be disarmed.

131. Will the States give up to Congress their last Resource, the Command of the Militia?

132. Will the Militia Laws be as mild under the genl. Govt. as under the State Govt. Militia? Men may be punished with Whipping or Death. They may be dragged from one State to any other.

133. "Congress guarantees to each State a *Republican* Form of Govt." Is this a Security for a free Govt? Mr. Adam's Defence. 86 Poland is a Republic.

134. Can even the Shadow of State Govts. be continued if Congress please to take it away?

134. The Senate and Presidt. may dismiss the Representatives when once a standing Army is established with Funds; and there this Government will terminate.

135. Mr. Findlay—The Objections of the Members from Fayette are founded, important, and of extensive practical Influence. Tax and Militia Laws are of universal Operation.

136. The Militia will be taken from Home, and when the Militia of one State has quelled Insurrection and destroyed the Liberties; the Militia of the last State may at another Time be employed in retaliating on the first.

137. No Provision in Behalf of those who are conscientiously scrupulous of bearing Arms.

138. Mr. Smilie—As Citizens we are all equally interested. Let us have a friendly, free and fair Discussion.

139. Mr. Findlay—The Power of regulating Elections remains to be considered.

140. Art. 1, s. 4, as to the "Place" of Elections, struck the Public more suddenly and with more Force than any other. The "Time" may be justified.

141. Congress may say that none shall vote by Ballot.

142. The *Modes* of Election will be appointed in such Way as to give the greatest Influence to Govt.

143. The "Places" of Elections are of more Importance than the Time or Manner.

144. The States were competent as to the Places by their Knowledge and Responsibility. This is intrusted by our Constitution to the State Legislature.

145. This can have no *virtuous* or *pure* Use.

146. The *Place* of Elections may be removed so as to take it out of the Reach of the lower and midling Classes of Men.

147. By this Clause the Government may mould and influence Elections as it shall please.

148. This Govt. may go into the Channel of Monarchy, but more likely of Aristocracy.

149. Under the present Confederation, Congress have not both the Power of raising standing armies and the Means of paying them.

150. I could not contrive a better plan [than] this, for introducing Aristocracy.

151. Mr. Smilie—Mr. Adams says there is in all Societies a natural Aristocracy. Letter 53, p. 362. Three Branches of Government in every Society. The Executive ought to have a Negative on the Legislature.

152. The People of the U. S. thought a single Branch sufficient for Congress, which is not a legislative but a diplomatique Body, etc., ib.

153. Letter 55, 372.

In Convention, 7th Dec., 1787, A. M.

154. Mr. Whitehill—The Vice-President will be an useless and perhaps a dangerous office, as he will be more blended with the Legislature and will have a Voice when the Votes are equal. Salaries may depend on his Vote.

155. The Power of Congress to fix the Time of choosing the Electors of the President is improper: We have no Power to oblige Congress to act.

156. The Power of the Senate to make Treaties is dangerous.

157. The Extent of this Government is too great. It cannot be executed. We have proved it to be a consolidating Government.

158. Mr. Findlay—Only a Part of the Executive Power is vested in the President. The most influential Part is in the Senate, and he only acts as *primus inter pares* of the Senate; only he has the Sole Right of Nomination.

199. The officers of Government are the Creatures of the Senate: The Senate should not therefore be the Judges on Impeachments.

160. The great Objection is the blending of executive and legislative Power: Where they are blended there can be no Liberty: Mr. Adams says so. This great Subject is better understood by the People and attended to by the Legislature than any other: It is my Duty to insist, and I will insist, that the Distribution of Power in the present System be amended.

161. Mr. Whitehill—Why is the Sovereignty of the People always brought to Voice? There are 13 Sovereignties in the United States, and 13 different Governments: Why knock down all Distinction of different Governments.

162. The judicial Department is blended with and will absorb the judicial Powers of the several States; and Nothing will be able to stop its Way.

163. The Supreme Court will have very extensive Powers indeed: They must be an extension of the United States.

164. There must be a great Number of inferior Courts in the several States. One for a large State would not be enough.—Shall an Action for 5 or 10 be brought in it? There ought to be one in every County. The Number of judicial officers will be multiplied.

165. Appeals will be to the Supreme Court, which will put it in the Power of the wealthy to oppress the poor.

166. The Powers will be too extensive for the Safety and Happiness of the People: Justice cannot be administered.

167. Any Kind of Action may by Contrivance be brought into the federal Courts.

168. There may be Courts of Equity as well as Law.

169. Can the federal Courts give Relief to the Complaints of the People in proper Time. The State Courts have much Business. How much more will the genl. Courts have?

170. The general Courts may alter the Rights of Dissent and the Division of real Property. They may establish the Rights of Primogeniture.

171. The Trial of *Crimes* is to be by Jury, therefore the Trial of civil Causes is supposed not to be by Jury.

172. We preserved the Trial by Jury against the Attempts of the British Crown.

173. I wish for the Honour of the Convention this had not been omitted.

174. Art. 3, s. 2, "The Laws of the United States" Laws may be made in *Pursuance* of the Const," tho' not agreeably to it: The Laws may be unconstitutional.

175. Treaties may be so made as to absorb the Liberty of Conscience, Trial by Jury and all our Liberties.

176. "Citizens of another State" must mean *all* the Citizens.

177. There is no Line drawn in the judicial Department, between the genl. and State Govts.

178. Houses may be broke open by the officers of the genl. Govt. They will not be bound by this Constitution.

179. Mr. Smilie—In common Law Cases there ought not to be an Appeal as to Facts. Facts found by a Jury should never be re-examined.

180. I doubt whether there has not been an Intention to substitute the civil Law instead of the common Law.

181. There may be Danger in the Execution of the judicial Department as in the Case of a rigorous Collection of direct Taxes.—A Quarrel between a Collector and a Citizen would drag the Citizen into the Court of Congress.

182. The Courts must be very *numerous* or very *few*. Either will be inconvenient. They must be numerous.

183. If the State Govts. are to continue, the People will not be able to bear the Expense of them and the genl. Govt. Will this save Expense?

184. Mr. Findlay. The Convention, no doubt, thought they were forming a Contract or Compact of the greatest Importance.

185. The Judges are better for the Guard of Juries in all possible Cases. The Mistakes of Juries are never systematical. The Laws can never be so enacted, as to prevent the Judges from doing wrong.

186. I admit that it would have been impossible to have accommodated the Trial by Jury to all the States: But Power ought not to have been given applying to such *internal* Objects.

187. There might have been a Declaration that the Trial by Jury in Civil Cases as it hath hitherto been in the several States, or in the State where the Cases arose.

188. The Jurisdiction will, I believe, be chiefly appellate, and therefore chiefly without Jury.

189. The States can make "no post facto Laws, etc," therefore there was no Occasion for introducing the Clause "between Citizens of different States."

190. This Clause may produce Doubts in the Dealings between Citizens of this State and New Jersey.

191. "Compensation" is a new Form: Does it denote Salary or Perquisites? These should be incapable of holding offices under the States, or other Offices under the genl. Govt.—They may hold Sinecures. I have only lately discovered this Objection.

192. A Treaty is not constitutionally guarded. It may be superior to the Legislature itself. The House of Representatives have Nothing to do with Treaties.

193. Mr. Smilie—I cannot see the great Difficulty of securing at Cost the Substance of Jury in civil Cases.—It ought [to] have been said that the Legislature should make Regulations for the Trial by Jury in them.

194. Whatever is not given is reserved. The Trial by Jury is given in criminal cases, therefore reserved in civil Cases.

195. The Judges may be bribed by holding other Offices.

In Convention, 8th December, 1787.

196. *Mr. Smilie—This System puts the Govt. in a Situation, in which the Officers are not responsible.

197. Every Door is shut against Democracy.

198. It was the Design and Intention of the Convention to divest us of the Liberty of Trial by Jury in civil Cases; and to deprive us of the Benefits of the common Law.

199. The Word Appeal is a civil Law Term and therefore the Convention meant to introduce the *civil* Law.

200. On an Appeal the Judges may set aside the Verdict of a Jury.

201. Appeals are not admitted in the Common Law.

202. If a Jury give a false Verdict, a Writ of Attaint lies, or the Verdict may be set aside. A Writ of Error lies as to Matters of Law, but on that Writ the Facts are not re-examined.

203. †3 Bl., 378—concerning Trials by Jury.

204. 3 Bl., 392. The *Expense* of civil Law Proceedings.

205. 3 Bl., 390, 391. The Propriety of new Trials.

206. 3 Bl., 452. Chancery frequent[ly] directs the Trial of Facts by a Jury.

207. 3 Bl., 336. Trial by Witness is the only Mode known to the civil Law.

208. ‡The Case of Fossey av Cunningham, New York. Appeal to the Governour and Council — Reasons of the Chief Justice for the Conduct of the Judges.

209. "All the Appeals we have yet had, have been in Error."

210. If such an attempt was made in England, what would the People or that Country do? It would set the whole Nation in a Flame.

211. Securing the Trial by Jury in criminal Cases is worse than saying Nothing.

212. The Convention might have said that Congress should establish Trials by Jury in civil Cases.

213. Mr. Whitehill—Are we to trust all to Judges, who will have their Favourites?

214. There is no Security by the Constitution for People's Houses or Papers.

* New Hampshire.
† At the Will of Parlt.
‡ The Question here was—whether Instructions from the Crown could, or were meant to alter the Law.

215. Farener's Letters. Let. 9. The King cannot punish till a Person be found guilty by his Peers, Excellence and Description of Trial by Jury in criminal Cases.

216. These Privileges (described in the Letter) are not secured by this Constitution.

217. The Case of Mr. Wilkes and the Doctrine of general Warrants show that Judges may be corrupted.

218. A wicked Use may be made of Search Warrants.

219. If such Men execute as forward this Constitution, all Alterations will be for the worse.

220. The People will not submit to this Govt.

221. Art. 6, Clauses 2 and 3 are concluding Clauses that the State Governments will be abolished.

222. * The Oath here required is contrary to the Oath required by the Constitution of Penna. No Member of Assembly will hereafter take the latter Oath.

223. The next Thing will be to call Conventions to alter the State Governments.

224. All our Constitutions may be altered by Treaties made by a few Senators.

225. This lordly Domination will not do.

226. Our greatest Liberties will, by this Constitution, be sacrificed to the Will of Men.

227. The Trial by Jury is given up to the Will of Congress.

Mr. McKean—I have read as well as heard the Objections mentioned here in the Centinel, Brutus, Cincinnatus.

228. Mr. Findlay—The State has had but two Months to consider this System.

229. Trial by Jury is not secured in civil Cases as in criminal ones. It is at the Mercy of the Legislature.

230. By the appellate Clause, an appeal lies from the Verdict of a Jury, a Thing hitherto unknown.

231. Personal Liberty cannot be enjoyed without Trial by Jury.

232. All the northern Countries have been zealous of Freedom. Sweden till lately had Trials by Jury, and certainly a free Govt. well balanced, consisting of four Branches.

233. Trial by Jury is inconsistent with a complete Aristocracy.

234. The Lower Class of People will be oppressed without Trial by Jury.

235. This Part is explanatory of other Parts of the Plan.

236. The People never expressed a Wish to give up the Trial by Jury.

237. In Penna. the Trial by Jury must be by a Jury of the proper County.

238. Mr. Smilie—In all Times a Minority contending for the Rights of Mankind have been treated with Contempt.

239. The People should be represented by Juries in the Administration of Justice.

* New H. Bils. R., s. 20, 21.
Mass. B. R. s. 15.

240. 3 Bl., 380. Every new Tribunal without Jury is a Step towards an Aristocracy.

Mr. Findlay—

In Convention, Monday, 10th Dec., 1787, P. M.

Mr. Findlay—As to the Trial by Jury in Sweden. Mod. Un. His., Vol. 33, p. 21, 22, Juries remain *in Office for Life*. 3 Bl., 349, *380*, **381.**

Mr. McKean.—

1. Consider Objections.
2. Give Reasons in Favor of the Plan—Objections.
1. Elections not frequent enough.
2, N[umber] of R[epresentatives] too few.
3. Senate have too many blended Powers.
4. Congress, Times, etc., Elections.
5. Powers of Congress too large.

Appropriations too long.

6. Whole of the Ex. Power not lodged in Presdt. alone.

V.-Pres. should not have a vote in Senate.

7. Compn. of Judges may be incidentally increased.
8. No Bill of Rights.
9. A consolidating Govt.—not a federal one.

[10.] An Aristocracy.

I. Elections frequent enough.

The different Durations of Parliament.

Service should be longer than that of Representatives.

II. The Representation is large enough.

Before 25 years the Number will be doubled.

III. None of the simple Forms of Govt. are the best.

There is no Writer of Reputation but has allowed that the Br. Gov. was the best in the World before the Emancipation of U. S.

When a Judge, etc. is impeached, it is probable that none of those who appointed him will be present. The Danger lies from the Desire of Removal.

In Penna., Ex. Council *appoint* and *impeach* Officers.

IV. Art. 1, s. 4.

Every House is Judge of Qualif. and Elections.

Are not *all* the States interested in the Elections?

V. Power of *internal* Taxes not too great.

Foreigners may *compel* Paymt. of their Debts.

Have we not had Experience enough of Requisitions?

Is it not necessary that Congress should have a Power of raising and supporting Armies?—and the Command and Discipline of the Militia?

"All Laws necessary & proper," etc., this liable to no first Exceptions.

"This Const." etc., shall be the Supreme Law.

"Importation" etc. Subject of Applause.

VI. In Penna. there is no Responsibility in Council because the Prest. has given up his Rights of Nomn. and they appoint by Ballot, and therefore are not responsible.

There is scarce a King in Europe that has not some Check upon him in the Appt. of Offices.

VII. Offices to Judges' Relations the same as to themselves.

There might be Improvements in the Institution of Juries ; particularly as to the Mode of appointing them.

The House of Lords have an appellate Jurisdiction in Law and Fact.

Appellate Jurisdiction from Orphans' Courts.

In the Eastern States, Causes tried by Juries are removed on Appeal.

VIII. What Occasion for a Bill of Rights when only delegated Powers are given ? One possessed of 1000 As conveys 250, is it necessary to reserve the 750 ?

Kock. on Gov., p. 2, s. 141, 152.

IX. I shall not quarrel about Names.

X. An Aristocracy is the best Security against external Force.

Consequences of Accepting.

Strengthen the Governt.—Assistance from the People of all the States.

settle and perpetuate our Independence.

Encourage our Allies—and make *new* Treaties, break our Parties and Divisions, invigorate Commerce, Shipbuilding.

The Clause of Amendment Art. 5.

This is the best System the World can now produce.

Mr. Findlay—The Principle of our Argument not stated—consolidating Govt.—In Connection with this Principle were all our Argnments.

Mr. Smilie—Those who clap and laugh are not the People of Pennsylvania. If the Gallery was filled with Bayonets, it would not intimidate me.

It is a great Misfortune that another State has been before us in the Surrender of their Liberties.

In Convention, 11th Dec., 1787, A. and P. M.
Mr. Wilson—

In Convention, 12th Dec., 1787, A. M.
Mr. Findlay—Sovereignty—Vat., p. 9, 19.

Locke on Gov., p. 13.—There is but one Supreme Power, viz., the legislative ; but is accompanied with a Trust, and there is still an inherent Right and Power in the People for self-preservation. But this inherent Power can never be exercised till the Government be dissolved.

Confederation, p. 11, s. 10.

Mont., 6, 9, c. 1. Confederate Republic.

There should have been a Council of Advice to the Presdt. responsible to their Conduct.

The Senate and Presdt. *may* make a Monarchy.

The Power of *regulating* Elections includes the Power of *Elections*.

It is not unreasonable to suppose that this System may be made better.

Mr. Smilie—The Case of the Active.

Are not the Persons to be entrusted with Power, Parties to this Govt?

British Liberties, p. 98, 99, 21.

In Convention, 12th Dec., 1787, P. M.

Mr. Smilie—Powers undefined are extremely favorable for the Encrease of Power.

If this was an explicit Declaration that the People had a right to alter this System, all Matters would be easy.

The Rights of Conscience are not secured.—Priestcraft useful to all tyrannical Govts.—Congress may establish any Religion.

Aristocracy is the Govt. of the few over the many.

The Govt. cannot be excluded—because the same Means must be employed for this Purpose as are necessary to execute a Despotism.—But Discontent and Opposition will arise in every Quarter: If executed at all it must be by Force: The Framers of this Constitution must have seen that Force would be necessary.

This will be the Case; and if this be so, we have struggled and fought in vain.

Since the Peace there has been a Set of Men from N. H. to Georgia who could not bear to be on the same Footing with other Citizens. I cannot tell how many of these were in the Convention.

Congress, by the Powers they have already, have contributed to throw Things into Confusion to produce the present great Event.

A Change of Habits is necessary to relieve the present Distress of the People: The Adoption of the present System will not accomplish this.

If this Constitution is adopted, I look upon the Liberties of America as gone until they shall be recovered by Arms.

Mr. Hartley—

Dr. Rush—

Mr. Chambers—

Mr. Whitehill—

Mr. McKean--

REPLIES OF MIFFLIN AND MORRIS TO CENTINEL.

[The attacks made on Robert Morris and Thomas Mifflin, by anonymous writers in the "Freeman's Journal" and the "Independent Gazetteer," caused no small excitement at the time, and were thought serious enough to be answered. As these charges of fraud, undoubtedly false, were also made by "Centinel," and are given in the body of this book, the editors think it no more than common justice that the answers of Morris and Mifflin to the charges referred to by "Centinel" should also be given.]

Mr. Oswald. In the "Freeman's Journal" of yesterday, among other names of Public Defaulters, in the most licentious manner held out to the public without any shadow of proof, we have the name of G—l M—n (meaning no doubt the present worthy and public spirited Speaker of the honorable House of Assembly of this State), in the words following, viz: "G—l M—n, the quartermaster-general of the Continental army, is almost the first of the list. I tremble to relate the prodigious sums that these wicked Antifederalists suppose him indebted to the public.

"The sums supposed by the enemies of the new government, that three delinquents owe the public, would pay the taxes of our state for three years to come, under a mild and equitable government. I have annexed them to their names for your information :

	Dollars.
Robert the Cofferer	400,000,
Billy in the big house	100,000,
G—l M—n, the quartermaster-general	400,000,

Total 900,000."

The following certificate from the Commissioners of the chamber of accounts, will show that on the settlement of the accounts of General Mifflin as quartermaster-general, there were only 3,203 continental dollars, equal in value to about forty-two dollars specie.

"Philadelphia, 23d October, 1781.
"We. the underwritten late commissioners of the chamber of accounts, do certify, that the accounts of Thomas Mifflin, esquire, late quartermaster general to the army of the United States, were a long time since presented for settlement: that from the state of his general account, there appeared to be a balance due to the United States in the year 1780, of three thousand, two hundred and three continental dollars; and that he informed us he had an account to produce for expenses while in the department which was not included in the aforesaid account. Had it been charged, it is probable, the balance would have appeared in his favor.
"We likewise certify, that we have examined the said general account, and excepting a few trifling errors, the whole of his charges appeared to have been for the public service in

(786)

purchases for the use of his department, and payments made to his deputies; and that the said account, with the vouchers thereto, appeared as perfect and satisfactory as any accounts that have hitherto come before us, but that the accounts of his deputies have not been examined so as to ascertain the exact balance, or to judge on which side it may fall.

"WILLIAM GOVETT,
"JOHN D. MERCER.

"The original of the above, General Mifflin hath lodged with me, and I certify the same to be a true copy.   JOSEPH NOURSE,
"*Late Assistant Auditor-General.*"

On this licentious and rude attack of one of the first characters under the American revolution, a friend of his wishes to state the following facts, which can be authenticated from public documents, viz:

1. Since the date of the above certificate, General Mifflin has been twice at New York to settle his accounts with Congress, but a general rule of that body, not to settle with the principal of any department without a previous settlement with all the deputies, has hitherto prevented the final adjustment of his accounts.

2. Several of the deputies have lately settled their accounts, and some few of them have declared that they are not in debt to Congress, and at present not in circumstances to attend at New York for the purpose of final settlement; but General Mifflin does not consider himself in any degree responsible for any of his deputies, as scarce any of them were appointed by himself, or by his direction, or at his request; and they generally drew for their own expenditures.

3. General Mifflin received his pay in a very depreciated state, and since the adjustment of his accounts by the commissioners as above, he has been obliged to pay several sums in specie, which he had not charged at all, or only in continental money, and he has a very considerable balance now due him by the continent.

4. To show the public sense of General Mifflin's services, let it be remembered that he was appointed quartermaster-general in August, 1775, resigned in May, 1776, and in September, 1776, a committee of Congress made a request that the commander-in-chief would direct General Mifflin to resume the quartermaster-general's department, which, like a true patriot, on account of the difficulty of the times, he did without any rigid regard to his own interest, and in Pennsylvania there is a cloud of evidence of the exertions he made for the public service in the moments of extremest danger.*

To the Printer of the Independent Gazeteer, *Philadelphia.*

Richmond, 21st March, 1788.

Sir: From some of your Gazettes which have lately reached me, and particularly from one of the 13th instant, I find that I am charged as a public defaulter to a very considerable amount. This assertion is made to support a charge against the Federal constitution, which those writers say is calculated to screen defaulters from justice. Without pretending to inquire whether the constitution be, in this respect, misunderstood or misrepresented, I readily agree that if, on fair investigation, that fault shall really appear, an amendment ought to be made.

* From the "Independent Gazetteer," March 6, 1788.

I stand charged in a two-fold capacity: first, as a Chairman of Committees of Congress, and secondly, as Superintendant of the Finances. But it so happens that in neither of those capacities did I ever touch one shilling of the public money.

At an early period of the revolution, I contracted with the committees to import arms, ammunition, and clothing, and was employed to export American produce, and make remittances, on account of the United States, for the purpose of lodging funds in Europe. To effect these objects I received considerable sums of money. The business has been performed, but the accounts are not yet settled. Among the various causes which have hitherto delayed the settlement, I shall only mention here that I have not yet been able to obtain the required vouchers for delivery of articles in different parts of America, nor the duplicates of some accounts, and other needful papers, which were lost at sea during the war. It was my intention to have gone in person to New York, where alone (since the removal of Congress) this business can be finally adjusted; but circumstances unexpected obliged me to come to this country. I therefore employed a gentleman to proceed on the settlement of those accounts, but during the investigation, obstacles arose which he was not sufficiently acquainted with the transactions to remove; and as some of the deficient vouchers are to be obtained in this state and South Carolina, he came on hither, and is now in pursuit of them. I have indeed been less solicitous on this subject than otherwise I should have been, from the conviction that there is a balance in my favor, so that no charge could justly lie against my reputation. Nor could my interest suffer by the delay; for the date of a certificate to be received for the balance was immaterial.

As Superintendant of the Finances, I have no accounts to settle. As I never received any of the public money, none of it can be in my hands. It was received in, and paid from the public treasury on my warrants. The party to whom it was paid was accountable; and the accounts were all in the treasury office, open (during my administration) to the inspection of every American citizen. The only point of responsibility, therefore, in which I can possibly stand is for the propriety of issues to others by my authority. It is true that I caused a statement of the receipts and expenditures to be made and printed, but this was not, by any means, intended for a settlement with Congress, but to be transmitted by them (if they should think proper) to the several states; for I have ever been of opinion that the people ought to know how much of their money goes into the public treasury, and for what purposes it is issued. Perhaps some persons may remember, that in conformity to this opinion, I caused the receipts (even during the war) to be published (monthly) in the Gazettes; and the expenditures, as I have already mentioned, were open to public inspection. This mode of conduct was reprehended by some, and perhaps justly. My fellow-citizens will judge whether it looks like the concealment of a public defaulter. As to the suggestion that the United States in Congress were influenced by me to neglect the duty of calling me to account, I shall not attempt to refute it. Every man who feels for the dignity of America, must revolt at such an insult to her representatives.

Before I conclude, I think it necessary to apologize for having written this letter, to all who may take the trouble of reading it. A newspaper is certainly an improper place for stating and settling public accounts, especially those which are already before the proper tribunal. But I thought it in some sort a duty to take notice of charges which, if not controverted, might have influenced weak minds to oppose the constitution. This was at least the ostensible reason for bringing me forward on the present occasion. With what decency or propriety it has been done, I leave to the reflection of the authors. Their exultation on my "losses and crosses" is characteristic. To every pleasure which can arise from the gratification of such passions they are heartily welcome; and the more so, as I hope and expect the enjoyment will be of short duration. ROBERT MORRIS.*

* From the " Independent Gazetteer," April 8, 1788.

INDEX.

Printed on paper that is acid-free and meets the requirements
of the American National Standard for Permanence of Paper
for Printed Library Materials, z39.48-1992 ∞

Cover design by Louise OFarrell
Gainesville, Florida
Printed and bound by Malloy, Inc.
Ann Arbor, Michigan